CIVIL WAR TO THE BLOODY END

NUMBER NINE:

Canseco-Keck History Series

Civil War to the Bloody End

The Life & Times of
Major General
Samuel P. Heintzelman

Jerry Thompson

Texas A&M University Press
College Station

First edition

The paper used in this book meets the minimum requirements of the American National Standard for Permanence of Paper for Printed Library Materials, Z39.48-1984. Binding materials have been chosen for durability.
♾ ♻

Library of Congress Cataloging-in-Publication Data

Thompson, Jerry D.
Civil war to the bloody end : the life and times of Major General Samuel P. Heintzelman / Jerry Thompson.— 1st ed.
p. cm. — (Canseco-Keck history series ; no. 9)
Includes bibliographical references and index.
ISBN-13: 978-1-58544-535-6 (cloth : alk. paper)
ISBN-10: 1-58544-535-5 (cloth : alk paper)
1. Heintzelman, Samuel Peter, 1805–1880. 2. Generals—United States—Biography. 3. United States. Army—Biography. 4. United States—History—Civil War, 1851–1865—Biography. 5. United States—History—Civil War, 1861–1865—Campaigns. I. Title. II. Series.
E467.1.H495T47 2006
973.7′3092—DC22

2006005040

For
Ceci and John Keck

"I have no hesitation in leaving my reputation . . .
in the hands of the future historian."

SAMUEL PETER HEINTZELMAN
Washington Daily National Intelligencer
August 9, 1865

Contents

Illustrations

FIGURES

MAPS

PHOTOGRAPHS

Introduction

SAMUEL PETER HEINTZELMAN was a refined and cultured family man, a patron of the arts, lover of Shakespeare and the opera, amateur astronomer, meteorologist, geologist, naturalist, inventor, violinist, and a better-than-average cartographer.[1] A respected career military officer who spoke three languages, he fought bravely in Mexico, established Fort Yuma along the Colorado River in 1850, and won the Cortina War along the Rio Grande in 1859–60. A tough disciplinarian rarely loved by his subordinates, he could be argumentative, proud, prickly, self-centered, and excessively vain. As an uncompromising Unionist, he rose to the rank of major general of volunteers in command of the III Corps of the Army of the Potomac during the Civil War. In the forefront of the fighting at First Bull Run and during the 1862 Peninsula Campaign at Yorktown, Williamsburg, Seven Pines, Savage's Station, and Glendale, and later at Second Bull Run, he might well have come to command the Army of the Potomac had he been more resolute, radical, and politically astute.

Details in this biography would not have been possible had Heintzelman not cared to compile and preserve valuable personal journals and pocket diaries as well as assorted papers and military records, all of which provide a rare glimpse into his life and a most crucial period of nineteenth-century American military history. His pocket diaries and journals alone comprise over 3,300 handwritten pages and close to a million words. They begin with the innocent and idealistic thoughts of a young and determined Pennsylvanian German boy on the plain at West Point in 1822 and end in 1872 with the somewhat embittered recollections of an aged and physically broken old general. Except for a six-week lapse in 1844, following his marriage to a Buffalo, New York, socialite, and a second five-week omission after being wounded at First Bull Run in July 1861, the journals are continuous from 1825 to 1872. Daily entries vary from a few sentences to several hundred words.

A serious deterrent to any scholarly study of the Heintzelman journals and papers has been the inability of scholars to read Heintzelman's difficult handwriting. Although his penmanship was legible when he entered West Point, it grew progressively worse over the decades that followed and at times became almost unreadable, especially during periods of fatigue and stress.

Creola Blackwell, who meticulously transcribed Heintzelman's Fort Yuma journals (January 1, 1851, to December 31, 1853) complained of the "tedious undertaking" and said that reading Heintzelman's writing was "akin to translating a foreign language."[2] While attempting to read portions of his journals in 1865, Heintzelman himself complained that "the writing is so bad that I can't immediately make out the words. I have left out letters, sylab[b]les and words and frequently spelled words wrong. I should have each day read off what I wrote and corrected it."[3] Discouraged by the difficult and time-consuming task of trying to read the journals, a number of scholars appear to have turned away. One exception was Diane M. T. North, who transcribed, ably edited, and published the journal dated August 3, 1858, to January 29, 1859, when Heintzelman was on a leave of absence at Tubac and Cerro Colorado in the newly acquired Gadsden Purchase; his sometimes dramatic 1859–60 journal of Texas and the Cortina War has also been published. Another scholar fascinated by Heintzelman was the Arizona physician and historian Benjamin Sacks, who mined the general's Civil War journals for his study of the creation of Arizona Territory. Sacks, who hoped to transcribe and annotate the Arizona journal, was one of the first to realize the historical value of these day-by-day accounts. What Heintzelman's writing lacked in "literary luster" was "more than compensated for by the precise information it supplies," he concludes. It was Sacks who first referred to Heintzelman as a "Second Father of Arizona Territory." Even more valuable are the journals, notebooks, and papers covering the Civil War. As expected, a number of prominent Civil War historians, including Stephen Sears, William C. Davis, and John J. Hennessy, have consulted Heintzelman's journals.[4]

Heintzelman bound the journals for 1825–41 in three volumes. Later the remaining journals were also bound, thereby creating a total of ten volumes of daily events covering forty-seven years. In 1913–14 these ten volumes, along with six boxes of army orders, maps, and correspondence, were deposited in the Library of Congress by Mary Lathrop Heintzelman, the general's only daughter, and by a grandson and West Point graduate, Capt. Stuart Heintzelman. In 1953 the Heintzelman Papers, including the diaries and journals, were converted to a gift by Dorothy Heintzelman

Mannan, a stepdaughter of Stuart Heintzelman. Unfortunately, only five of the lengthy personal letters, numbering perhaps a thousand or more, from Heintzelman to his wife appear to have survived, while the correspondence from Margaret Heintzelman to her soldier-husband is also apparently lost to history.

CIVIL WAR TO THE BLOODY END

ONE

Duty, Honor, Country

FOR MOST OF HIS LIFE, Samuel Peter Heintzelman sought a thorough understanding of his Pennsylvania-German ancestry. After graduating from West Point in 1826, he returned six times to the small southeastern Pennsylvania town of Manheim, where he had been born, to query elderly friends and relatives and visit the Old Lutheran Burial Ground, where he carefully copied the names as well as the birth and death dates of deceased family members. Upon visiting the cemetery in October 1842, he seemed proud that the "tombstones of our family are still standing."[1]

Heintzelman was born in the quaint rural farming community of Manheim in the early morning hours of October 30, 1805. The son of Peter H. Heintzelman and Ann Grubb Heintzelman, he was baptized three weeks later by the minister of the Trinity Lutheran Church in nearby Lancaster. His grandfather, Heironimus Heintzelman, a native of the Bavarian city of Augsburg, had followed two older brothers, Baltasar and John, across the North Sea to England in the mid-eighteenth century. Although the older brothers remained in England, where they became prominent merchants, in 1758 Heironimus was commissioned an officer in the "Royal Americans" during the French and Indian War. After a rough voyage across the North Atlantic to Halifax, Nova Scotia, the Royal Americans sailed south to Philadelphia, where they were sent west to garrison the recently captured Fort Duquesne, now renamed Fort Pitt, in the tangled wilderness of western Pennsylvania at the confluence of the Allegheny and Monongahela rivers. After the war Heironimus, who anglicized his name to Jerome, moved to the small village of Manheim in east-central Pennsylvania, where he met and married Catherine Elizabeth Wagner, the daughter of an itinerant Lutheran pastor.[2]

Samuel Peter also learned that his grandfather had been one of the first "inhabitants in Manheim" and that he had "kept a tavern" under a "large white oak tree." Heironimus's second son, Peter, Samuel Peter's

Heintzelman residence on South Prussian (now South Main) Street, Manheim, Pennsylvania. Manheim Historical Society.

father, was born in Manheim on September 30, 1768, and became a merchant, postmaster, and a person of some importance in the small village. On September 8, 1799, Peter married Ann Elizabeth Grubb, daughter of an influential Pennsylvania ironmaster. He purchased property and built an impressive two-story brick home on South Prussian Street (what became South Main Street). At Manheim, on the edge of the Amish country among rolling hills, quaint farmhouses, and fertile valleys, seven children were born to Ann and Peter Heintzelman.[3]

The young Samuel Peter received a limited education from private tutors and the parochial school of the Manheim Lutheran Church. Sadly, his mother died at the age of forty-one in 1812, two weeks before Samuel Peter's seventh birthday, from what were certain to have been the effects of childbirth. After visiting her grave twenty-one years later, he wrote, "The sight of Mother's tombstone brings melancholy reflections although she died almost before I can recollect."[4]

After presenting Rep. James Buchanan of Lancaster with a letter from a local teacher certifying that he was competent in English grammar, arithmetic, and algebra, Heintzelman was able to obtain the obligatory congressional recommendation necessary for appointment to the U.S. Military Academy at West Point. Buchanan wrote Secretary of War John C. Calhoun that the seventeen-year-old was the son of a "very respectable German" and "intelligent beyond what I would have expected from a boy of his age." Ten prominent Manheim citizens, including Samuel Peter's father, signed a letter to Calhoun affirming that the young man had an "unblemished moral character" and a "strong and healthful constitution." Receiving the news of his acceptance to West Point, Samuel Peter wrote a formal acknowledgment to the secretary of war to say that he was "highly honored" at being accepted. Representative Buchanan also took the time to write the Manheim lad, "As I have used all my influence . . . I hope that your conduct will be such as to reflect honor on your parents and your country and make me reflect with pleasure that I have been instrumental in procuring your appointment."[5]

After taking a steamboat up the Hudson River and disembarking at the small wharf on the west bank, the young man was marched up the steep hillside to meet the post adjutant and take the entrance exam. On July 1, 1822, Samuel Peter Heintzelman officially entered the U.S. Military Academy. Proclaimed academically qualified, his name was inscribed in a large book, and he marched across the parade ground to the South Barracks. There he was given a pillow, bucket, broom, brush, blankets, a washbasin, and a gray uniform. Three cadets were assigned to each room in the three-story barracks. The rooms, with no running water and no heat in winter except what a small fireplace could provide, were Spartan at best. The young men carried in their own wood from a yard near the barracks. They used a shelf over the fireplace for books and personal items. Most rooms had a table and three chairs, though some cadets used boxes, barrels, or trunks to study on. Beds were common, but many students slept on the floor. Candles or the flames in the fireplace provided the only light.[6] There was always the danger of fire, so cadets were organized into fire companies and required in winter to keep buckets of water in their room next to the hearth.

Heintzelman would never forget the endless marching required of the young "plebes." New cadets were drilled, drilled, drilled some more, and then drilled again. There was also the verbal harassment, often brutal, inflicted on the new arrivals by the older cadets, sometimes in the middle of the night, all of which was part of a well-established tradition at West Point. Despite the harassment and the physical rigors required at the academy, young Heintzelman took great pride in his appointment. Largely based on the French Ecole Polytechnique, West Point was one of the greatest military and civil engineering schools in the world.

The typical day at West Point began with reveille at 5 A.M., after which rooms were prepared for inspection. Drill commenced twenty minutes later and continued until breakfast at 7 A.M. Monday through Saturday, classes were held from 8 A.M. until lunch at 1 P.M., after which classes resumed and continued until 4 P.M. At 4:30 P.M. there was more drill followed by the evening parade and then supper. Evenings were devoted to study until 10 P.M., when candles had to be extinguished.[7]

Three-fourths of each day was consumed in the study of French, mathematics, natural philosophy, engineering, and military tactics. The heart of the curriculum was mathematics and French. Mathematics, the language of science, was necessary as a prerequisite for civil engineering. French was deemed valuable since most of the advanced texts in military science were written in that language. Supporting the core curriculum was drawing, chemistry, and mineralogy. Miscellaneous subjects consisted of English grammar, geography, history, rhetoric, natural law, constitutional law, and political economy.[8]

At West Point Heintzelman struggled academically, especially with chemistry, which had been added to the curriculum only a few years prior to his arrival. Driven by the dream of a career in the military and determined not to fail, he placed a blanket over his window at night so that the flickering flame of a candle would not reveal his studying past "lights out." In fact, he often would study until three or four o'clock in the morning or until fife and drum awoke the cadets. Only five feet, six inches in height and weighing less than 120 pounds, the "plebe" from Pennsylvania was also at a disadvantage when daily activities required feats of strength. Decades later a West Point classmate would remember young Heintzelman as "attentive to his studies and duties, tho' not considered to be a brilliant man in his intellect or abilities. He was uniformly courteous and gentlemanly in his deportment and manners and was well liked by all who knew him."[9]

The superintendent of West Point during these years was Col. Sylvanus Thayer, a dedicated administrator who had rewritten the curriculum and who brought order and discipline to the academy. Young Heintzelman studied mathematics with Charles Davies, a talented professor who helped make West Point the best mathematical school in the United States. Cadets called Davies "Tush" because of his protruding front teeth; after he energetically helped put out a fire at the South Barracks, "Rush" was added to his nickname, thus becoming "Rush-Tush."[10] A prolific writer and a favorite of the cadets, "Rush-Tush" authored a number of scientific and mathematical texts, ranging from basic arithmetic to calculus, that were widely used at colleges throughout the country.

French was taken with Claudius Berard, an excellent instructor who had prepared his own text, *A Grammar of the French Language*. Jared Mansfield, senior faculty member, was professor of natural and experimental philosophy. Extremely nearsighted and growing old, he was respected and beloved by most of the cadets.[11] David B. Douglass was professor of civil and military engineering. A Yale graduate and a superb scholar, Douglass had difficulty in communicating orally, and the cadets found his classes tedious and boring. During his last two years at West Point, young Heintzelman fell under the influence of Dennis Hart Mahan, who was known throughout the army for stressing the Napoleonic maxims of war. The commandant of cadets was Maj. William J. Worth, who taught them the little flourishes of arms and execution that gave meaning to the seemingly endless drill.

Heintzelman was fortunate to be a part of the academy's golden age that produced some of the most illustrious names in American history. His class at West Point included a tall, slender young man from Kentucky who had been appointed from Louisiana named Albert Sidney Johnston as well as another young cadet from Louisiana, who found religion at West Point, by the name of Leonidas Polk. There was also a dedicated Virginian named Joseph Eggleston Johnston. Three years later another Virginia lad arrived by the name of Robert E. Lee as well as a cantankerous and rebellious young Mississippian fresh from Transylvania University in Kentucky named Jefferson Davis.

In the frigid winter of 1824–25, during his third year at West Point, young Heintzelman began keeping a diary, a practice he would religiously continue for the next forty-seven years. With the thermometer well below zero, the Hudson River frozen solid, and the wind whipping the snow across the parade ground and around South Barracks in huge drifts, he quietly recorded the rigors of academic life at West Point. "We recited today in chemistry and did rather bad," Heintzelman wrote in early 1825. "Recited today in philosophy and did not do well by any means," he noted one day later. While studying Latin and Greek in Manheim, he had never heard of many of the subjects he would be exposed to at West Point, such as political economy, optics, pneumatics, dynamics, statics, hydrostatics, hydrodynamics, and hydraulics. Less than two weeks later, however, after being examined in natural philosophy, the young man boasted that he "did not miss a word. I did better than anyone in my section."[12]

Cadets found the annual examinations by the Board of Visitors particularly rigorous. Each was tested for an hour in each subject. For Heintzelman the 1826 examination of the Board of Visitors, with Sam Houston, a young congressman from Tennessee as president, was particularly memorable. Samuel Peter did not do well in mineralogy, which had been added to the curriculum in 1821, though he was fascinated by the subject and often found time to roam the rugged, forested hillsides around West Point and along the banks of the Hudson in search of rocks and minerals. "I took a walk today with several others along the bank of the river as far as Cornwall, about 4 miles from the Point, the scenery was sublime beyond description," he wrote.[13] For him climbing to a rock promontory called the "Crow's Nest" for a view of the academy and the Hudson River was always exhilarating.

Despite hours of dreary study and rote memorization of endless facts required in many of his classes, there was time for sketching, dancing, fencing, and, in the cold winter months, ice skating on a shallow hollow near South Barracks. There was also a pond behind the superintendent's quarters and one at Buttermilk Falls, just downriver. In the dead of winter, one could even skate on the Hudson River. The arduous life at West Point was sometimes broken by letters from brother Henry with news from Manheim. On other occasions Henry would send a copy of the *Manheim Free Press.* Infrequently, letters also arrived from sisters Juliana and Maria. During moments of leisure, the young cadet obtained the use of a telescope and frequently gazed at the moon. He was even more fascinated when, in the clear night sky, he was able to catch a glimpse of Jupiter and the red planet's three moons. In the fall and spring, cadets also gathered for an occasional game of what they called "foot-ball."[14]

Cadet Heintzelman took particular pride in being elected to the academy lyceum. He also played chess, practiced on a flute he purchased for four dollars, and began recording daily high and low temperatures in his journal, a habit he would continue with pleasure for the rest of his life.[15] He also joined other cadets in helping raise five thousand dollars for the erection at the academy of a statue of Gen. Thaddeus Kosciuszko, the Polish hero of the American Revolution who had designed the defenses at West Point and who had done much to advance the art of military engineering.

There was the constant fear of being dismissed from the academy. With a simmering nervousness rooted in intellectual insecurity that seemed to almost reach paranoia at times, Heintzelman watched as cadet after cadet was forced to leave. "Today 17 of the fourth class were informed that their services were no longer required at the Military Academy," he confided to his journal in January 1825. During his final year along the Hudson, he was rooming in South Barracks with Charles Landon Carter Minor and Hugh Weed Mercer, two cadets from Virginia, when a fire broke out in a nearby room. Although firemen quickly contained the blaze, Heintzelman's room was so badly damaged by water that he was forced to move into one down the hall with Martin Philip Parks and Francis Littleberry Dancy, two cadets from North Carolina.[16]

It was while Heintzelman was at West Point in October 1824 that tragic news arrived in a letter from Manheim. Samuel Peter's father was dead at the age of fifty-six. With both parents now gone, it was a crushing psychological blow to the young man. The rigors of academic life at West Point, however, allowed little time for self-pity and bereavement. In fact, it would be more than a year before he would be able to visit his father's grave in the Old Lutheran Burying Ground back in Manheim.

In late spring, early fall, or even during summer when not confined to camp, Heintzelman would flee to the nearby woods and hillsides and lounge under a tree to read Shakespeare. Although he often would lay his book aside to pick wild berries or gather grapes, Samuel Peter was a prolific reader who took great pride in owning books, many of which he would carry with him to distant and remote military posts on the far fringes of the American frontier, for the rest of his life.

There were more-formal pleasures at West Point as well. One of the biggest ceremonies came in the middle of summer camp on July 4, with patriotic speeches, a festive and colorful parade, followed by the cadets firing a thirteen-gun salute and assembling in the post chapel to hear a reading of the Declaration of Independence. There was also an abundance of patriotic toasts during which many of the cadets became "tipsy." A few of them, Samuel Peter disgustingly recorded on July 4, 1825, became so drunk that they could not stand erect, much less perform guard duty.[17]

In August 1825, the cadets assembled at the riverbank to greet and then pass in review for the Marquis de Lafayette, who had been invited by Pres. John Quincy Adams and the nation to tour the United States. The aging old general rode up the hill from the landing in an open carriage, after which a cadet battery fired a twenty-one-gun salute, and the young men paraded in full dress uniform. Refreshments were served at a reception, during which Lafayette presented the academy with one hundred books. Two months later the cadets assembled again, this time to greet the Duke of Saxe-Weimar, a "large, sorry looking chap," Heintzelman recorded, who, with a "whole parcel of German officers," arrived to visit classes, inspect the barracks, and review the curriculum.[18] A really festive ceremony came in late October 1825 with the completion of the Erie Canal, or what Heintzelman called the "Grand Canal." Cadets paraded and cheered as 24- and 18-pounder guns fired from both banks of the Hudson River.

In the summer the cadets headed into camp, where they lived in wall tents, drilled endlessly, and executed military tactics. In the heat and humidity and with no horses available, they seemed to sweat incessantly as they pulled artillery pieces from place to place. But summer camps could be dangerous. Once while preparing an artillery piece for firing, the gun went off prematurely, shattering the arm of one cadet. Another accidentally shot himself in the hand while attempting to fire his pistol. Cadets were formed into companies, with upperclassmen serving as officers. They would thus advance through the ranks much as in the Regular Army. Each morning and afternoon cadets were inspected in ranks under arms. But after the rigorous summer encampments, there were semiweekly dances or "balls," where all the "beauties of the land" were invited. "None of them were too handsome," young Heintzelman wrote of the girls in the summer of 1825.[19]

The young men were frequently arrested for leaving the academy at night for forays to Benny Havens' tavern in nearby Buttermilk Falls. The aspiring soldiers made the one-mile trek not only for drink but also for food. Cadets were also arrested for fighting, drunkenness, and the less serious offenses of playing cards and missing reveille. Even the studious Heintzelman was caught with cards and was known to occasionally miss reveille. But there were also more serious infractions. When a drunken cadet was caught stealing, he was ordered before a court-martial, given sixty days of solitary confinement, and drummed off the post to the tune of the "Rogue's March."

Anything Heintzelman did paled in comparison to what happened during Christmas, 1826. Many cadets resented the fact that Superintendent Thayer had issued orders banning the serving of liquor at any time, including the traditional Christmas and Fourth of July celebrations. As a result, several southern cadets, led by Jefferson Davis, circulated the news that they would explain "the mysteries of eggnog" on Christmas Eve. The intoxicating party started after midnight in North Barracks. Before long, drunken cadets were reeling from room to room, shouting and banging on doors. One fired his musket, and others soon drew swords. Pandemonium followed. Attempts to break up the party were met with defiance and violence. Seventy or more cadets, fully one-third of the corps, were implicated in the drunkenness and violence. Twenty-two were arrested, of whom nineteen were tried by court-martial and sentenced to be dismissed, though seven were later pardoned by Pres. John Quincy Adams.[20]

Through hard work and dedication, traits that would characterize his lengthy military career, Heintzelman graduated in May 1826, a respectable seventeenth in a class of forty-one. The top student, William H. C. Bartlett, would become one of the academy's most respected graduates and professor of natural and experimental philosophy (physical science) at West Point. As he pledged himself to duty, honor, and country, a bright military career seemed to loom on the horizon for the young soldier from Manheim. After hearing one last inspirational sermon from Chaplin Charles P. McIlvaine, Heintzelman filled his trunk with books and departed by steamer for New York City. With no money, he was forced to sell his pay accounts for five months (an accepted practice of going into debt by obligating funds) and, with ninety-seven dollars in his pocket, arrived in New York, where he immediately bought a ticket to the opera. Along with nine other recently graduated cadets and holding a four-month furlough, Heintzelman departed three days later by stagecoach for Philadelphia, where he took time to attend the theater and visit an aging uncle before going on by stage to Lancaster. After spending some time with Henry, who had found employment at a store in Lancaster, he excitedly hurried on to Manheim, where Maria joyously greeted him at the family home on South Main Street. Hearing that her brother had arrived in town, Juliana hurried over from Wrightsville for hugs and congratulations. Samuel Peter seemed gratified to learn that a number of neighbors were anxious to see him.[21] Observing him for the first time in four years, some residents of Manheim even remarked on the manner in which the young officer strutted about town.

In Manheim Heintzelman was disappointed upon discovering that no Independence Day celebration had been scheduled. He also wanted to travel to Lancaster for a memorial service in honor of John Adams and Thomas Jefferson, who had died within hours of one another on July 4, but he was too ill to do so. Instead he continued to read Shakespeare and even borrowed money from Maria for passage to New York City to see a performance of *Macbeth*.[22] Such was the beginning of a lifelong love of the theater and of the great English dramatist and poet.

Much of July was spent anxiously awaiting orders from army headquarters. Like most cadets, Heintzelman had hoped for a career in the prestigious Topographical Engineers. He knew, however, that such appointments were rare and only went to the brightest graduates. Nevertheless, while still at West Point he had approached Superintendent Thayer with the idea of obtaining a position in the engineers. Thayer was encouraging but asked young Heintzelman to await orders at Manheim. The young graduate was excited, though somewhat disappointed, when on August 2 the long-awaited orders arrived, announcing his commission as a second lieutenant and assigning him to the 3rd Infantry. Moreover, he was being sent west, half a continent away, to Belle Fontaine, Missouri, the first fort established by the United States west of the Mississippi River.

In October 1826 Lieutenant Heintzelman said goodbye to friends and relatives and made his way north by stage to Buffalo, New York, where he caught a Lake Erie steamer to Cleveland; then through Ohio by stage, past the rough frontier towns of Columbus and Cincinnati; and finally by steamer down the Ohio River and up the Mississippi River to St. Louis, Missouri. In St. Louis he found that Belle Fontaine, on the right bank of the Missouri River four miles above its mouth, was being abandoned and that he was being sent instead to Jefferson Barracks, south of St. Louis. After a "dull Christmas" at his new post, the young lieutenant was ordered farther west along the Missouri River to help garrison the newly established Fort Leavenworth. By the early fall of 1827, however, he was ordered to Fort Mackinac, on Mackinac Island in northern Michigan Territory. At St. Louis he booked passage on a steamboat up the Ohio River to Cincinnati, where he headed overland by stage to Detroit, then across Lake Huron to Michilimackinac and a cold and foreboding Fort Mackinac. At the fort, which guarded the strategic Straits of Mackinac between Lake Michigan and Lake Huron, the young lieutenant sat out the cold and snowy winter of 1827–28. Bored, lonesome, and somewhat depressed, he spent endless hours reading, taking singing lessons, and playing his flute. The following summer he was sent to Fort Gratiot near Detroit, at the entrance to the St. Clair River on Lake Huron. Shortly after arriving at his new station, Juliana wrote from Manheim to say that their younger brother, Henry had fallen seriously ill. A few days later Heintzelman briefly recorded the heart-wrenching news that his only brother was dead at the age of twenty: "I received a letter from Sister Juliana. Brother Henry died on 12 Nov. at Lewistown, Mifflin County, Penna. of consumption. I have answered sister's letter. He was much beloved."[23] Of the immediate family, only his two sisters remained.

Lieutenant Heintzelman spent a second frigid Michigan winter, this time gazing at the world through the frosted windows of the officer's quarters at Fort Gratiot. Although there was time for visits to Detroit, wolf hunting, and weekly church services, he complained again of loneliness and frequently brooded over his future in the military.[24] Observing the widespread drunkenness of the men at the fort, a chronic transgression that characterized life at the isolated military posts on the frontier, he continued to develop an intolerance for anyone who overindulged in alcohol, and though he drank moderately himself, his contempt for those who abused alcohol would only grow with the passage of time.

It was while stationed at Fort Gratiot on October 8, 1830, that a confrontation with a drunken private placed a blot on Heintzelman's otherwise spotless military career. Several enlisted men, who were habitually drunk, were in the habit of disobeying orders and challenging authority. While serving as officer of the day and with several citizens looking on, Heintzelman ordered one of the privates, Thomas Ablett, whom he charged with mutinous conduct, placed in irons and confined to the guardhouse. When the private, recalcitrant and unruly, continued his verbal abuse, Heintzelman grabbed a board and struck Ablett over the head several times, knocking him senseless.

Lieutenant Heintzelman's general court-martial convened at Fort Hamilton, a blockhouse post along the Pecatonica River just north of the Illinois-Wisconsin border, on June 17, 1831. Presiding over the court was Brig. Gen. Hugh Brady, a seasoned veteran of the 2nd Infantry. No sooner had the trial convened than alarming news arrived that several hundred Sac and Fox Indians, who had been pushed onto the prairies west of the Mississippi River, were on the attack. In particular, a party of Sac warriors under Chief Black Hawk, known as the "British Band" because they had served with the British during the War of 1812, had crossed the Mississippi River and were burning settlers' houses. The frontier was in panic, and the army was on the march. Soldiers from Fort Hamilton were being rushed to Fort Winnebago to replace those sent in pursuit of Black Hawk and his warriors. Departing with the Fort Hamilton garrison was General Brady as well as other members of the court, primarily aging veterans of the War of 1812, most of whom were senior artillery officers. When Capt. William Hoffman of the 6th Infantry was selected to replace Brady, Brig. Gen. John Roger Fenwick was designated as the new presiding officer. The trial was also moved to Fort Gratiot, where witnesses would be more readily available.[25]

When proceedings began on July 3, 1831, the charges were read, after which the prosecution called several witnesses, including Capt. Waddy Vine Cobbs, Asst. Surgeon Henry A. Stenecke, and two corporals, all of the 2nd Infantry. The four men recalled how they had seen Heintzelman, in anger, strike Ablett on the head with the board. They all admitted under cross-examination, however, that the private was drunk at the time and that he was not only resisting arrest but also making "much riotous noise" as well as "violent gestures" with "his fists clinched." "Don't strike me! If you do, you shall never strike another man," Cobbs recalled Ablett telling Heintzelman. Moreover, the soldier had not been seriously injured. In fact, there was "only a little blood from a slight scratch on the forehead." Although no witnesses were called in his defense, Heintzelman did deliver a dramatic summation. "It is with sorrow," he told the court, that "I find myself arraigned . . . , charged with violations of the laws." He admitted that the accusations were "grave and serious" and that he did strike Ablett after the private had been restrained, but the blows were struck "under great provocation" after "every means had failed to check the boisterous and mutinous clamor and conduct of the aggrieved individual." In conclusion, the lieutenant told the court that he would "cheerfully submit to any censure . . . trusting that it will not be beyond the measure of my offense." Within a few minutes and with little hesitation, the court-martial found Heintzelman guilty of striking Private Ablett but concluded that he had not done so "repeatedly." Because of the "peculiar circumstances of the case," Heintzelman was ordered to "be privately admonished by the commanding general of the department."[26] On July 3, after a trial that lasted less than a day, the court adjourned *sine die* to prepare for Independence Day ceremonies. Two weeks later Lieutenant Heintzelman was restored to duty.

In the late summer of 1828, Heintzelman obtained a leave to visit what remained of his family in the East. He scurried across Lake Erie to Buffalo by steamer, then on to Rochester, Albany, West Point, and down the Hudson River to New York City. Next he went to Philadelphia to visit a cousin before going on to Washington for a tour of the city. By late September he was back in New York at army headquarters, where he urged Gen. Winfield Scott to extend his leave by six months, a common practice at the time. Scott agreed to the additional leave, but not before he had given the young lieutenant a stern lecture on his behavior at Fort Gratiot. An "officer must control his temper," the general sternly warned. It was a verbal reprimand Heintzelman would long remember, one that would serve him well at numerous military posts in the American West. From New York the lieutenant steamed up the Hudson River to spend his twenty-sixth birthday, and a homecoming of sorts, at West Point. With winter approaching, he hurried back to New York and Philadelphia, then west through the fall landscape to Lancaster and Manheim, where he made a pilgrimage to the Old Lutheran Burial Ground, visited briefly with Rep. James Buchanan, socialized with relatives, and began an investigation into how his father's land in Manheim had somehow wound up in the hands of an uncle. After a "dull" and snowy Christmas with sisters Maria and Juliana at Lewistown, in the rugged foothills of the Allegheny Mountains northwest of Harrisburg, he was back in Washington by early January 1829 for art exhibits at the capitol and *William Tell* at the theater. Becoming "heartily tired of Washington," the young officer traveled south to Norfolk and Richmond for a few days. Although fearing that he had contracted cholera while visiting a hospital, he soon returned to Washington to see the great Shakespearean actor Edwin Booth in *Iron Chest* and fraternize with fellow officers.[27] He also purchased a thermometer for twenty dollars so he could record daily temperatures.

Early in 1829 Heintzelman learned that he had been assigned temporarily to the Topographical Engineers and was to report as soon as possible to Col. Stephen Long at Philadelphia. Traveling partly by horse-drawn cars on what travelers were calling a "rail road," by early September 1832 he reported to Long at Philadelphia, where he would remain for almost a year working to complete a survey of the Tennessee River and other Trans-Appalachian waterways. The young lieutenant learned much from Long, a seasoned explorer and man of science who had led an epic expedition across the Great Plains to the Rocky Mountains in 1819–20. In Philadelphia Heintzelman also found time for horticulture exhibits, tours of the Geological Society, and weekly visits to the theater to see *Cinderella, Lion of the West, Romeo and Juliet, Little Red Riding Hood, Alexander the Great*, and *The Hypocrite*. There were also weekly flute lessons from a man named Cuddy, the "best flute player in the country," and a visit to a local flute factory. With future trailblazer Lt. Lorenzo Sitgraves he went to the Academy of Fine Arts to see David's *Napoleon Crossing the Alps*. On Sunday he regularly attended religious services at the Lutheran, Catholic, Unitarian, or Presbyterian church or at the Quaker Meeting House. There was also time for the Italian opera, lectures on meteorology, astronomy, discussions on the origins of the earth, and a ghoulish recitation in which the skull of a mail robber, who had been hanged the previous year, was on display. Heintzelman became skilled at chess and went out of his way to challenge anyone interested in the game. Caught up in the political fervor of the times, he attended a large rally of Jacksonian Democrats and carefully scrutinized Andrew Jackson's written response to South Carolina's threat of nullification.[28]

By March 1832 he was able to visit sisters Maria and Juliana back in Manheim, again making a short pilgrimage to the Old Lutheran Burial Ground. With Maria's assistance he spent two days (much to the biographer's trepidation) burning family papers, some of which dated back to the eighteenth century. While there he attended services in German at the local Lutheran church. Although he had learned German as a child, he had lost command of the language while attending West Point and had difficulty in understanding the sermon.[29] Although rudimentary, his knowledge of German would serve him well in a frontier army that was partly composed of German immigrants with little knowledge of English.

By late March 1832 he was back in Philadelphia for the theater, a "silent meeting" at the Friends' Meeting House, a lecture at the Academy of Natural Sciences, an art exhibit at the Masonic Hall, and a ride on the new Germantown Railroad. In early July he steamed up the Hudson River for a brief visit to West Point before going on to Saratoga Springs to see the *Merchant of Venice*, eventually making his way west to Buffalo and a carriage ride to that sublime watery spectacle, Niagara Falls.[30]

By the late summer of 1833, Lieutenant Heintzelman was back at Fort Gratiot to begin a survey of Lake Huron. Most of the winter would be spent, however, in completing a report on the previous summer's work. Confined to the fort in the frigid weather, Heintzelman practiced on his flute and continued his French lessons. By the summer of 1834, he was back at Michilimackinac and then on to Fort Brady at Sault Ste. Marie.

With a cholera epidemic raging in Detroit, he remained isolated at the fort, where he complained that his only companions were drunken Frenchmen, "half-breeds," and Indians. All that seemed to excite his imagination was an Indian "pipe dance" and the "brilliant" Aurora Borealis.[31]

Frigid and uneventful winter evenings were spent playing euchre (a card game involving two, three, or four persons) and reading books on the American West. Heintzelman regularly attended temperance meetings and listened attentively to the stormy debates that followed. He was also learning to play the violin. As was becoming his custom, he used the last day of the year for personal retrospection in his journal: "I am pretty much [in] the same situation as last," he wrote on December 31, 1834. In the new year, though, he promised to "gain more knowledge—book knowledge." Fort Brady, he concluded, was "one of the least desirable in the army." Civilians living near the post were "not the most refined," and the fort was often "full of squaws." On January 2, 1835, while keeping meteorological data for the American Philosophical Society and the Franklin Institute, he noted that it was minus 23 degrees Fahrenheit and that the river was frozen solid.[32] Good news came during the traditional Jackson dinner on January 8, 1835, however, when he learned that he had been promoted to first lieutenant.

After exploring and mapping Goulais Bay on the Ontario side of Lake Superior in March 1835, Heintzelman moved across the lake to spend several months surveying the Michigan side. On leave by late summer, he headed east by way of Green Bay, Chicago, Detroit, and Montreal to Philadelphia, where he stopped to attend a horticulture exhibit and spend a depressingly dull thirtieth birthday all alone, "sick and not an individual in the city but myself knows that it is my birthday."[33]

By November 1835 a war with the Creeks had erupted in Georgia and Florida, and the young officer was ordered south as an assistant quartermaster. After passing through Washington, Norfolk, and Charleston, he was at the St. Francis Barracks at St. Augustine by early December. Although dolphins at play in the warm waters of the Atlantic offered a striking contrast to the ice and cold of Sault Ste. Marie, Heintzelman remained ill a large part of the time.[34]

In April 1836 he was sent up the coast to Darien, Georgia, to assist with equipping the poorly trained and badly disorganized Georgia Militia. Adapting himself to the southern way of life, Heintzelman agreed to serve as a second in a duel, but when the confrontation failed to materialize, he instead attended a lecture on the subject of "colored people" and later visited nearby St. Simons Island, where seven hundred slaves labored mercilessly on a large rice plantation. Not particularly critical of the "peculiar institution," he seemed to admire the plantation's overseer, who was an "admirable manager" and had experienced "no runaways."[35]

By early June 1836 he was at Hawkinsville in south-central Georgia, where the state militia were continuing to rendezvous. Here he gained another glimpse of slavery when he observed "a negro trader . . . half drunk trying to sell half a dozen young negroes, not more than six or seven years old." They "looked as indifferent as cattle, when their good and bad qualities were detailed," he noted.[36] The Pennsylvanian's views on slavery were evolving rapidly.

Still complaining of illness, he spent the remainder of 1836 and much of 1837 at Columbus, Georgia, and at Chattahoochee and Apalachicola, Florida. During most of 1838–39 he was at Tallahassee, but by late 1840 he had moved to St. Marks, at the head of Apalachee Bay, to investigate claims filed by the Florida Militia for forage, food, and transportation. One of the few consolations of his lengthy service in the Southeast was being promoted to captain in November 1838. By the summer of 1841 Heintzelman was ordered back to Tallahassee and then to St. Augustine again. During the summer of 1841, eighteen hundred dollars was stolen from a safe in the quartermaster's office by an undisclosed thief, a loss for which the captain was held responsible.[37] Reimbursing the army for the lost funds, which would take several years, proved to be a serious strain on the meager finances of a young officer.

Although "a little older and perhaps a little wiser . . . , I do not see that my condition has changed much," Heintzelman dejectedly wrote on New Years' Day, 1842. "Still the struggle is for happiness and it is not to be found. Here I am in a miserable village [and a] dirty noisey [*sic*] tavern. Scarce a soul with whom to hold the least communion. The world will still go on and I hope for better times, even should I die in despair. I do not think Florida will see me another year."[38]

While there were occasional horse races; a few old newspapers to read, chess, dominoes, backgammon, euchre; and a German lesson now and then, the captain was bored with an endless pile of militia claims and Florida in general.[39] After fifteen years in the army, all he had managed to acquire in personal wealth were assets of six hundred dollars in books, paintings, and engravings; a small piece of property he had purchased in Niles, Michigan; and a sixty-dollar interest in a house and lot in Tallahassee. More and more he thought of applying for a year's leave of absence to visit Europe. Although considering marriage, Heintzelman concluded that the uncivilized Florida backwoods was not the best place to find a bride. At a "Cracker Ball" he found none of the women "pretty or very interesting." There was one southern belle, however, a Miss Veatch, with whom he became infatuated. Later, while passing through Georgia on his way to Washington, he shared a railroad seat with her and admitted being "sad at the thought of losing her" and being hurt when she failed to return his advances, instead expressing a desire to correspond with another officer and passenger, Maj. Charles Mapes. Jilted, Heintzelman was unable to sleep for days. "I can hardly believe we will never meet again," he confessed.[40]

Florida and Miss Veatch gradually faded from the captain's mind after his assignment to Washington, for in the capital was an exhibit by a passionate and aspiring Pennsylvania-born artist named George Catlin. Heintzelman's imagination of the West came alive through Catlin's work as he gawked at portraits of Pawnee, Kaw, Blackfoot, Mandan, and Lakota Sioux chiefs; the colorful paintings of their rituals; and the seemingly endless expanses of the Great Plains. The exhibit also included buffalo robes, colorful buckskins, war clubs, peace pipes, and various other artifacts of a proud culture. Heintzelman also enjoyed a visit to the Capitol to see the statue of George Washington and a short trip down the Potomac River to Mount Vernon, where he collected a "sprig" from a tree near Washington's tomb. Meeting a cousin of the first president, he was ushered through the mansion and even shown the keys to the Bastille, once presented to Washington by the Marquis de Lafayette. Although everything at Mount Vernon was "neglected and going to decay," General Washington and the patriots of the American Revolution were the captain's heroes, and in his eyes they would always remain larger than life.[41]

Although continuing to compile claims by the Florida Militia, he was able to visit the Executive Mansion, or what would later be called the White House, where he had a conversation with an unimpressive John Tyler, the black sheep of the Whig Party. Later at the National Institute he listened to speeches by President Tyler; Joel Poinsett, the embattled first American minister to Mexico; and John S. Preston, a leading South Carolina states' rights Democrat. At the theater Edwin Booth "overdid his part" in *Richard III*.[42]

By late July 1842 Heintzelman was ordered to Racine, Wisconsin Territory, on court-martial duty. On his way west he managed a short visit with Juliana and her merchant-husband at Wrightsville in York County, Pennsylvania, before continuing on by way of Wheeling, Virginia, to Circleville, Ohio, where he visited his two other sisters. Maria, though contemplating marriage, remained single and was living alone in a rented house. Elizabeth had wed a watchmaker-turned-farmer named Haller, and the two were busy raising six children, four boys and two girls, on a small farm near Circleville. Through the years the army officer would express a growing intolerance of Haller, not only because of the family's poverty and squalor but also because of his brother-in-law's stubborn reluctance to educate his children.[43]

Continuing north and west by stage, he stopped in Columbus to see the noted Braham singers at a local dingy theater. "The wife is, I think, without exception the largest and fattest woman I ever saw. Her bosom sticks out a 'foot,'" he chauvinistically remarked with little inhibition. By steamboat past Cleveland, he reached Detroit and a familiar Fort Mackinac a few days later. In late summer it was on to Milwaukee and Racine. With the court-martial adjourning after only a few hours, Heintzelman went to the office of the Topographical Engineers to gaze at Jupiter and Saturn through a telescope. Later in Chicago there was the theater and in Detroit, an engaging lecture on "animal magnetism."[44]

Back in Circleville, Ohio, he convinced Maria that she should accept a marriage proposal from a respectable older gentleman in the village, and after a long conversation with the prospective groom, a Colonel Keffer, they made plans for a simple ceremony the coming Sunday. Maria's savings, they agreed, would go to support the Haller children. Finally, on the evening of August 28, 1842, Samuel Peter stood by as Maria, "calm and collected," was married at the local Episcopal church. After the hastily arranged ceremony, he watched in amazement as the bride retired for the evening to sleep with her sister, Juliana, while the groom, "confused and awkward," retired alone.[45] The next day Samuel Peter and Juliana, along with the oldest of the Haller children, who would be going to school in Wrightsville, Pennsylvania, departed by stage for points east.

Back in Washington Heintzelman received orders sending him to Buffalo, where he was to assume command of Company D, 3rd Infantry and resume his duties as assistant quartermaster. But first there was time for a short visit to Boston, where every sight brought "a thousand recollections of the Revolution." He walked to historic Faneuil Hall and ascended the Bunker Hill Monument, "a most conspicuous object," by "steam to the top." He visited Harvard College in nearby Cambridge and saw the tree "under which Washington assumed command" of the Continental Army in 1775. At Roxbury Continental artillery entrenchments still scarred the earth. At Lowell he toured factories "full of girls," some of whom were "very pretty and neatly dressed." There was also the theater and afterward a visit to see the "night owl."[46]

After a short stay in Washington the captain headed northwest for a nostalgic visit to Manheim, where little remained of the Heintzelman orchard, though the old family home still stood on Main Street. Friends pointed out where he and his brother, Henry, had carved their names on a tree twenty-two years earlier. By November he was back in Washington for a short stay before traveling to Klingerstown, Pennsylvania, to visit an aging uncle, whom he quizzed into the night about his family's German ancestry. Back in Washington there were the usual socials and an outing to Capitol Hill to hear President Tyler's annual message to Congress. At the theater James H. Hackett, probably the finest Shakespearean comedian of his day, portrayed Falstaff in the *Merry Wives of Windsor.* Lectures on Shakespeare and Lord Byron also proved interesting, as did a visit to see "Professor Morse's Electro Magnetic Telegraph." Heintzelman also began reading J. G. Bennett's *Mormonism Exposed* and, sharing the prejudices of the day, became convinced that "such a vile sect never before existed on the face of the earth." Face to face with Mormons in Arizona and California a decade later, he would radically alter his views. At the Executive Mansion on Christmas Eve, 1842, he found the tall, skinny, sharp-featured President Tyler to be "quite affable." Yet Christmas Day was the "dullest" Heintzelman had "spent for many a year."[47]

In early January 1843 he was among the standing-room-only crowd at the Unitarian church that heard Lucretia Mott speak "well and distinctly" on "abolition, ill treatment of Indians," and the "rights of women." In the throng he noticed an imposing and stately Gen. Winfield Scott—"his head towering above all." There was also an exciting speech on the "Oregon Question," a "charity sermon for orphans" at the Presbyterian church, and later an interesting lecture on "Luther and the Reformation."[48] Admitting he was living beyond his means, Heintzelman continued to attend parties, usually at the homes of superior officers.

In April 1843 he was on a steamer for Philadelphia on his way to Buffalo when he spotted Secretary of State Daniel Webster. After stopping in New York for the theater, Heintzelman caught a second steamer for Albany, stopped to see the state prison at Auburn and the falls at Rochester, then continued across a snowy landscape to Buffalo, where he reported for duty on the nineteenth. Socially and culturally, Buffalo proved to be more exciting than Washington. Heintzelman rode out to see Niagara Falls again. He also attended the theater several times a week, seeing Edwin Forrest, the first great tragedian of the American stage, in *Damon and Pythias*, *The Gladiator*, and *Richelieu.* At the Presbyterian church a seventy-year-old Polish colonel and aide to Marshal Ney at Waterloo lectured on "Napoleon and Josephine." Ex-president John Quincy Adams, elegant and intellectual, arrived, to be followed by a large "rabble," for a speech in the park. With a shrill voice and his hands shaking with age, Adams was well received by the hundreds of Whigs and abolitionists in the crowd. He was introduced by a local Whig congressman, attorney, and soon-to-be president of the United States, Millard Fillmore, who expressed a desire to see Adams back in Congress. In Buffalo the young captain also purchased a horse from Fillmore for $125. During two weeks in August, he visited Rochester; Fort Ontario at Oswego; the falls of the Genesee River; the site of the Battle of York, where the famous western explorer Gen. Zebulon Montgomery Pike had been killed; and Sackets Harbor and Fort Henry near Kingston, Ontario, where he walked along the ramparts and sketched the fort in his journal. Back at Buffalo he stood in a crowd of some three thousand at an Anti-Slavery Society rally to hear Henry Highland Garnet, an escaped slave from the eastern shore of Maryland, deliver an abolitionist speech. Unimpressed, the captain remarked that the meeting was little "better than a farce" and that Garnet and others "spoke treason."[49]

"Things get along with me in the old way," he wrote on his thirty-eighth birthday in 1843. "If I ever intend to marry it is now." A slender and petite Albany socialite named Margaret Stuart had caught his eye. Margaret, along with her sisters Caroline and Elizabeth were staying with a married sister in Buffalo, Mary Stuart Norton, in fashionable Park Place. In his journal Heintzelman noted seeing "Miss Margaret," who was "quite handsome," and how the two had spent a "couple of hours . . . very agreeably." A week later they played euchre until midnight, and by December they shared sleigh rides in the Buffalo snow and wintry walks through the streets and parks of the city. With a touch of jealousy, Heintzelman remarked that he had "scarcely ever been to see Misses Stewart [Stuart] without meeting gentlemen there." After walking home with Margaret and Caroline from the Unitarian church on New Years' Eve, 1843, he complained of their "impolite habit of going off with gentlemen to one side, pairing themselves."[50] In particular, Margaret had retired to the library with a young topographical engineer named James W. Abert. Yet the next day Heintzelman spent the "evening agreeably" with Margaret and Caroline at the Stuart home at 31 Park Place.

In early February 1844, upon learning that the Stuart sisters were scheduled to return to Albany, he wrote of being saddened to "have them leave," for they were "the most pleasant family . . . in Buffalo." But the women remained, and Heintzelman enjoyed parties three and four times a week, more sleighing, sermons at the Unitarian church, a masked ball at which he wore his coat inside out, German songs at the theater, a concert by a Spanish guitarist, and as usual, euchre. In the spring the sleighing gave way to buggy rides, walks through the public parks and gardens, and quiet evenings at the barracks. In June 1844, with the arrival of Margaret's mother (also named Margaret) from Albany, rumors circulated that the couple were to be married. Despite his obvious affection for Margaret, Heintzelman remained hesitant and insecure. "I have been so out of heart a dozen times," he wrote, "I have resolved to give her up, then next time I saw her my resolutions were all scattered to the winds. . . . I will persevere."[51]

On July 4, 1844, the couple attended the traditional salute at the garrison and a dance in the evening. Two days later Heintzelman escorted Margaret to the theater to hear Edwin Forrest "rant as usual" in *Othello.* Later, however, he met the thirty-eight-year-old actor and took pride in escorting him about Buffalo. Nevertheless, his every thought was on Margaret Stuart, and in October 1844, following an incident in which she took the arm of another officer during a "beautiful moonlight night," Heintzelman was seized by a fit of jealousy and at last mustered the courage to propose: "I saw Miss Margaret . . . and offered myself and after proper maidenly reflection was accepted. I have to ask her mother, but have no doubt she will give her consent." Even after Mrs. Stuart had assented and a wedding date had been set, the shy captain remained apprehensive and nervous about marriage to the pampered Albany socialite. "I do not like so many persons as they intend inviting," he complained. "I believe I would not be married at all rather than marry at a large party."[52]

On December 5, 1844, with the Stuart family and a number of Buffalo's leading citizens in attendance, Margaret Stuart and Samuel Peter Heintzelman were married. He was thirty-eight; she was twenty-five. Departing on the train immediately afterward, the couple spent their wedding night in Syracuse before going on to Albany, where Margaret introduced her officer-husband to several old schoolmates. From Albany the newlyweds steamed down the Hudson River past West Point to New York City for a "delightful" three-month honeymoon. They took long walks in the snow, visited the theater, and attended gala dinners, including one hosted by Lt. Col. Bennet Riley, Heintzelman's regimental commander. While they were in New York, and after Margaret had been ill for two days, she confessed to a serious affliction she had suffered since childhood that sometimes incapacitated her for days.[53] Her confession did little to thwart her husband's love, which would only grow with the passage of time.

The couple departed New York on March 12, 1845, for Boston, where they toured the State House on Boston Common and Faneuil Hall and took a carriage ride in the snow to the top of Bunker Hill. By early May they were back in Buffalo, where life at the garrison carried them into early summer. There Heintzelman purchased fifty shares in the Ontonoga Mining Company.[54] Always the aspiring entrepreneur, mining would dominate a large part of his life, and dreams of getting rich would send him into the far reaches of the Desert Southwest thirteen years later.

TWO

To the Halls of Montezuma

In early summer 1845 the Buffalo press reported that the Republic of Texas' impending annexation to the United States was quickly coming to a head. Little did Capt. Samuel Peter Heintzelman know then that these events were to profoundly change his life. In mid-September, confessing that they would miss their servants, the captain, Margaret, and Margaret's sister Caroline departed Buffalo for Fort Gratiot, Michigan, where Heintzelman was to continue as assistant quartermaster and company commander. From the Detroit newspapers he learned that Mexico had declared war on the United States, though this had been expected for some time and did not create "much excitement." The war, he came to realize, meant his certain transfer, though exactly to where he did not know. To complicate matters, Margaret was pregnant and unlikely to accompany him, but he did not want her to return to Buffalo, confessing, "I want to get her away from her family and teach her to depend upon herself." Later he was pleased to learn that he was being ordered to Detroit. Although the post was a "miserable place," Margaret was able to go along. The couple rented a comfortable house in town, and it was there that their first child was born on December 29, 1845. "Yesterday at 20 minutes past 4, I was made a father," the captain recorded. "Margaret has a son. He is a fine hearty child and weighs 8½ pounds. Both are doing well."[1] Named Charles Stuart, he would share many of his father's adventures in the West, graduate from West Point in 1867, and serve with dedication and honor in the U.S. Army.

Even more exciting news arrived from Texas in early May 1846. On April 24 a company of U.S. dragoons had been surrounded and either killed or captured by the Mexican Army not far from the banks of the Rio Grande. When the United States declared war three weeks later, there was "great excitement throughout the country," Heintzelman recorded.[2] Receiving orders to report to Louisville, Kentucky, he was certain that he was to be part of an expedition sent across the Great Plains on the Santa Fe Trail to far-off New Mexico.

Leaving Margaret and their newborn son in Detroit, Captain Heintzelman arrived in Louisville to find the town a beehive of excitement and activity. A local factory was turning out twenty army tents a day, and agents scurried about contracting steamboats to carry men and supplies on the Gulf of Mexico and the distant Rio Grande. Indiana, Ohio, and Kentucky volunteers were arriving daily, and recruiting officers hurried east to enlist even more men. During one incident there, the captain stood by as a band of drunken recruits and town gamblers fought a bloody duel with Bowie knives. Two weeks later, following a confrontation with local ruffians at a "brandy house" in which several prostitutes shot and wounded four bluecoats, sixty other recruits arrived, tore a hole in the side of the building, and rushed inside, where they ripped up the floor, tore the roof off the house, pushed over a chimney in which a "bully" had taken refuge, broke all the windows, and cut up the women's dresses and beds. More-sobering realities of war came when the badly wounded from the opening contests of the war along the Rio Grande at Palo Alto and Resaca de la Palma began to arrive on steamboats from New Orleans and Texas.[3]

Continuing as assistant quartermaster, Heintzelman spent most of his time procuring horses, mules, and wagons as well as corn, hay, and oats from the Kentucky countryside. He also made arrangements for the manufacture of wagons at the state penitentiary. In so doing he visited a number of small villages and towns, where he found the uncivilized and crude personal habits of the Kentucky backwoodsmen anything but alluring. There "every man uses his knife in every dish. They put the butter knife to one side and use their own . . . the only way is to help yourself to as much of everything you want at once," he complained.[4]

In Louisville he also watched a "number of negroes, very well dressed, lounging about." He wondered what they could be doing until he saw a sign: "A Garrison . . . Negro trader." Heintzelman admitted that he "never realized the odious trafic [*sic*] as I did when I saw that sign."[5] He was slowly but surely becoming more sensitive to the horrors of the "peculiar institution."

In September 1846 word arrived by courier from the Desert Southwest that Gen. Stephen Watts Kearny, without a shot being fired, had taken Santa Fe. On the Pacific Coast the Bear Flag Revolt had put most of California under American control. Yet despite a war that was gradually engulfing his life, Heintzelman's days in Louisville were pleasant. "I am a quiet, sedate, married man, the head of a family. . . . It is called the prime of life," he caustically recorded on his forty-first birthday.[6]

Just as hundreds of gamblers were arriving in Louisville for the annual horse races in early October 1846, the captain was ordered to accompany a small fleet of steamboats to New Orleans. Pleasant autumn days were spent reading *History of the French Revolution* as he steamed down the Ohio and Mississippi rivers toward the gulf. On the wharf at Vicksburg, in an incident that would be vividly etched in his mind for years, Heintzelman watched silently as a slave was brutally beaten with a riding whip. Passing Natchez in the night, he arrived at New Orleans two days later and, after the steamboats were turned over to the army, received orders sending him to Washington.[7]

On a "dirty disagreeable boat" Heintzelman steamed back up the Mississippi past Baton Rouge and Natchez and into the Ohio River to Louisville and Cincinnati. By stage through the night, then on a train with a group of zealous Quakers, and finally across Lake Erie on the vessel *Great Western*, he arrived in Detroit on November 21 to find Margaret buoyant and Charles bright-eyed and healthy. Within days he headed on through the rapidly changing late fall landscape to Washington, where he arrived in time to see the bullet-riddled battle flag of the Tampico Battalion triumphantly displayed at the Adjutant General's Office. After less than two weeks in the capital, he scurried west again by train and stage, past the picture-book village of Harpers Ferry to Wheeling, Virginia, and down the Ohio River to Guyanadotte, where several volunteer companies were preparing to depart for Mexico. Reflecting on the war, he commented: "No one to thank but Mr. Polk and the anexation [*sic*] of Texas. It has changed the fate of many and will that of many more." Later, after studying Polk's "Declaration of War," however, he reconsidered: "I begin to think we are not so much in the wrong as I once believed."[8]

In mid-December 1846 Heintzelman briefly visited Circleville, Ohio, where he found Maria in good health but her husband, Colonel Keffer, looking old and tired. Riding out to see Elizabeth and her ever-increasing family at the Haller farm, he found them getting along "in the worst possible manner." Haller would "always be a poor shiftless fellow and live from hand to mouth," he concluded. When Haller refused to allow his eldest son, William, to return to live with Juliana near Philadelphia, where he could continue his education, Heintzelman was furious; "I am provoked every time I think of him."[9]

Back in Guyandotte, while waiting for orders he was sure would take him to war, the captain purchased two books on Mexico and began studying Spanish. At the worst tavern he had "been in for many a day," a "perfect barn" frequented only by rowdy and ignorant drunks, he spent a boring and uneventful Christmas, 1846, and an equally mundane New Year's Day, 1847. Continuing to study Spanish, he arrived in Washington just in time to receive orders sending him to Hamburg, South Carolina. Days later he entered the "Kingdom of South Carolina where all the passengers are required to give their birthplace, ages, and occupations." Such was evidence, he concluded, that "the nullifiers are afraid of the abolitionists."[10]

Although it was not his first sojourn into the South, Heintzelman was becoming increasingly critical of the region's most infamous institution. At a large slave market in Hamburg, he watched as "30 boys from 8 to 18 years of age" were "marching about on the common for exercise" as well as "some girls—all young and numbering about 100." A few days later, after returning from Augusta, where the citizens had refused to "allow a slave market," he saw another "specimen of this southern domestic institution, a gang of seventy slaves, men, women, and children, marching in twos across the bridge," all destined for the New Orleans slave market. "I felt sorry for them," he confided. A week later he watched as two "negro traders" ordered forty women and children about "in a very brutal manner." The following month he saw another forty slaves marching through the town in chains, "miserable wretches, carrying their bedding and with blankets under their arms."[11]

Continuing to assist in equipping the badly disorganized volunteers, many of them drunk and disorderly, the captain remained in Hamburg until late January 1847. Riding west past Griffin, Georgia, in the rain and over bad roads to Tuskegee and Natasulga, Alabama, he arrived at Mobile in early February to hear the news of more American victories in Mexico. Moreover, the 2nd Infantry under Gen. David Twiggs had seized the port of Tampico. Taking a "miserable route for a sick man" back across Georgia and up the Atlantic coast, Heintzelman was back in Washington by mid-February 1847.[12]

Walking down Pennsylvania Avenue to the Capitol, he gawked at Benjamin Wier's *Departure of the Pilgrims from Holland* and the *Landing of Columbus*. In the Senate he listened as some of the great men of the era stood to debate the pivotal issues influencing the nation. John C. Calhoun of South Carolina "growled" at a northern senator who was ridiculing "southern chivalry." Daniel Webster's words "were not much but the manner was most decided."[13] Compared to the Senate, the House of Representatives was a "scene of confusion." Overshadowing Washington's rough politics was always the news from Mexico. Apprehensive and attentive crowds, many of them illiterate, gathered daily on street corners to listen to the latest news read from the city's newspapers. Gen. Zachary Taylor had won a great victory at Buena Vista in the arid mountains southwest of Saltillo, Mexico, they learned, and by early April 1847 Gen. Winfield Scott was ashore at Vera Cruz and pushing inland toward Mexico City.

Sent to Worcester, Massachusetts, on recruiting duty, Heintzelman found the town to be "a great anti-slavery, anti-war, anti-everything" place, and after several days he was able to recruit only a single Irishman. After touring Samuel Colt's new arms factory near New Haven, Connecticut, in anticipation of procuring one of the new revolvers, which were revolutionizing warfare, the captain and Colt sat down over "wine and liquor" at a local hotel until 4 A.M., by which time Colt became quite intoxicated.[14] It was the beginning of a long, yet strained, relationship between the two men. Still at Worcester on the first anniversary of the Battle of Palo Alto, Heintzelman read that General Scott had defeated a large Mexican Army under Gen. Antonio Lopez de Santa Anna at Cerro Gordo along the road to Mexico City and was continuing to push through the mountains toward the Mexican capital.

Dispatched to Syracuse, New York, Heintzelman hurried across the snowy Berkshires to the Hudson River at Albany and through the Mohawk Valley to Buffalo, where in late May 1847 he was reunited with Margaret and Charles. Full of mischief and giggles, Charles was walking for the first time. Able to enlist only eight recruits at both Utica and Syracuse, the captain was back in Buffalo when word arrived that General Scott, after a series of bloody battles at Contreras, Churubusco, Molina del Rey, and Chapultepec, had taken Mexico City.[15]

Heintzelman was still in Buffalo on July 26, 1847, when Solon Lathrop, a Buffalo businessman and a friend, wed Margaret's younger sister, Elizabeth. After cake and wine, the newlyweds departed for their honeymoon at Niagara Falls.[16] Two hours later Samuel Peter said goodbye to Margaret and one-year-old Charles and left for war. Three days later in New York City, he was finally able to purchase one of Colt's six-shooters, then, on the afternoon of August 4, along with three hundred recruits of the 2nd Infantry, he sailed for Mexico. Two weeks after leaving New York, with many of the officers and men now seasick, he spotted the green-tinted Sierra Madre on Cuba's eastern shore as the ship slipped into the tropics. With the temperature well over 100 degrees, the Pennsylvanian spent most of his time on deck, reading books on military tactics and trying to learn Spanish. On September 6, 1847, after a "long and tedious voyage," two towering Mexican peaks, the cloud-shrouded El Cofre de Perote and the snow-capped 18,640-foot summit of Pico de Orizaba, appeared through the mist on the distant horizon. Landing at Vera Cruz, the captain managed a quick visit to the city and the historic fortress of San Juan de Ulloa before setting out with four companies of the 2nd Infantry along the National Road for Jalapa and Mexico City. The first night after moving inland, at the village of San Juan, he was met by a company of mounted Louisiana Volunteers escorting an empty wagon train to the coast. Six days later, five miles from the National Bridge and halfway to Jalapa, the column went into camp at another small village, El Paso de Ovejas. At 2 A.M. on September 14, just as Heintzelman had retired to his tent for the evening, a band of 180 guerillas led by a local priest and concealed in a graveyard on a nearby hill fired into the camp. While running from his tent barefoot in the darkness, he stumbled over a tent peg and badly sprained his ankle. Although the sniping continued intermittently through the night, only one American was killed and another wounded in the attack, which was, he speculated, in retaliation for the army having plundered and burned several nearby ranches.[17] Not far from the National Bridge the next day, two American soldiers were found dead, their decomposed bodies stripped and mutilated.[18]

In the stifling heat of the Tierra Caliente near Plan del Rio, with the young recruits near exhaustion, the column caught up with a larger force commanded by Gen. James H. Lane in search of guerrillas. A young Maryland volunteer recalled that when Heintzelman's column arrived, the new arrivals "threw themselves on the ground in front of our quarters, a musket was accidentally discharged, and two of the men severely wounded." Continuing toward Jalapa, the devastation from the combat became even more evident to the soldiers: every house along the road had been burned, and the countryside was in ruin. With his men fatigued and weakened by yellow fever and scurvy, Heintzelman arrived at the hillside town of Jalapa on September 19. "A great many of our men are sick, and the duty upon all of us who are well is very heavy," one recruit scribbled in his dairy.[19] With yellow fever continuing to rage through the ranks, the captain ordered his men to burn all their tents and even some of their clothing.

While entering Jalapa, the saddle on Heintzelman's horse slipped, and he accidentally fell off his mount onto the rocky hillside road. Uninjured but embarrassed, he seemed more concerned about his cased violin that had tumbled out of one of the baggage wagons. With its flowers and climate of perpetual spring, Jalapa was a welcome site. When the frightened residents came forth to say that they were not harboring guerrillas and to plead that their homes not be burned or plundered, the captain assured them they would not be molested.[20]

After eleven days of rest and recuperation, Heintzelman and his men departed Jalapa in good spirits. The road climbed steadily into the Sierra Madre, past deep gorges, through groves of ponderosa pines, and across beds of red volcanic cinders to a rugged 8,000-foot pass beneath the 14,049-foot summit of El Cofre de Perote. The mountain's green slopes, towering above the American conquerors much as they had Spanish conquistadors centuries before, were mystically shrouded in clouds. On October 4, after crossing a large cultivated plain rich in corn and barley, the men of the 2nd Infantry looked up to see the U.S. flag floating over the colonial fortress of Perote. The citadel brought bitter memories to some in the American Army, for it was here that many of the men of the ill-fated

1842 Texan Mier Expedition had died in prison. Heintzelman took time to ride out to the "castle" to see "the bones of the Texans shot there."[21]

Leaving Perote, he was less than a mile from the rustic town of Huamantla on October 9 when a courier raced up to say that some three thousand green-clad Mexican lancers had overrun the town and that Capt. Samuel Walker, legendary Texas Ranger, had been killed by a sniper. Ordering his men to "double quick" into the town, Heintzelman found Walker lying on the plaza, "shot above the eye and in the right breast."[22] Seeing the dead Texan, the Americans went into a frenzy and "killed every Mexican they saw." The "beautiful town" was plundered and "dead Mexicans [lay] about in every direction." Along with other officers, Heintzelman completely lost control of the men, who were caught up in the pillaging. Drunk and bent on destroying everything in sight, many of the soldiers remained in the town until well after dark. "Such a drunken lot I never saw. . . . I could do nothing with them," he confessed. Homes of wealthier Mexicans were robbed and the goods given to the poor women of the town. After making camp some two miles beyond, only half of his men could be persuaded to leave Huamantla. "We are a strange people," the captain concluded.[23]

Although two of Santa Anna's aides had been captured, Heintzelman's role at Huamantla, the last battle of the war, was slight. Nevertheless, he was later brevetted a major for his heroism in the fight. With the passage of time, the battle would be magnified in his imagination into a much larger event. For much of his life, Heintzelman would celebrate every October 9 with a joyous toast.

Three days after leaving Huamantla, the Pennsylvanian helped raise the American flag over the old colonial city of Puebla. Although Puebla had fallen to General Scott's Army of Occupation much earlier, Mexican guerrillas concealed in a nearby cornfield had ambushed a company of soldiers. Discovering the bodies of seven of these Pennsylvanians, hacked to pieces by the guerillas, sent the Americans again into a rage. White flags were everywhere, but Heintzelman watched helplessly as the soldiers ran wild well into the night, sacking every house and business, much as they had done at Huamantla. Even a number of churches were plundered and desecrated. "From the little respect we paid their saints and images, I do not wonder they call us barbarians," he poignantly wrote.[24] While condemning the plundering, he did not hesitate, nor did several other officers, in confiscating the items taken from the drunken soldiers and using them for his personal use.

Heintzelman remained at Puebla for two weeks. Besides constantly struggling to keep his men sober, he found time to attend a gala fandango and experienced two minor earthquakes that rattled the city. He also recorded how an American teamster, who had murdered a wagon master, was hanged in the *zocolo.* The Mexicans "looked on in wonder," he wrote, while "our people laughed and joked." At several churches he listened "to the singing of . . . priests and boys." There was always time for the theater as well as a visit to the Bishop's Palace to view a number of magnificent paintings. The captain also rode out to the ancient ruins of Cholula, where he spurred his horse to the top of a giant pyramid for a magnificent view of the Mexican countryside. Never, he wrote, had he seen "anything to compare with it."[25] The smoking, snow-capped 17,800-foot summit of Popocatepetl glistened in the western sky, while to the east the brown-tinted volcanic spire of Malinche dominated the skyline, and far on the eastern horizon the silver-crowned Pico de Orizaba, the third-highest mountain in North America, towered majestically above the clouds.

Frustrated with his inability to converse in Spanish, he spent several hours each night studying. Reminders of home came in a letter from Margaret containing a lock of Charles's hair, "fair, fine, soft and silky." Leaving Puebla in early December 1847, Heintzelman was in Mexico City less than a week later. With the war all but over, he took quarters in the quaint village of Tacuba, just south of the city. Here, with the help of a Mexican servant boy he hired for a few pesos, he proceeded to lead a gentlemanly life of leisure. Evenings were spent writing lengthy letters to Margaret, sisters Maria and Juliana, studying Spanish, and reading William H. Prescott's *Conquest of Mexico.* Each day the captain rode into Mexico City to visit the theater, the "largest and finest" he had ever seen.[26] At Contreras, Churubusco, and Chapultepec he walked over the bloodied ground where the Americans had swept the Mexicans from the field and brought the war to an end.

At San Cosme, at the gates of Mexico City, a young lieutenant named Ulysses S. Grant showed him where the Mexican artillery had tried in vain to defend the capital. The captain also visited the Church of the Virgin of Guadalupe, the most sacred site in all of Mexico. At the bullfights matadors shook "a red cloth" and tormented "six poor looking small steers." At the Academy of Fine Arts he looked on as students worked at engraving, sculpting, and painting, while at the library at Chapultepec, just west of the city, he examined fifty books, all that remained of a collection of over six thousand, the rest having been taken or sold by the conquering Americans. He walked over Aztec temples and collected pre-Columbian artifacts, and at the Museum of Art he gazed at portraits of Fr. Miguel de Hidalgo and several Spanish viceroys, a bust of George Washington presented to the Mexican government by Joel Poinsett, a copy of the American Declaration of Independence, and some "picture writing of ancient Mexicans."[27]

On New Year's Eve, 1847, Heintzelman took time to write his usual retrospection in his journal: "How many heavy hearts has this war already made for the Army. Great events for some of us may happen before it ends. . . . I hear a band playing."[28] After the signing of the Treaty of Guadalupe-Hidalgo on February 2, 1848, he moved into the city and rented a large house from a wealthy Mexican widow, Faustina Fayuoga, at 2 Calle de Moneda.

Despite Winfield Scott's strict discipline, Heintzelman's lengthy journal entries indicate a personal disdain for the behavior of the conquering army, especially the volunteers. At Chapultepec he found a "poor Indian woman" who had been run over by a drunken American soldier. She was lying in the road with her face badly cut and her hand broken; in an act of kindness he took her to the 5th Infantry hospital and saw to her care. On another occasion he watched as another "poor Indian," stumbling along with a "skin of pulque" over his shoulder, was approached by an American who maliciously poked a hole in the liquor sack. Angrily, Heintzelman apprehended the soldier and ordered him to pay for the damage, a fee "rather dear for a little sport."[29] When the man pleaded that he did not have $1.75, the captain gave the Indian the money and the incident was forgotten.

In late March 1848, along with sixteen other officers, Heintzelman rode out to the old mining town of Pachuca, northeast of Mexico City, for a tour of the silver mines. From there the party continued through oak and pine forests to Real de Monte to visit a mine operated by an English company. Then the group continued farther into the mountains, past towering basalt cliffs, for a spectacular view of a two-thousand-foot-deep *barranca*, or chasm.[30]

Back in Mexico City, exciting news arrived from Buffalo: "My daughter was born on the evening of 27 Feb. and all doing well. . . . I got a lock of hair."[31] Neither mother nor father realized at the time that the newborn, christened Mary Lathrop, had been born with a deformity in one of her legs and that the child would be slightly crippled, walking with a limp for the rest of her life. Mary, nevertheless, was to become an important part of her father's life, vigilantly guarding his military reputation, especially in his old age, when she became a constant companion.

While serving as regimental commander and awaiting ratification of the treaty, Heintzelman attended several churches in Mexico City, regularly appeared at the theater, and hired a tutor to continue his Spanish lessons. He also persuaded his landlady to allow one of her servants, a small orphan boy named Jesús, to return with him to the United States.[32] He would be one of several American officers who returned with such boys as servants. Whether his efforts were an altruistic attempt to free the boy from peonage or a desire to have a personal servant is unclear.

On May 21 he watched as the Mexican Chamber of Deputies ratified the Treaty of Guadalupe-Hidalgo; a week later he stood by as fireworks lit the sky in celebration. Sick with boils but with Jesús by his side, Heintzelman departed Mexico City on June 6, 1848, in a mile-long column of bluecoats. Four days later, with "drums beating and colors flying," his convoy passed through Puebla. The Americans continued past Perote, down into the Tierra Caliente, and into the sweltering tropical heat of Vera Cruz, where on July 2 Heintzelman departed on a steamer for New Orleans. Still sick in the midnight darkness, he arrived at Algiers, opposite New Orleans, four days later. "The first human being I saw on shore this morning in this land of liberty was a slave," he sarcastically commented the next morning.[33]

At the end of the Civil War some eighteen years later, he would reflect back on the Mexican War: "I considered it a great outrage on our part and I saw a great many, most outrageous things in the conduct . . . , but as it was the government of the country, I gave it the benefit of my abilities."[34]

Although he had experienced little of the bitter fighting that had characterized a war that redrew the political map of North America, Heintzelman, like so many other officers, would take great pride in having served in Mexico. He would always cherish being a member of the Aztec Club, a fraternal organization for Mexican War veterans, which in 1848, at the age of forty-four, he considered himself to be.

THREE

Hell Burned Out

After spending a few days at Camp Jeff Davis in East Pascagoula, Mississippi, Brevet Maj. Samuel Peter Heintzelman was back in New Orleans in time to depart on the ill-fated steamboat *Sultana* for St. Louis.[1] At Jefferson Barracks plans were already underway for the departure of the 2nd Infantry for California. After considerable discussion, and with the officers requesting permission to travel by water, the regiment was ordered to depart by ship in the autumn from New York rather than travel overland on the long and fatiguing Oregon and California trails.

As new recruits arrived at Jefferson Barracks, Heintzelman stood by as the men were drilled three times daily. Complaining of an inflamed leg and foot injured in Mexico, he became bedridden and, out of boredom, cut off his beard for the first time in several years. The only consolation to the dreary garrison life in Missouri came when Margaret sent daguerreotypes of Charles and Mary from Buffalo. Although Mary's photograph was blurred, Charles appeared "handsome," with an "intelligent face and fine head."[2]

Caught up in the tumultuous politics of the era, Heintzelman read the proceedings of and seemed fascinated with the newly formed Free Soil Party that met in Buffalo. "If they would have kept that negro away, I would have liked it better," he commented. The "negro" was the escaped slave and leading abolitionist Frederick Douglass. Regardless, the Free Soilers were correct "about slavery," he concluded.[3]

Finally in early September 1848, with the "little Mexican" boy Jesús by his side, he made his way overland by stagecoach and across Lake Erie on the steamer *Pioneer* to Buffalo. Solon Lathrop was there to greet the captain at the dock, saying that Margaret and the children were well and anxiously awaiting his arrival. Joyously reunited with his family, he agreed that Mary would need an operation sometime in the near future to remove a "small spot" on her leg.[4] After considerable thought, he also agreed that

Margaret and the children, along with Caroline Stuart, would accompany him to California. It was an exciting time for the entire family, for the lengthy, even frightful trip around Cape Horn was certain to be one of the great adventures of the children's young lives.

In October 1848 the captain rushed ahead to New York to make final arrangements for the departure of the 2nd Infantry. Margaret, Caroline, and the children, with Solon Lathrop as escort, followed a few days later. Margaret had also hired a servant girl named Bridgett who, along with Jesús, would also be making the journey. On October 29 Heintzelman received final orders from Col. Bennet Riley, cautioning him to ensure that all rules regarding "troops on board of transports" be followed and to make sure the soldiers received the proper diet to avoid scurvy and "other ship diseases." In the brisk morning air of November 8, 1848, the *Rome*, with two companies of the 2nd Infantry onboard, weighed anchor and set sail for California. Only one day out of New York, Margaret, Caroline, the children, and both servants were already seasick. In heavy seas off Cape Hatteras, North Carolina, a few days later, Caroline became so weak that she could not even lift her head, remaining ill for several days. Although Margaret's spirits were lifted by a fine Thanksgiving dinner that included champagne and wine, she was too weak to celebrate the couple's fourth wedding anniversary a few days later.[5]

Besides caring for Margaret, Caroline, and the children, the captain spent much of his time on deck watching sharks, dolphins, and schools of flying fish as well as studying Spanish. He was also making a detailed chart, carefully logging each day's latitudinal and longitudinal progress. Despite being "at sea," he also worked to complete the usual monthly company muster rolls and returns required of a company commander. By December 12, 1848, the *Rome* was across the equator and into warmer summer water. During the long sea voyage in the cramped and stuffy quarters below deck, many of the young recruits, and even the older veterans, became restless and rebellious. On December 14 Heintzelman was forced to convene a court-martial to try a defiant sergeant. Another soldier was caught stealing food and severely punished. Some of the "thieving scoundrels" even consumed the "hospital wine."[6]

By late December the rocky, tropical Brazilian coast came into sight, and Christmas, 1848, was spent in the "magnificent harbor" of Rio de Janeiro, where the calm waters and "high abrupt conical hills," including Sugar Loaf, provided an idyllic setting. Seeing cathedrals, convents, magnificent gardens, and elegant villas while walking through the streets of the Brazilian city, Heintzelman could not help but think of his first impressions of Vera Cruz sixteen months earlier. In Rio de Janeiro the captain and his family visited the botanical gardens, a silver-and-diamond shop, and a larger basilica. He even treated the ladies and children to ice cream. From another American ship in the harbor, Heintzelman learned that "Old Rough-and-Ready," Gen. Zachary Taylor, Mexican War hero and wealthy Louisiana Whig, had been elected the twelfth president of the United States. The spirits of the men in the 2nd Infantry were heightened when they began hearing rumors of the discovery of gold in California.[7] Few officers, including Heintzelman, realized at the time the problem this historic event would cause the army.

On January 2, 1849, the *Rome* lifted anchor and set sail for Cape Horn and California. Passing into the cold and windswept waters of the South Atlantic, the ship began "rolling and pitching" off the coast of Argentina, and most of the passengers, especially two-year-old Mary, became sick again. During the storm, one man was washed overboard and lost. Several soldiers were caught stealing food again, and twelve of them were tied to the rigging of the ship and left in the cold. Although it was summer in the southern hemisphere, there was a terrible storm off Cape Horn. And despite the frightful seas, Heintzelman managed to celebrate the occasion of rounding the cape with a bottle of scotch whiskey. Two weeks later, off the Chilean coast, the weather grew warmer as the *Rome* slipped into Valparaiso harbor. To welcome the Americans, a band on a nearby English ship struck up "Yankee Doodle." In the city of endless terraces, Heintzelman purchased plums, peaches, pears, and apples and managed a quick visit to an Episcopal church. He learned from Colonel Riley that his two companies of the 2nd Infantry, after first making port at Monterey, were being sent to San Diego, instead of San Francisco as he had hoped. Before leaving Valparaiso, exciting news came with the receipt of a San Francisco newspaper containing a letter confirming the discovery of gold in California. Even greater excitement arose when several "massive ingots" from California were shown to the men.[8]

Back out at sea, the *Rome* crossed the Tropic of Cancer on March 25 and headed into the North Pacific. During the long voyage, Samuel Peter and Margaret observed the growing attachment between Caroline Stuart and a young army surgeon from Virginia named John Edward Summers. Late into the evening they were inseparable, playing cards, laughing, and conversing freely. In early April, off the southern California coast, the two were strolling on deck when the vessel gave a sudden lurch and both were thrown onto a skylight and injured.[9]

The *Rome* at last reached the picturesque half-moon harbor of Monterey, California, on April 6. Three days later the ship's crew defiantly struck out for the goldfields as the captain fired several shots from his "six shooter at the deserters." Although one sailor was wounded, the seamen were not deterred. Caught up in the excitement of the times, Heintzelman hoped that somehow he might be stationed in the gold country, but orders arrived confirming that he was being sent to San Diego. After a pleasant trip down the coast, the Heintzelmans arrived in the small seaside community just in time for a Mexican fandango.[10] After five months and fifteen thousand exhausting miles by sea, they were safely at their new home.

With a population of four hundred, the old village of San Diego, some five miles from the landing, was a collection of dilapidated adobe buildings amounting to little more than "a heap of ruins." Very much a frontier town, it was crowded with gold seekers, gamblers, destitute settlers, and about three hundred "Californios" and Indians. Although the captain was able to find temporary lodging, Dr. Summers and most of the men in the regiment were forced to pitch tents in the village plaza. After several days, Heintzelman found a house for Margaret and the children, but the dwelling was "intolerably dirty" and flea infested; Margaret was so "disheartled" and disgusted she wanted "to go into a tent." Three months later she was still complaining and now talking of returning to Buffalo.[11] Several months pregnant, she was also suffering from "morning sickness."

After endless cleaning, numerous repairs, and building furniture and beds, living conditions for the family became more tolerable. Always the agronomist, Heintzelman planted tomatoes and a small vineyard and bought a cow for fresh milk. In addition to Juan and Bridgett, he hired a free man of color named John, who proved a habitual drunk and of little assistance. Realizing that San Diego, with its fine bay, was certain to become a transportation hub for Southern California, Heintzelman purchased two lots near the beach for four hundred dollars. Later he would purchase sixteen additional lots.[12]

The trip around Cape Horn and the difficulty of adjusting to the harshness of life on the California frontier took its toll on Margaret. A little over eight months after arriving in San Diego, she began to experience labor pains late one evening and gave birth to a stillborn male. After fashioning a small wooden coffin and holding a hastily arranged funeral, the infant was buried on a hill near the beach beneath a large tree as the family stood by in tears.[13]

There was little time for the captain to mourn, however, for serious problems developed when men in the 2nd Infantry began deserting in hordes for the gold diggings. The officers could do little to stop the exodus as entire companies slipped away into the night. A month after arriving in San Diego, Heintzelman recorded how nine of his men, some of them drunk, deserted, one in broad daylight after breakfast. Even the soldiers guarding the camp left for the goldfields. In all, 390 men, 72 of whom were apprehended, deserted within weeks after the 2nd Infantry arrived in California. A few of those who were apprehended were either

San Diego, California. Bartlett, Personal Narrative of Explorations and Incidents.

whipped or chained, but still the desertions continued. Those caught inebriated were frequently placed in stocks, but this punishment did not help either. Heintzelman was so incensed that he put one "mutinous rascal" in irons and threatened to keep others in them "for many a long month."[14]

But after seeing a one-pound gold nugget, the captain too contemplated resigning to join a mining company. Months later he complained that he had "yet to get the first particle of gold." Jesús was so inflicted with gold fever that he dug a shaft behind the army quarters in search of the precious metal. Growing restless, he even tried to run away several times. Complaining that the boy had become "entirely worthless," Heintzelman first issued verbal threats but later tied him up and "made him promise to behave." He even thought of whipping the boy, but Jesús "begged too hard."[15]

In San Diego the romantic relationship between Dr. Summers and Caroline continued to blossom, and the two were soon spending "all their time making love." Not overly enthusiastic about the relationship, Margaret warned her sister that if their mother were present, she would not tolerate Caroline's constant visits to the surgeon's tent. Finally, after securing permission from Mrs. Stuart in Buffalo and obtaining the services of a parson from a ship anchored in the harbor, John E. Summers, twenty-seven, and Caroline I. Stuart, twenty-four, were married on February 20, 1850, in a simple ceremony at the Heintzelmans' small house, after which champagne and cake were served.[16]

Captain Heintzelman witnessed and objectively chronicled the decline of the native Californios. Capt. Edward R. S. Canby, assistant adjutant general, wrote confidentially from Monterey encouraging him to assist in gathering the prominent San Diego Californios for a meeting to select delegates to a convention to establish a government for the purpose of writing a constitution as a prerequisite to statehood. At times Heintzelman appeared to blindly accept the concept of Manifest Destiny and the Americans' determination to "root out everything *Californio.*" Such changes were the inevitable consequence of empire, he felt, yet he remained inwardly sympathetic to the Californios' plight and was especially sympathetic to those who befriended the Americans. The natives, he wrote, "already feel they are nothing along side the Americans." With two parties, one American and one Californio, competing for political control of the village, the newcomers easily prevailed, and with the formation of San Diego County, Heintzelman voted for the first time in his life.[17]

He was particularly saddened by the death of Spanish-born shipping agent Don Miguel de Pedrorena, "a kind hearted man and very friendly to the Americans and one of the first to embrace their cause." To Heintzelman, Pedrorena, who had served as customs collector at San Diego under the Americans during the Mexican War, had been a valuable link between the Californios and the newcomers.[18]

Life along the Pacific included picnics at the old mission of San Diego de Alcala, some five miles east of Old Town, where the priest complained to Heintzelman that someone had hidden the clappers to his bells. In the afternoon there were quiet buggy rides to the top of a hill to watch the ocean surf break on the shore and whales at play in the harbor. There were also quail, duck, and rabbit hunts and long walks along the beach with the children, while invitations to festive balls came from both the Americans and the Californios.

Both the Mexican Boundary Survey Commission under Gen. Pedro García Condé and its American counterpart, with Maj. William Hemsley Emory in charge, arrived on the coast to be greeted and entertained by the officers of the garrison. Heintzelman took a liking to the forty-six-year-old Condé, who visited with the Heintzelmans and spoke frankly of his family and his role in the recent war. Samuel Peter was saddened when the former secretary of war and navy, who had also served in the Mexican Congress, died of typhus at Arispe, Mexico, a year later.[19]

In April 1850, only one year after arriving on the West Coast, Heintzelman was ordered to Oregon on court-martial duty. Departing San Diego on the brig *Colonel Fremont,* he stopped at San Pedro and Santa Barbara before going on to San Francisco, where he found the harbor "filled with square-rigged vessels." Crews from many of the ships had left for the goldfields, and the ships lay abandoned and rotting at anchor. North to Oregon, he first stopped at Bakers Bay before steaming up the broad Columbia River to Portland and finally up the Willamette River to Oregon City. "The most conspicuous object" in Oregon City, he quickly noticed, was "a newly erected gallows, that mark of civilization—erected to hang five Cayuse Indians convicted for the murder of Dr. [Marcus] Whitman and a number of others." Although he was on court-martial duty at the time, a "great crowd assembled" on May 3, 1850, for the hanging. Inquiring into the specifics of the case, he became convinced that "the youngest of the Indians and perhaps two more were innocent." The entire episode, he wrote, was "a foul blot on the country."[20]

After two weeks in Oregon City, Heintzelman departed for the old trading post of Astoria at the mouth of the Columbia before going on to San Francisco. There he had a long conversation with Col. Persifor Frazer Smith, commander of the Department of the Pacific, and was told that he could expect orders soon to establish a post at the junction of the Gila and Colorado rivers at the Yuma Crossing of the Gila Trail. Smith also told him that a company called the "Gila Association" had been formed to "keep the ferry and trade" on the Colorado River.[21] Always the aspiring entrepreneur, Heintzelman "entered into it at once." With a reported ten thousand Sonorans and an equal number of Americans certain to use the ferry each year, he believed there was money to be made.

Arriving back in San Diego, he learned that Jesús, along with a soldier from the 2nd Infantry, had left in the night for the goldfields. A few days later, in November 1850, orders arrived directing the garrison to move to the old mission of San Diego de Alcala. Shortly thereafter Heintzelman at last received orders to "establish your command in the most eligible position in the vicinity of the junction of the Gila . . . as early as possible in order to give protection to the emigrants and to repress any hostile disposition on the part of the Indians."[22] After requesting information from Major Emory of the Boundary Commission as to the nature of the country at the junction of the two rivers, where two ferries were said to be operating, as well as the best route across the desert from San Diego, he led a reconnaissance across the mountains to Warner's Ranch and the headwaters of San Felipe Creek. Vallecitos, some 110 miles from San Diego, the last place where grass and water was available before entering the terrible heat and shifting sands of the 100-mile desert, was the best place for a

Mission of San Diego de Alcala. Bartlett, Personal Narrative of Explorations and Incidents.

subdepot, from which the new post could be supplied. By using the southern trail, Heintzelman calculated he could reach Vallecitos in six days from the coast, and by crossing into Mexican territory, he could reach the Yuma Crossing in less than fifteen days. Back in San Diego, problems erupted with an unruly artillery company commanded by Capt. John B. Magruder. Many of Magruder's men were drunk, and within days eight of his men stole a whaleboat loaded with provisions and left for the goldfields.[23]

The Yuma Crossing, thanks to American scoundrels led by the notorious and ruthless scalp-hunter John Joel Glanton, was in havoc. With twelve ruffians, Glanton had seized control of the ferry and was not only abusing the Yuma Indians but also said to be robbing and murdering helpless immigrants on their way to the California goldfields. On April 23, 1850, the Indians rose up in rebellion. Catching Glanton and his men in a drunken stupor, the natives killed and scalped most of the scoundrels and cremated their remains in a big bonfire. Four of Glanton's men escaped, however, and fled across the Colorado Desert with the news. As word of the "Glanton Massacre" spread to San Diego, Los Angeles, and points north, citizens demanded action. The undisciplined California State Militia headed for the Yuma Crossing, and Heintzelman feared their presence would "only lead to further difficulties with the Indians." When reports of additional killings along the Colorado River reached the coast, he wrote department headquarters expressing uneasiness with the situation: "Whites have commenced hostilities by abusing the Indian women and destroying their cornfields and vegetables. I very much fear this is the commencement of an Indian war which may continue several years."[24]

After sending one company ahead to Vallecitos, Heintzelman rode out of San Diego on October 23, for the Yuma Crossing with three additional companies of infantry. With supplies packed in broken-down wagons that had come across the continent from Saltillo, Mexico, he reached Vallecitos on November 3. There he took time to ride east some 60 miles to the shores of a large saline sea, the Salton Sink, to meet with the head chief of the Luiseños and some Yuma who were said to be interested in negotiating a peace with the bluecoats. Proclaiming success, the captain returned to Vallecitos, where he sent a small party eastward into the desert to dig out some wells. After a 110-mile fatiguing march across the Colorado Desert, 90 miles of which was difficult sand, Heintzelman successfully reached the Colorado River with two companies of the 2nd Infantry on November 27. A third company followed a few days later. In all, ninety-two enlisted men, two officers, and a medical officer reached the river. The soldiers pitched tents, and the captain set out to make life as bearable as possible. Brush arbors and picket fences, constructed of reeds found along the river, were placed around the tents for protection from the blistering sun and the wind. Orders were issued to keep all "liquor sellers" away, and when a Sonoran sold the men some whiskey, Heintzelman had him arrested. Construction of a temporary hospital was also started, and twenty-six different kinds of vegetables were planted in a garden near the river as well as peach, fig, and olive trees in a small orchard. With grapevines from San Diego, they also started a small vineyard. Hauling water from the river by

View up the Gila River from its junction with the Colorado River. Bartlett, Personal Narrative of Explorations and Incidents.

hand for irrigation proved to be excessively laborious, however. What was needed, the post commander concluded, were pumps.[25]

Although supply wagons from San Diego arrived weeks late, goat meat, beef, and mutton were sometimes available. More frequently, however, there was only bean soup. By Christmas, with vegetables no longer available, scurvy appeared among the men. Heintzelman also managed a flock of chickens, but coyotes that were so "bold at night" as to almost "come . . . into your tent" soon carried off the fowl. He also took time to write the secretary of war asking that Fort Yuma be made a double-ration post, a request that Col. Persifor Smith enthusiastically endorsed. With an additional company arriving at the crossing, Heintzelman optimistically concluded that the isolated outpost could, with some effort, "be made more desirable than the San Diego mission."[26]

Yet by late December the post was dangerously low on food. At the same time, its commander learned that teamsters on the coast had been unable to find forage for their animals, and it was doubtful the post could be supplied before spring. "In the meantime, we are left to starve," he dejectedly told headquarters.[27]

Before leaving San Diego, Heintzelman had persuaded the army to supply Fort Yuma by an all-water route by way of the Gulf of California and the Colorado River. By the end of the year, however, the 120-ton military schooner *Invincible*, bound for the Yuma Crossing, had not been heard from, and he feared the ship had been unable to enter the mouth of the river. In early January 1851 a friendly Cocopa Indian came into the post with a note from Lt. George Horatio Derby of the Topographical Engineers, who was onboard the *Invincible*. The schooner, which had left San Francisco on November 1, had arrived at the mouth of the river two days before Christmas and had made her way up the river thirty miles. Although he had little knowledge of the lower reaches of the river, Heintzelman calculated the ship was some sixty miles below the Yuma Crossing. With no meat or bread and desperate for supplies, he rigged a small raft with sails and, with six men and two civilians, set out downstream, hoping to reach the *Invincible* in two days. On the third day they met a lighter from the ship twenty-seven miles from the mouth of the river and reached the *Invincible* seven hours later.[28]

Although the skipper of the ship, Capt. Alfred H. Wilcox, had been able to guide the *Invincible* into the Colorado, shifting currents and a tidal bore buffeted the schooner until it lost its anchor and went aground. Finally able to free the vessel, Willcox piled the rations on some driftwood on the Sonora bank and sailed away. Unable to carry the vital supplies in the small raft, Heintzelman ordered 1st Lt. Edward Murray and nine men to open a wagon road through Mexican territory to the cache. By late January 1851 Murray's wagons had begun to arrive at the post with the badly needed items; at the same time, a train of eight wagons with foodstuffs arrived from San Diego. Back at Fort Yuma, Heintzelman sent Colonel Smith a lengthy report of his trip. He also mapped a portion of the lower river and sent a copy to Major Emory of the Boundary Commission. The Colorado was navigable, he concluded, though the channel was crooked and filled with shifting sandbars. He remained convinced that the best way to supply the post was by steamboat.[29] Although authorized to use armed escorts to accompany the supplies across Mexican territory, Heintzelman was prohibited from pursuing hostile Indians into the neighboring republic.

Besides drill, review, and the endless paperwork required of a post commander, Heintzelman began to keep a daily record of the rise and fall of the Colorado River. He also took time to visit with several bands of friendly Yumas, under the leadership of Cavallo y Pelo and Santiago. Primarily growers and gatherers rather than hunters, these Indians lived in small rancherias scattered along the Colorado and east along the Gila River. Generally avoiding the forbidding desert terrain beyond the flood plains

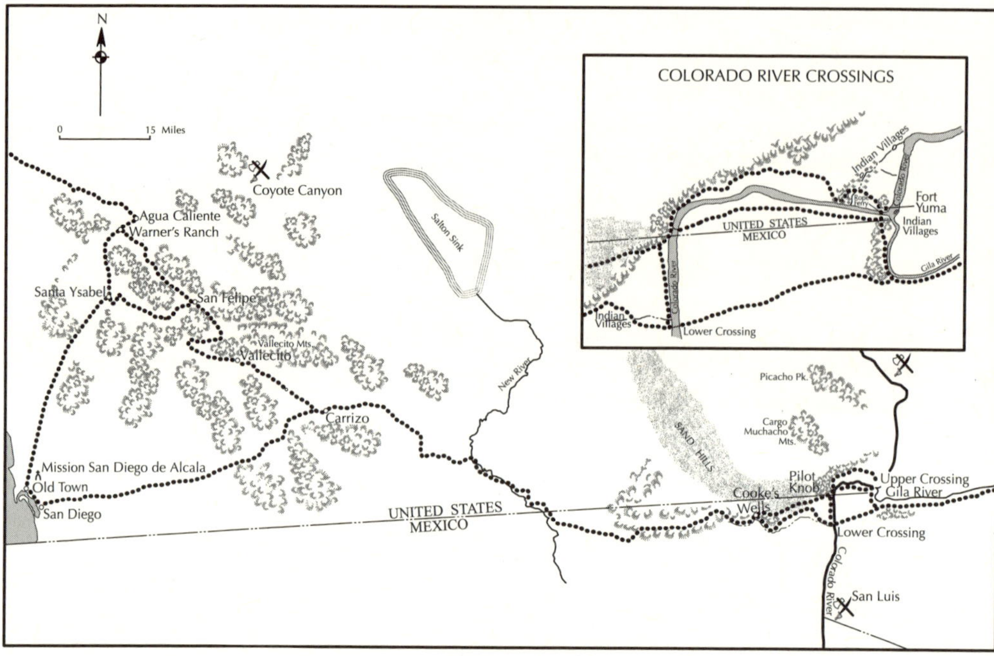

San Diego to Fort Yuma,
1850-1854

of the two rivers, the Yuma, or Quechan, planted wheat, maize, beans, pumpkins, and melons several times each year.[30]

"I had a visit this morning from four tribes of Indians and quite a talk," he wrote in February 1851. "I gave them some tobacco, meat and flour and they left quite satisfied." Having previously been given presents by the Boundary Commission, many of the Indians wanted gifts, but the captain had none, for which he expressed "much embarrassed." Learning that the Indians were fearful of being attached by the Maricopas who lived up the Gila, "I promised them our protection and shall endeavor to open a communication with the Maricopas and may be able to bring about a peace."[31]

With the Yumas' meager crops failing in the summer of 1851, the post was overrun with men, women, and children begging for something to eat. Some of them reported, much to Heintzelman's excitement, that south of the Gila in the arid mountainous wastes of Sonora was "plenty of gold" only "two days' journey from us." In April 1851, after a band of Indians, probably Mohaves, made off with "several animals from the post," the captain promised to "punish them severely" if they could be caught. Communication was also opened with other Indians, including the Pimas to the east and the Mohaves more than a hundred miles upriver.[32]

Determined to obtain a working knowledge of Spanish and interpret for himself, Heintzelman began reading an 1825 Spanish edition of the Bible, and he continued studying the language at every opportunity. Three months later he began reading William H. Prescott's classic *Conquest of Mexico*, also in Spanish, and found only a few phrases he did not understand. Hoping also to retain as much German as possible, Heintzelman conversed freely with German immigrants who arrived at the crossing as well as the numerous German recruits in his command. One day he visited with hundreds of Mormon converts on their way to the valley of the Great Salt Lake. He even borrowed a copy of "Joe Smith's bible" and concluded that the Latter Day Saints, whom he had once despised as a "vile sect," were "a determined go ahead people."[33]

During the second week of February 1851, Colonel Smith arrived at the Yuma Crossing in a dust storm. Although Smith was expected to inspect the post, the colonel was more interested in locating a permanent location for the fort. Using Heintzelman's small raft, the two ascended the Gila River for a short distance but finally settled on a relatively flat, rocky promontory known as Mission Hill about eighty feet in height on the north bank of the Colorado at its junction with the Gila. Both agreed that the site where Fray Francisco Tomás Garcés old mission, La Puerta de la Purísimo Concepción, had once stood was "the best point for the permanent post." A post here not only would provide some relief from the suffocating dust but also was safe from flooding. Moreover, by using a waterwheel, water could be raised from the rivers for storage and use at the fort. Smith also agreed with Heintzelman that a reliable steamship service was crucial so the garrison could be regularly supplied by way of the Gulf of California. After the colonel's departure, Heintzelman continued to scout out new locations, even ascending the Colorado fifteen miles, but he could find none better than that at the confluence of the two rivers. In early March he gave orders to move his small command to Mission Hill.[34]

In early 1851 an entomologist named Dr. John Le Conte, whom Heintzelman jokingly called "Bugs," reached the Yuma Crossing with a letter from Royce Oatman, an Illinois Mormon farmer of the Brewsterite sect, who was eight days west of the Pima villages on the "Hila" River and desperate for help. Having been "rob[b]ed" of his animals, Oatman, his wife, and their seven children were almost out of provisions: "Without help . . . I am confident we must per[r]ish."[35] Heintzelman dispatched "two men . . . and two pack mules and a few provisions . . . 100 or 120 miles up the river" to assist in "getting them in." Arriving on the scene, the two bluecoats found two graves covered with stones near an abandoned wagon on top of a ridge and a few carpenter tools strewn about. Still, Heintzelman could not believe the immigrants had been murdered. He would later learn the

Site of the Oatman Massacre. J. Ross Browne, Into the Apache Country.

grisly details. The Oatmans had pushed ahead of other immigrant parties and had been attacked by a band of either Tonto Apaches or Yavapais, though Heintzelman thought at the time the Maricopas were to blame.[36] Six of the family members had been killed, while two girls, Mary Ann and Olive Ann, had been carried off as captives. Lorenzo Oatman, a lad of sixteen who was left for dead, eventually made his way to the fort, where he provided details of the massacre.

Heintzelman was severely criticized by Dr. Henry Stewart Hewit, the post surgeon, Capt. Delozier Davidson, second in command, and Dr. Le Conte for not doing more to help the Oatmans. Hewit and Le Conte went as far as to write letters highly critical of his inactivity to the *San Francisco Alta California* and the *San Diego Herald*.[37] The letters were in reprisal, Heintzelman argued, for his refusal to provide Le Conte and Hewit with an army escort in their "gold speculations." In a lengthy response that appeared in the *Alta California*, he put part of the blame on Le Conte by saying that on February 21 a Sonoran who had accompanied the doctor on a scientific expedition into Sonora arrived at Fort Yuma with news that the party had been robbed by the Indians but not a word about the Oatmans. The attack had taken place on the south side of the river in Mexican territory by "Mexican Indians," Heintzelman further stated: "I had not the men nor the means to send a sufficient party so far on a hostile expedition; and if I had had ten thousand men, I have no authority to send an armed soldier into Mexican territory to chastise Mexican Indians." He had done everything that "humanity required and the means at my disposal permitted." Moreover, he had made "diligent enquiries of all the Indians" but could "get no trace of the missing girls." It was later learned that Mary Ann and Olive Ann had been sold by the Apaches to the Mohaves. In captivity Mary had died of starvation, but Olive, who was tattooed by the natives, survived and was ransomed five years later. Her story was dramatized across the nation. For months Heintzelman would continue to defend his actions, writing that "in the case of the Oatman family, I did all that the means at my disposal would allow and international law permitted."[38]

Well into 1851, Heintzelman conducted several reconnaissances in hopes of improving and shortening the trail east along the Gila River and west across the desert to San Diego. On one such excursion he ascended a five-hundred-foot peak near the post, probably Pilot Knob, for a view of the Colorado Desert and a "long line of shifting sand hills extending . . . far north." In the burning heat of May, he completed a lengthy expedition northwest into the desert for a view of a large brackish lake. The following year a French trapper and guide, Joaquin Antoine Jacques Leroux, arrived at the post telling of a spectacular "great canon" on the Colorado River far to the northeast, which was said to be some five hundred miles long with walls two thousand to three thousand feet high. The river, hemmed in by sublime perpendicular walls of rock hundreds of feet in height, as viewed from the rim of the canyon, appeared as "but a streak of foam."[39] There was no other area of the vast Mexican Cession as unexplored as the area north of the Gila Trail. Virtually unknown and unmapped, it was one sweeping terra incognita.

Despite the harshness of the environment, Heintzelman would always remain attracted to the beauties of the desert and the world around him. His naturalistic instincts notwithstanding, his main concern was the day-to-day operation of the post. Always a tough disciplinarian, he was determined to "break" the "lazy habits" of a number of the recruits who had recently arrived at the post. An even greater challenge came from Dr. Hewit, and even more so from the post quartermaster, Lt. Thomas William Sweeny, who had previously been arrested by civil authorities at San Diego. The Irish-born lieutenant, who came to America as a child with his widowed mother, was well known in the frontier army as "Fighting Tom" for his bravery during the Mexican War. He had fought heroically at Cerro Gordo and at Churubusco, where he was wounded in the groin and lost his right arm. Although many in the service admired Sweeny for his coolness, skill, and intrepidity, Heintzelman had never liked the brash and quick-tempered lieutenant. Hewit and Sweeny "agreed on one thing," he wrote, they hate "me most cordially."[40] Hewit possessed "a determination to do all in his power to annoy and embarrass me," the captain told department headquarters. He promised, nevertheless, to "bring them down to their proper places." In March 1851 Hewit preferred charges against Heintzelman, accusing him of cruel and inhuman conduct, neglect of duty, and being indifferent to the health and safety of the sick by not putting sheds over the men's tents and not providing a suitable hospital. In a test of wills Heintzelman preferred charges against Hewit, but the entire feud eventually faded into history when the Connecticut-born surgeon unexpectedly resigned from the army.[41]

Besides the difficulty of maintaining supply lines across the desert or by sea around Baja California, the terrible heat and the blinding dust storms made life along the Colorado miserable and immobilized the army. On January 27, 1851, Heintzelman recorded a temperature of 99 degrees, and by April 12 it was a blistering 108. Once in the bottomland by the river the temperature had reached a scorching 121 degrees. Besides the lambent heat, one soldier was bitten by a scorpion and another by a rattlesnake. By early March the captain yearned to leave the desert isolation and return to his family in San Diego: "How Sundays and the twilight make a man think of home. I am getting quite tired of such a life."[42]

Later that month Heintzelman concluded that the supply depot at San Diego simply did not have the means necessary to supply Fort Yuma, especially during the approaching heat of summer. The only way the post could be adequately provisioned, he continued to caution headquarters, was by water. Even the twice-monthly mail from the coast arrived days late, if at all. A wooden box containing the "burial remains" of Lt. Herman Thorn, a Mexican War hero who had drowned at the Yuma Crossing in October 1849, which Heintzelman had sent to the coast for shipment to his father in New York, had even been lost. By the end of April, the post was entirely out of beans, rice, sugar, and coffee, and only one barrel of flour remained. By June his superiors had also concluded that Fort Yuma could not be adequately supplied and that the post must be abandoned. Nevertheless, they also decided to leave Lieutenant Sweeny with ten men to guard the ferry some six miles downriver and protect immigrants on their way to California. Heintzelman even gave the brash lieutenant an extract from the Treaty of Guadalupe-Hidalgo, by which the United States agreed to prevent hostile incursions into neighboring Mexico. In addition, the Yuma Indians were to be treated with "justice and kindness" and whites prevented from occupying their lands.[43]

The day before leaving the river, Heintzelman called the Yuma chiefs together, telling them that the army was withdrawing, though he would not be gone long, and that he was leaving Lieutenant Sweeny at the river for their protection. Sweeny's small force was more than sufficient, he speculated, to guard the public property and to prevent any of the immigrants "passing through the country from committing any outrages on the Indians and the latter from retaliating." At daylight on June 5, the captain led his three companies of the 2nd Infantry 125 miles westward across the desert to Santa Ysabel on the eastern slopes of the mountains. There, with sufficient shade, wood, water, and grass, along with fresh fruits such as peaches, apples, grapes, and vegetables, he was sure that in a few months the men could recover from their terrible ordeal at the Yuma Crossing.[44] After only two months at Santa Ysabel, however, Heintzelman and his men were ordered to San Diego, where they remained throughout the summer.

While he was at San Diego, a delegation of Yumas and Cocopas came to seek his counsel. In particular, the Yumas were hopeful that Heintzelman would assist them in removing their two principal chiefs, Santiago and Cavallo y Pelo. The two chiefs were hostile toward the military, and some feared a general war. For several months Heintzelman had heard rumors that Santiago was endeavoring to unite the Yumas against the army. After lengthy discussions, he told the Indians that he did not have the authority to depose their chiefs but that they should return home, "call their tribes together and if they saw fit to depose these chiefs and elect others."[45] He falsely assumed that the majority of the Indians in southern California were content to live in peace. To foster their friendship, he continued to press the government into providing presents—while at Fort Yuma, the only thing he had been able to give them was some tobacco, which came from his "private stores."

In early October several immigrants arrived in San Diego from the Yuma Crossing with hastily scribbled notes from Lieutenant Sweeny saying that he was low on provisions, his men were suffering from scurvy, and he was expecting an attack from a large number of Indians who had surrounded his camp. Heintzelman could scarcely believe what he was reading. "There is not the slightest foundation for the reports in circulation about their hostility," he told headquarters. When it was confirmed that four Americans had been killed at the crossing, he finally became convinced that the Yumas were indeed on the warpath. Taking the shortest possible route across the mountains, Capt. Delozier Davidson, with sixteen men and a supply train of mules and wagons, proceeded to the Colorado River with all deliberate speed.[46]

Heintzelman was distracted in mid-December 1851 when news arrived in San Diego that a band of Cahuilla Indians had raided Warner's Ranch and Agua Caliente, across the mountains to the east, and that he was being ordered into the field with three companies of men. In the days to come, he came to quickly conclude that the Yuma hostilities were only part of a much larger uprising of Native Americans in southern California. In fact, the entire desert frontier was ablaze. At a watering hole in the desert, he learned that Captain Davidson had reached the Yuma Crossing but had abandoned the river on December 6, and much to his disgust, all of the captain's personal belongings, including his small library, had been left behind and presumed destroyed.[47] With the army quitting the river, a portion of the Boundary Survey escorted by Capt. Louis S. Craig had also fled west to San Diego. Although Davidson argued that he was out of provisions at his camp six miles downriver near Pilot Knob and was about to be attacked by an overwhelming force of Indians, Heintzelman did not "see the necessity of abandoning the post."[48] When the *San Diego Herald* reported that Sweeny had been attacked by eight hundred Yumas, the captain found the news preposterous. His disdain for Sweeny and Davidson would grow to a point where he would find reasons to prefer charges against both.[49]

Heintzelman's immediate concern, however, was the Shoshonea-speaking Cahuilla Indians. Even the alarm among the Californios in San Diego was "very great." So widespread was the panic that he met with town and county officials and agreed to furnish arms and ammunition for the protection of San Diego should the rebellion spread across the mountains. With five companies of the 2nd Infantry, a company of the 1st Artillery that was rushed south from Monterey, Indian trader and rancher Jonathan Trumbull Warner, and the Indian agent for southern California, Dr. Oliver M. Wozencraft, Heintzelman pushed his small force east into the desert in hopes of locating the raiders. By December 20, with Warner as a guide, he had reached a site only a few miles from where scouts said the Cahuillas were camped. From a dry camp in the desert near the upper end of Borrego Valley, the soldiers were in formation before sunrise the next morning, and with a steady rain falling, they rode into the semiarid mountains only to be attacked in a narrow defile called Coyote Canyon by about one hundred Cahuillas under Chief Chipule. The Indians were poorly armed with bows and arrows and a few old rifles and were easily repulsed, losing six warriors killed, including Chipule and another chief named Cecili, and then pursued deeper into the mountains.[50] When a cache near a Cahuilla rancheria was found to contain items from Warner's Ranch, the soldiers torched the nearby Indian village.

Later an Indian woman appeared on a nearby hill requesting a parley. Realizing they were outnumbered and outgunned, the Indians agreed to capitulate, and runners were sent to bring in all the principal chiefs, especially those from San Ysidro who were accused of murder in the raid on Warner's Ranch. With Warner as interpreter, Heintzelman immediately called a council of war to decide the fate of the four leaders implicated in the killings.[51] After several hours the Indians were pronounced guilty of murder, arson, and robbery, and all were sentenced to death. The next day the four men, Juan Bautista, Francisco Mocate, Jacobo (Quisil), and Luis, alcalde at Agua Caliente, were informed of the verdict. One of the warriors begged for mercy, but the others "took it very well," Heintzelman recorded in his journal. In a slight drizzle on a bleak Christmas morning, the four were dragged out and, kneeling before hastily dug graves, with the soldiers and glum-faced Indians looking on, executed by firing squad. The men "fell and were dead in a few moments." Heintzelman was greatly relieved that the "disagreeable duty" was over.[52]

After burning more Indian huts, the bluecoats rode triumphantly out of the mountains in a heavy rain. In camp at Temecula five days later, Heintzelman, Warner, Captain Magruder, and the other officers celebrated the new year with a "nice supper of ribs and choice broth." Later the men gathered around a fire for eggnog as the always jovial and half-drunk Magruder provided the entertainment. Two days later Heintzelman was back in San Diego with his family. Colonel Smith wrote from Benicia to congratulate him on the success of an expedition that had been "planned with judgement and executed with promptness." Smith could think of "no more important service . . . rendered by the troops on the Pacific coast, than that just accomplished under your direction."[53] In hopes of obtaining an additional brevet, Heintzelman would magnify the fight with the Cahuillas into a much larger conflict, much as he had done with the Battle of Huamantla during the Mexican War. He made extra copies of his report of the Cahuilla fight and sent them to Margaret for publication in the *Buffalo Commercial Advertiser.*

When orders came directing him to reestablish Fort Yuma, he agreed with Margaret that she and the children should return to Buffalo. It was particularly heart wrenching for Samuel Peter to realize that he would not see his family again for two or even three years. It was one of those times he wished he had never pursued a career in the military: "I could not realize that Margaret and the children were going, but . . . I made up my mind not to see them again for some time."[54]

Before again heading for the Yuma Crossing, he pushed supplies across the mountains to Vallecitos and watched as the schooner *Sierra Nevada* sailed for the mouth of the Colorado River with more supplies and a company of the 2nd Infantry. With four companies of the 2nd Infantry and a company of dragoons commanded by Capt. George Stoneman, 160 men in all, Heintzelman left San Diego on February 8, 1852. At Cook's Wells in the desert, about twenty miles before reaching the river, Heintzelman sent Stoneman and his dragoons downstream from Yuma Crossing to seize a ferry that was being operated by the Indians. All Stoneman could find, however, was a small scow much farther south.[55] After a fatiguing sixteen-day march, Heintzelman was back at the Colorado River, "worse off than when we first occupied the post last winter," yet he vowed to scour the country and "punish the Indians if they or their villages can be found."[56] Seeing the post burned, his small boat sunk, the garden withered and trampled, and his grapevines and peach trees dead, Heintzelman became convinced that Captain Davidson was a "notorious coward." In fact, he could not "find words to express" his "contempt for the coward who abandoned the post." With the army now at war with the Yumas, the fort had become a place of peril and "perfect exile." What "a life this is to lead," Heintzelman wrote, "far away from all you love and uncertain when you will join them."[57]

By spring 1852 the blinding sandstorms so common to the area, "burning like the blasts from a furnace," temporarily halted all army operations. "It has been blowing a gale and sand flying on the desert," the post commander recorded. Two weeks later, with the temperature dropping from 100 degrees to 57 degrees in two hours, one of the worst storms he had ever seen swept over the area, flattening and ripping the men's tents to shreds. Even Heintzelman's buggy "was sent flying" in the heavy wind. "Such clouds of dust I never saw before," he declared, "it is worse than any description I can give. To realize it you must feel the sand and dust in your eyes and over everything about you." With such natural challenges, most of the men became preoccupied with just surviving. Rations remained short, and considerable time had to be devoted to the construction of temporary brush shelters to help shade the tents from the burning sun. The captain spent great effort in drilling and training his soldiers, most of whom, he told department headquarters, "appear never to have had a firearm in their hands before they reached San Diego."[58]

From the time he first arrived at the Colorado River, Heintzelman realized that Fort Yuma was one of the most isolated posts in the entire West, that his success was dependant on the army's ability to supply the post by water; sending wagons overland across the desert was simply too long and perilous. "After a steamboat reaches this post and it is demonstrated beyond a doubt that we can be supplied by water, there will no longer be a need for a depot at San Diego," he postulated. Such a steamer could reach not only the Yuma Crossing but also even the "great canyon" far upriver. With dependable water communication and transportation, Fort Yuma would become the best route to the Mormon settlements of Deseret at the Great Salt Lake. Moreover, he concluded, the men at Yuma could enjoy "the comforts of civilized life."[59] Somewhat of a visionary, Heintzelman predicted that settlers could be attracted to the area, where wheat, cotton, corn, and sugar could be grown in the fertile soil along the two rivers.

In early February 1852 the *Sierra Nevada* arrived at the mouth of the Colorado River with ten thousand rations and was able to make its way upstream sixty miles. There two fifty-foot-long lighters were constructed.[60] Due to the fast current of the river, however, it would take more than a month to pole the boats upstream to Fort Yuma. While trying to ascend the river, one of the flatboats was swamped by the bore of the river and its entire cargo lost. With a new load, the lighter was eventually able to make it all the way to the Yuma Crossing, while the second boat was forced to unload at Ogden's Landing, far downriver.

Realizing that most of the supplies would still have to be brought overland, Heintzelman sent Capt. Edward H. Fitzgerald with a detachment of forty dragoons and a mule train to escort the wagons to the post. After traversing the boggy Yuma Valley, Fitzgerald went into camp in the desert eighteen miles away only to have eight of his men and a civilian teamster attacked and besieged for eighteen hours by as many as three hundred Yuma warriors. All but one of the men guarding the dragoon's animals were killed, as were four of the Indians in what was called the "Battle of San Luis." Leaving the men unburied, Fitzgerald fled back to the fort with the tragic news. At the head of a hastily arranged burial detail of sixty men, Heintzelman went back into the desert and found the corpses stripped and devoured by buzzards. In retaliation he became even more determined to undertake an aggressive campaign against the Yumas. He also requested permission to cross his men into Mexico, if necessary, in pursuit of the hostiles. The fight, in which the Yumas bragged that they had driven "the Americans from the river and killed their soldiers," gave the Indians "much confidence," Heintzelman was forced to admit.[61] He realized it would be sometime before he could reduce the size of his garrison, as department headquarters had hoped he could do.

By August a second schooner, the *Capacity*, had arrived at the mouth of the Colorado River, and by late September it too had made its way upriver to where the *Sierra Nevada* had anchored. More importantly, the men of the *Capacity* began assembling a sixty-five-foot-long, sixteen-foot-wide, twenty-five-horsepower sidewheeler called *Uncle Sam*. By late November word came that the *Uncle Sam* was headed upriver with thirty-two tons of supplies. "I am looking for her every moment," Heintzelman excitedly told department headquarters.[62]

Although delayed by mechanical problems and forced to stop each day for several hours to cut mesquite to feed the steamer's small boiler, early on the morning of December 3, after fourteen days on the river, the *Uncle Sam* arrived at Fort Yuma to the elation of the post commander and his men. To celebrate the momentous occasion, Capt. James Turnbull, skipper of the *Uncle Sam*, took Heintzelman and the other officers on a short jaunt up the Gila and Colorado rivers. The small steamer, more of a tug than a steamboat, then departed but on Christmas Day returned with more supplies. By late January she had made two more provisioning trips, and in early April she made yet another. On June 22, however, the *Uncle Sam* sank at her moorings five miles below the post. Heintzelman sent several men with ropes and blocks to try and raise the vessel, but they were unsuccessful. During the next two years, the post would be regularly supplied by steamboat. In fact, the Colorado was "far superior to the Ohio," Heintzelman concluded, and if "iron could be introduced by this river," a southern route would be the most practical for a transcontinental railroad.[63]

Late in March, largely in retaliation for the defeat at San Luis, Heintzelman sent two detachments of forty men each under the command of Captains Fitzgerald and Davidson some seventy miles upriver to destroy a Yuma village. The Indians had detected the advance, however, and by means of smoke signals and runners had abandoned several rancherias before the arrival of the bluecoats. Only twenty Yumas were spotted, and only one old man was captured. A few days later a short expedition by the dragoons up the Gila found only a few Indian trails. Shortly thereafter Lt. Frederick Steele led forty men in a third expedition up the west bank of the Colorado and was able to catch a small band of Indians off guard, killing several Yumas, though most of the Quechan escaped into the heavy vegetation along the river banks, from which they swam to the opposite shore.[64] After destroying several fields of green wheat, Steele returned to the fort.

Nevertheless, by late April the Yumas had become so bold as to prowl around camp "day and night." Heintzelman had hopes of apprehending some of the Indians, but there were not even enough horses or mules to make a meaningful scout. Besides, his recruits remained too rowdy and undisciplined for any effective military engagement. When travelers arrived to report a large party of hostile Indians some forty miles up the Colorado, he did send thirty men seventy miles upriver, but they could find no sign of hostiles before returning. Still, Heintzelman was forced to maintain constant pickets.[65]

In mid-May Lieutenant Sweeny led twenty-five men in a foray downriver to attack a small Yuma village, killing one warrior, wounding an Indian woman, and burning the village and a large quantity of clothing and provisions. In a second scorched-earth expedition, Lt. Henry Bascom Hendershott destroyed two small Yuma villages, killed two Indians, and burned several small wheat fields. In a third scout, led by 1st Lt. George Pearce, only days later, the soldiers killed three Yuma warriors and wounded Chief Pasqual. In this encounter one woman was wounded and a child, Heintzelman wrote, "unfortunately drowned." The morale of the men was recovering rapidly from the disaster at San Luis, he informed department headquarters.[66]

In daytime temperatures averaging 105 degrees, small scouts continued to hunt for hostile Indians well into May. With twenty men each, Sweeny and Lt. James Curtis searched upriver again but could find no Indians and only a few abandoned rancherias. In early June, when an express rider galloped into the post reporting that he had been attacked by a large force of Cocopas, Heintzelman sent out the entire garrison. On another occasion, one scouting party crossed the river and moved up the Gila River while a second scoured the river bottoms above and below the post.[67]

By June the heat had become so intense that it was virtually impossible to undertake any offensive operations. In July Lieutenant Curtis did lead a small scout downriver, but after losing one man from heatstroke returned to the post. By this time the annual floodtide had reached the post, sweeping away the garden that Heintzelman had carefully planted. The heat and the flooding made any scout up the Gila River to the east equally impossible. As soon as the water began to recede, the captain replanted the garden, and in ten days the seeds had sprouted. He sought to grow "something green" in hopes of "arresting the scurvy," which had begun to spread among some of the older soldiers.[68]

With the burning heat intensifying, the garrison remained largely inactive well into early summer. Regardless, little could be done until July, when the crops of the Yumas would begin to mature as a result of the spring floods that "fertilized" the small floodplains of the Colorado "as those of the Nile." Hostilities with the Yumas came to a climax in late August, when Ambrosio Armijo and a number of "Nuevo Mejicanos" who were headed for California approached Yuma Crossing with nine thousand head of sheep. Armijo had first run into problems at the Pima villages when the Pimas and Maricopas ran off a large part of his herd. Pushing slowly west along the Gila, he was nearing the Colorado when his party ran into a band of thirty Yumas, who tried to intimidate his herders and drive off more of his sheep. Armijo immediately sent an urgent message across the river requesting protection. Without hesitation, Heintzelman dispatched Lieutenant Sweeny with fourteen men. No sooner was Sweeny across the river than he sent a message that the Yumas were threatening to attack him and had already killed one of Armijo's men. In fact, the Indians were said to number as many as eight hundred warriors and were reported to also include Apaches, Mohaves, and Maricopas.[69]

With his entire force, Heintzelman crossed the river to confront the Indians. Well past midnight he pushed his men up the Gila River, hoping to locate Sweeny and the camp of the Nuevo Mejicanos. But in the thick brush of the valley floor, the troopers became lost after the moon went down and were forced to bivouac for the night. "My intention was to reach the Mexican camp, learn the position of the Indians and attack them at daylight—before they knew we had crossed the river," Heintzelman reported. When sunup brought the burning desert heat, he learned that he had passed Armijo's camp during the night and sent the bluecoats back down the Gila. The soldiers had gone less than a mile when a large party of Yuma were seen approaching. "A warm discussion arose among'st them," Heintzelman recalled, "some wishing to fight and others to run."[70]

Concerned that his men were on foot while the 100–150 Yuma and Cocopa warriors were mounted on "fine horses" and possessed "a perfect knowledge of the country," Heintzelman sent out one of the sheep herders to contact the Indians to determine their true intentions, but the man became frightened and returned. Hoping to outmaneuver the hostiles, the captain sent one company to flank them, but when the Yumas and Cocopas spotted the men, they immediately opened fire with rifles and a flight of arrows. With the thermometer at 110 degrees, Heintzelman gave the order for his entire command to advance, whereupon the Indians scattered. In this encounter two infantrymen were wounded with arrows and two Indians were also wounded, one of them being tall and rawboned Chief Pasqual. With the Indians in retreat but the bluecoats unable to pursue, Heintzelman ordered his men back to the fort. The march had progressed only a short distance when one of the Nuevo Mejicanos rode up to say that the Yuma chief José María wanted to meet with the captain. During the tense confrontation, the Yuma chief expressed "great pleasure" at seeing him and proposed a truce until the Indians could gather their crops, at which time they would come into the fort to sign a peace treaty. Heintzelman bluntly told the chief that if the Indians truly wanted peace, now was the time. They agreed that José María should consult with the other Yuma leaders first and come into the fort in a few days.

The next day José María appeared again, saying that he was not responsible for the violence along the Colorado River and that Vicente, another chief, was the one who had incited the Yumas. Convinced that José María represented only one small band, Heintzelman gave him an ultimatum. The principal chiefs had ten days to come into the post to make peace or the army would attack them. He reminded José María that he had made peace with the Indians two years earlier. The Yumas and Cocopas should declare what they prefer, for the captain stated that "peace or war was a matter of indifference to us, that we were sent here to punish the bad and that I would do so."[71]

Ten anxious days passed at Fort Yuma, and no Yuma or Cocopa appeared. Knowing that the Indians were beginning to gather their crops and that they could be easily found, Heintzelman prepared to move against them. "I have deemed it advisable not to delay," he told headquarters.[72] Capt. George Andrews was sent upriver with twenty men and a flatboat of provisions while Heintzelman prepared to leave the next day with eighty men and twelve days' rations on pack mules. Just as he was leaving, however, three Yuma warriors made their appearance at the crossing, saying that other Indian leaders would arrive at the post within a few days. Still Heintzelman ordered his men into the field, determined to force a peace.

By September 29 he was already sixty miles upriver in what he thought was Utah Territory, hoping to surprise an Indian rancheria reported to be eight miles distant. Moving before daylight, as was his custom, the soldiers were turning the point of a large sand hill when they learned that the Indians had detected their approach and fled farther upriver. Continuing to push his men upstream, where an even larger Yuma village was reported, he observed large fields of ripe wheat, but all the rancherias were abandoned. On several occasions Indians were seen in the distance, and Heintzelman spurred his horse ahead of his men, trying to halt some of them in hopes of persuading them to contact their chiefs, but the Indians ran into the tall reeds along the river. After making camp for the night, Tómas Chiuj, the Santa Ysabel chief and Heintzelman's guide, was able to contact several older Yumas, who said their principal chiefs were several days' journey upriver. That night some of the Yumas shot a few arrows into the camp and set fire to the grass nearby. Meeting Captain Andrews and the supplies, Heintzelman was preparing to continue up the Colorado when he was approached by a "fine old man" who said that his name was Huttami, the supreme civil chief of the Yuma, that his word was law and he was "for peace."[73]

On October 2 four other Yuma chiefs came into camp professing peace, whereupon Heintzelman demanded that Santiago and Cavallo y Pelo, the two principal chiefs, be sent for. Both were "old and good for nothing" and far upriver, the Indians replied. A few days later José María came into camp proclaiming himself the primary chief. Realizing that most of the leaders were indeed far upriver and that if he continued his pursuit, "there was not the slightest probability of my catching them," Heintzelman ordered his men back to the post. "I could have destroyed many of their fields and harassed their people" and "driven them further up the river and created much distress, but it is not probable I could have arrived at a different result," he wrote. Besides, "the punishment would have fallen on the least guilty and particularly on a branch of the tribe who have always lived on that part of the river. Their desire now is to gather their crops and then to reestablish themselves in our neighborhood to plant as before, agreeing when our animals stray to return them and exchange their productions for what we have to give."[74]

Well into 1853 Heintzelman would continue to negotiate with the Yumas, and by late spring large numbers of the Quechan had returned to plant their crops along the river above and below Fort Yuma. Violence flared in May 1853, however, between the Yumas and the Cocopas. In one raid the Cocopas surrounded three Yuma rancherias, killing Chief Macedon, four men, and ten women and children while making off with twelve prisoners and the Yumas' horse herd. The Cocopas, on foot and on horseback, also attacked José María's camp, killing three men and slaughtering twenty-three women and children. "This appears to have been a most unprovoked and wanton aggression on the part of the Cocopa," Heintzelman concluded.[75] Although the violence had occurred on Mexican soil, he sent out a party of two officers and thirty men with a few Yumas to burn the dead and determine, if possible, the cause of the violence. Within days José María arrived at the post to report that the principal chief of the Cocopas had released some of the women and children, but the majority of Cocopa warriors had fled into the mountains with most of their captives.

The Yumas later joined with the Cuchanos for a retaliatory raid against the Cocopas in which seven Cocopa warriors and four women were killed.[76] A few weeks later as many as 250 Yuma warriors and some of their allies stopped at the fort on their way to attack the Cocopas. So many Indians were in camp that some of the soldiers became greatly alarmed.

After considerable effort, Heintzelman was finally able to establish a meaningful peace with the Yumas, and hundreds of Indians began to appear at the post. Part of his success was due to Tómas Chiuj, the Indian chief he brought from Santa Ysabel. Tómas, who spoke Quechan and Spanish and had lived among the Yuma, had worked for the Boundary Commission.[77] Many of the Yumas brought corn, pumpkins, melons, and squash as gifts or to sell. Heintzelman rode out to visit several of their villages and carefully compiled a forty-three-page handwritten report on the different Indian tribes of the area, mentioning their numbers, customs, and religions, as well as climatic data, including the highest and lowest temperatures at Fort Yuma for 1852. So impressed was the adjutant general by the lengthy paper that he forwarded it to the secretary of war, who sent it on to Congress, which published it in the *Congressional Record*.[78] Heintzelman befriended many of the Yumas who came into the fort, including one woman with a mixed-blood child.

During a windstorm in October 1852, disaster struck Fort Yuma. Hearing the ringing of the fire bell, Heintzelman rushed out to find several buildings engulfed in fire. A baker in Company H had left one of the large bread ovens open, and coals from it had blown against the side of the kitchen. The kitchen was soon engulfed in flames, and the wind-whipped fire spread to the company quarters and another kitchen. Heint-

Fort Yuma, Arizona. Author's collection.

zelman was busy fighting the flames when he realized that the recently completed commissary storehouse was also on fire. Only two hours earlier an ordnance train had arrived from San Diego with a large supply of ammunition. Fearing an explosion, several of the officers and men had retreated to the opposite end of the parade ground. Captain Davidson, instead of assisting in saving the ordnance, had dragged his trunk out of his tent and retreated even farther to the top of the hill outside the post. In the flames and dust, Heintzelman persuaded a few men to join him as he rushed through the flames to save forty boxes of cartridges and two barrels of powder. "The fire was all around me before I got all the ammunition," he wrote. Since he had ordered the men to concentrate on saving the ordnance, only a small quantity of foodstuffs, including beans, coffee, flour, and meat, were salvaged. Another serious loss was a large portion of the post and company records. When Colonel Smith wrote to praise him for his "presence of mind and daring intrepidity" in saving the supplies, Heintzelman forwarded a copy of the letter to Margaret in Buffalo for publication in the local press.[79]

A month later a violent and horrific earthquake shook the area, toppling newly erected rock and adobe walls, frightening the garrison, touching off landslides in the nearby mountains, and crumbling the banks of the Colorado River, even slightly altering its course. Even more spectacular was the eruption of an enormous geyser some forty-five miles to the south, clearly visible from the fort, which sent a "beautiful snowy jet more than a thousand feet into the air . . . above the tops of the mountains like a white cloud."[80] Three months later Heintzelman visited the site and recorded the temperature in several ponds around the base of the geyser, which was continuing to erupt every fifteen or twenty minutes, at 118–170 degrees. Later in the year he was fortunately absent when lightning struck his new quarters, dislodging adobes, "splitting the door frames [and] knocking off the casing."[81]

Although most supplies now came by ship around Baja California, basic necessities at the post remained scarce. A garden was again planted in the bottomland near the post, but the Colorado soon washed it away. Many soldiers were without proper clothing and were shoeless. "I never saw men in so destitute a condition," Heintzelman noted. "Some have not a change of clothes to their backs, no blanket and their shoes worn out." The lack of "clothing, shoes in particular, for the recruits is a great embarrassment," he informed department headquarters.[82]

A few of the men at Fort Yuma succumbed from disease and were buried in a small cemetery Heintzelman established "amongst willows and mesquite" at the base of a nearby hillside. Recruits continued to arrive, but many were unable to bear the loneliness and hardships of life there and deserted into the arid and foreboding expanses of the desert. If apprehended, they were whipped, branded, placed in irons, or drummed out of the service. Many were never seen again, though the bleached bones of a few were later found in the desert.[83]

Heintzelman was particularly shocked when Capt. Louis S. Craig was killed by deserters near New River in the Colorado Desert. Spotting two men on foot in the waste and realizing who they were, Craig called on them to surrender. When the deserters refused, the captain, accompanied by two sergeants, followed the men five miles, trying to "induce them to submit." The two finally stopped, turned about, and defiantly declared that "the matter must be settled." Handing his revolver to one of his sergeants, Craig dismounted, unbuckled his sword, dropped it to the sand, and advanced toward the men, "telling them he was unarmed." When one of the sergeants rode off to retrieve the captain's mule, which had strayed off into the desert, one of the deserters shot Craig while the second fired at the other sergeant, wounding him in the leg and killing his mule. As Craig bled to death in the desert, the assailants rifled his pockets, took the revolver from the sergeant, and rode off toward Mexico on their captured mules. Although Heintzelman was sure the men had escaped into the mountains of Baja California, the two deserters, Cpl. William Hayes and Pvt. John Condon, were captured by friendly Indians. Imprisoned at

San Diego, they were court-martialed, found guilty of murder, and hanged before a large crowd.[84]

A contributing factor to the large number of desertions was the fact that many of the men were running around shoeless and nearly naked. Although clothing and new shoes were eventually issued, desertions continued. In fact, Heintzelman learned that several men were waiting only for the new shoes before fleeing in mass, even forcing "their way through" if necessary. "This mutinous spirit is deeper than I anticipated," he wrote in his journal. "I learned tonight that forty men have sworn to desert in a body." He even warned department headquarters that "a mutinous spirit has manifested itself among'st the recruits." To ward off trouble, Heintzelman had the men's ammunition seized, issued limited rations, and ordered several sergeants to keep a close eye on those suspected of plotting a revolt. After placing one of the "ring leaders" in chains, the spirit of insubordination subsided, and tensions at the post returned to normal. But enlisted men were not the only disgruntled soldiers along the Colorado. Captain Davidson as well as Lieutenants Hendershott, Sweeny, and Curtis asked Pacific Division headquarters in San Francisco for transfers to Oregon or anywhere else away from Fort Yuma, where they had "been living in this extremely hot climate and on little else but salted provisions."[85]

In the heat of early June 1852, John Russell Bartlett and the Mexican Boundary Commission, after a fatiguing journey of twelve days across the Colorado Desert in temperatures as high as 114 degrees, arrived at Fort Yuma to a cheerful reception. Heintzelman shared his quarters with the controversial Rhode Islander and helped ferry the commission's animals and baggage to the south bank. He also ordered Lt. George H. Paige and twenty-five men to accompany Bartlett as far as the Pima villages. "I am much pleased with Major Heintzelman who has given us a most hospitable reception, and rendered me great aid," Bartlett wrote. By early July he had visited with the Pimas and was at the Maricopa villages, where he planned a short expedition up the Salt River before pushing east to El Paso del Norte. Despite previous promises by the War Department, however, Bartlett was embittered that Lt. Amiel Whipple and the Topographical Engineers refused to provide a sufficient escort.[86]

Well into 1853, construction at the fort continued. Buildings, laid out over the old Spanish mission, were constructed of adobes made by Mexican laborers. At the same time, Heintzelman continued to explore and map the area up and down the Colorado River and east and west along the Gila Trail. Hearing rumors of gold in the mountains of Sonora and upriver on the Colorado, he frequently turned lengthy desert reconnaissances in search of hostile Indians into prospecting forays. Heintzelman's position at Fort Yuma, a friend would write many years later, "gave him great opportunities for gaining information about the mineral resources of Arizona."[87]

While many of the men and officers at the fort spent their leisure time drinking and frequenting a busy house of prostitution, Heintzelman, who was now commanding the entire Southern District of California, spent his time reading and playing chess and euchre. He read books on the Mexican War as well as a new publication entitled *Uncle Tom's Cabin*, an instant bestseller that he found anything but "extraordinary." Frequently while sitting in a tub of water to escape the heat, he reread Prescott's two-volume *Conquest of Mexico*, again in Spanish, as well as Miguel de Cervantes's *Don Quixote*. In the uninterrupted and seemingly endless heat, he wore the "scantiest possible wardrobe" and at night even tried sleeping naked on the roof of his quarters.[88]

To improve life at the desolate and isolated post, Heintzelman persuaded headquarters to allow him to hire a chaplain. Since two of the officers, the post sutler, and half of the soldiers were Catholic, a priest should be sent, he wrote the Bishop of California at Monterey. The priest, who the major hoped could speak Spanish, would be paid forty dollars a month and would also serve as schoolmaster. Two months later, however, he was disappointed to learn that a priest could not be found for the desolate outpost.[89]

At Fort Yuma, letters from Margaret and friends in the East were always welcome.[90] Newspapers from San Francisco and San Diego were available, but they arrived weeks late. Sometimes Margaret sent newspapers from Buffalo or New York City, but they took several months to arrive. The captain continued to send copies of his reports for publication in the *Buffalo Commercial Advertiser*, hoping that such favorable exposure would assure him an additional brevet.

Samuel Peter wrote Margaret several hundred letters while he was at Fort Yuma, a small part of the thousands of lengthy letters he would write her from forts and army camps during his antebellum career. Unfortunately, fewer than five of these letters, spanning over thirty years, have survived. One eight-page letter, dated November 1, 1852 (and numbered "26"), which was written amid a violent dust storm, provides considerable insight into their warm and loving relationship. Heintzelman was excited that daguerreotypes of both Mary and Charles had just arrived, though he was disappointed that he could not tell how much the children had grown and that they were posed with such a "grave look."[91] He seemed pleased that Margaret was well and teased her not to be afraid of getting too fat. Samuel Peter himself had gained 7 pounds since the hot weather had abated and now weighed almost 130 pounds. In the recent presidential election held at Fort Yuma, he expressed surprise that the Whig candidate, Mexican War hero Gen. Winfield Scott, only garnered five votes, while the Democrat, Franklin Pierce of New Hampshire, received thirty-two votes.

Always the entrepreneur, Heintzelman invested in the "Colorado Ferry Company," which was in operation at the crossing; a sheep and cattle ranch at the junction of the rivers; and a small San Francisco business, all while also maintaining his more-important mining interests. His investment in the ferry, which he later sold, proved to be one of his few profitable ventures.[92] But his involvement in the local economy went far beyond that of other officers, not only at Fort Yuma but also at many of the military posts he would serve at in the West over the years to come. For the remainder of his life he would be the soldier-entrepreneur.

Among his responsibilities, Heintzelman kept busy assisting an ever-increasing stream of destitute immigrants and gold seekers wandering out of the desert from the east. One such party, on its way to California, reached the left bank of the river and sent a note to the fort saying that a woman in the group was about to give birth and needed the post surgeon. Heintzelman later learned that the woman, after giving birth to a healthy daughter, crossed the ferry to dance the night away before departing for the Pacific the next morning.[93]

Sonora and New Mexico herdsmen such as Ambrosio Armijo, heading for the goldfields with flocks of sheep numbering as many as twenty thousand, were not the only ones to arrive at the Yuma Crossing. There were also ever increasing numbers of zealous Mormons bound for Utah. Heintzelman met yet another important figure in American history when a party of mountain men led by the legendary Christopher "Kit" Carson came riding out of the desert from the west on their way home to New Mexico.[94]

Unwelcome rowdy filibusters, blinded by Manifest Destiny and determined to conquer large parts of northern Mexico, gathered at the river. Although the "grey-eyed man of destiny," thirty-year-old William Walker, was able to seize La Paz in Baja California, he was far less fortunate in his attempts to claim Sonora. Two small parties from Walker's ill-fated invasion arrived at Fort Yuma on foot, desperate and hungry. The bulk of the expedition, numbering as many as one hundred men, were some fifteen miles below the post trying to cross the river with a small cannon and a small herd of cattle. All of them were said to be suffering from "want of provisions, shoes and clothing." Heintzelman learned from the stragglers that Walker's plan was to strike the Gila above the junction, push east to the Pima villages, then turn southwest to Tucson before continuing on to Santa Cruz, Sonora, and eventually the capital, Hermosillo. "My own impression is that the expedition will have to disband or starve," he wrote. Many stragglers from the Walker expedition continued to trickle into the post for weeks as the grandiose scheme did indeed flounder in the desert. Yet when orders arrived to arrest as many of the filibusters as possible, all the captain could find were two young misguided teenagers.[95]

In May 1854 Andrew Belcher Gray, who was surveying a possible railroad route along the 32nd Parallel, arrived at Yuma Crossing. He wrote of Heintzelman, who welcomed him and shared with him his own "notes and sketches" of the region, his "hospitality and generous assistance . . . can never be forgotten."[96]

By far the most fascinating frontier traveler to arrive at Fort Yuma was the "Great Western." Well over six-feet tall, the notorious Sarah Bowman had fought Mexicans at Fort Brown, Texas; followed Gen. Zachary Taylor's men into Mexico; and had gone west with the army. Said to have been the "greatest whore in the west," she opened a mess hall and later a brothel at the crossing. Heintzelman estimated Bowman's age at fifty and described her as "a large, tall, fearless looking woman." In the scorching summer heat of 1854, with the thermometer at 117 degrees, he even accompanied the Great Western, who was really thirty-nine, along with her husband and one of her adopted daughters, up the Gila River by steamer for a pleasant picnic in a grove of cottonwood trees.[97]

In the heat of early June 1854, Col. Joseph King Fenno Mansfield, inspector general of the army, arrived at Fort Yuma. After looking over the buildings, the waterworks, and the sidewheeler *General Jesup*, which was anchored at the post, the gray-bearded, no-nonsense colonel watched as Heintzelman's men drilled and performed target practice. "I believe the colonel was well satisfied with what he saw," Heintzelman reported. Indeed, Mansfield recorded that the men "gave a very handsome drill and some target firing." Moreover, the post commander was "entitled to great credit for the improvements in the roads and for the manner he . . . supplied the post with water."[98]

One party of miners reaching the Yuma Crossing in June 1854 included a young Kentucky adventurer named Charles Debriell Poston and a German mining engineer, Hermann Vollrath Ehrenberg, who had survived the Goliad Massacre during the Texas Revolution. After prospecting for four months in the Sonoran Desert, they had discovered several rich veins of silver in the mountains west of Tubac and had specimens of ore to prove it. At the crossing Poston and Ehrenberg began surveying a town site called "Colorado City," a precursor of present-day Yuma.[99] At the same time, exciting news arrived from the East. The United States, in hopes of building a Pacific railroad, had purchased from Mexico 29,640 square miles of territory south of the Gila River in present-day Arizona and New Mexico for $10 million. In the next decade, both Poston and the Gadsden Purchase would become important parts of Heintzelman's life.

After three years at the post, Heintzelman's thoughts drifted back to Buffalo and his family. In one "vivid" and terrible dream, he saw his family swept away in a frightful storm. Finally in June 1854, after more than four years in the Southwest, word arrived that he was being relieved by Maj. George H. Thomas of the 3rd Artillery.[100] Heintzelman was especially touched when several hundred Yumas, including Chiefs Pascual, Cavallo y Pelo, and José María, assembled to bid him a fond farewell. After selling his furniture and some household items to the Great Western, he rode west across the desert with a drunken escort to San Diego, departing from there in early July for San Pedro, Monterey, and the foggy, ship-jammed harbor of San Francisco.

Anxious to visit the goldfields himself, Heintzelman hurried off in a "miserable" boat with several Chinese men and women to Sacramento and Marysville, then on by stage to Sutter's Mill and Grass Valley, and finally going deeper into the Sierra Nevadas, where he inspected some mills and several large diggings, including the famous "Gold Hill." There he collected a few gold nuggets and even caught sight of the cottage where the voluptuous dancer Lola Montes lived.[101]

Back in San Francisco, he attended the theater and a "magnificent gambling house" before departing for New York via Nicaragua. Steaming past Cape Lucas at the southern tip of Baja California in calm seas and by Acapulco in the night, he spotted the Nicaraguan volcanoes in the early morning mist as the ship put into a balmy San Juan del Sur. Carried ashore by natives through the tropical waves, he found the U.S. flag flying and Nicaragua in revolution. Convinced that the Americans, filibustering precursors to William Walker, were "fighting for freedom," he gave his sword and belt to one of the revolutionaries.[102]

On muleback he continued inland past grass huts where natives offered to sell everything from lemonade, liquors, and tropical fruit to monkeys, armadillos, and parakeets. Crossing a calm Lake Nicaragua on a crowded, rickety steamboat with no place to sleep or even sit down, he reached the village of San Carlos, where the Rio San Juan flowed out of the lake and a small sternwheeler waited to take passengers downriver. Forced to disembark at a series of rapids on the river, he walked through a pouring rain to another small sternwheeler that carried him past groves of coconut trees to Greytown on the Caribbean. "Gentlemen can get along," he wrote, "but this is not at present the route for ladies."[103]

On September 1, 1854, Heintzelman boarded the *Star of the West* and a week later was off Cape Hatteras, North Carolina, in heavy seas. Twelve days after leaving Greytown, he arrived in New York. After telegraphing Margaret in Buffalo, he hurried off to see sister Juliana in the Brandywine Valley of southeastern Pennsylvania. But he soon returned to New York to sit for the spectacled Mathew B. Brady's daguerreotype camera at his studio on Broadway. Later he went shopping with Julia Brady, attended the theater and the opera, and the next day set off for Buffalo for a joyous reunion with his family. The children were fine, though Mary had grown so much that he scarcely recognized her. Margaret, however, was thin and did not look well. Although the family was still in mourning for Eddie Summers, who had died unexpectedly, Heintzelman was able to celebrate his forty-ninth birthday with cake and bourbon. And despite Margaret being somewhat subdued on their tenth wedding anniversary, the couple went on a sleigh excursion, attended an eggnog party at Christmas, and held a small celebration for Charles on his ninth birthday.[104] After four years in the Far Southwest, it was good to be in the East again. It was a joyous time for the forty-nine-year-old brevet major and his family. Yet even greater adventures and dangers awaited him in the Desert Southwest.

FOUR

Arizona and Silver

IN FEBRUARY 1855 HEINTZELMAN TRAVELED to New York City, Philadelphia, and finally Washington, where he met with Charles Poston to discuss the prospect of opening silver mines in the Gadsden Purchase and the future of Colorado City, "our city." Poston had continued to prospect the vast expanses of the Sonoran Desert and was certain that some mines near Tubac, though previously worked by Spanish miners, would yield vast riches. In the capital Heintzelman also met with Secretary of War Jefferson Davis, the real inspiration behind the Pacific railroad and the Gadsden Purchase, who surprisingly "made no allusion" to their "former acquaintance." After a brief tour of duty at Carlisle Barracks, Pennsylvania, where he was responsible for the training of cavalry recruits, he was able to obtain a four-month leave of absence and return to Buffalo. Later, while visiting his sister Juliana at West Chester, Pennsylvania, he received orders cutting short his leave and sending him to Jefferson Barracks, Missouri, which had been his first duty post after graduating from West Point. With a cholera epidemic sweeping the St. Louis area, most of the army personnel had fled, and Heintzelman was concerned that he too would come down with the dreaded disease. Not satisfied with his new assignment, he fired off a request to the adjutant general in Washington asking that he be compensated for transporting his baggage to St Louis, mostly his books, amounting to $101.[1]

Back in Washington in March 1855, his mood improved considerably when Gen. Winfield Scott praised him for his services at Fort Yuma and promised him a seven-month leave of absence. Shortly thereafter he learned that he had been promoted to full major in the 1st Infantry.[2] Perhaps his long hours of dedicated service had paid off after all. Never had his future in the army looked brighter.

By the early summer of 1855, he was back at Carlisle Barracks. With the vast majority of his veteran sergeants transferring to the more prestigious 1st and 2nd Cavalry, Heintzelman bitterly complained to Washington that he did not have a "single suitable man for a non-commissioned officer."[3] Col. Edwin Sumner had sent him a corporal, but with recruits arriving daily, the situation was becoming increasingly chaotic.

In the late summer of 1855, Heintzelman was appointed superintendent of the Western Recruiting Department and sent to Newport Barracks, Kentucky, on the south bank of the Ohio River opposite Cincinnati. He had been in the Bluegrass State for only a few months when he was ordered to Fort Leavenworth, Kansas Territory, for the court-martial of Lt. Col. William Reading Montgomery, who was accused by the proslavery faction in Kansas of appropriating a portion of the Fort Riley Military Reserve for private purposes. At Fort Leavenworth in the days before the court convened, Heintzelman spent time socializing with Colonel Mansfield and a West Point classmate, Albert Sidney Johnston, as well as enjoying dinners at the quarters of Bvt. Maj. Henry Hopkins Sibley and his wife, Charlotte. After the court-martial found Montgomery guilty and ordered that he be dismissed from the service, Heintzelman was sent 130 miles west to Fort Riley for a second court-martial. This trial was for James Simons, an assistant surgeon from South Carolina, who was charged with leaving his post during a smallpox epidemic. The emotional case, which was heard in a cold and unpleasant hospital tent, revealed a grisly story of how fifty-nine soldiers had died of smallpox, seven of them in a single day.[4] Even the wife of 1st Lt. Lewis A. Armistead, a young officer in the 6th Infantry who was stationed at the post at the time, perished in the deadly outbreak.

It was while he was at Forts Leavenworth and Riley that Heintzelman became well acquainted with another member of the courts, Lt. Col. Robert E. Lee, who had been two years behind him at West Point. The two became close, and in the evenings after dinner they frequently took long walks together and conversed freely. When Simons too was found guilty and dismissed, Heintzelman and Lee rode back to Fort Leavenworth in mid-November, booking a stateroom on a Missouri River steamer bound for St. Louis. Boarding the vessel, the two officers watched in amazement as a flirtatious widow arrived with the four-week-old body of her deceased husband. Heintzelman noted that the widow was listed on the passenger list as "Mrs. —— and corpse." In Jefferson City Heintzelman and Lee put on their cloaks and "took a walk through the town and to the State House."[5] Reaching St. Louis in the night, the two parted. They would soon meet again in Washington, then four years later in Texas.

From St. Louis Heintzelman caught the train for Indianapolis and Cincinnati. Back at Newport Barracks in December 1855, there was time to celebrate Margaret's birthday, their eleventh wedding anniversary, Christmas, and Charles's tenth birthday. Most of his duties at the post were routine, and with two servants catering to their every need, the family settled into a two-story house and a comfortable lifestyle. The major watched, however, as eight soldiers who had been found guilty at a court-martial were publicly whipped and, a week later, as another six were drummed out of the service. Although he was a strict disciplinarian, he had always found such scenes unsettling. At Newport Barracks he also served with Dr. Charles Stuart Tripler and Lt. H. B. Hendershott, Lt. A. F. Bond, and Lt. I. N. G. Whistler on several boards of inspection to examine recruits, almost all of whom were found unfit for duty. One was rejected because of epilepsy, two others because of lameness, one with a protruding hernia, and yet another who possessed a "sluggish intellect." Another recruit had a "feebleness of constitution," while one had a "chronic enlargement of both testicles." One young man who appeared before the board had lost all of his front teeth, while another was blind in the right eye. One recent arrival had "constitutional syph[i]lis" and another a "deformed heart," while a "drunkard" was rejected, not because of his continual inebriation, but because of a "chronic inflamation of the right eye" and his "ulcerated legs."[6]

By January 1856 the Ohio River was frozen solid, allowing for ice skating and leisurely walks across its surface to the opera, theater, and a guitar concert in Cincinnati. There Andrew Gray, who Heintzelman had known at Fort Yuma, persuaded him to invest $1,000 in the Texas Western Railroad. Heintzelman also greeted Charles Poston, who brought important "information as to the silver mines in the Purchase." The major introduced Poston to Thomas and William Wrightson, brothers who edited the *Railroad Record*, a publication advocating the development of western railroads. Encouraged by the meeting, Heintzelman and Poston made plans to establish a mining company. Able to persuade the Wrightsons and other Cincinnati businessmen to invest in the venture, Heintzelman was selected president on May 24, 1856, and plans were made to send Poston with a party of men back to Arizona, where he would meet Hermann Ehrenberg, purchase the silver mines in the mountains west of Tubac, and begin mining. In August 1857 the Sonora Exploring and Mining Company was incorporated in Ohio with capital stock listed at $2 million.[7]

With his stock speculation and various business investments failing to yield a profit, the family financial resources were seriously depleted, and Margaret became moody and withdrawn. "We have had frequent quarrels but never so frequent as of late and never so bitter. The great offence is my speculations in railroad and mining stocks and the losses in California. I can't see where this will end," Samuel Peter confided to his journal.[8] The two were able to reconcile their differences, however, and with money borrowed from his sister Maria, he continued to invest in railroads and mining.

Heading west to Arizona, Poston paused to write encouraging letters from Franklin (El Paso), Texas, and from Las Cruces and Mesilla, New Mexico Territory, where he proposed a scheme to buy the Hugh Stevenson Mine in the Organ Mountains, east of Las Cruces, along with a tract of land in the Mesilla Valley for twenty thousand dollars. By late 1856 an illustrated pamphlet with a map and sketches of different sites in the Gadsden Purchase was ready for distribution. In January 185, Poston wrote that he had reached Arizona and that, despite the fact that his party, due to death and illness, was reduced to four, he had taken possession of "17 veins of silver within 10 miles of Tubac" on which ten Mexican miners were already at work. He also expected to acquire the nearby silver-rich Rancho Arivaca. A month later Frederick Brucknow and Charles Schuchard, who were hired as mining engineers, were reporting sixteen veins of silver, some of them two to four feet thick, within a mile of Cerro Colorado, seventeen miles west of Tubac. Heintzelman also began corresponding with Sylvester Mowry, a young and ambitious lieutenant stationed at Fort Yuma who was promoting mining in the Gadsden Purchase, sending him several reports of the Sonora Exploring and Mining Company.[9]

By April 1857, promoting the mining company was consuming much of Heintzelman's time, so much so that a discharged soldier, Thomas G. Hibben, wrote Secretary of War John Floyd complaining of the major's neglect of duty. According to Hibben, "the Commanding Officer paid more attention to his silver mines than he did to his command." Moreover, "being a german himself, he gave office to germans to such an extent that I almost tho't I was in a foreign army and not Uncle Sam's." On a trip to Washington, Heintzelman tried to sell stock in the Sonora Exploring and Mining Company to several officers and friends, including Robert E. Lee, John B. Magruder, and officers at the Mexican Boundary Commission office. He also met and exchanged information with Lt. Joseph Christmas Ives, who was planning an expedition by steamboat up the Colorado River from Fort Yuma. Continuing to promote mining in Arizona, he spoke briefly with Pres. James Buchanan but was disappointed that the tall and ruggedly handsome president did not remember recommending him for West Point thirty-five years earlier.[10]

Back at Newport Barracks, he continued meeting with the Wrightson brothers and became even more convinced of the riches to be had in the Southwest. When one of the post surgeons at Newport Barracks was rumored to have said he was greatly exaggerating the amount of silver in Arizona, Heintzelman was visibly perturbed: "We must stop his mouth."[11]

Heintzelman's interests in the Arizona mines were overshadowed on August 25, 1857, by the birth of his second son, Henry Summers, who was named after Margaret's deceased nephew. Samuel Peter recorded in his journal, however, that the infant did not seem well and did not breath properly. A month later the child fell seriously ill "from pain in the bow[e]ls."[12] For months to come, Henry's frail condition occupied much of the family's attention.

But exciting news continued to arrive from Arizona. Hermann Ehrenberg wrote encouragingly about the mines and sent a map he had skillfully drawn of the Gadsden Purchase and Sonora. Mowry, who had resigned from the army to promote his own Sopori Mining Company, wrote regularly to say that he was coming to Washington to lobby in person for the creation of a Territory of Arizona, separate from New Mexico. Mowry wanted to see Jefferson Davis, and he was hoping that Heintzelman would accompany him. Poston wrote that the main shafts at Cerro Colorado, which he had named the Heintzelman Mine, were reported to be "quite rich."[13]

In October 1857 Heintzelman was back in Washington to meet with William H. Emory, John Butterfield, and Edward Beale, all of whom had valuable information about Arizona. By November he had rented a room at the corner of 16th and F streets and had resumed lobbying on behalf of Arizona. He met with Sen. William M. Gwin of California, who agreed to introduce a bill to organize Arizona Territory, and the two went to see President Buchanan. Heintzelman once again reminded Buchanan that he too was from Lancaster County, Pennsylvania, and that it was the president who had helped him obtain an appointment to West Point. Once again he was disappointed that Buchanan did not recall having done so. Moreover, he wrote, "The Pres't don't know much about Arizona."[14]

Although Mowry shared his correspondence, including a letter from Ehrenberg saying that the Heintzelman Mine was the "richest in the world," the major found this Arizona adventurer to be self-centered, excessively egotistical, and unworthy of trust: "I don't think Mowry intends to do anything to have me remain here and I shall not rely upon him." Mowry somehow had "managed to get himself as authority for much that is said. . . . He gets information from me and others and gives it as his," Heintzelman complained.[15]

In Washington Heintzelman talked with Lt. Robert W. Eagle of the 2nd Cavalry, who had just arrived from Texas. He also met with Maj. William W. Chapman, army quartermaster and a stockholder in the lead and silver mines at Vallecillo, Nuevo León, Mexico. Chapman gave him several copies of a brochure describing the Mexican mines and proposed that his own company and the Sonora Exploring and Mining Company exchange stock.[16] He also took Heintzelman to see Samuel Colt, the "pistol man." Colt appeared interested in the Arizona mines, but Heintzelman was fearful that Mowry would persuade him to invest in the Sopori Mining Company instead. On December 19, 1857, however, Heintzelman spent the evening with Colt and reported that he was "quite taken with our mining Co." Colt offered $10,000 for $100,000 in stock, and Chapman persuaded Heintzelman to accept it.

Heintzelman remained in Washington through Christmas, 1857, as he continued to promote a territorial bill for Arizona. By January 2, 1858, he was in Hartford, Connecticut, to meet with Colt at his large armory. Although despondent and subdued by the death of his only son ten days earlier, Colt gave Heintzelman a check for $10,000.[17] Returning to New York, he met with Major Chapman, then in Washington with Illinois senator Stephen A. Douglas, the "Little Giant" and chairman of the Committee on Territories.

In late January Margaret wrote from Buffalo that their infant son, Henry, was seriously ill with whooping cough. Samuel Peter hurried north and then west through a bleak wintry landscape to find the child near death when he arrived. In early February one-year-old Henry rallied briefly, but a few days later he was so ill that his grandmother insisted that he be baptized as soon as possible. Although many in the family gave up hope, Samuel Peter refused to admit that his son was dying and thought the "poor little fellow looked so much better." On February 12, however, the doctor said the child could not be helped and that he might die at any moment. Grief stricken, Margaret was unable to care for the child and took to her bed. Samuel Peter and Margaret's sisters sat up all night with the infant. "I was in hope he would pass off in the night, but he stood the wary hours," Heintzelman wrote. Then, "yesterday he gradually became more quiet," his condition "failing rapidly," and at "20 min of 4 died." It was one of the saddest moments in Samuel Peter's life. He had "held one of his little hands" as the boy "died in his mother's arms." Following a hastily arranged funeral ceremony in the parlor of the Stuart home, with Mary, Charles, and Margaret in tears, Henry Summers Heintzelman was buried next to Eddie Summers in the Lathrop family plot in Buffalo's Forest Lawn Cemetery.[18]

A week later, with a despondent Margaret and his remaining children by his side, Samuel Peter was back in Washington at Willard's Hotel at the corner of Pennsylvania Avenue and Fourteenth Street, continuing to promote the Arizona bill. On February 25 he visited with Senator Gwin, who had just introduced a measure to organize the territory. Mowry and Colt were there to help too, and they called on Senator Douglas and showed him reports from the Sonora Exploring and Mining Company.[19] Heintzelman also met with John R. Bartlett and called on Sen. Benjamin F. Wade of Ohio, whom he thought could be helpful.

With new regiments of infantry being contemplated by the War Department, Heintzelman also pressed friends, including colleagues and associates from Cincinnati along with prominent citizens of Buffalo, to write President Buchanan urging his promotion to a colonelcy of one of the new regiments. Vigorously advocating this, former Pennsylvania governor and U.S. senator William Bigler, joined by Reps. J. Glancy Jones, Allison White, and Owen Jones, wrote Secretary of War John B. Floyd to urge that Heintzelman be appointed, not only because of his thirty-one years in the army but also because "the services rendered by Major H. [was] one of a character so highly meritorious as to entitle him to this mark of favor."[20]

Disappointed that he was not given a promotion, in late March 1858 Heintzelman returned west to Cincinnati for a meeting of the Sonora Exploring and Mining Company, and it was there for the first time that Solon Lathrop suggested that he obtain a year's leave so the two could go to Arizona.[21] Back in Washington eight days later, excited about this idea, Heintzelman went with Colt to see Sen. Jefferson Davis, a southern expansionist who was viewed as the key supporter in the effort to create Arizona Territory. Davis, who had previously served as secretary of war under Franklin Pierce and had always been interested in Arizona and westward expansion, promised he would do everything in his power to help the major obtain a leave. If Heintzelman was able to go to Arizona, Colt suggested that Margaret and the children should stay in Hartford, an idea Margaret vehemently rejected. By early April, with his leave still not approved, Heintzelman wrote Maj. Irvin McDowell, assistant adjutant general, "asking to visit the silver mines in the Gadsden Purchase," where the Sonora Company was preparing to place "in operation our reduction works." In more than twenty-five years of military service, except for a four-month leave after returning from California in 1854, Heintzelman had received only two short leaves of just more than seven days. Even then, he complained, one leave was cut short when he was ordered to take command of the depot at Jefferson Barracks during the height of a cholera outbreak. He had no desire to be absent from his regiment, but at the present time, his presence was "not of much importance."[22]

At a private dinner for Secretary of War John Floyd on April 12, Colt continued to press for Heintzelman's leave. Samuel Peter's determination to go to Arizona caused a serious rift in his marriage, and after Floyd assured him he would be given a leave, he confided to his journal how Margaret had complained late into the evening "in the most unreasonable manner about my going to the Gadsden Purchase." The two quarreled well past midnight, and Margaret became "very nervous." She had previously written to his sister Maria saying that if Samuel Peter went to Arizona, she would be "left with the children to shift for themselves."[23]

On April 29 Heintzelman received the desired twelve-month leave of absence, but when he showed the paper to Margaret, relations between the two further deteriorated. She "says I may go my way and she will go hers. . . . [S]he will not live at West Chester [or] Buffalo . . . and does not say where." But Samuel Peter remained adamant: "I go to the mines. . . . What will happen afterwards it is difficult to tell. . . . She says she will not write to me anymore."[24]

Undoubtedly, Heintzelman's decision to go west threatened to break up his marriage. So strained did his relations with Margaret become, he thought he would have to either give up hope of going to Arizona or sacrifice his fourteen-year marriage. Margaret remained bitter and uncompromising for weeks but finally agreed to go to Newport Barracks to live during his absence. In a Washington hotel room, with the children so excited at the prospect of returning to Kentucky they were singing, Samuel Peter vividly recorded what happened next: "Finally I threw my arms around Margaret and she could not resist the appeal. She said all was passed and we could commence anew . . . we have passed a happy day."[25]

Back at Newport Barracks in early May, Heintzelman was able to rent a house and arrange for the children's education. It was also decided, largely due to the insistence of Dr. Charles Tripler, surgeon at the post and a close friend, that Mary must have an operation on her leg as soon as possible. Determined not to leave for Arizona "until all is well," Samuel Peter watched anxiously as Tripler and two other surgeons performed the lengthy procedure. Mary had sensed what was about to transpire, and she had hid herself in her room in horror. Moreover, the surgeons began the operation before she was completely under the chloroform, and she began to scream hysterically. Finally able to continue after administering additional sedation, Tripler reported finding an "orifice" and began scraping the bone of her leg. Later, as the effects of the chloroform lessened, Mary again began to scream in pain. "She abused the doctors," Heintzelman wrote, thinking "they were going to hurt her."[26] For the ten-year-old girl, the experience was both painful and traumatic. She would be on crutches for a year, continue to have problems with her leg, and walk for the remainder of her life with a noticeable limp.

In late May 1858 Heintzelman said goodbye to his family and left for New York, where he met with Major Chapman to continue discussion of the Arizona and Mexican mines. He also dined with Colt, who presented him with a new pistol. After ten days and 1,991 miles on the steamer *J. C. Stevens*, he arrived in Colon, Panama, where he caught the newly completed Panama Railroad, which sped travelers through the isthmus rain forest in less than five hours. Reaching the Pacific at Panama City, he made his way through the crowded port for a look at the city's old Spanish fort and the cathedral. Leaving Panama on June 17, again by steamer, he paused in Acapulco, Mexico, to visit the American consul and walk over the ruins of yet another Spanish fort. "What a place to live in," he wrote after seeing the unsanitary conditions of the coastal town.[27]

Eleven days after leaving Panama, he arrived in San Francisco to find Solon Lathrop and Hermann Ehrenberg anxiously awaiting his arrival. After purchasing a shotgun and supplies, Lathrop and Heintzelman left a few days later for Monterey, San Luis Obispo, Santa Barbara, Los Angeles, and San Diego, where they arrived in a heavy fog at daylight on July 7 to be greeted by several old friends. The town remained much as Heintzelman had remembered it, "overrun with loafers and drunken men." A week later, after spending several days in a dirty room in soiled and filthy beds, the two men left in a mule-drawn wagon for Fort Yuma. Crossing the desert in the scorching heat of summer, they arrived at the Colorado River after a ten-day trek. "Near 106° yesterday. It has been a cool summer," Heintzelman wrote.[28] Halting only to walk over the parade ground and inspect some of the newer buildings at the fort, the two crossed the Colorado on the ferry and headed east along the desolate Gila Trail. Pausing at Oatman Flats to view the graves of the Oatman family, they pushed on in excruciating summer heat to the Pima villages and Maricopa Wells, where they were able to purchase forage and melons. They then set out across the eighty-mile "Great Desert," past giant saguaro cactus and the naked spire of Picacho Peak, for Tucson.

With good grass, ample water, and a cooling summer rain to make the trip more bearable, they reached the desolate village of weathered adobe on August 14, 1858. Two days later they took a crude road south through the desert past the mission of San Xavier del Bac to Tubac, where they found Poston expecting their arrival. Here amid the ruins of an old Spanish presidio on the west bank of the Santa Cruz River, the headquarters of the Sonora Exploring and Mining Company had been established in a weather-beaten rock-and-adobe building. Floating above the walls was the banner of the company, bearing the insignia of a hammer and pick. A few weeks later, after returning to Tucson briefly, Heintzelman departed Tubac in a four-mule wagon over a rough makeshift road past forests of ocotillos, through the rugged Tumacacori Mountains, to the Heintzelman Mine, located beneath the barren south face of Cerro Colorado, in all some seventeen miles west of Tubac.[29] Standing on a rise of rolling land isolated from the neighboring mountains, the conical hill of reddish-colored igneous rock was visible from miles away.

Except for brief visits to Fort Buchanan, Tucson, and Tubac, Heintzelman would remain isolated at Cerro Colorado for the next four and a half months, living in primitive frontier conditions in a tent, though on one occasion he does mention sleeping in the corner of the "carpenter's shop, on a broken cot, with a keg of powder under the side." Each month, as army

Tubac and the headquarters of the Sonora Exploring and Mining Company. J. Ross Browne, Into the Apache Country.

regulations required, he reported his whereabouts to Adjutant General Samuel Cooper: "Tubac, Gads. Purch., via San Antonio, Texas."[30] Arising every morning before daybreak, he set an example of hard work and self-sacrifice for everyone at the mine to emulate. Lathrop, who was sick a large part of the time and lost forty pounds, remained at Tubac in charge of the company's business transactions. Heintzelman frequently complained of his partner's illness and seemed resentful of his more comfortable surroundings, while he was forced to endure more-austere conditions.

At Cerro Colorado Heintzelman's initial optimism quickly soured. Poston had estimated that ten men could mine over $2 million in silver in one year. Even Brucknow thought it would yield at least $700 a week. Selected ore from the mine was said to be worth as much as $2,000 a ton. But as Heintzelman quickly learned, the operation rarely yielded more than $300 a week, barely enough to pay expenses. He also discovered that the company was $10,000 in debt and that Poston, who had been appointed manager with the title of colonel but now in poor health, had spent needless amounts of money on the company's headquarters.[31] With little capital, Heintzelman hoped the creditors could be stalled until the mine, with new machinery brought from the East, could be made profitable.

The Sonoran miners, who had been recruited from south of the border, he discovered to be lazy, unreliable, and frequently drunk. Often condescending and ethnocentric, Heintzelman could not understand why they drifted off to visit their families in the small villages in northern Sonora

Heintzelman Mine at Cerro Colorado. National Archives.

or to Tucson for fiestas and religious holidays. The difficulty of obtaining reliable workers was compounded by the inability of the company to regularly pay and feed the miners. By October forty men were toiling at Cerro Colorado for twelve to fifteen dollars a month, yet by late November they were on strike, not for higher wages but for more beans and salt. Moreover, thieves often carried away the more valuable ore; one man was caught with thirty-six pounds of it. Although Heintzelman let off this culprit, he threatened to whip the next man caught stealing.[32]

Work at the Heintzelman Mine went slowly. It took a month to construct a furnace that should have taken a week to complete, and yet it was poorly built and inoperable a large part of the time. Since the mine was in one of the most isolated and desolate reaches of the Desert Southwest, logistics proved even more difficult than what Heintzelman had experienced at Fort Yuma. For example, basic necessities such as nails had to be shipped all the way from San Francisco. Foodstuffs often ran short and on occasion were nonexistent. He reported living on beans, squash, pumpkins, and even horse meat.[33]

On October 27 H. J. Olds became the first employee to die at Cerro Colorado, expiring at noon and buried at sunset. Several of the German mining engineers came down with malaria and lead colic. Soldiers from Fort Buchanan, on the eastern side of the Santa Rita Mountains, tried to protect the miners from raiding Apaches, but the Indians killed the camp cook, among others. The War of Reform in Sonora and the chaotic nature

Heintzelman Mine and Works at Cerro Colorado. J. Ross Browne, Into the Apache Country.

of Mexican politics did not help either, nor did American filibusters, who continued to gather along the border, promoting and threatening an invasion of Sonora.[34]

In November 1859, as workers reached what was thought to be one of the richest veins at Cerro Colorado, Heintzelman's mood heightened, and he reported "getting out the richest and most abundant" ore. But the next day the "fine looking ore" turned out to be mostly copper, yielding only $400 a ton in silver. A month later, with much work still to be done, he admitted that he was homesick and "disheartened." Furthermore, the company's debt in San Francisco was at $6,292, and there was only $1,000 in the company account. Although anxious to join his family at Newport Barracks, Heintzelman was hesitant to leave until William Wrightson, who was heading west with a large train of supplies and machinery as well as the type and press for a weekly newspaper, arrived at Tubac. Wrightson had pushed west through Texas' vast trans-Pecos into the Mesilla Valley in southern New Mexico and struck out through the heart of Apache country for Tucson, only to be slowed by two feet of snow at Apache Pass. Double-hitching his teams, he struggled through the pass to reach Cerro Colorado on January 5, 1859.[35]

After appointing Lathrop as acting director of mining for the company, and with a sack of ore as samples for eastern investors along with shells and a dead snake for the Smithsonian Institution, Heintzelman departed Tubac in an ambulance with one of the mining engineers, Charles Schuchard, the day after Wrightson arrived. In Tucson three days later, the two men bought seats on the Butterfield Overland Stage for "the states," and with some "rather hard looking characters," including a common gambler, a "broken down" New York City political boss, and an Arkansas farmer, they headed east. Spotting a few Apaches and slowed by ice and blowing snow at Apache Pass, they sped on past the towering spire of Cooke's Peak and through rain and snow to the Rio Grande at Mesilla. Three days after leaving Tucson, the stage paused at El Paso before rattling east through barren badlands, beneath the naked face of El Capitan and the towering summit of Guadalupe Peak, through scrubby mesquite and the upper fringes of the Chihuahuan Desert to the Pecos River, across the Llano Estacado, and into the night. After passing half a dozen stage stations, Heintzelman's group reached Fort Chadbourne on January 16 and Fort Belknap two days later. Eleven days after leaving Tucson, he was at Fort Smith, Arkansas.[36]

In terrible cold the stage bounded on through the Ozarks past Fayetteville to Springfield, Missouri. During the trip, the mercury dropped to minus 5 degrees, and in the unprotected stage several apples Heintzelman was carrying in his coat pockets froze solid; for weeks afterward he would complain of frostbite. At Springfield the owner of the line, John Butterfield, came aboard for the final leg of the trip to St. Louis. After a bone-jarring and fatiguing journey across half a continent, Samuel Peter arrived at Newport Barracks to be joyously welcomed by Margaret and the children.[37]

Margaret's aging mother and her younger sister, Matilda, were at Newport Barracks too. Afterward he made visits to the nearby garrison to see old friends, went shopping in Cincinnati, and had meetings with Thomas Wrightson. Heintzelman had been at Newport Barracks for less than a month when he set out for Washington. Sharing a room with an old friend from California, Maj. John B. Magruder, at Willard's Hotel on Pennsylvania Avenue, he continued to lobby for the creation of Arizona Territory. After two hour-long meetings with Secretary of War Floyd, he reported a "pleasant talk . . . about Arizona and Sonora." In discussing the region Heintzelman had a distinct advantage, being one of the few individuals in the capital who had ever been there. While in Washington he also learned that the army would be sending him to Texas. He also met with Samuel

Colt, and the two agreed on a slate of officers to be presented at the forthcoming business meeting of the Sonora Exploring and Mining Company in Cincinnati. They also agreed that since Heintzelman would be on duty in Texas, Colt should be chosen as president since he "understands the management" of the company. In a second meeting a short time later and obviously envious, Heintzelman confided in his journal that Colt was "a most unreasonable man and one I don't care to do business with."[38]

From Washington Heintzelman went on to New York to see Maj. William Chapman and attend a meeting of the Vallecillo Mining Company. A shaft at the company's mines in Nuevo León, Mexico, had collapsed, but workers were busy sinking a second. After visiting with sisters Juliana and Maria at West Chester, Pennsylvania, within a week he was back in Washington, where he continued to promote Arizona. Heintzelman also rode down Pennsylvania Avenue to listen to several fiery debates in both the House of Representatives and the Senate. Back at Newport Barracks, he worked on his annual report for the meeting of the Sonora Exploring and Mining Company. Although the report was well received, the directors decided to reincorporate the company under the laws of the state of New York. They also agreed to organize a subsidiary company, the Santa Rita Mining Company, of which Heintzelman was elected a director.[39] While he would never return to Arizona, the mines of the Sonora Exploring and Mining Company would continue to dominate his entrepreneurial interests and a large part of his life. By early March 1859, Heintzelman began to prepare for the long trip to the Lone Star State.

FIVE

Texas and the Cortina War

IN THE EARLY SPRING OF 1859, the Heintzelman family began to feverishly pack for the long journey to Texas. Margaret and the children seemed excited about going to the infant Lone Star State; Margaret in particular was hoping the Texas sun would help ease her rheumatic pains. When Samuel Peter placed an ad in a Cincinnati newspaper for a male servant, several individuals applied, and Zachary Jackson, a free man of color, was hired for one year at fifteen dollars a month. In early April, with two wagonloads of household goods and personal belongings, the Heintzelmans boarded the paddle-wheeler *Switzerland* and steamed for New Orleans. Two days later they were at Cairo, Illinois, and into a flooded Mississippi River that swept their boat rapidly downstream. After stopping briefly at Vicksburg, the *Switzerland* put in beneath the bluffs at Natchez, where the family walked ashore to clip roses. Arriving in a crowded and bustling New Orleans on April 16, they made their way to the elegant St. Charles Hotel.[1]

During four balmy days in the Crescent City, there was time for sightseeing, shopping, and a night at the opera to attend Gaetano Donizetti's *La Favorite*, a tragic love story in four acts set in Santiago de Compastela, Spain. Compared to the "splendid house in Cincinnati," the New Orleans opera house was a "small dingy affair," Samuel Peter disappointingly wrote. On Palm Sunday there was a visit to St. Louis Cathedral on Jackson Square and a carriage ride along the shores of Lake Pontchartrain. The family also booked passage to Indianola, Texas, on the steamer *Texas*, and after all the baggage had been loaded and Charles had gotten his dogs aboard, the Heintzelmans departed early the next morning.[2] After three hours on the Mississippi River, the *Texas* steamed into the gulf and headed down the coast. On the open seas a violent norther lasting through the night engulfed the small vessel. As their boat was tossed about on the stormy waters, Margaret and the children became violently sick. But just before daylight, the storm appeared to subside somewhat, and the family was able to sleep.

When they awoke, the *Texas* was easing into the dock at Galveston. There the family walked ashore and rented a carriage for a "drive on the beach and all over town." Galveston, the largest city in Texas, was a "pretty flourishing place," except for the dreaded yellow fever that frequently struck. Departing Galveston at sunset the same day, the *Texas* continued down the coast through the night and into a windswept Cavallo Pass at the north end of Matagorda Island. Steaming across Lavaca Bay, the *Texas* docked at Indianola, the largest supply depot for the army in the state. Going ashore, Major Heintzelman was able to book a room at the fashionable Casimir House, only one block from the pier that jutted out into the bay and a short distance from the army depot. Indianola, he thought, was "a nice little town."[3] Locating Capt. Alexander W. Reynolds, quartermaster at the depot, he was able to obtain the use of an ambulance and a wagon, as well as horses and mules, for the overland journey to San Antonio. Much of the family's baggage would be left behind for shipment later.

With Jackson driving the wagon and Samuel Peter the ambulance, the Heintzelmans struck out the next morning across a marshy "hog wallow prairie" to the small village of Chocolate. Pausing only briefly, they hurried on to Victoria, where they took rooms at the elegant Globe Hotel, a modern brick structure on the main plaza.[4] After crossing the Guadalupe River the next day, the family took the wrong road and missed going to Yorktown. Although pushing hard across a seemingly endless coastal plain, the travelers were hit by a rain-and-hail storm and were forced to spend the night on the open prairie near a small creek. Beds were made in the wagon for Samuel Peter and Margaret, while the children slept on the bare earth underneath. After spending an unpleasant night fighting fleas, they continued on the next day to the San Antonio River and Helena, a rough frontier community where they found a room at a "miserable place" with only cornbread and bacon to eat. Margaret complained vociferously that the accommodations were the worst she had even seen. There two of the horses became sick, and Jackson was left behind to lead the mounts while the Heintzelmans continued on. "Half starved," at midday they stopped by the roadside, where a Mexican woman agreed to boil a dozen eggs, and with a few oranges they had brought from the coast, they managed a small meal.

Finally on Sunday, May 1, after six hard days on the road, the weary travelers reached San Antonio, where they took rooms at the Menger Hotel, a short distance from the Alamo and army headquarters. Although fatigued, they were still excited about being in Texas. At the hotel, letters were waiting from Solon Lathrop and Samuel Peter's sister, Maria. Within hours Heintzelman wrote the adjutant general in New York of his arrival in Texas, and the next day he reported to headquarters.[5] In particular,

Heintzelman was anxious to see department commander Brig. Gen. David Emanuel Twiggs, or "Old Davey" as he was known in the frontier army. Ever since he had first met Twiggs four years earlier at Jefferson Barracks, he had admired the seventy-one-year-old general, a veteran of the War of 1812. Twiggs had performed admirably in Mexico a decade earlier and had an excellent reputation in the frontier army. At the time, however, he was reported to be in ill health and indisposed. Heintzelman was able to visit with other officers, nevertheless, and was told that he was being sent to either Camp Cooper, on the northwestern frontier of the state, or to Fort Duncan, southwest of San Antonio along the Rio Grande.

After several days in San Antonio, headquarters recommended that Heintzelman go in person to Fort Duncan, located on the Mexican border, and determine if Lt. Col. Gouverneur Morris, who commanded the 1st Infantry on the frontier and at the post, would be taking leave, as he had previously indicated. If so, Twiggs was intent on stationing the major at the post. Leaving Margaret and the children at the Menger Hotel, Heintzelman left in the stage for Eagle Pass. With only one other person onboard, the coach rattled west from San Antonio, stopping for dinner at the small Alsatian village of Castroville on the west bank of the Medina River before continuing west in a light rain to the village of D'Hanis for the night. After a sleepless night fighting fleas again, he boarded the stage early the next morning to continue west. After stopping briefly at Fort Inge on the east bank of the Leona River, by sundown and with fresh mules, the stage was across the Nueces River and headed south. Throughout the night, providing a "cool and pleasant" ride, the stage clattered on, arriving in the small, sun-baked adobe village of Eagle Pass at sunrise on May 7.[6]

Established shortly after the end of the Mexican War on the left bank of the Rio Grande upriver from where the old "Camino Real" crossed the river, Fort Duncan was part of a chain of forts protecting the newly established border as well as the vast western frontier of the Lone Star State. Another chain of primitive outposts helped guard the San Antonio–El Paso Road, also known as the Lower Military Road, all the way to Franklin (El Paso) in far West Texas. After walking over the grounds, Heintzelman concluded that Fort Duncan afforded adequate accommodations and that Margaret and the children would probably be comfortable there. After Fort Yuma, anything looked good. In the evening he listened to the band of the 1st Infantry perform some lively tunes, and the next morning he visited with Lieutenant Colonel Morris, who confirmed that he would be taking leave. As far as Morris was concerned, the sooner Heintzelman took command of Fort Duncan, the better. While socializing with several of the officers over tea, the major looked up to see the post engulfed in a dust storm that swept violently into the valley and evoked unpleasant memories of life at Fort Yuma. The storm was followed by pounding hail as large as a "hen's egg" that even knocked a small calf to the ground.[7] Hoping to return to San Antonio as soon as possible, he was forced to spend a second night at the fort when storm clouds again appeared on the horizon. Leaving at sunrise the next morning, the stage chattered across the eastern fringes of the Chihuahuan Desert and by early afternoon was already past Fort Inge. Three miles west of the Sabinal River, the stage ran into a herd of army camels out of Camp Verde, a curiosity on the frontier at the time. After spending the night at Sabinal, Heintzelman was back in San Antonio by sunset the next day.

Anxious to depart for Fort Duncan, the major learned that the remainder of his baggage would not be arriving from the coast for over a week. In the meantime he went again to army headquarters to see Twiggs but was told the general was deathly ill and was not expected to survive for long. In San Antonio Heintzelman met with Frederick Brunckow and Charles Schuchard, both German engineers of the Sonora Exploring and Mining Company, who complained that they had not been paid for their services in Arizona. Moreover, they were convinced that in Heintzelman's absence, Colt was bent on gaining control of the company. Additional bad news arrived in a letter from Lathrop at Tubac saying that hostile Apaches had made off with eight mules belonging to the company. As director of the mines at Cerro Colorado, Lathrop was spending much of his time lobbying for military protection, even writing to Secretary of War John B. Floyd to warn of the tenuous situation on the Arizona-Sonora border, enclosing a newspaper clipping from the *Tubac Weekly Arizonian* authored by "one of the most intelligent gentlemen in this country" on the increasingly intolerant situation.[8] More than a thousand miles to the east, there was little Heintzelman could do.

On May 24, with their baggage finally arrived from the coast and with Margaret and the children still excited about being in Texas, the family set out for Fort Duncan. Not waiting for the slower-moving baggage wagons, Heintzelman pushed on to Castroville the first day. A second day in the heat brought them to the Rio Seco at D'Hanis. The violence of the Texas frontier became evident when a party of Mexicans rode up, proudly displaying an Indian scalp and a woman prisoner as trophies of war.[9] Unable to find any shade at the crossing of the Frio River, Heintzelman decided to continue on to Fort Inge, where the family made camp by the tree-shaded banks of the Leona River just below the post. There they picked up an escort of six bluecoats before turning west to Turkey Creek, the last stage station on the road to the border. With Margaret sick, the party arrived at the Rio Grande early in the evening of the following day. Lieutenant Colonel Morris had already departed, so Major Heintzelman issued orders early the next morning assuming command of the post. There were more reminders of life at Fort Yuma with the approach of the long and hot summer so common to South Texas. During his second day on the border, Heintzelman recorded a temperature of 106 degrees in the shade. With the arrival of the remainder of their baggage from Indianola, Samuel Peter and Margaret were shocked to find several of their household items badly damaged. The family crockery was shattered, and an illustrated Bible she had recently purchased was water damaged. The major also discovered that his new saddle and bridle were water soaked.

In the evenings there were serenades by the regimental band. After riding around the post a few days later and not seeing a single "blade of green grass," Heintzelman concluded that he did not like Fort Duncan after all.[10] Equally bad was Piedras Negras, a "miserable Mexican town" across the river.

Not long after arriving at Fort Duncan, and much to Heintzelman's surprise, orders arrived from General Twiggs to abandon the post. At the same time, Fort Brown at Brownsville, Ringgold Barracks at Rio Grande City, and Fort McIntosh at Laredo were also ordered evacuated. Troops were needed farther west to guard the San Antonio–El Paso Road and to combat the growing Indian problem on the northwestern frontier of the state. There was no hint at the time that leaving the southern border of the state unprotected would come to haunt Twiggs and thrust Heintzelman into the forefront of Texas history. On June 4 the major learned that he was being sent to Camp Verde in the Hill Country northwest of San Antonio. Within a few days the Heintzelmans had again packed and secured their baggage, and on June 18, with "few regrets," they left the border for Camp Verde. Back along the stage route, north and then east, they eventually turned into the Hill Country; across the Medina River at the small frontier community of Bandera; and, passing through the narrow and rocky confines of Bandera Pass, separating the Guadalupe and Medina valleys, they reached Camp Verde after seven long days on the road.[11]

Camp Verde had been established on July 8, 1856, on the north bank of Verde Creek in Kerr County. Called "Little Egypt," the post had become the headquarters for the Camel Corps in Texas.[12] Several distinguished frontier officers, including Heintzelman's West Point classmate Albert Sidney Johnston, had previously commanded there. In the heart of the Hill Country, with abundant water and shade, mild summers, and good grazing, the post was one of the most desirable in Texas, if not in the entire trans-Mississippi. Lined by ancient cypress trees, the crystal-clear waters of Verde Creek meandered their way past the post before joining the larger Guadalupe River. Camp Verde was strategically located to guard Bandera Pass as well as the villages of Bandera to the south and Kerrville to the north.

Heintzelman found Camp Verde to be dilapidated, and within days he had hired carpenters and painters to help improve the looks of the post as well as its living conditions. At the commander's residence, there was much washing, cleaning, and whitewashing to be done. Heintzelman also set out to put the camp's garden in cultivation. Sod was spaded and lettuce, squash, tomatoes, cucumbers, corn, and watermelons planted. With an abundance of deer, turkey, and bear in the verdant hills nearby, fresh meat was also available.[13] In the months to come, fishing excursions to Turtle Creek, four miles to the north; a short walk to Verde Creek; or a ride downstream to the much larger Guadalupe River became routine. Samuel Peter rigged up a shower for his family to bathe, and for the more adventuresome, there was swimming in a large pool in the limestone bed of Verde Creek. With servants catering to their every need, it was one of the few times the entire family was together for any length of time during his antebellum career. The summer of 1859 proved to be a pleasant respite the Heintzelmans would not soon forget.

With the band of the 1st Infantry arriving from Fort Duncan, evening concerts became an enjoyable routine at the post. Socializing with other officers as well as settlers in the area was also common. In particular, Heintzelman enjoyed evening buggy rides through the nearby countryside. He relished short jaunts down Verde Creek to Zanzenberg for visits with Dr. Charles de Ganahl, a wealthy, Austrian-born slaveholding physician, and his wife, Virginia. The Ganahls had built a large residence not far from the banks of the Guadalupe near what became the small village of Center Point. Another lasting friendship developed with Dr. Andrew Jackson Foard, the Georgia-born post surgeon, whom he came to admire and respect. Heintzelman also spent a lot of time corresponding with officials of the Sonora Exploring and Mining Company and trying to sell stock to officers at the post or to anyone who would listen. Still, the garrison was somewhat isolated, and the weekly mail that arrived from San Antonio by way of Zanzenberg was always anticipated with considerable excitement.

In his spare time Heintzelman also corresponded with the editors of *Scientific American* to put forth the idea of using a kite to secure a line and then a cable for construction purposes over the top of the yet-to-be-completed Washington Monument. He had also been thinking of devising a double pulley, which he felt would lift far more weight than a single pulley. Contemplating a patent for the device, he even enclosed a sketch. Heintzelman was also contemplating the idea of a transcontinental telegraph by which a plow would be used to harrow a slight rut across prairies and mountains into which a telegraph wire coated with "gutta percha" (a rubberlike substance) would be placed. He also developed the idea of attaching rubber tubes to oceangoing vessels that could be inflated during storms to prevent the ships from floundering or sinking. He was able to obtain a patent for a similar floating device that would allow cavalry to cross rivers and streams.[14]

At Camp Verde the only real excitement came when small bands of hostile Comanches raided farms and ranches in the vicinity, driving off horses and mules and carrying off captives. So daring were these Indians that they even rode through the village of Bandera. Thirty-five citizens of the small community wrote Rep. Alexander J. Hamilton and sent a petition to Pres. James Buchanan outlining the "horrible atrocities and outrages" in the area and pleading for protection. In response to the Comanche forays, Heintzelman sent out small detachments in pursuit, but with no effective cavalry force at the post, the 1st Infantry soon lost the raiders' trail in the rocky and rugged Hill Country terrain. So ineffective was the infantry at pursuing the more mobile and elusive Comanches that in the early fall of 1859, with the Indians becoming bolder, Company I, 2nd Cavalry, consisting of seventy-nine men and commanded by Lt. Wesley Owen, established a temporary camp at Turkey Creek, some four miles north of Camp Verde.[15]

Heintzelman was fortunate to have the dedicated and skilled services of José Policarpio Rodriguez, a veteran guide for the army in Texas. In fact, he was as dependent at Camp Verde on Rodriguez as he had been at Fort Yuma on Tomás Chiuj. Rodriguez had served the army on the western frontier since the time of the Mexican War, and he was widely regarded as one of the best Indian fighters and trackers in Texas.[16] Heintzelman developed a deep admiration for Rodriguez, and the two would spend many pleasant hours together hunting and fishing.

Despite the healthy climate of the Hill Country, Margaret remained ill a large part of the time. More family complications came in August when Charles was kicked by a horse and both bones in one of his legs were broken; for two months he would be unable to walk.[17] There was also earth-shattering news from Virginia that some saw as an ominous and frightful warning of a rapidly approaching national crisis. On November 8, 1859, a radical abolitionist named John Brown, with eighteen zealous followers, raided the picture-book town of Harpers Ferry, Virginia, hoping to instigate a slave uprising that would spread down the crest of the Appalachian Mountains like a dagger into the heart of a morally decadent, slave-holding South. Although seven of the raiders escaped when U.S. Marines under Col. Robert E. Lee and 1st Lt. J. E. B. Stuart arrived and stormed the engine house where Brown and a handful of his men had taken refuge, Brown was captured and later hanged as fifteen hundred soldiers and hundreds of spectators, including an actor named John Wilkes Booth, looked on in silence. Facing death with dignity, Brown won millions of admirers in the North.

News from the East would soon be eclipsed by news from the Rio Grande frontier. While Heintzelman was on his way to Camp Verde from Camp Ives, he was overtaken by a courier dispatched from department headquarters in San Antonio with news of trouble on the Texas-Mexico border.[18] The major was to take command of nine companies of infantry, artillery, and cavalry, to assemble at old Fort Merrill on the lower Nueces River, as soon as possible and march immediately to Brownsville.

An angry and defiant Tejano ranchero, Juan Nepomuceno Cortina, had seized Brownsville, touching off a small war along the Rio Grande. As the hot Brownsville summer passed into fall and Heintzelman remained comfortably at Camp Verde with his family, the simmering ethnic discontent in the lower Rio Grande Valley erupted in the early morning hours of September 28, 1859, when Cortina led seventy-five heavily armed raiders into the darkened streets of the border town. The sharp crack of pistol and rifle fire, interrupted by shouts of "Viva Cheno Cortina," "Viva la Republica Mexicana," and "Mueran los Gringos," echoed off the two-story buildings along Elizabeth Street, where soon six men lay dead at the hands of the Cortinistas.

Many on the border blamed General Twiggs for Cortina's success, saying that he never should have allowed the forts along the Rio Grande to be abandoned, especially Fort Brown at Brownsville, thus leaving the border totally defenseless for three hundred miles. Now, with Cortina's continued success and his defeat of the Brownsville militia and the Texas Rangers, the general was convinced the army had to act. On November 12, 1859, he telegraphed the War Department that Cortina had murdered one hundred Americans and was on the march for the Nueces River with eight hundred men. The next day Heintzelman received orders placing him in command of the "Brownsville Expedition" and sending him scurrying for the border. Specifically, the major was to "employ whatever means [necessary] to meet the exigency of the case, to disperse the forces of Cortina and restore quiet to the frontier." In Twiggs's mind the task required a senior officer with drive and determination, and Heintzelman, he concluded, was just that individual. In addition to Heintzelman's nine companies, two companies of light artillery and three of infantry from Fort Leavenworth, Kansas, along with six companies of infantry from as far away as Fortress Monroe, Virginia, were to depart "with all speed to the Rio Grande." Four days later Twiggs wired Washington again to say that Cortina was certain to have from eight hundred to fifteen hundred men. Affairs along the lower Rio Grande had come to eclipse the recent events at Harpers Ferry, at least in the Lone Star State. Twiggs was especially concerned about the security of the large military arsenal at Brazos Santiago, where two complete field batteries and $125,000 in ammunition were stored. The cannon, howitzers, and mortars (some of them 32- and 24-pounders) "had probably been taken . . . by Cortina," the general reluctantly concluded.[19]

At department headquarters in San Antonio, more-reliable news arrived from the Rio Grande. By the second week of November, Twiggs informed Washington that he was "disposed to think the Cortina affair" was "greatly exaggerated." Four days later he assured the War Department that the rumors from Brownsville were "mostly false."[20] Consequently, orders sending troops to the border were countermanded. Heintzelman, however, was still being sent to Brownsville, but the size of his forces was to be scaled back.

Saddling his horse a few hours before sunset on Sunday evening, November 14, Heintzelman rode hard through the Hill Country during a bitterly cold night. Pausing only to water his mount and get something to eat at sunrise, he was at army headquarters by noon the next day, having ridden sixty-five miles in seventeen hours. In San Antonio he learned that several companies of Texas Rangers, including one commanded by William G. Tobin that had been recruited in the city, were already on the march. Riding in a buggy followed by three supply wagons and a sizeable escort, Heintzelman left San Antonio after three days. Splashing across the Medina River, his small party took the Laredo Road by mistake and spent several hours aimlessly meandering through the chaparral before finally locating the right route. Continuing to hear rumors of bloodletting along the border, the men arrived at Fort Merrill on the Nueces River at high noon, four days after leaving San Antonio, to be greeted by Richard King. There Heintzelman paused for several days while companies from various frontier posts could join the expedition. In all, his command would consist of two batteries of light artillery acting as infantry under Lts. Douglas Ramsay and William Montrose Graham, a company of the 2nd Cavalry led by Capt. George Stoneman, and two companies of the 8th Infantry headed by Capts. Arthur Tracy Lee and Charles Downer Jordan. The other companies of the 8th Infantry, one company of the 2nd Cavalry, and a battery of artillery were to first rendezvous at Fort McIntosh at Laredo before moving down the Rio Grande to join Heintzelman. While camped at Fort Merrill, the major also learned that General Twiggs, convinced that much of the news he was hearing from Brownsville was false, had decided to scale back the size of the force even more.[21] Heintzelman, nevertheless, was to proceed to Brownsville as soon as possible with the units at hand.

After celebrating Thanksgiving in a light rain on November 25, the expedition broke camp early the next morning and moved downriver to San Patricio, where they purchased supplies and forage before turning south to the small village of Banquete and then to King's Rancho, where King provided the expedition with fresh mutton. Continuing south, the expedition entered the vast expanses of the Wild Horse Desert, where the column was slowed when the mule teams began to falter in the shifting sands. With water scarce, Heintzelman continued to push the column farther south. Closer to the Arroyo Colorado, the expedition began to see deserted ranches, the first signs of the violence that had beset the border, the owners having fled and leaving only a few chickens and pigs behind. On December 2 the soldiers were still north of the Arroyo Colorado when they were hit by a fierce Texas norther. "The air was quite warm," Heintzelman remembered, when suddenly "a dense fog came down from the north, rolling over and over repeatedly," and by nightfall it had begun to freeze.[22] Camping beside the road in a cold rain, the men awoke the next morning to find their tents stiff as boards and the ground covered with snow and sleet. Near the Arroyo Colorado, with the expedition's animals badly jaded from the long march, Heintzelman sent Lieutenant Ramsey ahead to Brownsville to procure corn. After crossing the arroyo on a ferry, and with the road still muddy and the chaparral dense, Heintzelman, fearful of an ambush, ordered the men to keep their rifles loaded and to be ever watchful.

Reaching the Palo Alto prairie, Heintzelman ordered a pause to allow the animals to graze, after which the column pushed on past the Resaca de la Palma battlefield. Finally, in the freezing cold of December 6, a few minutes before midnight, the tired and fatigued column of bluecoats rode past several flimsy barricades and uneasy sentinels to be joyously welcomed by several sleepy and frightened Brownsville townsmen. From Camp Verde Heintzelman had ridden 332 bone-weary miles.[23]

The leading citizens of Brownsville were frightened and panicky, and the Texas Rangers, who had arrived three weeks earlier, had only acerbated the situation, Heintzelman astutely observed. The night after Captain Tobin and his ninety men arrived from San Antonio, sixty-year-old Tomás Cabrera, one of Cortina's chief lieutenants and who had been captured by the Cameron County sheriff, was dragged from the Brownsville jail and lynched by a frenzied mob in Market Square. When Cortina received word of the death of his friend, he was said to have hanged three captives he was holding at Rancho del Carmen. In a vicious firefight a few days later on the edge of the Palo Alto prairie, three rangers were killed while four others were badly wounded. The bodies of the dead rangers were found the next day stripped and mutilated.[24]

Burying their dead, Tobin and his men rode to the small village of Santa Rita, upriver from Brownsville near Cortina's camp, where they joined other rangers in torching many of the small jacales in the community. Dragging along a 24-pounder howitzer and vowing to "exterminate Cortina," Tobin led his men upriver a few days later. Within sight of the camp near Rancho del Carmen, the rangers were met by a "galling fire of round shot, grape and canister." Realizing that Cortina was "strongly entrenched and fortified," and fearful of being attacked on both flanks, Tobin retreated in confusion, "hotly pressed" by the Cortinistas. Although sixty of his men refused to fight and returned to Brownsville, Tobin again marched out the next day only to be repulsed a second time. Back in Brownsville, as many as one hundred rangers decided they had had enough of the Cortina War, and they departed for the Nueces River. "It was a wise decision," Heintzelman wrote, for in "their disorganized condition, an attack would have brought certain defeat."[25]

Inspired by his repulse of the rangers, Cortina issued a second *pronunciamiento* on November 23, promising to end the impunity with which Anglos had killed Mexicans in Brownsville and Cameron County as well as the chicanery and intimidation that had resulted in many Mexicans losing their lands and becoming second-rate citizens in a land that had once been theirs. More confident than ever, Cortina came to see himself as the spokesman for all "Mexican inhabitants of the State of Texas." At this point Heintzelman would write, "Cortina was . . . a great man; he had defeated the 'Gringos,' and his position was impregnable; he had the Mexican flag flying in his camp, and numbers were flocking to his standard."[26]

Heintzelman found the rangers disorganized, poorly trained, and undisciplined, and he came to place little faith in their abilities as an effective fighting force. Moreover, he did not trust them and despised their richly deserved reputation for indiscriminately killing both Mexicanos and Tejanos. Only a few days after arriving in Brownsville, Heintzelman sent Captain Stoneman to the ranger camp to drill the Texans for several hours. Consequently, one hundred of the more zealous rangers excitedly rushed off to annihilate Cortina but fled back to Brownsville when they were fired on.[27]

From his quarters at Fort Brown, Heintzelman patiently gathered information on Cortina. Although the rangers were certain that Cortina had at least 620 men, Heintzelman concluded that Cortina probably had no more than 300 or 350 at the most, 100 of whom were mounted and all poorly armed. Much of his information came from Mayor Stephen Powers and Edmund J. Davis, district judge for South Texas. Davis, who estimated Cortina's strength at 260, drafted a sketch of the defenses at Rancho del Carmen and even offered to send a spy into the camp to gather information.[28]

While waiting for additional artillery pieces to arrive from Brazos Santiago, Heintzelman had time to socialize and walk about town. He also crossed the ferry to Matamoros, meandered across that city's plaza, and visited with José María Jesús Carbajal, revolutionary, filibuster, and one of the most influential men on the border. Heintzelman was much taken by the Kentucky-educated Carbajal, who spoke fluent English. He was particularly impressed with his knowledge of Mexican politics and the border. Carbajal was certain Cortina had no more than two hundred men. Convinced that he could easily defeat Cortina, Heintzelman began preparing to march on his fortifications early on the morning of December 13. Waiting for the moon to rise shortly after midnight, he hoped to reach Rancho del Carmen by daylight.

Departing Brownsville via the river road one hour behind schedule, Heintzelman was met two miles outside of town by 125 rangers. He was hoping to use the Texans for reconnaissance, but they were fearful of being ambushed and refused to move through the dense chaparral that lined the road. Reaching Cortina's brush fortifications near Rancho del Carmen, the rangers once again hesitated until Judge Davis persuaded several men to follow him forward. Finding the position abandoned, Heintzelman and several officers rode forward to examine the ten-foot thick mesquite parapets.[29] Axemen came up to chop their way through the brush, and the army again moved forward, with the rangers at last on the flanks and in front of the main column.

Two miles beyond Rancho del Carmen, at a second small ranch the guides called La Ebonal, Heintzelman spotted one of Cortina's men in the distance defiantly waving a flag. Within seconds, the Cortinistas fired a "four pound ball" down the road. "I immediately had our guns unlimbered and returned the fire," Heintzelman recorded in his journal. As Lt. Thomas Crook Sullivan and Company C, 1st Artillery went into action, the major found his artillerymen terribly inexperienced, never having fired live ammunition before. The shots from their howitzers flew well beyond Cortina's fortifications and did little more than stir up clouds of dust and smoke. Not until Heintzelman sent one of his men up a tall mesquite tree with a spyglass to direct their fire did the artillerymen achieve any degree of accuracy.[30] At the same time, the Cortinistas continued to fire their small cannon filled with grape and canister. One piece of canister hit the pommel of Judge Davis's saddle, while another ripped into a man's thigh. Yet another shot killed a mule before slamming into the ammunition wagon, which burst into flames.

Heintzelman calmly ordered the rangers to dismount and advance on one flank while the regulars moved forward on the other. In the meantime the artillery held the river road in the center. In the dense chaparral neither flanking movement made much progress, and the Cortinistas soon moved to the attack. Hoping to seize the artillery, they "marched up to

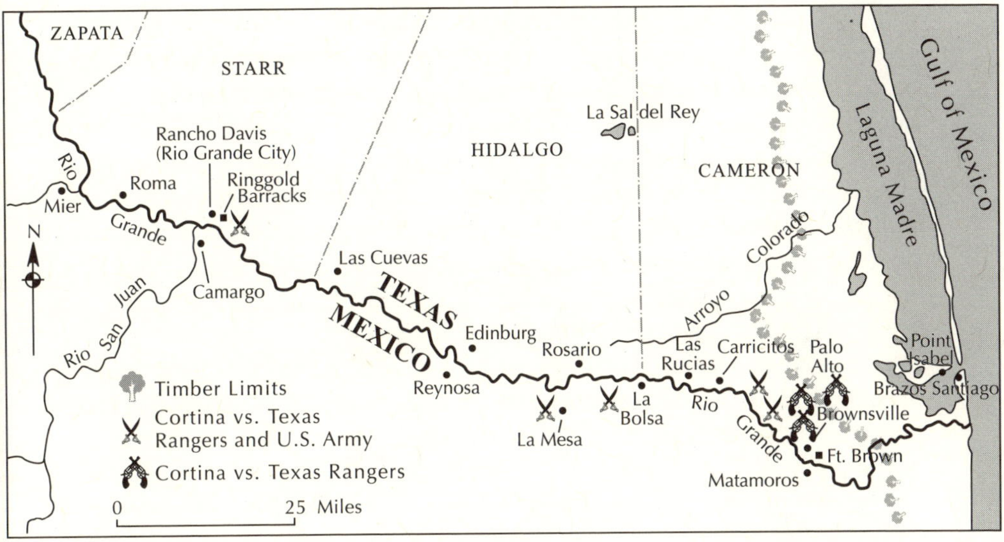

Cortina War,
1859-1860

near the lines . . . , bold and fearless, crying out *'Gringoes! Viva Cortina!'"* But the superior firepower of the bluecoats soon sent them reeling. Eight of Cortina's men lay dead on the field. One ranger was killed and two were wounded, while two of the regulars suffered wounds.[31] With the Cortinistas now in retreat, Heintzelman ordered a two-hour halt for his men to rest and regroup.

Heintzelman later learned that Cortina had not been at La Ebonal. Hearing that a company of rangers was approaching the border, he had taken two hundred of his men to Los Indios, north of Brownsville, hoping for an ambush, while Teodoro Zamora, his chief lieutenant and former county commissioner and chief justice of Hidalgo County, was left in command.[32]

Hearing the roar of artillery in the direction of the Rio Grande, Cortina had ridden hard to rejoin his small army. Pushing upriver again, Heintzelman soon encountered the Cortinistas, who again tried to make a stand only to retreat in haste, many abandoning their arms and provisions as they fled. Four miles up the road to Edinburg and Rio Grande City, the Cortinistas made yet another stand at the ranch of Jesús León. There the rangers, emboldened by their previous success and supported by the regular infantry and the artillery, routed Cortina's men and threw them back. Although most of the Cortinistas fled up the river road, a few panicked and bolted for the Rio Grande and safety in Mexico. During the fighting, one of the rangers was mortally wounded, while another man's arm was shattered above the elbow when his gun accidentally discharged. Riding up to the De León ranch, Heintzelman reported seeing eight Cortinistas dead from artillery fire; the exact number of dead, however, was difficult to determine since several of them had been blown to pieces. One of the prized seizures at the ranch was a barrel of beer. Afterward Heintzelman ordered a second halt to rest the animals and let the men have water and something to eat. Maj. John S. Ford and his company of rangers, near Brownsville, had heard the artillery in the distance and had raced upriver, but only joined Heintzelman's command after the fighting was over.[33]

In a light winter drizzle, Heintzelman again ordered his small army to advance. At a fork in the road near Cortina's Rancho San José, a trail led off into the chaparral, where they discovered Cortina had dragged one of his cannons. Fifteen miles from Brownsville, with the rain becoming heavy, Heintzelman decided to bivouac for the night. At 8 A.M. the next morning, after being delayed for more than an hour by the rangers, who were slow to break camp, the column had no sooner taken up the march than Mexican bugles were heard in the distance. Hastily pushing forward, none of the Cortinistas could be found, however, and the major, convinced that Cortina's small army had been dispersed, called a halt and ordered the troops back to Brownsville, hoping to encounter some of Cortina's men along the way. Retreating downriver, the rangers burned a number of abandoned ranches along the road. Although Heintzelman ordered the fires extinguished, many of the small houses were burned to the ground. "The Rangers were burning all—friends and foes," he confided to his journal. "We would undoubtedly have done better without the Rangers."[34]

Riding ahead of his men, Heintzelman was back at his quarters at Fort Brown by early evening. The next day he was besieged by visitors congratulating him on his success. But there were rumors, many of them greatly exaggerated, that Cortina was preparing to take the offensive again. Some said the wily revolutionary was near Point Isabel threatening to burn the small seaside village and seize the customhouse and several steamers that lay at anchor. To complicate matters, Heintzelman learned the rangers were feuding among themselves: some wanted Tobin as their commander, while others preferred Ford. Heintzelman had taken a liking to Ford, who insisted on discipline in his ranks and, perhaps because of his long years on the Texas frontier and experience during the Mexican War, appeared to have the respect of his men. In contrast, Tobin did not know how to command his men, whom he allowed to run wild.

A council of war decided to send one ranger company to Point Isabel, while others would scout north to Los Fresnos and Las Norias. Captain Stoneman with his company of the 2nd Cavalry would be sent upriver on a reconnaissance.[35] With his forces in the field, Heintzelman was invited to a formal dinner in Matamoros with Mexican military officers and dignitaries, including Carbajal and José Silvestre Aramberri, the former governor of Nuevo León. After dinner he was taken on a carriage ride to Aramberri's headquarters to sip wine and review seven hundred Mexican troops on parade.

Back in Brownsville, he had a long talk with the influential Mexican consul, Manuel Treviño, about Cortina and affairs in general. Henry Clay Davis, prominent merchant at Rio Grande City, also rode into town. Having used the Mexican side of the river to reach Brownsville, Davis brought additional information on Cortina. Stoneman and the rangers also reported back to say that all evidence indicated that Cortina was continuing to retreat upriver toward Edinburg, burning and plundering as he went. Ford was sure that he was at Rancho Bastón in Hidalgo County with some five hundred men. Stoneman also reported that his troopers had found a prominent Mexican known to be sympathetic to the Brownsville establishment hanged in the chaparral. They later learned that Tobin's rangers had done the dastardly deed, leaving the poor man dangling with his feet only a few inches from the ground.

At noon on December 21, with 150 regulars and 198 rangers, Heintzelman began a march upriver. With the rangers moving through the chaparral to guard the flanks, by 3 P.M. the column was at the village of Santa Rita. Through the rain the next day, the small army reached Rancho Carricitos near Las Rucias, where the opening shots of the Mexican War had been fired fourteen years earlier. Receiving reliable information that Cortina was in the process of barricading the brick ranch house at Rancho Bastón, Heintzelman gave orders to push upriver with all deliberate speed, hoping to catch him by surprise. On December 23 the bluecoats and the rangers reached the ranch to find "fences, corrals, and *jacales* burned, the house sacked, and the enemy gone."[36] Continuing along the road into Hidalgo County, more and more ranches, especially those of prominent ranchers, were found to be burned and destroyed and their livestock driven into Mexico. Even those residences that were not burned were abandoned, their owners having fled across the river. The few that did remain standing were presumed by the rangers to be owned by Cortinistas or at least their sympathizers, and the Texans put them to the torch.

On the march upriver the rangers killed an armadillo and presented it to Heintzelman for a Christmas Eve dinner. On Christmas Day his small army marched into Edinburg, the county seat of Hidalgo County, to find the town abandoned and in a wretched condition. The customhouse, post office, and all county offices had been plundered and sacked. Pushing on to the village of Las Cuevas, Heintzelman learned that Cortina, with 350 men, was at Rio Grande City, the county seat of Starr County, "his men drinking and looting."[37]

Heintzelman became convinced again that by a forced march he could catch Cortina off guard and inflict a decisive defeat. Leaving Las Cuevas shortly after midnight on December 27, with the rangers riding ahead as scouts in the silence and darkness, the major pushed his men hard, hoping to reach Rio Grande City at daylight. Three miles below Ringgold Barracks, the main column overtook Ford and the rangers, who reported that Cortina was still in the town. Heintzelman's original plan called for the rangers to outflank the Cortinistas by a wide movement through the chaparral and hills north of town to gain the road leading upriver to Roma and escape. The regulars would then deliver a frontal knockout blow. "You must be extremely cautious; do not stir Cortina up," Ford remembered Heintzelman saying.[38] Guided by H. Clay Davis, who knew the area well, Ford led two companies of rangers off into the darkness. The chaparral proved to be too dense and the terrain too rugged, and Ford became convinced that it would be impossible to turn Cortina's flank. Hearing the rumble of the artillery carriages, the Texans soon retreated to the main road to join the regulars. Having passed several small jacales whose inhabitants were likely Cortina sympathizers, any element of surprise had been lost.

Advancing along the main road at sunup, the rangers ran into Cortina's pickets near Ringgold Barracks, and a vicious firefight erupted. Brisk fighting continued for more than half a mile in a dense fog as the Texans pushed the Cortinistas back toward Rio Grande City. On the outskirts of town, a number of the Cortinistas commenced to snipe at the advancing rangers from the tops of several rock-and-adobe dwellings while two artillery pieces hurled grape and canister at them. With eighty men, Ford charged to within forty yards of Cortina's two artillery pieces, but finding the guns heavily defended, the rangers dismounted and led their horses off into a grove of mesquite trees. In the dense fog it became difficult to determine friend from foe. With Cortina's bugler sounding "charge" in the heavy morning air, several Cortinistas opened a galling fire while his cavalry came close to outflanking the Texans. Sixteen rangers were wounded, while several Cortinistas were killed. "Many a charger galloped off, carrying an empty saddle," as "Cortina's bold riders were left on the ground," Ford wrote many years later.[39] Pressed on three sides, the rangers were contemplating falling back when the white-topped wagons of the regular infantry appeared on the horizon.

With reinforcements arriving, Ford ordered a second charge. Observing the regulars rushing forward to support the rangers, the Cortinistas fled through the town. And they kept going. Cortina's main camp just above Rio Grande City was overrun as many of his men retreated along the river road toward Roma. Others escaped into the chaparral and soon disappeared into the fog. Some ran for the river, leaving provisions half-cooked. Stoneman's dismounted company of the 2nd Cavalry caught up with a number of the Cortinistas as they were crossing the Rio Grande. The regulars' Sharps carbines proved most effective, and at least six of Cortina's men were killed in the river. Along the road to Roma, a second band of Cortinistas was attacked and fled for the river, and ten more were killed. Along the road to Roma, Cortina tried several times to make a stand, losing men with each effort. Five miles above Rio Grande City, where the road crossed a large ravine, he tried one last time to rally his men, but the rangers charged and captured one of his guns. A mile upriver and still pressed hard, Cortina abandoned his second gun and all his ammunition. With about forty men five miles below Roma, Cortina left the main road and fled across the river. For ten miles he had been driven from every position. Riding forward at a gallop, Heintzelman gave orders to "press the pursuit," but he found the ranger "companies all broke up, and strewed along the road, with most of the officers in advance."[40]

During the fighting at Rio Grande City, fifteen rangers were wounded, some of them seriously, while there were no casualties among the regulars. Heintzelman estimated that out of a total force of 590 men, Cortina lost 60 killed; Ford was sure the number was at least 200. So hastily had Cortina retreated from Rio Grande City that he abandoned all of his records, including lists of the names of his men.[41]

"We made a great march and surprised them," Heintzelman proudly wrote. "Fifty miles and a fight is a pretty good business." The major had "won golden opinions from all for his skill as a commander, and his high-toned bearing as a gentleman and a soldier," Ford told Gov. Sam Houston. Having "defeated Cortina, dispersed his forces, captured his artillery, ammunition, baggage, etc.," was one of the crowning achievements of Heintzelman's military career.[42] In the weeks and months to come, he came to take great pride in his decisive defeat of Cortina at Rio Grande City. One of his officers, Capt. Arthur Tracy Lee of the 8th Infantry, who fancied himself a poet and an artist, even managed a lighthearted poem entitled "The Rout of the Black Cortina: A Legend of the 'Rio Bravo del Norte'":

> The Heintzelman, five hundred strong,
> Fresh from the land of doodle dandy;
> With Texas Rangers, five miles long,
> Came Sweeping up the Rio Grande.
> And gaily rode the Heintzelman,
> Not he of fear or death e'er dreaming;
> Rode proudly as the Ritter Ban

With trumpet blast, and banners screaming.
Vive Americana!

The Heintzelman, he flashed his blade,
The red legs held their brass guns handy;
The Rangers yelled out "Who's afraid?"
As they swept up the Rio Grande.
Vamos, pasearse, hi![43]

Although Cortina was soundly defeated at Rio Grande City, Heintzelman was forced to send Stoneman and Ford to Roma when rumors swirled that the elusive revolutionary was on the opposite bank with forty men threatening to burn the town; Heintzelman followed one day later. With the regulars and rangers in control of the Texas bank of the river, Ford was anxious to enter Mexico and pursue Cortina. Heintzelman, however, remained critical and distrustful of the rowdy Texans. In the days following the battle, the rangers at Ringgold Barracks were reported to be in a "disgraceful state of affairs" and were said to be shooting "all the dogs and killing all the chickens, not only in town but in the neighboring ranches."[44] So disgusted was Heintzelman that he contemplated writing Governor Houston asking that they be withdrawn from the border. He also realized that he would not be able to proceed up the valley of the Rio Grande to Fort Duncan as he had originally planned. In fact, he concluded that the Cortina War would probably keep him on the lower river for months, and it would be weeks before he would be able to join his family at Camp Verde.

To complicate matters, Cortina remained active and elusive. One of Captain Stoneman's guides reported that Cortina and a small force were at Ciudad Guerero, some forty-five miles upriver. One day later he was said to be at Rancho Bastón on the Texas side of the border with three hundred men. Another, more reliable report said the Cortinistas were scattered all along the Rio Grande from Matamoros to Camargo, "unarmed and ragged." Yet on January 1, 1860, reports reached Heintzelman that Cortina was at Mier with thirty "well armed and well mounted men," who were said to be his bodyguard. One day later he was reported to be at Camargo. There was little doubt, Heintzelman realized, that Cortina was regrouping and remained active and dangerous. "His defeat at Rio Grande City," Ford admitted, "had not caused his admirers to lose confidence in him. They supposed he would retrieve his fortune and fame by some happy stroke, and woo fortune to his side once more."[45]

At Roma, a small town built on a high bluff overlooking the Rio Grande at its head of navigation, Heintzelman took a vacant room in a two-story rock building near the plaza overlooking the south bank of the river. From his window he could gaze across the Mexican desert to the mountains in the distance, where he knew the Vallecillo silver mines were located, less than one hundred miles to the southwest. When a man gave him a sample of the silver ore from the Dolores Mine at Vallecillo, Heintzelman's capitalistic instincts began to get the best of him, and he set out to devise a way to visit the site, something he had wanted to do every since he had arrived in Texas. Any visit to the mines was a dangerous and imprudent undertaking since the roads leading from the Rio Grande into the Mexican interior were known to be infested with Cortinistas. Bandits, who often murdered with impunity, were also known to operate in the vicinity. Moreover, bands of Lipans and Comanches frequently raided the small ranches south of the border, carrying off captives and plunder. Despite the dangers involved, Heintzelman lay his uniform aside and, hiring a buggy and a driver, set off for the silver mines.[46]

Wearing civilian clothes and passing himself off as one of the proprietors of the Vallecillo mines who knew little Spanish, he thought, would be a sufficient ruse. There is no evidence that Heintzelman informed army headquarters in San Antonio or even his subordinates of his dangerous Mexican sojourn. His capture or death in Mexico would certainly have been a major embarrassment to department headquarters as well as to the War Department and even the State Department in Washington. Capturing the commander of the Brownsville Expedition could also be a major coup for Cortina and could easily escalate into an international incident with dire consequences.

Hiring a guide, Heintzelman crossed the river and rode upriver to the village of Mier, then across what he called a "miserable country," finally reaching the mines after an eighty-three-mile, bone-rattling ride over rough roads to be greeted by Albert Lowry, director of the mines, whom he had first known as a quartermaster in the 2nd Dragoons during the Mexican War, as well as Samuel M. Jarvis, assistant director. At Vallecillo Heintzelman took a quick tour of the Jesús María and the Dolores, two of the bigger mines, but he did not have time to go down the shafts of either. He did take note of the thousands of dollars in mining equipment, broken and rusty, that had been laboriously transported from New York to Brownsville, up the Rio Grande to the Roma landing by steamer, and then overland by mule train. After a short stay, he was safely back in Roma by January 7.[47]

Remaining another ten days at the river village, Heintzelman concluded that Cortina did not pose a significant threat, and after leaving a company of the 1st Artillery at Ringgold Barracks, he gathered a small cavalry escort and headed for Brownsville. In pleasant weather with warm days and cool nights, he stopped occasionally by the roadside to pick flowers. A few Tejanos, possibly Cortinistas, were sometimes spotted at a distance, but they spurred their horses off into the chaparral. Consequently, he became even more convinced that Cortina had "the active sympathy of all the lower class of the Mexican population." At Las Cuevas his party was met by a Tejano express rider carrying a message hidden under his saddle. Two members of the Texas legislature, Richard H. Taylor and Ángel Navarro, were being sent to Brownsville by Governor Houston to "inquire into the cause, origin and progress of the disturbances" on the Rio Grande.[48] Below Edinburg at San Rosario three days later, a second rider rode up, this time with messages hidden in his shoe. He had been robbed on the way and reported that Cortina was on the north side of the river again.

By the evening of January 21, 1860, Heintzelman was back in Brownsville at his quarters at Fort Brown, having completed the 127-mile trip from Roma in five days. One of his first orders of business was to meet with Navarro and Taylor. Two companies of rangers were enough to protect the lower valley, he frankly told the commissioners. Moreover, Tobin's command should be mustered out and sent home. In Brownsville he also had a lengthy visit with Francisco Yturria, a wealthy and influential cross-border merchant who knew as much about the region as anyone. Heintzelman also visited with a charismatic Samuel A. Lockridge, a leading filibuster and veteran of William Walker's ill-fated Nicaragua adventure. Lockridge, a Mississippian by birth who had fought gallantly with the rangers at Rio Grande City, told Heintzelman confidentially of elaborate plans by a growing force of spirited filibusters to invade Mexico.[49]

Heintzelman made a brief trip to Point Isabel to tour the customhouse and inspect the arsenal at the bayside hamlet. He also climbed the lighthouse and took a steamboat ride to Brazos Island before returning to Brownsville to begin work on a lengthy report to department headquarters. He also met with Gen. Guadalupe García, commanding the Mexican military along the Rio Grande, who said his forces on the frontier were under orders to cooperate with the Americans and capture Cortina, if possible. García also hoped to complete an agreement by which either army could cross the Rio Grande while in pursuit of bandits. "I told him that if he took care of his side we would of ours," Heintzelman noted in his journal.[50]

In early 1860 Cortina remained as elusive as ever, and Heintzelman worried that affairs in the lower valley would somehow inaugurate a war between the United States and Mexico. If only Mexican authorities would apprehend or control the revolutionary. There was increasingly less doubt in his mind, however, that the Mexicans had any interest in seeing Cortina arrested. Although he had known from the time he first arrived in

Brownsville that the crafty and wily Cortina had considerable support on both banks of the river, the major now realized that even high-ranking military and civilian officials were also sympathetic to his cause and duplicitous in what they were telling the Americans.

Cortina was frequently seen in Matamoros, and it was well known in Brownsville that he was drawing his supplies and arms from the city. In fact, Heintzelman came to conclude that a number of Cortinistas were even frequenting Brownsville. Reports continued to arrive at Fort Brown that Cortina was on the American side of the river with a sizeable force and was recruiting men into his ranks, though authorities in Matamoros insisted that he had departed for Ciudad Victoria. Heintzelman wrote General García, hoping to pressure the Mexicans into capturing Cortina or at least curtailing his activities. "I will make them squirm," he confided to his journal. Not taking any chances, he sent Stoneman's company of the 2nd Cavalry and Ford's rangers to scout the area along the river all the way from Brownsville to Rio Grande City. Upriver some forty miles, Stoneman's cavalry ran into a number of Cortinistas rustling cattle on the Texas side of the river and killed seven of them.[51]

Heintzelman was in bed reading on the evening of February 4, 1860, when an excited express rider galloped into the post at 10:30 P.M. to say that the steamboat *Ranchero*, on its way downriver from Rio Grande City and carrying $300,000 in coin, had been attacked at La Bolsa, a big bend in the Rio Grande some thirty-nine miles above Brownsville. Onboard were some rangers, most of them sick; a few regulars; several women and civilians; and the two cannons that had been captured from Cortina at Rio Grande City. Prior to the attack, Tobin's rangers, escorting the boat downriver, had skirmished with the Cortinistas, who had crossed the river at Las Rucias and intercepted the U.S. mail, cutting open the mailbags and rifling through the contents.[52]

In retaliation for the attack on the *Ranchero*, Ford crossed the river with forty-nine men and commenced a vicious firefight with one hundred Cortinistas at Rancho La Bolsa, during which a number of Mexicans were killed and wounded. In the approaching darkness Cortina had "tried to halt his panic-stricken men," Ford remembered years later, but as the crafty revolutionary turned in the saddle, the ranger captain ordered his men to open fire: "One shot struck the candle of his saddle, one cut out a lock of hair from his head, a third cut his bridle rein, a fourth passed through his horse's ear, and a fifth struck his belt. He galloped off unhurt."[53] Before crossing back to the north bank, the rangers torched the ranch and corrals.

Weeks later Heintzelman would learn, much to his dismay, that the *Ranchero* had not been fired on from the south bank of the river and that the rumors circulating in Brownsville and appearing repeatedly in the jingoistic *Brownsville Flag* were false. In reality the steamer had been caught in a crossfire between the Cortinistas on the Mexican side and the rangers and Stoneman's cavalry on the Texas side of the river. On April 29 he wrote to headquarters in San Antonio expressing regret that a number of these falsehoods had crept into his official reports: "I have the verbal testimony of persons who stood at the time on her hurricane deck, saw the smoke, heard the reports of the guns and the whistle of the balls, as they passed over their heads."[54]

Hearing that Ford had crossed the river, Brownsville went "wild with excitement," Heintzelman reported. In their jubilation a party of heavily armed and frenzied filibusters were in the process of crossing the river to seize the ferryboats tied up along the Mexican side of the river when the major reached the scene. After considerable effort he was able to convince the ruffians "of the folly of their act."[55]

Heintzelman was very much afraid that the rangers would retaliate for the alleged attack on the *Ranchero* by plundering ranches on the south side of the river. He was also concerned that Ford would be lured deep into Mexico and ambushed: "It is of utmost importance that you preserve the most rigid discipline among'st your troops so that no injury that can be avoided is done to the inhabitants, or their property. Do not allow yourself to be drawn from the river but confine your operations strictly to the protection of the boat." The major also heard rumors that Tobin's rangers, who had been ordered to Brownsville to be discharged, were intent on crossing the river and sacking Reynosa and Camargo, even Matamoros.[56]

As a result of the fighting at La Bolsa, General García led a small expedition upriver from Matamoros to apprehend the elusive revolutionary but returned to say that he "saw nothing of Cortina," though Heintzelman heard that the general had actually been in Cortina's camp. García did report that Cortina, with sixty-seven men, was at Rancho La Mesa, not far from La Bolsa. With Stoneman's 2nd Cavalry leading the way, Ford's rangers splashed across the Rio Grande yet again. Upon reaching the ranch, Stoneman and Ford hoped to conceal their horses in the chaparral and surround the ranch on foot. Within half a mile of La Mesa, however, one of Cortina's sentinels spotted the Americans and was able to sound the warning. Riding into La Mesa with guns ablaze, the Americans mistakenly attacked twenty-seven men of the Matamoros Guardia Nacional. The only casualty was a woman who was closing a door and fired on by some rangers, falling mortally wounded. Although both Stoneman and Ford were certain the Guardia Nacional was "acting in concert" with Cortina, Heintzelman found the entire incident embarrassing.[57]

When it was reported that Cortina had fled to the Rancho Maguey, some twenty-four miles south of Matamoros, Stoneman and Ford spurred their horses in that direction. Nearing the ranch and hearing gunfire, the Americans charged the ranch at a gallop, only to be met by a party of Mexicans peacefully celebrating St. Joseph's Day. Although one man fled into the brush and was killed by the rangers, Cortina was gone. Returning to the Texas side of the river, Stoneman and Ford calculated that they had ridden 140 miles in forty-eight hours. Although the incursion into Mexico had frightened some of the people in Matamoros, Heintzelman felt the results were good and that the Mexican authorities might finally do something about Cortina.[58]

Hearing of yet another American incursion, General García wrote Heintzelman requesting that the American commander "take measures as to prevent the likes from happening again." In response, Heintzelman promised García he would inquire into what had happened at both La Mesa and Rancho Maguey. The fiascos at the two ranches, however, did not deter Ford and his rangers. Ford next took aim on Reynosa and Old Reynosa, the most anti-American communities along the river and each a hotbed of Cortina sympathizers; in fact, an entire company of Cortinistas had been recruited from the two communities. During the night, Ford and his rangers splashed across the river at Rancho Tabasco and rode downriver to Old Reynosa, hoping to surround the town before their enemy could escape. If necessary, Captain Stoneman, who was encamped at Edinburg, would cross the river there with his two companies of cavalry. Failing to find any Cortinistas in the town, though, Ford rode downriver to Reynosa, where he found four hundred angry citizens, including a number of men from neighboring ranches, preparing to defend the central plaza. A bloody confrontation appeared imminent. Denying that any Cortinistas were in town, defiant and heavily armed residents demanded that Ford retreat back into Texas. "What an outrage on a friendly government," Heintzelman wrote upon hearing of Ford's imprudence.[59]

In Brownsville Heintzelman was elated to learn that Lt. Gen. Winfield Scott, upon reading the major's initial reports from the Rio Grande, was recommending him for a brevet as lieutenant colonel. The victory at Rio Grande City, General Scott wrote, was a "brilliant affair." With the Cortina War winding down, Heintzelman found time for leisure and a carriage ride to the Resaca de la Palma battlefield with several ladies and officers. Capt. Arthur T. Lee showed him where the American and Mexican dead had been buried. Lee even found the spot where he had buried one of his men and presented the wife of Capt. James B. Ricketts with a tooth from the skeleton as a souvenir. The ladies also gathered spring flowers from the battlefield before returning to Fort Brown.[60]

But Heintzelman devoted much of his time at Fort Brown in reading back issues of Brownsville newspapers; interviewing prominent Cameron

County officeholders, the town's merchant elite, and many of the large landowners; and preparing a lengthy report on the origins and history of the Cortina War. This amazingly objective document, which was published in the *Congressional Record*, accurately details the major events of the conflict. "The whole country," Heintzelman writes, "from Brownsville to Rio Grande City, one hundred and twenty miles, and back to the Arroyo Colorado, has been laid to waste." Fifteen Americans and eighty "friendly Mexicans" lay dead, while Cortina lost an estimated 151 men killed with countless wounded. "It will be a long time before the ill-feeling engendered by this outcome can be allayed," he continued. While Cortina was clearly to blame for the violence, Heintzelman concluded, the "citizens of Brownsville are not entirely guiltless."[61]

In addition to preparing his report, Heintzelman spent endless hours compiling depredation claims. Merchants including H. Clay Davis and John P. Kelsey at Rio Grande City along with leading Rio Grande Valley ranchers Thaddeus Rhodes, Mifflin Kenedy, Charles Stillman, Salome Young, Nestor Maxan, William Neale as well as numerous small ranchers and farmers, many of them Tejano, would eventually submit claims, many greatly exaggerated, amounting to $336,879.[62]

On March 7 Heintzelman learned that six additional companies were being ordered to the border. Moreover, Col. Robert E. Lee, who had temporarily replaced General Twiggs in command of the Department of Texas, was to take charge of the forces along the Rio Grande with authority to cross into Mexico.[63] Heintzelman thought his dispatches had made it clear that such action was unnecessary, and he was sure the orders sending Lee to the border would be countermanded. Nevertheless, on March 25 orders arrived telling the major to meet the colonel at Ringgold Barracks. At noon three days later, Heintzelman departed Brownsville with Captain Stoneman's cavalry and Capt. Arthur Lee's company of the 8th Infantry, who were to be stationed at Ringgold Barracks. Riding up to twenty miles a day, the column reached Edinburg in three days and Ringgold Barracks on the morning of April 2, where Heintzelman found Colonel Lee waiting. Although he personally liked Lee, who had ably served on General Scott's staff during the Mexican War, he was envious of the Virginian, whose ancestry included two men who had signed the Declaration of Independence and whose father was the famous "Light Horse Harry" Lee of Revolutionary War fame. Yet he realized that Lee was one of the most promising officers in the army at the time.

With a company of the 2nd Cavalry, Lee had marched south from San Antonio to Fort McIntosh at Laredo. Two days south of San Antonio, he heard that Cortina was near Eagle Pass, and Lee headed for Fort Duncan instead. Finding Cortina, whom Lee referred to as a "myth," nowhere in the vicinity, he joined a second company and turned downriver for Laredo. While Heintzelman was sitting out a rainstorm in Brownsville, Lee had suffered through a rare and excruciating snow-and-ice storm near Laredo.[64] Some of the bluecoats had bought whiskey in the "miserable town" of Laredo and had become so drunk that when the storm hit they died of exposure.

Over dinner at Ringgold Barracks, Lee told Heintzelman that his orders were to stop the violence along the border at any cost. He was to sternly warn the Mexican authorities that they must do everything possible to stop Cortina from raiding into Texas, and if they were unable or unwilling to do so, Lee was to invade Mexico. After dinner the two old warriors and West Point classmates sat for several hours on the front porch of the post commander's quarters, discussing the volatile situation on the border. Heintzelman privately felt that it was he who had suppressed the violence along the border, yet the colonel would claim the credit. Nevertheless, he had not seen Lee since the spring of 1855, when the two were on court-martial duty at Fort Leavenworth and Fort Riley and had shared a steamboat ride down the Missouri River, and he was happy to see the Virginian.

On April 3 Lee sent a letter across the river to Camargo addressed to the governor of Tamaulipas, Ándres Treviño. Without mentioning Cortina, he asked the governor to "break up and disperse the bands of banditti which have . . . sought protection within Mexican territory." The Americans were informed, however, that Treviño was in Tampico, and he probably would not receive the letter for another six weeks. Leaving Ringgold Barracks for Brownsville, Lee and Heintzelman went into camp at Edinburg four days later, and Lee sent a second similar letter across the river to the civil and military authorities in Reynosa, demanding they "break up and disperse the bands of banditti within your jurisdiction." The next day the alcalde, Francisco Zepeda, replied that he was under similar orders from Mexican authorities. Yet he took the opportunity to complain about the previous incursion into the town by Ford and his rangers. Finally, arriving in Brownsville on April 12, Lee wrote General García demanding the immediate arrest of the Cortinistas who were known to be in Matamoros.[65]

With three artillery companies at Fort Brown, two companies of the 8th Infantry at Ringgold Barracks, and four companies of the 2nd Cavalry at various locations along the river between Brownsville and Rio Grande City, Lee and Heintzelman agreed that the rangers were no longer needed for security. The "frontier on the river [is] quiet," Lee wrote from Brownsville, thanks to Heintzelman, who had "conducted with much ability the military operation on the Rio Grande."[66]

Leaving Ringgold Barracks at noon on April 6, Lee and Heintzelman hurried downriver, the two riding together in the colonel's ambulance.

During the trip Heintzelman found it irritating that Lee arose every morning at 4 A.M. to break camp an hour later. Although he admired Lee greatly, he also seemed peeved that the colonel constantly asked for advice, though placed in command along the Rio Grande. Near Edinburg, Lee became somewhat alarmed at an incident Heintzelman perceived as minor. Revelers at a noisy fiesta in Reynosa fired into a camp of rangers on the opposite bank. The Texans opened fire in turn, seriously wounding two citizens. The rangers, Heintzelman wrote in his journal, "evidently intend to make war if they can." Lee sent Capt. Albert G. Brackett across the river with a white flag and the same stern message previously delivered to Governor Treviño. Brackett found the plaza barricaded, the citizens armed, and several cannons loaded, yet the alcalde, Zepeda, insisted that "all good Mexicans" wanted the "most pleasant relations" with the Americans. Mexican customs officials as well as the men and women of the town were "unable to go to the river for water, since they had repeatedly been fired on from the north bank," Zepeda went on to complain.[67]

By the second week of April, Heintzelman was back in Brownsville. He found the town quickly filling up with filibusters, many of them members of the shadowy Knights of the Golden Circle, a secret, ardent, states' rights, pro-southern, and anti-Catholic organization that was hoping to create a slave empire in Mexico. "There are a great many strangers in town. Some came by water and others by land," he recorded.[68] The adventurers told him there would soon be two thousand members in town.

Wild rumors as to Cortina's whereabouts continued to arrive at Fort Brown, but most were either easily dismissed hearsay or outright fabrications. Some said the wily ruffian had left the border for good and had taken his family into the Burgos Mountains near Ciudad Victoria, far to the south. Other reports placed him in camp at the Rio Grande, upriver from Matamoros.

Heintzelman continued reading the newspapers from New York and New Orleans, especially the articles foreshadowing the approaching secession crisis. Finding it increasingly difficult to foster national party unity, the Democrats had met at Charleston, South Carolina, to select a candidate for president. Northern supporters of Stephen A. Douglass and southern radicals refused to compromise, and following a series of heated debates, delegates from eight Southern states walked out as the convention collapsed. Although he continued to hope for a national reconciliation, Heintzelman was becoming increasingly pessimistic that a rational compromise could be found.

With the border violence abating, the major made an occasional trip across the river to Matamoros for dinner and a quiet evening at the theater. On Sundays Heintzelman accompanied Colonel Lee to either the Presbyterian or Methodist church, neither of which he found very inspirational. Finally, on May 2 orders came relieving Heintzelman from command of the Brownsville Expedition. After five months on the border, he was anxious to return to Camp Verde to see Margaret and the children. Convinced that he had done more than anyone to bring some semblance of order to the region, he was hurt and miffed that leading citizens were planning a party to honor Ford and his Texas Rangers. "I felt that I had done something for the town," Heintzelman wrote, and yet "no one had recognized it."[69] Brownsville in May 1860 was very different from the town into whose barricaded streets he had ridden five months earlier, and he remained convinced he deserved some of the credit for the improvement.

Delayed in Brownsville with rumors of renewed Cortinista activities, he wondered if the elusive border raider might ever be apprehended. With wagons greased, mules foraged, and provisions of ham, eggs, potatoes, and coffee securely packed, he was anxious to get away. Not waiting for Colonel Lee, who was returning to department headquarters in San Antonio, Heintzelman left the border on May 7, riding past the Palo Alto battlefield on the fourteenth anniversary of the engagement. In his haste the major and his small party became lost in the dense chaparral north of Brownsville and did not get back on the main road until they were forced to hire a guide. After crossing the Arroyo Colorado ferry, they plunged into the blistering heat of the Wild Horse Desert.

Four days from the border, Colonel Lee caught up with Heintzelman's party.[70] Riding once again with the colonel in his ambulance, Heintzelman reached King's Rancho on May 12, where the column was joined by Ford and his rangers, who were also returning north. Early on the morning of May 17, after 264 miles and ten days on the road, Heintzelman was back in San Antonio. Margaret and the children arrived that afternoon, and in the evening there was a big party at the Menger Hotel, though Margaret, after the bumpy ride from Camp Verde, was too tired to attend. After a week in San Antonio shopping and visiting friends at army headquarters, the Heintzelmans left for Camp Verde. Riding past the small villages of Boerne and Comfort, the major was soon back at his original post.

While settling into his old routine, Samuel Peter continued to worry about Margaret's delicate health. Once in the early summer heat, she fell into a frightening stupor, and the next day she had a high fever and became delirious. His wife remained ill for several days, and Samuel Peter was forced to keep a watchful eye on her health for months.[71]

Nevertheless, he found time to catch up on the activities of the Sonora Exploring and Mining Company, including having to pay two thousand dollars in assessments, which proved to be a considerable strain on the Heintzelmans' budget. Letters arrived from friends in the East, and

Comanches staged an occasional raid, but such incursions were few, and the Indians were becoming less of a threat to the Hill Country. In late August Samuel Peter made the sixty-three-mile ride into San Antonio with Charles so that his son could catch the stage for Gambier, Ohio, where he would be attending college. For several months he had worried about his son's education and regretted that Charles had "not studied more while in Texas."[72]

As one of the hottest summers in memory passed into the pleasant days of fall, the major went on hunting and fishing expeditions with José Policarpo Rodriguez, who had established a ranch near Bandera, not far from Camp Verde. And news constantly arrived from the Rio Grande. Jeremiah Galvan, a prominent Brownsville merchant who Heintzelman had befriended while on the border, wrote to say that troops were still on patrol for Cortinistas. In fact, three of Cortina's men had been caught on the Texas bank of the Rio Grande and arrested, but they had managed to bribe their Brownsville jailer and escape into Mexico. In July Captain Stoneman wrote to report that although the *Brownsville American Flag* was saying the Rio Grande was in turmoil, everything was "perfectly quiet . . . since the departure of the Rangers." Cortina had not "been heard from for a long time—and no one appears to know where he is or what he is doing."[73] Ironically, though not surprisingly, some of the Cortinistas had joined forces with a few former rangers as well as members of the Knights of the Golden Circle in stealing cattle and horses on both sides of the border.

In late November Major Heintzelman was ordered north to Fort Mason on court-martial duty. Taking thirty men and two wagons, he rode across the Guadalupe River to the bustling frontier German community of Fredericksburg, then on to the Llano River and Fort Mason, where he was warmly greeted by the post commander, Maj. Earl Van Dorn, who had just been appointed to the rank. A hard-living Mississippian, Van Dorn had gained a reputation on the Texas frontier for his fights with hostile Comanches. Several other officers, mostly from the 2nd Cavalry, including Andrew Porter, Joseph Minter, and Joseph McArthur, had also assembled at Mason. In five days the court was able to dispose of several minor cases and adjourn on December 4.

Returning to Camp Verde and learning that he had been granted a long-sought sixty-day leave with permission to apply for six months, the family began to pack for the long trip back east.[74] As was the custom at frontier posts, personal belongings, especially household items, were sold to members of the garrison. Heintzelman did carefully pack his small library, including the books on military theory and practice that had been a part of his baggage for several years. Before leaving, the family awaited the arrival of Solon Lathrop from Arizona, who would accompany them east.

Heintzelman was still at Camp Verde on November 6, 1860, when Abraham Lincoln was elected president of the United States. The Republican Party had made little if any effort to win votes in the South and especially in Texas, where Lincoln was not even on the ballot. In the Hill Country, populated mostly by German Texan Unionists, the news did not cause much of a furor. In other parts of Texas, however, the reaction to Lincoln's election was immediate, as a torrent of intense passions swept the state. In Austin, Houston, Galveston, and elsewhere, mass gatherings cheered as liberty poles were raised and the Lone Star flag unfurled. Angry crowds demanded that Governor Houston call the legislature into session to consider secession. Reflecting much of the sentiment in Texas, Rip Ford wrote from Austin to say that there was "considerable excitement." Still Ford, who was "for the Union" as long as Texans were treated "as equals," did not "think extreme measures [would] be advocated." In late November, three weeks prematurely as it turned out, Heintzelman learned that South Carolina had seceded. "It is sad news" was his only comment.[75]

On December 16, with all their personal belongings securely packed in a wagon and Margaret and Mary riding in a carriage, the Heintzelmans left Camp Verde on a cold and misty morning. In San Antonio two days later, the major met with General Twiggs, who bluntly announced that the Union had been dissolved. It was evident that the growing and heated debate over secession had spread from isolated military posts to army headquarters in San Antonio. When pressed on the issue, Twiggs, a Georgian known to be sympathetic to secession, would only say that he was "certain the Union is gone."[76] Heintzelman also met with Colonel Lee, who was on his way to Fort Mason, but if Lee expressed any thoughts on secession, Heintzelman did not bother to record them in his journal.

Leaving San Antonio early on the morning of December 21, the Heintzelmans and Solon Lathrop struck out southeast across the Texas coastal plain. After four days on the road, the travelers arrived at Victoria for a dull Christmas with only a bottle of wine to celebrate. In a drizzling rain in Indianola a day later, the major heard rumors that South Carolina was indeed on the verge of secession. Many at the seaside port, despite the pro-Union efforts of Governor Houston, were excited that Texas might soon follow. Able to book passage on the steamer *Austin*, the Heintzelmans steamed from Indianola in a pouring rain on December 28.

The trip up the Texas coast was frightening. In a furious storm the *Austin* pitched and rolled and was tossed about on the open sea. Passengers were unable to walk about without being thrown to the deck; Samuel Peter was injured in such a fall. It was impossible to eat, and dishes in the dining room were thrown to the floor and shattered. Most of the one hundred cattle that were aboard had to be thrown over the side. After three frightening days on the stormy gulf, the *Austin* entered the Mississippi River and calmly eased into the docks at New Orleans. Although able to book passage onboard a second steamer, the *Chancellor*, bound for Louisville, Heintzelman also found time for an omnibus ride through the Crescent City to the army quartermaster office, where he drew two months pay.

On a depressingly cold and dreary day, with a light rain continuing to fall, Samuel Peter read in the New Orleans newspapers that on December 20, 1860, South Carolina had indeed seceded. There was wide-scale speculation that other Southern states, including Mississippi, Florida, Alabama, Georgia, and Louisiana, would soon follow. "The friends of the union are losing all hope of preserving it," he lamented.[77]

After twenty months in Texas, Major Heintzelman was happy to be returning to the East. He would always take great pride in his tour of duty in Texas and his role in the Cortina War. With secession fever sweeping the South and the nation on the verge of war, however, a most uncertain future loomed for the fifty-five-year-old major in the U.S. Army.

SIX

Debacle at Bull Run

NEW YEAR'S DAY, 1861, WAS chilly and unpleasant as Heintzelman made his way through the crowded streets of New Orleans to the St. Charles Hotel. He had come in search of Samuel Lockridge, the Nicaraguan adventurer and his friend from the Cortina War. Lockridge, however, could not be found and would die in February 1862 while leading a charge against Federal forces at the Battle of Valverde in distant New Mexico Territory.[1]

In the secessionist winter of 1860–61, the fate of the nation occupied Heintzelman's every thought. Although South Carolina had left the Union by the time he reached New Orleans, he remained confident that the "Cotton States will not prevent the Government's going on as usual." It was a pity that "they did not go long ago. It is better to be rid of them." Failing to locate Lockridge, and two days after arriving in New Orleans, Samuel Peter, Margaret, Mary, and Solon Lathrop departed for Cincinnati on the paddle-wheeler *Chancellor*. Steaming past Baton Rouge, the major was happy to "see the starry flag still flying from the staff at the barracks." Upriver at Vicksburg, he rushed ashore at dusk to learn the latest news from Charleston and Washington. In the rain at Memphis, he could learn little, but in the mist and cold at Evansville, Indiana, on the Ohio River, he read in a Cincinnati newspaper that Pres. James Buchanan had decided to reinforce several of the forts in the South. "It is too late," he reflected in his journal. "It should have been done six months ago."[2]

Although a branch of the Underground Railroad ran near his boyhood home of Manheim, Heintzelman had never embraced the abolitionist cause. Yet on the question of secession, he was a determined and uncompromising Unionist, with little sympathy for the defiant and belligerent South, especially South Carolina. "I would reinforce the forts and blockade the ports of the seceding states," he wrote.[3]

Arriving in Cincinnati, Heintzelman took the opportunity to visit old friends and attended a meeting of the Sonora Exploring and Mining

Company, at which the company decided to lease the Arizona mines to Charles Poston. With Lathrop departing by stage for Buffalo, the Heintzelmans continued by train and then carriage north and east to Gambier, Ohio, to see Charles at Kenyon College. "He looks very well and has grown much," Samuel Peter proudly confided to his journal.[4] Two days later in a bitter and biting cold, the travelers left for Buffalo, and after a brief respite in the snowbound lakeside city, the major was back in Washington, D.C.

With additional Southern states leaving the Union, the capital was a beehive of confusion and rumor. Events were moving fast. A number of officers, including his friend from Fort Yuma and the frontier Col. J. K. F. Mansfield, arrived from Texas to say the Lone Star State was on the verge of secession. In fact, Mansfield, after visiting forts in the trans-Pecos and along the Rio Grande frontier, had been forced to cut short his inspection tour. Despite the urgency of the situation, Heintzelman applied for an extension to his leave. After his exemplary services in Texas, he was told, there was no doubt it would be granted.[5]

In late February 1861 the major received orders assigning him to a general court-martial to convene at Newport Barracks, Kentucky, the first week of March. Capt. John Pope was charged with violating the Fifth Article of War for making derogatory remarks about President Buchanan during a speech in Cincinnati. A friend of the president-elect, and related to Mary Todd Lincoln by marriage, Pope had castigated Buchanan for his inaction and ineptness in dealing with South Carolina and the seceding states.[6] Three weeks later, however, Buchanan had agreed to dismiss the charges, and Heintzelman was notified, much to his delight, that his services were no longer needed.

In early March 1861, as President-elect Abraham Lincoln slipped into the capital incognito by train at dawn, Washington took on a somber but excited atmosphere. Rumors abounded that secessionists were plotting to abduct or even assassinate him. Heintzelman professed little enthusiasm for the gangly Lincoln and seemed surprised when large crowds gathered to gawk at the strange-sounding prairie lawyer from Illinois. With Margaret at his side a few days later, he visited briefly with Mary Lincoln. Although pleased with the soon-to-be first lady's demeanor, he seemed surprised that when being introduced, she "had no glove on and put out her hand."[7]

The day after the rough man from Illinois arrived in Washington, the telegraph wires were alive with news from Texas. General Twiggs had "surrendered the arms and supplies . . . of the troops to the State of Texas," Heintzelman learned. "If I were with troops, I would not obey such an order. I cannot believe it."[8] In the weeks that followed, army officers would continue to arrive from Texas with details of what had happened. The more he learned, the more disgusted Heintzelman became. He had once admired and respected the aging and infirm commander of the Department of Texas, but no longer. To the loyal officers in the army and the Northern press, the Georgian now became known as "Traitor Twiggs."

While in Washington, Heintzelman conversed freely with several prominent politicians, including Louis T. Wigfall and John Hemphill, secessionist senators from Texas who lingered in the capital, along with the pro-Southern delegate from New Mexico Territory, Miguel A. Otero. In walking the halls of Congress, Heintzelman continued to lobby for the creation of Arizona Territory. He was also hoping his commendable service during the Cortina War would warrant an additional brevet, as Gen. Winfield Scott had recommended. When Thomas Wrightson arrived with news of renewed Apache attacks in Arizona, the major rushed with him to the Capitol to ask that troops be sent to protect the mines.[9]

By late February, with Lincoln's inaugural approaching, citizens began to converge on Washington. A heavy spring rain had turned the grass from winter brown to green, and the streets now oozed with ankle-deep mud, but the tall chestnuts and elms on many of the main thoroughfares of the city had yet to bloom. Hotels overflowed with the president-elect's friends and supporters, many of them coarse men from the frontier Midwest. In the evening large crowds congregated at Willard's Hotel, the grand five-story edifice at Pennsylvania Avenue and Fourteenth Street. Yet trepidation and gloom abounded, and everything seemed in disarray and in flux.

Only days before Lincoln's inauguration, Heintzelman was received, along with several other officers, including General Scott, by clean-shaven President Buchanan at the Executive Mansion. Buchanan thought secession illegal but said that the government could not force a seceding state back into the Union. In introducing the officers, Scott remarked that Heintzelman was "a Pennsylvanian and one of the best soldiers in the army." Despite traitors such as Twiggs, Scott reminded Buchanan that most of the officers were loyal. Moreover, the United States possessed "one of the best arm[ies] for its size in the world."[10]

On Inauguration Day, March 4, 1861, it rained early, but the day turned cool and clear as a large and excited crowd gathered on the streets of Washington. With Solon Lathrop and Margaret, Samuel Peter made his way from Willard's Hotel down Pennsylvania Avenue to the Capitol, past armed guards, sharpshooters on the roofs of many buildings, and cannon on the Capitol grounds. In anticipation of a confrontation with secessionists, Lathrop had even strapped on two pistols. After seeing Margaret to a seat in the balcony on the east portico, beneath the still unfinished Capitol dome, Heintzelman was able to get "a good view of Lincoln." Proclaiming that secession was the essence of anarchy and certain to lead to civil war, the new president's well-received address proved to be one of the most important in American history. A lady in the crowd put it best, Heintzelman thought, when she referred to Lincoln's conciliatory yet forthright remarks as "a steel hand in a soft glove."[11]

The day after Lincoln's inauguration, Heintzelman met the courtly Colonel Lee at General Scott's headquarters; Lee felt badly about secession and the prospect of war, Heintzelman recorded. Two weeks later the Heintzelmans rode across the Potomac River for a social visit with the Lees at their spacious columned mansion atop Arlington Heights. While Mary Custis Lee, crippled with arthritis, showed Margaret the "old fashioned home" and its "beautiful view," their soldier-husbands reminisced for over an hour about Texas, the Cortina War, and Twiggs's surrender. Lee, who disapproved of slavery and secession, had been in San Antonio at the time of the one-sided negotiations and capitulation, "gave me much information about the disgraceful surrender," Heintzelman wrote. Lee "told the commissioners they could not get the arms from the troops without fighting for them."[12] It was evident that had Colonel Lee been in command of the Department of Texas in February 1861, the Civil War most likely would have begun in the Lone Star State, and the entire course of events that followed, including Lee's resignation, may have been radically altered. But all that was unrealized speculation in March 1861.

In early April Heintzelman was appointed superintendent of the Eastern Recruiting Department and sent to Fort Columbus on Governor's Island in New York harbor. After a short visit to Buffalo, he was on a train to New York City when he learned that at 4:30 a.m. on April 12, Confederate guns had fired on Fort Sumter in the harbor of Charleston, South Carolina. Six days later, on the anniversary of the Battle of Lexington, he read that a Baltimore mob had attacked several companies of the 6th Massachusetts Regiment en route to Washington. When the melee was over, four soldiers and twelve civilians lay dead. Not long after the major arrived, a reporter told him that four more Southern states, including Lee's Virginia, had seceded. "These are stirring times," he wrote. "There never was such excitement in the country and such unanimity of feeling."[13]

The War Department became increasingly concerned about holding on to Fortress Monroe at the tip of the Virginia Peninsula, between the James and York rivers, and all the recruits that had been undergoing drill and training on Governor's Island were to be armed and sent to the strategic and symbolic bastion by steamer as soon as possible. While still in New York, Heintzelman was called to the Astor House, where Vice President Hannibal Hamlin of Maine sought his advice relative to the national crisis.[14]

On May 2 the major was summoned back to Washington, where he was appointed acting inspector general and placed under the command of Col. J. K. F. Mansfield in the newly created Department of Washington. Certain that he was to be part of a major campaign in Virginia, he left early the next morning by train for the Federal capital. Arriving in Philadelphia four hours later during a pounding rainstorm, he missed his connecting train but was able to board a second one carrying the 7th New York Volunteers. At Wilmington, Delaware, "U.S. flags were flying," and at Perryville, at the head of Chesapeake Bay on the Maryland shore, an unnamed Pennsylvania regiment was seen flying their flags as they prepared to embark by steamer for Washington. After a five-hour steamboat ride down the bay to Annapolis, he noted that many in the Maryland capital were at their doors and windows and "looked sullen."[15] Leaving that city by train at dusk, he noticed the road was lined with Federal pickets. At railroad bridges along the route, hastily deployed soldiers, guarding against Maryland secessionists, were bivouacked and heavily armed. By late morning Heintzelman was back in Washington.

Surrounded by slave states, the Federal capital was quickly taking on the look of an armed camp. Citizens lived with open ponds and effluvia in the streets, cattle and even horses roamed at large, and health and sanitation were nightmarish. Hot and humid in the summer and cold in the winter, Washington was anything but pleasing. In addition, the residents' sympathies were mostly with the South. In fact, it was said that there were Rebel spies on every street corner, most of whom were inept and did little more than read the newspapers. In the city by the Potomac, there were more brothels than boarding houses.[16] Yet Heintzelman enjoyed being in the place where some of the most important decisions in the history of the Republic were made daily.

Not long after his arrival, Heintzelman and several other officers visited Lincoln at the Executive Mansion. "The president shook my hand as if I was an old and particular friend," he recalled. At Willard's Hotel, where he had again taken a room, he was awakened at 3 A.M. with the cry of "fire" and the smell of burning pine. Fleeing downstairs in a panic, he was told that an adjacent tailor's shop was in flames. Back in bed, he was awakened again with assertions that the hotel was indeed in flames. It was first feared that the hotel could not be saved, especially since the Washington firemen, many of them Southern sympathizers, had failed to respond. Consulting with General Mansfield, Heintzelman hurriedly summoned the New York Zouaves, firemen by profession, who, dressed in their bright red baggy pants similar to the French Algerian Zouaves, broke open the engine houses, brought the equipment to the scene, and began pumping water on the flames. Within an hour the fire was under control, and by dawn it was out. Mansfield had the Zouaves, who had gained a reputation in Washington for their rowdiness, assemble to personally congratulate them, after which Henry A. Willard provided breakfast for the New Yorkers.[17]

Although he continued to make the rounds at social gatherings, as inspector general there was much work to be done. Volunteer regiments constantly arrived from all parts of the North. The arms of the 3rd New Jersey Regiment were so bad and antiquated that he had them condemned. A day later he found that the newly arrived 8th Massachusetts had "the dirtiest muskets" he had ever seen.[18] The next day he rode out with General Mansfield to watch Col. Daniel Butterfield's 12th New York drill on Franklin Square, and he was a bit more impressed. Washington was alive with activity and spirits ran high. Many in the green militia units were worried that the war would be over before they could get involved. It was an exhilarating time to be in Washington, and though he feared for the future of the Republic, Heintzelman was excited and proud.

Hoping for promotion to colonel and perhaps even brigadier general, he carefully and skillfully nurtured his political connections. At the War Department at Seventeenth Street and Pennsylvania Avenue, he learned that his long-sought brevet to lieutenant colonel for his fight with the Cahuilla Indians in the mountains of southern California had been approved. With Washington quickly filling up with new regiments, he pressed hard for a promotion. During the second week in May, he met briefly with Sen. Thurlow Weed, powerful New York senator and political boss, who was scheduled to have dinner with General Scott, Col. Charles P. Stone, and the influential Edwin Stanton. While Weed pressed Scott on Heintzelman's behalf, Stone reminded the old general of Heintzelman's bravery in saving the provisions and ammunition during the fire at Fort Yuma. "I presume I will get a colonelcy," Heintzelman optimistically wrote upon hearing the details of the meeting. When William B. Franklin and Montgomery C. Meigs, both captains, were made colonels four days later, Heintzelman was furious, writing that such appointments were a "great outrage" and "disgraceful." In a fit of anger two days later, upon hearing that Maj. Irvin McDowell was made a brigadier general, he rushed to see President Lincoln but was told he was out. The next day he pressed General Mansfield to see Scott about the matter. Finally, on May 27, not long after assuming his duties as inspector general, Heintzelman was handed a letter, dated nine days earlier, promoting him to colonel in the Regular Army and giving him command of the 17th Infantry; three days later he was brevetted a brigadier general of volunteers.[19] Even then he seriously contemplated turning down the promotion to hold out for a higher one.

On the morning of May 22, Mansfield told him that Union forces could be expected to take the field at any moment. The next afternoon he met again with the white-bearded fifty-eight-year-old general and was informed that he was to have command of five regiments, mostly New York troops, a battery of artillery, and Company I, 2nd Cavalry, which had recently arrived from Texas.[20] Heintzelman was to take his brigade across the Long Bridge spanning the Potomac River that very night and occupy Alexandria and Arlington Heights; five other regiments would cross the river by way of the towpath on the aqueduct that carried the Chesapeake and Ohio Canal across the river from Georgetown.[21] Protected by the gunboats *Pawnee* and *Pocahontas*, the exotically clad, baggy trousered 1st New York Zouaves would cross by steamer and seize Alexandria.

Although not wanting to invade the Old Dominion prior to that state joining the Confederacy, Lincoln and Scott were determined to seize the high ground on the southern shore of the Potomac in a secret three-pronged strike devised by Mansfield.[22] Particularly galling to many in the capital was the fact that a Rebel flag could be seen flying atop the roof of the Marshall House, a popular tavern in Alexandria. Other Rebels on Arlington Heights, near Lee's Arlington mansion, were known to be spying on Federal military activities, and at night the campfires of the pro-Southern militia could be seen dotting the Virginia bank of the river. Rebel artillery atop the heights, Mansfield concluded, could even shell government buildings in Washington two miles away.

On the afternoon of May 23, Heintzelman notified his five regimental commanders to be prepared to cross the river "at a moment's notice." A few hours later orders came to assemble his men at the Washington end of the Long Bridge, and at 2 A.M. the next morning, he proudly wrote, "the first operation against the rebels in front of Washington" commenced.[23] By moonlight and accompanied by a small squad of cavalry from the District of Columbia and guides acquainted with the area, Heintzelman rode across the river at the head of the 12th New York. Without firing a shot, the Rebel militia guarding the Virginia side of the bridge fled into the woods. As his brigade occupied the Virginia shore, including Arlington Heights, Heintzelman rode with the 25th New York two miles west along the Columbia Turnpike toward Four Mile Run. As a "beautiful morning" dawned mild and sunny, the New Yorkers had already made camp when residents in the area awoke.

Although the operation was to have been conducted in secrecy, Washington had been full of rumors of a Federal advance for days, with word quickly spreading to the Virginia bank of the Potomac. Consequently, some seven hundred Rebel infantry, expecting the approach of the Union troops and greatly outnumbered, did little more than exchange a few shots before fleeing along the Orange and Alexandria Railroad toward Manassas Junction, burning bridges as they headed west into the countryside.

The Federals followed, burning what bridges that were left and capturing thirty-five straggling cavalrymen.

During the occupation of Alexandria, Heintzelman learned, Col. Elmer E. Ellsworth of the 11th New York Fire Zouaves had been killed with a shotgun by the angry proprietor of the Marshall House when the dashing and popular twenty-four-year-old officer had tried to remove the Confederate flag from the roof. The man had then been bayoneted by one of the Zouaves. Ellsworth, the only casualty of the operation, was to become the Union's first martyr.[24] A favorite of the president, his body lay in state at the Executive Mansion as thousands in the capital mourned. "Remember Ellsworth" quickly became a patriotic slogan for the Union Army.

Only days after crossing into Virginia, Heintzelman galloped upriver to Colonel Lee's Arlington mansion, where he found a company of his men comfortably bivouacked under the big trees on the front lawn. Lee, who had been offered command of the Union Army, was gone. Resigning his commission, he had grudgingly decided to cast his fate with his native Virginia. Heintzelman was not surprised. Lee's overseer said the mansion was vacant and that the Lees, having removed most of the paintings and furniture, had gone south to Richmond. It was there in the newly designated Confederate capital that the colonel was given command of the Virginia militia. After breakfast the next day, Heintzelman again rode to Arlington House. This time Lee's overseer, with tears in his eyes, reported that some of the soldiers "had shot his pet rabbits and chickens and frightened his wife." It was "provoking to hear these things," Heintzelman recorded.[25]

Four days after crossing to the Virginia bank of the Potomac River, he received official orders placing him in command of a brigade of troops consisting of the 8th, 12th, and 25th New York Regiments. Largely responsible for the Virginia defenses of Washington, Heintzelman set out to erect an intricate system of earthen fortifications and familiarize himself with the southern approaches to the capital. Despite having taken the offensive, he remained apprehensive about the combat readiness of the rapidly growing Union Army. Turning private citizens into soldiers was proving to be a monumental task. These amateurs possessed a military innocence and a naiveté the colonel had not seen in the Regular Army. Many of the recruits did not even possess the slightest notion of what war was about or know how to use a rifle. "Everything appears to be badly managed," he complained. Nevertheless, he had little doubt as to the ultimate triumph of the Union. Spending endless hours inspecting the untrained regiments that arrived almost daily, Heintzelman often slept in the field with his clothes on. "I lay down in my spurs last night," he wrote in June 1861.[26] Yet he frequently returned to the city to be with Margaret and Mary and to meet with Gen. Irvin McDowell, the forty-two-year-old newly appointed commander of the Army of Northeastern Virginia. Yet Mansfield cautioned Heintzelman about spending too much time in Washington, saying that he could lose his chance for promotion if Federal forces were attacked during his absence.

In early June Heintzelman learned that on the road from Hampton to Yorktown on the Virginia Peninsula, not far from Fortress Monroe, Federal troops on a night march had blundered upon entrenched Confederates at a hamlet called Big Bethel and had been decisively repulsed. Rebel forces under Maj. Gen. John B. Magruder, Heintzelman's hard-drinking friend from the southwestern frontier, had unleashed a fierce artillery barrage on the advancing column, throwing the Federals back and inflicting more than seventy casualties. Southerners were elated, even displaying souvenirs of the engagement in Richmond store windows. In the North there was embarrassment. "It was badly managed," was Heintzelman's only comment.[27] But the news from northwestern Virginia was better. At Philippi five Union regiments commanded by Maj. Gen. George Brinton McClellan overwhelmed a Confederate force and carried off several enemy battle flags.

In late June and early July, skirmishing in the area south and west of Washington, especially around Fairfax Court House, became a daily occurrence. Although the Union Army had become a formidable fighting force, Heintzelman remained fearful of being surprised. His scouts reported that the Rebels had as many as twenty thousand men in close proximity to Manassas Junction and Centreville on the Warrenton Turnpike, and by using the Orange and Alexandria Railroad they could get within twelve miles of the Federal camps and fortifications and "readily make an overwhelming attack on us."[28] After carefully reconnoitering the Confederate positions, however, Heintzelman became convinced that any such attack could be easily repulsed, especially if he could bring on a battle near the Potomac under the muzzles of the large Federal guns. As more and more volunteer regiments arrived, he became increasingly confident. At the same time, information arrived at his headquarters from Virginia Unionists, who along with secessionists freely traversed both the Federal and Confederate lines. Most of the information was either unreliable or insignificant, but on occasion there was intelligence he deemed significant. Rebel deserters also drifted into the Union lines with information on troop concentrations and movements. But secessionists were also providing information on Union positions and troop strengths to the Rebels. Heintzelman was besieged with requests for permission to travel beyond the lines. Many were from known secessionists, including a few prominent citizens of Washington and Alexandria. Realizing the danger of allowing vital information to reach the Rebels, he began restricting such passes and eventually disallowed them altogether. Civilians were also prohibited from touring the fortifications, a common practice ever since the army had occupied the Virginia bank of the Potomac.

In early June General McDowell, who had never commanded an army in the field but who had taught tactics at West Point, showed Heintzelman a telegram from General Scott putting into motion a movement west along the Orange and Alexandria Railroad and the Little River Turnpike. Within a week Heintzelman was to be prepared to move. As was the case with many senior officers in Washington, he realized that the Federal troops were too green and inexperienced for any major engagement with the Confederates. But as President Lincoln, responding to the drumbeat in the North to take Richmond, told McDowell, "You are green, it is true, but they are green also; you are all green alike."[29] Such an advance was necessary, Scott argued, as a diversion so that Maj. Gen. Robert Patterson's eighteen-thousand-man army in the Shenandoah Valley could not only hold Gen. Joseph E. Johnston's ten thousand Confederates in check but also attack and secure the arsenal at Harpers Ferry. Yet the sixty-nine-year-old Patterson was simply too old and slow to hold his own against Johnston. Nevertheless, by taking Union forces by rail as far as Vienna and then marching thirteen miles, the Confederate Army in and around Centreville could be easily defeated, Heintzelman optimistically concluded.

He also agreed with General McDowell and most of the politicians in Washington that Federal forces must move south and capture the new Confederate capital of Richmond before July 4, but he continued to worry that his troops were still ill-prepared. He also came to question Scott's resolve. "I had a long talk with McD[owell]. He thinks that Gen. Scott does not care to invade Virginia," Heintzelman wrote, adding that "McD speaks very sensibly about the way affairs are conducted."[30]

On June 14 he rode to the camp of a Pennsylvania regiment and was surprised to see Lincoln's carriage and to learn that the president was preparing to review the troops. "It is rather an extraordinary proceeding to have a review of my troops without my knowledge," he commented. Although caught off guard, he accompanied Lincoln, Secretary of War Simon Cameron, and Secretary of the Treasury Salmon P. Chase in inspecting the troops and the nearby earthworks. Later that month Heintzelman met McDowell on Pennsylvania Avenue and was told that he was being given command of a division and "that an advance was contemplated of three columns of 10,000 men each and a reserve of 10,000 more." Contemplating the Federal advance, Heintzelman devised a plan of his own that would surprise the Rebel forces at Manassas Junction by sending a "floating force" of ten thousand men down the Potomac to land on the

Virginia coast, race inland, and cut the railroad from Richmond to Manassas. He presented the plan to McDowell, who liked it, and a few days later presented it to General Scott. Scott also liked the plan but concluded that it would take too long to arrange the ships necessary for such a large number of men.[31]

A telegram arrived on July 15 directing Heintzelman to meet General McDowell in Washington as soon as possible. Crossing the Potomac on the early morning steamer with two other division commanders, Brig. Gen. Daniel Tyler and Brig. Gen. David Hunter, he was told to be ready to move the next day. At a final council of war at McDowell's headquarters at Arlington House, a young officer remembered seeing Heintzelman: "He came up the slope with an alacrity consistent with his character; his eyes flashing and his whole demeanor inspiriting."[32]

Plans called for Heintzelman to march along the Old Fairfax Road leading west from Alexandria, well south of the other two columns. Moving south of the Orange and Alexandria Railroad, he would cross Bull Run at Union Mills Ford, five miles south of Centreville, and move on Gen. Pierre G. T. Beauregard's right flank at Manassas Junction. Specifically, he would advance to Wolf Run Shoals or to Brentsville and, if possible, cut the railroad in the rear of Manassas. Heintzelman spent all afternoon meeting with his brigade commanders to arrange the details of the march. "I believe that we have now done all we can do [in] the short time left us to prepare," he confessed.[33]

Heintzelman's 3rd Division of the Army of Northeastern Virginia consisted of three brigades of ninety-five hundred men each. Leading the 1st Brigade was Brig. Gen. William B. Franklin, a thirty-seven-year-old fellow Pennsylvanian from York, southwest of Manheim, who had graduated first in his class at West Point in 1843 and had compiled a distinguished antebellum career in the Topographical Engineers. Commanding the 2nd Brigade was Col. Orlando Bolivar Willcox, an 1847 West Point graduate who had served in Mexico and the trans-Mississippi before resigning his commission in 1857 to practice law in Detroit, Michigan; he had returned to the army in 1861 to command the 1st Michigan Infantry before being promoted to brigade commander. From Maine, Col. Oliver O. Howard, thirty-one, had graduated from West Point in 1854 and had spent much of his antebellum career teaching mathematics there.

Considerable confusion prevailed before Heintzelman's division could get underway. Despite several requests, no horses could be found for his guides. Arrangements for the artillery also slowed the column. In addition, the 11th Massachusetts was delayed by a lack of sufficient rations. Other distractions came when William McKee Dunn, a Republican congressman from Indiana, demanded that he be allowed to accompany the command.[34] After horses finally arrived for the guides and a final meeting with McDowell to go over the marching orders, Heintzelman was prepared to march.

For thirty-five years, ever since he had graduated from West Point, he had sat at remote western outposts and dreamed of commanding a great army in battle. Now his aspirations had reached fruition. On July 16, 1861, thirty-seven thousand men, the largest army ever assembled in North America to that time, headed southwest from Washington, and Heintzelman led a large part of it. Winding its way like several giant serpents across the Virginia countryside, the Army of Northeastern Virginia struck out for the junction of the Manassas Gap and Orange and Alexandria railroads, where twenty thousand Confederates commanded by the flamboyant General Beauregard, a Louisiana Creole and hero of Fort Sumter, was known to be waiting.

Leaving Alexandria at ten A.M. on Tuesday, July 16, Heintzelman's column maneuvered its way southwest along the roads that would lead him to Manassas Junction, over rolling hills, across small creeks, and through dense woods with tangled brush. Sweltering in the Virginia heat and humidity, many of the soldiers stopped to pick blackberries or forage for pigs or chickens at the small farms along the route. The advance was slowed even more by narrow roads amounting to little more than dirt tracks that squeezed the column to a snail's pace. With a "continual succession of delays," by nightfall the column had traveled less than eight miles.[35] In fact, the last of the division did not get into camp until one hour before sunup the next morning.

At daylight the march was resumed, only to be slowed when skirmishers in advance of the column found the Virginia forests almost impenetrable. The lack of reliable maps also hindered the march, as did mistakes and errors of judgment. Upon reaching a small creek, the advance brigade came to a halt when men in the leading company insisted on crossing a small log bridge single file. Realizing such a crossing would take hours, Colonel Howard rode forward and ordered the men to wade across the creek. Frequently along the route, the artillery became stalled on steep inclines. In addition to these obstacles, Confederate axmen had also felled hundreds of large trees that further slowed the march. Bringing up the rear of the column, Heintzelman frequently gave orders to hurry the pace.

On the second day scouts brought word that Rebels were entrenched at both Fairfax Station and along the road to Sangster's Station. Reaching Elzey's, Heintzelman sent Franklin's brigade toward Sangster's Station, while Willcox's brigade was dispatched down the road to Fairfax Station. For the first time, Union skirmishers were beginning to encounter Confederate pickets, most of whom were caught off guard and quickly chased into the woods. Good news came when Willcox sent word that he had reached Fairfax. Manning the small earthworks there, the 1st Alabama had fled toward Bull Run, a winding stream bordered by steep, wooded banks, behind which the Rebels were reported to be entrenched in large numbers. Eleven Alabama stragglers, including a sergeant and a corporal, were captured. Besides finding rations half-cooked and fires still burning, Willcox seized a Rebel flag, one of the first such banners captured during the Civil War. Other fleeing Rebels left behind barrels of flour and sacks of corn as well as clothing and fresh beef and bacon. Had Willcox been able to surround the enemy three hours earlier, Heintzelman surmised, at least three thousand Confederates could have been taken.[36] From Fairfax Station in the late evening, smoke could be seen in the distance along the Orange and Alexandria Railroad, indicating the retreating Rebels were burning yet another railroad bridge.

After remaining behind at Elzey's for several hours, Heintzelman took to the saddle and led his two remaining brigades to Sangster's Station. There he too could see the smoke from the burning bridges. Reaching Sangster's after the long and fatiguing march, he was so exhausted that he forgot to contact General McDowell as instructed. This was a mistake that Heintzelman would repeat later in the war under even more critical circumstances. With their supply train, which had departed Alexandria two days after the march commenced, having yet to arrive, the men were without provisions and had no alternative but to forage from the Virginia countryside. One foraging party was sent "out to get beef, but [they] could get nothing but an old cow."[37] Learning that many of the provisions issued to his men in Alexandria had been discarded when they were thought to be too heavy, the general was forced to send an officer back along the route to recover as many of the supplies as possible.

Early the next morning a courier raced into camp with a note from McDowell asking Heintzelman to report his location. Then shortly before noon McDowell arrived in person with his staff.[38] After a lengthy discussion, he decided that the plan of attack should be altered since the terrain did not permit an easy crossing of Bull Run at Union Mills Ford. Heintzelman now was to wheel his 3rd Division about and move on Centreville. Ordering Willcox to leave the 4th Massachusetts at Fairfax Station and to join the division with the rest of his brigade on Little Rocky Run, one mile east of Centreville, Heintzelman left Sangster's Station and reached the main Federal force on the Warrenton Turnpike at dusk.

On his way he learned that Beauregard had evacuated Centreville without firing a shot and that General Tyler had moved forward to demonstrate against the Rebels camped on the west bank of Bull Run, forcing them to conclude, it was hoped, that the Federal army was moving directly on Manassas Junction. Reaching Bull Run without incident and seeing only a few enemy pickets, Tyler was tempted by the idea of capturing Manassas himself. Not realizing that Beauregard had more than half of his army directly in his front, Tyler, in what Heintzelman called a "disgraceful affair," attacked "without orders," only to be repulsed and thrown back in confusion, suffering seventy-six casualties.

In camp one mile east of Centreville, with his supply train yet to arrive, Heintzelman ordered a number of cattle and hogs seized from nearby farms and butchered to feed his hungry men. That evening in a heavy rain, he took shelter in an abandoned farmhouse not far from General McDowell's headquarters. Strong coffee and pickets firing at regular intervals permitted little sleep that night. The next morning he was ill, but by early afternoon he felt better. His headquarters was crowded with civilians from Washington, including Reps. Dunn of Indiana and Charles B. Hoard of New York as well as Secretary of War Simon Cameron, who conversed with Heintzelman in German. Also arriving at division headquarters was the general's photographer friend, Mathew Brady. The thirty-nine-year-old bushy-haired little Irishman, with pointed beard and big nose, had brought his huge camera and plate holder in a wagon shrouded with black cloth and fitted with chemicals. Brady was hoping to do what had never been done before—make a photographic record of a battlefield.[39] Carriages of other spectators were drawn up near headquarters as if at a county fair.

On July 19 a scout from the 1st Massachusetts went beyond Wolf Run and became involved in a firefight with a Confederate picket. In another encounter, seven Rebel cavalrymen were surrounded and captured while carrying their flag. At Centreville late on the afternoon of July 20, McDowell called his generals together. With several congressmen present as well, the commanding general spread several maps on the dirt floor of his tent and put forth his plan for a Union victory. A bold plan based on speed and avoiding a frontal attack, McDowell would offer a textbook feint by sending General Tyler along the Warrenton Turnpike against the stone bridge spanning Bull Run, while Heintzelman's division, along with that of General Hunter, would march upstream some two and a half miles toward a low-water crossing called Sudley Ford. About halfway to the ford, Heintzelman would lead his division along a secondary road to Poplar Ford, a little-known crossing of Bull Run, sweep southward, and strike Beauregard's exposed left flank. Once across Bull Run, the Manassas Gap Railroad could be cut to prevent the arrival of Confederate reinforcements from the Shenandoah Valley. "The plans were detailed, but no opinions asked," Heintzelman wrote. "I asked a few questions to understand what I had to do."[40]

With three days' rations in their haversacks and drums beating, the 3rd Division broke camp near Centreville at 2:30 in the morning darkness of Sunday, July 21. In the lead was Franklin's brigade, consisting of the 5th and 11th Massachusetts Infantry along with the 1st Minnesota Infantry and Capt. James B. Rickett's Company I, 1st U.S. Artillery, with six guns. Two companies of the 1st Minnesota deployed forward to act as skirmishers. The commander of the 4th Pennsylvania notified Franklin that his regiment's term of enlistment had expired that very day and the men was refusing to go forward.[41] Willcox's 2nd Brigade, composed of the 1st Michigan Infantry and the 11th and 38th New York Regiments along with Capt. Richard Arnold's Light Company D, 2nd U.S. Artillery, with four guns, followed Franklin. Bringing up the rear was Howard's 3rd Brigade—the 3rd, 4th, and 5th Maine Regiments and the 2nd Vermont Infantry. Organized in Burlington, the 2nd Vermont had arrived in Washington only days earlier.

With General Tyler's brigade clogging the road at Centreville, Heintzelman's column came to a complete halt. For three hours in the confusing darkness, the division waited. Finally realizing the situation, General McDowell raced forward to order Tyler's men off the road so the divisions of Hunter and Heintzelman could pass. Since Tyler had the shortest distance to travel, it was obvious that he should have gone last, one of several strategic mistakes made by Union forces that fateful day.

Less than a mile down the Warrenton Turnpike by 5:30 A.M., with his men stumbling along in the twilight and already two hours behind schedule, Heintzelman came to Cub Run, a small stream spanned by a single rickety bridge. Just beyond the span the long column turned off the main road to the northwest as Col. Ambrose E. Burnside's brigade of Hunter's division led the way. General Hunter, who was lame, followed in a carriage. Leading the march, the 2nd Rhode Island Infantry was slowed when skirmishers on both sides of the path had difficulty moving through the dense underbrush and woods; the artillery also slowed the column. The army was further delayed by a number of puzzling forks in the road. At one crossroads the lead regiment took the wrong path and marched several miles before discovering the mistake. By early morning the army that was to cross Bull Run at daylight was still hours from that goal. "What a toilsome march it was through the woods!" Chaplain Augustus Woodbury of the 1st Rhode Island wrote. "What wearisome work in clearing away the fallen trees, which now and then obstructed the path." In anticipation of a Federal advance through the area, Confederates had cut down hundreds of large trees along the route, and more time was consumed by axmen clearing the route. The trail through the woods was "much obstructed," a private in the 2nd Rhode Island recorded, "and hard work we found it."[42]

Heintzelman called the route to Sudley Ford a "country road." Maj. Alonzo F. Bidwell of the 1st Michigan Infantry remembered the march as "thick with dust, and where but a scant supply of water could be obtained." None "but an immediate eye-witness can fully realize the real sufferings of the men during the march," Col. Mark H. Dunnell of the 5th Maine wrote. "The best, stoutest, and bravest men failed, and fell by the roadside." Yet Lt. Col. Francis S. Fiske of the 2nd New Hampshire found tranquility and beauty in the Virginia countryside: "I wish I could adequately describe the loveliness of this summer Sabbath morning. In the midst of war we were in peace. There was not a cloud in the brazen July sky; a gentle breeze rustled the foliage over our heads, mingling its murmurs with the soft notes of the wood-birds; the thick carpet of leaves under our feet deadened the sound of the artillery wheels and the tramp of men." One Rhode Island officer was so impressed with the dense woods and fields of ripening corn that he could not help but remember the poetry of the English Romanticist William Wordsworth. Farther along the route in a clearing in the forest, "at the door of a log hovel stood a woman who so loved the 'sacred soil'" of Virginia, Fiske recorded, "that she bore much of it on her person; she told us that there were enough Confederates on ahead to wipe us all out, and that her old man was one of them."[43]

Reaching a fork in the narrow track, guides, who frequently appeared confused, came forward to say that the army could take a shorter trail closer to Bull Run, but it would expose the column to Rebel artillery on the opposite bank and give away the flanking movement. What the guide did not say, or did not know, was that the more circuitous route added four or five miles to the already long trek. The advance was further delayed by innumerable puzzling forks in the twisting and narrow path.

It was now morning, and as the sun rose above the Virginia countryside, farm families began to appear on horseback and in buggies, some making their way to the Methodist church at Sudley Ford, where services were abruptly cancelled. Unable to find the road leading to Poplar Ford, Heintzelman decided to continue on to Sudley, almost six miles from where he had left the Warrenton Turnpike.[44] Still moving at a snail's pace in the intensifying summer heat, many of his men were already exhausted. By 11 A.M. the division was five hours behind schedule. Spurring his horse across the Catharpin Run ford, Heintzelman halted the column moments later at Bull Run to allow the rear of Hunter's division to pass and his own men a brief rest to fill their canteens. In the heat and humidity, a few of them jumped into the cooling waters of the creek. Other fatigued soldiers fell out beside the roadside for a nap in the shade.

On the south bank of Bull Run, General McDowell overtook the column. Riding in a carriage and accompanied by his staff, he passed in haste, heading down the Sudley Springs Road toward Manassas Junction. The constant pounding of a Union 30-pounder Parrott gun back along Bull Run indicated that fighting had commenced. Across the stream other sounds of gunfire and smoke made evident to Heintzelman that Hunter's division had engaged the enemy. He could also see heavy clouds of dust in the direction of Manassas Junction, indicating, he thought, that Rebel reinforcements were being rushed forward to meet the Union envelopment.[45]

By the time Heintzelman was across Bull Run, the battle was well underway and going well for the Federals. At the head of the division, he had proceeded less than a few hundred yards down the Sudley Springs Road, past the two-story brick church and near Sudley Mill, when several officers came galloping up. Maj. Malcolm McDowell of the engineers, brother of General McDowell, along with one of the commander's aides, Capt. H. G. Wright, reported that Hunter was being heavily pressed by Rebel forces and on the verge of being outflanked. Heintzelman hastily brought forward Col. Willis A. Gorman's 1st Minnesota and Col. George Clark's 11th Massachusetts, both from Franklin's 1st Brigade. Proceeding hastily along the Sudley Road, Captain Wright led the 1st Minnesota to the left of the road, while Major McDowell and Heintzelman took the 11th Massachusetts toward Matthews Hill and the sound of battle. With the exception of the 1st Michigan and a battery of artillery, which were left to guard the rear, the remainder of the division received orders to follow as soon as possible. Dashing to the front, Heintzelman learned that Hunter, at the head of a Rhode Island regiment, had suffered a severe wound in the left cheek and neck and had been carried from the field; now Col. Ambrose E. Burnside of the 1st Rhode Island had assumed command of the division.[46] Hunter had hoped to celebrate his fifty-ninth birthday with a great Union victory.

Able to advance for more than a mile before reaching the fighting, Heintzelman watched as Confederate regiments on Matthews Hill, after a furious defense, began to pull back. Although retreating in disorder, Col. Nathan G. "Shanks" Evans had stopped the Union advance for over two hours. But Federal lines seemed confused, and Heintzelman could find no one who seemed to be in command. Within minutes, General McDowell, who was now on horseback, rode up and ordered him to press the retreating Confederates. With the Rebels retreating from the crest of Matthews Hill, Heintzelman sent Col. Samuel C. Lawrence's 5th Massachusetts of Franklin's brigade to attack the Rebel's left flank in hopes of seizing their artillery. As the defenders fell back across the Warrenton Turnpike to Henry House Hill and fresh Union brigades arrived at the front, the tide of battle was clearly turning. Heintzelman, like McDowell, was sure the Union Army was on the verge of a great victory. One more push and the day would be won. As his line surged forward, McDowell was heard to shout: "Victory, Victory! The day is ours." The battle was quickly becoming a rout.

Forming on the Union far right, Heintzelman pushed his men past the Stone House on the Warrenton Turnpike and across Young's Branch, a small western tributary of Bull Run less than three miles from the Manassas Gap Railroad, in an attempt to move against enemy units on Henry House Hill from the northwest. Henry House Hill, named after Isaac Henry, a retired naval surgeon whose aging eighty-four-year-old widow and two semi-invalid sons still lived on the hill, rose gently from the Warrenton Turnpike and contained open grassland dotted with trees. South of the hill and to the east, though, stood a dense woodland. Much closer to the Warrenton Turnpike stood a second dwelling, Robinson's House. Home of a freeman, the clapboard cottage had been built at the top of a grassy lane lined with split-rail fencing.

With the Confederates in retreat, McDowell ordered two of his veteran batteries, commanded by Capts. Charles Griffin and James B. Ricketts, forward to a position near the Henry House, where they could fire on the Southern line forming on the far crest of the hill. Both Griffin and Ricketts expressed concern that their guns would be too exposed, but they were assured of infantry support from the New York Zouaves. "Mark my words, they will not support us," the veteran Griffin told his artillery chief, Maj. William Farquhar Barry. "Col. Heintzelman now came in person and directed the battery to cross a field to our left and open fire," Col. Orlando Willcox remembered. As the guns approached the crest of the hill, Confederate sharpshooters opened fire from Henry House. In response, Griffin, a former instructor of artillery tactics at West Point, ordered his men to open fire on the house.[47] One shell smashed through the wall and into the bedroom where the widow Judith Carter Henry was lying, almost severing one of her feet and sending wood splinters into her face and stomach—seriously wounded and in great pain, she died a few hours later, the only woman killed in the battle. For half an hour the nine rifled and two smoothbore Federal guns furiously dueled with thirteen Confederate cannon at less than three hundred yards.

Observing the Rebel lines on Henry House Hill and hoping to turn the tide of battle, Heintzelman concluded that the Confederate left could be outflanked. Ordering forward Col. Noah Farnham's 11th New York (Ellsworth's Zouaves), he spurred his horse out in front of the Union line, yelling, "Here they are, here they are!" In their bright red trousers, the Zouaves, accompanied by a company of U.S. Marines, came on in good order. Heintzelman personally led the New Yorkers across a field and through scattered pines at double-quick time to where they could see

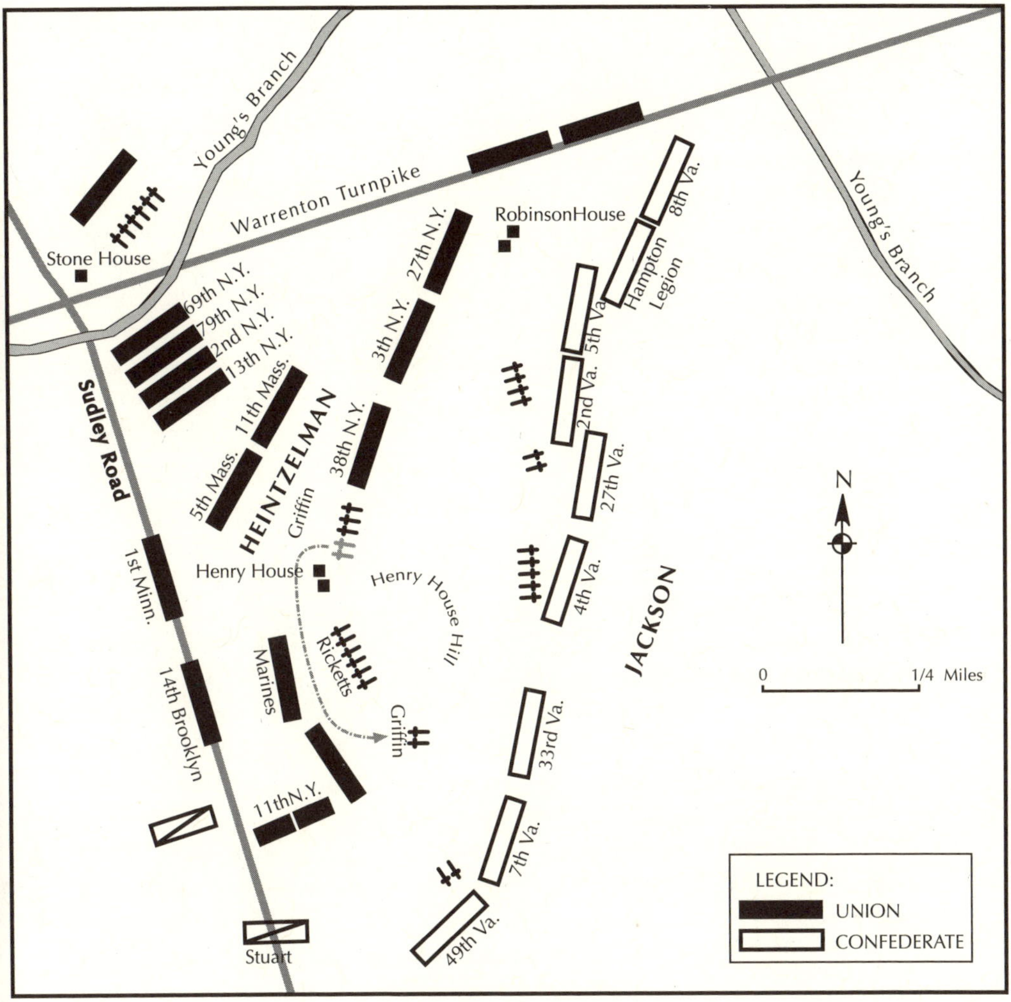

Henry House Hill
First Battle of Bull Run,
July 21, 1861

the soldiers holding the center of the Southern line, in "citizen dress," drawn up in good order in a grove of small pine trees in an old field. At first he thought the Southerners were Federal reinforcements just arrived at the front. Realizing his mistake, he turned on his horse and shouted to the Zouaves, "There are the Secession troops, charge them." Dropping their knapsacks, the men rushed forward. But when "both parties came in sight of each other," he remembered, the Rebels "fired and the Zouaves ran and I believe the enemy also." At the same time he was leading the advance on the Confederate flank, about thirty or forty of Col. J. E. B. "Jeb" Stuart's 1st Virginia Cavalry galloped onto the scene. Stuart's Black Horse Cavalry, whom Heintzelman noticed did not have a single black horse among them, came dashing down a road that cut through the woods on the extreme Union right. "Catching sight of the charging cavalry," the Zouaves "broke ranks to such a degree that the cavalry dashed through without doing them much harm." As the Rebels slashed and hacked their way through the retreating New Yorkers, the Zouaves unsaddled nine of the Rebel horsemen. At the same time, a company of the 1st U.S. Cavalry, commanded by Capt. Albert V. Colburn, opened fire on the Southerners. In their charge and retreat, forty-nine Zouaves were killed and seventy-five wounded, almost all of them on Henry House Hill.[48] Although Colonel Farnham fought bravely, as did several of the officers in the regiment, many of the enlisted men were mentally shaken when their friends were struck down with horrid wounds and died in unbelievable agony.

Amid the fury and chaos on Henry House Hill, Confederate colonel Arthur C. Cummings ordered an attack by his 33rd Virginia Regiment, part of two thousand Old Dominion troops Brig. Gen. Thomas J. Jackson, an eccentric former teacher at the Virginia Military Institute, had hurried to the scene. Ironically, the Virginians were clad in blue uniforms. Seeing the Rebels charging out of the woods from the east, Captain Griffin ordered his gunners to open fire with canister. Noticing the blue uniforms of the Virginians, however, Major Barry shouted at Griffin, "Captain, don't fire there; those are your battery support." Griffin growled back, "They are Confederates, as certain as the world, they are Confederates." Barry was still insisting the soldiers were Federals when the Virginians raised their rifles and fired a deadly volley into the battery from less than seventy yards. Both horses and gunners were struck down by the deadly fire of the massed musketry. "That was the last of us," Griffin would later say. "We were all cut down."[49]

To Griffin's left, just north of Henry House, the balding and bearded Captain Ricketts was hit four times, fell from his saddle, lay unconscious amid the wreck of his own battery, and when he regained consciousness, found himself a prisoner. Another artillery officer, Heintzelman's friend from the Rio Grande 1st Lt. Douglas Ramsay, was killed in the Rebel charge, along with most of his men.[50] In the fierce fighting the Virginians swarmed around Griffin and Ricketts's ten guns and drove what remained of the Zouaves and the marines down the hill.

Sensing the battle slipping away, Heintzelman raced about on the battlefield trying to rally his troops in hopes of regaining the cannons. Shouting and cursing, he made the same mistake as McDowell of sending in regiments individually rather than slamming in entire brigades. He first brought up Col. Willis A. Gorman's 1st Minnesota Infantry. Heintzelman had known the rotund Gorman during the Mexican War, and he considered the Minnesotans the best-trained and best-disciplined soldiers in his division.[51] With zest, the soldiers threw down their haversacks, blankets, and canteens, and gallantly charged up the grassy, open slope to the crest of the hill, retaking the guns. During the charge, Heintzelman spurred his horse forward to a position in front of the regiment and within easy pistol shot of the Rebels, perhaps mistaking some of Jackson's blue-coated Virginians for Federal reinforcements. Realizing his error, though, Heintzelman turned in the saddle and, with his "peculiar nasal twang," calmly called out, "Fire once, boys, then charge, and you've got 'em." Within seconds, a Minnesota private recalled, "The whole rebel line opened fire upon us, and we—nearly every man of my regiment, I believe—went down flat upon the ground to avoid the deadly shower of lead they sent among us." The 1st Minnesota, in "considerable confusion," was thrown back with 180 casualties, Heintzelman remembered; several of Gorman's men simply "ran away."[52] Unlike the Zouaves, however, most of the Minnesotans retreated in good order, and they were one of the last Union regiments to leave the field that day.

Heintzelman next brought forward two of General Franklin's Massachusetts regiments and Colonel Willcox's 1st Michigan. Moving in columns on the far right, Willcox was seen to wave his cap in the air as his men cheered. Despite a destructive fire from Rebel artillery and infantrymen concealed in the woods just behind the hill, the "regiment moved bravely on" as the men loaded and fired with coolness and precision. Heintzelman watched as the cannons were retaken, only to be lost again as the Virginians counterattacked with a savage viciousness. The Rebel fire became "continuous from every quarter, their infantry advancing on us through the woods in great force, our officers and men falling all about us," Maj. A. F. Bidwell of the 1st Michigan wrote.[53] Henry House Hill became an inferno of fire, smoke, confusion, and death as the Federals again fell back in "considerable confusion." Some men, frightened and disoriented, fled in terror, while others, forgetting to remove their ramrods from the barrels of their rifles before firing, sent the rods sailing toward the Confederate lines like arrows. When the smoke cleared, Colonel Willcox had been wounded and captured, and the hillside was strewn with the dead and dying. In all, the 1st Michigan had nine officers and 108 men killed, wounded, or missing. After the repulse, in the terrible heat and humidity, the Minnesota and Michigan regiments, joined by a few Zouaves, took cover in a wooded area from which they directed a devastating fire on the Rebels.

At the head of Lt. Col. Edward Brush Fowler's 14th Brooklyn Chasseurs (Red-Legged Devils) from Hunter's 2nd Division, Heintzelman was again able to recapture the Federal guns, but after taking several volleys of deadly musketry from Confederates concealed in the woods, the New Yorkers "broke and ran," leaving the guns again in Rebel hands. While retreating, the Chasseurs kept up a scattered but ineffective fire. "I considered it useless to attempt to rally them," Heintzelman wrote. At this time, as the general was between the two lines, he was hit by a spent Minié ball in the right arm about two inches below the right elbow. There was so much confusion on the battlefield, though, that he would always wonder if he had not been hit by friendly fire. At first the arm was numb and there was little pain, and Heintzelman continued to dash about trying to bring order to the retreating Federal regiments. Later, in considerable pain, he rode to the rear to find a surgeon. Dr. William S. King, his friend from the Texas frontier, rode forward and successfully cut the ball from his arm, bandaged the wound, and placed the arm in a sling.[54] Days later Heintzelman noticed that his uniform on his left side had also been pierced by a Rebel ball.

Still refusing to retire or seek further medical assistance, the general again rode forward. At 3:45 p.m., after joining Colonel Howard's brigade of Maine and Vermont men, Heintzelman led the last futile Union advance. Exhausted by the long marches and the burning heat of early summer, the New Englanders were sent reeling back by a heavy Confederate fire. Around 4:30 p.m. the tired and jittery Federals, many of them hungry and thirsty, began retreating as their lines collapsed. At that point the fifty-five-year-old Heintzelman continued to race back and forth, swearing mightily, as he tried to rally the men. Howard remembered seeing him scurrying about, his wounded arm flapping in a sling, as he raced his horse "up and down, trying to restore order." The general "spoke to me sharply, and told me to reform my lines. He did the same to other brigade and regiment commanders."[55]

Near the Warrenton Turnpike, Heintzelman gallantly tried to assemble a line with a section of Capt. Richard Arnold's Light Company D, 2nd Artillery, scattered units of the U.S. cavalry, and remnants of some infantry regiments. "In this I utterly failed," he admitted. On one occasion he came upon two New York regimental color bearers who were carefully furling their banners. "One man held the staff, one the spear head, and one each [the] outer corner of the silk," he recalled. Grinding his teeth, the general inquired in language more forcible than polite what the men were doing. When they replied that "they were going home," he angrily responded "that he was damned if they were" and ordered them to "unfurl their flags and march to the support of their imperilled comrades." The men grudgingly unfurled their flags, but when he rode off to encourage another regiment, he looked back to see the New York units "retreating and slowly disintegrating."[56] Riding back along the Sudley Springs Road, Heintzelman sent several of his staff officers to rally the troops beyond Bull Run, but most of the men were so panic stricken and the retreat so chaotic that such endeavors were futile. The retreat degenerated into anarchy.

At Sudley Church, on the rise above Bull Run, Heintzelman assisted in placing a few of the wounded in wagons and ambulances for evacuation, but most soon fell into the hands of the advancing Rebels; one cavalry company even crossed the stream and seized an ambulance full of the wounded. "When I got across Bull Run, I found that not a Regt. could be rallied, nor even a company," he later wrote in disgust and embarrassment. Finally realizing the battle was lost, he too took up the retreat. As part of the Union rear guard, Heintzelman joined five companies of regular cavalry and Captain Arnold's Company D, 2nd U.S. Artillery as "a few secession cavalry followed."[57]

Back along the same road that had taken them through the woods to battle that day, the Federals retreated, with the Rebels close on their heels. More than once Heintzelman ordered Arnold to wheel his artillery about and fire rounds of canister at the pursuers, which "sent them scampering away, and kept them at a respectful distance during the remainder of our retreat."[58] At dusk near the Warrenton Turnpike, he found a Rebel artillery battery enfilading the road. While Arnold ran the gauntlet in front of the Rebel guns, Heintzelman and his staff took to the fields and the woods.

For many the retreat now disintegrated into panic. On the Warrenton Turnpike at Cub Run, there was complete chaos and confusion. Here the road was blocked by an overturned army wagon disabled by Confederate artillery fire. While men waded across the creek in water up to their armpits, Arnold's guns had to be abandoned as the artillerists joined the straggling column of shattered soldiers and terrified civilians who soon clogged the roads leading to Washington.

Civilians only added to the confusion of the retreat. Several congressmen and citizens, including a number of women and children, had encamped earlier that day near the battlefield, hoping to enjoy a Sunday picnic while watching what was certain to be a Union victory. Women with parasols and picnic lunches had been strolling leisurely about as their children scampered across the green hillsides when the first fleeing Union soldiers straggled into sight. Finally realizing the full extent of the disaster, they panicked and fled for Washington. Rep. Alfred Ely of New York was not so fortunate. Captured, badly treated, and almost shot, he would spend five months in a Confederate prison.

By 8 P.M. in the growing darkness, Heintzelman was back at Centreville, where he had to be helped from his horse only to collapse from exhaustion.

After seventeen continuous hours in the saddle, his feet were so numb that he was unable to walk. After a drink of whiskey, a cup of strong coffee, and half an hour's sleep, however, he revived and hurried on toward Washington. Making his way along the twenty-mile road to the capital, he came to realize more completely the full extent of the Union defeat in the war's first great battle. The once-proud army had become little more than a demoralized rabble mob. Wrecked baggage wagons were everywhere. Fatigued, humiliated, and frightened soldiers refused to take orders and staggered along into the darkness, many without their weapons. Riderless horses raced about while wagons carrying the dead and wounded rambled on toward Washington. "Such a rout I never witnessed before," Heintzelman wrote. The march was further complicated when drenching rain turned the road into a morass. "We found the road full of fugitives and wagons, but not a regt. in good or any order," he recalled.[59]

In their headlong flight, hundreds of unnerved soldiers threw their rifles down by the side of the road and fled toward Washington. Three-fourths of the Zouaves disappeared during the retreat. A young private in the 2nd Rhode Island Infantry, one of the last regiments to leave the battlefield, vividly described the retreat along the Warrenton Turnpike: "I suffered untold horrors from thirst and fatigue but struggled on, clinging to my gun and cartridge box. Many times I sat down in the mud determined to go no further, and willing to die to end my misery. But soon a friend would pass and urge me to make another effort, and I would stagger on a mile further. At daylight we could see the spires of Washington, and a welcome sight it was." Many of the men in the Union ranks had been on their feet for thirty-six hours without anything to eat. Reaching the Potomac, they had marched over fifty miles that day.[60]

In the darkness, confusion, and drizzling rain, Heintzelman reached the Long Bridge to be greeted by the friendly faces of the 21st New York, a regiment from Buffalo, who gave him a tumbler of whiskey and helped him across the Potomac. Having been all night on the road, he arrived home at sunup the next morning and again had to be helped from his horse. Alarmed and frightened, Margaret sent for Dr. Eugene H. Abadie, their friend from Texas. At last, after twenty-eight hours in the saddle, his wound was properly dressed, and he collapsed from exhaustion.

For six weeks Heintzelman was unable to use his right arm, which was fractured and terribly swollen. In fact, for the rest of his life he never completely regained the use of the arm, and for the remainder of the war he could not lift his sword. Unable to turn his wrist, he was also incapable of writing, and his daily journal was discontinued during those six weeks. In the days that followed the disaster at Bull Run, visitors came to see him, inquire about the extent of his wound, and wish him well. When word reached Buffalo of his injury, one western New York resident rushed a box of ointment to the capital for his use.[61]

The day after the battle he sent his staff back to the Virginia side of the Potomac to try and reorganize his division, but the disorder and confusion were simply too great. "The disorganization after the battle was frightful," he recorded, and for over a week he "feared for the safety of the city." To Heintzelman there was little doubt that the Rebels could have overrun the defensive works along the Potomac outside Washington. There was little he and his staff could do, for "the panic was great."[62]

Of the 470 Union soldiers who died at First Bull Run, 188 were from Heintzelman's 3rd Division. Total casualties in the division amounted to 1,581. Hardest hit was Howard's 3rd Brigade. Although it had seen the least fighting, suffering only 50 dead, the three Maine regiments and the 2nd Vermont had 622 men missing. Willcox's 2nd Brigade was hit hard too, suffering the largest number of killed; 48 died in the 11th New York Zouaves alone. In Franklin's 1st Brigade, the 1st Minnesota had also suffered heavy casualties, losing 42 men killed and 108 wounded.[63] Bull Run was an enormous battle, the largest in American history to that point, yet the ghastly bloodletting on the rolling plains of Manassas was only the beginning.

SEVEN

Red Mud of Virginia

WITH WASHINGTON GRIPPED BY FEAR and panic following the Battle of Bull Run, many in the capital became increasingly apprehensive about the future of the country. Demoralized and wounded soldiers were everywhere, and gloom settled over the city like a shroud. No longer were lighthearted bands marching along Pennsylvania Avenue or regimental banners snapping in the wind. Bull Run had been a humiliating defeat for President Lincoln, General Scott, General McDowell, General Heintzelman, and the entire Federal Army. The battle also destroyed any illusion of a short war. Along with several other senior officers, Heintzelman feared that those who had anything to do with Bull Run would be sacked. "Every mother's son of you will be cashiered," he told several prominent officers.[1]

Despite the crushing defeat, Heintzelman would always remain proud of his performances during the battle. He had fought bravely and had done everything in his power to halt the Confederate onslaught. Yet he remained dismayed at the lack of resolve he had seen among the Union rank and file. "Raw troops," he observed, "cannot be expected to stand long against an unseen enemy."[2] Still somehow the pieces of the shattered army had to be put back together if the Republic was to be saved. In time he would come to see Bull Run as the event around which a Northern consciousness would emerge; out of defeat would emerge a better army, one capable of winning the war. After Bull Run there was no turning back.

Heintzelman was still at his home in Washington recuperating from his wound when he learned that General McDowell had been replaced by mustachioed thirty-four-year-old Maj. Gen. George Britton McClellan. On August 2, 1861, with his arm still in a sling, Heintzelman reported to his new commander. A week later, largely through the efforts of the Pennsylvania congressional delegation, he was made a brigadier general of volunteers and placed in command of a brigade of troops consisting of the 5th Maine; 16th, 26th, and 27th New York; and a battery of artillery.

But in the rush to create a large army, other officers, many younger and junior in rank, were being promoted over him. "If I had not been so unfortunate in my mining speculations, I would resign at once," Heintzelman bitterly wrote in his journal.[3] Yet he continued to visit with influential and friendly congressmen and senators who were likely to influence the composition of the quickly forming Army of the Potomac.

Even the news from Arizona was bad. In early October he read in the *New York Times* that Charles Poston's brother, John, had been murdered by Mexicans not far from the border. "All our business is ruined and the Americans driven out of the country," Heintzelman despondently declared. A month later William Wrightson arrived in the capital with details of an escalating and bloody Apache war in the Desert Southwest.[4] With the Heintzelman Mine at Cerro Colorado inactive and largely abandoned, the general began to concentrate more of his attention on the Vallecillo silver mines. He was concerned, nevertheless, that the small Rebel army at the Rio Grande, or perhaps revolutionary forces in Mexico, would cut all communications with or even seize the mines, and his investments would be lost. At every opportunity he promoted the idea of sending Union troops to Texas and the Southwest.

But there was little time to dwell on reverses in Arizona and Texas. On the banks of the Potomac, concerns were immediate and pressing. Late into the fall he watched patiently as the handsome and charming McClellan shaped and molded the Army of the Potomac into a formidable fighting force. Within three months he had trained and armed 134,000 soldiers. By late December the army numbered 220,000 men and more than five hundred cannons. Newspapers praised the new commander as the "Young Napoleon," the army called him "Little Mac," and McClellan reveled in such pronouncements. Although twenty-two years older than his commander, Heintzelman admired McClellan's energy and hard work. From the beginning he realized the charismatic and popular general was exceptionally bright and a master organizer. "Little Mac" had fought well in Mexico, been a military observer in Europe, and become a successful railroad executive. Nor was he put off by McClellan's excessive egotism, conceit, and contempt for views other than his own, traits that did not endear him to others. Heintzelman did frequently find it difficult to meet with McClellan, whom he found to be obnoxious and something of an elitist. In such instances he was forced to settle for consultations with Col. Randolph B. Marcy, McClellan's father-in-law, likeable chief of staff, and renowned western explorer. At the same time, Heintzelman continued to press for an appointment as major general of volunteers, and he was gratified when friends from Buffalo, New York, prepared a memorial on his behalf. When he learned in the process that a brevet as lieutenant colonel had been previously denied him by Millard Fillmore, he hurried off a letter to the former president and friend, inquiring as to the reasons.[5]

In the latter months of 1861, the city that had been in disarray and disorder following the defeat at Bull Run now became a disciplined armed camp. Gone were the drunken soldiers roaming Pennsylvania Avenue and the demoralized officers who filled the saloons at Willard's Hotel. Many of the three-month volunteers who had fled the field at Bull Run had gone home, and other troops who had cowered along the banks of the Potomac were now busily drilling eight hours a day. Moreover, thousands of zealous new recruits arrived by train each week.[6]

As the reinvigorated Federal Army took shape, several close friends came to Washington. On August 12 Dr. Charles Tripler arrived, having been appointed chief medical officer. Closely examining Heintzelman's injured arm, he confirmed Dr. Abadie's initial diagnosis: the arm was indeed fractured at the elbow, and it would be some time before it would properly heal. Also arriving in Washington was Solon Lathrop, Heintzelman's closest friend and confidant, who had obtained a captain's commission in the 17th U.S. Infantry.

Inspecting the defenses of the capital, McClellan found the approaches vulnerable and dispatched Heintzelman to construct and maintain a more secure defensive line south of the Potomac that stretched for eight miles from the mouth of the Anacostia River to Franconia. In fact, McClellan was determined to surround Washington with a series of impregnable fortifications. On both sides of the Potomac, numerous farms were seized, their orchards and vegetable gardens transformed into massive earthworks. Eventually forty-eight forts, lunettes, redoubts, and batteries, mounting three hundred guns, would ring the capital. A few of these fortifications, such as Fort Runyon on the Virginia bank of the Potomac at the Long Bridge, had been built prior to Bull Run. As part of Heintzelman's command, Forts Craig, Woodbury, and Corcoran were constructed to guard the western approaches to Arlington Heights, while smaller outposts, including Forts Ward, Ellsworth, and Blenker, were hastily designed to guard the approaches to Alexandria. During the third week of November, construction began on redoubts and trenches guarding the Fairfax and Leesburg Turnpike approaches to Alexandria. In front of the massive nine-acre earthworks christened Fort Lyon, two New York regiments went to work digging a twelve-foot-deep ditch and felling trees for abatis.[7] With Washington thus successfully fortified, Heintzelman hoped McClellan would be free to take his army into the field.

Heintzelman set up headquarters in the large two-story Ballenger House near Fort Lyon. The house was actually made up of three parts. In a large and roomy two-story frame structure, his staff worked on the first floor, near the telegraph office, while the second story made up the sleeping quarters. In the older, smaller white-columned middle structure, the general worked and slept. A smaller octagon-shaped structure in the rear was used as a kitchen. The secessionist owner, fleeing south to join the Confederate Army, had removed all of the furniture, so Heintzelman and his staff worked from makeshift wooden tables. Only a few hundred yards away stood the high earthen walls of Fort Lyon, beneath which acres of tangled abatis made any approach difficult. The leading Northern newspaper correspondents of the times all visited Fort Lyon, as did the distinctive English novelist Anthony Trollope, whom Heintzelman reported to be a "snob-nob."[8] From the piazza of Ballenger House, a splendid view of a large stretch of the Potomac was possible. When not at home in Washington, Heintzelman often gathered here with his staff for long conversations late into the night.

Directly in front of Fort Lyon in the Virginia countryside lay the camps of the ever-increasing Confederate Army. Heintzelman's scouts detected enemy outposts on the Little River Turnpike at Prospect Hill, west of the Chain Bridge, as well as on the Leesburg Turnpike at Munson's Hill. Other patrols said the Stars and Bars could be seen floating in the wind atop Upton's Hill, just north of the Leesburg and Alexandria Turnpike. The Rebels were also reported to be guarding the Fairfax Turnpike west of Alexandria. Union patrols also found large enemy camps at the village of Falls Church and at Lewinsville. Heintzelman was also concerned that if Confederate batteries on the Virginia side of the Potomac downriver from Washington were not destroyed, the capital would be effectively blockaded.

At Fort Lyon Heintzelman worked to build a competent and loyal staff. His adjutant general, someone he had known in the antebellum army for many years, was Capt. Chauncey McKeever. A career officer from Maryland and a strong Unionist, McKeever had graduated fourteenth in his West Point class of 1849 and had served in the 3rd Artillery for over a decade. Heintzelman had confidence in McKeever, whom he later promoted to major. Capt. Isaac Moses, assistant adjutant from New York, had attended West Point but had not graduated. The general would later find him lacking in energy. From Vermont, Lt. Leavitt Hunt had been in the 38th New York Infantry before Heintzelman persuaded the young lieutenant to join his staff as an aide. Hunt was said to have been a "leading spirit in gaiety and a very brave and efficient officer." Lt. Granville Johnson, a Bostonian in the 99th Pennsylvania, was recruited as chief aide, while Margaret's nephew, Lt. Henry Norton, transferred from the 63rd New York Infantry to also become an aide. French-born John Jefferson Milhau, an assistant surgeon in the army since 1851, was appointed medical director. Capt. Samuel McKelvy, a native of Pittsburgh, served

Ballenger House, Heintzelman's headquarters at Fort Lyon, Virginia. Sketch by Robert Knox Sneden. Virginia Historical Society.

ably as commissary and chief quartermaster. From the 1st Maryland Infantry, Prussian-born William Heine was made chief topographical engineer. Assisting Heine as a cartographer was the all-observing and skilled Robert Knox Sneden, a young private from the 40th New York Infantry who kept a detailed diary and provided countless sketches of the scenes and events that would soon engulf General Heintzelman and the Army of the Potomac.[9]

Heintzelman watched as the promising but untried McClellan continued to build and reshape the army defending Washington. As a division commander, he too attempted to instill in his men the kind of discipline he had maintained in Mexico, California, and on the Texas frontier. When the 52nd New York was reported to be in a state of mutiny, he threatened to remove the commanding colonel and take command of the regiment himself. When two other regiments, the 2nd Maine and the 79th New York, did indeed mutiny, he had the ringleaders arrested, hauled before a court-martial, and when found guilty, sent to the Dry Tortugas, off the southern tip of Florida, to serve out their terms at hard labor. When a Vermont boy, William Scott, fell asleep on sentry duty at the Chain Bridge, he was tried by court-martial and sentenced to be shot. The case created so much sympathy in Washington, however, that the lad was pardoned by President Lincoln. A short time later Pvt. William H. Johnson of the 1st New York Lincoln Cavalry was found guilty of desertion and shot by a firing squad.[10] He was the first soldier to be executed in the Army of the Potomac.

By September Heintzelman had regained much of the confidence he had possessed in the weeks prior to Bull Run. Although the Confederates had pushed their lines to within fifteen miles of Washington, he was convinced that any attack on the capital could be easily repulsed. Yet the Rebels in northern Virginia continued to pose a threat. On September 11 a patrol skirmished with Union forces near the Virginia approach of the Chain Bridge, only a short distance above Georgetown. Fearful of being attacked, Heintzelman sent his own patrols into the field to the west and south of Washington to detect any Confederate movement toward the capital. On his fifty-sixth birthday, September 30, 1861, he learned that a poorly planned reconnaissance had ended badly when two Union regiments mistakenly fired on one another and several men had been killed and wounded. Three weeks later he sent Brig. Gen. Israel B. Richardson, with two regiments of infantry accompanied by a company of cavalry and a small artillery battery, on a reconnaissance in force toward the Occoquan River, south of the capital. Taking the Telegraph Road, Richardson discovered that the enemy had evacuated Pohick Church and Accotink Village but were still in force along Accotink Run.[11]

Three weeks later, when four hundred Confederate cavalry reoccupied Pohick Church and advanced against his pickets, Heintzelman sent Richardson's brigade along with those of Brig. Gens. John Sedgwick and Charles Davis Jameson by different roads in the direction of the church. Leaving Fort Lyon at daylight, Heintzelman overtook the column only to be told that the Rebels had evacuated the area the night before. Determined to make contact with the enemy, he pushed several regiments forward to the Occoquan River. After crossing Accotink Run, Capt. Henry B. Todd of the Lincoln Cavalry sent out a squad of seven men, who were attacked while in the process of plundering a local residence. One man was mortally wounded, four were captured, and three managed to escape. Heintzelman was furious that the captain had allowed his men to straggle and plunder in the face of the enemy. Todd, who was captured in the encounter, wrote his report from a Richmond prison.[12]

A much larger setback came a few days later when McClellan sent Brig. Gen. Charles P. Stone and part of a division across the Potomac northwest of Washington on a reconnaissance to determine the strength and movements of a Confederate brigade reported to be in the area around Leesburg. On October 21 Stone crossed the river only to be ambushed at Ball's

Bluff. Forced down a steep embankment and driven into the river, more than two hundred bluecoats were shot, drowned, or wounded as they tried to swim to safety; seven hundred Federals were captured.[13] Among the killed in this fiasco was a popular Republican senator from Oregon and close friend of President Lincoln, Col. Edward Baker. One of the consequences of Ball's Bluff was the creation by Congress in December 1861 of a joint committee to investigate "the conduct of the present war." The committee, which came to be dominated by Radical Republicans, would not only investigate Ball's Bluff but also Bull Run, and in the coming months they would prove to be a major detraction to the military prosecution of the war, occupying much of Heintzelman's time and attention.

Heintzelman shared McClellan's love of martial pageantry and ceremony. Accompanied by Charles, who had arrived from Kenyon College, he delighted in the parades and reviews the commanding general used to lift and maintain morale in his ever-increasing army. Most reviews were staged on the commons east of the Capitol. But one large review took place in the Virginia countryside at Taneytown the third week of September, during which Heintzelman met with the Prince de Joinville, a French aristocrat and member of the royal family that had gone into exile in England following the Revolution of 1848, and the nobleman's two nephews, the Comte de Paris and the Duc de Chartres, both princes of the House of Orleans. Exiles from the regime of Napoleon III, all three were staunch supporters of the Union cause, and they had come to Washington to offer their services to McClellan. Although the Prince de Joinville was said to possess impressive credentials, to Heintzelman he looked "like any ordinary Frenchman."[14]

Reviewing the well-disciplined regiments, Heintzelman could not help but reflect back on the poorly disciplined soldiers he had led prior to Bull Run: "When I saw these troops march by, I thought what a change has taken place since then. How much better prepared we are now." Riding out again in early October to watch a review of four cavalry regiments and one hundred artillery pieces, he thought it the "largest force of the kind ever together in this country." At another large assembly on a muddied parade ground a few days later, at which time President Lincoln and Secretary of State Seward reviewed a large force of cavalry and artillery regiments, the limber box of one of the artillery batteries exploded, seriously wounding four men but only frightening the president and secretary of state. During a grand review in late November, Heintzelman seemed pleased when President Lincoln rode forward to shake his hand. The president, the general proudly recorded, said "that he wished to shake hands with me and that he would never forget me." At the same review Seward also came forward and "put out his hand." Five days later, at a reception at the Executive Mansion, he conversed freely with the president on a variety of topics.[15]

In the late fall and early winter of 1861, Heintzelman became privy to McClellan's growing disrespect and contempt for the president. Once he rode to McClellan's headquarters to find Lincoln going over a map and "making remarks, not remarkably profound, but McClellan listened as if much edified." When Heintzelman retired to an inner room, Lincoln and McClellan continued to discuss military matters. The president spoke so loud that all those gathered in the outer room could hear him tell McClellan that he had decided to place Maj. Gen. Henry W. Halleck in command in the western theater. Later, after McClellan had seen Lincoln to the door and the president had disappeared into the night, the commander of the Army of the Potomac turned and remarked, "Isn't he a rare bird?"[16] It was evident McClellan did not respect Lincoln as a man or a leader.

At the same time, Heintzelman was becoming involved in the heightening debate over the disposition of runaway slaves. At Fortress Monroe, Virginia, the bald and sleepy-eyed Maj. Gen. Benjamin Franklin Butler, whom Heintzelman had met in Washington in early September, was defiantly refusing to return runaways to their masters. Heintzelman thought Butler courageous and that his actions should be applauded. To him, the Fugitive Slave Law was no longer valid since runaway slaves had simply become "contraband of war." When one visitor to his headquarters inquired why he was refusing to return runaway slaves, Heintzelman responded that he "refused to be either a slave catcher or slave driver." He later told Sen. Edgar Cowan of Pennsylvania, "I informed Virginians who came to me for their fugitive slaves, that they could not take them and that I expected the war would last so long that they would have any left." For the rest of his life he would always take pride in the fact that he was one of the first Federal commanders who refused to return slaves to their masters. As hundreds of escaped slaves made their way into his lines in northern Virginia, some with valuable information on Confederate troop strengths and locations, Heintzelman persisted in giving them safe haven and flatly refused to return them to bondage. As a result, a number of Northerners, including many abolitionists, wrote to congratulate him on his "refusing to catch negroes." Although he was no abolitionist, Heintzelman came to see the runaways, or "Contrabands," as valuable war assets. In some instances slaves who reached the Federal lines were sent back into Rebel-held areas of northeastern Virginia as spies and given sizeable rewards for the information they provided. As a soldier, "I had nothing to do with slavery," Heintzelman wrote many years later. "I then believed and still believe that slavery was a curse to the white man."[17] He was among a small cadre of Union generals, including Benjamin Butler, John C. Frémont, and David

Hunter, who struck at the institution of slavery long before the Contraband Act, Emancipation Proclamation, or the Thirteenth Amendment to the Constitution.

During the pleasant days of fall, Heintzelman heard his name mentioned as the commander of an expedition to be sent to Texas. Lone Star Unionists had fled across the Rio Grande by the hundreds to congregate in Matamoros, Mexico, where they had made their way to the mouth of the river to find passage to Washington. Arriving in the capital, they pleaded with Lincoln and anyone who would listen that troops should be sent to their state. In December 1861 Jeremiah Galvan, Heintzelman's Brownsville merchant-friend from the Cortina War, arrived in Washington, and the two spent a pleasant evening together. "He gave me much information about Texas," the general wrote. "There are no guns at Brazos, but Ft. Brown has been repaired. There were two companies on the Rio Grande when he left, but I understand they have dwindled down to 87 men." Galvan said there were "few Secessionists in Brownsville," and the Texas Unionists wanted Heintzelman "to come with Union troops to relieve them." Moreover, his friend continued: "The Texans have not received a barrel of flour or a bag of corn from the Confederates. . . . They are ripe for a revolt." Although Heintzelman contemplated offering his services for the reclamation of Texas, he realized that the war in the East would soon be reaching a climax, and if McClellan faltered, he would be in line to command the Army of the Potomac. Any chance of greatness lay in Virginia, not on the remote Texas frontier. "Our course now is to press the war on every side," he wrote.[18]

Mingling with the Washington social and political elite and frequently visiting the Executive Mansion, the petite and strong-willed Margaret did everything possible to advance her husband's career. "She thinks McClellan is against me, but Congress [is] in my favour," Samuel Peter reported. Early in 1862 he learned that Lincoln had dismissed his Pennsylvania friend from Lancaster, Simon Cameron, the corrupt secretary of war, and replaced him with the tough-minded Edwin M. Stanton, who was brusque, irritable, tireless, and a dedicated antislavery Democrat. "The report is that Mr. Lincoln told Cameron he would have no more of the d——d cheating going on in the War Department," Heintzelman recorded.[19]

Also that fall, as the roads in Virginia became dry and hard, Northern newspapers, including Horace Greeley's influential *New York Tribune*, and a host of politicians clamored for the Army of the Potomac to take the offensive. But McClellan, who was excessively secretive about his intentions, refused to move. As autumn gave way to the biting cold and snow of winter, it became evident that the army would not be moving anywhere until spring. Instead of advancing, the nearly 150,000-man-strong Army of the

Potomac was busy building log huts for winter quarters. A number of senators and representatives, as well as the president himself, came to not only question McClellan's resolve and strategy for winning the war but also his proslavery pronouncements. Consequently, Heintzelman came more and more to envision himself as "Little Mac's" possible successor. Even if McClellan remained in overall command of Union forces, Heintzelman began hoping that he could personally lead the Army of the Potomac against Richmond and end the war. Due to his personal aspirations, it was inevitable that he would become involved in the rough-and-tumble world of Washington politics. McClellan was a conservative Democrat in a city where liberal Republicans held power. Although he had never delved into politics, Heintzelman was seen as being far more moderate.

In an army dominated by conservative Democrats, his refusal to return fugitive slaves caught the attention of a number of prominent Radical Republicans. A few days before Christmas, 1861, at the National Hotel at Sixth Street and Pennsylvania Avenue, Heintzelman met with Sen. Zachariah Chandler of Michigan, a blunt Radical Republican and ardent foe of slavery, who promised to use his influence to assist Charles in obtaining an appointment to West Point. "He locked the door and we had a talk of two hours on the affairs of the Army," Heintzelman recorded. Questioned about McClellan, the general went as far as to say that his commander had never called a council of war or consulted him on strategy or "any military subject." Although he had made a number of suggestions to McClellan, his recommendations had largely been ignored. Chandler did not "want me to speak of our interview," he confided to his journal.[20] At Fort Lyon Heintzelman also met secretly with Sen. Benjamin Franklin Wade of Ohio, another Radical, who was suspicious of McClellan and critical of his refusal to advance against the Rebels. He had first come to know Senator Wade as chairman of the Committee on Territories, when he had lobbied for the Territory of Arizona. Growing up poor, Wade had been one of the founders of the Republican Party. A Radical in the true sense of the word, he wanted slavery abolished, women liberated, and labor reformed. He had fought slaveholders with his fists and now called for a no-holds-barred prosecution of the war.

Both Chandler and Wade, as well as Vice President Hamlin and others in power, approached Heintzelman with the idea of a command separate from McClellan. When the two senators first appeared at his house in Washington and Margaret had learned their true intentions, she had turned them away, saying that her husband would not compromise his integrity. "I declined to intrigue against my commander," Heintzelman would later write. But in the weeks ahead, as Washington politics became even more partisan and convoluted, he drew closer to the Radicals.

In contrast, McClellan made no secret of his contempt for abolitionists, the idea of emancipation, and Radical Republicans in general. At the same time, Heintzelman realized that McClellan had learned of his meetings with the Radicals. Suspicious of his subordinate's intentions, McClellan never developed the "cordial intercourse as there would other wise have been," Heintzelman admitted.[21]

It was becoming evident that McClellan did not want to fight the kind of war the Radical Republicans were demanding. To the general and his followers, both in and out of the army, the war was not about slavery or reshaping the South in the North's image but about saving the Union, a view they shared with President Lincoln. "Help me to dodge the nigger," McClellan wrote a friend. "I am fighting to preserve the integrity of the Union. . . . To gain that end we cannot afford to mix up the negro question."[22] There was little doubt a dangerous polarization was rapidly developing between the Radical Republicans and McClellan, and Heintzelman was in danger of being caught in the crossfire. Yet he realized that the Radicals were desperate to replace McClellan with one of their own, and he aspired to be their man.

The Joint Committee on the Conduct of the War, created in December 1861 and led by Radical Republicans Wade and Chandler, both of whom were zealots and intensely partisan, proved to be a threat to any conservative Democratic general. Striking at McClellan, who had Lincoln's reluctant support, through his subordinates, they were relentless in pushing the Radical agenda. The first victim of the committee was General Stone, a proslavery Democrat who became a convenient scapegoat for the disaster at Ball's Bluff. Perceived to be disloyal and in sympathy with the South, Stone was grilled before the committee in secret sessions without the right of counsel and subsequently arrested by Secretary of War Edwin Stanton, who was in league with the Radicals. This caused a considerable amount of mortification in the Army of the Potomac. To Heintzelman, Stone's arrest and imprisonment was "as high-handed an outrage against personal liberty as could have been enacted during the Middle Ages."[23] Placed in solitary confinement at Fort Lafayette, New York, Stone remained there for 189 days without being granted a trial. Although not wanting to alienate his Radical friends in the Congress, Heintzelman was convinced that Stone was irresponsible but loyal. Later released without ever being charged, Stone's military career was nevertheless in ruins. With Wade wielding the committee's gavel, he and other senators went on to destroy the reputations of several Union generals, especially West Point–educated Democrats.

Consorting privately with the Radicals on several occasions, Heintzelman consistently portrayed himself as more liberal than his private papers and journal indicate. Although secure about his position in the army and privately aspiring to an independent command, even of the Army of the Potomac should McClellan falter, he was the second person summoned by the joint committee. With Chandler leading the questioning on Bull Run, the hearing proved to be overly friendly. Chandler wanted to know how many men Heintzelman had prior to the campaign and how many men he had on the day of the battle. When asked his opinion on why Union forces had been defeated, Heintzelman offered a few explanations. "There were a number of causes," he said. "In the first place, the delay of Friday and Saturday at Centreville was one efficient cause. Another cause was the three hours lost at Centreville on Sunday morning." His conclusions pretty much confirmed those of the committee. The battle had largely been lost because of the unnecessary delays at Centreville, which had allowed Confederate reinforcements to arrive at Manassas Junction. In his journal Heintzelman recorded his reaction to the questioning: "I met the committee and was introduced to all. We at once went to work. They wanted to know about Bull Run and then asked a great many questions about the present conduct of the war. I gave my opinions freely, though I hesitated about operations, as there had never been a council of war and I did not know o[u]r force or resources or those of the enemy."[24] But it would not be his last appearance.

Only days later the worst pessimism Washington had seen since the dark days following Bull Run settled over the capital. On November 8, much to Heintzelman's pleasure, Capt. Charles Wilkes of the USS *San Jacinto* stopped the British mail-packet *Trent* bound from Havana to the British West Indies. Onboard were Confederate commissioners James M. Mason of Virginia and John Slidell of Louisiana, bound for London and France, respectively. Captain Wilkes, who became a hero in the North, apprehended Mason and Slidell and spirited them off to a Union prison in Boston. Prime Minister Viscount Palmerston was furious, and Britain dispatched reinforcements to its North American fleet and even sent an expeditionary force to Canada. To many an Anglo-American war seemed imminent. Realizing such a conflict would be disastrous for the Union cause, Lincoln, using a maritime technicality, ordered Mason and Slidell released on Christmas Day.

A week later, late on the evening of December 31, as Heintzelman sat to write his last journal entry for the year, he seemed to reflect the sober mood in the capital, yet he remained upbeat: "I hope soon to be in bed and forget all our troubles. I hope long ere the coming year is gone our whole country will be at peace." At a grand reception at the Executive Mansion the next day, the first day of 1862, Samuel Peter and Margaret mingled with members of Lincoln's cabinet, the diplomatic corps, Supreme

Court justices, and officers of both the army and navy. "A striking feature of the scene was the great number of gay uniforms," a correspondent for the *New York Times* wrote. "Generals, Colonels and Majors were plenty as blackberries, while Captains and Lieutenants were multitudinous. If our soldiers prove as useful as they are ornamental, nothing more could be desired of them."[25]

With the dawning of a new year, more than a million men remained locked in mortal combat all the way from Virginia to New Mexico Territory. In northern Virginia the early winter snows turned the roads into quagmires. Pvt. Robert Sneden described conditions in late January 1862: "We have had several storms . . . [and] about sixteen inches of snow now covers the ground, making it very uncomfortable camping out. . . . The roads and camps [are] six and eight inches deep in red mud and slush. . . . As a defense to the enemy, this Virginia mud is all as good as several regiments."[26]

With the army bogged down in knee-deep mud and snow, its high command remained mired in gloom and appeared paralyzed by a strange inertia. McClellan fell ill with typhoid fever and took to his bed for weeks. In the prolonged bad weather, Marcy too became sick, and McClellan's senior commander, Maj. Gen. Edwin V. "Bull" Sumner, was injured when his horse fell on him. Heintzelman feared Sumner would not survive, though even if he did, that he would never ride or command troops again. Mary was unable to walk, and Dr. Tripler was called to operate on her leg again. Margaret was sick much of the time, and Samuel Peter too came down with what was probably the flu. On February 20 Lincoln's eleven-year-old son, Willie, died of typhoid, or what the physicians called "bilious fever," and the Executive Mansion was plunged into mourning. Mary Lincoln bordered on insanity, and the president was despondent. Many in Washington questioned the course of the war, if not the very future of the Union.[27]

With the growing stalemate and inactivity, Heintzelman became increasingly restless and frustrated. "Why don't we advance somewhere?" he wrote. But when Senator Chandler again spoke of getting him a command separate from McClellan "to go South," his spirits were lifted. A week later there was "strong talk of an advance," and Heintzelman was sure he would be placed in command. "The Penna. delegation and some if not all [of] the Maine [delegation] will urge me for the command of an expedition South," he commented, noting that even Vice President Hamlin "recommends me."[28] Sen. Henry Wilson of Massachusetts, a formidable Radical Republican and chairman of the powerful Committee on Military Affairs, also sought Heintzelman's advice. During this time, he and the other Radicals in Congress continued to question the loyalty of a number of McClellan's generals. Wilson pushed for immediate emancipation and wanted the South made over in the image of the North. Besides Wilson and Chandler, Heintzelman went out of his way to nurture a relationship with Sen. Ira Harris of New York.

As early as November 1861, Heintzelman had begun to work on a plan he thought would go a long way toward winning the war. He would assemble thirty thousand men at Fortress Monroe at the head of the Virginia Peninsula, "ostensibly to go South, take them up the James and York rivers, silence the batteries at Yorktown, land above and capture Gen. Magruder's forces. There I would be in a condition to advance on Richmond or night attack Norfolk by landing on the Nansemond River, or go again South. A demonstration like this would carry off a large portion of the rebel army now at Centreville and Manassas. It might be made one of the most brilliant events of the war. The expedition could not fail." Repeatedly unable to see McClellan, he presented the plan to the army's chief of staff, Randolph Marcy (now a brigadier general), who thought "it a good move."[29]

In order to avoid the Rebel forces at Manassas Junction, McClellan also favored a large amphibious operation that would embark from Annapolis. Avoiding the Rebel guns along the lower Potomac, his army would steam down Chesapeake Bay, then up the Rappahannock River, disembarking at Urbanna, before advancing rapidly on Richmond, fifty miles away. But when it became evident that McClellan would not move until spring, Heintzelman too came to seriously question his commander's resolve. McClellan "may be a great general," he wrote, "but so far I have not seen it exhibited in his acts."[30] Although Little Mac was idealized by the troops, Heintzelman was sure he himself could do a better job.

All the while the skirmishing around Pohick Church, Fairfax Court House, and along the Occoquan River continued. In late January 1862 a reconnaissance from the 37th New York Infantry attempted to capture a squad of the 1st Texas Infantry, which had taken refuge in an abandoned two-story farmhouse along the Occoquan. Heintzelman was awakened in the night at Fort Lyon by a heavy knocking on the door and told that the Federals had captured "30 Texas Rangers" and killed nine more, suffering only one casualty themselves in what the courier characterized as "a very handsome affair." He later learned, however, that the affair had been "badly managed" and the New Yorkers had, in fact, retreated after suffering several casualties and killing only one of the Texans.[31]

Finally, in February morale in the North was lifted with good news from the West. Brig. Gen. Ulysses S. Grant had seized Forts Henry and Donelson, important Rebel fortifications twelve miles apart on the Tennessee and Cumberland rivers in northern Tennessee. With the capture of the two forts, just as Heintzelman predicted, the Confederates were forced to evacuate the Tennessee capital of Nashville. On the six-month anniversary of Bull Run, Heintzelman was reflective and optimistic: "In every quarter our affairs look most promising. I feel confident that this rebellion will be a small affair by May."[32]

While in Washington, he somehow found time to continue lobbying for the creation of a Territory of Arizona. After meeting Poston in the rotunda of the Capitol in late February 1862, the two men dined with Ohio representative John A. Gurley, after which they retired to the congressman's room to "discuss Arizona affairs and our mines." With Poston a few days later, Heintzelman went to see Rep. James M. Ashley of Ohio, chairman of the House Committee on Territories and a friend of the Sonora Exploring and Mining Company, who agreed to "report a bill for the Ter. of Arizona."[33]

Heintzelman also continued to use his influence with senators and the president to obtain an at-large appointment for Charles at West Point. His son, who was not yet sixteen, had received little education while in Texas, but he had done well at Kenyon College. In late January 1862 Samuel Peter went with Margaret to the Executive Mansion to urge Lincoln to appoint Charles. While the president would make no promises, he asked the general to put the request in writing and "he would attend to it.[34]

Always interested in scientific innovation, Heintzelman befriended the thirty-year-old New Hampshire–born aeronaut and balloonist Prof. Thaddeus Sobieski Constantine Lowe, who was experimenting with hydrogen-filled balloons near Fort Lyon. Lowe had attracted considerable attention in 1859 when he had tried three times to fly across the Atlantic. In April 1861, a few days after the surrender of Fort Sumter, he did balloon some nine hundred miles from Cincinnati, Ohio, to Unionville, South Carolina, only to be promptly arrested as a Union spy. Released, he hastened to Washington to offer his services to the Union Army. Impressed with his energy and knowledge, Lincoln named him chief of army aeronautics. Meeting with Lowe for the first time in February, Heintzelman too was impressed, and he recommended that Lowe make an ascent near Pohick Church to observe the Confederate camps and outposts along Bull Run.[35]

At a deserted and ransacked Pohick Church, the general watched as Lowe sent his balloon five hundred feet into the cold wintry sky. On a second ascent with Heintzelman aboard, he let out all the rope, and they reached a more impressive height of one thousand feet. "I there had a fine view," a "beautiful sight," Heintzelman recorded. With a snowstorm near Manassas, though, he could see little in that direction, but across the Occoquan and in the direction of Wolf Run Shoals, he spotted the rising smoke from several Confederate camps, both large and small. To the east he could clearly see Washington and even the unfinished dome of the Capitol. Downriver he sighted a Union gunboat flotilla and watched with great interest as the vessels fired three shots at Confederate fortifications on the south bank of the river. "I could see the smoke and hear the reports," he wrote, as he watched the gunboats steam even closer to the Virginia bank.[36]

Finally fed up with McClellan's unwillingness to move, Lincoln issued orders directing the Army of the Potomac to attack the Confederates at a point on the Orange and Alexandria Railroad southeast of Manassas. In response, McClellan was forced to reveal his "Urbanna plan." Hearing out the general, Lincoln was reluctant to approve, believing such an operation would leave Washington vulnerable to a sudden Confederate strike. After refining some details of his original plan in response to the president's concerns, McClellan still proposed to load the Army of the Potomac on transports, steam down the Potomac River to Chesapeake Bay, then to the mouth of the Rappahannock and up to Urbanna. By late February 1862, Heintzelman was meeting more regularly with McClellan to discuss the proposed operation.

At an assembly of all twelve division commanders at army headquarters on Pennsylvania Avenue at Jackson Square on March 4, the generals debated McClellan's plan for several hours. When the army commander excused himself, they discussed the intricacies of the plan late into the afternoon. Although the proposed operation was better than no plan at all, since it would at least put the Army of the Potomac in motion, Heintzelman was concerned about "crossing two rivers in the face of the enemy." Failure at either the Mattapony or the Pamunkey "may bring disaster," he warned the other generals. But the most serious concerns were raised by Brig. Gen. John G. Barnard, the army's chief engineer, who was doubtful that "the Federals could transport enough men to the Rappahannock by water, land them, and fortify a new base on hostile ground before the Rebels reached the scene from Manassas and assaulted the bridgehead." The three senior commanders, Heintzelman, Sumner, and McDowell, along with Barnard argued for a less ambitious plan that would have the army advance on the Confederates via the Occoquan River, less than two days' march from Washington, and by threatening the railroad lifeline to Manassas, force the Rebels to come out of their entrenchments and meet the Army of the Potomac on the open field.[37]

Later Chief of Staff Marcy took Heintzelman aside to say that the operation was in jeopardy due to a political plot by the Radicals to replace McClellan. Although clearly wanting to command the Army of the Potomac himself, and perhaps privy to actual plans to remove McClellan, Heintzelman would only say that it was a terrible time to change commanders. Later at a cabinet meeting, Lincoln frankly told McClellan that he still had second thoughts about the Urbanna plan. The president even repeated rumors he had heard that it was little more than a treasonous plot to remove the Army of the Potomac from Washington and that many in the capital, both in and out of his cabinet, thought the general was doing little more than placating the Rebels. Incensed and indignant, McClellan asked for an apology and then hurried to army headquarters, where he hastily assembled his twelve division commanders. After a thorough discussion of the plan, and after McClellan and Marcy had left the room, the generals had a spirited debate for several hours and then voted 8–4 in favor of the Urbanna operation. Those voting in the affirmative, most of whom owed their positions to McClellan, urged the four dissenters, Heintzelman, Sumner, Barnard, and McDowell, to make the vote unanimous. When the minority refused, it "excited considerable feeling," Heintzelman recorded.[38]

Meeting with Lincoln, Stanton, and McClellan at the Executive Mansion later in the afternoon, the generals continued to debate the plan. During the discussion, Heintzelman learned that McClellan, as early as September 1861, had revealed his plan to both General Franklin and Brig. Gen. Fitz John Porter, evidence, he concluded, that he was not one of McClellan's confidants or favorites. Lincoln continued to express his concerns "that if so large a force was taken away," Washington would not be safe. Adjourning at 6:30 P.M., the president promised a decision on the plan the next day. As promised, with all the generals assembled at 10 A.M. the following morning, Lincoln announced that he was approving the operation, but with conditions. He had "decided to send 50,000 men to the Chesapeake as soon as possible to be followed by 50,000 more," providing the Confederate batteries along the lower Potomac could be silenced.[39] Determined to have the last word, Heintzelman prepared a "short memorandum" for Secretary of War Stanton, but when he found the secretary discussing the plan with several other generals, he gave the memorandum to Lincoln instead.

At the same time he authorized the campaign, Lincoln also gave final approval to the idea of dividing the Army of the Potomac into corps. Several months earlier Heintzelman had learned of this idea, and throughout the winter Stanton and others had repeatedly assured him that as a senior general, he was certain to have one of the corps commands. On February 18, 1862, a brusque and often excitable Stanton told him that although he favored the adoption of the *corps d'armee*, McClellan was reluctant; Little Mac wanted to test the army in the field to see who would make the best commanders. At the meeting Heintzelman told Stanton that McClellan had never discussed military matters with him. Such information, he undoubtedly knew, would undermine McClellan's influence with both Stanton and Lincoln.[40] Despite McClellan's desire to choose the commanders himself, Lincoln named each of the five senior generals, McDowell, Sumner, Keyes, and Heintzelman, as corps commanders. Three of the four generals, including Heintzelman, had cast votes against the Urbanna plan, and McClellan was fearful they would undermine his authority.

Heintzelman was given the III Corps, consisting of three divisions of three brigades each along with four batteries of artillery.[41] Commanding the 1st Division was Fitz John Porter, a New Hampshire–born son of a prominent naval officer. A veteran of the Mexican War, Porter had spent six years as an artillery instructor at West Point prior to the war. He was dignified, handsome, autocratic, and intensely loyal to McClellan. Massachusetts-born Brig. Gen. Joseph Hooker, hard drinking and profane, commanded the 2nd Division. Ten years younger than Heintzelman, Hooker had fought Seminoles in Florida and had served under both Gen. Zachary Taylor and Gen. Winfield Scott in Mexico, where he won three brevets for his gallantry. In 1853 he had resigned and settled at Sonoma, California, where he had taken up farming, before rejoining the army at the beginning of the war. A fine-looking man, Hooker was tall, florid, and beardless. Commanding the 3rd Division was New York–born Brig. Gen. Charles S. Hamilton, an 1843West Point classmate of Grant. Hamilton too had fought in Mexico before resigning in 1853 to run a flourmill at Fond du Lac, Wisconsin.

Seeing the commander of the III Corps for the first time, at least one officer, Col. Charles Shiels Wainwright, chief of artillery in Hooker's division, was not impressed. "Ugly as his pictures are, they flatter him," Wainwright wrote. To the New Yorker, Heintzelman was "a little man almost black, with short coarse grey hair and beard, his face one mass of wrinkles, he wears the most uncouth dress and gets into the most awkward positions possible. He talks way down in his throat too, having lost his palate, so that one can hardly understand him. I was much disappointed in him; could not see any signs of a great man."[42]

In the early days of a turbulent March 1862, the Urbanna plan came into serious question after disheartening news arrived from Hampton Roads near Fortress Monroe. At Norfolk across the bay, Confederates had managed to salvage an old wooden frigate, the USS *Merrimack*, that had been burned to the waterline. They equipped her with armor and ten guns, renamed her the CSS *Virginia*, and sent her to attack the blockading Federal fleet. On March 8, while Lincoln was meeting with his cabinet and the generals at the Executive Mansion, the *Virginia* steamed out into the bay to battle the Union ships. Off Hampton Roads she rammed and sank the USS *Cumberland*, set on fire and destroyed the USS *Congress*, and then drove the USS *Minnesota* aground. Over 250 U.S. sailors and marines were killed or wounded, and every wooden frigate off Fortress Monroe awaited its fate the next day.

Hearing the news from Hampton Roads, President Lincoln and the War Department went into shock. Stanton feared the *Virginia* would steam up the Potomac and shell the Executive Mansion, or it might even attack Philadelphia, New York, or Boston. Certainly any plan to move the Army of the Potomac by water would have to be put on hold. But then good news arrived from Hampton Roads. When the *Virginia* steamed out to do battle the next day, the USS *Monitor*, a small and uniquely designed ironclad with a revolving turret conceived and built by an ingenious Swedish inventor named John E. Ericsson, waited for her. Heintzelman had first heard of the strange little ship from Lincoln weeks earlier, and he was optimistic she would do well. At 6:45 P.M. the Washington telegraph went wild with news of an epic naval battle. After four and a half hours of combat, the *Monitor* had forced the *Merrimack* to withdraw.

Any further discussion of the Urbanna movement, however, became moot when more startling news reached Washington in early March. Overextended, his camps racked by sickness and disease, Gen. Joseph E. Johnston had withdrawn his 42,000-man Confederate army from east of the Blue Ridge Mountains to a position south of the Rappahannock River, where it could easily oppose any landing at Urbanna.[43]

As the Rebels slipped out of their entrenchments around Manassas and Centreville, the forts along the Potomac below Washington, complete with their big guns, were also abandoned. At Manassas Junction Union scouts found the charred hulks of locomotives and freight cars as well as smoldering storehouses and hundreds of tons of supplies, including smashed barrels of flour, vinegar, molasses, and pork, scattered across the landscape. Here more Confederate guns lay spiked and abandoned. At Centreville they found a number of "Quaker guns," logs shaped like cannons to confuse the Federals. Late on the evening of March 11, Heintzelman received a message from army headquarters summoning him to Washington early the next day. With Johnston's army on the move, McClellan had decided to send the Army of the Potomac to occupy the area around Manassas. At noon Heintzelman hurried back across the river to help prepare the advance. The long-anticipated spring offensive was underway.

With many of the soldiers elated that at last they were going into the field, Heintzelman again received orders to meet McClellan, this time at Fairfax Court House the next day. In the shabby parlor of an abandoned farmhouse, McClellan called his second council of war in less than a week. Johnston's movements necessitated abandoning the Urbanna plan, he told his generals, but he was simply not willing to hurl the Army of the

Potomac against the Rebels, who were certain to be entrenching on the south bank of the Rappahannock. Instead, he would take his army and steam down Chesapeake Bay past Urbanna to the Virginia Peninsula, that narrow finger of fertile soil between the York and James rivers, and disembark at Fortress Monroe. Similar to what Heintzelman had suggested months earlier, the new design called for offering a feint against Norfolk, seizing Yorktown, and then advancing some seventy miles up the Peninsula to Richmond.[44]

With all four corps commanders endorsing this new plan, the largest amphibious operation in U.S. history to that time was soon underway. Some 121,500 men, 14,592 animals, 1,150 wagons, forty-four batteries of artillery, and seventy-four ambulances would be sent via water to the Peninsula. Four hundred Union ships of every description, including ocean-going vessels, river steamers, and even barges and tugs, most having already assembled for the Urbanna movement, would take the Army of the Potomac to the Peninsula. Heintzelman's III Corps was to be the first to embark for Fortress Monroe.

On March 16 the general watched as the hills about Alexandria became dotted with a thousand little campfires as the men of his corps began gathering for embarkation. Several regiments bivouacked in the muck near his headquarters at Fort Lyon "The mud is a foot deep . . . and water everywhere," a staff officer recorded. When Heintzelman later learned that most of the men were forced to spend the night in a cold rain while their officers were comfortably housed in Alexandria, he became enraged. This was such a blatant disregard for the welfare of the soldiers that he swore that had he been present, he "would have . . . arrested all of [the officers]." Nevertheless, on a "raw, cloudy and uncomfortable" day, Heintzelman rode to the docks at Alexandria and watched as the first of General Porter's men boarded the ships. But Heintzelman found everything in disarray. The Quartermaster Department had confused the capacity of some of the vessels, and the troops embarked at a snail's pace, causing many of the ships to depart hours behind schedule. The next day he watched again as the III Corps continued to depart for the Peninsula. The following night, however, a terrible storm swept over Washington and Alexandria, and the next day was raw and even more unpleasant. On March 20 he again rode down from Fort Lyon to Alexandria, there to see President Lincoln and General McClellan. He was not surprised when Little Mac arrived more than an hour behind schedule. It was all, he thought, part of McClellan's growing disrespect for the president. Regardless, the commanding general had "better be punctual in these uncertain times," Heintzelman reflected in his journal.[45]

In a dense fog and drizzle at noon on March 21, the headquarters flag of the III Corps was struck at Fort Lyon. Wagons carried tents and everything Heintzelman and his staff would need to the wharf at the foot of King Street in Alexandria. The general had selected the *Kent*, one of the newer and faster steamers then in service, for passage to Fortress Monroe. A fleet of white steamers lay at the docks, crowded with blue uniforms. The sun glistened brightly off the men's muskets and bayonets as the vessels pulled away from shore and steamed downriver, accompanied by loud cheering, bands playing, and the noisy salute of the large guns at Fort Lyon. Within minutes the fleet was "lost in the haze beyond Fort Washington and Mount Vernon."[46]

The *Kent* did not depart until 6:30 P.M. Onboard were more than one hundred officers of the III Corps as well as newspaper correspondents, including Ed Hall of *Frank Leslie's Illustrated*, Thomas B. Gunn of the *New York Sun*, and Samuel Wilkeson of the *New York Tribune*.[47] Margaret and Charles were also making the voyage, which to some seemed more like a pleasure excursion that a military operation. In a clear, cold, and moonlit night, Samuel Peter remained on deck with Margaret, Charles, and many of the officers until well after midnight.

Since the *Kent* had left Alexandria late, it was not until early morning that it overtook the remainder of the flotilla. Steaming in two long columns, most of the vessels were no more than sixty feet apart as bands continued to play and whiskey flowed freely. The armada seemed to fill the lower reaches of the Potomac. In fact, for the next three weeks, the Potomac would churn with activity as the invaders shipped vast numbers of men, animals, and cannons to Fortress Monroe. Heintzelman ordered the *Kent* to stop briefly at Budd's Ferry on the Virginia bank of the river so that maps could be taken ashore for General Hooker, who would embark with his division in a few days. Here only two weeks earlier, Confederate guns had pounded Federal ships on the river.

By 8 P.M. the *Kent* had overtaken the fleet once again. The moon was out, and the lights from hundreds of vessels reflected off the smooth waters. The mouth of both the Occoquan River and Quantico Creek were clearly visible as the dark, black pine trees from the Virginia headlands threw eerie shadows on the water. Easing into the broad Chesapeake, the *Kent* steamed by the mouth of the Rappahannock River, past Urbanna, then around New Point to the York River and the aroma of more Virginia pines. Smoke visible from the forest indicated, one Federal thought, that "the 'Yankees' had come at last to investigate matters for themselves."[48] Guided by the Old Point Comfort Lighthouse and the frowning massive walls of polygon-shaped Fortress Monroe, the *Kent* slipped into the crowded and bustling wharf near the fashionable Hygeia Hotel. Ironically, the revetments of Fortress Monroe, the largest coastal fortification in North America, had been constructed under the supervision of a young U.S. Army lieutenant in the early 1830s named Robert E. Lee.

Walking ashore at midmorning, Heintzelman was greeted by seventy-eight-year-old Maj. Gen. John E. Wool, who invited Samuel Peter, Margaret, and Charles to dine with him that evening. He greatly admired the white-haired, no-nonsense Wool, a veteran of the War of 1812, who was beginning his fiftieth year in the army. Along with division commander General Hamilton, Wool took the family on an inspection of the *Monitor*, or what Heintzelman and Southern newspapers were calling a "Yankee cheese box on a raft." Walking onboard, one could clearly see the indentations in the ship's revolving gun turret made by shot from the *Virginia* less than two weeks earlier. "She appears to be perfectly invulnerable," Heintzelman noted.[49] Not far away, the mast of the sunken *Cumberland* jutted out of the murky water with flags still flying. Later, with Margaret retiring to the Hygeia Hotel, Heintzelman took a long walk with General Hamilton across the moat and along the massive ramparts of the enormous masonry fortress. There he stood and watched as Union vessels, bringing everything from horses and fodder to cannon and munitions, arrived without pause. As soon as one steamer was unloaded, it eased away from the dock and another took its place. Such hustle and bustle would go on for two more weeks.

As the men of the III Corps moved slowly across the narrow causeway connecting Fortress Monroe to the mainland, some of Heintzelman's staff rode up to say that his headquarters would not be ready for another day, so his first night on the Peninsula was spent in the Hygeia Hotel. When Margaret and Charles returned to Washington by way of Baltimore a few days later, the general rode across Hampton Creek on a hastily assembled pontoon bridge to his headquarters amid the ruins of Hampton village, three miles from Fortress Monroe. Dating back to 1610, the town had been a fashionable resort for wealthy Virginia planters until it was burned by Heintzelman's old friend from San Diego and the California Indian wars, John Bankhead Magruder, now a general in the Confederate Army. Rumor was that Magruder had heard the Yankees were intent on turning Hampton into a settlement for runaway slaves.[50]

The cluster of six tents that made up III Corps headquarters was near Main Street, close to the burned-out ruins of the courthouse. There a telegraph connected Heintzelman to Fortress Monroe. Nearby stood the ruins of St. John's Episcopal Church. White marble tombstones in the churchyard, many of them marking the resting place of officers of the antebellum army and navy, had been knocked over and smashed by Magruder's army. "We found the town in utter ruin, nothing but tumble down walls and

Heintzelman's headquarters in the ruins of Hampton, Virginia. Sketch by Robert Knox Sneden. Virginia Historical Society.

blackened chimneys, which stuck up in all directions amid charred timbers and debris of all kinds," Heintzelman's cartographer, Pvt. Robert Sneden, wrote.[51] Day and night in the drizzling rain, one blue-clad regiment after another moved slowly across the pontoon bridge and through the ruins of the town to make camp in the large green fields beyond. Within hours white army tents and supply wagons dotted the horizon in every direction.

Much to Heintzelman's disgust, some of the Union soldiers began to dig into the tombs in the churchyard. Coffins were unearthed and skeletons scattered about as the grave robbers scavenged for jewelry, souvenirs, or anything valuable. But more ominous were the reports of skirmishing in the direction of Big Bethel and the first casualties of the Peninsula Campaign. While camped at Hampton, Heintzelman watched as the regiments of General Keyes's IV Corps arrived, followed by Professor Lowe with two of his large balloons. "I don't think that this campaign will be a long one," he optimistically recorded. "We will soon have so overwhelming a force that it will carry all before it."[52]

Three days before leaving Washington, Heintzelman had been given detailed and explicit directions by McClellan. As soon as the divisions of Porter and Hamilton were ashore, he was to push out three to four miles where wood and water could be easily obtained. One division should take a position on the road from Newport News to Yorktown, while the other would bivouac along the road leading from Fortress Monroe to Yorktown. McClellan's main concern was that Heintzelman would push too far forward and divulge the true initial objective of the expedition, Yorktown, some twenty miles up the Peninsula, rather than Norfolk. Nevertheless, strong reconnaissances were to go forward to "ascertain the position of the enemy and his pickets." Moreover, he cautioned, "make no important move in advance until we are fully prepared to follow."[53] Even before the campaign was underway, McClellan was in a defensive mode.

On March 26, with a light snow blanketing the callow fields of the Peninsula, Heintzelman met with Porter to arrange a reconnaissance in force in the direction of Big Bethel. That town had a symbolic importance, for it was there that Federal forces had been soundly routed prior to Bull Run in the first battle on Virginia soil. McClellan, however, rejected any idea of an immediate full-scale advance up the Peninsula toward Yorktown, for he was hoping the Confederates could still be lured into thinking that the real objective was Norfolk. Nevertheless, the next day Heintzelman rode out to join Porter. By noon the advance had encountered only a few enemy pickets, while two hundred Confederate cavalry fled toward Yorktown.[54] By 10 P.M., after bringing in several prisoners and contrabands, Heintzelman was back in camp. He would later learn from several Rebel deserters that Magruder, with his army of eight thousand Confederates, was waiting in battle formation just down the road. From what intelligence he could develop, Heintzelman was sure that Magruder had no more than fifteen thousand to twenty thousand men at Yorktown. History would prove that the Confederates had even fewer. If not for McClellan's stern order not to make any movement that would give away the Union objective, Heintzelman was sure that "we could have cut off [Magruder's] retreat and occupied Yorktown."[55]

Back in camp, and with the Army of the Potomac continuing to arrive in large numbers, Heintzelman took the time to ride over to Newport News to see his old friend from the frontier, the former inspector general Joseph K. F. Mansfield. After being transferred from the Washington defenses to Newport News, the gray-bearded and aging Mansfield, who had seen more of the American West than anyone since the days of the fur trappers, was itching for a combat command.

One of Heintzelman's first casualties on the Peninsula was his black horse. The animal had stepped on a nail while being loaded at Alexandria and had developed lockjaw. "I was up till after midnight with my horse," the general wrote in late March. "I took the blankets off my bed to keep him warm, but he died at 2 A.M. It is a great loss I can't replace. He had a great many good qualities."[56]

On April 1 General Marcy advised Heintzelman by telegraph that McClellan was expected to arrive at Fortress Monroe that evening and that he should have his corps ready to advance immediately. When McClellan arrived on the steamer *Commodore* late in the afternoon two days later, Heintzelman immediately rode to the wharf to see him. Onboard the vessel, the two sat up until 2 A.M. discussing the intricate details of the advance, which would begin the next morning. At 6 A.M., with Porter's 1st Division in the lead, the III Corps broke camp and moved along the road toward Big Bethel and Howard's Bridge. The terrain, McClellan cautioned, was to be thoroughly examined by "advance guards, flankers and patrols." Should Heintzelman get within striking distance of Yorktown, McClellan gave strict orders "not to attack unless you see that the rebels are actually evacuating the place."[57]

General Hamilton's 3rd Division followed Porter an hour later. One of the objectives was to isolate and force the surrender of the Rebel batteries at Ship Point on the York River. In the push up the Peninsula, Heintzelman was also given command of Brig. Gen. John Sedgwick's division of the II Corps. Simultaneous with the III Corps advance, General Keyes would move his corps along the James River Road on Heintzelman's left, while McClellan would bring up the rear with the reserves. If Keyes could reach the Halfway House, he could cut off the garrison from Yorktown, which would be certain to retreat, McClellan speculated. Heintzelman and Keyes were to communicate frequently with one another during the march. Hopefully, the III Corps would be able to get as far as Howard's Bridge, while McClellan would establish his headquarters at Big Bethel.[58] Only thirty-six hours after arriving on the Peninsula, McClellan was, at last, on the offensive.

Yet McClellan received aggravating news from Washington. Lincoln had decided, after McClellan's departure, to retain General McDowell's I Corps to defend the capital. Such news drove Little Mac, who was convinced that Lincoln's decision dangerously imperiled the campaign, into a "towering rage." Heintzelman too was disgusted. "At what a time to do such a thing. It is a great outrage," he confided to his journal.[59] Yet the campaign went forward.

Back in camp, forty rounds of ammunition were issued each soldier along with three days' rations, with orders to be prepared to march at daylight the next morning. During the night, a terrible storm swept the lower Peninsula, dousing campfires and leaving virtual ponds of water everywhere. At III Corps headquarters in Hampton, the lightning cracked and the thunder reverberated off the blackened walls of the town. Terrified horses and mules screamed and tore at their tethers. Sleep was impossible.

A major disadvantage for Heintzelman and the III Corps was the lack of reliable maps. A few charts had been obtained from General Wool, while others were duplicated from those previously drawn by General Butler's engineers and scouts. All proved to be inaccurate. Both he and McClellan were surprised to learn that the Warwick River lay athwart their intended path and that the Rebels had fortified the west bank all the way from Yorktown to the James River. The best maps available were coastal surveys brought from Washington, but these were only accurate for areas close to the banks of the James and York rivers. We must "march and fight on unknown ground," Sneden complained.[60]

Before daylight on April 4, 1862, with the abandoned peach orchards glowing pink with the first blossoms of spring, the III Corps broke camp and commenced pushing up the muddy roads of the Peninsula. Cavalry led the advance, followed by seemingly endless columns of infantry. Teamsters cursed and lashed at their mules as supply trains slowly crept along the murky roads behind the soldiers. "On to Richmond" was joyfully shouted from one regiment to another.[61] Leaving Hampton at midmorning and accompanied by his staff and a cavalry escort, Heintzelman overtook the slow-moving infantry, and within minutes he was at the head of the advance. In the rear the artillery, ammunition trains, and commissary wagons crept along the main road, while the divisions of Hamilton and Porter advanced in columns on both sides.

Here and there in small clearings, abandoned log cabins were visible, but no civilians or animals were to be seen. It was as if the entire countryside had been abandoned. By noon, advance regiments of the III Corps were already at Little Bethel, a miserable and dirty little hamlet consisting of three abandoned houses and a few old barns. Three hours later, as the bluecoat cavalry approached Big Bethel, Confederate horsemen fled up the road toward Howard's Bridge, leaving behind more abandoned log houses and sheds that they had used as barracks. Piles of dirty straw, broken boxes and barrels, and dirty and ruined clothing littered the structures. A sickening stink seemed to permeate everything. Billowing smoke in the direction of Yorktown indicated that the Rebels were burning farmhouses on their retreat. Confederate deserters and escaped slaves came forth to say that Magruder had no more than eight thousand men. Heintzelman remained fearful that this entire army would escape up the Peninsula. At 1:30 P.M., in the mud and rain, the column reached Howard's Bridge on the Poquoson River, pushing back Confederate pickets as they advanced. All along the west bank of the river, the Rebels had dug entrenchments.

The march continued into the darkness, with fires built by the roadside to guide the men. When the mud slowed the column to a crawl, many of the soldiers bivouacked by the roadside to resume the march early the next morning. The "gorgeous uniforms" of the Army of the Potomac "were splashed all over with the beautiful red mud of Virginia," Sneden noted. The next day, when McClellan and his staff passed the column, there was a "great cheering from the troops." On April 6 the column continued past Grafton Church before again bivouacking in the rain. Pushing the III Corps forward the following day over marshy ground, Heintzelman reached a point where he could ride forward and see across an open and treeless plateau the ramparts of Yorktown. "The enemy's force is much larger than we anticipated and better fortified," he admitted.[62] The general established his headquarters at an abandoned sawmill in what was to become the center of the Union line. From here he had a good view of Yorktown and the extensive and impressive network of trenches that guarded the town. Heintzelman continued to speculate that Magruder had no more than 8,000 men. With 53,000 Union soldiers in the vicinity, 42,000 of them combat ready, he was anxious for a knockout blow.

Heintzelman was well aware of the historic and strategic importance of the old tobacco town. Twenty miles up the Peninsula from Fortress Monroe and the main roadblock on the road to Richmond, Yorktown had been the scene of General Washington's celebrated defeat of Lord Cornwallis during the American Revolution. Washington had always been one of his childhood heroes, and just as the Americans and French had forced Cornwallis to surrender in 1781, Heintzelman and his III Corps would force Magruder and his defiant Rebels to capitulate in 1862. Going over copies of maps of the Revolutionary War battle, Heintzelman took pride in knowing that his headquarters was where the Marquis de Lafayette had established his own eighty-one years earlier.[63] In fact, Magruder was using some of the remnants of the British earthworks for his defenses. Reinforced by thirty thousand sandbags stitched together by the women of Richmond in less than thirty hours, the Yorktown earthworks were fifteen feet thick in places and stretched for over four miles. In fact, Magruder's fortifications were not limited to Yorktown but reached fifteen miles across the Peninsula from the York River to Mulberry Island on the James River. Although formidable, Heintzelman was convinced that the Confederate lines could be easily broken. The weakest point, he thought, was the earthworks at Lee's Mill on the Warwick River five miles south of Yorktown.

With the Union forces facing Yorktown now numbering seventy-five thousand men and another thirty thousand soon to arrive, Heintzelman grew restless with McClellan's reluctance to attack the besieged Rebels. Perhaps taking his cue from President Lincoln, who was also becoming impatient with the slow-moving commander, Heintzelman urged an immediate assault. When McClellan refused, he went in person to ask for permission for a strong reconnaissance to probe what he perceived to be weak spots in Magruder's defenses. McClellan remained reluctant, however, first wanting a more thorough study of the defensive lines. "General Heintzelman says that he could with his command storm the whole line of works there and shut the enemy up in Yorktown by seizing the road in the rear of that place which leads to Williamsburg," Sneden wrote in his journal. "But by McClellan's orders, no general is permitted to bring on a battle until all our forces are up. One corps alone could take the place in an hour."[64]

On April 11 Hooker's division arrived in front of Yorktown and went into camp near III Corps headquarters. A few weeks later, with his entire corps intact for the first time, Heintzelman complained bitterly that a "siege was determined upon without my being consulted."[65] As McClellan visited III Corps headquarters several times during the operations at Yorktown, Heintzelman came to better know "Little Mac," and he started to question even more his commander's lack of resolve.

Magruder had only ten thousand men at Yorktown. But using his natural panache and theatrical flair, he fooled both McClellan and Heintzelman by astutely stage managing his little army. The soldiers were constantly marched to and fro and ordered to cheer at regular intervals, as if reinforcements had just arrived, thus giving the impression that they were more numerous than they actually were. Cannons were frequently fired, drums were beat late into the night, and one Rebel regiment was marched from Yorktown to the James River and back six times. "By the constant beating of drums in Yorktown at different hours of day and evening we surmise that the enemy are receiving reinforcements," Sneden wrote. Magruder had also installed several "Quaker Guns," a ploy that had been effective at Manassas. Before long, Heintzelman too had become convinced that "the enemy's force is much larger than we anticipated and better fortified."[66]

In late April Heintzelman was surprised to learn that General Hamilton was being relieved of his command. When Hamilton had asked for permission to storm the Confederate defenses and McClellan had turned him down, he had retaliated by loudly complaining that his division was being overworked, while the troops of Fitz John Porter, McClellan's favorite general, were left idle. When he wrote several letters to army headquarters in Washington that were deemed disrespectful, Hamilton was recalled.[67] He was replaced by the dashing and debonair Brig. Gen. Philip Kearny. Nephew of Gen. Stephen W. Kearny and independently wealthy, the new division commander had lost his left arm during a cavalry charge at Churubusco in the Mexican War. In 1859 he had fought in Italy with

Napoleon III's Imperial Guard at Solferino and Magenta and had been awarded the Legion of Honor. Ten years younger than Heintzelman, Kearny had also studied war at the cavalry school at Saumur, France.

A notorious drinker with a loose tongue, Kearny would prove to be one of the more able and respected generals, not just in the III Corps, but in the entire Army of the Potomac. Tall, lean, and handsome, his reddish beard neatly clipped and his kepi slanted in the French manner, he cut a dashing figure. Although Heintzelman never questioned Kearny's bravery (Winfield Scott called him the "bravest man I ever knew"), he disliked his flamboyancy and had concerns that he would be "troublesome."[68]

Heintzelman would come to consider Kearny daring and resourceful, but the respect was never mutual. From the beginning of their relationship, Kearny, especially in his private letters, relentlessly and savagely ridiculed his superior. As a military thinker, not only were Heintzelman's skills passé, he was "as stupid as an effete ossified small brain." On another occasion Kearny told his wife that his commander had "neither courage nor brains." Heintzelman had not been "with the army that won Mexico," he complained, and his "small quanteen [*sic*] of brains have been fossillized [*sic*] by near 40 years of small garrison routine at the head of 100 foot [soldiers], in some western outpost."[69] While the supercilious Kearny was equally disrespectful toward other corps commanders, especially Sumner and Keyes, he hated McClellan, whom he considered a coward.

Near III Corps headquarters, Professor Lowe frequently sent his balloons high into the Virginia sky. On April 6 Heintzelman wrote of having a "fine view of the [Rebel] works from the balloon." Three days later thousands of Union soldiers swarmed out of their camps in the woods to see a yellow-colored balloon rise abruptly to an elevation of nine hundred feet. On it was painted a large portrait of General McClellan. Within minutes the ramparts of Yorktown swarmed with Confederates, also gazing at the balloon. For three hours Lowe and several officers observed the Rebel defenses through spyglasses as they carefully sketched the outline of the enemy parapets, even the exact number of guns and their bearings.[70]

A few days later the cry that a balloon had broken loose from its moorings echoed throughout III Corps headquarters as Heintzelman and his staff rushed out of their tents. The sole occupant, General Porter, sailed gracefully and swiftly off toward Yorktown and the Rebel lines. As the balloon passed over headquarters, men shouted, "pull the valve," but at sixteen hundred feet, Porter could not hear them. Heintzelman watched as the Rebels opened fire on the balloon as it neared their lines. Crouching in the gondola, Porter began to frantically throw as many sandbags overboard as possible. As the sphere soared to greater heights, an upper-air current sweeping inland from the York River caught the balloon and sent it sailing back toward the Union lines and into the woods. Just before crashing to earth, Porter was seen to jump into a large tree. Emerging from the woods near III Corps headquarters, he was not injured but very embarrassed. Some of the Union soldiers joked that the general had advanced up the Peninsula a lot faster than McClellan. "The Rebels would have been delighted to have got the balloon with Fitz-John in it. We at headquarters did not care as long as they did not get the balloon," Sneden sarcastically wrote.[71]

The following day a large balloon rose to seven hundred feet from behind the enemy's works at Wynn's Mills on the west bank of the Warwick River, not far from Heintzelman's headquarters. Lowe hurried forward to scornfully pronounce the craft as an inferior and very dangerous hot-air balloon, one he had seen in Charleston, South Carolina, before the war, and that it was likely to catch fire. After only a few minutes, the balloon was hauled back to earth.[72] Several days later, early in the morning, the Rebel balloon again ascended to a height of two hundred feet, at which point a man was seen to fall out head first to earth.

By April 20 Lowe was also sending a second balloon, the *Intrepid*, high into the sky. With telegraph wires attached, it often reached heights of eighteen hundred feet. Anxious to see the Yorktown defenses himself, Heintzelman proved to be one of Lowe's most frequent aeronauts. Several times the Rebels tried in vain to shoot the balloon out of the sky with artillery. Although unsuccessful, many of the shells impacted to within fifty feet of Heintzelman's headquarters tent. From what the general and Lowe could see, combined with what Rebel deserters were saying, Heintzelman had no doubt the Yorktown garrison was being steadily reinforced, speculating that the army had grown to as many as 100,000 men, and that Gen. Joseph E. Johnston was now in charge. From Lowe's balloon it was also evident that Gloucester, on the opposite bank of the York River, was also being reinforced. "A day or two after we arrived, we could have forced their lines," but by the third week of April, it was too late, he concluded.[73]

As a young officer, McClellan's forte had been engineering. He had been with General Scott at the siege of Vera Cruz during the Mexican War and had observed the prolonged siege of Sevastopol during the Crimean War. If there was one thing the commander of the Army of the Potomac knew, it was siege warfare. McClellan had "siege operations on the brain," Sneden sneered. Although he consistently overestimated the number of Yorktown's Confederate defenders, the general never doubted his superiority in artillery, especially heavy artillery, and the ability of his army to drive the Rebels out.[74]

Late in the afternoon of April 13, about three hundred Confederates and almost as many slaves suddenly appeared with picks and shovels from behind the Yorktown parapets. Escorted by several squadrons of cavalry, they moved into a large peach orchard and began to construct a line of rifle pits well ahead of their main defenses. Within thirty minutes Heintzelman ordered out a battery of horse artillery. The bluecoats galloped up to a position on the opposite side of the orchard and opened fire. With shells bursting around them, the Rebel horsemen beat a hasty retreat back into the Yorktown defenses, with the laborers close on their heels.[75]

By late April the Union forces before Yorktown equaled in size the ninth-largest city in the United States. As the siege continued, Union engineers cut roads through the forests of the Peninsula for the long trains of supplies that came up from Fortress Monroe. In the rain and mud, many of the old roads had to be corduroyed with thousands of small logs. At the front, hundreds of miles of parallel and advance trenches were dug into the red Virginia earth by thousands of Union soldiers. Both officers and men, working mostly at night, complained of the long hours and the tedious, backbreaking work; to help relieve their aches and pains, the men were given an extra whiskey ration. The III Corps "will now have to do more digging than fighting," young Sneden complained.[76] Standing in ankle-deep mud and water, many men became ill, and the corps hospital was soon overflowing. With twelve to fifteen men dying daily, soldiers scoured the sawmill for boards for coffins and small headboards. At the same time, Union laborers looked up to see as many as three thousand slaves, taken from the numerous plantations on the Peninsula, working on the Rebel fortifications.

As the Union trenches crept closer to the Rebel parapets, Heintzelman sent forward the 1st U.S. Sharpshooters, commanded by Col. Hiram G. Berdan, who was considered by many to be the best marksman in the country. Equipped with .45-caliber target rifles with four-power scopes accurate up to five hundred yards and wearing forest green uniforms for camouflage, every man was said to be a crack shot. During the siege, Berdan's sharpshooters performed some of the most deadly work, killing many Confederate gunners in the Yorktown defenses and even some of the slaves.

To support the siege, lumbermen from the 4th Maine worked to fell trees and haul them in ox-drawn wagons to the steam sawmill at III Corps headquarters, which operated day and night. While much of the lumber was hauled off for mortar platforms, the sawdust was used to make clean paths in the mud around headquarters. From the roof of the sawmill, Heintzelman also established a signal station. Unable to use flags at night, the men quickly mastered the use of torches. Smaller trees were cut and put up around headquarters as blinds. To hinder the sighting of the Confederate artillery, Heintzelman ordered all lights to be distinguished by

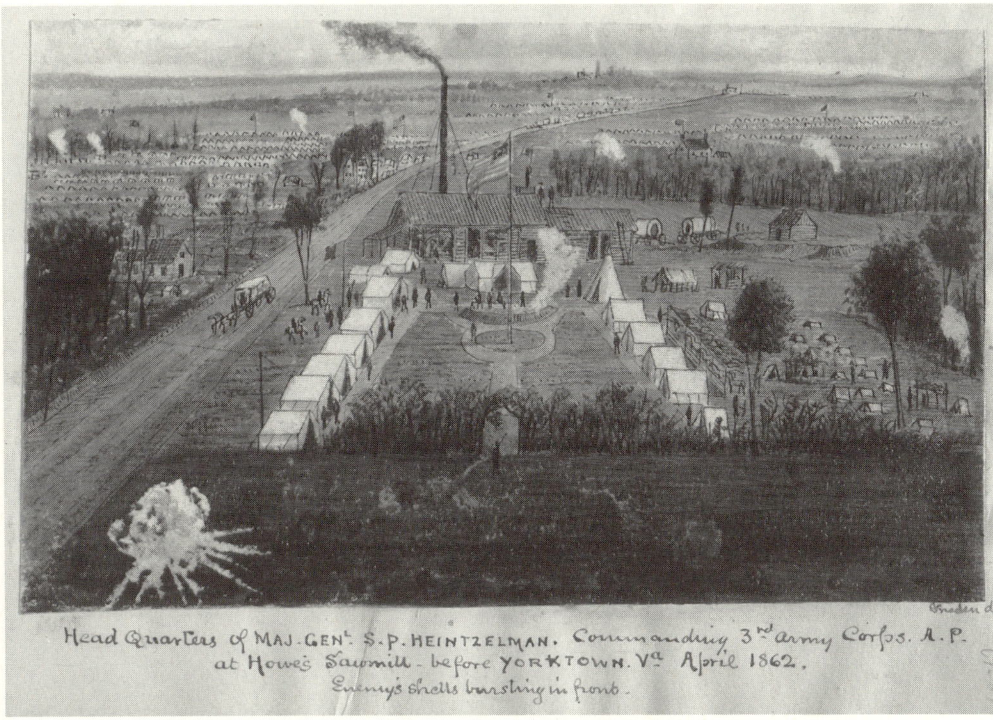

Heintzelman's headquarters before Yorktown. Sketch by Robert Knox Sneden. Virginia Historical Society.

8:30 P.M. At a log fire in front of his double-wall tent, the general would sit with his staff until nearly midnight, discussing strategy and tactics, while Chauncey McKeever, his chief of staff, sent couriers galloping about with orders.[77]

Earlier, 1st Lt. Orlando G. Wagner of the III Corps engineers was reconnoitering in front of a Federal artillery position when he was struck in the shoulder by a large piece of shrapnel from an exploding Rebel shell and badly wounded. Due to the heat, Wagner was carrying an umbrella and attired in his dress uniform, with much gold lace, and thus was deliberately targeted by Confederate gunners, some speculated. From Pennsylvania, Wagner, who had seen action in western Virginia early in the war, had been commissioned into the Topographical Engineers after graduating fifth in the West Point class of 1858. He had been welcomed into Heintzelman's staff when Lt. Wilhelm Heine transferred to the staff of Brig. Gen. David B. Birney. Wagner, whose collarbone was also broken, was brought into headquarters on a stretcher and then carried to the III Corps hospital, where his arm was amputated. Four days later, he died.[78]

Closely observing the artillery barrages during the siege, Heintzelman came to conclude that the artillery was having a profound effect on the weather. After first arriving at Yorktown, he noticed that after several shots were fired, "small detached clouds appeared, joined and floated away."[79] In reality, it was evaporation from the heavy rains that fell two out of every three days during the siege that helped form the small clouds.

Union morale was lifted the second week of April with the arrival of additional Federal ironclads on the York and James rivers. Spirits soared even more with exciting news from the West. In a great two-day battle not far from the banks of the Tennessee River in early April, Maj. Gen. Ulysses S. Grant had turned back a large Confederate army under Gen. Albert Sidney Johnston, the South's most respected field commander. During the battle, General Johnston was shot in the leg and bled to death, while his second in command, Gen. P. G. T. Beauregard, was rumored to have lost an arm. The twenty-three thousand casualties at Shiloh were roughly the same as at Waterloo and more than those of all previous American wars combined. On the evening of the second day, the Confederate army, licking its wounds, limped back toward Corinth, Mississippi. Nothing in the previous American experience remotely compared to Shiloh. Heintzelman heard that his antagonist from Fort Yuma, one-armed Col. Thomas W. Sweeny, while leading a brigade at Shiloh, was rumored to have received three wounds. As the bloodletting at Shiloh slackened, Island No. 10 near New Madrid, Missouri, fell to Union gunboats, opening the Mississippi River as far south as Memphis, Tennessee. A few weeks later equally exciting news came from the Deep South. Heintzelman learned from a Rebel prisoner that sixty-year-old Adm. David G. Farragut, born in Tennessee and married to a Virginian, had run a fleet of Union vessels past the forts of the lower Mississippi River and seized New Orleans, the world's largest cotton port and the South's biggest city.[80] The infant Confederacy seemed to be reeling and in retreat everywhere.

Although Heintzelman often nurtured friendships with the numerous newspaper correspondents who crowded his headquarters, Samuel Wilkeson of the *New York Tribune* proved to be a problem. Wilkeson, who was sharing the general's tent, wrote several articles critical of McClellan, and Heintzelman feared the articles would further damage his relationship with his commander. The *Tribune* was also publishing confidential information and accurate maps that could compromise the Union positions before Yorktown. He was greatly relieved when Wilkeson departed. Correspondents from the *New York Herald* were less troublesome, though their cartographic coverage of the Yorktown siege exceeded that of any other newspaper. So accurate was the *Herald* that on April 22, for example, the newspaper published a full-page map detailing Confederate earthworks and fortifications and even noting the placement of a number of Rebel cannon. Also arriving at III Corps headquarters was Alfred R. Waud, the skilled artist for *Harper's Weekly*. Frequently demanding passes to visit the front lines, other reporters were little more than nuisances.[81]

Although Heintzelman questioned McClellan's tactics, he too remained confident in the ultimate success of the army. By late April no less than seventy heavy rifled pieces, including several 13-inch seacoast mortars, each weighing more than eight tons and capable of firing 220-pound shells 4,300 yards, were in place. The huge guns had been brought on canal boats up the York River and then up Wormley's Creek to be laboriously hauled ashore. Fourteen batteries of heavy cannon, each pulled by twenty mules, were also in place. In all, Heintzelman estimated, there were 295 guns ready to open fire on the Yorktown defenses. More than six hundred wagon loads of powder, shot, and shell were required to stock one of the battery magazines. Capable of raining "7,000 pounds of metal on Yorktown's defenders at each blow," McClellan had the Confederate defenders easily outgunned.[82] In fact, the Union firepower facing Yorktown exceeded anything the world had ever seen. By early May McClellan was prepared to unleash a rain of iron and steel on the Confederate defenders, concentrating the heaviest of his guns on Yorktown and a portion of the Confederate lines just outside the town. Gunboats anchored in the York River were also preparing to join the shelling. McClellan set May 6 as the date for the massive bombardment, which was to be followed by a monumental frontal assault. On the right wing, the III Corps was to carry the brunt of the attack.

In preparation for the assault, an inspection of the trenches late one evening found the commanders of the 105th Pennsylvania and the 9th Massachusetts asleep while on duty. Particularly disturbing was the fact that Colonel Cass of the 9th Massachusetts, who was sleeping in one of the magazines, was in charge of the entire right section of the trenches. Angered, McClellan wrote Heintzelman demanding that the two colonels explain "their criminal neglect of duty." If necessary, they were to be arrested. Moreover, if the officers were not prepared to sacrifice their personal safety for the security of the army, McClellan asserted, they were to be replaced.[83] Had the two been enlisted men, they probably would have been shot.

On the evening of May 2, 1862, at about 11 P.M., only days prior to the planned attack, the Rebels opened the most devastating bombardment yet seen. A rhythmic barrage of shells exploded near the sawmill and among the tents at corps headquarters, blowing holes in the ground five feet deep. Heintzelman's telegraph tent was knocked down as red-hot shrapnel shredded several other tents. While the shelling was at its height, the general "sat in front of his tent whittling a piece of wood and was the most composed of us all, though one solid shot went but a few feet over his head," Sneden remembered. Actually, Heintzelman was sitting with Professor Lowe in front of his tent. "The general and I were sitting together, discussing the probable reasons for the unusual effort to destroy the balloon," Lowe recalled, "when we were both covered with what appeared to be tons of earth, which a great 12-inch shell had thrown up. Fortunately, it did not explode. I suggested that the next morning we should move the balloon so as to draw the foe's fire in another direction, but the general said that he could stand it if I could. Besides, he would like to have me near by, as he enjoyed going up occasionally himself." The Rebel barrage was nothing, Heintzelman said, "as compared with the sight I would look down upon . . . when our great mortar batteries would open their siege-guns on the fortifications."[84]

"I did not lie down until after midnight and had scarcely been asleep," he wrote a few days later, when he was awakened by the sound of musketry and drumming from inside the Yorktown defenses. Instantly alert, he asked Professor Lowe to take the *Intrepid* up for a look. In the pitch darkness, Lowe could see little except for a building on fire near the wharf on the York River. Not long afterward, flashes of fire burst forth from the Rebel guns on the parapets. Other large fires began to appear in the town as loud explosions reverberated from a number of enemy positions. The shadows from the flames were clearly visible on the parapets. Even larger fires erupted on the Yorktown docks as piles of lumber and supply sheds went up in flames, lighting up the York River. Slowly the cannonading grew weaker. A few batteries on the Warwick River fired a few round shots, then all became quiet. At 4:30 on Sunday morning, May 4, word reached corps headquarters that the Rebels were abandoning their fortress. In a second ascent in the *Intrepid*, Lowe confirmed that the Confederates were indeed evacuating the town. At first light and after only a few hours of sleep, Heintzelman and Lowe made yet a third ascent. "At first the general was puzzled on seeing more wagons entering the forts than were going out," Lowe recalled many years later. "But when I called his attention to the fact that the ingoing wagons were light and moved rapidly, while the outgoing wagons were heavily loaded and moved slowly, there was no longer any doubt as to the object of the Confederates." While recording his impressions of the same scene, Heintzelman said that clouds of gray and black smoke obscured a large part of the Rebel defenses but that he could not see a single soldier in them. "We could not see a gun on the rebel works or a man . . . all quiet as a grave," he wrote.[85] Soon the Rebel army was gone. With fifty-six thousand men, Johnston had slipped away in the night.

Bugles sounded in the camps of the III Corps and throughout the Army of the Potomac as thousands of soldiers scurried about to move on the Rebel works. Yet many, including Heintzelman, were disappointed that after so much work the Confederates had been allowed to slip away in the night. "All the fine [Union] guns stood up in the different batteries with ammunition piled in them for a forty-eight hour's continuous bombardment as monuments of McClellan's imbecility and 'fortification on the brain,'" Sneden bitterly wrote.[86] Indeed, of the fourteen batteries of heavy cannon, thirteen had not fired a single shot.

Heintzelman watched from the balloon at 6:30 A.M. as Federal skirmishers rushed forward to enter the abandoned earthworks. They were followed by the 20th Massachusetts, whose color bearer planted the Stars and Stripes on the Yorktown parapet. "Our flag can now be seen floating over the rebel parapets," Heintzelman announced.[87] Within minutes thousands of Union soldiers appeared on the plateau in front of Yorktown as regimental bands began to play and flags were carried forward. Back on the ground, the general ordered his III Corps to gather three days' rations in haversacks in preparation to pursue Johnston. But by 9 A.M. no orders had been received from McClellan, so Heintzelman rode over to army headquarters, where he learned that Brig. Gen. George Stoneman, with his cavalry and some horse artillery, alone would be sent in pursuit.

Heintzelman later rode up to examine the captured defenses, only to be told by a Union sentinel that the retreating Confederates had mined the entrance to the earthworks and that several men had already been killed by booby-traps. Despite the dangers, Heintzelman walked along the parapets, past underground shelters and bombproofs, all the way to the York River. The defenses "were absolutely in a filthy condition," he wrote. After inspecting the fifty-six large naval guns the Confederates had been unable to scuttle, the general hurriedly "pushed on."[88] He was relieved that Yorktown had at last been taken, but there was frustration that it had taken thirty crucial days.

With Hooker and Kearny by his side and bands playing and flags waving, Heintzelman proudly led his corps through Yorktown. From the forty unpainted and weatherworn houses in the town, a few elderly slaves emerged from hiding. Several wounded and dying Confederates were found in a makeshift hospital as Union soldiers began putting out the fires. "Not a live chicken or pig could be found in the place," Sneden wrote. Many in the III Corps were infuriated when they learned that the corps's telegraph operator had entered the Confederate telegraph office only to trip on a wire attached to a torpedo shell that blew off both his legs. The young soldier died in agony within minutes. Along the main road leading through town and in houses and along the parapets, other live shells were found planted with fuses attached. "Several other men were killed and some wounded before we could teach our men caution," Heintzelman wrote.[89]

In retrospect, Heintzelman would realize that Yorktown was the first indication of McClellan's shortcomings as a field commander. He himself had learned that there was a big difference between leading a few hundred men on the Texas border in pursuit of a band of Mexican irregulars, or even a division on the plains of Manassas, to commanding a corps of more than thirty thousand in the rain and mud of the Virginia Tidewater. Unlike McClellan, Heintzelman was willing to take risks, but like "Little Mac" he had a tendency to magnify the difficulties before him. Although he had led the III Corps with skill and courage at Yorktown, he had exercised little control over his division commanders. In the weeks and months to come, he came to severely criticize McClellan for his hesitancy in moving against Yorktown. Yet much of Heintzelman's criticisms came about only as afterthoughts. He too had greatly overestimated the number of Confederates defending Yorktown and also had a tendency to vacillate. Yet he was determined to lead the III Corps into Richmond.

Heintzelman never passed up the opportunity to have his photograph taken, usually at Mathew Brady's studio in Washington, D.C. Many cartes de visite of Heintzelman survive today in archives and private collections. Top left: U.S. Army Military History Institute; upper right, Library of Congress (BH831-926); lower left and right, author's collection.

During and after the Civil War, Heintzelman was depicted in numerous lithographs and steel engravings in a variety of books and periodicals. Author's collection.

Heintzelman (wearing a kepi in front of column) poses with his staff for the camera of Mathew Brady at Robert E. Lee's Arlington House early in the war. Library of Congress (USZ62-119499).

Placed in command of the III Corps of the Army of the Potomac, Heintzelman established his headquarters at the Ballenger House at Fort Lyon near Alexandria, Virginia. He lived and worked in the white middle structure behind the main building. Library of Congress (B811-2305).

Brig. Gen. Fitz John Porter's headquarters at the Allen's farmhouse near the Williamsburg Road during the siege of Yorktown in May 1862. Camped in the background is part of Heintzelman's III Corps. Library of Congress (B815-370).

On August 7, 1862, in the tangled woods near Berkeley Plantation not far from Harrison's Landing, Virginia, Heintzelman and his staff posed for the camera of Alexander Gardner. Library of Congress (U5Z62-124357).

With family and friends at a convalescent camp in Virginia not far from the Potomac River, Heintzelman stood for this photograph on October 4, 1863. The woman seated and looking away from the camera has mistakenly been identified as Mary Todd Lincoln. Margaret Heintzelman is standing in the doorway next to her husband. Library of Congress (U5Z62-124356).

Heintzelman and his friend Maj. Gen. Dan Sickles near Washington four months after the great Union victory at Gettysburg. In command of Heintzelman's old III Corps, the controversial Sickles had lost his right leg during the fighting in the Peach Orchard on July 2, 1863. U.S. Military Academy at West Point.

On June 21, 1865, on the fourth anniversary of the First Battle of Bull Run, Heintzelman (eleventh from left in kepi) gathered with veterans atop Henry House Hill for the dedication of a twenty-one-foot tall red sandstone marker. On Heintzelman's left is Maj. Gen. Orlando B. Willcox, who fought bravely in Heintzelman's division during the battle. U.S. Army Military History Institute.

Heintzelman poses with prominent Union veterans Gen. Philip H. Sheridan (with cane, third from right) and Adm. David G. Farragut (seated fourth from left) at a reunion in 1870. Chicago Historical Society.

EIGHT

A Crisis in Our Affairs

Within hours of the evacuation of Yorktown, Stoneman's cavalry rode in pursuit of the retreating Rebels. In the mud and rain, Brig. Gen. William F. "Baldy" Smith's 2nd Division of the IV Corps and General Hooker's 2nd Division of the III Corps followed the cavalrymen along the Lee's Mill and Yorktown roads toward Williamsburg. Hooker, who had arrived from Budd's Ferry on the Potomac only days earlier, was spoiling for a fight. While Fitz John Porter's division remained behind to occupy Yorktown, General Kearny's 3rd Division, III Corps followed Hooker up the Peninsula. McClellan was hoping that Stoneman's cavalry, along with Hooker's division, could push forward to a position near the Halfway House, a colonial wayside tavern on the edge of the woods seven miles from Williamsburg, where they could cut off the Confederate retreat. "Everyone was joyous to be once more foot loose in pursuit of the enemy," Private Sneden recorded.[1]

During the winter, General Magruder had erected a large earthen redoubt at the junction of the Yorktown and Lee's Mill roads in front of Williamsburg, which he proudly christened Fort Magruder. Although not as large or as formidable as the defenses at Yorktown, it had parapets nine feet thick and a ditch in front that was ten feet wide and nine feet deep. Fort Magruder proved to be an imposing bastion and key to any defense of Williamsburg. In front of the fortress, Confederate axmen had felled a wide belt of timber. To further impede any advance, numerous rifle pits were dug and abatis constructed to shelter field artillery. A crude line of fieldworks, consisting of thirteen smaller redans and redoubts, stretched across the Peninsula on both sides of Fort Magruder.[2]

Following with his staff along Lee's Mill Road in a light rain on the morning of May 4, Heintzelman could hear firing in the direction of Williamsburg. At the same time, a hastily scribbled note arrived from General Stoneman saying that he had engaged the enemy's rear guard, which had entrenched. If he were to carry the Rebel defenses, he badly needed infantry. Reaching the Halfway House, Heintzelman found the road clogged by an abandoned Rebel wagon train, the wagons turned over on their sides and the wheels cut to pieces.[3] Dead mules were everywhere. The head of Hooker's division had been stalled here too when Smith's division filed into the main road from a crossroad. Galloping his horse forward for more than a mile, Heintzelman met Hooker, who complained mightily about the situation.

Nevertheless, Hooker suggested that he take his division to the left by way of Cheesecake Church, a half-mile to the rear, cross over to Telegraph Road, and attack the Confederate right flank. Heintzelman agreed but told him "not to let Sumner get into Williamsburg first." By 5 P.M. Heintzelman had reached the Adams House on the Yorktown Road, where he found Sumner, Smith, Stoneman, and Brig. Gen. Winfield Scott Hancock in consultation; within minutes General Keyes joined them. Heintzelman was surprised to learn that McClellan had placed the sixty-five-year-old Sumner, as senior corps commander, in charge of the pursuit.[4] Sumner said Fort Magruder was formidable, but he thought it could be taken with the bayonet.

That night, before final arrangements for an assault on the fort could be made, several Union regiments got lost in the swamps and woods and were forced to wait until daylight to continue their advance. In the darkness and heavy rain, Sumner himself became lost and was forced to spend the night in the woods, coming close to being captured by a Rebel patrol.[5]

Heintzelman spent the night at the Adams House, sleeping on a sofa while thousands of tired and hungry Federals huddled outside in the darkness and rain.[6] During the night, orders arrived for Sumner from General McClellan, who was still at Yorktown. Since Sumner could not be found, Heintzelman opened the orders, which officially placed the old general in command of the pursuit. Sumner arrived at daylight to say that he had concluded the Confederate left flank, where two earthworks were thought to be abandoned, could be easily turned and should be attacked immediately.

With the meeting concluded, Heintzelman rode off to join Hooker on the Union left. It was now 11 A.M., and the six-mile ride in the rain through the soggy woods, without maps or a guide, took an excruciating two hours. Along the way he could hear the reverberating sound of artillery and the cracking of musketry, and he confessed to "great anxiety." All along the road were abandoned Confederate wagons and equipment stuck in the mud. Reaching the front, Hooker rode up to say that his division was being overwhelmed and that he had already suffered heavy casualties. Surprisingly, "Fighting Joe" asked that he be allowed to retreat. With memories of Bull Run reverberating in his consciousness and realizing what was at stake, "I would not hear of it," Heintzelman recalled years later, though he admitted at the time that "our affairs did not look very promising."[7]

Hooker had advanced the previous night along the Hampton Road in the darkness and rain until his men had become exhausted. At 11 p.m. he had been forced to call a halt in the middle of the road, where his division bivouacked in the rain and mud. Resuming the march before daylight the next morning, Hooker had looked up to see the "venerable spires of Williamsburg" in the distance and a formidable Fort Magruder in the foreground. He had attacked at 7:30 that morning by sending the 1st Massachusetts and 2nd New Hampshire into the felled timber on the left and right of the Hampton Road in front of Fort Magruder, hoping to drive the Rebels from their rifle pits. At the same time, Hooker had thrown the 11th Massachusetts and the 26th Pennsylvania forward on the right to seize the Yorktown Road, pushing an artillery battery forward to within seven hundred yards of Fort Magruder. No sooner had the Union guns emerged from the woods, however, than a devastating fire was opened from Fort Magruder and one or two other redoubts, killing several of the gunners and most of their horses.[8] Hooker had been forced to plea for volunteers from the infantry to rush forward and work the guns.

Although he was successful in driving the Confederates from several small earthworks, Hooker was outnumbered and hard pressed, and he pleaded for reinforcements. He had sent Heintzelman a note to that effect, but as it turned out, the messenger arrived at Sumner's headquarters after Heintzelman had departed. "I have had a hard contest all the morning," Hooker wrote, "but do not despair of success. My men are hard at work, but a good deal exhausted." Hearing Hooker out, Heintzelman sent an aide racing to General Kearny, who was waiting with his division at Cheesecake Church, with orders to bring up his brigades as fast as possible. A second messenger speed to Sumner asking for additional reinforcements. Heintzelman would later learn that Sumner had not bothered to respond to his request, even though three divisions remained inactive on the Union right. For the rest of his life, he remained critical of both Keyes and Sumner for their inactivity that day. "Who ever heard that Keyes did anything at Williamsburg? Or Sumner? We came near being defeated from their inactivity," he wrote in his journal a year later. He was also critical of McClellan for keeping Porter in Yorktown. Almost paranoid and certainly suspecting a sinister political plot at the cost of the blood of his men, Heintzelman speculated that McClellan wanted him defeated and "disgraced."[9]

With Hooker's three brigades facing Maj. Gen. James Longstreet's

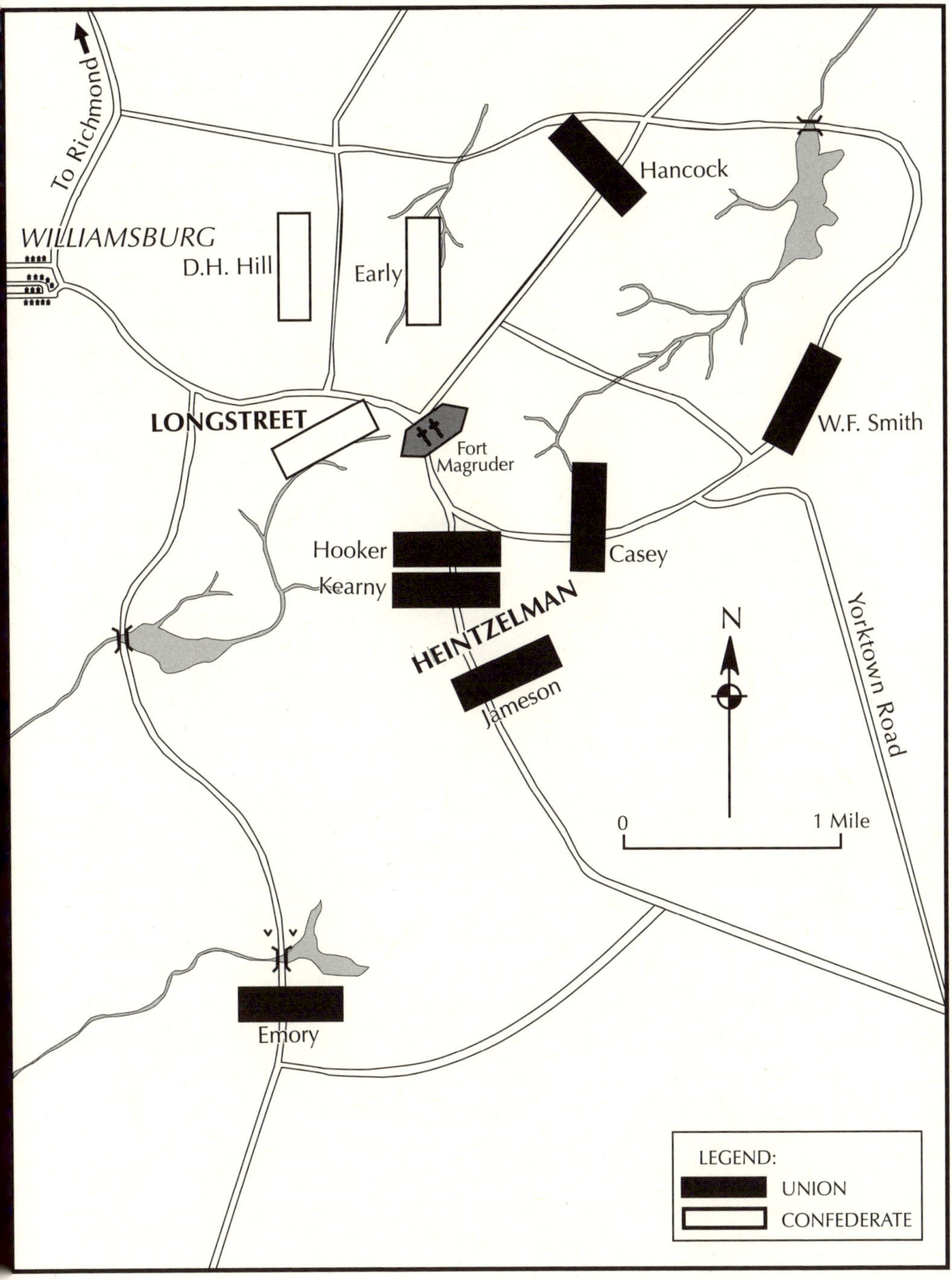

Battle of Williamsburg,
May 5, 1862

entire division of six brigades, the Battle of Williamsburg, in Hooker's words, "had swollen into one of gigantic proportions." The battle "raged furiously in our front," Heintzelman later scribbled in his notebook. "Our men would be driven back and then recover their ground." Hundreds of able-bodied bluecoats followed the wounded to the rear, and stragglers seemed to be everywhere. Few could be induced to rejoin their regiments. At the front Hooker's men were critically short of ammunition. Heintzelman hoped to bring forward more artillery, but the only place he could find to deploy the guns exposed the artillerists to a dangerous crossfire. All the while, Rebel guns at Fort Magruder maintained a steady fire on the woods. "The shells kept bursting near me killing and wounding several men," Heintzelman wrote.[10]

With the Union advance stalled and Hooker's division hard pressed, Heintzelman met with Col. William Averell of the 3rd Pennsylvania Cavalry and concluded that the Confederate right flank could be turned and any possible Confederate retreat blocked. Moreover, any Union advance in that direction was certain to relieve the pressure on Hooker. Brig. Gen. William H. Emory, commanding the Union Cavalry Reserve, was sent with a battery of horse artillery to Whitaker's Mill, one mile south of Fort Magruder on the Union far left, where Emory could also prevent a Confederate attack on the Union left. Although he was reinforced, Emory advanced but a short distance before concluding that his force was inadequate to attempt such a movement, and he fell back.[11] Yet another opportunity had been lost.

As the attack on Fort Magruder raged, the Confederates continued to enjoy the advantage of position and initiative, and the tide of battle seemed to be flowing against the Federals. Fearing that Hooker's lines were beginning to collapse, Heintzelman sent messenger after messenger urging Kearny to "hurry up." Many of Hooker's men were now out of ammunition, and they had fallen back into the dense woods, only to be followed by the Rebels, and more intense fighting ensued. A battery of three Parrott rifles and one 12-pounder howitzer was overrun and captured by the 19th Virginia. Another Union battery was abandoned, but the guns were so mired in the mud that the Rebels could do little with them.

"General Hooker and his division gallantly sustained themselves against a much superior force from early in the morning until near 3 o'clock," when they began to give way, "having expended nearly all their ammunition," Heintzelman reported. Many of the Federals were totally exhausted, not only from "the long march through the rain and mud" but also by the "labors of the siege of Yorktown."[12] Yet for over eight hours, Hooker and his men had attacked and then valiantly held off a determined Rebel counterattack.

Hit particularly hard was the 2nd New Hampshire of Brig. Gen. Cuvier Grover's 2nd Brigade. Commanding the regiment, Col. Gilman Marston would always remember what he perceived as treachery by the Rebels at Williamsburg. Amid the fighting, a Confederate captain extended a white flag while crying out, "Don't fire, don't fire; we are friends!" Believing they were about to surrender, a Union officer ordered his men to cease firing, "whereupon the whole body of the enemy suddenly fired upon him, killing him instantly and also several of his men." Another incident, involving the 11th Massachusetts of the same brigade, Heintzelman also found incredulous and inglorious. With the fighting particularly fierce and the two forces less than fifty yards apart in the dense woods, a Rebel officer suddenly displayed a white flag, crying out, "Don't fire on your friends." When Pvt. Michael Doherty came forward to seize the flag, another Confederate officer was heard to yell out, "Now, give it to them." As musketry belched forth, Doherty was seriously wounded, though not before he had shot the Rebel officer through the heart.[13] Many of the Federal wounded were bayoneted by the Rebels, Heintzelman also claimed. In addition, a captain in a New Jersey regiment was found not only to have been bayoneted but also to have had his ears cut off as souvenirs.

Despite suffering heavy casualties, many of Hooker's men held their ground. Throwing their knapsacks aside and having depleted their ammunition, they relied only on their bayonets and the stocks of their muskets. Yet there was a constant stream of soldiers to the rear, not only the wounded but also hundreds of stragglers, frightened men in blue who simply gave up. Some feared that the battle was looking like another Bull Run. "Even the elements were combined against us," Heintzelman wrote. "The smoke and rain were driven by the wind into the faces of our men." The general raced about on the battlefield, much as he had done at Manassas, desperately trying to rally his fatigued and beleaguered men. "I made every exertion to rally them and partially succeeded," he later scribbled in a notebook. In the dense woods "a man could scarcely be seen at a greater distance than 60 yds." Fearing defeat, Captain McKeever sent two squadrons of the 3rd Pennsylvania Cavalry to either side of the road, with orders to fire on stragglers and force them back into battle.[14]

"The rain, the sight of the wounded, the re-enforcements still behind, all conspired to depress everybody," Heintzelman confessed. "No efforts I could make would move them. I ordered the drums to beat, but the drums were wet, and did not give forth cheerful sounds. I saw some brass instruments. I ordered the musicians to play, but it was only part of a band." A young private in the 8th New Jersey remembered seeing the general "call out in stentorian tones through his nose for the band to strike up an air. In a few moments a miserable remnant of the tooters rallied and made a number of sickly efforts at Yankee Doodle with their bazoos, which, instead of infusing courage into our hapless systems, sent a cold chill down our back and set our teeth aching."[15]

Finally, one of Heintzelman's staff officers, Lt. Granville Johnson, looked around and found more musicians. "Putting them together, the band struck up a patriotic air. This inspired new life into all. The men collected and began to cheer. The strains were wafted through the old forest, and made themselves heard by our weary troops above the roar of the battle, and inspired them with fresh vigor to perform new deeds of valor," Heintzelman informed McClellan.[16] It was a defining moment in the Battle of Williamsburg.

Capt. Selden Page of the 11th Massachusetts was watching as a man on horseback rode up to the band of the 1st Massachusetts, who was standing by the roadside. The man, who had a nasal twang, called out: "Come boys! Play something lively to cheer these boys up." A member of the band defiantly called out, "Who are you?" "I'm General Heintzelman, and I am going to win this fight," came the reply. The general spotted a bugler sitting on horseback and rode up to him. "Come my man, play something to cheer these boys up," he said. "I can't play anything but the calls," the bugler responded. "Well," said Heintzelman, "Toot! toot!—you can toot, can't you?" The band played "something lively," Page wrote, and the bugler "tooted."[17]

All accounts of the incident agree that Heintzelman was able to gather musicians from several regimental bands and ordered them "to play patriotic airs," which he hoped would lift the spirits of the men. "Play! Play! It's all you're good for," he shouted. "Play, damn it! Play some marching tune! 'Yankee Doodle' or any doodle you can think of, only play something." Within minutes the discordant airs of "Yankee Doodle" and then "Three Cheers for the Red, White, and Blue" were heard above the thundering sounds of battle. Amid the fighting, another soldier remembered hearing "The Flag of the Free." Another bluecoat thought the music worth a thousand men. "It saved the battle," he flatly declared.[18]

At three in the afternoon, as the tide of battle was turning against the III Corps and Hooker's lines were beginning to give way, Heintzelman looked up to see Brig. Gen. Hiram George Berry gallop up at the head of his 2nd Brigade, Kearny's division. Although the men had marched nine miles through rain and mud, they did not hesitate to enter the fight. The Confederates were on the verge of seizing yet another battery when, with a loud cheer, Berry and his men charged into them and threw them back in confusion. Within an hour Brig. Gen. Charles D. Jameson's 1st

Brigade had also arrived on the field. Chauncey McKeever had met Kearny a mile from the front with orders to hurry forward. "We dropped our knapsacks . . . & in obedience to orders from Gen. Heintzelman, ran the 3 miles at double quick thro' mud & water knee deep," a soldier in the 40th New York remembered.[19]

Within minutes the dapper General Kearny galloped up. Mud-spattered and spoiling for a fight, he had pushed his men through the rain and muck, past several companies of slow-moving infantry and supply trains that were bogged down in the mire. Overjoyed to see him, but worried that he had been in command for only three days, Heintzelman inquired if he might not require Hooker's assistance. "General, I can make my men follow me to hell," Kearny responded.[20]

Hooker's division was ordered to the rear to regroup and resupply. In front of Fort Magruder, Kearny deployed Berry's 3rd brigade to the left of the Williamsburg Road and sent Brig. Gen. David B. Birney's 2nd Brigade to the right. The 5th Michigan, with bayonets fixed, drove the Confederates back into their rifle pits, killing 143 of the Rebels, 63 of whom were shot through the head. Within minutes the 38th New York came charging down the road and took the rifle pits. With Heintzelman now on the offensive, Jameson's 1st Brigade, composed of the 57th, 63rd, and 105th Pennsylvania and the 87th New York, arrived just at Longstreet, having received reinforcements too, launched a counterattack to turn the Union right. As the battle continued to rage, General Kearny charged wildly into the fray, jerking the stump of his left arm as he did when excited. In front of his men, with the reins of his bridle between his teeth, the general waved his saber above his head with his remaining arm. With his aides and his staff by his side, Kearny then rode into the open field ahead of the Federal lines, as if on parade, and leisurely galloped along the entire front, hoping to discover the concealed positions of the Rebels. Two of his aides were shot from their horses, but Kearny rode back to his men and shouted, "You see, my boys, where to fire!"[21]

Kearny would be remembered that day for personally leading the charge of the 2nd Michigan Infantry that retook the captured Federal guns and hurled the Rebels back. During the fighting, Lt. Charles B. Haydon remembered seeing Heintzelman on horseback by the roadside excitedly encouraging the 2nd Michigan to the attack. "He swung his hat, hurrahed for Michigan most lustily and swore as hard as ever saying, 'Give them hell. God damn them, give the steel, don't wait to shoot.' He was more enthusiastic than I ever supposed he could be."[22]

It was evident that the arrival of General Kearny and his 3rd Division had turned the tide of battle. "I cannot find words to express my admiration of their gallantry," Heintzelman wrote.[23] No one in the Army of the Potomac, including Hooker and Hancock, was more courageous than Philip Kearny. But as Heintzelman realized, and as the coming months would prove, Kearny was bold and impetuous to the point of being reckless.

Heintzelman would always remain convinced that had Porter been on the scene with his division, "I would have turned the enemy's right flank and been in Williamsburg before dark." As a soggy darkness crept over the battlefield and the fighting sputtered to a close, Heintzelman, who was totally exhausted, built a small fire for himself back in the woods. Out of rations and hungry, other soldiers also gathered in the darkness. About midnight the rain ceased, and he composed a short note to McClellan, whom he assumed was still at Yorktown, requesting reinforcements. Hooker had suffered so severely that his division could no longer be relied on. For most of the night, Heintzelman had heard the movement of Confederate forces behind their works, and he was sure that Longstreet, a South Carolinian and perhaps Joe Johnston's most trusted lieutenant, was receiving reinforcements and determined to make a stand. Heintzelman also sent an urgent dispatch to Sumner, again pleading for reinforcements and asking that the II Corps commander attack the Confederates in his front: "Cannot you also attack him at daylight on his left and in your front?" he asked. "I fear greatly that unless he is strongly pressed I will not be able to maintain my position. May I rely upon your aid to sustain me?" If he were to hold Longstreet, the III Corps needed at least an additional division before morning. In the early morning hours, the general was awakened from a slumber by one of McClellan's staff, who rode up to say that the commanding general was at the Adams House. The aide had been looking for Heintzelman for several hours. In fact, an infantry company had been sent to open communications with the III Corps but had been unable to penetrate the woods and swamps. The aide said that on the Federal right, near the York River, General Hancock's 1st Brigade, 2nd Division, IV Corps had smashed the Rebel right flank in a heroic twenty-five-minute bayonet charge. More importantly, Heintzelman was not to renew the attack in the morning without orders. In McClellan's eyes it would always be Hancock, not Hooker or Kearny, who was the hero of the Battle of Williamsburg.[24]

After sleeping in his clothes in the drizzling rain, Heintzelman rode forward with Kearny, Jameson, and Barry before daylight the next morning. Despite what Heintzelman had concluded, Kearny said several of his reconnaissances during the night and early morning indicated the Rebels had been withdrawing toward Williamsburg for several hours.[25] Riding closer to the enemy works, Heintzelman could see through his field glasses only a few Rebels in the defenses, and within minutes they too were gone. The sun was out, the rain was gone, and so were the Confederates. He watched calmly as the 4th Maine and 105th Pennsylvania, preceded by skirmishers and with flags waving, entered Fort Magruder. Men of the 4th Maine raised the Stars and Stripes over the abandoned earthworks as a loud cheer reverberated through the woods and along the Williamsburg Road. In the abandoned fortress a silk Rebel flag, inscribed "Pickens Guard" and "Presented by the Ladies," was found, which Heintzelman proudly presented to the men from Maine.

Realizing that the Confederates were in full retreat, both cavalry and horse artillery were sent in pursuit. When two Rebel infantry regiments and some cavalry tried to make a stand in front of Williamsburg, he sent forward more infantry and some artillery under General Jameson to clear the road. Seeing the Union advance, the Rebels hastily retreated through the town, abandoning two field pieces, five large siege guns, several wagons, and hundreds of small arms. A short time later McClellan rode forward to congratulate Heintzelman on the victory. After giving orders to collect the wounded and bury the dead, the two rode triumphantly into Williamsburg.[26]

The Battle of Williamsburg took a heavy toll on the III Corps, especially Hooker's division. Of the 8,000 men "Fighting Joe" led into battle, 1,551, or nearly 20 percent, were either killed, wounded, or missing. Brig. Gen. Francis E. Patterson's 3rd Brigade, composed entirely of New Jersey troops, had suffered 526 casualties, 42 of them officers. Brig. Gen. Nelson Taylor's 2nd (Excelsior) Brigade of New York troops was badly battered, with every regiment losing at least 100 men; with 330 casualties, the 7th New York suffered the heaviest regimental loss. In fact, Hooker's division suffered close to 70 percent of Federal casualties at Williamsburg. But what angered both Heintzelman and Hooker for months was the fact that while Hooker's division was being so badly bloodied in front of Fort Magruder, over 30,000 Union soldiers stood idle within an hour's march of the battlefield. In Kearny's division the 5th Michigan was hit hardest, losing 144 men. In the 38th New York, 88 men had been lost, including one-third of the regiment's officers. Of the 9,000 Confederate defenders, five brigades of General Longstreet's division, 1,052 men were lost. Although he was never given credit for the role the III Corps played in the victory, Heintzelman would always consider it his crowning achievement during the Civil War. Williamsburg, he would later write, "was the first battle of the Army of the Potomac and gave it its character."[27]

Heintzelman soon discovered that Longstreet had abandoned most of his badly wounded. With the arrival of the Union wounded, every available space in the old colonial capital, including all the town's churches and William and Mary College on its western edge, were put to use. Citizens graciously offered their homes to the medical staffs, and yellow hospital flags appeared everywhere. It seemed that the community had become one immense infirmary. Heintzelman's close friend, Charles S. Tripler, medical director of the Army of the Potomac, estimated that about 700 Union soldiers and 333 wounded Confederates were in the town. To assist the Confederate wounded, many of whom died hourly, Longstreet sent his chief surgeon, S. D. Cullen, along with a team of doctors back to Williamsburg under a flag of truce to assist the Union physicians.[28]

After sending out reconnoitering parties on the roads leading up the Peninsula toward Richmond, Heintzelman established his headquarters near the eastern end of town at Waller Street in the two-story home of John C. Mercer, a surgeon in the Confederate Army who had moved his family to Lynchburg.[29] After all the bloodletting, the Federals took time to rest and regroup. The general found time to clip some roses, tulips, and lilacs from Mercer's flower garden and relax over a glass of lemonade. From the physician's office near the main residence, he wrote Margaret a long letter and started work on his official account of the battle, a report that would eventually number twenty pages. He even found time to write letters relating to the Arizona silver mines.

While in Williamsburg, Heintzelman learned that during the fighting, the Prince de Joinville had returned from the front and told McClellan, quite excitedly, that there were three "old women" in command and that they were doing nothing. Moreover, if Little Mac was to save the day, he should take command himself as soon as possible. Although the prince later denied that Heintzelman was one of the "old women," it was obvious he was referring to him as well as Sumner and Franklin. Heintzelman also learned of the return of Samuel Wilkeson of the *New York Daily Tribune*, whom he welcomed back to corps headquarters. As he continued to work on his lengthy report, the general shared his account with the journalist, who offered "literary corrections." Largely based on Heintzelman's report, the tireless, opinionated, and dedicated Wilkeson wrote a lengthy "glowing account" of the Battle of Williamsburg for his paper.[30]

Still aspiring to command the Army of the Potomac, Heintzelman rushed a copy of his report to Margaret in Washington, hoping that it would reach army headquarters and find its way into newspapers before that of other corps commanders. If Margaret released the report to the public, he would be in violation of army regulations, but there was no rule against allowing someone to read it, he calculated. Besides, he was "confident Sen. Ben Wade would ask for it in due time." He also wrote several Radical senators urging them to persuade Lincoln "to act at once" by sending reinforcements to the Peninsula. He badly wanted to command the Army of the Potomac, even if it meant undermining McClellan. Appreciating what had happened to General Hamilton for his earlier criticisms, he fully recognized that discretion was essential. Heintzelman regretted that no reporter had witnessed the fierce fighting on the Union left during the Battle of Williamsburg. All that was being published was McClellan's version of the action, which was a glorification of Hancock and somewhat critical of his corps commanders. "There is great indignation at Gen. McClellan that he don't give us credit for the great battle," Heintzelman wrote. A few days later General Kearny and his brigade commanders, Jameson, Birney, and Berry, appeared at corps headquarters with a copy of the *Philadelphia Inquirer* containing a telegram from McClellan that gave all the glory to Hancock. "They and their divis. are very indignant and some officers talk of resigning," Heintzelman recalled.[31] Berry suggested that the general write his friend, Vice President Hamlin, with a more accurate account of what had transpired on the Peninsula.

The next day Heintzelman went to see McClellan, who graciously agreed to draft a telegram to the War Department offering a more balanced account of the battle. Little Mac even agreed to allow his corps commander to make corrections in the final draft. Although Heintzelman was angry with McClellan for slighting his corps, Kearny was outraged. In a letter to Oliver S. Halsted, an active lobbyist, socialite, and regular member of Mary Lincoln's salon, Kearny proclaimed McClellan to be "the first commander in history . . . to ignore those under him, who not only have fought a good fight, but even saved his Army, himself and his reputation."[32] The commander's failure to recognize the gallantry of others was due to his personal weakness and insecurity, Kearny was convinced. His scathing letter eventually made it to Lincoln, further damaging McClellan's reputation with the president.

Although other Union generals were coming to despise newspaper correspondents, Heintzelman continued to welcome them into his camp and see to their needs. If favorable reports of him and the III Corps were published, especially in the big Philadelphia and New York newspapers, his career was certain to be enhanced. He was especially excited when *Frank Leslie's Illustrated Newspaper* published a "most flattering notice" of his conduct at Williamsburg. At the same time, however, the *New York Times* printed a letter from an unnamed officer in the III Corps calling him an "authoritarian coward."[33] In response, Captain McKeever wrote the newspaper in protest, demanding to know the name of the officer, at the same time assuring Heintzelman that if the individual could be identified, he would be driven from the army. So inaccurate were the accounts of the fighting, one newspaper even stated that Heintzelman had been killed, a report Samuel Peter prayed Margaret had not seen. There was little time, however, to respond to such accusations and distortions.

The Battle of Williamsburg had served in many ways to make Heintzelman overconfident. The action, he concluded, had shown McClellan that his subordinate could "be trusted with operations." More importantly, the battle might just be "the finishing stroke to the rebellion." As a result of his success, Heintzelman was slowly gaining a reputation of being a real hero, and his star was on the rise. Because of his hard fighting, inexorable Unionism, and uncompromising determination to win the war, he was becoming known throughout the North and even cheered in wild patriotic speeches at such places as the Cooper Institute in New York City.[34] Back home in rural Manheim, he was known simply as "Sourdough Sam." Although many other Civil War commanders, both North and South, gained colorful sobriquets during the conflict, his was certainly one of the more unique.

For six hours on May 9, 1862, with flags waving and regimental bands playing "Dixie" as well as patriotic Northern airs, long lines of Union troops, accompanied by hundreds of white-topped wagons, poured down Williamsburg's Duke of Gloucester, Francis, and Nicholson streets. "I don't know what the Secessionists must have thought," the general wrote.[35] The name "Williamsburg," he proudly announced to his troops, could be sewn on the battle flags of the III Corps. But Richmond was still fifty miles away.

As the III Corps departed Williamsburg and began inching its way up the Peninsula, Kearny led the way. With few guides and a smattering of reliable maps, he was followed by Hooker's 2nd Division. When General Keyes's IV Corps clogged the only road leading toward Richmond, the III Corps fell hours behind schedule; at the end of the first day, they had marched only six miles. The next day the army moved past Ewell Hall, the home of Benjamin Ewell, president of William and Mary College, who had gone off to join the Confederate Army; then past Olive Branch Church; and finally bivouacking at the hamlet of Burnt Ordinary.[36]

Although the weather was warm and pleasant, the roads were badly rutted, and the III Corps moved slowly. Abandoned Confederate wagons were everywhere, evidence of the haste with which the enemy had fled toward Richmond. By May 11, eighteen miles from Williamsburg, Heintzelman reached Barhamsville, where the road leading to Richmond forked and where he established III Corps's headquarters in a large abandoned farmhouse nearby. Along the way, he learned that the day after the battle, less than five miles from where he was camped, Brig. Gen. William B. Franklin, one of McClellan's favorites, had taken Eltham's Landing at the mouth of the Pamunkey River across from West Point, the eastern terminus of the York River Railroad, which led directly to Richmond. Hoping to block the Confederate retreat, Franklin's infantry, supported by five gunboats, had landed in pontoon boats. A four-hundred-foot-long floating wharf was swiftly assembled, and by torchlight the division's artillery and supplies had been hauled ashore. After establishing picket lines in the pinewoods around Eltham Plantation, Franklin waited for three divisions from Yorktown to join him. On the morning of May 7, in the woods not far from the Union camp, Franklin's advance ran headlong into Brig. Gen. John Bell Hood's Texas Brigade, reinforced by six regiments. Thrown back in fierce fighting, the Federals lost 186 men; Hood's casualties amounted to 48.[37]

Better news arrived from down the Peninsula with word that the Confederates had been forced to evacuate Norfolk. Moreover, on the night of May 10, they had abandoned the large Gosport Navy Yard. Realizing the James River was too shallow for the *Virginia* to reach Richmond, the ironclad had been blown up before dawn the next day, an ignominious end for the pride of the Confederate Navy. A flotilla of Union gunboats, including the *Monitor*, was now proceeding up the James River toward Richmond, less than seventy miles away, which both sides now considered imperiled. The thirty-eight thousand citizens of the city began to panic when the Confederate government, clearly understanding the gravity of the situation, began packing up.

By May 10, after taking part of his army up the Pamunkey River from West Point Landing, McClellan had established his headquarters at the historic White House Plantation. With five hundred tons of supplies arriving daily, the vast four-thousand-acre estate became an enormous supply depot. Five locomotives and eighty railcars were pulled ashore for use on the Richmond and York River Railroad to supply the army in its drive on Richmond. Heavy ordnance, including the big guns from Yorktown, was brought on barges and canal boats to the landing, where they were loaded on railroad cars to be hauled to the gates of the Confederate capital. So massive was the Union buildup that army camps stretched for more than two miles along the Pamunkey River, all the way to Cumberland Landing.

White House Plantation was the home of Col. William Henry Fitzhugh "Rooney" Lee, son of Gen. Robert E. Lee. Heintzelman noted that in the hall of the main house, Mary Custis Lee had left a small sign saying that it was here that George Washington had courted the widow Martha Custis and asking the "northern troops not to desecrate it." As a result, a strong guard was posted around the house. "We take good care of the property of traitors," the general sarcastically commented.[38]

After spending three days in Barhamsville, orders came to move the III Corps eight miles closer to Richmond. With pickets well in advance, Hooker advanced on one road while Kearny moved his division along another. Unable to ride on horseback because of inflammation in his left foot, Heintzelman was forced to take to a carriage. Once again he came to question why McClellan was moving so slowly. Sharing his corps commander's concerns, Kearny began to refer to Little Mac as the "Virginia creeper." Yet the men in the ranks idolized McClellan. "They will follow wherever he shall lead, or go where he directs, knowing full well that his interests are fully identified with theirs," one soldier wrote.[39]

After two hours and eight miles in the rain over roads that were as bad as ever, the column finally reached Slatersville. All along the way, they encountered evidence of a desperate and demoralized Confederate army. Everywhere gardens and smokehouses had been raided by the hungry and dispirited Rebels. A number of the dwellings in the small community, including the Slater House, where Heintzelman established his headquarters, bore evidence of a fierce skirmish that had erupted two days earlier when General Stoneman's cavalry encountered the rear guard of Johnston's retreating army.[40]

Two weeks after leaving Williamsburg, Heintzelman finally reached New Kent Court House, where only three elderly women and two wounded Confederates could be found. He set up corps headquarters in the deserted home of a local attorney, Telemachus Taylor. Colonel Averell's 3rd Pennsylvania Cavalry had chased a Confederate rear guard out of New Kent Court House the day before. But before leaving, the Rebels had burned several of the buildings in the small settlement, including the county jail. Much to Heintzelman's displeasure, he found that Union soldiers had looted the courthouse, carrying off irreplaceable deeds and other legal documents. These men, he realized, had no respect for abandoned property thought to be owned by secessionists who had joined the Rebel army. The wide-scale destruction by the III Corps caused McClellan to write Heintzelman asking that every effort be made to "prevent depredations upon . . . persons and property." With the weather growing warmer, McClellan did not even want fence rails burned. Although many of the planters on the Peninsula had fled to Richmond with their slaves, more and more blacks straggled into the Union camps. As "contrabands," they were put to work as cooks, servants, and laborers. "The boys . . . make themselves at home if the folks are away, and visit their cellars, tasting the vintage of each, while the blacks belonging to the plantations are busy baking hoecake, receiving any loose change in return," one soldier wrote home. "We have taken possession of three flourishing mills full of grain, and the farmers are apt to wake up in the morning and find themselves minus of pigs and chickens," a New York artilleryman wrote from the small crossroads of Mechanicsville.[41]

While Heintzelman was at New Kent Court House, orders arrived announcing the reorganization of the Army of the Potomac effective immediately. Angered at the conduct of his corps commanders at Williamsburg, McClellan diluted the authority of Heintzelman, Sumner, and Keyes by reducing their corps to only two divisions. Two new units were created for his favorite generals: Fitz John Porter would command the V Corps, while William B. Franklin would take command of the VI Corps. "The gen. has pretty well broken up these Army Corps," Heintzelman complained.[42] As the campaign progressed, he had come to realize that McClellan was confiding in Porter and Franklin more and more, while ignoring the more experienced commanders.

By May 21 the III Corps had reached Baltimore Cross Roads, only eighteen miles from Richmond, where the staff established headquarters in the two-story home of Tazewell Tyler, a relative of former president John Tyler. The Tyler family had fled only an hour before the Union advance guard reached the village, leaving two older slaves and a male servant behind. All the furnishings were still in the residence, even the silverware on the dining-room table. Books were lying about as well as "a trunk of female apparel." The officers were amazed to see in one of the hallways a "polished skull" on a table, "across the forehead of which was printed in black, block letters 'A YANKEE.'"[43]

From Baltimore Cross Roads, Heintzelman rode four miles through the woods to Tunstall's Station to see McClellan at his new headquarters. When Little Mac arrived an hour later, a very frank discussion ensued. With the Confederates demoralized by Yorktown and Williamsburg, McClellan was sure the Army of the Potomac could be in Richmond in forty-eight hours if he could have General McDowell's forty thousand men. Both McClellan and Heintzelman continued to believe, however, that the defenders of the Rebel capital outnumbered the Army of the Potomac. Although President Lincoln remained convinced that Washington would be inadequately defended if McDowell marched south, Heintzelman was certain the best defense of the Union capital would be the fall of Richmond. He also learned from McClellan that any hope of a seaborne assault on Richmond had been dashed at Drewry's Bluff, seven miles down the brown waters of the James River from the Confederate capital. There on May 14 a small squadron of heavily armored Union vessels led by the

Galena and followed by the *Monitor* had approached the Rebel-held fortification on the south bank of the river through a heavy mist. In a four-hour battle, which Heintzelman called a "gunboat affair," that rattled windows in Richmond, the warships had been badly battered by heavy Rebel guns firing down on them from the cliffs ninety feet above the river. The *Galena* was struck by as many as fifty shells, set on fire, and forced to pull off down the river, followed soon after by the rest of the squadron.[44] Safe now from a naval assault, Richmond would have to be taken by land.

With the expected arrival of McDowell, McClellan had decided to place the right wing of the Army of the Potomac, consisting of Sumner's, Franklin's, and Porter's corps, north of the Chickahominy River ("Chicken-and-Hominy" to some of the Federals), while the left wing, composed of the III Corps and Keyes's IV Corps, would cross the river and push against Richmond from the east. By constructing additional bridges across the Chickahominy, McClellan would, once the assault had begun, shift the bulk of his army to the south bank and attack from the east. If necessary, the large siege guns from Yorktown would be used to lay siege to the city. Playing on his subordinate's vanity, McClellan told him that one of the great battles in the history of the world was imminent, and Heintzelman was certain to play a leading role in what was sure to be a great Union victory. "I think if I am to do the fighting, I might have some of the honors," he confided to his journal.[45]

At Baltimore Cross Roads the next day, Heintzelman wrote a letter to Senator Wilson outlining McClellan's plans for taking Richmond. "We have now arrived at a crisis in our affairs," he told the Massachusetts senator. But reflecting McClellan's optimism, he was sure Richmond could be taken. The Army of the Potomac must be reinforced, though, since General Johnston's army was thought to number as many as 130,000 men. "With the fall of Richmond our capital will no longer be threatened and the rebel Confederacy will virtually be at an end," he assured Wilson. It was of the utmost importance that the senator urge Lincoln "to act at once."[46] When General Berry arrived at III Corps headquarters, Heintzelman urged him to write (one Maine man to another) Hannibal Hamlin asking that the vice president urge Lincoln to rush reinforcements to the army as soon as possible.

As Union forces moved closer to Richmond, Heintzelman and Little Mac learned that Stonewall Jackson was running wild in the Shenandoah Valley. Marching his "foot cavalry" four hundred miles in a month, the pious, blue-eyed Jackson, a bundle of oddities and eccentricities, had surprised and decisively defeated Maj. Gen. Nathaniel Banks at Winchester and pursued him all the way to the Potomac. The Rebels were expected to make a dash for Harpers Ferry, and Lincoln was fearful they then would march on Washington. Consequently, he was reversing his decision releasing McDowell to join the Army of the Potomac. McClellan protested, but the president was adamant.

Better news came from the Union right flank when General Franklin telegraphed that his VI Corps was within five miles of Richmond. Through field glasses, his men could see the streets and lampposts in the Rebel capital. On the extreme right Porter's V Corps had reached Mechanicsville, only five miles northwest of Richmond, from where the spires of the city's numerous churches could also be seen. Porter's bluecoats were even keeping time by the chiming of church bells and the striking of public clocks in the capital.[47] As the Army of the Potomac inched closer to Richmond, Heintzelman came to think Richmond might fall without a fight.

General Marcy wrote to say that pickets were across the Chickahominy River and that Keyes's IV Corps was expected to cross at Bottom's Bridge, which engineers had rebuilt. On the morning of May 24, Heintzelman too guided his III Corps across the Chickahominy. He established corps headquarters in a deserted farmhouse nearby, where he received orders from McClellan placing him in command of all forces south of the river. McClellan also asked that Heintzelman make every effort to open communications with Union gunboats at City Point on the James River.[48] From army headquarters at Cold Harbor, he also informed him that the Richmond and York River Railroad was now operational all the way from White House Landing to the Chickahominy and carrying seven hundred tons of supplies a day.

With the narrow, tree-lined river at flood stage from heavy rains, McClellan was concerned about his army being divided. To maintain communications with the corps south of the river, engineers went to work constructing eleven bridges across the Chickahominy over a twelve-mile stretch. The high waters along the twisting river had inundated the bottomlands, and endless corduroying was required to cross wagons to the south bank.

As Keyes advanced his 15,678 soldiers west along the Richmond and York River Railroad and the Williamsburg Road, Heintzelman's men followed. Meeting with Keyes, he learned that only a few Confederate pickets had been spotted and everything was quiet. "I don't think that we are in the least danger of an attack," Heintzelman wrote.[49]

Cautiously avoiding any contact with the enemy, a small cavalry scout had made contact with the *Galena* on the James River near City Point, as McClellan had directed. The redoubt atop Drewry's Bluff, which was being called Fort Darling, was reported to contain a battery of thirty guns and a garrison of five thousand men. Although the troops were stationed on the south bank of the river, Heintzelman remained concerned that his left flank was badly exposed. But with the railroad bridge across the Chickahominy now repaired (eighty feet of it had been burned by the retreating Rebels), railroad cars began bringing supplies directly to the front. The enemy had made a serious mistake, he thought, by not completely destroying the bridge and ripping up the tracks.

Although deserters came into the Union lines saying that Longstreet's division was badly demoralized, the Confederate general was preparing to resist any advance on the capital from south of the Chickahominy. Heintzelman and Keyes, nevertheless, decided to push Brig. Gen. Silas Casey's division of the IV Corps forward to a position near the crossroads of Seven Pines on the Williamsburg Road. There Casey's men began constructing defensive works.[50] A thirty-six-year veteran of the old army, the white-haired Casey was well respected for having written a manual on infantry tactics. If attacked, he was ordered to hold "at all hazards."

On May 29 III Corps headquarters was moved three miles west to Savage's Station, five miles from Bottom's Bridge. Along the railroad at what was called Laurel Hill, Heintzelman pitched his headquarters tent on the front lawn of George M. Savage's plantation. A leading secessionist, Savage had sent his three daughters to South Carolina to escape the war, and though the Union Army was the last thing he hoped to see in his front yard, he shared some ripe strawberries with Heintzelman, the first the general had seen since leaving Texas.[51]

When Federal engineers made a thorough examination of the area around Seven Pines, it was decided to relocate Casey's division to a more advantageous position three-quarters of a mile farther west to the crossroads leading from Seven Pines to Old Tavern. There rifle pits were dug and abatis put into position. Although handicapped by a shortage of shovels and axes, work was even commenced on a pentagonal redoubt for six pieces of artillery. With the heavy rains, the work went slowly, however, but when finished, Casey's front lines extended for more than a mile from north of the Williamsburg Road to a point across the Richmond and York River Railroad at Fair Oaks Station. North of Fair Oaks, an impenetrable wilderness of mosquito-infested swamps and dense woods extended three miles to the Chickahominy River.

No sooner was Casey in position than a sharp skirmish ensued in which a major in a New York regiment, whom Heintzelman remembered as a sergeant in the 2nd U.S. Infantry in Texas, was killed. More ominous was the fact that on the night of May 30, Casey's pickets reported hearing cars running all night on the Richmond end of the railroad. In yet a second skirmish the next morning, Lt. James B. Washington, one of Joe Johnston's aides, was captured. The following day Casey's pickets again engaged Confederate scouts. All the while the green and badly equipped Federals continued to entrench, though a heavy thunderstorm put a stop to the work.[52] Casey would always insist that he was not surprised by the Confederate attack that hit him the next day.

On the opposite side of the river sat General Sumner's 17,000-man II Corps. In Casey's rear, in a second line of defenses, was Brig. Gen. Darius Couch's 7,000-man division, covering Seven Pines and the Nine Mile Road as far as Fair Oak Station. Like Casey, Couch's men were busy entrenching. Kearny, with about 6,500 men, was bivouacked another mile in the rear of Couch.

Unknown to Heintzelman, General Johnston, commanding the Confederate forces defending Richmond, was preparing to strike the isolated Union corps south of the swollen Chickahominy River with a large part of his 82,000-man army. Criticized for his indecisiveness and lack of resolve thus far in the war, Johnston, who had simply run out of room to retreat, hoped to smash the Federal left wing with three divisions of nearly 40,000 men before McClellan could get reinforcements across the river. He had originally planned to strike the right wing of McClellan's divided army, but after a reconnaissance on May 30 showed Casey to be vulnerable, Johnston decided to send Maj. Gen. Daniel Harvey Hill with 8,500 men in four brigades directly east on the Williamsburg Road to Seven Pines. At the same time, Maj. Gen. Benjamin Huger would lead his division of three brigades east on the Charles City Road, passing over the head of White Oak Swamp to strike the flank and rear of the Union line. General Longstreet, supported by Brig. Gen. William Henry Chase Whiting's division, would lead the attack along the Nine Mile Road, running parallel to the Williamsburg Road. Although Johnston's plan seemed simple, it would miscarry from the start.

A raging and violent thunderstorm, which began at five o'clock on the afternoon of May 30, dumped more than three inches of rain in two hours on the two armies east of Richmond and continued throughout the night. Lightning lit the Virginia sky, and thunder echoed through the camps and dark woods. A quartermaster in a New York regiment was killed by lightning, as were four men in a Rebel camp. The storm, Samuel Wilkeson of the *New York Tribune* recorded, "was the most furious full of rain and explosions of lightning I ever saw. Not a regiment, not a company, not an officer was exempt from its chilling and exhausting effects." A *New York Times* reporter described it as "deluging the earth with rain, converting the spongy soil into a nearly impassable bog, and raising the waters of the Chickahominy so as to carry away one of two bridges." Johnston saw the storm as godsend. Heintzelman remembered only that "it rained in torrents."[53] Both armies passed a miserable night, unable to cook any meals. The heavy rains turned the Chickahominy into a raging torrent that threatened McClellan's communications and isolated the 31,500 men of Heintzelman and Keyes south of the river.

Although Johnston had not revealed his plans to either Pres. Jefferson Davis or his military adviser, Gen. Robert E. Lee, there were so many Southern soldiers on the march that on Sunday, May 31, crowds began to gather early on the hills east of Richmond to watch a battle they knew would determine the fate of their city. Although the II and III Corps were stacked up from beyond Seven Pines to Bottom's Bridge, Heintzelman realized the Union forces south of the Chickahominy were in a hazardous position, fearing the possibility of the very attack that Johnston planned. The general telegraphed McClellan for permission to advance the III Corps to a position that could be better supported in case the enemy struck. He became even more concerned when Keyes sent a note saying that "rebel pickets were around him [Keyes] in a semicircle." He was particularly concerned about Casey's green troops, who were in a vulnerable position west of Seven Pines. Casey "urged me to let his division occupy the advanced lines. After I had examined these . . . I gave my consent although Gen. Keyes objected to it," Heintzelman later remembered. At 4 P.M. on May 30, he sent Capt. Leavitt Hunt to Kearny with orders to move two brigades forward along the railroad to a position three-quarters of a mile west of Savage's Station. After leaving a sufficient force to guard the crossings of the Chickahominy, Hooker was ordered to follow Kearny as soon as possible.[54]

Shortly after noon on May 31, Casey was sitting in front of his tent when several artillery rounds passed over his head, crashing into some trees near the Seven Pines crossroads. These signaled the beginning of the Battle of Fair Oaks. Within minutes pickets of the 103rd Pennsylvania, who had never been in combat before, were hit head on by a fierce Rebel attack, and they fled in panic to the rear. So ferocious and swift was the Confederate assault that the regiment's flag was riddled and the staff shot to pieces. At the same time, a withering artillery fire raked Casey's unfinished redoubt. Brig. Gen. Innis N. Palmer, commanding the 3rd Brigade, was so surprised by the attack that he bolted from his tent, leaving his midday meal and his personal belongings behind. As large numbers of General Hill's soldiers came screaming out of the woods in columns, Casey's green troops were overwhelmed. "We commensed firing and we kept fighting and falling back till they got almost around us then we had to retreat back . . . we lost every thing that we had but what we had on," a soldier in the 81st New York wrote.[55]

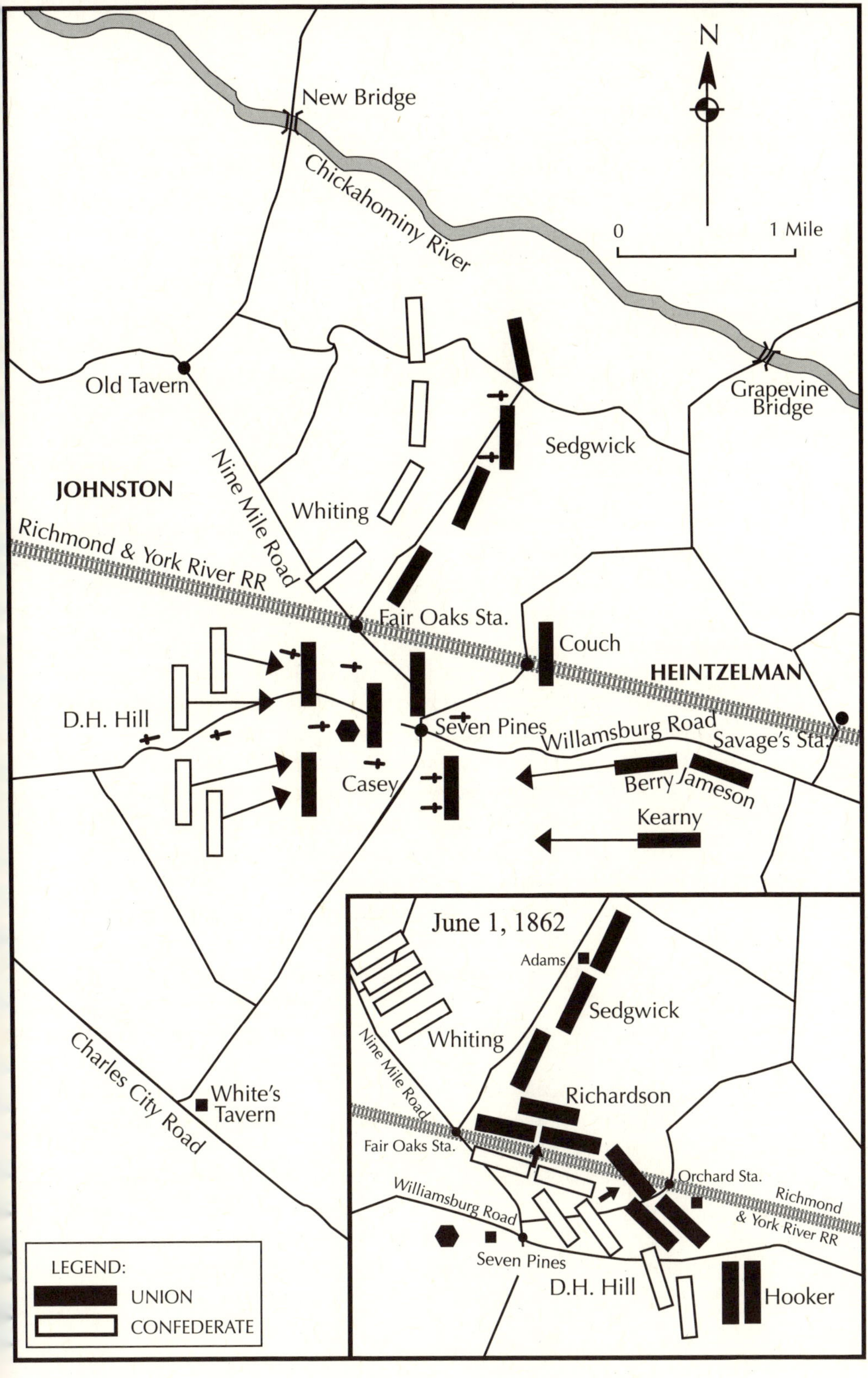

Battle of Seven Pines
May 31, 1862

Not only was Casey's headquarters overrun but his personal baggage was captured as well; several of his letters were later published in Richmond newspapers. Many of the gunners in the redoubt were shot down by Confederates firing from behind trees on the fringes of White Oak Swamp. With the quarter-mile-long earthwork virtually surrounded and the division suffering heavy casualties, the defenders inside began to scamper for safety. Capturing the redoubt, its guns were turned on the retreating bluecoats as the white-haired Casey tried repeatedly to rally his fleeing troops. Hit particularly hard was the brigade of Brig. Gen. Henry M. Naglee, which had been posted north of the Williamsburg Road. Realizing that Casey was under attack, Keyes sent the 55th New York and the 10th Massachusetts to the front, but they were easily repulsed by the Rebel onslaught. During this attack, the Confederates claimed to have captured four regimental colors as well as Casey's garrison flag. Heintzelman speculated, however, that the flags were found boxed up in camp and had probably never been unfurled.[56]

Heintzelman was at his headquarters at Savage's Station at 1:30 P.M. when he heard the booming of artillery to the west. Realizing the firing was heavier and more concentrated than anything he had heard in several days, he dispatched two aides, Captain Hunt and Lieutenant Johnson, to the front. Shortly after 2:30 P.M. Hunt and Johnston, after having met with General Keyes, excitedly raced up to headquarters to say that Casey had been hit by a massive frontal attack. He had already lost as many as 164 men killed and 884 wounded, and his division was in retreat. The entire front must be reinforced immediately to prevent a disaster.

North of the Chickahominy, McClellan, who was suffering from malaria and bedridden, had also heard the firing and immediately wired Heintzelman inquiring as to the nature of the action. With no word yet from his aides, there was little he could tell his commander: "No report has been received from Genl Keyes yet, therefore I presume there is nothing serious."[57] Not willing to take any chances, McClellan wisely telegraphed General Sumner to be ready to advance the II Corps across the river, if necessary.

As the Rebels continued to press their attack along the Williamsburg Road, Heintzelman became concerned that General Couch's division would also be overrun. With Couch pleading for at least two brigades of reinforcements, Heintzelman responded by ordering General Birney's brigade of Kearny's division to advance west along the road. Shortly after 2:30 P.M., with the Rebels still on the attack and after hearing Hunt and Johnson's report, the general told Chief of Staff McKeever to issue orders rushing all available troops from the III Corps forward. "So soon as I was satisfied that the attack was serious I sent a staff officer to appraise Gen. Sumner of it and this officer met one of his aides to offer me Gen. Sumner's assistance," Heintzelman later recalled.[58] He also began issuing a rash of orders. "You will allow no men . . . wounded or otherwise, to pass to the rear of the entrenchments. If found necessary you will fire upon them," he wrote General Naglee, who was in command near Burnt Chimneys. He also telegraphed McClellan the alarming news from the front and, with his horse already saddled, galloped off toward the sound of the fighting. Near a large field less than half a mile west of his headquarters, Heintzelman watched as large numbers of Casey's men came streaming east along the Williamsburg Road, and he came to realize the full extent of the Union collapse. These troops simply "did not fight well," and their retreat "had a most dispiriting effect," he bluntly reported to McClellan. From army headquarters north of the Chickahominy, Little Mac immediately ordered Sumner across the river with his II Corps.[59] Still smarting from criticism received for his inactivity at Williamsburg, Sumner had already taken the liberty of marching his corps to the bridges crossing the Chickahominy.

As Heintzelman rode toward the fighting, he continued to encounter large numbers of panic-stricken men and boys in blue falling back in considerable disorder. The closer he got to the front lines, the more soldiers he encountered and the more confusing the scene became. A member of the 40th New York recalled seeing "a vast crowd of stragglers, with many wounded . . . piling along the road in Bull Run style." Spotting the 2nd Michigan Infantry from Berry's brigade, Heintzelman became enraged, thinking the regiment to be in full retreat. Discovering instead that it was en route to the front, he ordered the unit deployed as a provost's guard to arrest anyone found retreating. Within an hour the regiment had arrested more than one thousand men.[60] In fact, the stream of fleeing bluecoats eventually stretched all the way to Bottom's Bridge, where a guard from the 3rd Michigan had to be posted. Although more than a thousand men were stopped there, perhaps a thousand others, most of them from Casey's division, were already across the Chickahominy. One of the roads leading to the front was so crowded with retreating soldiers that a regiment from Hooker's division, rushing to the front, had to use their bayonets to force their way through the mass of nervous and frightened men. Not realizing that Sumner was on the march, Heintzelman sent an urgent request for immediate assistance from the II Corps. His courier was quickly met by a member of Sumner's staff, who had been dispatched to see if Heintzelman needed assistance.

The fighting was fierce at Seven Pines when the general reached the front. Meeting with Keyes, he was told the specifics of what had happened.

Although Casey's artillery was lost and a large part of his division had fled the battlefield, three of his regiments, the 92nd New York, 104th Pennsylvania, and the 11th Maine, from the brigades of Naglee and Palmer, had gallantly rallied under heavy fire. Less than a mile from where Casey had been attacked, the Union regiments had even counterattacked before being overwhelmed by the sheer numbers of Rebels continuing to pour out of the woods.

Heintzelman was met by his *Tribune* friend, Samuel Wilkeson, who agreed to serve as a volunteer aide. The general would remember the journalist as calm and courageous under fire, someone who was "conspicuous in . . . aiding" and "rallying the men." Wilkeson behaved with the "greatest gallantry" that day, Heintzelman remembered.[61]

Still advancing, the Rebels soon ran into Couch's division. Unlike Casey, the slight and frail Couch personally led a counterattack, only to be cut off and almost surrounded. With three regiments and an artillery battery of four guns near Fair Oaks Station, Couch made several attempts to break out and join the rest of his division at Seven Pines. In the fierce fighting two of his regimental commanders were killed. With many of the Federals low on ammunition in the increasingly bitter struggle, Heintzelman was repeatedly "urged to consent to the troops falling back." Realizing many of the men under fire were veterans of Bull Run, he feared any retreat would cause a general panic. During the fiercest of the fighting, it was said a New York colonel came galloping up with two companies and earnestly inquired where to deploy his men. "If it is fighting you want," Heintzelman was heard to say, "just go in, colonel; there is plenty [of] good fighting all along the lines." As he had done so successfully at Williamsburg, Heintzelman hastily organized as many regimental bands as possible and had them "stationed on the road, and despite the dreadful roar of cannon and musketry," a corporal in the 105th Pennsylvania remembered that "the strains of the National Airs could be heard cheering us on."[62]

By three o'clock Heintzelman and Keyes had successfully reformed the Federal battle lines near Seven Pines. Within minutes Kearny reached the front with two of his brigades. Fearful of being attacked on his left and rear, Heintzelman sent Kearny, at the head of Berry's brigade, into the woods to the left of the Williamsburg Road, hoping the dashing one-armed general could outflank the advancing Confederates and capture their artillery. General Jameson was sent to the right to support Brig. Gen. John J. Peck's brigade, which was reported to be under heavy attack.[63] At the same time, General Birney was ordered to advance along the railroad.

Dashing out in front of his men, just as he had done at Williamsburg, General Kearny had his bay horse shot from under him, though not before he threw the 63rd and 105th Pennsylvania across the Williamsburg

Road, not only halting the advancing Rebels but also pushing them back several hundred yards. Kearny's aide-de-camp, George W. Mindil, said the Confederate attack "was spirited and the resistance stubborn, every foot of ground being obstinately and desperately contested." One soldier in the 105th Pennsylvania of Jameson's brigade in Kearny's division, who was badly wounded and left on the battlefield for two days, vividly recorded the fierce fighting and many of the conversations he heard that day. One soldier lying at the foot of a tree, picking with his fingers at the stump of a leg torn off, was heard to say, "Go in boys, I'm sorry I can't go with you." Another soldier was heard to say, "You fellows will get enough of it in there." Another bluecoat yelled out, "Hurry up boys, they need you over there."[64]

During the fiercest of the fighting, the Confederates were exposed "to a galling fire in front, as well as to a most destructive fire in [the] flank." Despite losing 233 men killed and over 800 wounded, Kearny was able to regain the ground that had been lost that morning. Fortunately, the dashing division commander had reconnoitered what he called "that secret, locked-up country of forests and swamps" a few days earlier and knew the terrain well. In fact, he was so far in advance of the remainder of his division that he feared being cut off. With darkness approaching, he was in a precarious position, and there was little alternative but to withdraw.[65]

At about five o'clock, General Longstreet, having taken the wrong road, finally arrived on the field to reinforce Hill. Again the Confederates advanced against the Union line, and again the Federals bent but did not break as Heintzelman ordered two of General Peck's regiments from the right to redeploy. While Jameson tried to rally his men, his horse was hit three times and fell on him. Men of the 63rd Pennsylvania had to lift the animal off of the general, who was carried to the rear.

With three regiments near Savage's Station, General Couch was hoping to hold out until reinforcements could arrive. Suddenly at 5:30, with much of the fighting becoming hand to hand and the Confederates within yards of seizing his guns, a long line of blue-clad reinforcements came streaming out of the woods from the north. Help had come from an unexpected source. As the vanguard of the II Corps thrust across the Chickahominy, Brig. Gen. John Sedgwick had crossed his eight-thousand-man division of three brigades at Grapevine Bridge. Although many of McClellan's spans had been swept away by the river's raging waters, Grapevine Bridge, named for the inch-thick vines that choked the nearby banks, remained largely intact. Marching to the sound of the guns through the swampy bottomlands in mud up to their knees, Sedgwick's men were viewed as godsent.

Although two of Sumner's divisions were eventually able to cross the Chickahominy, only one of the II Corps's artillery sections, the six guns of Lt. Edmund Kirby's Battery I, 1st U.S. Artillery, made it to the south bank.

Kirby was itching for an opportunity to avenge Bull Run, and though frequently bogged down in the mud, his battery had eventually reached the scene of the fighting. Following the infantry, the lieutenant placed his guns on a slight rise in front of a peach orchard near Fair Oaks Station and poured a deadly crossfire into the Confederates' lines. With reckless abandon, the determined Rebels charged the battery three times over open ground, determined to seize Kirby's guns. General Magruder was said to have recognized among the Union ranks not only his former subordinate in the old army but also some of the enlisted men, and he swore that the guns would be taken. When Kirby's artillerists ran short of grape and canister, they began firing shell and case shot without fuses, "so that, like canister, they burst leaving the muzzles with the lethal effect of giant shotguns."[66] The charging boys in gray were seen to "stagger, reel, then fall back" as the gunners, supported by infantry, took a deadly toll. Before the sun set, Kirby and his men had fired 343 rounds at the Confederates. Bull Run had been avenged.

Racing to and fro behind the front lines, Heintzelman was able to rally as many as eighteen hundred men from various regiments and sent them back to the front. The general "was everywhere, encouraging the troops by his coolness and bravery, and giving his orders to meet the ever-shifting positions of the field," an officer in the III Corps later recalled. With the Rebels still on the attack, Heintzelman feared that the Union center was near collapse. In the intense musketry he was almost killed and had his horse was shot from under him.[67]

On the Federal left flank south of the Williamsburg Road, Kearny's troops held their position, with each man firing as many as sixty rounds, then resupplying himself with cartridges from the dead and wounded. The division remained in position until dark and then fell back about a mile. Flashes from the hundreds of muskets could be seen all across the front as darkness descended on the battlefield. Then the "fire gradually slackened and ceased."[68] Heintzelman was able to create a defensive position along some unfinished rifle pits about a half-mile in the rear of the main line. Sixty artillery pieces were placed at strategic locations to repulse a renewed Rebel attack he was sure would come the next morning. But with Sumner reinforcing his right flank and Kearny fighting well on the left, the general felt far more secure than he had only hours earlier.

Heintzelman was furious at General Birney, who had been ordered to advance along the Richmond and York River Railroad with his New York and Maine troops. For reasons never fully explained, Birney halted a short distance after beginning his march. A second order and a third were sent directing him to come up, but the general failed to engage the enemy.

Had he done so, Heintzelman wrote, "I believe we would have driven back the enemy and have recaptured our artillery lost before I came on the field." Birney was placed under arrest for disobeying orders and replaced by Col. John Henry Hobart Ward of the 38th New York.[69]

After seven hours of horrendous combat, darkness crept through the woods and over the bloody battlefield, and again it began to rain. Only the gallantry of General Kearny and the steadiness of Couch's division, combined with the timely arrival of Sedgwick on the extreme right, had saved Heintzelman's corps from complete collapse. The dead and wounded lay scattered throughout the woods and fields. Teams of fatigued blue-clad soldiers gathered as many of the injured as they could find. Some of the severely wounded had been propped up by their comrades to prevent them from drowning or suffocating in the mud and water. All were sent to the field hospital at Savage's Station, many to be evacuated on the railroad to White House Landing. Yet for days every farmhouse in the vicinity was crowded with the wounded.

J. J. Marks, a minister assigned to the III Corps, remembered the ghastly scene as the wounded filled all the barns, sheds, outhouses, and hundreds of hastily erected tents at Savage's Station, where Heintzelman's chief of commissary, Captain McKelvy, had twenty bales of hay brought forward for the casualties to rest on. All night long, lanterns could be seen burning as the surgeons went about the task of amputating arms and legs. "Every few moments there was a shriek of some poor fellow under the knife," Marks recalled. "Others begged that some board might bear their name and be placed at the head of their grave." One dying soldier took his gold wedding ring and gave it to the minister, asking that it be sent to his wife. Among the wounded there were also a number of Confederates who had been badly injured, captured, and brought into Savage's Station. "I found a little boy apparently not more than twelve years of age," Reverend Marks remembered, his "long hair thrown back from a beautiful forehead, enabled me to see by the lantern light a very childlike face. His right leg had been amputated above the knee, and he was lying motionless and apparently breathless, and as white as snow. I bent over him, and put my fingers to his wrist, and discovered a pulse. I immediately said to my attendant: 'Why, the child is alive.' 'Yes Sir,' said he, opening his eyes, 'I am alive; will you not send me to my mother?' 'And where is your mother,' said I, 'my child.' 'In Sumterville, South Carolina,' he replied. 'Oh! Yes, my son, we will certainly send you to your mother.' 'Well, well,' said he, 'that is kind; I will go to sleep now.'"[70]

From late in the afternoon until two hours before midnight, Heintzelman telegraphed McClellan every thirty minutes. "Hold firm and repulse every and any attack. Recapture, if possible, any guns taken. Keep me fully informed of all that passes. Let me send to Washington as soon as possible the news that all is right," McClellan responded at 5 P.M. "Our loss in killed and wounded is considerable," Heintzelman informed his commander an hour later and continued to blame Birney for his misfortunes during the heaviest of the fighting. At 10 P.M. he telegraphed again, saying that he had food for three days and ammunition was being rushed from north of the Chickahominy River but that he badly needed entrenching tools.[71] An hour later McClellan decided the urgency of the situation required that the two should meet face to face at Dispatch Station on the Richmond and York River Railroad, two miles northeast of Bottom's Bridge, as soon as possible.

In the darkness Heintzelman thought of crossing at Bottom's Bridge on horseback but eventually decided to catch the train instead. Meeting with his commander at midnight, he found McClellan pale and weak. He was sure, he told Little Mac, that the Rebels would renew the attack the next morning, but with more reinforcements arriving from Sumner's II Corps and by deploying Hooker's division, he was confident they could be repulsed. McClellan "repeated and earnestly questioned me as [to] my ability to hold our position. I assured him that I could hold them against any force the rebels could bring against me," Heintzelman recorded. "I felt perfectly secure."[72] By 3 A.M. he was back at Savage's Station.

On the first day of the Battle of Seven Pines, the Confederates had suffered more than 5,000 casualties, while Union forces lost 3,828 men. "We have lost a great number killed and wounded," Heintzelman admitted. But a single casualty was to alter the course of the foundling Confederacy. At dusk Heintzelman's West Point classmate, Gen. Joseph Johnston, arrived on the battlefield near Fair Oaks. It was there, Johnston was sure, that the battle would be decided the next day. The Virginian was about two hundred yards north of the railroad station sitting on his horse atop a small knoll when he was hit in the right shoulder by a musket ball, and he was seen reeling in the saddle. Seconds later a shell exploded directly in front of him, sending a large fragment slamming into his chest and knocking him off his horse. Unconscious, the general was thought to be mortally wounded and was carried along Nine Mile Road on a stretcher by his staff. Although regaining consciousness just as President Davis arrived on the scene, Johnston was in great pain and was carried to his headquarters, where he was placed in an ambulance and taken to Richmond. Although he had broken ribs and other serious injuries, his wounds were not life threatening, but he would be out of action for six months. As the future would dictate, the musket ball and shell fragment that wounded Johnston at Seven Pines were the worst Federal shots of the war. Replacing Johnston was Heintzelman's friend from the Texas frontier Robert E. Lee, who would eclipse his predecessor in military prowess and turn the war in Virginia from one of defense for the Confederacy to one of offense.[73]

Fortunately for the Federals, the Confederate battle plan from the beginning had become botched and confused. Twenty-two years later Heintzelman would learn the specifics of Johnston's plan, and he became convinced that had everything gone as Johnston had hoped, the III Corps would "have been overwhelmed by numbers." Few "battles ever go entirely as their generals plan them," a prominent historian of the Peninsula Campaign has written, "but seldom does a battle stray so far from plans as Seven Pines on May 31, 1861."[74]

On Sunday, June 1, Heintzelman was awakened at dawn after only a few hours' sleep by the sound of musketry near Fair Oaks Station and realized that the battle was being renewed, just as he expected. Borrowing Captain McKeever's horse, he galloped off in the fog and rain toward the firing. Reaching the front at 7:30 A.M., he found the fighting was already heavy. Maj. Gen. A. P. Hill had hurled three brigades against Union forces north of the railroad and east of Fair Oaks Station. There Sedgwick had been reinforced by three brigades of Brig. Gen. Israel Richardson's division of the II Corps. Richardson had also brought across the Chickahominy the remainder of Sumner's artillery, fifty guns in all. Posted along the railroad tracks facing south, he had linked up with Kearny's and Hooker's divisions of the III Corps. General Howard commanded the 1st Brigade of Richardson's division, leading his men across the railroad and into the woods to force the Confederates all the way back to the Williamsburg Road. Only an hour after reaching the front, Heintzelman was able to wire McClellan that he was "driving the enemy back" and that the Rebels were in retreat on both sides of the railroad.[75] The contested ground had been gained at a heavy cost, however, as 60 percent of the casualties suffered on the second day of the Battle of Fair Oaks would be in Richardson's three brigades.

During the Federal advance, General Howard, who had fought well at Bull Run, had two horses shot from under him and was hit twice in the right arm, which was amputated the next day. After the operation, Kearny, who had lost his left arm in Mexico, tried to console the abolitionist from Maine: "I am sorry for you, but you must not mind it; the ladies will not think the less of you!"[76] Howard was said to have laughed and remarked that at least the two of them could buy their gloves together. They then exchanged a handshake with the hands left them.

As the low-lying clouds and drizzle gave way to bright sunshine, Brig. Gen. Daniel E. Sickles's Excelsior Brigade of Hooker's division, consisting of five New York regiments, also drove back the Rebels.[77] After one or two volleys of musketry, the 71st New York launched a vicious bayonet charge that sent the Confederates reeling. In the advance Col. John Cochrane's 65th New York Irish Regiment even captured the flag of the 23rd North Carolina. Before 2 P.M. General Casey's camp had been reoccupied.

To the south Heintzelman sent two of Hooker's brigades in a sweeping attack on the Rebel right and watched as Fighting Joe ordered his men to fix bayonets. Hooker formed the 5th and 6th New Jersey Regiments in the shape of a huge V, with the point toward the enemy, and personally led them in a furious charge between the Williamsburg Road and the railroad. The Federals "drove the enemy with the bayonet in gallant style more than a mile," Heintzelman gleefully wired McClellan. "The enemy is repulsed wherever he has appeared."[78] With his other two brigades committed to guarding Bottom's Bridge and the crossings of the Chickahominy and no reserves nearby, Hooker was reluctant to advance farther.

During the Federal counterattack, a hotel omnibus from Richmond carrying Confederate wounded to the city was captured with several "contrabands," who said the Rebel infantry, cavalry, and artillery were falling back everywhere. By two o'clock in the afternoon, Heintzelman had regained all the ground that had been lost the previous day, the combat now sputtering and grinding to a halt. He would later blame Kearny for his own reluctance to order an all-out attack on the retreating Rebels. "Gen Kearny rode up to me and begged me to stop," Heintzelman wrote. "He had no reliance on my reserves and thought if we were repulsed it would go hard with us and also said Gen. McClellan would in a day or two make a general advance and a premature advance would interfere with his plans."[79]

In the bright sun of mid-afternoon, McClellan and his staff appeared on the field to the wild cheers of the boys in blue. When applauded by one New Jersey regiment, Little Mac doffed his kepi in recognition: "Boys, you have licked them, right, left, and center, and we're going into Richmond." The general also took time to congratulate the commander of the III Corps: "You have done what I expected. You have whipped the enemy," Heintzelman remembered him saying. Later in appreciation, McClellan rewarded him with a straw hat, a small token of a job he thought well done. Yet Heintzelman resented the fact that too many in his command saw the popular McClellan as the hero of the battle and the reason why the Rebels had been driven back on the second day. That night Heintzelman retired to his tent at Savage's Station, where he slept "soundly notwithstanding the groans of the wounded lying around my tent."[80]

The next day, after riding along his entire front and seeing his men now entrenched, Heintzelman felt the III Corps was at last secure. Nevertheless, a telegram arrived from Marcy saying that observations from

Lowe's *Intrepid*, which had gone up at McClellan's headquarters four miles north of the battlefield, indicated there were still large concentrations of Rebel troops on Heintzelman's left and that he and Sumner should remain on the alert.

Although the first day of the Battle of Fair Oaks, or Seven Pines as the Rebels called it, had favored the Confederates, the Federals had undoubtedly won the contest the second day. Casualties were about equal on June 1, the Confederates losing 1,132 men and the Federals 1,203. With the fighting over, more Union wounded were taken in ambulances to the large field hospital at Savage's Station, where surgeons again continued the ghastly task of amputating arms and legs. Heintzelman watched as many of the patients were loaded onto boxcars and sent down the Peninsula to White House Landing, where steamboats and hospital ships waited to take them to hospitals throughout the North. "I am getting use[d] to the amputations and groans. I hear them all the time," he confessed.[81]

There was also the gruesome task of recovering and burying the dead from both armies. Four hundred Federals alone were buried near Seven Pines. A soldier in the 5th New Jersey remembered seeing dead Confederates "still laying where they fell on the second day after the battle, and [they] presented a horrible sight. They had swelled to double their natural size, and as a consequence their clothing had burst, thus exposing their bodies to the sun, and turning them as black as ink." There were so many shallow graves in proximity to the Union camps in the woods west of Savage's Station that every morning soldiers were forced "to clean the grounds of worms, that had been washed from the graves during the night by the rains." Moreover, when the rain "washed the dirt from the shallow graves, every morning a detail was sent out to cover up arms, legs and heads that had protruded from the ground during the night."[82] The battlefield was not only strewn with the dead, friend and foe alike, but also hundreds of small arms, caissons filled with ammunition, baggage wagons, and subsistence stores.

A few days later, while continuing to search for the wounded, some of whom had been lying unattended for more than forty-eight hours, a Union patrol advanced into the woods on the left of the Williamsburg Road near Seven Pines and came to an abandoned house near a small pond. In and around the water were the ghastly remains of over one hundred dead Confederates, "poor fellows, wounded, who had crawled there for a drink of water and were left to die." In the dense and tangled woods, many of the Rebel dead were never found.[83]

After the battle Heintzelman rode over the scene of some of the fiercest fighting. "A number of rebels are still unburied and some few of our own men," he observed. "We have collected nearly all the wounded. Some have been lying out two days. It is a hor[r]id sight, a battle field two days after the fight in the month of June." A *New York Times* reporter, while walking over the battlefield near Casey's original position, found the stench intolerable. In a space not forty feet square, fifty-seven Rebels lay dead. Some of "the dead rebels were found with pieces of paper pinned on their clothing, giving their name, with a request that they might be properly buried and their graves marked, so that when the war was over their remains could be found by their relatives and friends."[84]

In and around Seven Pines and Fair Oaks Station, the stench from hundreds of dead artillery horses was so unbearable that the corpses had to be burned. For days afterward, men from the III Corps were reluctant to go near the area west of Seven Pines because of the unbearable rankness from decaying horseflesh.

On June 3 Wilkeson of the *New York Tribune* returned to III Corps headquarters looking for his nephew, who was reported missing. After examining the last spot where the young soldier had been seen, he found the body, and Wilkeson had the "melancholy satisfaction" of burying his brother's son. John Wilkeson, father of the dead soldier, arrived at Savage's Station a week later not only to retrieve the remains but also to look for a brother who was in the III Corps and reported missing.[85]

At midnight on Sunday, June 1, from his forward camp, dashing General Sickles of Hooker's 2nd Brigade could hear the long roll being beat in the Rebel camps and a Confederate officer ordering his regiment into line. Three hours later he heard the tapping of assembly and the sound of Rebel artillery moving to their rear, the noisy retreat of the entire enemy army.[86] At daylight the next morning, Heintzelman sent out a small patrol that found the Rebels gone, and by 6 A.M. he was able to wire McClellan that his pickets were half a mile beyond where Casey had been attacked two days earlier.

With the Confederates in retreat, Hooker, with seven regiments of infantry and one of cavalry, was ordered out to locate the whereabouts of the Rebels south of the Chickahominy. Heintzelman asked Sumner to support Hooker, but the II Corps commander declined, saying that he was reluctant to do so without first receiving orders from McClellan. By noon Heintzelman telegraphed McClellan that Hooker was four miles from Richmond and had only encountered a few pickets. "What order shall I give General Hooker for tonight?" he asked. "He is advancing with great caution." To Heintzelman's surprise, orders were quickly received to recall Hooker.[87] This reconnaissance in force would be the closest the Army of the Potomac would get to Richmond prior to the collapse of the Confederacy in April 1865.

Realizing that the Rebels were in full retreat, Heintzelman was anxious to press them, but McClellan, who was shocked by the mangled corpses he witnessed at Seven Pines, was reluctant. Exhausted and still in ill health, Little Mac wanted to move his entire Army of the Potomac across the Chickahominy before moving on Richmond. Besides, General Porter was opposed to any lightning assault on the capital. In any case, such an attack would have been uncharacteristically bold and out of character for McClellan.[88]

Heintzelman would always be convinced that "the capture of Richmond itself was not beyond possibility." The bloody Battle of Fair Oaks, he wrote General Kearny's aide-de-camp, Capt. George Mindil, in 1874, "opened to us the road to Richmond, and that my move on Monday, had it been supported and followed up, we would have found it so." He always claimed that he was preparing his corps to pursue the Rebels into Richmond and that he only needed McClellan's blessing to do so. "I believe in following up a defeated army," he continued.[89] This ease with which the Army of the Potomac could have marched into Richmond, however, appears to have been little more than an afterthought.

Fair Oaks wrought carnage that could scarcely be imagined. In assessing the fighting, Heintzelman admitted that his corps had been badly mauled, but on the second day he had driven the Rebels back and recovered the ground lost the first day. The enemy, he insisted, had suffered far worse. He was correct. In this battle, the biggest and bloodiest thus far in the East and the largest in the war to that point except for Shiloh, Confederate casualties amounted to 6,134, with 980 men dead, while the Army of the Potomac suffered 5,031 casualties, with 790 dead.

Their backs now against Richmond, little had been gained for the Confederates at such a terrible cost. Yet the Army of the Potomac was no closer to capturing the city. Moreover, McClellan had become more cautious than ever, and his army began to dig in deep. Certain that the Confederates would remain in their earthworks, more and more guns and equipment were hauled forward for what McClellan expected to be a lengthy siege. The Union grip on Richmond was to make the siege of Yorktown seem trivial.

For his gallantry on the first day, Heintzelman was later brevetted a brigadier general in the Regular Army. As had been the case at Williamsburg, he had fought well but it was his able division commanders, Kearny and Hooker particularly, who had provided most of the thunder and much of the glory. "Bull" Sumner had also done well, acquitting himself for Williamsburg. Small of stature and with a raspy, almost inaudible voice, Heintzelman simply did not have the commanding presence on the battlefield exercised by Kearny or Hooker. Once again, especially in the early stages of the fighting, Heintzelman's indecisiveness and tendency to vacillate almost proved disastrous. Once committed to battle, however, no one was tougher, braver, or had more resolve than he. When McClellan's dispatch telling of the "Great Battle Before Richmond" reached Washington and was read aloud to "several successive crowds" at Willard's Hotel, there was the "wildest excitement and cheers for Gen. McClellan and Heintzelman and the Union."[90] In the Federal capital his star continued to rise.

Although the bloodletting had not altered the position of the two armies, Fair Oaks was to change the course of the war. A few miles to the west in the Confederate capital on the afternoon after the battle, without ceremony, Jefferson Davis named Gen. Robert E. Lee commander of what Lee would call the Army of Northern Virginia. Lee, who had been chief military advisor to Davis, would lead the most famous of all Confederate armies for the remainder of the war.

NINE

Seven Harrowing Days

DESPITE THE BLOODBATH AT FAIR OAKS, the III Corps remained an effective fighting force, and Heintzelman was confident that the Army of the Potomac could still take Richmond and end the war. In fact, his lines were so close to Richmond that one of his pickets climbed a tree west of Seven Pines and sketched the capital, complete with Confederate flags, which he sent to Margaret in Washington.[1] Yet McClellan sat frozen astride the Chickahominy, still pleading with Lincoln for McDowell's Army of the Rappahannock to join him in a final push against the Rebels. With Jackson still active in the Shenandoah Valley, though, Lincoln agreed only to release twelve regiments of the Pennsylvania Reserves commanded by Brig. Gen. George McCall.

Only days after Fair Oaks, rain again swept over the Union camps. "The whole country is flooded," Heintzelman wrote. "Our flank and front are perfectly covered by mud and water."[2] Confederate lines stretched for eight miles east and northeast of Richmond, and McClellan, sobered and intimidated by the recent battle, responded by digging in and rebuilding his bridges over the Chickahominy River. Using the Richmond and York River Railroad, he continued to bring up his large siege guns. After shifting his army to the south bank of the Chickahominy, he would shell Richmond and, if necessary, carry the city by assault.

Arriving back at headquarters on the afternoon of June 2, Heintzelman was shocked to see orders placing General Sumner in overall command of the II, III, and IV corps. "What does this mean?" he asked, fearing McClellan might be setting him up as a scapegoat for Union failures on the Peninsula. "We are better off than we were two days ago. We have lost heavily, but the rebels still more," he surmised. Although Heintzelman was no longer Keyes's superior, both McClellan and Sumner sent him orders for Keyes's IV Corps to follow. When Sumner issued orders he found trivial and meaningless, he persuaded McClellan to issue a second dictate "for Sumner not to interfere with my corps."[3] The command structure of the Army of the Potomac seemed to be in confusion.

Some of Heintzelman's most reliable intelligence on the Rebel army came via Richmond newspapers seized from prisoners and civilians. Two newspapers with "some valuable information" came from a woman who wandered into the Union lines "looking for her cow." On June 12 he read in the *Richmond Whig* that fifty-five-year-old General Lee, whom McClellan thought weak and cautious, had replaced the badly wounded General Johnston in command of the army defending Richmond. Heintzelman was always convinced, both during and after the war, that Johnston was a far better general than Lee, both as a tactician and as a strategist. He also read the Rebel version of Fair Oaks. President Davis claimed a great victory, saying that after the battle Heintzelman had asked permission to recover and bury the Federal dead. "How can a man put his name to such lies?" he angrily wrote in his journal.[4]

In the heat and humidity at corps headquarters at Savage's Station, distinguished guests and dignitaries arrived on the Richmond and York River Railroad to be greeted and entertained. Two weeks after Fair Oaks, several members of Congress, including a friend from the Committee on the Conduct of the War, Sen. Benjamin Wade, visited headquarters. Wade, Heintzelman wrote, "is bitter against the rebels and wants to deprive them of their property." Sen. Henry Mower Rice of Minnesota dropped by as did Rep. Frederick Augustus Conkling of New York and Sen. Ira Harris, also from New York, who brought along his wife and daughter. Senator Rice humored the general by saying that he had seen a piece of paper posted on a bulletin board in Washington saying that McDowell was preparing to defend Willard's Hotel, which was of "great strategic importance," but that he needed reinforcements. "This ridicule will kill him," Heintzelman concluded.[5]

Friends and politicians from Pennsylvania visited as did members of the Women's Central Relief Committee and the Sanitary Commission. High-ranking European military advisors, dispatched by their respective governments to observe the impending siege of Richmond, also showed up at headquarters. Gen. Juan Prim y Prats, who McClellan described as a "dark-faced, black-haired, bright, young looking man of 45," and a large retinue of Spaniards were entertained by Heintzelman and his staff and provided with eleven horses and an escort for a tour of the front. The Brazilian ambassador to the United States, Miguel María Lisboa, also came for a short visit. Heintzelman gave him one of his recently completed journals to take back to Washington to give to Margaret for safe keeping, fearing that it might be lost. More-frequent visitors included François Ferdinand Philippe Louis Marie d'Orléans, the Prince de Joinville, and his two youthful nephews, the Comte de Paris and the Duc de Chartres.[6]

Heintzelman now seemed obsessed with fears of another massive Confederate frontal attack. Awakened two or three times a night with alarming news from his pickets, he slept uneasily in his uniform. On more than one occasion, upon reports that his position was under attack, entire regiments were aroused and sent scurrying through the mud and woods into the night, only to discover the reports were exaggerated or even false. Mentally fatigued, the general sometimes noted his insecurity and frustrations in his journal: "I am awkwardly situated, as I don't know how far my command extends and I cannot do properly what is expected of me."[7] In the suffocating summer heat of the Virginia Tidewater, he became excessively miffed when he realized his headquarters tent had been pitched downwind from George Savage's hog pens.

With Wilkeson of the *New York Tribune* continuing to act as his unofficial editor, Heintzelman began collecting reports from his brigade commanders and then writing and revising his own lengthy report on the Battle of Fair Oaks. General Keyes's account, he thought, was exceptionally well written and thorough. That of General Kearny, however, was too full of "I." Brig. Gen. Henry M. Naglee's version of the actions of the 1st Brigade of General Casey's 2nd Division of Keyes's IV Corps was "the most extraordinary report" he had ever seen. Naglee, he commented, "did everything and no one else anything."[8]

Heintzelman was not surprised when, in the third week of June, a court-martial found Gen. David Birney innocent of the charges he had preferred against him. Birney's exoneration was largely due to the fact that Heintzelman's orders to him had been lost. Moreover, Kearny had given orders of his own than contradicted those of the corps commander. Regardless, the Southern-born, slavery-hating Birney was a "coward" in Heintzelman's eyes, or at least someone who avoided "close contact with the enemy."[9]

While on the Peninsula, Heintzelman continued to covet command of the Army of the Potomac, and his journal entries are tainted with egotism and cynical self-interest. If he were to ever command the army, though, McClellan would have to be removed, and if the Radicals took Little Mac down, Heintzelman must be careful that he did not go down with him. Still, he seemed elated when the *New York Tribune* reported a petition was circulating in Washington "signed by many Senators and Representatives praying for the promotion of Gen. Heintzelman to a Major Generalship in recognition of his gallantry . . . at Williamsburg." Pressed to make the appointment, especially by Pennsylvania's congressional delegation, President Lincoln agreed that Heintzelman was a "good egg" and that he "deserved it." Much to the general's chagrin, however, Lincoln did nothing. At the same time, he discovered that McClellan was opposed to the promotion, and when he inquired as to the reasons why, he was told by the always diplomatic General Marcy that Little Mac was only waiting for the right time. Later, when he rode over to McClellan's new headquarters east of Savage's Station to confront him, Little Mac complained that Margaret, who had become a regular guest of Mary Lincoln at the White House, had been speaking against him in Washington. Besides, McClellan asserted, there were bigger problems to worry about. He was particularly bitter, Heintzelman noted, that Lincoln was not answering his letters and telegrams, and when the president did respond, the replies were blunt and unsettling. "What a state of affairs! How can our cause succeed having such narrow minds at the helm?" Heintzelman responded.[10]

Margaret wrote from Washington to say that Texas Unionists were continuing to urge the president to send an army to the Lone Star State to assist "Union men" who were being persecuted, even hanged, and that they wanted her husband to command the expedition. "They say they don't believe the Texas Rangers would fight against me and all the Union men would join," Heintzelman noted in his journal. Although he was honored by the confidence the Texans placed in him, he did not care to go to Texas, a minor sideshow, for he believed the war would be won or lost in the East, not in the vast expanses of the Southwest.[11]

At 9 P.M. on the evening of Friday, June 13, just after Heintzelman had retired for the evening, Captain McKeever rushed in to say the telegraph was alive with news that the army's right flank had been turned by Confederate cavalry. The Rebel horsemen had already reached Tunstall's Station on the Richmond and York River Railroad in the Union rear, and the telegraph lines to Fortress Monroe had been cut. Sending some of his own cavalry to help guard Bottom's Bridge, Heintzelman seemed concerned about the safety of the vast Union depot at White House Landing.[12] Over the next two days, details of exactly what had happened trickled in to headquarters. General Lee had sent the twenty-nine-year-old Brig. Gen. James Ewell Brown "Jeb" Stuart on a daring reconnaissance. Selecting 1,200 men from four regiments, Stuart led a half-mile column around General Porter's right flank at Mechanicsville. At Old Church, a village south of the Pamunkey River, his horsemen had overrun and burned the camp of the 5th U.S. Cavalry, and at Tunstall's Station they had torched supply wagons and shot up a supply train. Riding through the night, the Rebels rebuilt the partially destroyed span over the Chickahominy River at Forge Bridge, southeast of Seven Pines; continued south across the Peninsula, cheered on by women who offered flowers; and then turned northwest to return to Richmond and be hailed as heroes. In three days Stuart had ridden 130 miles around the entire Army of the Potomac. Stuart's aging father-in-law, Brig. Gen. Philip St. George Cooke, was sent in pursuit, but he was unable to overtake his dashing son-in-law. To Heintzelman the Rebel raid amounted to "bad business."

The general was at corps headquarters on the evening of June 24 when he received a telegram from McClellan saying that the Confederates were continuing to entrench near the small hamlet of Mechanicsville on the Union right flank. Unaware that Lee was preparing to take the offensive with his army of ninety thousand men, the largest in the history of the Confederacy, McClellan had devised a plan calling for an advance by the Union center to secure Old Tavern, a short distance east of Richmond. Hoping to inch closer to capital so that his large-caliber guns could bombard the city, Little Mac ordered an advance on the morning of June 25. Heintzelman was to lead the III Corps west from Seven Pines along the Williamsburg Road while Sumner's II Corps anchored his right flank north of the Richmond and York River Railroad, beyond which Franklin's VI Corps held the line all the way to the Chickahominy River.

The next morning, with a light drizzle falling, Heintzelman was in the saddle by sunup and already at Casey's old redoubt a thousand yards west of Seven Pines. Orders went out for General Sickles's Excelsior Brigade and General Grover's brigade, both from Hooker's division, to advance along the Williamsburg Road. On the left Brig. Gen. John Cleveland Robinson's brigade of Kearny's division was to march at the same time. Moving across the headwaters of White Oak Swamp in the early morning mist, Sickles and Grover were slowed both by stiff Confederate resistance as well as by the swamps and dense vegetation; in many places their men were forced to wade through waste-deep water. So sluggish was progress through the heavy woods that Heintzelman was forced to send Birney's brigade to support the right wing.[13]

The Excelsior Brigade was initially delayed when the men had difficulty getting through their own abatis and the large number of trees felled in their front. Then they encountered determined opposition from the Rebels. In fact, the Federals were counterattacked several times, once by the 1st Louisiana Infantry, which lost 135 of 355 men, the highest number of casualties in any regiment on the field that day. The 71st New York, the only regiment in the Excelsior Brigade that had not seen combat at Williamsburg, panicked when someone in the ranks shouted that they were flanked and must retreat.[14] Only after considerable effort did Sickles restore order.

Much of the fighting this day was over the same ground that had been contested during Fair Oaks, and the stench from decaying horseflesh was so putrid as to be nearly unbearable. In the dense woods the opposing forces were sometimes within fifty feet of one another. Here the fighting

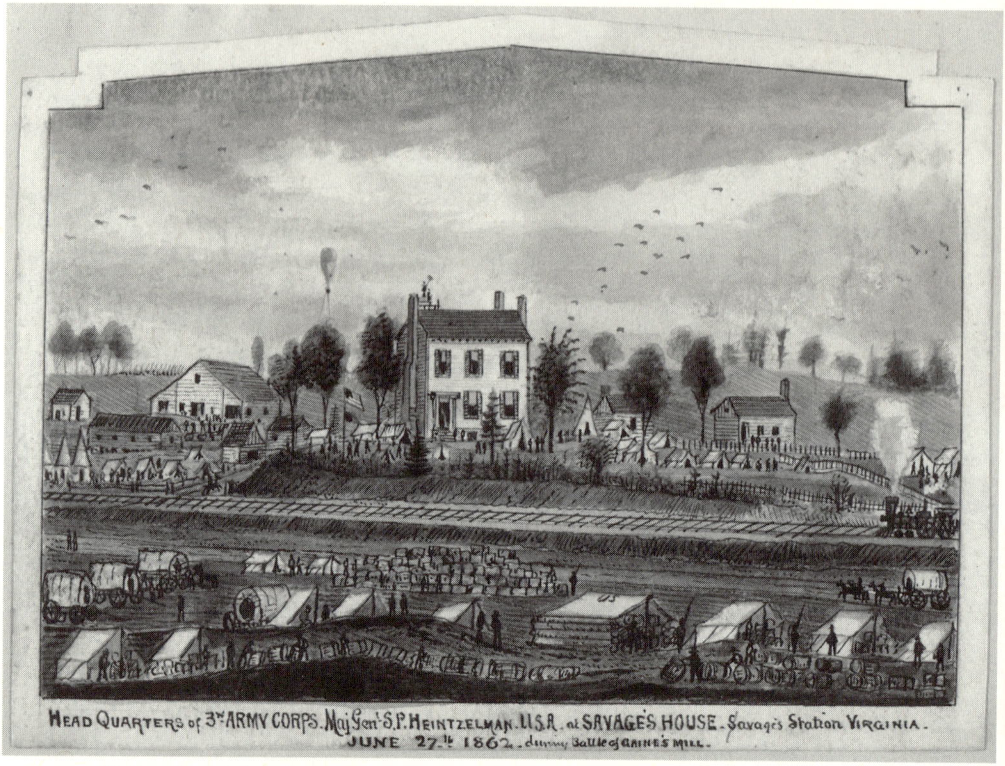

Heintzelman's headquarters at Savage's Station at the time of the Battle of Gaines's Mill. Sketch by Robert Knox Sneden. Virginia Historical Society.

raged for over three hours, and Hooker was able to advance less than half a mile. The battle in his sector was sharp, Grover reported, "varied by dashes of the enemy to break our front at different points." Overestimating the size of his enemy, as he was prone to do, Heintzelman telegraphed McClellan that Hooker's division was outnumbered and encountering stiff resistance. In what Hooker later asserted was a "misapprehension of my true condition," McClellan issued orders halting the advance and ordering a retreat. Hooker and most of the officers were taken aback and baffled by the order. Sickles protested that he was driving the Confederates back at the moment it arrived. In fact, the 73rd New York had advanced as far as a place called Brick Chimney beyond King's Schoolhouse on the edge of the woods at an intersection on the Williamsburg Road. Grover either never got the word to retreat or found that "he was too engaged to obey it and stayed where he was." At 1 P.M. McClellan appeared on the field with his staff and a large cavalry escort. The commander took off his coat and climbed a tree to view the Confederate positions and take some notes.

Back on the ground and still under enemy fire, he decided to renew the attack.[15]

With a battery of the 4th Artillery, Capt. Gustavus Adolphus DeRussy, chief of artillery in the III Corps, drove the enemy out of the woods along both sides of the Williamsburg Road and across a large open field. At about 5:30 P.M., with the Federals steadily advancing over ground they had contested and won only hours earlier, McClellan received an urgent dispatch from Fitz John Porter that Rebel forces were massing on his far right, north of the Chickahominy River, and he galloped off in haste, leaving Heintzelman in command. Everything was quiet for thirty minutes until the Rebels abruptly launched a vicious attack on Kearny's right, causing part of the Union line to give way. In what he called the "Engagement of the Orchards," Heintzelman was able to rush forward enough reinforcements to blunt the Confederate advance and force back the enemy. "This is the hour for which we have been longing," Kearny told his men as the Federals once again surged forward. "We'll see you in Richmond, General Phil," a soldier shouted back. "That's the spirit," Kearny replied.[16] By 9 P.M. the fighting had diminished, and Heintzelman returned to Savage's Station. The III Corps had fought well, and he considered the battle a victory. Although the occasional sound of musketry and artillery could be heard well into the night, the fighting had largely subsided. At the conclusion of the Battle of Oak Grove, or King's Schoolhouse as some called it, the III Corps was six hundred yards closer to Richmond.

Union casualties, mostly in Hooker's division, included 68 dead, 503 wounded, and 55 missing. Maj. Gen. Benjamin Huger's Confederates suffered 66 killed, 362 wounded, and 13 missing. Once again railroad cars took the Federal wounded to White House Landing, while army surgeons, working by lanterns through the night, went about the ghastly task of amputating arms and legs. Fearful of being attacked by Confederate reinforcements the next day, McClellan sent Heintzelman three informal orders basically repeating what he had telegraphed earlier. If attacked in force, the III Corps must fight from their entrenchments, in front of which the timber was to be cut, which would allow Union forces to utilize their advantages in artillery and musketry, and the III Corps could hold off a superior force.[17] Fearful that his left flank would be turned, Heintzelman spent an uneasy night, half-asleep in his uniform; the next day his men began to dig in again. But with Lee's daring attack at Mechanicsville June 26, the little-known Battle of Oak Grove became merely the beginning of the Seven Days Battle, one of the most decisive weeks of the war.

The day after Oak Grove, Heintzelman was at the front at daybreak, finding his pickets jittery and many of the regiments fearful of a Confederate attack. By sending a man up a tree with a spyglass, however, he learned that the enemy infantry and artillery were gone. "I felt more disposed to believe the enemy afraid we would attack them and that they were concentrating troops to repel us," he wrote.[18]

Certain of an attack north of the Chickahominy, McClellan telegraphed his corps commanders south of the river asking for reinforcements. Saying that he could hold his position "with four brigades for twenty-four hours," Heintzelman offered two brigades, despite the fact that most of his men were "so tired and worn out that I fear they would not be in a condition to fight after making a march of any distance."[19] Franklin and Sumner refused to assist, however, saying that the Rebel forces in their front were simply too strong for any of their troops to be released.

Had Heintzelman and McClellan known that the bulk of Lee's army was north of the Chickahominy preparing to strike the exposed Federal right flank at Mechanicsville, they might have launched an all-out assault south of the river and probably broken through to Richmond. Generals Magruder and Huger, who commanded Rebel forces south of the Chickahominy, had fewer than twenty-five thousand men. Here along lines that stretched over four miles, the Confederates were outnumbered more than three to one. But as he had done at Yorktown, Magruder deceived the Union generals by constantly repositioning his forces and staging noisy artillery barrages. On the evening of June 13, for example, Union pickets reported seeing a strange array of signal lanterns, Roman candles, and rockets along the Rebel front lines, an obvious attempt, Heintzelman concluded, "to deceive us as to their movements."[20]

At Beaver Dam Creek, near the small crossroads village of Mechanicsville, on June 26, Lee's attack on McClellan's right flank went as badly as Johnston's assault at Fair Oaks. Hoping to drive the Federals out of their defenses, Lee was counting on the timely arrival of Stonewall Jackson's 18,000-man army of "foot cavalry" from the Shenandoah Valley, which was scheduled to attack Porter's right and rear early that morning. Moving his command 120 miles by rail out of the valley, Jackson then marched his men up to 36 miles a day in the heat. Personally exhausted himself, he misunderstood Lee's orders, fell six hours behind schedule, and then failed to show at all. Impatient and not willing to wait, Lee sent the divisions of A. P. Hill, D. H. Hill, and James Longstreet to attack Porter's 5th Corps, dug in on the high ground beyond Beaver Dam Creek, only to be bloodily repulsed. Of the 56,000 men he had hoped to deploy, hardly 11,000 went into action. In his first major battle, Lee had failed miserably. The Rebels lost 1,484 men killed and wounded, while Porter suffered fewer than 400 casualties.

Upon arriving at Porter's headquarters, McClellan was ecstatic, wiring Washington of yet another great victory. But the Union right flank remained exposed. Knowing that Jackson had yet to bring his three small divisions into action, McClellan ordered Porter to withdraw his corps during the night. In reality, Little Mac lacked the will to fight, and he was somewhat unnerved. Although Lee had taken a beating at Beaver Dam Creek, and Confederate dead and wounded were again pouring into Richmond, he had seized the initiative.

Porter withdrew his command four miles to a strong line just east of Gaines's Mill, a gristmill owned by a fire-eating secessionist named William G. Gaines. Just as he had done at Beaver Dam Creek, the general was able to deploy his divisions on high ground, this time beyond Boatswain's Creek. He positioned the artillery on the heights and ordered his troops to quickly build crude breastworks and dig rifle pits. With A. P. Hill leading the attack, Lee hurled his army of 57,000 men against Porter's 34,000 Federals. On the afternoon of June 27, Heintzelman could hear the sounds of heavy guns beyond the Chickahominy. "The firing is very steady and continues although it is getting dark," he wrote. "There must be quite a battle."[21]

Enjoying much more unity of command than at Mechanicsville, Lee brought up Longstreet's division on the Confederate right, followed by Jackson, who was late again. Committing all his reserves, Porter successfully repulsed attack after attack, the enemy assaults being disjointed and poorly coordinated, and inflicted terrible casualties among the Southerners. At 7 P.M., willing to gamble everything, Lee was finally able to muster his forces for an all-out attack. Gen. John Bell Hood's Texas Brigade of Maj. Gen. W. H. C. Whiting's division launched a ferocious bayonet charge that broke the Union center. Although half of the men in the 4th Texas, which Hood bragged that he could "double-quick to the gates of hell," were killed or wounded, the tide had turned. With the center broken, Porter's flanks began to collapse. Hardest hit was the 4th New Jersey, with only 83 of 680 members escaping death or capture. The battle then turned into a rout. The greater part of two Union regiments were cut off and captured as the Rebels pressed their pursuit and repulsed a counterattack by the 5th U.S. Cavalry. The Federals also lost twenty-two pieces of artillery.

With night descending over the battlefield and both armies exhausted, the fighting stopped. In the darkness the shattered V Corps, leaving their badly wounded behind, staggered across the Chickahominy, burning the bridges in their retreat. Only the timely arrival of two brigades from Sumner's II Corps saved Porter from complete disaster. Gaines's Mill would be remembered as the bloodiest and costliest battle of the Seven Days. Porter had lost 894 men killed, 3,114 wounded, and 2,829 captured. Lee's casualties were even higher, with 1,483 killed, 6,402 wounded, and 108 missing.[22] In all, the two armies lost more than 15,000 men in nine hours of fighting. McClellan was now convinced that the Peninsula offensive had failed; his confidence shattered, he was near panic.

As the fighting raged north of the Chickahominy, Heintzelman continued to hold the line west of Fair Oaks south of the river. In fact, 64,000 men in blue sat idly by while Porter was being routed only miles away at Gaines's Mill. Shortly before midnight on June 27, Heintzelman recorded how McClellan summoned his corps commanders to his headquarters. "On the other side of the Chickahominy the day is lost," he told them. Before a bonfire of blazing pine knots in front of his tent, McClellan, who never questioned Allan Pinkerton's Secret Service estimation that Lee had 200,000 men, offered two alternatives for his generals to consider. One was to concentrate the army north of the Chickahominy and hurl it at Lee in one decisive battle. "But if we were defeated," Heintzelman conjectured, "the Army and the country would be lost."[23] A second alternative was more viable, McClellan argued. The Army of the Potomac must be evacuated from in front of Richmond and moved south to the James River, where it would have the advantage of a new supply base and the protection of a flotilla of Union gunboats. What Heintzelman and the other corps commanders did not know was that this council of war was an exercise in pseudo-democracy. Prior to the meeting, McClellan had already decided to abandon the campaign.

Upon hearing that McClellan was ordering a retreat, both Hooker and Kearny, bypassing Heintzelman, rushed to army headquarters to protest. Kearny was so verbally abusive in talking of cowardice and treason that some were surprised that McClellan did not have him arrested for insubordination. Kearny and Hooker, whose pickets were less than five miles from the Rebel capital, argued that if an attack were pushed south of the Chickahominy, Richmond could be captured. If Heintzelman was privy to the vociferous protests of his division commanders, he failed to make mention of it in his journal.[24]

Early on the morning of June 28, the Army of the Potomac began withdrawing to the James River. Keyes's IV Corps and Porter's V Corps were to move in advance to establish defensive positions at Malvern Hill, not far from the banks of the James, while the three remaining corps would slow Lee's anticipated advance. Pulling back from positions west of the Seven Pines battlefield, the III Corps left campfires burning along the picket lines to deceive the Rebels. Complicating the movement was the fact that most roads in the upper Peninsula radiated out from Richmond west to east, and there were few dependable roads running north to south.

Northeast of Heintzelman's headquarters at the vast two-square-mile military depot at White House Landing, all was chaos as valuable supplies were loaded on barges towed by steamers for transfer to the James River. Dozens of soldiers and civilian workers frantically sought a place on the overcrowded vessels as vast quantities of valuable foodstuffs and military equipment that could not be transported went up in smoke. Rail cars and five locomotives also were set afire. During the evacuation, vengeful soldiers of the 93rd New York burned the historic White House Plantation house—all that remained were two towering chimneys among the ashes. The railroad bridge on the Chickahominy as well as Bottom's Bridge of the Williamsburg Road were torched too.

East of Richmond, long columns of men and animals, the latter hauling field guns and wagons, began streaming east on the Williamsburg Road before turning south to the bridges over White Oak Swamp. During the "change of base," the 99,000 men of the Army of the Potomac took with them 281 pieces of field artillery, twenty-six heavy siege guns, as many as three thousand wagons and ambulances, and 2,500 head of beef. Heintzelman was up before dawn on the morning of June 28 and rode off in the fog to spend most of the day sending off his artillery and supply wagons in what he called a "stampede." To Hooker, the Army of the Potomac retreated like a parcel of sheep. Like Kearny, he despised McClellan. Sumner was so defiant that he refused to retreat until McClellan sent one of his aides with direct orders telling him to do so, even threatening to have Sumner arrested should he refuse.[25] Retreating over the ground west of Fair Oaks that had been won with so much blood made no sense to many of the bluecoats in the III Corps.

Heintzelman's greatest regret in retreating from Savage's Station was that 2,300 sick and wounded soldiers had to be left behind. There was simply no way to evacuate them. The Rebels had gained possession of the Richmond and York River Railroad on the north side of the Chickahominy, and the last train had stopped running at 11 A.M. on June 28. So many sick and wounded were left at the huge field hospital that they filled every room on both floors of Savage's plantation house, the adjoining slave quarters, out buildings, and more than one hundred army tents, even overflowing onto the grounds, placed under large trees and along the railroad tracks. Exhausted surgeons worked in front of their tents and in the main house, amputating arms and legs by the hundreds. "The walls and floors were spattered with blood and dozens of officers were lying on the floor in hallways awaiting their turn. Some were moaning in pain, while others were fast asleep. A general feeling of despondency prevailed," Sneden recorded.[26] Fortunately, a number of Union surgeons and attendants stayed behind to care for the men. Ironically, even though McClellan had given orders that anyone who could not walk would have to be left behind, five hundred empty ambulances would be going south to the James River (to be used for the wounded from future battles, some speculated). Hobbling on improvised crutches, only three hundred of the sick and wounded managed to get away. In the intolerable heat, though, they were frequently spotted by the roadside and in the woods, where they stopped to rest and adjust their bloody bandages.

While meeting with Sumner, Sedgwick, Franklin, and a number of their staff officers, all of whom it was said were "taking the situation cooly," Heintzelman agreed that the vast stores of ammunition in Savage's barn and coach house and stacked all around the train station would have to be destroyed. "When I reached General Heintzelman's tent," Reverend Marks remembered, "I found everything foreshadowed an immediate removal . . . orderlies hurrying backwards and forewards in the wildest haste—surgeons, commissaries, colonels, crowding for directions and help." The general was said to have "issued the orders with all the calmness of one familiar with the greatest dangers." He sent Lt. Henry Norton, his nephew and aide, with some cavalry and the 15th Massachusetts to supervise the destruction of the depot. After moving the wounded, the buildings were set on fire. "Shells went screaming and bursting in the air. Volumes of white smoke, mixed with flying timbers, enveloped the house and grounds for ten minutes," Sneden observed. Savage's large icehouse caught fire, melting twenty tons of ice. Seventeen cars filled with tons of shot and shell and hundreds of barrels of gunpowder were also set ablaze. The engine attached to them was set in motion by the engineer opening the throttle, then jumping from the train to escape. As the cars began to explode along the tracks, the train went plunging off the partly destroyed railroad bridge over the Chickahominy. Thousands of dollars in sutler's supplies were stacked two-stories high and consigned to the flames; one Bostonian said the pile of supplies was as big as Faneuil Hall. Barrels of whiskey exploded, as did a warehouse filled with bacon. Huge black plumes of smoke went bellowing into the clear sky. Although the 15th Massachusetts spent all day in the hot sun destroying the valuable supplies and sutler's stores, a Georgia soldier later bragged that in the ruins at Savage's Station, "you could find anything from a siege gun to a cigar."[27]

Realizing the Army of the Potomac was retreating to the James River and not down the Peninsula, Lee decided to send his entire army to destroy the retreating Federals. General Magruder, who had been holding the Confederate line east of Richmond, would advance east toward Fair Oaks and Savage's Station along the Richmond and York River Railroad and strike the Union rear with fourteen thousand infantry, while Stonewall Jackson would cross the Chickahominy at the repaired Grapevine Bridge and move south to link up with Magruder's left. Fresh from their victory at Gaines's Mill, Longstreet and A. P. Hill would cross the Chickahominy

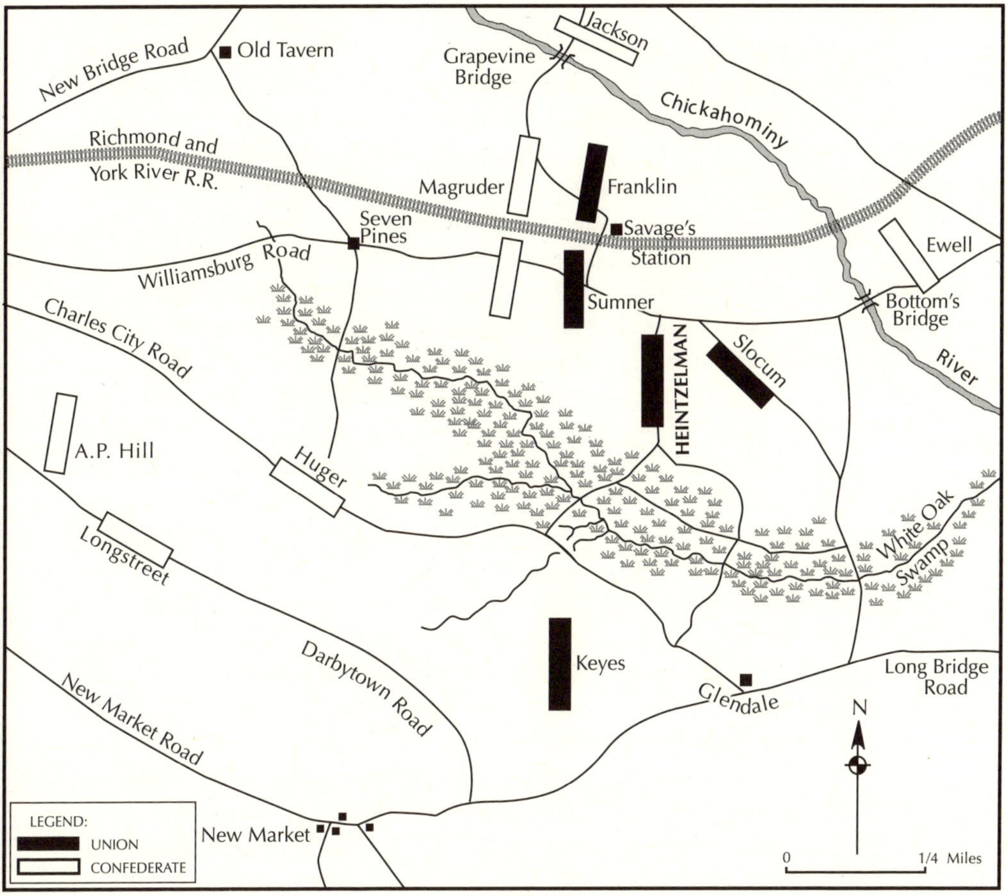

Battle of Savage's Station,
June 29, 1862

downstream with their divisions, join General Huger, and intercept McClellan south of White Oak Swamp.

White clouds of battle smoke appeared above the treetops three miles east of Fair Oaks Station at 11 A.M. on June 28, signaling that Magruder had smashed into Sumner's II Corps. Heintzelman rode rapidly to the front to find large numbers of Sumner's troops fleeing. Realizing that his right flank was dangerously exposed, he immediately ordered Hooker and Kearny to withdraw and reform their lines just west of Savage's Station.[28] Supported by forty cannons, the Federal infantry stopped the Rebel advance in its tracks. The artillery, in particular, inflicted terrible losses on Magruder's gray-clad infantry. But the fierceness of the Rebel attack also cost Sumner.

The 5th Vermont, which had charged a regiment of Rebels concealed in the woods south of the Williamsburg Road, lost 209 of its 428 men.

In the woods just west of Heintzelman's headquarters, Sneden met "lines of wounded men hobbling toward Savage's Station by the railroad tracks. Many had been so badly wounded they sat on the ground to die." Ambulances and wagons "were all full of dying and desperately wounded men. Thin streams of blood ran out the sides and bottoms of the vehicles."[29] At 5 P.M. Rebels yelling like Comanches appeared in the woods to the west. Suddenly a strange-looking railroad car followed by flatcars with Confederate sharpshooters on board and protected by cotton bails, all pushed by a locomotive, appeared in the clearing. Mounted on the first flatcar was a 30-pounder railroad gun, protected by a hood built of iron. One shot from the cannon struck the remains of Savage's ruined icehouse. When a Union regiment approached the rear of the armored train, intending to tear up the track, the train suddenly retracted a half-mile backward, all the while continuing to fire. Nicknamed the "Land Merrimack" and built by the Confederate Navy, it was the first armored railroad battery ever used in warfare. Proving too cumbersome in practice, it was never used again.

Having seized large quantities of whiskey in the Federal camps, many of the advancing Confederates became intoxicated. With Jackson nowhere in sight and darkness engulfing the battlefield, a final Rebel push sputtered, and Magruder called off the attack. By 9 P.M., with the Rebels in possession of Savage's Station, the fighting ended. But by battling Magruder to a near stalemate, Sumner had bought McClellan valuable time. The contest for Savage's Station, nevertheless, had cost the Federals some 919 men, while Magruder lost 444.[30]

Caught up in the maelstrom at the rear were Heintzelman's III Corps and half of Franklin's VI Corps. With McClellan in advance of the army's retreat, the corps commanders were left largely on their own. Heintzelman met with Franklin, who reported that the Confederates were beginning to cross the Chickahominy. Two hours later a cavalry officer galloped up to say the Rebels had successfully repaired several bridges on the river and were crossing in large numbers.

For years to come, considerable controversy raged over Heintzelman's withdrawal of his III Corps from Savage's Station. McClellan would later assert that Heintzelman misunderstood his orders and withdrew prematurely. Regardless, convinced that Sumner and Franklin had ample forces to withstand any attack, Heintzelman, without consulting either general, issued orders for the III Corps to move across White Oak Swamp. It was a near fatal tactical blunder, undoubtedly the biggest mistake he would make during the entire war. On the defensive, then and later, Heintzelman tried to rationalize his decision. He had been given a map by one of McClellan's aides, he said, and even shown the route the III Corps was to take in the retreat. By remaining he "would have been no aid to General Sumner, as he already had more troops than he could defile through the narrow road in his rear, and the road I took covered his left flank." To have held his position until dark, and after Franklin and Sumner had fallen back, would have exposed his right flank and rear, and his only line of retreat would have been cut off. "I would have lost my entire corps," Heintzelman asserted. Having little respect for the sixty-five-year-old Sumner and considering him somewhat of an alarmist, the digression may not have been inadvertent. Afterward, Sumner was so incensed that Heintzelman had not bothered to inform him of his withdrawal that he refused to speak to the general.[31]

At sundown, just as the Rebels were approaching Savage's Station, Heintzelman and his staff departed in haste, leaving their tents standing for the wounded. Despite the obvious chaos, Samuel Peter would write Margaret a few days later that the "withdrawal was made splendidly." Guided by fugitive slaves, he decided to take the road leading toward Brackett's Ford instead of the main road south from Bottom's Bridge. For more than a mile, the rear guard was closely pressed by advance parties of Rebels until one last assault was bloodily repulsed by Federal artillery firing canister. Just past Linden Farm, where Heintzelman once had his headquarters and where now stood a Union hospital, the column turned south toward White Oak Swamp and the James River. As the retreat continued into the night, the men of the III Corps entered a dense pine forest—and great confusion. Masses of troops and wagons crowded the road. Teamsters lashed and swore at their mules. Hundreds of wounded men, along with disoriented stragglers, hobbled along. In the darkness the fatigued soldiers threw down their haversacks, blankets, overcoats, and much of their equipment. So many garments were discarded along the route that one soldier remembered the roadside being "literally blue with clothes." There was "a great deal of property lost and destroyed on the retreat. I saw more provisions lost than you can raise on your farm in your lifetime," a soldier in the 81st New York wrote his brother.[32] Without canteens, some men drank the muddy water that collected in the ruts left by the passing artillery.

In the heart of White Oak Swamp, at midnight it began to rain as lightning flashed and the thunder roared. Horses pulling a large siege gun gave out, and the cannon had to be spiked and abandoned. In the green mire of the swamp, Heintzelman and his staff slowly followed Hooker's division across Brackett's Ford at White Oak Swamp Creek. At 3 A.M. the rain stopped, and at sunup on June 29, Heintzelman struck the Charles City Road a mile north from where it entered the Quaker Road at Glendale. For him, badly fatigued and unable to concentrate, the Union retreat from in front of Richmond, along with the disheartening and fatiguing march through the night, constituted the darkest hours of his military career since the flight from Bull Run. It was one of the few times in his life that Heintzelman did not have the mental energy for daily entries in his journal.

By 10 A.M. Monday, June 30, the rear guard of the Army of the Potomac was safely across White Oak Swamp. By this time McClellan's retreating and battered command stretched for ten miles all the way to Malvern Hill on the James River. The focus of attention now was the hamlet of Glendale, a dangerous bottleneck where the army was vulnerable to attack. There the Charles City Road to Richmond intersected the Long Bridge Road that ran north through White Oak Swamp to Bottom's Bridge on the Chickahominy. A third road, the Quaker Road, led south to Malvern Hill. Lee realized that Glendale offered him an excellent opportunity to cut off the Army of the Potomac from the James River and destroy it, and he planned to descend on the village with ten of his eleven divisions, 71,000 men in all. Advancing with an overwhelming force in several columns, he would split McClellan's dispirited Federals and destroy them.

Reaching Glendale at sunup, Heintzelman set up his headquarters at the Nelson House on Quaker Road, just south of where Sumner had established his headquarters. He also had breakfast with McClellan before Little Mac rode off for the James River. The commanding general was, Heintzelman would say later, perhaps "the most extraordinary man I ever saw. I do not see how any man could leave so much to others; and be so confident that everything would go just right."[33] Hoping to slow the advancing Rebels, he departed only after giving orders to blow up the bridge over White Oak Swamp Creek, northeast of Glendale, and to fell trees across the road south of the bridge and along the Charles City Road toward Richmond.

At the bridge Stonewall Jackson's "foot cavalry" caught up with the Federal rear guard of Israel Richardson's division of the II Corps and Gen. "Baldy" Smith's division of the VI Corps. Repairing the span, which the enemy had only partly destroyed, Jackson pressed the Federals hard. Although the 63rd Pennsylvania, supported by artillery, charged and drove the Confederates back three times, Jackson kept coming.

Realizing that another bloody battle was imminent, Heintzelman rode off to deploy the III Corps. He first positioned Kearny's three brigades on the right to guard any advance along the Charles City Road. Kearny had been dangerously exposed but had fallen back closer to Glendale to what was thought to be a much stronger position. In fact, he was so secure, Heintzelman noted, that he could "advance upon Richmond." General McCall's division of Pennsylvania Reserves from Keyes's V Corps, which had borne the brunt of the fighting at Gaines's Mill, anchored the center of the Union lines west of the Charles City and Quaker roads. Hooker's dependable division anchored the left flank, in support was Sedgwick's division of Sumner's II Corps. Complicating the Federal command structure was the fact that McClellan, his courage completely eroded, was already four miles away on the James River.[34]

At 2 P.M. one of General Birney's aides raced up to the Nelson House to report that the Confederates were advancing in force on the Charles City Road, and by 3:30 P.M. Heintzelman could detect the sound of artillery and musketry. "The Rebel yells could be heard above the crashing musketry and the sharp report of the rifle cannon. A line of battle smoke a mile long showed over the tree tops, with the puffs of bursting shells still higher in the air," Sneden recalled. At 5 P.M. A. P. Hill slammed into McCall's troops and, with bayonets fixed, seized two artillery batteries, including the German Light Artillery, which had been recruited from the German population of New York City. The Virginians also overran the 12th Pennsylvania, shattering McCall's left flank. The badly fatigued Pennsylvania regiments were fighting their third battle in five days, and all twenty-six of their guns now were either captured or abandoned. In less than an hour, McCall's entire division had given way, suffering more than a thousand casualties; the Confederate onslaught also forced Kearny's left to give way. "If anyone tells you that the rebels will not fight, just tell them to come down to this neck of the country and try them on," a soldier in the 7th Pennsylvania wrote his family.[35] But the extent of McCall's collapse at Glendale would be debated for decades.

Learning of this potential disaster, Heintzelman spurred his horse toward the Union center, arriving just in time to see the Pennsylvanians falling back out of the woods into an open field. For a while he was doubtful if the III Corps could hold its position. Hastily consulting with Sumner, they decided to send Sedgwick's division into the breach left by McCall. At the same time, Heintzelman sent Captain DeRussy's 4th Artillery into position on Sedgwick's right to shell the advancing Confederates. On the east side of the Quaker Road, not far from the Nelson House, at the edge of the woods near another battery, Heintzelman sat on horseback observing the fighting with "Bull" Sumner. As he watched the Rebels advance across an open field, the Confederates opened fire with musketry, and he was hit on the left wrist by a spent Minié ball that inflicted a "severe contusion." For several days he would be unable to use the wrist. At first he thought it was broken but discovered that it was only badly bruised. Seconds later Sumner too was struck in the arm by a spent ball while a second shot grazed the back of one of his hands.[36]

West of the Quaker Road, McCall's retreat also exposed the Union right flank, but Hooker and his three brigades held fast. With guns posted on high ground and infantry in front, the Federals took a terrible toll on Hill's Division as it advanced out of the woods. As the Rebel attack was seen to fizzle, Hooker attacked "in the handsomest manner with great slaughter." Simultaneously on the Union right, the Rebels renewed their attack on Kearny's division, only to be repulsed too with great loss. The Federal artillery, consisting of six guns of Capt. James Thompson's Battery G, 2nd U.S. Artillery and a two-gun section of a Rhode Island battery, took an appalling toll by hurling spherical case at the charging Rebels. When the Confederates charged a second time, Thompson switched to canister and then to double rounds of canister. "I never saw such slaughter," Capt. Charles B. Haydon of the 2nd Michigan wrote. "The head of the column seemed to sink into the ground. Beyond a certain point they could not come." Kearny's lines became frayed but held. A third Confederate assault was heroically repulsed by the 63rd Pennsylvania and part of the 37th New York.[37]

In brutal, bloody hand-to-hand combat, Kearny was able not only to halt Hill's breakthrough but also to mount a savage counterattack that drove the Confederates back. In the heat of battle, Kearny, who always led from the front, found himself surrounded in the smoky woods and was almost captured or killed by enemy skirmishers. After several hours of fighting, darkness settled in, and the bloodletting abated. But even during the night, small units from the two armies continued to blunder into one another. The Federals noticed the red glare of torches moving through the woods as the Confederates searched for their wounded. And over the hum of insects and the calls of the whippoorwill was an eerie, dreadful sound. "The unbroken, mournful wail of human suffering," Hooker wrote, "was all that we heard from Glendale during the long dismal night."[38]

The ground around R. H. Nelson's farm was covered with the dead and dying. The Union wounded filled Willis Methodist Church, where they lay on the pew cushions on the floor as surgeons feverishly worked to save lives by amputating legs and arms, tossing the shattered limbs into a pile in the corner of the church. More surgeons in tents also commenced the grueling and ghastly task of emergency amputation. At Glendale, Lee lost 3,673 men, including 638 dead, 2,814 wounded, and 221 missing, while the Federals suffered 3,797 casualties, including 297 dead, 1,696 wounded, and 1,804 missing; among the captured was General McCall himself. The Confederate wounded were again carried into Richmond, while ambulances took the Federals to Haxell's Landing on the James River, four miles to the south. In this pivotal battle, 51,000 Confederates, men Lee had intended to throw into the fray, did not fire a single shot. More important was the fact that he lost his last chance to stop the Union retreat to the James.[39]

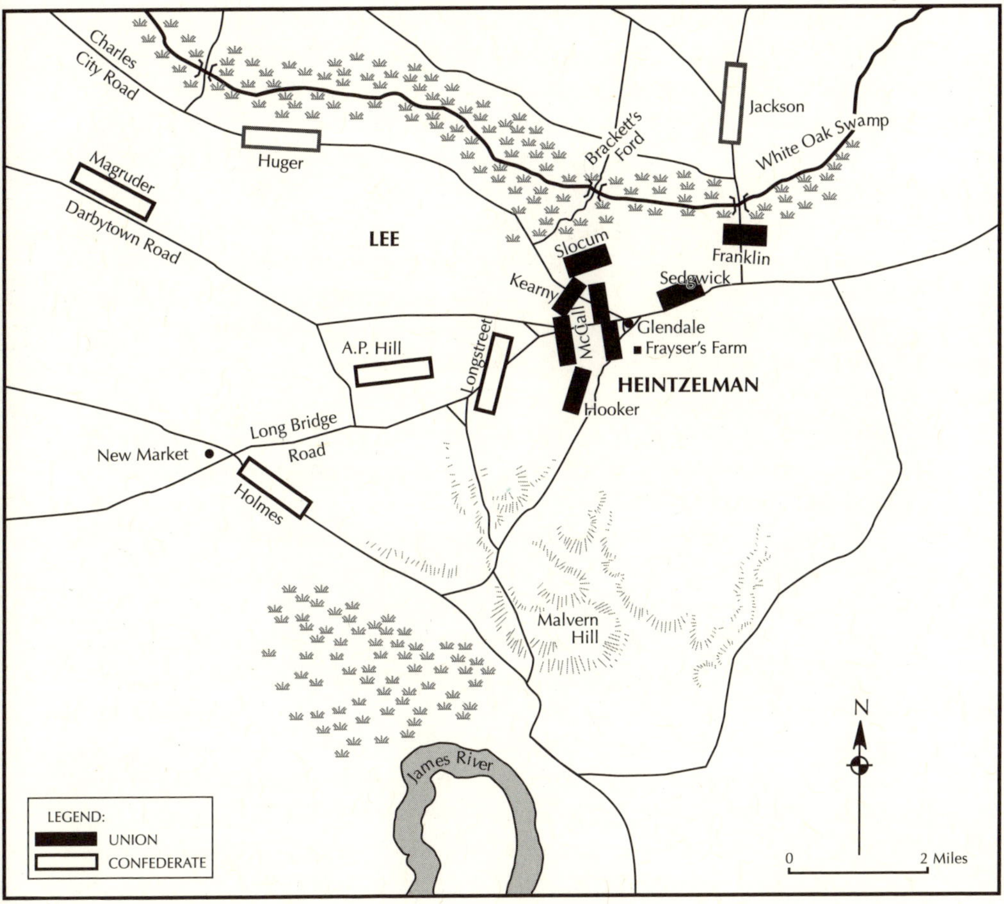

Battle of Glendale,
June 30, 1862

At sunset Heintzelman sent one of his aides to McClellan with a detailed oral report of the bloody events of the day. Although the Confederates had failed to break the Union lines, Heintzelman feared that Lee would renew the attack with fresh reinforcements in the morning, and he warned McClellan that his men were "worn out" and could not hold. The III Corps was also in need of ammunition and provisions, and he asked for permission to withdraw. To make sure that the general received his report, he sent it separately by three of Little Mac's own aides. At the same time, Heintzelman received the alarming news that Franklin, who had been holding the bridge over White Oak Swamp Creek northeast of Glendale, had withdrawn. "I could not believe it," he wrote. His entire right flank and rear were now exposed. Lt. Leavitt Hunt was sent racing to find Franklin and "beg him to hold on a little."[40] When the aide returned at midnight to say that Franklin could not be found and that most of his men were in retreat, Heintzelman quickly met with Brig. Gen. Henry W. Slocum of the VI Corps, who had been supporting Kearny on the far right. The two agreed that they "could not wait any longer," and though they had not heard from McClellan, the situation demanded a general withdrawal. Slocum would lead the retreat, followed by Kearny and then Hooker. Not wanting to make the same mistake he had made at Savage's Station, Heintzelman rode off in the darkness to tell Sumner in person of his decision. A note was hastily sent to McClellan as Sumner prepared to follow Hooker south to the James.

Leaving the Nelson House in the darkness at 1 A.M., Heintzelman made the three mile ride to Malvern Hill with his staff in little more than an hour. Immediately reporting to McClellan, who was at Porter's headquarters, with the details of the Battle of Glendale, he was told to consult with Porter and Brig. Gen. John Gross Barnard, the army's chief engineer, to determine where the III Corps should be deployed. Finally able to find the two generals in the darkness, they agreed that nothing could be done until daylight. Heintzelman was surprised that everyone at Porter's headquarters "knew but little of the country." Sleeping on the ground in his clothes until daylight, he sent several of his staff to find Hooker and Kearny. Once the two division commanders had been contacted, he rode back to Porter's headquarters, and Barnard showed him where the III Corps should deploy. Leaving his staff officers to position Hooker's and Kearny's troops, he rode with McClellan around the entire Union line to the James River, where the *Galena* and *Mahaska* were anchored. The tents of III Corps headquarters were pitched under some trees on the lawn of the Haxall House near a small bridge spanning Turkey Creek, within a half-mile of the gunboats. Although he acknowledged that the Army of the Potomac was in a "very strong position," he feared the lines were too weak and that Lee could overwhelm them if he concentrated his forces on a particular salient. "The line I thought too long for our number of troops but we could not well occupy less."[41] The day opened hot and sultry, and it was 10 A.M. by the time he returned to the crest of the hill where Porter had established V Corps headquarters.

Malvern Hill is a small plateau, a mile and a half long, three-quarters of a mile wide, and more than one hundred feet high at its crest. Separated from the James River on the south by a strip of swampy ground, it is also protected on the north and west by Turkey Creek and on the east by Western Run. By using signal flags, Porter could communicate with the gunboats anchored on the James. The location was ideal for defense. Here the entire Army of the Potomac was formed in a rough semicircle, or U, on the northern crest of the plateau. Facing north, McClellan had placed three divisions of infantry and numerous batteries of artillery in a long line, ahead of which Berdan's deadly sharpshooters took position in rifle pits. Behind the northern crest near the century-old Malvern House was the army's artillery reserve of nearly 100 guns and 14 siege cannon. In all, the Federals amassed as many as 250 guns on Malvern Hill.

While Heintzelman hurried to deploy his corps, he engaged in a shouting match with General Kearny. Heintzelman had just posted one of Kearny's artillery batteries when the one-armed New Yorker rode onto the scene and ordered the battery moved to another location. Shortly afterward, the corps commander returned to find the artillery in a different location, angrily inquiring who had ordered it moved. "On being told he rode brim full of wrath for Gen. K.," Captain Haydon wrote. "You countermand another order of mine and I will have you arrested, Sir," Heintzelman shouted. "Arrest my ass, God damn you," Kearny replied as he rode off, never turning to look at his commander. "Heintzelman looked after him very earnestly for near a minute," Haydon recalled. "A faint smile came over his features and he himself turned around and rode slowly off leaving the battery where he found it."[42] When the deployment concluded, Kearny's division was on the left, Brig. Gen. Darius Couch's division of the V Corps stood in the center, and Hooker's division held the right. Even before his men were in position, Heintzelman could hear the sound of Confederate artillery. Once again, Lee was preparing an attack.

Observing the Union forces before him, Lee was certain, as Longstreet suggested, that by placing forty to sixty guns on a small nearby knoll and one hundred more in a field on the left, the Federals could be pounded into such disorder by the enfilading artillery that the lines could be carried by frontal assault. No sooner had the Rebel artillery gone into action than they were silenced by the vast array of Union guns massed on the slopes and crest of Malvern Hill as well as the Union gunboats lobbing in shell after shell from the James. The Rebel batteries, brought up one by one, were easily disabled. Moreover, less than thirty Confederate guns had been brought forward, while ninety remained in the rear. Frustrated by missed opportunities at both Savage's Station and Glendale, Lee sought to flank the Union position but was unable to do so. By mid-afternoon the crescent-shaped Confederate line, stretching for more than a mile, had become ragged and disjointed.

Having marched for eighteen hours the previous day, Magruder's Division arrived late and exhausted. "Prince John," who was said to be drinking heavily, misunderstood a message from Lee and ordered a massive frontal assault by his infantry at 4:45 P.M. A long line of gray soldiers advanced

Heintzelman's headquarters during the Battle of Malvern Hill. Sketch by Robert Knox Sneden. Virginia Historical Society.

across a meadow and through a wheatfield and, with a yell that could be heard above the crash of the musketry, advanced to within 150 yards of the Federal guns. Union artillerymen, stripped to the waist in the sultry air, opened up a firestorm of steel that cut down the Rebels by the hundreds. Like a scene from some ghastly inferno, "the whole side of Malvern Hill seemed a vast sheet of fire," Sneden marvelled.[43] So dense was the smoke from the thousands of guns and muskets that the two armies became obscured from each another.

Seeing Magruder's men charging up Malvern Hill through the smoke, D. H. Hill sent his five brigades along a half-mile front directly into the mouth of the Union guns. Rapidly moving up the long slope with incredible valor, the gray-clad infantry was repulsed with terrible losses. The Confederates "advanced at a run with terrifying yells, heard all above the crash of musketry and roar of artillery," Sneden wrote. Confederate battle flags rose and fell as the Southerners went down before a withering storm of canister and grape. So effective were the Union guns that they cut huge swaths through the charging ranks—with favorable acoustics, it was said the thunder from the artillery could be heard at Staunton, all the way across Virginia to the Blue Ridge Mountains, one hundred miles to the west. The long line of Union infantrymen held their fire until the remaining Rebels appeared through the smoke, then unleashed a deadly volley of musketry. The 3rd Alabama had advanced to within two hundred yards of the enemy guns but lost six color bearers and half its members. "Our men poured a single crashing volley of musketry and charged the enemy with the bayonet," Sneden recalled. "We drove them back handsomely with great slaughter," wrote Heintzelman, who would remain convinced for many years that the god of battles was with the Army of the Potomac that day.[44]

Porter, whose corps bore the brunt of the Rebel onslaught, was fearful that his lines would be broken, as had happened at Gaines's Mill, and he sent out an urgent plea for reinforcements. Sumner sent Brig. Gen. Thomas Meagher's Irish Brigade to bolster the V Corps, while Heintzelman rushed Sickles's Excelsior Brigade. "By Jove! if Porter asks for help," the III Corps commander was heard to say, "I know he needs it and I will send it." Porter would later recall Heintzelman's willingness to assist him in a time of crisis: "I had served under General Heintzelman up to the capture of Yorktown, and I appreciated his act as the prompting of a thoughtful, generous, and chivalrous nature." For his part, Heintzelman would always believe that if he and Sumner had not sent reinforcements, the day would have been lost. Moreover, if the Confederates had threatened his own right flank, Sickles's brigade could never have been sent. As daylight faded into dusk and the sky grew dark and cloudy, Magruder brought up a fresh brigade and launched one last desperate assault on the Union lines. As Lee watched from a blacksmith shop across the road from the Methodist parsonage in the Rebel rear, the Southerners advanced out of the smoke and gloom, and once again the guns on the crest of the hill, along with the gunboats on the James River, unleashed their deadly missiles into the advancing infantry, saturating the open ground with canister and grapeshot. Stumbling over their dead comrades, the Rebels gallantly rushed forward only to be forced back into the woods with heavy casualties. It was Southern valor against Northern firepower, and the guns won. "Hundreds of poor maimed wretches were continually crawling on hands and knees across the open, many of whom were killed before they regained shelter in the woods," Sneden observed.[45]

In the darkness of 9 P.M., amid the cries of the wounded and the rumblings of wagons and artillery, the sound of musketry slowly died away. In the camps of the III Corps, the reverberations from the Federal artillery and gunboats that continued to pound the Rebel lines were heard for another hour. The burning fuses from the lobbed shells produced fiery arcs against

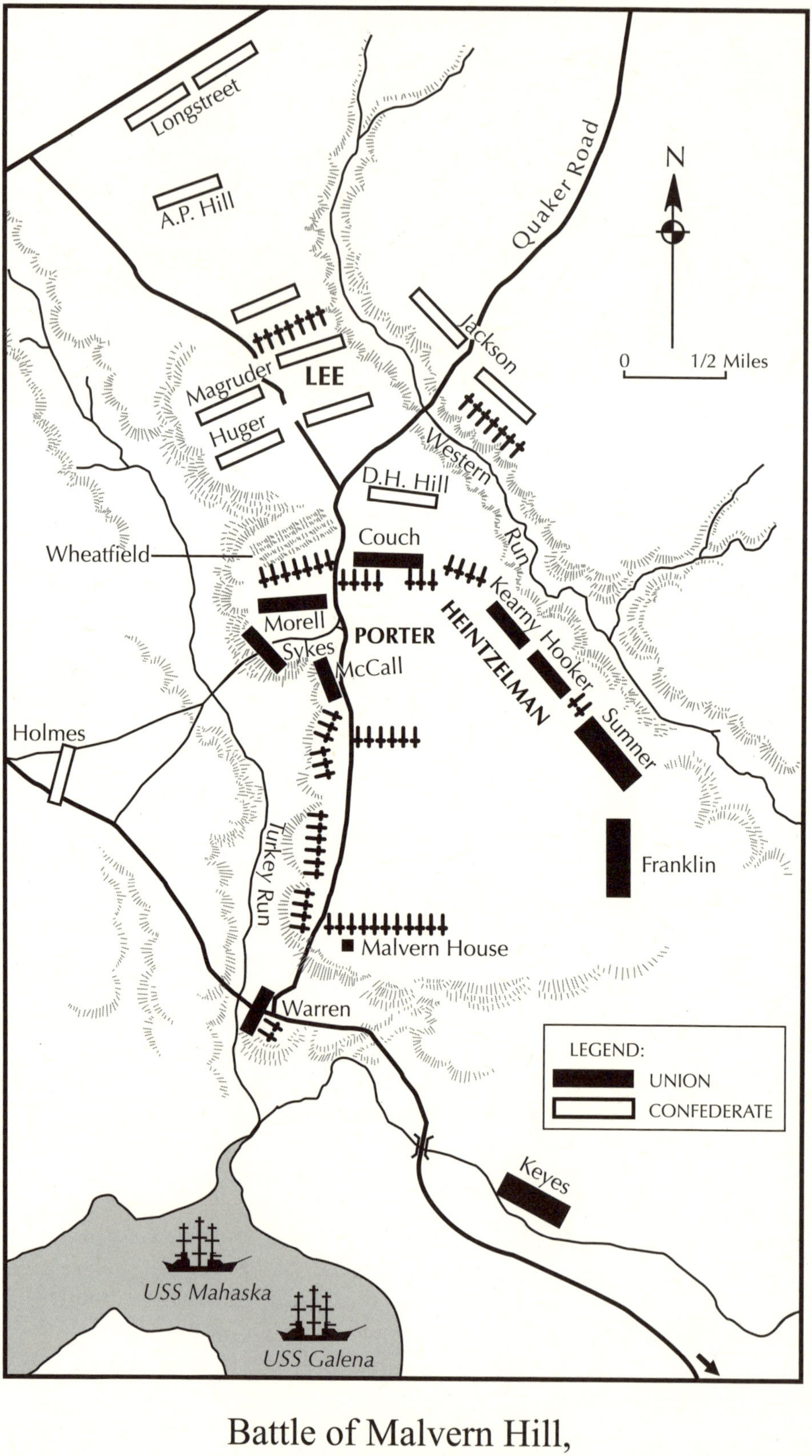

Battle of Malvern Hill,
July 1, 1862

the dark clouds. In the eerie darkness red flashes from the gunboats and the glare of hundreds of small Union and Confederate campfires seemed to reflect on the low-lying clouds. When the shooting finally stopped, numerous torches and lanterns could be seen slowly moving about on the slopes of the hill as Confederate surgeons and soldiers searched for the wounded.

Piles of dead and dying Rebels lay on the slopes of Malvern Hill. In all, Lee lost 5,355 men in this final battle, while the Army of the Potomac suffered 3,214 casualties. Among the Rebels who had fallen that day, "enough were still alive and moving to give the field a singular crawling effect," Colonel Averell wrote. "The battlefield at the foot of the slopes presented a shocking sight of dead, dying, and mangled corpses," Sneden observed, "while the numerous dead and wounded horses were crawling and kicking in death agony among them." The mutilated bodies of the Confederate dead on the bloodstained grassy slopes and in the woodlands below presented a ghastly scene that many in Lee's army would never forget. For days afterward thousands of wounded boys in gray and butternut could be seen hobbling along the roads toward Richmond. In the Union rear the scene was equally appalling. At Malvern House, which had been converted into a hospital, Federal surgeons worked at a frenzied pace. Piles of amputated arms and legs lay in a horrible "heap near the house . . . thrown out of the windows by the assistants."[46] When it became full, surgeons hastily established improvised field hospitals in nearby barns, under trees, and in sheltered ravines.

The frenzied Seven Days Battles ended on the bloody slopes of Malvern Hill. To Gen. D. H. Hill and thousands of men and boys in both armies, the action there was not war, but murder. Superiority in artillery had saved the Army of the Potomac and dealt Lee a stunning check. During this week of nearly constant combat, the eastern equivalent of Shiloh, Confederate casualties amounted to an appalling 20,614 men, while McClellan placed his losses at 15,849.[47]

At Malvern Hill, the newly christened Army of Northern Virginia had been badly bloodied, yet the Army of the Potomac, following McClellan's orders, fled as if it had been routed. The dead were left unburied, and many of the wounded were abandoned, despite the fact that numerous empty wagons were hacked to pieces to prevent them from falling into enemy hands. After carefully examining a number of maps of the area below Malvern Hill, Heintzelman issued orders shortly after midnight for the III Corps to pack up and move out. As before, many of the officers in the corps questioned the orders to retreat, cursing McClellan with every breath. Kearny went as far as to denounce Little Mac again as a traitor and a coward.[48]

In rain and darkness, the exhausted and demoralized III Corps filed down the rear slope of Malvern Hill and into the woods in silence. With Colonel Averell's 3rd Pennsylvania Cavalry as a rear guard, fires were left burning on the crest of the hill to deceive Lee's Rebels, and the bridge over Turkey Island Creek was burned. Before daylight Heintzelman also departed Malvern Hill. The roads were crammed with slow-moving infantry, cavalry, wagons, artillery, and ambulances. Many soldiers became separated from their comrades and crept along with strangers. Several lost or threw away their knapsacks and only had the clothing on their backs. In the mud and disorder, mule teams had to be double and then treble hitched, the crack of whips echoing through the night. An hour after midnight heavy rain came down as thunder roared and vivid lightning flashes lit up the woods. A covered wagon carrying Heintzelman's personal belongings had gone less than a mile when it was run into by an artillery gun and hopelessly wrecked. Both of the wagon's axles were broken, and the general's maps, clothing, demijohn, and other personal items were strewn about in the mud of the road; within minutes teamsters consumed the whiskey in the demijohn.[49] Plunging on through the tangled Virginia countryside for five miles, the James River at Harrison's Landing began to emerge with the dawn.

For the remainder of his life, Heintzelman would never forget this retreat. Simply put, it was another low point in his long military career and as bad as the march through White Oak Swamp only days earlier. Knowing the fate of a nation rested with the Army of the Potomac and on McClellan's shoulders, he was despondent and depressed for days, convinced that the army should have held its position before Richmond. Rumors that Great Britain and France had decided to recognize the Confederacy did not help his mood. Unable to locate McClellan's headquarters, he rode to Riverside Plantation, the home of William Mortimer Harrison. Although a strong secessionist, Harrison invited the general and his aides inside for breakfast.[50]

In the heat and humidity of the swampy lowlands at Harrison's Landing, many of the wounded who had been carried from Malvern Hill were struck down by gangrene or malaria. But July 4, 1862, brought bright sunshine, and a general inspection was ordered for 10 A.M. One soldier remembered the fine appearance made by the "long lines of infantry with shining muskets and bayonets." Bands that had been silent for weeks played while General McClellan and his corps commanders rode along the lines. The men cheered and placed their caps on the points of their bayonets. At noon all three hundred guns of the Army of the Potomac fired a salute, as did the gunboats nearby. The deafening roar of so many guns shook the earth, and the sound reverberated up and down the James River for miles.

In the evening Capt. Chauncey McKeever brought out a cake his wife had sent from Baltimore, and in the woods at Harrison's Landing, the general and his aides dined on chicken, accompanied by whiskey punch, and the cake that was to have been consumed to celebrate the fall of Richmond. Festivities continued well past midnight. The next day Heintzelman's spirits were lifted when he received a telegram from Secretary of War Edwin M. Stanton notifying him that he had been promoted to major general of volunteers and given a brevet as brigadier general in the Regular Army.[51]

On July 8 Heintzelman put on a clean uniform and went to greet President Lincoln, who arrived at Harrison's Landing on the steamer *Ariel*. Lincoln had come to urge McClellan to resume the offensive. In the dust and 98-degree heat, McClellan and Heintzelman rode around the lines with the president as the gunboats on the river fired a salute. Heintzelman was somewhat embarrassed when Lincoln was not enthusiastically received by the rank and file, some of the men simply forgetting to cheer as they had been directed. "The President looked ungainly on horseback," young Sneden wrote. "He wore a high silk hat and his black clothes were covered with dust."[52] While watching this, one soldier feared Lincoln's long legs would become entangled with those of his horse, and the two would come tumbling down together.

Later, with Lt. Henry Norton, Heintzelman rode down to the wharf and went onboard the *Ariel* to be interviewed by the president. When Lincoln asked him how many men remained in his corps, Heintzelman said he was not sure, but he would guess about fifteen thousand. The president also inquired as to the health of the III Corps and what condition the general thought Lee's army was in. Heintzelman said that his corps was improving daily and that he was not sure about Lee's command. When Lincoln asked if the Army of the Potomac could be withdrawn safely from the Virginia Peninsula, Heintzelman replied that it could be done, but "to withdraw the army would be to ruin the country."[53] Along with Porter and Sumner, he urged the president to overrule McClellan and order an immediate advance on Richmond. After sharing a glass of wine, Heintzelman watched as Lincoln departed for Washington.

Not long after Lincoln's visit to Harrison Landing, Maj. Gen. Henry Halleck, an excellent strategist and administrator, arrived to assess the military situation. "Old Brains," as Halleck was known, had recently arrived in Washington from the West, where he had enjoyed tremendous success, to become general in chief. He had come to inform McClellan that he could have no more than twenty thousand reinforcements; if that were not enough, the Army of the Potomac would have to be withdrawn.

A few weeks later Heintzelman staged a grand review of the III Corps, hoping to improve the men's morale. Bands played and battle flags were unfurled, as the troops appeared in their new uniforms and, for the first time, white leggings. Many of the regimental bands performed late into the evening. One that appeared at Kearny's headquarters was so bad that the general gave them a gallon of whiskey "to go away." At Harrison's Landing Heintzelman frequently met with Hooker and Kearny, who both wanted the army to move on Richmond. Yet the exact whereabouts of Lee's army remained something of a mystery. At least two hundred Confederate cavalrymen could be seen across the river at the sprawling Maycox Plantation, which the Federals mistakenly thought to be the home of proslavery ideologue and Southern nationalist Edmund Ruffin. With a spyglass, Rebels could be seen in the cupola of the main building observing the Union camps across the river. The previous night the Rebels had pulled eight artillery pieces onto the grounds of the plantation and shelled the Union camps. As a result, eighteen hundred Federals crossed the James and burned Maycox Plantation and all the outbuildings to the ground. Axmen even cut down all the trees.[54]

While at Harrison's Landing, the army was able to rest and regroup. The men also found time to bathe in the James River and feast on ripe watermelons.[55] Yet in the wilting heat, boredom engulfed the army, and in their misery many turned to alcohol. In the endlessly hot days and nights, swarms of insects constantly annoyed the soldiers, and disease and death became common in the ranks. At one time as many as twelve thousand men were reported to be either sick or still recovering from their wounds.

The respite at the James River also allowed Heintzelman the opportunity to painfully reappraise some of the major battles of the Peninsula Campaign. Although McClellan had been unwilling to order a direct attack on Yorktown, he could easily "have forced the Rebel lines" and isolated the garrison. Little Mac, Heintzelman thought, had been influenced by Fitz John Porter into ordering the siege. With sufficient reinforcements at Williamsburg, the general was sure he could have overrun Fort Magruder. At Seven Pines there was little doubt his III Corps had saved the entire left wing of the Army of the Potomac from collapse.

In the days after Lincoln's departure, the corps commanders continued to urge an advance on Richmond. McClellan remained convinced, however, that Lee had over 200,000 men defending the city and that any such move would result in a catastrophe. Anticipating Ulysses Grant's 1864 strategy, Heintzelman urged McClellan to cross the James and seize Petersburg. From there the army could march on Richmond from the south. "We should have taken Petersburg two weeks ago," he confided to his journal in late July.[56] McClellan not only refused to entertain the idea of advancing on Petersburg but also was flatly unwilling to move on Richmond.

The only common ground Heintzelman found with his commander was that the Army of the Potomac needed at least 50,000 reinforcements.

Heintzelman remained apprehensive, as he had told Lincoln, that a withdrawal from the Peninsula would destroy the army's morale and plunge the country into political uncertainty. Growing even more intolerant, he urged McClellan to go to Washington to meet with Halleck and Lincoln and determine what action the army should take. When the general declined, Heintzelman even offered to go himself and applied for a leave of absence, which was promptly denied. With McClellan's indecisiveness came continued endemic demoralization. Hooker, as well as a number of other high-ranking officers in the III Corps, openly talked of resigning. There were even rumors that McClellan himself would resign. As far as Heintzelman was concerned, his commander had left the once-grand army in a "sad state of affairs." Yet Little Mac remained immensely popular with the rank and file. "When the soldiers see McClellan," a recruit in the Pennsylvania Reserves wrote from Harrison's Landing, "they jump up and cheer him and cheer as long as he is in sight."[57]

Although he was fearful of going outside the chain of command, Heintzelman was so disgusted with McClellan's leadership that he sent Margaret to the Executive Mansion to complain to Lincoln. On the evening of August 8, she saw Lincoln and diplomatically, but tersely, told the president of her husband's concerns. The next day she sent Lincoln a note in which she copied Samuel Peter's recommendation from one of his private letters. A simple glance at the map, the general argued, would convince anyone that by crossing the Army of the Potomac to the south bank of the James, Lee could be forced to abandon Petersburg. "If these troops [of the Army of the Potomac] are withdrawn and carried beyond Washington, I dread the consequence," he wrote. "I fear that one third will desert among them many officers." So many men would leave that it would be impossible to control those who remained. "I fear whole Regiments will disband." The army "must advance or the country is ruined," he continued. "Fill up our ranks and send us raw troops—anything but retreat." Margaret was also able to obtain an interview with Stanton, in which she learned that the secretary of war had never received her husband's report of the Battle of Williamsburg.[58] Margaret did not know, and Lincoln and Stanton did not divulge in their conversations, that the decision had already been made to withdraw the Army of the Potomac from the Peninsula.

With indecisiveness at Harrison's Landing, the resolve that Heintzelman had seen in the army during the early days on the Peninsula continued to dissipate. His mood reached a new low when General Stoneman returned from Washington to say that Lincoln thought the English and

French were likely to intervene on behalf of the Confederacy and that reinforcements were out of the question. Samuel Peter also worried about Margaret, whom he knew to be frail and "nearly sick from anxiety and uncertainty." He even regretted having not "gone to Texas and freed it from Secessionists."[59]

On July 18 the rain began again, and three days later Heintzelman was taken ill with malaria. Quinine was of little help, and all his body servant, George Washington, could do was watch as the general became weaker and weaker. He was still sick when news reached Harrison's Landing that Lee was moving the bulk of his army north. "I fear the worst," was his only response. Continued Confederate successes, he explained, would pressure Lincoln into negotiating with the South. Somehow Heintzelman came to conclude that the president had "some secret designs" that might be detrimental to the country. "I have lost all faith in him," he wrote. In early August Alexander Gardner, "Mr. Brady's artist," as Heintzelman called him, arrived at III Corps headquarters in the tangled woods northwest of Berkely Plantation, where the general and his staff proudly posed for the camera. In Gardner's photograph one can see a fatigued and ruffled, though still resolute, general.[60]

Having recovered from malaria, his spirits were lifted when he learned that Maj. Gen. John Pope was preparing to advance on Richmond from the north with his newly created Army of Virginia. With two armies advancing on the Confederate capital, Richmond could surely be taken. He did not know that Lee, confident that McClellan was no threat, had already sent General Jackson north to confront Pope. Two weeks later Lee also moved north with the bulk of the Army of Northern Virginia.

By August 3 Lincoln became increasingly concerned about Pope's army and the security of Washington, and he issued orders immediately withdrawing the Army of the Potomac from the Peninsula. As these arrived at Harrison's Landing, Hooker retook Malvern Hill with his division, drove a small Rebel force back toward Richmond, and captured one hundred prisoners, inspiring McClellan to tell Halleck that "with re-enforcements I could march this army" into Richmond "in five days."[61]

On August 10 orders went out to cook five days' rations and be prepared to march. With little or no understanding of the bigger events that were about to engulf them, most of the rank and file were sure they would soon be advancing on Richmond. There was one final review in which the III Corps displayed their red diamond corps badges for the first time. They were the first unit in the Army of the Potomac to use distinctive patches for identification.

Several hundred contrabands as well as the sick were hurried aboard steamers, and everything that could not be taken was burned. At 6 A.M.

on August 15, bugles sounded, tents were struck, and the III Corps was in motion. Each man carried a haversack full of rations and sixty rounds of ammunition. Riding past the slow-moving infantry, Heintzelman was heartily cheered by his men, who were happy to at last be on the march.

Leaving the heat and humidity of Harrison's Landing with a squadron of cavalry as an escort, Heintzelman led his III Corps across the Peninsula by way of Charles City Court House toward Yorktown. Hundreds of contrabands followed on foot and in broken-down wagons and farm carts. Along the route the farms and plantations were virtually abandoned, with only a few women to be seen. Some begged for tobacco and snuff. With husbands in the army and many of their slaves having run away, they were both sullen and defiant. "I say, have you some fine 'bacca to give a lady?" Sneden remembered one woman saying. "Why don't you 'uns let us alone?" another defiantly called to the Federals.[62]

Breaking camp each morning at 5:30 A.M., the III Corps moved slowly across the Peninsula. By August 16, the lead columns were at Brahamsville, and the next day Heintzelman reached the Williamsburg Stage Road. With cavalry protecting his left flank, he was already at Williamsburg on the afternoon of August 18 and established headquarters on the green near William and Mary College. There the wagons were unloaded for the first time since leaving Harrison's Landing. Fearing that his men would plunder Williamsburg, the soldiers were ordered to stay in camp and not enter the town. In the stifling heat and dust, the corps pushed on to Yorktown the next day. Although the men were prohibited from leaving the line of march, Heintzelman, Hooker, Kearny, and Sickles rode over to see Fort Magruder. Rains had eroded the parapets, and a heavy growth of weeds and vines covered what had been bare earth. Strewn about the ground were rusty canteens, broken muskets, cartridge boxes, and the skeletons of horses and mules. Of greater interest were hundreds of stakes indicating the resting places of the many soldiers killed in the battle. Sadly, the rain and sun had obliterated the names of the dead.

At Halfway House, only bare chimneys remained. After passing through Yorktown, corps headquarters were established outside the fortifications near the steep banks of the York River. When this location proved unsuitable, they moved to a better and dryer location. Here whole regiments took the opportunity to swim and bathe in the river. Looking over the burned-out and ruined buildings used as his headquarters during the siege and reflecting on the immense amount of toil and sweat that went into the Union entrenchments before Yorktown, the cursing of McClellan began all over again.

On August 19 Heintzelman received an urgent telegram from McClellan, who was at Fortress Monroe, urging that the III Corps depart as soon as possible. "Make use of every vessel that arrives at Yorktown, both during the night and day, to embark your troops," he directed.[63] Two days later, with regimental bands playing, long lines of troops began making their way to the ships. By 11 A.M., along with two hundred men of the 105th Pennsylvania, Heintzelman and his staff went aboard the *Long Island*, and at noon the steamer pulled away from the docks and headed down the York River in a light drizzle. As the III Corps steamed away, bands again played, and the men, many of them drunk, cheered loudly. Many thought the scene resembled their embarkation from Alexandria months earlier.

But conditions in the Army of the Potomac were very different in August 1862 than they had been only four months earlier. The Peninsula Campaign had failed miserably. Thousands of lives had been lost, yet the Confederate capital stood as defiant as ever. Now, with Lee on the march, Washington must be secured.

TEN

Failure at Second Bull Run

ON AUGUST 21, 1862, the III Corps of the Army of the Potomac was en route from Yorktown. Steaming on Chesapeake Bay in a heavy swell, many of the soldiers became sick. By early afternoon the *Long Island*, carrying General Heintzelman and his staff, was past the mouth of the Piankatank River, and by 4:30 P.M. the entrance to the Rappahannock came in sight. Original orders called for the III Corps to land at Aquia Landing, the terminus of the Richmond and Potomac Railroad some ten miles northeast of Fredericksburg, but Heintzelman was directed to telegraph General in Chief Halleck for final orders before disembarking the troops.[1] Arriving off Aquia Creek a little after nine o'clock on the morning of August 22, a telegram arrived sending the III Corps to Alexandria instead. Continuing up the Potomac River past Pohick Bay and Mount Vernon, the *Long Island* reached Alexandria at 1:30 the same afternoon. Waiting at the dock was Col. John C. Kelton, one of Halleck's aides, with orders to hurry the III Corps to Warrenton Junction on the Orange and Alexandria Railroad southwest of Manassas as soon as possible. The advance guard of Lee's Army of Northern Virginia, racing north from Richmond, was already across the Rappahannock, Kelton said.

For three days the III Corps continued to disembark and march up Alexandria's King Street to a large open field below Fort Lyon. Corps headquarters was established nearby, not more than a thousand yards from the city's old slave pens. Despite the urgency of the situation, Heintzelman took time to visit with Caroline Summers, who along with her surgeon husband, had taken up residence in Alexandria. The visit was cut short when Caroline said that Margaret had been ill for several days. Hurrying across the Potomac, Samuel Peter found his wife confined to her bed and unable to keep anything in her stomach. Their son Charles was there, and Margaret was being seen by Dr. Summers, who said her condition was not serious. Still, Samuel Peter worried about his wife's delicate health and urged her to leave the capital, perhaps going north to stay with Juliana at West Chester, Pennsylvania.[2]

In Washington Heintzelman visited with Secretary of War Edwin Stanton, and the two had a frank talk about the rapidly developing crisis in northern Virginia. The general was leaving Stanton's office when Chauncey McKeever (now a major) handed him a telegram. General Pope had telegraphed that Stonewall Jackson had turned his right flank, forcing him to pull back from the Rappahannock. It was essential that Heintzelman take his III Corps and join Pope's Army of Virginia at Warrenton Junction as soon as possible. Hurrying over to the Halleck's office, he continued discussing Pope's predicament and going over several maps of the area around Warrenton. Returning to Alexandria by the next boat, he rode out to headquarters, where soldiers of the III Corps were continuing to arrive from the Peninsula. He learned that Pope had concentrated most of the rolling stock near Manassas and that it would take several days to get the entire III Corps to Warrenton. Moreover, most of his artillery, ammunition, and supplies would have to be transported by wagon train. Almost all III Corps horses would have to be left behind, and each man would only be allocated forty rounds of ammunition and three days' rations.[3]

Returning to Washington, Samuel Peter found Margaret still ill. At Pennsylvania Avenue's "Newspaper Row," he had a lengthy conversation with Douglas Wallach, proprietor of the *Washington Evening Star* and brother of Richard Wallach, mayor of the city, in which he learned that the newspaperman had "given up on McClellan." Still delayed at Alexandria, he returned a third time to the capital to visit with Dr. Summers and check on Margaret's condition. In the stifling late-afternoon heat of August 25, the III Corps finally began boarding cattle and freight cars for Warrenton Junction, where Pope had established his headquarters.[4] Nevertheless, Heintzelman was frustrated with the delay in getting his horse and those of his staff aboard. Finally underway, the train had not gone more than two miles when it stopped to take on more soldiers. There were more delays along the route, and Heintzelman did not reach Warrenton for several hours.

Once arrived, he and his staff established III Corps headquarters in a large grove of pine trees not far from General Pope. Heintzelman found the situation confused and chaotic. "No one appeared to know what to do, or think it necessary to do anything," he observed, complaining of how "he and his troops had been hurried down here on the cars without horses, ambulances, baggage, or artillery." In addition, the men were "naked, with only their arms and their clothes." Yet he shared Pope's optimism that the III Corps, combined with the three corps of the Army of Virginia, could easily repulse any serious Confederate advance. "The Rebels have lost the opportunity to defeat Pope," he wrote. "Our reinforcements are coming in position too rapidly. . . . I don't think the Rebels will be able to make any more offensive movements in this direction."[5]

Summoned to Pope's headquarters, Heintzelman found the general sitting in a large wicker chair, smoking a cigar and anxiously awaiting his arrival. Pope was tall, burly, long-bearded, and an outspoken critic of McClellan. A loyal Kentuckian and West Point graduate, he had served ably under Halleck in the West. Bragging that his headquarters were in the saddle, he had arrived in the East to win the war. Heintzelman thought Pope boisterous and a braggart. In turn, Pope came to see Heintzelman as indecisive and weak; in fact, he respected "Fighting Joe" Hooker and the dashing Kearny far more. Part of Pope's attraction to those generals was the fact that they too hated McClellan. Although he was not impressed with his new commander, Heintzelman liked the approach he brought to the war in Virginia. Wanting to make the Confederates feel the pain of the conflict, Pope had commenced confiscating Rebel property. He also threatened to execute guerrillas and arrested those who assisted and harbored them.

By August 26, all of the III Corps had arrived at Warrenton Junction. At a council of war that evening, Kearny, his tongue well lubricated, launched into a tirade, denouncing McClellan and going as far as to say that any plans should not include Porter and the V Corps, charging that Porter, a McClellan partisan, was not dependable. Ironically, when Porter arrived at Pope's headquarters a few hours later, Kearny complained to him that Pope was badly mismanaging the campaign.[6]

Holding the III Corps in the vicinity of Warrenton Junction, Pope was waiting to hear from the other corps commanders in both the Army of Virginia and the Army of the Potomac before making any decisive move against Lee. After retiring on the evening of August 26, Heintzelman was awakened with news that the Confederates were moving on the Union left and that Pope was sending the III Corps to Weaversville, a small hamlet three miles south of Catlett's Station. Heintzelman could not find Weaversville on any map and confessed that he had never heard of the place; without a reliable guide, he did not "know where to go." Just as the corps prepared to march, news arrived that a small band of the Rebels had taken possession of the Orange and Alexandria Railroad in Pope's rear. Twenty minutes later, believing the attack to be a small cavalry raid, Pope wrote Heintzelman to "put a regiment on a train of cars and send it immediately to Manassas to ascertain what has occurred."[7] Marching orders quickly went out for Col. Harman J. Bliss's 3rd Excelsior Regiment (72nd New York) of Hooker's division to move by train toward Manassas and repair the railroad tracks and the telegraph line, if necessary. A train could not be found, however, and the regiment was forced to wait for transportation in the darkness until well past midnight.

Moving past Catlett's Station and across Kettle Run at night, the 72nd New York had advanced to within half a mile of Bristoe Station when they first encountered Rebel pickets. Colonel Bliss responded by throwing a company forward as skirmishers and flankers. He could tell by the light from two derailed and burning trains that the enemy was in possession of the station. After the Confederates had torn up the track and derailed one train, a second train, speeding down the line from Warrenton Junction toward Alexandria, had ploughed into the first. In the early morning light, the Confederates spotted the advancing bluecoats and deployed infantry on one flank and cavalry on the other. Fearing that he would be overwhelmed and cut off, Bliss ordered the regiment back to Kettle Run, where he telegraphed Pope. With large numbers of Confederates continuing to advance along the railroad and artillery shelling his command, Bliss again retreated, taking with him two companies of the 105th Pennsylvania posted as pickets at Kettle Run.[8]

At midnight on the evening of August 26, even-more-alarming news reached Pope. To the west as many as 10,000 to 15,000 Confederates were pouring through Thoroughfare Gap in the Bull Run Mountains. Although Pope contemplated moving his command to the Rappahannock to link up with the remainder of the Army of the Potomac, he feared that such a move would dangerously expose Washington. He decided instead to concentrate his forces in the vicinity of Centreville or Manassas Junction and strike at what he thought to be the advance of Lee's army. With as many as 66,000 men, he would overwhelm Jackson, who was thought to have less than 25,000 men.[9] In reality, Pope was disorganized and utterly unprepared for Jackson's dash around his flank.

Hearing the artillery fire from Kettle Run on the Orange and Alexandria Railroad in his rear, Pope sent Col. David Hunter Strother with orders for Heintzelman to send two brigades to investigate. Strother remembered the III Corps commander that morning as "a knotty, hard-looking old customer with a grizzled beard and shambling one-sided gait . . . a man of energy and reliability." Heintzelman moved with Kearny's division and part of Maj. Gen. Ambrose E. Burnside's IX Corps, commanded by Maj. Gen. Jesse Lee Reno, over a meandering country road to Greenwich, a small hamlet north of Catlett's Station some ten miles west of Manassas. At the same time, Hooker advanced along the Orange and Alexandria; Porter followed with his V Corps. Marching in terrible heat with little cavalry and almost no artillery, Hooker advanced across Kettle Run only to smash into Maj. Gen. Richard Stoddard Ewell's three brigades of Rebels at Bristoe Station. Upon their approach, the Federals were "saluted with a volley of musketry that rattled through the leaves like hail," a private in the 5th New Jersey remembered.[10] Hooker, who was mounted on a magnificent white charger, sent three regiments along the railroad while he personally lead two others in a flanking movement to the left. General Grover's brigade of New Yorkers moved to the right of the railroad. In the center the 2nd New York and 8th New Jersey suffered heavy casualties while moving against two reinforced regiments of Louisiana troops concealed in dense woods.

In what became known as the Battle of Kettle Run, the fighting went well for the Rebels until an undetected Federal column crashed into Ewell's right. After more than an hour of intense combat, with the Confederates on the verge of being overwhelmed, Ewell, who was thought to be Lee's ablest division commander, ordered a retreat back along the railroad toward Manassas Junction. Left behind were a number of dead in a large stone house that had served as a makeshift hospital during the fighting. Burning the bridge over Broad Run and forming his regiments in successive lines, Ewell was able to hold off Hooker's pursuit of his exhausted men. Although the exact Union casualties at Kettle Run were never determined, it has been estimated that Hooker lost as many as 300 men killed and wounded. Heintzelman would only say that Hooker "had a hard fight with them and the Excelsior Brigade lost heavily." Ewell counted his losses at 144 killed and wounded.[11]

Hearing that Hooker had engaged the Confederates, Heintzelman sent the rest of his III Corps toward the sound of the fighting. Lead regiments reached Bristoe Station just as the last shots were fired around sunset. As had been reported, the Rebels had torn up rails, even heating and twisting them around trees, and destroyed all the bridges on the Orange and Alexandria, including the trestle over Broad Run. In the darkness Heintzelman could distinctly see a huge fire glowing on the horizon toward Manassas Junction, and he began pushing his Federals in that direction.[12] At 1 A.M. an aide from General Kearny galloped up to say that the division was in possession of Manassas Junction and that Jackson and his Rebels had fled west along the tracks of the Manassas Gap Railroad.

Most alarming was the fact that Jackson was now between Pope and Washington. "I don't know what we are going to do," Heintzelman despondently commented. In the rain two hours later, the general arrived to find the large Federal supply base at Manassas destroyed and several railroad trains still burning. One of the largest depots in the country, covering over one square mile, was a total ruin. Two rail sidings, each a mile long, were lined with burning boxcars. "Ten locomotives laid on their sides with running gear destroyed. . . . The whole railroad track smoked for 1,000 yards," Sneden noted. Wooden sheds, warehouses, stacks of ammunition, tarpaulin-covered piles of foodstuffs such as coffee and sugar, shoes, boots, and blankets had all gone up in smoke. More than fifty thousand pounds of bacon, one thousand barrels of corned beef, two thousand barrels of salt port, and two thousand barrels of flour were destroyed. Sutler's wagons full of luxuries such as oranges, lemons, candy, fine wines, whiskey, and expensive cigars had all been destroyed or carried off. "The whole plane as far as the eye could reach was covered with boxes, barrels, military equipment, cooking utensils, bread, meat, and beans," Colonel Strother remembered.[13] Needless to say, the Rebels had helped themselves to a cornucopia of food and equipment compliments of the Union Army.

Receiving orders to pursue Jackson, who was thought to be in force at Centreville, Heintzelman came to realize that this surprise raid was a prelude to a major battle. With Jackson still between Pope and Washington, he could not understand why troops were not pushed forward from the capital. Leading the III Corps, Kearny reached Centreville to find only a single Confederate regiment, which offered little resistance before falling back toward Bull Run. Scouts said Jackson had taken up a position along an abandoned railway line northwest of the Sudley Road, not far from the old Bull Run battlefield. In the growing darkness Heintzelman bivouacked with Kearny's division near Centreville, while Hooker's division spent the night south of Bull Run. At 11 P.M. he could hear the distant rumble of guns near Groveton, four miles to the west. It was evident that contact had been made with Jackson, and at 1 A.M. Pope sent orders for Kearny to advance toward Groveton, make contact with the enemy pickets, and wait for daylight, at which time he would be joined by Hooker's division. Not realizing that Lee and Longstreet were approaching, Pope was convinced that Jackson was attempting to retreat and probably trapped. For some unknown reason, which neither Kearny or Heintzelman ever explained, Kearny did not move toward Groveton until daybreak.

Early on the morning of August 29, Heintzelman could see a large cloud of dust over the road to Leesburg, but he did not know if it indicated that the Rebels were retreating or advancing. After establishing headquarters at Island Ford on Bull Run, he could hear the sound of guns from across the stream. At 9 A.M. he rode southwest along the Warrenton Turnpike to find the stone bridge over Bull Run destroyed by the Rebels. Hurrying on toward the sounds of the guns, he found Maj. Gen. Franz Sigel's I Corps already engaged and slowly pushing the Confederates back toward Sudley Church. Kearny's division moved into position on the Union far right, while Hooker, who arrived an hour later, took his division to the left, just north of Groveton and the turnpike. Kearny was ordered to advance but failed to move, and the order had to be repeated. "The orders to General Kearny were to attack immediately," Heintzelman wrote, but "there was so long a delay that I sent him a second order to move at once. The message brought me was that he was delaying to care for his division. Why it took so long I never learned, but I only know that the reply I got was very unsatisfactory."[14]

Finally advancing up a slight incline northwest of the Sudley Road, Kearny was able to drive the Confederates back toward Sudley Church, where the Rebels made a determined stand and even launched a counterattack. At 1:45 P.M. Pope arrived on the field and set up his headquarters on the summit of Buck Hill, just north of the Stone House at the junction of the Warrenton Turnpike and Sudley Road. Despite the urgency of the situation, Heintzelman took time for a nostalgic ride over to the spot on the Bull Run battlefield where he had been wounded the previous summer.[15]

On the right Hooker too was attacking, but his advance was uncoordinated and ineffective. From the beginning, one of the biggest problems facing Heintzelman and the Union command was knowing exactly where the bulk of Lee's army was located. "There was great doubt about the position of the enemy," he admitted. At 3 P.M., as the center of Hooker's line began to falter, Grover's 1st Brigade, consisting of three Massachusetts regiments and one each from New Hampshire and Pennsylvania, launched what Heintzelman said was one of the "most gallant and determined bayonet charges of the war."[16] With the Confederates strongly posted behind an unfinished railroad grade, General Grover was given the task of driving them out of their strongly fortified position and gaining, if possible, the woods in the Rebel rear.

"Pieces were loaded, bayonets fixed, and instructions given for the line to move slowly upon the enemy until it felt his fire, then close upon him rapidly, fire one well-directed volley, and rely upon the bayonet to secure the position on the other side," Grover, a thirty-three-year-old West Point graduate from Maine, wrote. "Many of the enemy were bayoneted in their tracks, others struck down with the butts of [their] pieces, and onward pressed our line." Yet as the Federals surged forward, they ran into "a terrible fire from a second line" of Rebels, which was thrown back into a third line of defenders.[17] Fighting alone with no sign of support and his men exhausted, Grover's center and left began to falter. In response, the general personally led the 16th Massachusetts in a desperate flanking movement. Pressed in front and on both flanks and pounded by a devastating fire of canister, the regiment sustained heavy casualties, and it too began to fall back. Retreating to the railroad embankment, Grover and his brigade were soon back where they had started.

In twenty minutes Grover had come close to breaking the Rebel lines and turning the tide of battle. "Men never fought more gallantly or efficiently," he later wrote. "Striking examples of personal gallantry were

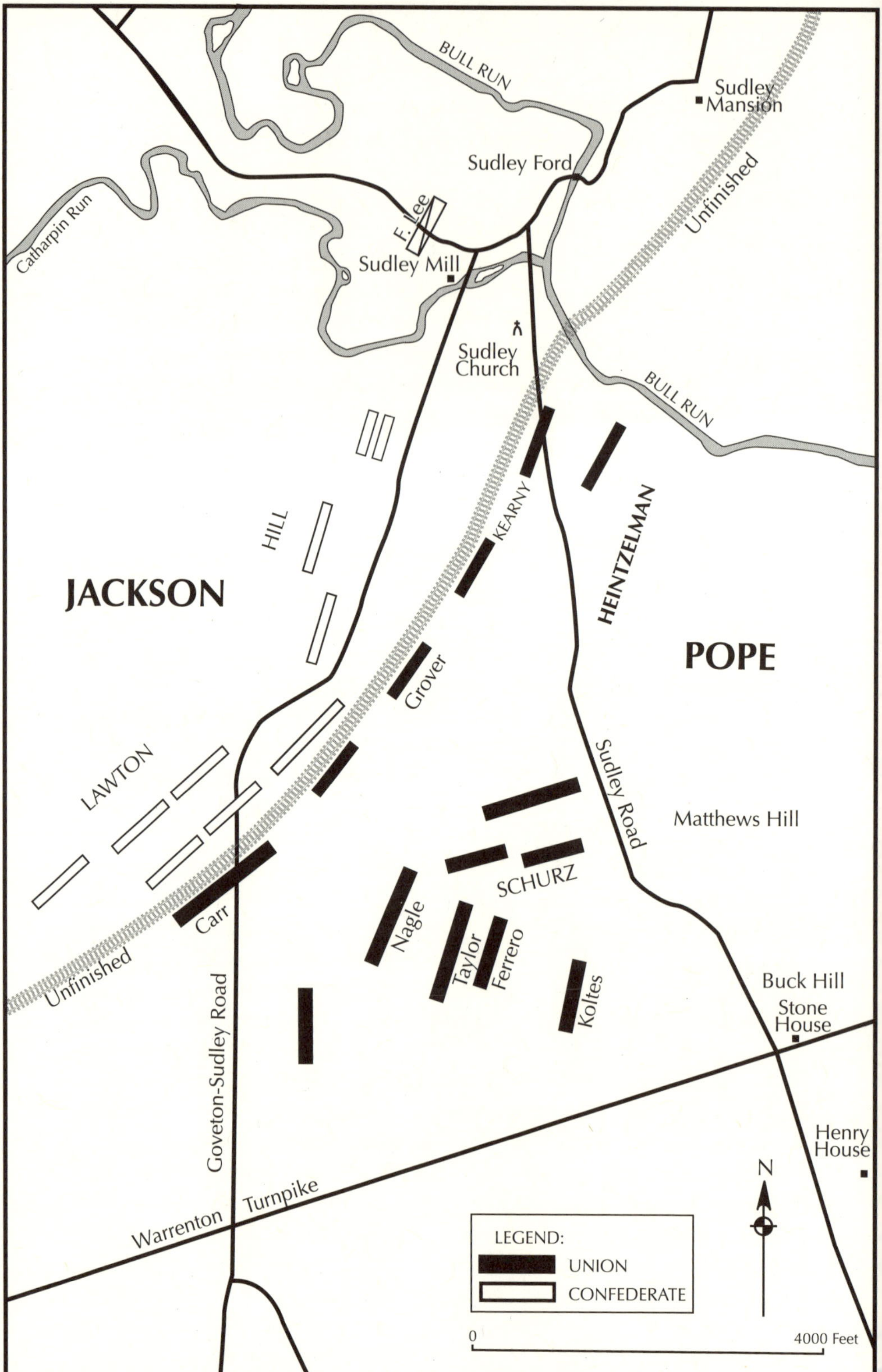

Second Battle of Bull Run
August 29, 1862 (PM)

unusually numerous." But the brigade was badly bloodied. Of the 2,000 men he took into battle, 484 were lost. Hardest hit was the 2nd New Hampshire, with 138 casualties, though the 11th and 16th Massachusetts also suffered, losing 113 and 110 men respectively.[18] Other Union brigades on the right followed Grover's attack, but their advances were disjointed and uncoordinated, and they were far less successful. By 3:30 P.M. many of the regiments on the Union right had begun to fall back.

Finally, at 5 P.M., Kearny advanced through the woods against the Rebel far left, hoping to turn Jackson's flank. As he had done on the Peninsula, the impetuous general rode out in front of his men, with bridle reins in his remaining hand. "Fall in here, you sons of bitches, and I'll make major-generals of every one of you," he was heard to yell.[19] Just as Grover had done earlier, Kearny threw the Rebels, most of them South Carolinians of A. P. Hill's division, back beyond the railroad embankment to the top of a small knoll. There, at dusk, fresh Virginia and North Carolina regiments came crashing down the slope in a vicious counterattack, the 3rd Division was hurled back, and the fighting subsided. Kearny's attack during the late afternoon of August 29 was the largest of the day, and he too had come close to breaking the Rebel lines. That night, with no rations available, the men of the III Corps went hungry as they bivouacked on the battlefield. The first day of the Second Battle of Bull Run had ended. On the far left Porter's V Corps had failed to engage the enemy, while back at Alexandria, Sumner's II Corps and Franklin's VI Corps, along with a mountain of supplies, remained with McClellan.

During a council of war at Pope's headquarters atop Buck Hill late that evening, everyone agreed that the Rebels had been decisively defeated. Reports had even reached Pope that the Confederates were retreating, probably through Thoroughfare Gap in the Bull Run Mountains. "It was now concluded," Heintzelman wrote, that the enemy "had left and we should pursue." At midnight Pope agreed that the bulk of his army should be "immediately thrown forward in pursuit of the enemy and press him vigorously during the whole day."[20] In reality, however, Jackson had not retreated at all but had simply compacted his lines by moving men from his left to his right. Pope's impending great victory was a great illusion.

August 30 dawned bright and clear. At a hastily called meeting of corps commanders and generals atop Buck Hill at 7 A.M., everyone was in remarkably fine spirits despite the horrendous casualties of the previous day. No one seemed to know that fresh enemy units were continuing to arrive on the battlefield. In fact, Pope, who was still fuming at Porter's inactivity the previous day, was refining details of how to pursue the supposedly retreating Rebels. After an hour of intense discussions, all agreed that the best plan would be to send Heintzelman's III Corps of the Army of the

Potomac and McDowell's III Corps of the Army of Virginia against the Confederate left near Sudley Church, where Kearny had enjoyed short-lived success the previous day. Reconnoitering west along the Sudley Road, the two corps commanders dismounted to examine on foot the thick vegetation along Bull Run and the woods bordering the road. As far as Heintzelman could tell, there was no evidence of the enemy being in force. In fact, several positions held by the Confederates the previous day had been abandoned. While riding back to Buck Hill, Heintzelman and McDowell were met by Pope. "I know what you are going to say," Pope blurted out, "the enemy is retreating."[21]

German-born Franz Sigel, who held the center with his I Corps of the Army of Virginia, also confirmed that the Rebels had evacuated their positions to his front. Although the generals agreed on a basic plan of attack, there is no evidence that Pope issued any orders initiating such an assault, nor did any of the corps commanders.[22] In fact, as the day progressed, Pope grew increasingly indecisive, and Heintzelman became more and more impatient, though he offered no plan himself except that there should be an advance on the Federal right.

Leading the assault on the Sudley Springs Road were the troops of Brig. Gen. James B. Ricketts's division. The thrust here had not gone far before Rebel skirmishers were encountered. As the day turned hot and dusty, the Union advance again floundered. At the same time it was learned that a large Confederate battery had secured a position overlooking the road. The Rebels had not evacuated their lines but were still on the field in large numbers, Heintzelman now realized. If fact, with General Lee assuming direct command on this wing, General Longstreet, with Hood's Texas Brigade in the forefront, launched a massive attack on General Porter on the Federal left.

By 4 P.M. desperate combat had extended all the way to the III Corps on the right. During the fierce fighting, the left and center of the Federal line broke in several places as the Confederates came on again and again. On the right Hooker was able to advance several hundred yards through some woods in his front before the attack sputtered and collapsed. At the height of the action, Private Sneden, who rushed maps to Heintzelman on the battlefield, wrote that the general "looked very much used up from constantly being in the saddle." At 4:30 P.M., as the fighting continued to rage along the entire line, Pope sent Colonel Strother racing to Heintzelman asking that two brigades from General Ricketts's division be sent immediately to the imperiled left. Heintzelman flatly refused, saying that he was in too critical a position and any weakening of his lines could lead to a disaster. Instead he offered a brigade of Brig. Gen. John F. Reynolds's Pennsylvania Reserve, which was to his rear.[23]

By 6:00 P.M., with Jackson now pressing the attack too, it was readily evident that the tide of battle had turned dramatically against Pope. The Federal right, stretching from Henry House Hill north to Poplar Ford on Bull Run, was beleaguered and fragmented. After ordering his artillery to fall back, Heintzelman was sitting astride his horse in the growing darkness near the front lines when a large Rebel force charged and opened a devastating fire on the confused Federals. Not more than twenty yards behind the lines, he was engulfed in the frantic fighting and later marveled that he was not killed or wounded. As the III Corps fell back beyond the Sudley Springs Road, Heintzelman admitted that he too was forced "to retreat rapidly."[24] As the determined Confederates pressed forward, the key on the right of the lines became Henry House Hill, for Confederate artillery there could command any route of retreat along the Warrenton Turnpike. Only a stubborn defense on the hill, he realized, would prevent the battle from becoming a complete disaster.

As twilight engulfed the battlefield, Heintzelman's command structure collapsed in the confusion and bedlam, and he not only became separated from his staff but also lost contact with both Hooker and Kearny. Neither on the Peninsula nor at First Bull Run had he and his troops been so vulnerable. With only a single orderly by his side, it was a helplessness Heintzelman had not experienced before and one that he would not soon forget. For most in the Union Army, the issue was no longer one of defeat, but of survival. In his official report of the battle written weeks later, Heintzelman did not dare mention the degree to which he had lost control of his corps. In his journal he was far more forthright.

Demoralized, fatigued, and hungry, his men fell back in the heat and dust across the repaired stone bridge over Bull Run. As the cavalry rallied to form a rear guard, the infantry waded across the creek both above and below the bridge. From III Corps headquarters at Island Ford, Sneden observed the Union rout. With the sun going down behind the tall trees nearby, shells could be seen exploding high in the sky, and the "discharge of musketry and artillery was incessant and terrible in volume."[25] Dust from the retreating Union soldiers kicked up so much powder that the evening sun became a fiery red. By evening, long lines of stragglers could be seen winding their way across the Stone Bridge toward Centreville.

At 8 P.M. Pope sent an urgent hand-scribbled note to Heintzelman, to be opened by Hooker or Kearny, if necessary: "Retire to Centreville tonight with your command. If possible go by the way of Sudley's ford. [U]pon your arrival at Centreville, you will assemble your command on the north side to that town. Early in the morning proper positions will be assigned you."[26] With little hesitancy, Heintzelman, defeated and downcast, gave the orders to move his headquarters to the war-battered and desolate village.

On the battlefield Kearny rallied to guard the Federal rear. "It's another Bull Run, sir, it's another Bull Run!" he told Gen. John Gibbon of the Iron Brigade. "Oh! I hope not quite as bad as that, General," Gibbon responded. "Perhaps not. Reno is keeping up the fight. He is not stampeded. I am not stampeded, you are not stampeded. That is about all, sir, my God that's about all," Kearny replied. To his mind, nine-tenths of the army had run away "like sheep."[27]

All along the Warrenton Turnpike in the early evening, Heintzelman could see the broken and rotting wagons that had been left during the retreat following the First Battle of Bull Run. The road was again crowded with lines of wagons and ambulances, dead mules, wounded stragglers, and thousands of confused and demoralized men in dusty blue uniforms. Many of the soldiers took to the woods and fields. Reports that a large Rebel cavalry force was advancing on Sudley Springs Road did not help. In the retreating mass of humanity under a gentle rain, near where the Warrenton Turnpike crosses Cub Run and close to where he had tried to rally another defeated army thirteen months earlier, Heintzelman was once again able to halt "some cavalry and sent it out to obstruct the road and hold it until all our troops had passed."[28] Covering the retreat, Kearny, with regiments from Reno's division and Gibbon's "Black Hat Brigade," did not leave the battlefield until 10 P.M. By midnight his rear guard was across Bull Run.

The scene Heintzelman left behind was beyond description. Including both armies, more than three thousand men lay dead on the bloodied ground along with fifteen thousand wounded. As a young Confederate cooked breakfast on the battlefield the next morning, he remembered counting "at least one hundred dead men" within eyeshot, "six within twenty feet of my campfire."[29] For the next two days, long lines of ambulances streamed toward Washington.

For Heintzelman, Second Bull Run was eerily similar to First Bull Run. In both battles the Federals had fled the field in panic. "The troops did not fight well," he confessed in his journal. Although his shortcomings as a field commander were more evident here than at any time on the Peninsula, he placed the blame for the humiliating defeat on Pope. "It was evident neither officers or men had any confidence in Pope, nor much in McDowell," he wrote. Weeks later he would recall the chaos and confusion that cost the Federals five times the casualties of First Bull Run: "We had plenty of troops,, but they were not handled with any skill. They were marched and counter marched. I got several orders and had I obeyed them, our right would have been turned and our retreat cut off. I have not 5,000 men left in my two divisions."[30]

Reaching Centreville at 11 P.M., the extent of the bedlam in the Union ranks became even more evident as Heintzelman struggled to deploy his III Corps in a defensive position north of town. Engineers worked throughout the night shoring up the defenses. "Lanterns were seen moving all night on the old Rebel forts at Centreville while the sound of hundreds of axes were heard on all sides," Sneden recorded.[31] The only good news during the entire day came when Lieutenant Norton arrived from Washington with word that Margaret, though bedridden and too weak to write, was recovering rapidly.

With his beaten and fatigued men, Heintzelman slept on the open ground that night. On August 31, after only a few hours of sleep, he awoke to a gray dawn and gentle rain and was able to find a small dwelling for shelter. At a council of war, he and other corps commanders told Pope than any offensive action was unthinkable. Hooker, for example, told Heintzelman that his division was so badly demoralized due to the severe losses sustained on the Peninsula and at Bull Run that it "was in no condition to meet the enemy." Centreville, like Malvern Hill, could be easily defended, but Heintzelman feared that Lee would simply move around the army's right, and he recommended that the Federals withdraw to the defenses of Washington. Moreover, with the army badly beaten and demoralized, he did not want to fight another battle with Pope in command. "Neither officers or men have the slightest confidence in Pope," he wrote. Although there were no orders to abandon Centreville, he concluded, "I know it must be done."[32]

A despondent Pope agreed that retreat was inevitable. Writing Halleck early on the morning of September 1, he complained that his cavalry was "completely broken down, so that there are not five horses to a company that can raise a trot." Pope knew the army was badly demoralized, but he put some of the blame on "officers of high rank in the Potomac Army, arising in all instances from personal feeling in relation to changes of commander in chief." There had been "constant talk, indulged in publicly and in promiscuous company, . . . that the Army of the Potomac will not fight; that they are demoralized by withdrawal from the Peninsula," he told Halleck.[33]

As the army regrouped at Centreville, Heintzelman moved his headquarters a mile to the east near some old Rebel fortifications and log houses.[34] Again he was summoned to Pope's headquarters and told that Lee was on the march and threatening the Union rear. Hoping to strike a fatal blow before the Federals could find shelter in the Washington defenses, Lee had renewed his offensive by sending Jackson and his "foot cavalry" across Sudley Ford and down the Little River Turnpike toward Fairfax Court House. Pope wanted Hooker's battered division to take position at

Fairfax Court House while Heintzelman, with the rest of his III Corps, would march north toward the Little River Turnpike at daylight the next morning. Less than an hour after he returned to his makeshift headquarters, a mud-splattered courier raced up with an urgent message from Pope. The Rebels were already attacking, and the III Corps must march immediately. Back at Pope's headquarters, with the army resupplied with 120 wagons of ammunition, the general was ordered to move east in the direction of Germantown and Fairfax Court House to protect the Union right flank and line of retreat.[35] At 4 P.M. Kearny was on the move, followed by Hooker's division.

Near the country mansion of Chantilly, not far from the small hamlet of Ox Hill on the Little River Turnpike two miles west of Germantown, Kearny's division and that of Brig. Gen. Isaac Stevens of the IX Corps ran head on into Jackson's three divisions moving east. At 5 P.M. in the fields and woods southwest of the turnpike, as dark storm clouds appeared in the western skies, the Battle of Chantilly, or Ox Hill as some called it, was fought in a torrential downpour. A brutal, seesaw struggle of attack and counterattack raged in the soaked woodlands and fields. Once again the sounds of combat could be heard twenty-two miles away in the nation's capital. During a lull in the fighting, with the rain still coming down in sheets and the lightening now dancing about in the early darkness, one-armed General Kearny, while leading the 21st Massachusetts, spurred his favorite black horse forward into a cornfield to reconnoiter with his "usual gallantry" and "reckless manner." Encountering several soldiers in the shoulder-high corn in the gloom of some trees, Kearny asked, "What troops are these?" The reply came back, "49th Georgia." Trying to bluff his way out of danger, he calmly replied, "All right," but as he wheeled his horse about, one of the Georgians yelled out: "That's a Yankee officer! Halt! Shoot him, fire on him." Another version has the Georgians calling out "Halt and surrender!" or "Surrender or die!" at which Kearny shouted back, as he gave his horse the spur, "Never by God!" Although hanging over his saddle Indian-style and dodging several bullets, the general's clothes were ripped, his saddle was hit, and he was struck in the lower spine, the bullet ranging upward and killing him instantly. Many surmised that had Kearny had the use of both arms, he could have escaped, since he could have thrown himself completely out of the saddle. Arriving on the scene, Jackson was said to have proclaimed: "My God boys! Do you know who you have killed? You have shot the most gallant officer in the United States Army. This is Phil Kearny who lost his arm in Mexico."[36]

Lee, who had known Kearny in Mexico and who respected his bravery, ordered the general's remains, along with his horse, saddle, and sword, returned to the Union lines under a flag of truce, where Heintzelman arranged for transportation to Washington.[37] Although he had frequently complained of Kearny's uncontrolled egotism, Heintzelman had never questioned his dedication and exceptional courage. His name would forever be "identified with . . . glory." Thinking of Kearny as the "Ney of the Union Army," young Sneden perhaps put it best: "No officer in the army was as much respected and known for cool bravery under fire. . . . Daring in judgement when a crisis occurred in battle, [and] leading charges in front of his command directly into the lines of the enemy regardless of personal danger," Kearny was undeniably one of the bravest individuals in the war, North of South.[38]

The two Union divisions lost upward of one thousand men, including General Stevens, who was also killed in the fighting, while Jackson had suffered casualties of around five hundred. Although the Federals had withdrawn, Lee was blunted in his attempt to get between Pope and Washington and destroy the Union army. As the rain continued at daylight the next morning, orders arrived for the III Corps to act as rear guard during the Union retreat. Hearing that Lee was again trying to turn Pope's right flank, Halleck ordered the whole army to fall back to defend Washington. Instead of retreating along the Little River Turnpike, Heintzelman took a wrong turn and was forced to traverse a less-traveled road to the south through Pohick Church. With his exhausted, dispirited, and hungry soldiers, he safely reached the outskirts of Alexandria by early evening, and within twenty-four hours his entire corps was safely bivouacked around Fort Lyon, many of the men in the same camps from which they had departed for the Peninsula five months earlier. After establishing his headquarters along the Old Fairfax Turnpike at the head of King Street, Heintzelman rushed off to see Dr. Summers at his office, where the general enjoyed the first decent meal he had eaten in weeks. Late in the evening he walked across the Long Bridge to Washington, and by midnight he was home. Consumed by anxiety, Margaret was still ill but feeling better.

Against the advice of his cabinet, Lincoln once again turned to McClellan. On September 2 Little Mac mounted his great stallion Dan Webster and rode out to Munson's Hill to meet the remnants of Pope's defeated army. When word reached the beleaguered Federals that their former commander was near, the long lines in blue began to cheer. Hearing that McClellan was back in command, Heintzelman seemed elated. Despite McClellan's many faults, "he has the confidence of the troops . . . and he would be received with enthusiasm by the whole army."[39] Perhaps Little Mac could restore morale in the army as he had done after First Bull Run.

Back in Washington, Heintzelman bluntly told Secretary of War Stanton what "had occurred and why," and he "did not spare Pope." Nevertheless, out of courtesy he also went to see the downtrodden and disgruntled

Heintzelman's headquarters, King Street, Alexandria, after the Second Battle of Bull Run. Sketch by Robert Knox Sneden. Virginia Historical Society.

Pope. A few days later at Willard's Hotel, where top-ranking Union officers often gathered at the bar, Heintzelman watched in amazement as several officers walked in and were cheered. When Pope entered, he was met with a depressing silence. From New York four months later, Pope tried his best to put his spin on the disaster. His account of the Second Bull Run Campaign amounted to more than sixteen thousand words and was one of the longest after-action reports written during the war. All he could say about Heintzelman was that he "performed his duty faithfully and honestly."[40]

It would be over six weeks before Heintzelman would write his official report of the Union debacle. Although he too tried to put a good face on what was clearly a stunning setback, there was no hiding the extent of the defeat. Moreover, the III Corps was now ineffective and would not be ready for service in the field for weeks, if not months. Of the 14,462 Union soldiers lost during the Second Bull Run Campaign, 2,238 were from Heintzelman's III Corps, of which 1,209 were from Hooker's 2nd Division and 1,029 from Kearny's 1st Division. Both divisions "are ruined from their heavy losses," he admitted. In all, twenty-three officers had been killed; in one of Hooker's regiments, five companies no longer had a single officer. Halleck perhaps put it best: "Our losses in these battles were very heavy both in life and materials."[41] Never had the cause of the Union seemed so hopeless.

Just as Heintzelman predicted, the battle so discredited Pope, who had boasted and failed, that he was relieved of command and sent off angry to Minnesota to fight the Sioux. McDowell asked for a court of inquiry, which eventually exonerated him. Ruined by his devotion to McClellan, Fitz John Porter became the scapegoat for the defeat. He was eventually court-martialed for disloyalty, disobeying orders, and misconduct in the face of the enemy and dishonorably discharged.

But Heintzelman was also to be a victim of Second Bull Run. One historian has gone as far as to say that his leadership during the battle was comparable to a "ninth-place finish in a horse race."[42] The general had indeed not done well. Age, confusion in the Union command, but most of all his lack of leadership all combined to discredit him. Although Heintzelman did not know it at the time, never again in the Civil War would he command a sizeable force in the field. On September 5, 1862, he was in Washington when he learned that he had been relieved as III Corps commander. A few days later he was placed in charge of Union forces defending Washington south of the Potomac. Only three months earlier he had been at the gates of Richmond, when Union prospects for ending the war looked bright. Now he was back in Washington, and like the country he fought so hard to save, his future seemed uncertain. As he waited in Washington, the hastily reassembled Army of the Potomac prepared to meet Lee's invasion of Maryland.

ELEVEN

A City of Shoulder Straps

For defense of the southern approaches to Washington, Heintzelman learned from Lincoln and Halleck that he would have the 17,700-man XXII Corps. As a result, he moved his headquarters from the Ballenger House at Fort Lyon to the Arlington House mansion. There Lee's female slaves, who had remained on the estate, were put to work cleaning the house with soap and water. Once again Heintzelman was able to spend more time with his family in the capital. Bad news came on September 14, 1862, however, when he received word from Caroline and Dr. Summers that their infant daughter, Matilda, had died of scarlet fever in Alexandria. After a hastily arranged funeral, the child's remains were placed in a vault so her body could be taken to Buffalo later for burial.[1]

On September 4 Heintzelman heard that Lee's 55,000-man Army of Northern Virginia was north of the Potomac and moving toward Frederick, Maryland. After meeting with President Lincoln at McClellan's headquarters, he was taken aside by General Marcy and told that "matters looked badly." Moreover, his old III Corps, which had been virtually destroyed at Second Bull Run, was in no condition to aid the Army of the Potomac. Even worse news came twelve days later with reports that Stonewall Jackson had taken Harpers Ferry. "They always outgeneral us," Heintzelman complained. In poor health and worried about the fate of the army, he was anxious and uncertain much of the time, often huddling with his staff late into the night. But then heartening news came of a victory at South Mountain. Three days later large crowds gathered to hear even better news from McClellan.[2] At Sharpsburg, Maryland, on September 17, in some of the worst fighting of the war, Lee had been turned back in what the North called the Battle of Antietam—the bloodiest single day in American history. More than twenty thousand men and boys lay dead or wounded in the narrow country lanes and the ripe cornfields of the Maryland countryside. Dead was Gen. Jesse Reno, who had fallen mortally wounded at Fox's Gap in South Mountain during the approach to Sharpsburg. And among the killed in the great battle was Heintzelman's venerable and respected friend from the western frontier, gray-bearded Joseph King Fenno Mansfield, who was mortally wounded while leading the XII Corps in the East Woods not far from the village of Sharpsburg. But with McClellan claiming a great victory, the North went wild with jubilation.

In the wake of Lee's defeat, Heintzelman did much more than defend the capital. In hopes of intercepting units of the Army of Northern Virginia as it limped back from the Potomac, he sent patrols deep into the countryside east of the Blue Ridge Mountains. For example, on September 22 Col. R. Butler Price's 2nd Pennsylvania Cavalry, with two companies of the 1st Vermont Infantry, advanced through Thoroughfare Gap in the Bull Run Mountains in hopes of intercepting a large Rebel supply train of several hundred wagons, escorted by the 6th Virginia Cavalry, heading for Ashby's Gap. Price reported that after "a short but severe struggle, the enemy broke in great disorder."[3] As the Rebel cavalry retreated back through Ashby's Gap, the Federals burned a few abandoned wagons and returned to Washington with some wounded prisoners. Three weeks later a second expedition captured eighty Confederates at Thoroughfare Gap.

In late September, after it was learned that the Rebels had rebuilt the Orange and Alexandria Railroad bridge over the Rappahannock River, Col. Nathaniel Collins McLean was sent with a brigade of the XXII Corps to Catlett's Station in hopes of destroying a locomotive and train reportedly running men and supplies as far north as Warrenton Junction. McLean arrived just as a train loaded with Confederates sped south toward Richmond. On September 29 Col. Joseph Kargé, with elements of the 1st New Jersey Cavalry and the 1st Pennsylvania Cavalry, was sent by Heintzelman to attack a small Confederate force that had regarrisoned Warrenton Junction. Kargé entered the town without serious opposition and discovered conditions that Heintzelman characterized as lamentable. Every dwelling was full of sick and wounded Confederates who were said to be dying at the rate of fifty a day. Although attended by forty Southern surgeons, many of the "poor sufferers were lying on the bare floor" and "literally decaying in their own filth."[4] As many as twelve hundred of the convalescent soldiers were given parole papers.

Throughout the fall of 1862, there were so many reports of Rebel cavalry operating both north and south of the Potomac and near the capital that Heintzelman could not keep track of them all. Patrolling the Virginia and Maryland countryside, his cavalry had to be on constant alert, as were the infantry and artillery manning the fortifications. In mid-October Union scouts reported that Gen. J. E. B. Stuart was at Leesburg with ten thousand cavalry.[5] "There is quite a scare in Washington. I have all my troops on the alert and the guards on the bridges increased," Heintzelman wrote. When Rebel cavalry captured a train near Manassas Junction, railroad engineers and laborers refused to return to work until the line was secured.

Much of the general's time was also consumed by meetings with Stanton, Halleck, and even Lincoln himself. Stanton seemed distracted, while Halleck complained that Lincoln was micromanaging everything. In the wind and dust of late October, Heintzelman and the president reviewed the troops at Alexandria, after which Lincoln pronounced himself satisfied. Later the two made a short visit to what was known as "Camp Misery," a huge, filthy encampment for army convalescents near Alexandria of which Heintzelman was in charge. Despite his new duties, he found time almost every day to ride across the Long Bridge to visit his family. Sisters Maria and Juliana arrived from West Chester for a short visit, and he gave them a tour of the fortifications.

After being in the forefront of the fighting on the Peninsula and at Second Bull Run, Heintzelman often seemed bored with his new assignment. At headquarters in Arlington House, problems also developed with his aides. "It appears to me that my staff is getting worse and worse every day. I can't have anything done unless I . . . give my personal attention," he complained. In early September McKeever, McKelvey, and Johnston fell ill, and Dr. John Milhau resigned. Solon Lathrop arrived after visiting relatives in Maine to continue as assistant inspector general. In reality, Lathrop remained the general's closest confidant and the most influential member of his staff. Lt. Col. Elias M. Greene, a New Yorker, joined as chief quartermaster, while Vermont-born Maj. Leavitt Hunt, who had fought well on the Peninsula, especially at Malvern Hill, became an aide-de-camp. Capt. Granville Johnson remained as an aide as did Capt. Henry Norton, while Capt. Carroll H. Potter was appointed as assistant adjutant general. Dr. George Taylor was recruited to replace Milhau, while Capt. E. C. Sturges headed the ambulance corps.[6] Heintzelman seemed overjoyed when the staff presented him with a new horse, which was, like the general himself, a veteran of the Peninsula Campaign.

In early November both Hunt and Johnson submitted their resignations, saying they could no longer work with recently promoted Lieutenant Colonel McKeever. "He has made himself so obnoxious," Heintzelman wrote of McKeever, that "no one will serve with him or have anything to do with him."[7] When the general confronted him with the accusations, McKeever found a position in the War Department and resigned. As a result, both Hunt and Johnson agreed to stay on. At Arlington Heintzelman frequently visited with General Porter, whom he asked to join the

XXII Corps, at least temporarily until the controversial general's status could be resolved.

Heintzelman seemed overly concerned about spies in the capital. "Every window curtain in Washington concealed two spies," he told Eunice Tripler, the wife of Dr. Charles S. Tripler. Once Mrs. Tripler and Margaret had gone to see Samuel Peter near Alexandria, only to be stopped by a sentinel several hundred yards from headquarters. When they asked why, they were told that someone might hear the telegraph and decipher the message. Tripler remembered the general telling her that at a meeting with the president and McClellan in early 1862, he had been forced to close all the doors and windows. Lincoln, Heintzelman thought, was "strangely obtuse to the danger of spies in the White House."[8]

In late October, with the Army of the Potomac finally on the move, McClellan began issuing a rash of orders stripping the Washington defenses of men and material. So many troops were being removed that Heintzelman became legitimately concerned. He had gone to bed on the evening of October 31, when the army commander telegraphed an order sending the entire XXII Corps to Thoroughfare Gap. So alarmed was Heintzelman that the city would be left defenseless that he rushed to Halleck to complain. After considerable discussion, the general in chief agreed to send most, though not all, of the troops McClellan wanted. With Maj. Gen. Nathaniel Banks, who commanded the Washington defenses north of the Potomac, absent in New York, Halleck asked Heintzelman to remain in the city.[9] Finally, on November 8, following McClellan's incessant quarreling with Lincoln and his lack of resolve in pursuing Lee, Little Mac was replaced by Maj. Gen. Ambrose E. Burnside.

Realizing that he was unlikely to ever command the Army of the Potomac, Heintzelman now began to give more thought to a proposed expedition to Texas. Edmund J. Davis, antebellum district judge from South Texas and an uncompromising Unionist who Heintzelman had come to know and trust during the Cortina War, wanted the general to lead an expedition to the Lone Star State. The judge was in Washington with a number of other prominent Texas Unionists to lobby Lincoln to authorize such a campaign. With a letter of endorsement from Heintzelman, Davis went to the Executive Mansion to see the president. "I find the administration unalterably opposed to any operation in Texas," he told Heintzelman after the meeting, "till after Richmond is taken and the Mississippi fairly opened." Undeterred, the judge also met with a number of Lincoln's cabinet officials, whom he hoped would be interested in Texas. Several unnamed cabinet members, Davis reported, had "small acquaintance with the state of feelings, the condition of affairs, and the ways and means in the South." Even worse was the fact that they seemed "to be indifferent to all information on these subjects." The Texas Unionists were not only "listened to with impatience" but also "dismissed with as much indifference as any of the ordinary crowd of office seekers."[10]

Although Davis left for the Rio Grande frontier to assist his family in their flight out of Texas, he returned to Washington to continue pressing for military action. If Heintzelman was not interested in commanding such a campaign, Davis was hoping the general would at least assist "in securing the appointment of some other officer who has seen service in Texas and knows the country and people." Davis thought either Gen. George Stoneman or Gen. Henry Jackson Hunt, both of whom had served with Heintzelman during the Cortina War, would "do very well," but he did not want John C. Frémont or well-known "Jayhawker" James Henry "Kansas" Lane, whom he had heard mentioned as possible commanders. "Nothing could be more disastrous to the Union cause in that state, than sending either of these men," he wrote. When Davis and his friends continued to press the issue, Heintzelman finally agreed that he would "go if they make it an object." His expectations rose in early November 1862 when he heard that Lincoln wanted to see him, thinking perhaps that a major command was in the offing, but the meeting turned out to be of little importance. Through discussions with Alexander J. Hamilton, an antebellum congressman and leading Texas Unionist who, like Davis, had fled to Mexico and had been commissioned a brigadier general and named military governor of Texas, he learned that General Banks was being considered for the Texas command. In early December 1862 Banks set sail, but his destination was a secret, though it was rumored that he was bound for South Carolina, not Texas.[11] Nevertheless, Heintzelman continued to meet with several leading senators as well as Secretary of War Stanton in hopes of obtaining a command by which he could redeem his rapidly waning military reputation.

In Washington Heintzelman expended considerable effort in trying to obtain an appointment for Charles at West Point. He solicited letters of recommendation from fellow officers, several congressional delegations, and Gov. Andrew Gregg Curtin of Pennsylvania. But delays and uncertainties abounded, and the family decided that Charles, now sixteen, should continue his schooling at Perth Amboy, New Jersey, and that Margaret should accompany him.[12] Although both Margaret and Mary were ill at the time, they left by train with Charles on September 17. Complaining of illness himself, Samuel Peter sought the medical assistance and advice of Dr. Summers.

Heintzelman met with William Wrightson, and the two continued to lobby for the creation of a Territory of Arizona. Poston was in the capital too but soon left for New York, where the Sonora Exploring and Mining Company had established its offices, before continuing on his way to Europe in hopes of selling the Arizona mines. "I am willing to sell them for almost anything," Heintzelman wrote, often displaying the rich silver ore he had brought from Cerro Colorado in 1859 to potential buyers. At the same time, he maintained his interest in both the building of a Pacific railroad and the further development of the Vallecillo Mines in northern Mexico (which he had visited during the Cortina War). He was hoping that a military expedition to Texas would help open the road "to our mines and get our silver-lead to market."[13] Yet there were rumors that French emperor Napoleon III had his eyes not only on Mexico but also on Texas. Moreover, French recognition of the Confederacy was almost certain.

Succeeding General Banks in overall command of the Washington defenses, Heintzelman was forced to devote more and more of his attention to the fearful conditions in the huge convalescent camp near Alexandria. With the onset of cold weather in the late fall and early winter of 1862, the mortality rate at Camp Misery became a scandal. As a result, the Sanitary Commission was forced to come to the rescue, with hospital tents, woolen shirts, and blankets. Yet in early December several congressmen visited Heintzelman, demanding that he improve conditions in the camp. Not only was the sanitation there abominable, but rumors circulated that several men had frozen to death as well. More wood and blankets were badly needed, the general admitted. When members of the Sanitary Commission complained to Stanton, the secretary of war called him to his office and, in Heintzelman's words, "took me to task." Investigating the conditions himself, he found they were not as bad as had been reported, yet the sick and wounded continued to die at an appalling rate. In January 1863 the dedicated and influential Dorothea L. Dix, who had been appointed superintendent of women nurses and had devoted her life to uplifting the mentally ill and poor, complained to Stanton of conditions in the camp. When Stanton ordered Heintzelman to meet with Dix, the general complained privately that he was not accustomed to having a woman interfere with his work. Moreover, he groused, Dix had not been to the camp in two weeks and thus had little knowledge of actual conditions there.[14]

By January 1863 the camp housed 8,108 men , and more patients arrived every day. Eventually, conditions at Camp Misery did improve. A new barracks, housing as many as 5,000 men, was completed, and many convalescents, fully armed and equipped with clothing, canteens, haversacks, and knapsacks, began returning to their regiments at the rate of several hundred a day.[15]

Along with Gen. John Barnard, chief engineer for the Washington defenses, Heintzelman was charged with enlarging and strengthening the earthen fortifications ringing the city. At Barnard's suggestion, many of the forts were renamed for fallen Union heroes, such as Mansfield, Reno, and Kearny. By February 1863 the total number of officers and men in the Department of Washington had reached 66,560. Of this number, more than one-third, fully 26,725 men, were assigned to the Washington garrison. Defending the capital now were 10,305 artillerymen with 826 pieces of both field and heavy guns and 16,420 infantrymen.[16]

By November 1862 the capital was again filled with hundreds of soldier straps. Many officers flocked to the city's numerous saloons. Relocating his headquarters from Arlington to Washington, Heintzelman was in a better position to feel the pulse of the struggling nation and hear the latest rumors emanating from the War Department and the Executive Mansion. From the leading newspaper correspondents there, many of them friends, he became privy to the latest news from the various fronts.

On December 3, 1862, Heintzelman received a summons to testify at both a court of inquiry that General McDowell had requested and the much publicized, heart-wrenching court-martial of General Porter. Two days later at the court of inquiry, he was quizzed by McDowell for almost an hour. There was little Heintzelman could say or add to the proceedings. He told the court he had known McDowell for many years and, though he had heard rumors of his drunkenness, he "had sat at the table for weeks at a time with him and have met him at various times and places" and had never seen him drunk.[17] Contrary to what he had often written in his journal, he told the court he had always found McDowell to be a competent commander.

On December 12, much to his displeasure and uneasiness, he appeared at General Porter's court-martial. When he had first come to know Porter during the Peninsula Campaign, he had disliked him and was somewhat envious, seeing him as McClellan's pet. Yet Porter had fought with distinction, especially at Gaines's Mill and Malvern Hill, and had been promoted to major general. Following the humiliating debacle at Second Bull Run, however, Pope had charged him with disloyalty, disobedience, and misconduct, and Heintzelman came to see him as a scapegoat for yet another embarrassing Union failure. There was little that Heintzelman could tell the court about Second Bull Run that related directly to the charges against Porter, since their commands had been on opposite ends of the battlefield. Most of what he had to say was general information relating to the conditions of the Orange and Alexander Railroad prior to the battle. In the end he was more critical of Pope than of Porter. Five weeks later, on a dreary and misty Washington day, Heintzelman was "disappointed and surprised" to learn that Porter had been found guilty and cashiered. He immediately went to see Porter, writing afterward in his journal that he felt very sorry for him.[18] Heintzelman remained convinced that Porter had done nothing wrong and had simply become an easy and tragic victim of a humiliating Union defeat and the Radical Republicans wrath toward McClellan.

With the Army of the Potomac on the march again, the capital was abuzz with news of fighting at Fredericksburg, Virginia, where it was said that Burnside had established a bridgehead across the Rappahannock. But then Heintzelman observed as the army attempted to censor the news, even keeping Lincoln sitting in suspense hour after hour at the telegraph office. At first the reports were only that the Army of the Potomac had been turned back, then it became evident that the Federals had suffered a resounding defeat. More than twelve thousand Union soldiers had been killed or wounded as Burnside hurled assault after assault against Lee's Fredericksburg defenses before staggering back across the river. "People look gloomy," Heintzelman wrote. "It will be as much as the president can do to maintain himself. . . . There is great dissatisfaction in the city." At Christmas, Margaret's mother arrived from Buffalo for a lavish Christmas dinner with Vice President Hannibal Hamlin. That evening, Heintzelman noted in his journal that the "disaster at Fredericksburg" was "disgusting and disheartening" and that Burnside was "solely responsible."[19]

Following the Union debacle at Fredericksburg, desertions in the demoralized Army of the Potomac reached two hundred a day. When Burnside moved to cross the Rappahannock above Fredericksburg, the entire army—men, guns, animals, and wagons—became stuck in knee-deep mud. Bogged down in the infamous "Mud March," Burnside came to Washington to offer his resignation, which Lincoln promptly accepted.

A few days later, in early January 1863, word arrived from Tennessee that the Confederate Army of Tennessee had been turned back at Murfreesboro, and Heintzelman's mood lightened. "I would almost have despaired had we been defeated," he wrote. But around this same time, there were reports of Rebel cavalry near the capital. Telegrams from Dumfries, south of Washington, indicated that as many as four thousand Southern horsemen, supported by infantry and artillery, had passed through Union lines. The next day the Confederates were reported to be north of the Occoquan River and headed toward Fairfax Court House. Heintzelman responded by sending Brig. Gen. John Joseph Abercrombie with all the cavalry he had in his Washington command to confront the Rebels. After a skirmish near Chantilly, the intruders retreated south, carrying with them forty prisoners, some of them civilians.[20] At the same time there was another report from Baltimore that Confederate cavalry had again crossed the Potomac.

New Year's Day, 1863, dawned mild and pleasant. As was the tradition with high-ranking government officials and generals in the army, Heintzelman walked down Pennsylvania Avenue at noon to pay his respects to the president and Mary Lincoln at the Executive Mansion. Next came a visit to Navy Secretary Gideon Wells, then down Pennsylvania Avenue again to see General Halleck. With Quartermaster General Montgomery Meigs, he also called on Secretary of State William H. Seward, and later in the afternoon he went to see Secretary of the Treasury Salmon P. Chase and Attorney General Edward Bates. The talk of the city was Lincoln's Emancipation Proclamation, the text of which had appeared in several newspapers. Many individuals expressed disapproval, though Gov. William Sprague of Rhode Island thought it "would have a great effect on Europe."[21] Most agreed that the proclamation was a "war measure" and that it should have a "decided success." Although it did not free all of the slaves, only those who were in the states and parts of the states then in rebellion, Heintzelman realized that the Emancipation Proclamation was one of the great documents of American history, a giant step forward, one from which the nation could never retreat. The war had evolved from a contest to preserve the Union into a struggle over the meaning of freedom. In the evening there was a public reading of the document as many African Americans in the capital huddled in prayer. At a sumptuous dinner with Mexican ambassador Matías Romero, Sen. Henry B. Anthony of Rhode Island, Judge Edwards Pierrepont of New York, Governor Sprague of Rhode Island, and Edmund J. Davis, a lively discussion of the proclamation continued well into the evening.

Following Burnside's resounding defeat at Fredericksburg, Heintzelman again aspired, at least in his imagination, to the command of the Army of the Potomac. Learning that General Hooker, who he had once called the bravest man in the Union Army, had attended two cabinet meetings and might be appointed, Heintzelman wrathfully turned on his old division commander. "What can they want with him?" he angrily wrote in a fit of indignation. Later, when Hooker was quoted as saying that he was the "the only general in the country competent to lead the armies of the Republic," Heintzelman indignantly retorted, "What vanity!" Indeed, Hooker was brave and able, but he was as vain as a peacock. Heintzelman had taken time to visit with the general while he was recuperating in Washington after being shot in the foot at Antietam. But when rumors swept the capital that Hooker was sure to replace McClellan, Heintzelman became even more incensed. "What a mistake and what an outrage!" he exclaimed. To him, there was "universal disgust at the prospect of Gen. Hooker's having command."[22] Heintzelman's own vanity would not allow him to envision anyone who had served under him ascending to command the Army of the Potomac.

When told in late January 1863 that Hooker was certain to replace Burnside, Heintzelman rushed to see Halleck, telling the general in chief that he would not serve under someone "whose whole reputation was gained under my command." Heintzelman wanted command of a separate department or he wanted to be relieved. Although cautioned by friends not to press Halleck too hard, Heintzelman went to see the general in chief a second time during a terrible snowstorm only to find Hooker present. Nevertheless, on February 2 Halleck reestablished the Department of Washington, and five days later Heintzelman assumed formal command of the XXII Corps. Headquarters were now moved to a building on the corner of 15½ Street and Pennsylvania Avenue adjoining Lafayette Park, opposite the Executive Mansion.[23]

With no immediate threat to the capital, Heintzelman spent much of January and February 1863 visiting with old friends, including Irvin McDowell. Maj. Gen. Edward Richard Spriggs Canby, who Heintzelman had known in Mexico and California, came to Washington, telling how he had chased Brig. Gen. Henry H. Sibley's grandiose dreaming Texans out of New Mexico Territory. Considerable time was also spent with John W. Forney, former clerk of the House of Representatives and proprietor of the *Philadelphia Press*, who had recently been named secretary of the Senate. Forney, who had also established the *Washington Daily Morning Chronicle*, agreed to publish Heintzelman's official report of the Battle of Williamsburg, though when it appeared in print, it was full of typographical errors.[24] There was also time to continue lobbying for an Arizona territorial bill and again show off his silver ore from Cerro Colorado. Poston came to Washington in early February, and the two went to see Sen. Lyman Trumbull of New York and Sen. Benjamin Wade. A few days later William Wrightson arrived from Cincinnati, and on February 17 Heintzelman held an "oyster supper . . . to talk Arizona."[25] The next day Heintzelman, Poston, Wrightson, and Wade made their way through rain and streets of mud to see Rep. John A. Gurley, a proponent of organizing Arizona and a principal candidate for governor of the proposed territory. After a lengthy meeting, they decided they should call on the president as soon as possible to push for the creation of the territory.

If Arizona Territory could be created, Heintzelman was sure the chances of troops being sent to the Desert Southwest would be greatly improved, and with troops in Arizona, the mines could be reopened. Stanton must be convinced, he thought, that at least two regiments, along with a third from California, were needed to secure the territory. When Stanton refused to go along with the idea, Representative Gurley and John Noble Goodwin of Maine, an ex-congressman who was hoping for a position in the Arizona territorial government, went to see Lincoln and Halleck. They "satisfactorily arranged about troops for Arizona," Heintzelman recorded.[26] Finally on February 20, 1863, the general learned that the Senate

The John B. Floyd residence, 15½ Street and Pennsylvania Avenue, Heintzelman's headquarters in Washington, D.C. Sketch by Robert Knox Sneden. Virginia Historical Society.

had passed the Arizona Bill by a vote of two to one; his persistent lobbying had at last achieved results. No other individual, except perhaps Poston, deserves more credit for the creation of Arizona Territory than he. In late February Heintzelman went with Wrightson to see Lincoln, who had signed the Arizona Bill four days earlier, in hopes of having Poston made superintendent of Indian affairs for the new territory. Well into March 1863, the Heintzelman residence continued to be a beehive of activity on behalf of Arizona.

On Capitol Hill the Committee on the Conduct of the War was busy delivering McClellan a *coup de grâce* that would prevent him from returning to command the Army of the Potomac or any other army. The Radicals were also hoping to destroy any political ambition Little Mac might have toward the presidency in 1864. On February 17, 1863, Heintzelman made his way down Pennsylvania Avenue to appear before the partisan committee. For three hours he was grilled on McClellan's leadership of the army during the Peninsula Campaign. At long last he had a forum in which he could publicly castigate his former commander. First, the siege of Yorktown, he vehemently asserted, was unnecessary. In fact, the III Corps alone could have taken the town shortly after landing at Fortress Monroe. Moreover, there should have been a vigorous pursuit of Rebel forces after the Battle of Williamsburg. Heintzelman also said that had McClellan allowed him to launch a more determined counterattack after the Battle of Seven Pines, he might well have led his corps into Richmond.

A close analysis of the testimony indicates that many on the committee were only using Heintzelman to discredit McClellan. Perhaps the most shocking revelation came when the general told the committee that during the latter stages of the Seven Days, McClellan had not been in overall command of the army. "Was the Seven Days' battle fought under the direction and orders of General McClellan," Rep. Daniel W. Gooch of Massachusetts asked, or did "each corps commander fight his own troops as he thought best?" "The corps commanders fought their troops entirely according to their own idea," Heintzelman replied. The committee "was a little surprised that Gen. McClellan did not consult with me and at his absence from the battlefield," he wrote that evening in his journal. Appearing before the committee two weeks later, McClellan contradicted much of what Heintzelman had said, arguing that the III Corps could not have taken Yorktown without a siege, nor could Heintzelman have taken Richmond following Seven Pines.[27]

Beginning in January 1863, Heintzelman was forced to devote a considerable amount of effort to a growing threat from a fearless and restless Old Dominion guerilla named John Singleton Mosby, the legendary "Gray Ghost of the Confederacy." Operating out of Fauquier and Loudoun counties, especially the area between the Bull Run and Blue Ridge Mountains, Mosby and his men were concealed, sheltered, and fed by Rebel sympathizers. Raiding east toward Washington and north into Maryland, he attacked small Union garrisons and cut Federal supply lines. On the night of March 8, 1863, Mosby and twenty-nine raiders rode through a breach in the Union picket lines between Centreville and Chantilly and slipped into Fairfax Court House. There they captured Brig. Gen. Edwin Henry Stoughton in his bed, raced back through the lines, and delivered him to Brig. Gen. Fitzhugh Lee at Culpeper Court House. Stoughton's capture was a major embarrassment for Heintzelman and the War Department.[28] On May 14, when Mosby's raiders were reported near Leesburg above Washington, Heintzelman ordered Brig. Gen. Robert Cumming Schenck at Baltimore to send out the 1st Michigan Cavalry to pursue the guerillas. But month after month, Mosby's "partisan rangers" captured Federal pickets at small Virginia hamlets such as Herndon Station, Aldie, Snicker's Ferry, Dranesville, and Chantilly.[29]

Well into 1863, Heintzelman continued to refight the Peninsula Campaign in his imagination. Although he would always question McClellan's strategy, he came to feel that Little Mac had been mistreated by the Committee on the Conduct of the War and that he was "a greater man than most people give him credit." In March word came that an aging General Sumner, after being relieved from command following the Battle of Chancellorsville, had died suddenly at Syracuse, New York. "He was a most gallant man and served the country faithfully for many years," Heintzelman wrote.[30] Although he had at times been critical of the old general, he had never questioned "Bull" Sumner's dedication to his country.

Most of all, Heintzelman wanted a field command and promotion to brigadier general in the Regular Army. When he went to see General Halleck to press his case in these matters, he was bluntly told by Brig. Gen. George W. Cullum, Halleck's chief of staff, that he was too conservative, or as Cullum put it, not "nigger enough." Rushing off to see Stanton, he found Gov. Andrew Johnson of Tennessee in the secretary of war's office, but when Halleck appeared, he left without further discussion. He even sent Governor Curtin to the Executive Mansion to make an appeal to the president. Lincoln told Curtin that Heintzelman was "a very good officer" but declined to make any promises. "I have never got a single thing I have asked [for from the president] and may as well give up asking," Heintzelman wrote. Later on Newspaper Row, he met Samuel Wilkeson of the *New York Tribune*, who revealed that the prevailing rumors were that Heintzelman was being sent to St. Louis.[31]

In the capital that spring, with the peach trees in full blossom, the general continued to work for an at-large appointment for Charles at West Point. But again Lincoln gave the application a lukewarm endorsement. "When the time comes," he would "make this appointment if not pressed . . . in other directions," Lincoln wrote. "I never asked him for anything but this," Heintzelman wrote. "I am going to press him harder," he continued, while setting off to solicit the influence of the Pennsylvania, New York, and Ohio congressional delegations. In the end, it was Margaret's friendship with Mary Lincoln that appears to have made a difference. On April 18, 1863, after a meeting with the first lady, the Heintzelmans were assured that their son would be appointed. Not long thereafter, Charles, who was still at Perth Amboy, received the coveted appointment.[32] The happy lad arrived in Washington, where he proudly accompanied his father around the capital. In early June Charles was off to West Point, from where he naively wrote within a few days to complain that the "plebes" were being harassed by the older cadets. Charles also asked for money. Although Samuel Peter sent five dollars and would continue to send funds during the four years Charles remained at West Point, he reminded his son that during his own four years he had spent at the academy in the 1820s, he had only received three dollars total from his family in Manheim.

By May the news from Virginia improved. The Army of the Potomac was across the Rappahannock again, and a victory was expected soon, "even if Hooker gets drunk," Heintzelman quipped. Four days later Heintzelman heard that "Fighting Joe" had "gained a great success." Three days after that, however, details of the Battle of Chancellorsville, in which Hooker was outmaneuvered and "badly whipped" by Lee and his smaller Army of Northern Virginia, dribbled into the capital, and again Northern morale plummeted. Hooker's repulse was "a great disappointment," Heintzelman wrote, for he "should have risked much before he retreated." Surprisingly, both Lincoln and Halleck did not know that Hooker had retreated across the Rappahannock until Heintzelman told them. His haughtiness toward the clean-shaven Hooker, who had fought so gallantly on the Peninsula, even motivated his sister-in-law Matilda to write a "sarcastic piece" about the defeated general.[33]

During the second week of June, Heintzelman learned that Lee had turned Hooker's flank and was again moving north, approaching the Potomac. "I of course do not believe it," he wrote. Two days later, though, when news reached Washington that advance units of Lee's army were indeed nearing the river, "great excitement" gripped the city. Although Lee's intentions were unknown, Heintzelman told Governor Curtin that he was certain Lee was intent on invading Pennsylvania with hopes of sending a political shockwave across the North that might reverberate into a negotiated end to the war. But the more he learned, the more he concluded that Lee's objective was probably just the Shenandoah Valley. "What a fearful condition our country is in," he concluded. Heintzelman's line of outposts along the Occoquan River was abandoned and its garrisons ordered back to the Washington defenses. Later that month the general watched as more and more of his own command was sent to bolster Hooker's army. Other regiments that had been assigned to the capital's defense steamed off to Norfolk and Suffolk to reinforce Maj. Gen. John A. Dix's command in eastern Virginia. With his cavalry gone, "the first indication of the approach of the enemy would be their appearance at our works," he told Halleck.[34] There were no Union forces, he complained, between the enemy and Fort Lyon.

Not only was Heintzelman's cavalry gone, but a large part of his infantry and artillery had also joined Hooker. So thoroughly stripped were the Washington defenses that it became a "great embarrassment." Moreover, with the construction of new forts, the number of men available for each became fewer and fewer. In consultation with General Barnard, they agreed that a detailed report should be compiled as soon a possible, outlining the weaknesses of the capital's defenses. By Barnard's calculations, there were not enough riflemen to protect the artillerymen in the sixty-two forts and redoubts south of the Potomac and the fifty-six north of the river. For example, Fort Mahan, which had been garrisoned by seven hundred men, now had a guard of less than one hundred, and when Halleck expressed concern that the bridges over the Potomac were inadequately guarded, Heintzelman was forced to place artillery batteries at both the Chain and Aqueduct bridges. More complications came in early June when a sixteen-hundred-pound powder magazine exploded at Fort Lyon, killing twenty-one men and greatly adding to the nervousness in the capital.[35]

The safety of Washington was dependent on Hooker's army, and neither Heintzelman nor Barnard knew where it was. If Lee was able to get between Hooker and the capital, there was little doubt that "a considerable body of cavalry might . . . dash into and destroy Washington," Barnard concluded.[36] A *coup de main* was a real possibility, he warned. Moreover, if Washington were attacked, the numerous secessionists in the capital would attempt to destroy the bridges over the Potomac and burn the public buildings. Heintzelman also worried that Mosby's guerrillas and other Rebel partisans operating in the vicinity would combine with Lee's advance cavalry units at Annandale, dash across the Potomac, and destroy the railroad between the capital and Baltimore. An even greater challenge was protecting the Orange and Alexandria Railroad. Heintzelman decreed that if citizens were caught damaging the railroad or any depots, they were to be impressed as laborers to repair the damage. If necessary, he would even remove secessionists living within ten miles of any damaged railroad and confiscate their property.

Heintzelman became so fearful of an attack on Washington that he organized all the employees of the Quartermaster's and Commissary Departments and requested permission to recruit citizens from the capital and Alexandria into home-guard units. He also organized one hundred army sutlers, who volunteered their services. When scouts reported J. E. B. Stuart and seven thousand cavalrymen were nearing Washington, Heintzelman began planning for an all-out defense of the capital that included recruiting more black troops and arming the city's numerous convalescents. Should Stuart attack, Halleck even urged him to place mounted batteries of artillery on the streets. Stanton vetoed this idea, however, arguing that "every possible means of security" had been adopted "against any sudden raid or incursion of the enemy, by day or by night." To calm the nerves of a populace in near panic, Heintzelman told Stanton that he had "taken all the precautions for the defense of the city and the public property which the limited means at my disposal will permit." So many men in Washington had been conscripted that Barnard asked that all laborers and experienced engineers be exempted.[37]

A few days later the capital was again thrown into panic when Stuart's cavalry broke away from Lee's army to strike at Fairfax, Annandale, and Dranesville before crossing the Potomac into Maryland, destroying part of the railroad west Washington, and cutting telegraph communication between it and the Army of the Potomac. When Stuart's gray-clad cavalry rode into Rockville, northwest of the city, at noon on June 28, churchgoers as well as schoolgirls from a local academy were terrified. Although the Confederates retreated from in front of the Union defenses, the city remained on edge. All of Heintzelman's staff were asked to remain at headquarters through the night, and when Rebel sympathizers in the city began to exalt, saying that "Lee will go into Pennsylvania surely this time," Heintzelman had them arrested and thrown in prison. So nervous were the soldiers that late one June evening, after Samuel Peter had ridden out with Margaret in a carriage to pick blackberries near the Chain Bridge and was returning in the twilight, he was shocked to hear the discharge of a cannon from one of the forts and a rifle shot go whizzing by the carriage.[38]

By late June long lines of soldiers began moving through the city day and night. "Great excitement prevails," Sneden recalled. As Lee's army reached Hagerstown, Maryland, heading north toward Harrisburg, Pennsylvania, Washington anxiously awaited the latest news from the Army of the Potomac. A Fourth of July Union League celebration in Philadelphia, at which Heintzelman was scheduled to speak, was promptly canceled as Governor Curtin and the city's mayor issued pleas for help. As expected, Heintzelman blamed Hooker for Lee's invasion of his native state, and he took every opportunity to criticize and castigate his former subordinate. When the headquarters of the Army of the Potomac was at Fairfax Court House, he recalled, Capt. Granville Johnson had been sent to consult with Hooker but had found "Fighting Joe" drunk. When the general later came to Washington to consult with Halleck and Stanton, it was said that he was drinking heavily. "There is universal dissatisfaction at Hooker. Why don't he confess his incompetency and resign?" Heintzelman wondered. There was "very little confidence felt in the army by the higher officers or by civilians in Hooker's abilities. I must confess that I fear some great blunder." Moreover, Lee had "no fear of any movement that he may make."[39]

Heintzelman was in Halleck's office on the morning of June 28 when he was told that if he needed to correspond with the Army of the Potomac, the headquarters of the army was at Frederick, Maryland, and that all communications should be addressed to Maj. Gen. George Gordon Meade, not Hooker. When asked what kind of a man Meade was, Heintzelman could only say that he was not well known but was "well spoken of." Regardless, there would be "great rejoicing at the removal of Hooker."[40]

On the afternoon of July 2, 1863, as Lee and Meade were locked in bloody combat at Gettysburg, Pennsylvania, the band of the 17th U.S. Infantry arrived at Heintzelman's residence to serenade him. His thoughts, however, were with Meade and the army at the redbrick town in southern Pennsylvania. There was little doubt in his mind that the Confederates would be turned back. "All I fear is that Lee will be able to make good his retreat to the Potomac," he wrote. On July 4, with the news that Lee had been decisively defeated, Heintzelman celebrated into the night. The "city is in fine spirits," he wrote, as a large crowd gathered on the grounds south of the Executive Mansion. The Declaration of Independence was read, and the Marine Band played the "Star-Spangled Banner." Early in the afternoon two days later, equally exciting news reached the capital from the West. The seemingly impregnable Confederate fortress of Vicksburg, Mississippi, had fallen to the resolute Ulysses Grant in one of the most successful campaigns of the war. It was only a matter of time before Port Hudson, Louisiana, the last Confederate stronghold on the Mississippi River, surrendered, Heintzelman concluded. The next day he ordered a hundred-gun salute fired from Fort Lincoln and Capitol Hill, and at noon the 17th Infantry band struck up a number of patriotic airs at his headquarters. Later the band of the 34th Massachusetts serenaded Lincoln, Stanton, and Halleck, after which all three offered a few patriotic words. "Captured battle flags were shown and paraded to deafening cheers and the booming of artillery," Sneden recalled.[41] Across the North, church bells rang and guns boomed a triumphant salute. After more than two years of war and bloodshed, Gettysburg and Vicksburg represented the turning of the tide. From here on, Heintzelman hoped, it would be a rapid decline for the Confederacy.

With Lee's army battered and in retreat, Heintzelman continued to worry that Meade would allow the Rebels to escape back across the Potomac and that Lincoln would somehow agree to a compromise with the South. Before any peace, the "Rebels must lay down their arms" and their "leaders must be punished and slavery utterly destroyed," he declared. Still, he maintained great respect for Lee, and when his bespectacled friend Mathew Brady gave him a photograph of the gray-bearded commander that had been taken from a Rebel prisoner, he seemed pleased. "He looks hard—as if he had not been kept well," Heintzelman commented.[42]

In the wake of the bloodletting at Gettysburg, the hospitals and many of the public buildings in the capital were again crowded with wounded. One casualty was Gen. Dan Sickles, who had commanded Heintzelman's old corps at Chancellorsville and had been badly wounded while leading it at Gettysburg. On the Union left in the vicinity of the Round Tops, and in defiance of direct orders, on July 2 Sickles had advanced forward into a peach orchard, inadvertently creating a salient that was overrun by Longstreet's corps, and it was there that the forty-four-year-old Sickles had lost his right leg. Although fighting bravely, the III Corps had been decimated. Heintzelman had always thought that Sickles was too close to McClellan, but he liked the controversial New Yorker, nevertheless. Within weeks Sickles was hobbling around the capital on crutches, making the rounds of the government offices and the Washington theaters. Had Heintzelman been at Gettysburg, Sickles said, he would have been proud of the III Corps.[43] On the second anniversary of First Bull Run, Sickles asked if the 17th Infantry band could play at his quarters in the evening, a request Heintzelman found self-centered, but one he readily agreed to.

He remained disappointed that Meade had not launched a vigorous pursuit of Lee's army. In fact, Meade admitted he did not even know where the Confederates had gone. With the Potomac at flood stage due to summer rains, the south bank of the river should have been occupied as soon after Gettysburg as possible, Heintzelman argued, and every effort made to occupy the Shenandoah Valley. Moreover, General Dix should be ordered "forward and take Richmond." But then there was news from New York City of bloody draft riots, and entire regiments had to be sent from the Army of the Potomac to suppress the violence. In Washington there was also dissatisfaction over the draft, and a regiment from Alexandria had to be brought across the river to patrol the streets. Heintzelman also sent two companies of black troops to guard the contraband camp. But when Gen. Silas Casey complained to Stanton that having black troops guard white convalescents was politically imprudent, the secretary countermanded the order.[44] In the capital there was a flood of new rumors. Meade had asked to be relieved, some said. Others insisted that General Grant had been ordered east to assume command.

On July 11 Heintzelman entertained Charles Poston and Thomas Wrightson. The next day he watched as the newly appointed governor of the Arizona Territory, John A. Gurley, left for Fort Leavenworth and the long trek along the Santa Fe Trail to the Desert Southwest. Meeting with Judge Davis and his wife, Anne Britton Davis, at Willard's Hotel on the evening of July 15, 1863, Heintzelman listened intently, with a rainstorm pounding outside, as Mrs. Davis related how she had been badly treated in Texas and how her husband had been abducted by Rebels on the south bank of the Rio Grande, carried across the river, and almost hanged on the prairie near Brownsville. In early September Heintzelman learned from Stanton that as many as twenty-five thousand men were being committed to an expedition to Texas. There was little doubt such a force "should sweep Texas in a very short time," he conjectured. Such a campaign would also "convince Louis Napoleon . . . not to interfere with us." Whoever commanded the force, Heintzelman and Davis agreed, should be "a man who has served in Texas and understands the country and its difficulties." Although few possessed such qualifications, he suspected that Ulysses Grant would be placed in charge. "I don't care to go to Texas much, but I want the command of a separate army," Heintzelman wrote. The only difficulty with the expedition that he could foresee was "the scarcity of water" in the Lone Star State. Later, when he learned that Grant was to assume a more exalted position, he speculated that either General Banks or General Franklin would lead the expedition, though neither, he felt, was "fit to command an army in Texas." The Union failure at Sabine Pass on September 8, 1863, was a direct result of the commander's unfamiliarity with the region. Anyone who would have "served in Texas . . . would have known better."[45]

More-immediate concerns, though, were with the small bands of guerrillas under Mosby that remained active in northern Virginia. Yet by late summer Washington appeared safe for one of the first times in the war, and he was able to attend a number of parties and lively "hops." In late August he accompanied Lincoln and Stanton to the Sixth Street wharves for an excursion down the Potomac to Rosiers Bluff on the sternwheeler *General Hooker* to inspect one of the latest Federal fortifications. There the party was welcomed by four companies of the 9th New York Artillery. After partaking of peaches, crackers, cheese, and champagne, the group returned to the capital.[46]

On the first anniversary of Second Bull Run, he took leave to visit the Army of the Potomac. With Governor Curtin, several aides, and a car full of distinguished guests from the Keystone State, the occasion was the presentation of a sword by the Pennsylvanians to General Meade. Catching the train at Alexandria, the party rambled down the Orange and Alexandria Railroad to Bealeton, where they were taken two miles through the woods to the camp of the Pennsylvania Reserves. The soldiers had constructed a large stage over which evergreens were hung. With several hundred officers and men present, the festivities included speeches and loud hurrahs for the Union. Accepting the sword, Meade said that at the Battle of Glendale, the Pennsylvania Reserves had not fought well, but they had matured as a combat force. In the evening there was a fine dinner at which time Heintzelman took the occasion to discuss the guerrilla problem in northern Virginia with Meade. "He agreed with me that they cannot be entirely got rid of," Heintzelman recorded.[47]

In early September, with Generals Cullum and Barnard and a twenty-five-man cavalry escort, the general enjoyed a pleasant sixteen-mile buggy ride upriver to view the Great Falls of the Potomac. A far more dangerous three-day excursion was made two weeks later when he accompanied a scout some thirty-five miles up the Potomac to the mouth of the Monocacy River. After visiting a cavalry camp, he spotted a "strong trail of horses" made by a party of at least sixty Rebel guerillas. Proceeding cautiously, the Federals learned from several Union sympathizers in the area that the guerillas had carried off a black contraband and were led by Elijah "Lige" V. White, one of Mosby's men, who with as many as 350 men, had been operating in and around Dranesville for months. Fearful that secessionist sympathizers would spread the word that a Union patrol was in the vicinity led by a major general, Heintzelman took the precaution of removing his shoulder straps, hoping that he would not become an easy target.[48] After three days the scout, fatigued and with jaded horses, was safely back in Washington, where Heintzelman issued orders for a much larger cavalry patrol to pursue White and his guerillas.

In late summer Mosby and his partisans renewed the intensity of their raids in the area between the capital and the Blue Ridge Mountains. Although Washington remained safe, the Rebels struck the Orange and Alexandria Railroad, burning bridges, disrupting lines of communication, and capturing hundreds of Union cavalry and infantry. On August 11, Confederates attacked a supply train of nineteen wagons at Annandale, only nine miles west of Alexandria. On August 28 they brazenly set fire to the Cameron Run bridge, only three miles from Alexandria. In early September guerrillas burned a bridge on the Orange and Alexandria even closer to the city. Three weeks later they set fire to the railroad bridge at Pope's Head, two miles west of Fairfax Station, then raided Burke's Station on the railroad, three miles to the east. In a bold strike on October 1, Mosby burned a railroad bridge less than a quarter mile from the fortifications guarding Alexandria. Another raid that same day resulted in the capture of several railroad workers near Springfield Station, eight miles west of the city. "Our bridges are constantly exposed, . . . none of them are guarded," Col. D. C. McCallum, superintendent of railroads, complained to Halleck in early October.[49]

When word reached his headquarters that "farmer guerrillas" had burned the bridge over Pope's Run near the Potomac, Heintzelman was called to Stanton's office and told in no uncertain terms that a sufficient force must be posted along the railroad. To inspect the situation himself, the general took a cavalry escort of twenty men, crossed the Aqueduct Bridge, and rode along the Columbia Turnpike to Annandale, where he then took the Little River Turnpike west to Fairfax Court House before turning south in the night to Fairfax Station and a camp of the 4th Delaware Cavalry. Riding west to Union Mills near Bull Run the next morning, few of the bridges that had been reported burned were actually destroyed. Continuing along the railroad, every span was found to be satisfactorily guarded. McCallum's assertion that the bridges were "constantly exposed" was a gross exaggeration, he concluded.

Crossing Bull Run to Centreville, Heintzelman was greeted by Brig. Gen. Rufus King and an artillery salute. King, who had 1,362 infantry in his small command, was charged with protecting the longest stretch of the twenty-three miles of railroad from Alexandria to Bull Run and maintaining a strong line of pickets in front of Centreville. Heintzelman was anxious to talk with him, since he had received earlier reports that some of his men had deserted and joined Mosby. In hopes of curtailing guerrilla raids, Heintzelman and King decided to reinforce the small Union army at Centreville and send more patrols into the area. What was really needed at the railroad bridges south and west of the capital, Heintzelman concluded, was a blockhouse at every bridge. Looking for an easy scapegoat, Hooker again came to mind. When "Fighting Joe" had withdrawn his army following the disaster at Chancellorsville, plans to construct blockhouses had been abandoned, many of the trains had stopped running, and the railroads were left unguarded.[50]

An even more embarrassing guerrilla raid came on the night of October 1, 1863. With 150 partisans, Elijah White struck a camp of the 16th New York Cavalry near Lewinsville, and without the New Yorkers firing a single shot in defense, the Rebel raiders killed two of the Federals, wounded two others, and carried off ten prisoners and over fifty horses. Hearing of the raid, Heintzelman dispatched Col. Carroll H. Potter with a large cavalry reconnaissance to Lewinsville. Potter reported that 1st Lt. W. J. Keays of the 16th New York had been grossly negligent in not posting pickets around the camp. Hearing the details of the raid, Heintzelman was furious, recommending that Keays "be summarily dismissed . . . or tried by general court-martial."[51]

When Halleck received McCallum's memorandum highly critical of Heintzelman's lack of resolve in dealing with Mosby and his guerrillas, the general in chief fired off a missive criticizing his inability in suppressing ongoing "guerrilla depredations." To Heintzelman the memorandum was yet "another offensive communication." He seemed to sense that his time was running out as commander of the Department of Washington.

Although his written rebuttal of McCallum's charges was diplomatic, in private he was furious. The fire on the bridge west of Alexandria had been discovered by soldiers working on the track, extinguished, and the bridge saved. The span at Pope's Run near Alexandria that White's guerrillas had set fire to also had been discovered and doused by an army patrol. The damage to the bridge over Cameron Run was "trifling" and had been repaired in a matter of hours. Moreover, the attack on Burke's Station amounted to little more than a minor skirmish in which a "wood party" drove off the guerrillas. Halleck had forgotten, Heintzelman continued, that during the entire war "the guerrillas have been operating on our communications all the way from the Potomac to Kansas." Moreover, he commented in his journal, if Halleck and Stanton were "not satisfied with my administration of this department, why don't they relieve me?" Besides, the troops assigned to guard the railroads were not even part of the Department of Washington. Yet into November Mosby continued to strike, raiding Catlett's Station early in the month and a Federal cavalry camp near Warrenton two weeks later.[52]

Heintzelman was also criticized for not maintaining discipline among his troops. By early October rumors had found their way into the newspapers that his days in Washington were numbered, Assistant Secretary of War Peter Watson frankly told him. Samuel Wilkeson, who was now writing for the *New York Times*, said that many in the War Department were angry that Heintzelman was not doing more to protect the railroads and in inspecting the capital's defenses. Either Stanton or Halleck, Heintzelman was convinced, was determined to replace him.[53] The *New York Times* said he was to be given a more active command. Another rumor was that Stanton had told Lincoln that Heintzelman had to be removed, at which time the president recommended that the decision be delayed until a position became available for the general elsewhere.

By September Heintzelman began suffering with boils on his legs and stomach. At the same time, he continued to complain of gout in both feet and rheumatism in both legs. So severe were his problems that he frequently could not put on his boots or walk for days at a time.[54] Although the boils were lanced and the gout improved, he was frequently unable to report to headquarters. On the afternoon of October 13, Halleck sent one of his aides to query the general as to when he would be able to take the field. Although Heintzelman said he would be ready in three or four days, that evening Maj. Gen. Christopher C. Augur handed him a letter from Halleck, dated October 14, saying that by directions of the president he was being removed from command of the Department of Washington and the XXII Corps. The letter stated the removal was temporary, but Heintzelman knew that his Washington sojourn had ended.

Although he had been expecting the news for several months, he was hurt and angry, blaming both Halleck and Stanton as well as, to a lesser degree, Lincoln. The president "had better look out for the state of Penn. [that] would run me for president," he warned in a fit of indignation.[55] To add to his exasperation, no one knew or would tell him where he was being transferred. Suspecting that he was deliberately being kept in the dark, he approached Wilkeson, who was privy to much of the information emanating from the War Department, but even he professed ignorance.

Shortly after receiving the letter, Heintzelman was assigned to court-martial duty in the capital. He now had time to devote to the impending sale of the Sonora Exploring and Mining Company and some of his stock in the Santa Rita Company and the Vallecillo silver mines. There was also the usual socializing, including dinner with Maj. Gen. James Abram Garfield, an antislavery Ohio Republican who had been elected to Congress. Heintzelman shared one thing in common with Garfield, they both distrusted Stanton. He stopped at Brady's Photographic Gallery, above Thompson's Saloon on Pennsylvania Avenue, to see the latest images from Gettysburg, where Lincoln had gone on November 19 to help dedicate a cemetery and deliver a short address. There was also a festival at the freedman's village and farm on the south bank of the Potomac, where he was surprised to see "quite a number of white people."[56] The general also rode down Pennsylvania Avenue in the mud to watch as the Statue of Freedom was hoisted atop the recently completed Capitol dome.

In early November 1863, when General Banks and seven thousand Federals successfully landed on Brazos Island and took Brownsville with little opposition, Heintzelman reminisced that it was he who had recommended this plan to Halleck. The expedition "should have been made before McClellan went to the Peninsula," however.[57] With the Union Army now in control of the lower Rio Grande Valley, Heintzelman again opened communications with his friend Jeremiah Galvan, who was back at his mercantile store in Brownsville.

On December 20, along with five other major generals—Silas Casey, Dan Sickles, Christopher Augur, Winfield Scott Hancock, and John McAllister Schofield—he served as an honorary pallbearer at the funeral of thirty-eight-year-old Maj. Gen. John Buford, a loyal and patriotic Kentuckian. Undeniably one of the best cavalry commanders in the Union Army, Buford had been badly wounded at Second Bull Run; fought bravely at Antietam, Fredericksburg, and Chancellorsville; and gallantly opposed the Confederate advance at Gettysburg on July 1, only to come down with typhoid fever and die in Washington nine days before Christmas. The funeral procession, twelve men abreast in a column that stretched for almost a mile down Pennsylvania Avenue, was one of the largest and most impressive ever seen in the capital. Buford's horse, with boots reversed in the stirrups, was led behind the hearse by two soldiers, while his black body servant walked behind.[58]

Along with other senior officers, he begrudgingly assembled at Halleck's office on New Years' Day, 1864, to make the accustomed pilgrimage to the Executive Mansion and the residences of Secretary of War Stanton and Secretary of the Navy Welles. Stanton asked that Heintzelman visit with him in a day or two. Expecting news of his new assignment, he rushed to Stanton's office early the next morning. First inquiring as to the general's health, Stanton went on to say that he was anxious to reassign him to a new command but wanted to first consult Lincoln. "I have since been thinking the matter over and can think of nothing but Texas," Heintzelman wrote in his journal that evening.[59] One day later he heard rumors that the president wanted him on the Rio Grande. "I am satisfied, though I did not care to go to Texas," he responded. A few days later he also heard that Seward and several New York politicians, largely because of his antebellum experience in Texas, were lobbying Lincoln to send him to the Mexican border. Brig. Gen. Lorenzo Thomas, the former adjutant general who had been removed by Stanton and sent to the Mississippi Valley to organize black regiments but who was back in Washington, approached him about renting his house since it had been rumored that he was being sent "out west." When Heintzelman expressed surprise, Thomas said that orders had already been issued sending him to Columbus, Ohio, to command the Northern Department.

Three days later Sen. John Sherman of Ohio confirmed that the general was indeed being sent to Columbus. "I had hoped it would be Texas," was Heintzelman's only response. As expected, the next day official orders arrived placing him in command of the Northern Department, consisting of the states of Ohio, Indiana, Illinois, Wisconsin, and Michigan.[60] When he asked Halleck exactly what his duties would be, the general in chief said that he would be in charge of five prisoner-of-war camps, two each in Ohio and Illinois and one in Indiana. Perhaps more importantly, he would also need to keep a keen eye on the troublesome Midwestern Copperheads, or Peace Democrats, who were proving to be a vexing and continuing problem for Lincoln and the Union war effort. Particularly strong in the "Butternut" counties of the southern Midwest, the Copperheads had aggressively campaigned against the war and any military appropriations. Not only were they unhappy with the war effort but also, true to their Jacksonian heritage, they disliked Republican economic policies, especially the national banking system.

Foremost among the Midwestern Copperheads was Clement Laird Vallandigham of Ohio. Descendant of a Virginia family and married to the daughter of a Maryland planter, Vallandigham eloquently argued in a variety of forums that Lincoln and the Republicans threatened the nation's values and traditions. Vehemently opposed to emancipation, he also argued that the "Republican war" had brought about a reign of terror as bad as that of the French Revolution. The North should stop fighting, declare an armistice, and invite the Rebel states to a peace conference. Proclaiming "The Constitution as it is and the Union as it was," he worked to have "King Lincoln" dethroned. Encouraged by Vallandigham and other Peace Democrats in Indiana and Illinois, Copperhead newspaper editors were openly encouraging desertions, which Lincoln and most Republicans considered treasonous. Indeed, desertions from Copperhead areas of the Midwest were on the rise.[61]

While Heintzelman was still in command of the Department of Washington following the Union disaster at Fredericksburg, General Burnside had been sent west to the Department of Ohio. From his headquarters in Cincinnati in the heart of Copperhead country, Burnside had issued an order stating frankly that "treason" would not be tolerated. When Vallandigham continued to denounce "King Lincoln," the "wicked war," the Emancipation Proclamation, conscription, and the suspension of habeas corpus, Burnside had him arrested.[62] A military commission followed suit by sentencing him to prison for the duration of the war. Ohio Copperhead newspapers howled against the government, while Peace Democrats, furiously and unanimously, nominated Vallandigham for governor. In Washington Lincoln found the entire affair embarrassing and commuted the sentence to banishment in the South. Shortly thereafter, Union troops escorted the controversial Copperhead across Kentucky to Gen. Braxton Bragg's lines in Tennessee.

After less than a month in Dixie, Vallandigham escaped on a blockade runner out of Wilmington, North Carolina, to Bermuda, where he made his way to Halifax and eventually to Windsor, Canada, opposite Detroit, and from there he began to campaign for governor. In the fall 1863 elections, with the nation's eyes focused on the Buckeye State, Vallandigham went down in a crushing defeat by more than 100,000 votes, while the Republicans won more than two-thirds of the seats in the Ohio legislature.

Although he was to proceed to Columbus at once, Heintzelman was still in Washington to attend a lavish party hosted by Seward on January 15. He also visited with Lincoln to thank the president for the new command. Lincoln replied that it was Stanton and Halleck, not he, who had made the decision.[63] Senator Wade revealed the next day that Heintzelman had earlier been considered for command of the Army of the Potomac, but Stanton had vetoed the idea, saying that the general was a good division or corps commander but did not have the leadership skills necessary to command such a large army in the field. Moreover, McClellan had earlier expressed serious doubts about Heintzelman's ability for such an independent command. As 1863 waned, a new year promised renewed hope for a final Union victory. But Samuel Peter Heintzelman would be far from Washington and the events that came to shape the history of a fractured nation.

TWELVE

Copperheads and Prison Camps

After being entertained by a band from Camp Misery and visiting briefly with Senator Wade, Heintzelman left Washington for Baltimore on January 17, 1864. After changing trains, he stopped again in Harrisburg, Pennsylvania, to see Gov. Andrew Gregg Curtin. Thought by many to be the best of the Northern war governors, Curtin was busily preparing for his own inauguration the next day, and the general paused only briefly. Continuing on the Pennsylvania Central to Altoona and across the Allegheny Mountains, through a cold and foreboding winter landscape, to Johnstown and across the Appalachian Highlands, Heintzelman arrived at the "dirty miserable . . . pig stye" train station at Pittsburgh the next day.[1] He read in the newspapers that Brig. Gen. John Hunt Morgan, the "thunderbolt of the Confederacy," had raided across the Ohio River into Ohio, destroying railroad trestles, bridges, depots, water stations, and Union supplies. A shrewd and fearless Kentuckian and the epitome of a cavalry leader, Morgan had gone on a wild twenty-four-day ride in the summer of 1863 through southern Indiana and Ohio that had ended in his capture and confinement, along with thirty of his men, in the Ohio State Penitentiary. But the incurable adventurer and legendary raider soon escaped to again take the saddle. Heintzelman realized that his command in Ohio was certain to be more challenging than he had envisioned. In a crowded and uncomfortable railroad car, the general continued west, reaching Columbus, Ohio's capital and railroad hub, at 3:20 A.M. on January 20.

After taking rooms at the Neil House, he rushed off to see Gov. John Brough, who had left a card at the hotel saying he was anxious to meet Heintzelman. Six years older than the general, Brough was unpolished but an able stump speaker and hearty campaigner with a wry humor and booming voice.[2] A War Democrat and a symbol of patriotism, Brough had switched to the Republican Party and easily defeated Clement Vallandigham in the contentious 1863 election. The governor told Heintzelman that he was not only worried about the Copperheads in his state but also subversive Peace Democrats throughout the Midwest, who were becoming bolder by the week. Of particular concern were the "Butternut" counties along the Ohio River, where antiwar sentiment was rampant. There Copperhead fears of emancipation were exacerbated by deep-rooted racism. Many laborers, especially Irish and German immigrants, were frightened that free blacks would take their jobs. In their excited imagination, the Copperheads also railed against miscegenation or any form of racial mixing.

Many of the Peace Democrats, Brough said, had joined secret antiwar societies and were continuing to conspire against the government. The filibustering Knights of the Golden Circle, an organization Heintzelman had come to know on the Texas-Mexico border during the Cortina War, had faded away only to be replaced by the Order of American Knights. There were also rumors that many of the Knights were being absorbed into the newly founded Sons of Liberty, with Vallandigham as supreme commander.[3] Rumors also persisted that the more radical Peace Democrats favored the overthrow of the Federal government and the creation of a Northwestern Confederacy that would seek an armistice with the South. From the time Heintzelman arrived in Columbus, Brig. Gen. Henry Beebe Carrington, Ohio's Copperhead-hating provost marshal, deluged him with letters saying that Ohio, Indiana, and Illinois dangled on a Copperhead volcano and that insurrection was imminent.

From the beginning Heintzelman became convinced that Governor Brough and General Carrington were greatly exaggerating the Copperhead threat in the Midwest, and he never came to appreciate the extent of sedition in such groups as the Order of American Knights or the Sons of Liberty. But much of what Brough and Carrington were telling him was true. Shortly after his arrival in Columbus, a handful of Midwestern Democrats did conspire to overthrow the governments of Indiana, Illinois, Kentucky, and Missouri. Led by Harrison H. Dodd, an Indianapolis printer, influential Indiana Peace Democrats and members of the Sons of Liberty schemed to seize arsenals, release Confederate prisoners of war, and withdraw the four states from the Union. The conspirators accepted money from Confederate agents and hoped to coordinate their efforts with Southern forces. The planned insurrection never came to fruition, however, when Dodd was persuaded by the leadership of the Indiana Democratic Party to call it off.[4]

One of Heintzelman's first responsibilities was to inspect Camp Chase, a large, sprawling prisoner-of-war camp four miles west of Columbus, which he found to be "crowded and very dirty." Although sensitive to Southern charges that prisoners were not being treated humanely, he thought many of the accusations were sensational and little more than propaganda. Yet he was anxious to see the camp, which had been established early in the war and named for the politically ambitious Salmon Portland Chase, former Ohio governor and current secretary of the Treasury. Confederates captured at Fort Donelson, Tennessee, and at Island No. 10 in the Mississippi River had been sent to Camp Chase, as had prisoners from other Union victories in the West. On taking an oath of honor, Confederate officers from the camp were permitted to roam the Ohio capital, even registering at hotels and receiving gifts of money and food. A few even attended sessions of the state legislature. But by the time Heintzelman assumed command at Columbus, complaints over lax discipline and administration at the camp had changed the situation dramatically. Rules were tightened, visitors prohibited, and mail censored. The parole and exchange system that had limited the number of prisoners held in such camps during the early months of the war had all but collapsed by 1864 after the South, angered by the Emancipation Proclamation, threatened to execute or enslave blacks captured wearing Union uniforms.

Shoddy barracks; low, muddy ground; and open latrines all contributed to a deterioration of sanitary conditions at Camp Chase. During the winter of 1863–64, just as Heintzelman took command of the department, a smallpox epidemic struck the camp, killing hundreds. Facilities that were intended to house no more than four thousand men were jammed with twice that number at this time, and prisoners were dying at a rate of several hundred per month. Visiting the officer's quarters, a "sorry place to be in," Heintzelman spoke with a number of Rebel officers and was "surprised to see so little apparent intelligence." What "a horrible life they lead," he concluded. Dressed in ragged gray or butternut, all were anxious to be exchanged. Spotting a former sergeant he had known in the antebellum army, but who had left and became a Confederate officer, he found it amusing when the man turned to a companion and, referring to Heintzelman, remarked, "there goes one of Uncle Sam's old ones."[5] At the infirmary he met briefly with Dr. William Shakespeare King, the Pennsylvania-born surgeon he had known at Fort Duncan on the Texas frontier and the physician who had cut the Minié ball from his arm at First Bull Run.

Less than a month after arriving in Columbus, the general learned from Governor Brough that Confederate prisoners at the Ohio State Penitentiary had secured knives and were planning an escape. Having never visited a prison before, he decided to go in person to inspect the penitentiary, which was located near the river in downtown Columbus. Built in the 1830s and occupying three blocks, the cold and damp three-story limestone structure, where disease was also said to be rampant, was the oldest penal institution in the state but was thought to be more secure than

Camp Chase. Several of the prisoners, "hard looking fellows" according to Heintzelman, were surprised when guards confiscated some ten knives and files. He was shown where, three months earlier, Morgan and six of his men, using knives secreted during mealtime, had dug holes in the bottom of their cells, crawled into an air shaft, and then tunneled their way to freedom.[6] Six weeks after visiting the prison and fearing another escape, he had many of the Rebel officers there sent east to Fort Delaware on Pea Patch Island, a mud shoal on the New Jersey side of the Delaware River opposite Delaware City, Delaware.

Chronically unhappy in Columbus, Heintzelman bombarded Washington with requests to move his headquarters to Cincinnati. From the time he had helped form the Sonora Exploring and Mining Company, he had a number of old friends in the Queen City, and he knew he would be content there. Halleck declined to respond, and when Heintzelman pressed the issue, the War Department flatly refused. Meanwhile, in Columbus he worked to build a competent staff. He also found time for billiards, euchre, and a number of social gatherings, which frequently lasted past midnight. He was also able to keep up with his mining interests as he watched the government for newly created Arizona Territory take shape. He seemed happy when Poston wrote from Fort Yuma to say that the Indians at the Colorado River remembered him with great affection.[7]

In the cold Midwestern winter, the general was often ill and spent much time reading newspapers and defending his actions during the Peninsula Campaign. George McCall, who had commanded the Pennsylvania Reserves at Glendale, took issue with what Heintzelman had written in his official report of the battle, and the two men exchanged several terse, yet diplomatic, letters. Heintzelman remained convinced that Richmond could have been taken, and on a cold February morning, with the thermometer at two degrees below zero, he wrote Maj. Gen. Benjamin F. Butler, commanding the Army of the James, urging a water expedition up the James River, followed by a quick overland thrust against the Rebel capital from the south. His mind remained on the war in Virginia, and when organizers for the Maryland State Fair wrote asking for a document of significance for display at the fair, he sent his Bull Run report, the first he had ever dictated.[8]

Later that month he was invited to the Sanitary Fair in Cleveland. Met by a regiment of troops at the train station, the general was escorted through the frost-coated streets to the Weddell Hotel. Marching to the opening ceremonies the next day, he listened to Rep. James A. Garfield speak for over an hour. With a thousand Ohioans in attendance, he too was invited to say a few words. Never comfortable at public speaking, largely because of his squeaky, low voice, Heintzelman was reluctant at first but then conceded, and afterward three cheers were given "for the hero of Williamsburg and Fair Oaks."[9] Although somewhat embarrassed by the attention, he now became convinced that Cleveland would make a better headquarters than Columbus.

Leaving the lakefront city the following afternoon, he caught the train west to Sandusky, Ohio, to inspect Johnson's Island, another large prisoner-of-war camp. Arriving in early evening, he was surprised at how the town had grown since he had last seen it in 1848, when he had returned from the Mexican War. Met by Brig. Gen. Henry Dwight Terry, commandant of the prison, he was told the ice was so thick on Lake Erie that it would be impossible to visit the island. Terry did give Heintzelman a carriage tour of the town, after which they visited the barracks of the 122nd New York. He had always liked and admired Terry ever since the two had been commanders in the Washington defenses early in the war and in the forefront of the fighting at Williamsburg and Seven Pines. Politely turning down an invitation from several leading ladies in the community for a formal reception in his honor, Heintzelman hurried back to Columbus, where he was surprised to see a dozen Rebel officers, on their way to Camp Chase, comfortably billeted at the Neil House.

He had just retired on the evening of March 2 when he was awakened with an urgent telegram from General Halleck. There had been a Copperhead insurrection at the small community of Paris in Edgar County, Illinois. The general in chief wanted Heintzelman to proceed there immediately and, in cooperation with the local authorities and the governor of the state, restore order as soon as possible. Leaving Columbus by train in the cold darkness three hours later, he traveled through the night, arriving at Indianapolis at noon the next day and immediately going to the Capitol to see Oliver Hazard Perry Throck Morton, Republican governor of the state. A skillful political opportunist, Morton said that from what he could learn, the revolt in Edgar County had been greatly exaggerated. Agreeing that the situation was not urgent, Heintzelman checked in to the Bates House, one of the dirtiest hotels he had ever seen, before booking passage on a freight train to Terre Haute, where he arrived slightly before daylight the next morning. There he changed trains and telegraphed Richard Yates, Republican governor of Illinois, of his arrival.[10] Yates wired back that he had already dispatched troops to Paris. Easily excitable, the governor was concerned about the antiwar sentiment in his state. Fearing that the Copperheads were striving to take Illinois out of the war, he had gained a reputation for arbitrarily arresting those he thought disloyal. In fact, when the state legislature passed a resolution calling for a national convention of reconciliation with the South, he boldly prorogued the assembly and ran the state by himself.

Leaving Terre Haute early the next morning, Heintzelman was at Paris by eight in the evening and learned the details of what had happened. After a gun battle between some veterans and twenty Copperheads, in which one man had been killed and three others wounded, the town was relatively quiet.[11] In the afternoon a company of soldiers from Chicago arrived, and when more bluecoats came the next day, he concluded the situation was under control and returned by train through Terre Haute and Indianapolis before arriving in Cincinnati.

There Heintzelman met with Thomas Wrightson to discuss Arizona and silver. He also crossed the Ohio River to Newport Barracks for a short visit with an old friend from the frontier, Col. Sidney Burbank. There he also met briefly with the Kentucky-born wife of Dr. Eugene Hilarian Abadie, a French-born Pennsylvanian whom he had known in Texas. Mrs. Abadie had gone out of her way to assist Charles when he had first arrived at West Point, and the general listened when she asked that he make every effort to assist her brother, William Nelson Rector Beall, a Rebel brigadier general who had been taken prisoner when Port Hudson surrendered on July 9, 1863, and was confined at Johnson's Island. Heintzelman also chatted with Solon Lathrop, who was on his way to Washington. Lathrop had always been his closest friend, and the two talked of him rejoining Heintzelman's staff.

While in Cincinnati, he learned that Lt. Gen. Ulysses S. Grant had only recently passed through on his way to Washington to assume command of the armies of the United States. There was also an account in the city's newspapers of a Copperhead "row" at Dayton, but the Ohio militia had easily suppressed it. Problems of a more personal nature came in an anonymous letter from Philadelphia containing a small newspaper clipping relating how Maj. Granville Johnson, one of Heintzelman's most trusted aides, had gone out of his way to befriend the notorious Rebel guerilla Basil Wilson Duke. Married to John Hunt Morgan's sister, the handsome and dashing Duke had been captured during the celebrated 1863 raid into Ohio and imprisoned at Columbus. When it was decided to send Duke and the other Rebel officers to Fort Delaware, Heintzelman sent Major Johnson to escort Duke east. Arriving in Philadelphia, the major took rooms at the fashionable Continental Hotel, where the two men enjoyed every luxury the hotel could offer, including cigars and plenty of liquor. While there, Duke had allegedly visited with several prominent Philadelphia Copperheads, who showered him with presents. The anonymous letter demanded that Johnson be cashiered forthwith. Although the major argued that he had arrived in Philadelphia too late to catch the steamer for Fort Delaware, that Duke had not received any privileges, and that the Philadelphia press had sensationalized the incident, the damage had already been done. When another telegram arrived from the War Department inquiring into the matter and asking what regiment Johnson belonged to, all Heintzelman could say was that he had served bravely on the Peninsula and was "a very conscientious officer."[12] Fearing that Johnson might be dismissed from the army, Heintzelman asked his aide for a full accounting of the circumstances under which he had assisted Duke so that it could be properly reported to Washington.

On the morning of March 28, Heintzelman received an urgent telegram from Springfield, Illinois. A "terrible affray" had occurred in Coles County in the east-central part of the state, where it was reported that Copperheads had killed two men of the 54th Illinois and wounded the regiment's colonel. In Moultrie County to the west, Copperheads were also said to be "rising."[13] The next day a second telegram arrived from Lt. Col. James Oakes of the 4th U.S. Cavalry, who had arrived at Charleston, a town Lincoln visited regularly when he rode the circuit as a young attorney and the site of one of the Lincoln-Douglas debates of 1858. Ten men, most of them soldiers, lay dead and some fifteen others were wounded. Oakes had arrested thirty Copperheads, some of them blood relatives of the president. An attack was expected to rescue the prisoners, and insurgents were said to be collecting in large numbers. "Troubles Continue. Forces of insurgents reported increasing," Oakes reported. "Have just asked for 500 men from Indianapolis. You had better come here in person," he continued. Realizing he had no time to ask for directions from Washington, Heintzelman ordered the 47th Indiana to board the next train for Charleston, taking along plenty of ammunition. No sooner had he telegraphed back for particulars than word came from Paris, Illinois, that the Coles County violence was continuing. If the Copperhead disturbances did not subside, Heintzelman warned, he would have troops "pounce on them."[14]

Days later, with the violence in Charleston finally subdued and the army in control, the general decided to again visit Johnson's Island to inspect the garrison there. On March 30 he departed for Sandusky, leaving the Illinois Copperhead problems somewhat in abeyance. With an all-out offensive in Virginia in the making, Halleck wanted to know how many men from the brigade stationed near the prison could be sent to the Army of the Potomac. With the draft progressing in the Midwest, orders arrived directing that all the draftees in the Northern Department be hurried to Washington. In fact, anyone who could be spared was to be sent to the front as soon as possible. For weeks Halleck and Grant continued to press him to get "every available man into the field."[15]

So many soldiers were heading east to join Grant and south to join Sherman that Heintzelman became particularly concerned about reducing the garrison at the prisoner-of-war camp at Rock Island, Illinois. Built on an island in the middle of the Mississippi River between Davenport, Iowa, and Rock Island and Moline, Illinois, the prison had become dangerously overcrowded. Of the six thousand prisoners who arrived in two feet of snow and a temperature of 32 degrees below zero in early December 1863, many had already contracted smallpox, while others had come down with pneumonia, with hundreds dying.[16] Only summer would bring relief, but by then an additional one thousand prisoners would have arrived.

When both Sherman and Grant continued to press for more soldiers, Heintzelman defiantly wired Washington in early July that the prison garrisons had been so reduced that not one additional soldier could be "spared from this department."[17] By August he was complaining that the number of prisoners in the five camps under his jurisdiction had risen to 23,646, many of whom were officers and "troublesome." Moreover, he only had 6,673 able-bodied men to guard them, barely enough to "prevent the prisoners from breaking out." In addition, newspapers in Columbus reported that Copperheads were not only congregating in Chicago for an open revolt but also secretly plotting to free prisoners at Camp Douglas as well as those on Johnson's Island.[18]

In Sandusky, Heintzelman calculated that, despite his earlier warnings that he did not have enough men, three regiments, the 122nd, 67th, and 65th New York, could be released to join either Sherman or Grant. With General Terry, he took a steamboat to the island for an extensive inspection of the prison. Prior to arriving on Lake Erie, he had been told that a hostile "armed vessel" was "lying in Canadian waters," but neither he nor Terry could uncover any information to support the rumors. There was, nevertheless, "an organized band" of Confederate refugees at Windsor, Ontario, across from Detroit, "watching for an opportunity to do us some damage."[19]

Since Johnson's Island was located two miles from Sandusky and one mile out in Sandusky Bay on Lake Erie, any escape would be difficult. The three-hundred-acre island was heavily wooded, with the compound of thirteen two-story wooden barracks built in a clearing of some fifteen acres on the southeastern end in late 1861. By early 1864 the prison had become overcrowded and filthy; on orders from Washington, rations had been cut. As a result, the most common pastime for the prisoners was catching and eating rats, which bred near the large open latrines only yards from the barracks. Although the health of the men at Johnson's Island was better than at most other prisons, pneumonia and smallpox were common. After walking through the barracks, prison yard, and hospital, Heintzelman admitted that the facility was dirty, but the prisoners were better off, he concluded, than those at Camp Chase. During his inspection, he took time to visit with sixty-two-year-old Confederate general Isaac Ridgeway

Trimble, a Marylander he had known decades earlier at West Point. Trimble had been in the forefront of the fighting during the Seven Days, was at Second Bull Run, and had been captured at Gettysburg, where he lost a leg. As promised, he also visited with Mrs. Abadie's brother, General Beall. Although a number of Rebel officers had complained to General Terry of being abused, some even saying that they had been robbed of their money, Trimble and Beall had "no complaints," only that "the confinement was irksome." There had "undoubtedly been some rascality" nevertheless, and Heintzelman promised an investigation.[20]

Back in Columbus the following day, news arrived that the Illinois Copperhead uprising had been successfully suppressed, and Heintzelman wired Halleck with the good news. A few days later he had an opportunity to see a number of Ohio Copperheads when they took rooms at the Neil House during the state Democratic convention. Privately, he sarcastically suggested that the Copperhead majority consider nominating Jefferson Davis instead of McClellan for president. "They are having a stormy time in convention," he wrote on March 23. "Vallandigham has many friends here." Although he had no desire to incite the Copperheads, when the *Cincinnati Enquirer* published an article that he considered treasonable, the general ordered mail agents not to distribute the paper.[21] Despite his efforts to curtail anything seditious, many Midwestern Republicans thought he was going out of his way to appease the Copperheads.

On April 16 he traveled to Indianapolis to meet with Governors Morton, Yates, and Brough. After checking in to the miserable Bates House again, where the food was equally as bad as the rooms, he attended a confidential meeting in which the subversive activities of the Order of the American Knights was discussed in detail. The Knights were active not only in the Midwest but also in Canada, where it was said as many as three thousand Copperheads were preparing to make a dash to free the Confederate prisoners on Johnson's Island. There was also the possibility, a detective said, that Lincoln's call for 500,000 new conscripts would cause wide-scale rioting throughout the region. The governors were also concerned that either General Morgan or Maj. Gen. Nathan Bedford Forrest and their cavalry would strike north of the Ohio River, creating even more chaos. In late March Morgan had attacked Paducah, Kentucky, and in the second week of April, Heintzelman read in the Columbus newspapers that Forrest had captured Fort Pillow on the Mississippi River forty miles above Memphis, mercilessly massacring both black and white soldiers after they had surrendered.[22]

After dinner the three governors decided to invite the governors of Michigan and Iowa to join them in Washington for a second meeting. Perhaps in the capital they could impress upon Lincoln and Stanton the seriousness of the situation in the Midwest. Later Heintzelman took time to ride out to Camp Morton, yet another prisoner-of-war camp. Constructed at the Indiana State Fairgrounds and named for the governor, the facility consisted of five large wood-frame barracks. Like other prisons in the Midwest, Camp Morton had become overcrowded, sanitary conditions had deteriorated, and life had become harsh and fragile. Large open pits near the center of the camp served as latrines as well as cultures for disease. Thirty-eight hospital tents housed over four hundred sick prisoners who had contracted everything from pneumonia to scurvy and intermittent fever.[23] To prevent escapes, a trench ten feet wide and six feet deep had been dug around the camp.

In Columbus several weeks later, General Carrington revealed additional details on the Sons of Liberty and Order of American Knights. The situation was indeed serious, Heintzelman agreed, requiring "immediate and energetic action." After informing Washington, he concluded that neither Lincoln, Stanton, nor Halleck "realize the gravity of these matters." On the evening of June 14 at the Neil House in Columbus, Lathrop arrived with an urgent telegram from Governor Morton asking that the department commander meet with the governor and General Carrington in Indianapolis the next day. Although ill, Heintzelman was up at dawn the next morning and on the early train for the capital. Arriving in Indianapolis, he spotted Carrington, who had just arrived from Louisville. Carrington was alarmed that Vallandigham had crossed into the United States from Canada and had already given a lengthy speech at Hamilton, Ohio, before returning to his hometown of Dayton, where he was scheduled to give a second speech.[24] In addition, the controversial Copperhead politician had said he was planning to attend the Democratic National Convention scheduled for Chicago in late August. In Indianapolis telegrams arrived from Col. John S. Potter, provost marshal for Ohio, saying that Governor Brough wanted Vallandigham arrested and that four companies of troops were being ordered out to assist. Heintzelman had just arrived at the hotel when Governor Morton came in. Urgent discussions ensued well into the night, at which time Morton agreed with Brough that Vallandigham should be apprehended. In recalling the political furor that followed General Burnside's arrest of Vallandigham, however, Heintzelman was reluctant to act without first hearing from Halleck. "The only thing I can see that should be done," he confided to his journal, was "to arrest Vallandigham and his attendants."[25] Yet he feared that such arbitrary arrests might bring on an open rebellion, and he was resentful that Governor Brough and Colonel Potter were giving orders to troops under his command.

Still procrastinating as to what to do, Heintzelman left the next day on the train for Columbus. At the station in Dayton, he heard that

Vallandigham was scheduled to speak in that city in the evening. While changing trains at Xenia, he mistakenly boarded the wrong carriage and wound up in Springfield instead of Columbus and was forced to spend the night. It took him most of the next day to make his way back to Xenia and then to the capital.[26]

In the end, Lincoln decided to follow a policy of watchful waiting. In mid-June he drafted a letter to both Heintzelman and Brough saying that if at any time Vallandigham posed a legitimate threat to the military, he should be arrested, otherwise "do not arrest him without orders; meanwhile report the signs from time to time." But for unknown reasons, Lincoln had second thoughts and never sent this letter.[27] Although there are no collaborating correspondence indicating that the president communicated his intentions to either Heintzelman or Brough, Lincoln's desire that Vallandigham be closely shadowed, yet not arrested unless it became absolutely necessary, was well known to Heintzelman. As Federal authorities hesitated and pondered what to do with Vallandigham, he lived quietly at Dayton and made no inflammatory speeches. When the *Cincinnati Enquirer* pleaded with Heintzelman not to arrest any Copperheads, much less Vallandigham, the general replied that he had "always been opposed to those arbitrary arrests in the loyal states."[28]

Meanwhile, Heintzelman's health grew progressively worse. Coughing up blood and complaining of rheumatism, he was also plagued by gout, which he blamed on an injury he had suffered seventeen years earlier in Mexico. He was so incapacitated that he was unable to walk for weeks at a time. But when Margaret and Mary arrived from Washington in early April, his spirits lifted and he became more active. The Italian opera came to Columbus, and the family went to see Bellini's *Norma.* They also attended frequent soirees and visited the circus, complete with dogs, monkeys, and trick horses. As spring eased into summer, the Heintzelmans took short train rides on the Cleveland, Columbus, and Cincinnati Railroad to the small community of Delaware along the Scioto River north of Columbus for overnight stays at the fashionable summer resort of White Sulphur Springs. There Margaret socialized with army wives and newfound friends, while Samuel Peter bathed in the strong sulphuric springs, hoping the medicinal properties of the water would ease his pains and ailments. His brief forays to the springs were some of his happier moments, though he complained that the owner of the springs, Joseph F. Culberson, was a Copperhead sympathizer.[29]

In Columbus he spent a lot of time in idle dreams, yearning wholeheartedly for a field command. When Margaret and Mary fell ill, he quietly watched from his hotel room on a beautiful day in early May as a recently trained and equipped Ohio regiment marched down the street with flags flapping and drums beating. "It made me feel sad to see them parading and I not in the field," he admitted. Somehow the war was passing him by, and all his military training had come to naught. In Ohio he had become more of a politician than a general. Although ill and crippled, if he were given command in the field, "I would be well in an hour," he wrote. Although Grant was driving hard against Lee in Virginia and Sherman was at the gates of Atlanta, "political prospects look gloomy," he reported. Learning that a few Radical Republican senators had met in Boston to consider an armistice, his mood reached an all-time low. If a truce were declared, he was certain that the war would be lost. "I have never felt so badly as I do now. No compromise, no armistice. Press the war till the rebels lay down their arms."[30] As Grant pushed his Overland Campaign deeper into Virginia, he also learned that his old III Corps of the Army of the Potomac had been absorbed into the II Corps.

When Margaret decided to visit her mother in Buffalo in late May, Samuel Peter decided to accompany her. With Mary at their side, they traveled north by train to Cleveland, then by the steamer *Atlantic* across Lake Erie in the rain and fog. After staying only twenty-four hours at the lakeside city visiting old friends, he returned to Cleveland on the *Comet*, then back to Columbus. In the state capital on the Fourth of July, he was awakened early in the morning by the sounds of drum and fife and the discharge of pistols and firecrackers. The streets were flooded with farmers from the countryside who had come in to celebrate the holiday, while townspeople scurried to the countryside for picnics.[31] By late September 1864 he was well enough to again visit Johnson's Island. He was especially interested in examining the specifics of a recent attempt to free some of the Rebel officers on the island. The prison was now quiet, though, and he soon returned to Columbus.

Almost daily the war in Virginia seemed to reach a new furor. Despite several Union successes, the newspapers carried long casualty lists, including the names of some old friends. On May 9 Heintzelman read where Brig. Gen. Alex Hays, who had commanded the 63rd Pennsylvania at Seven Pines and was wounded at Second Bull Run, had died in the tangled Virginia Wilderness four days earlier. In a nostalgic reflection he remembered how Hays had accompanied his small command across the mountains to Mexico City in 1847. A few days later he read where another friend, Brig. Gen James Samuel Wadsworth, had been shot off his horse during the Battle of the Wilderness and had died in a Confederate field hospital. On May 9 Gen. John Sedgwick, who had so ably commanded a division in Sumner's II Corps on the Peninsula and was wounded at Glendale and Antietam, was killed at Spotsylvania Court House.[32] Four days later he read that General Stoneman had been captured while leading a cavalry raid south of Atlanta. Ever since his days at Fort Yuma and tour of duty on the Texas border, he had thought highly of Stoneman, and he now worried that he would never see his friend again.

In his own department Heintzelman continued to question the extent to which Copperheads posed a threat to the Midwestern governors. Convinced that much of the intelligence on their activity was little more than malicious gossip, he refused any wide-scale arrest of Peace Democrats said to be associated with the Order of American Knights. In response, General Carrington warned openly that the Copperheads were on the verge of revolt. He also complained that Heintzelman and his staff were too "intimate with Copperheads."[33] When several boxes of ammunition addressed to known members of the Order of American Knights were intercepted, however, Heintzelman agreed to numerous arrests. He also issued orders forbidding the sale of rifles, pistols, ammunition, and gunpowder.

In Columbus serious problems continued to develop with his staff. Major Johnson, whom Heintzelman admitted was "impulsive and thoughtless," got into a fight with a restaurant owner over a bill and badly beat the man, after which the restaurateur had him arrested. Learning that a newspaper account of the affair had been sent to Washington, the general feared that Johnson would be dismissed. In Cincinnati Captain Norton became involved in a heated argument with an army quartermaster and beat that man so badly with a rawhide whip that he too was reported to Washington. Knowing the attack was "unjustifiable," Heintzelman thought that Horton would be dismissed. He also worried that the captain was spending too much "time with Copperheads."[34]

By the early summer of 1864, the closeness and mutual respect Heintzelman had once enjoyed with the Midwestern governors began to wane and crumble. Over dinner in Columbus, Governor Brough informed him of yet another Copperhead plot. This time the Peace Democrats, he said, were preparing to seize the arsenal in Columbus and release the prisoners at Camp Chase. When Brough declined to provide specifics, Heintzelman refused to act, and the governor "took great offense." Meeting later with Brough and provided with a few details, the general did agree to order a battery of artillery to Columbus and place an additional guard around the arsenal. Yet the governor felt that his integrity had been challenged. For weeks he remained aloof and distant while insisting on the arrest of any Copperhead he considered seditious. A few weeks later he bluntly told Heintzelman what Carrington had been saying all along: members of the department commander's staff "were too intimate with Copperheads." Heintzelman realized such rumors were rampant and tried to dispel them, but there was little he could do. He became particularly incensed when a lady approached him to "inquire whether most of my staff were not Copperheads."[35]

Visiting White Sulphur Springs, he heard more rumors about his staff being disloyal. Weekly accounts of small bands of Confederates raiding into the new state of West Virginia did not help either, nor did rumors that Morgan or Forrest were preparing to cross the Ohio River into southern Ohio or Indiana. The War Department seemed especially concerned about the security of the Baltimore and Ohio Railroad and the supply depot at Gallipolis, below Parkersburg, on the Ohio River.[36] Responding to repeated concerns, Heintzelman agreed to send two regiments of Ohio militia to guard the warehouses at the small town.

In late August, on the eve of the Democratic National Convention, Heintzelman received a report from Lexington, Kentucky, of a plot by disguised Rebel officers to release the prisoners at Camp Douglas. Two weeks later four hundred revolvers, 135,000 rounds of ammunition, and fifty kegs of gunpowder were confiscated from Copperheads in Indianapolis. Rumors were also rampant that two thousand prisoners had sworn to break out of Camp Morton. Convinced that a rescue attempt would be made at Camp Douglas in Chicago during the Democratic convention, Stanton directed Heintzelman to go to the city and determine the state of affairs. Although Stanton did not think it would be a good idea to have troops patrolling the streets, they should be positioned nearby, "ready to move at a moment's warning."[37]

With Lathrop by his side, Heintzelman left for Chicago in a crowded railroad car filled with a "hard set" of Democrats on the afternoon of August 28. At a packed Sherman House in the city two days later, he was immediately assailed by Copperheads who demanded to know why he had ordered in five thousand troops during the convention. Although he had never issued such orders, he seemed content to "let them believe so." A number of Peace Democrats also questioned his prohibition on the sale of weapons and powder. Despite this less-than-friendly reception, "I immediately put myself in communication with the leaders of the Democratic Party, and was satisfied that no danger need be apprehended," Heintzelman soon reported to Halleck.[38]

After visiting with Copperhead friends from Buffalo, the general rode out the next morning to inspect Camp Douglas. Located on the south side of the city, not far from the shores of Lake Michigan, it had been named for Stephen A. Douglas, Illinois senator and 1860 presidential contender, whose residence was nearby and who had died unexpectedly in June 1861. The camp was originally created as a rendezvous point to train and quarter soldiers recruited in the Chicago area, but out of necessity it had been turned into a prisoner-of-war facility. The sixty-acre compound was built on low ground that flooded with every rain in the summer, and when the ground froze and then thawed in the winter, the camp again became a vast sea of mud. Barracks there housed as many as eighteen thousand Confederates soldiers, Copperheads, suspected spies, and Southern sympathizers, all guarded by a garrison of some sixteen hundred bluecoats.

Escorted through the camp by Col. Benjamin Jeffrey Sweet, Heintzelman was impressed with the improvements that had been made recently, and he thought the camp was in "good order." After endless breakouts—seventy-five in November 1863 alone—Sweet had introduced a number of radical changes to stop the tunneling and escapes, ordering barracks elevated and an additional fence built around the perimeter. Yet Camp Douglas remained a place of acute misery. Many of the prisoners did not have adequate clothing, and in the previous winter more than a thousand had perished, many of them having frozen to death. Orders from Washington reducing rations, including the elimination of all vegetables, had led to a serious decline in the prisoners' health. Scurvy, smallpox, overcrowding, starvation, and the lack of adequate medical attention had turned the place into a living hell.[39]

While in Chicago, Heintzelman was invited to tour the Board of Trade, where he delivered a few remarks. As the Democratic delegates gathered in Chicago at the Amphitheater not far from the shores of Lake Michigan, wild rumors continued to circulate of alliances between Copperheads and Confederate agents in the Midwest. Talk of plots to free Rebel prisoners was also rampant. Some accounts claimed that major Northern cities were to be put to the torch and that resistance to the draft was certain to lead to open rebellion. Amid all of this intrigue, George McClellan, arguing against emancipation but in favor of a military victory, was expected to garner the party's nomination. The peace wing, campaigning for an immediate armistice, appeared to be in the minority, yet Governor Yates feared trouble. As Chicago seethed with excitement, hearsay persisted that Vallandigham and the Copperheads would bolt the convention if McClellan were nominated and attempt to establish a Northwest Confederacy.

Since McClellan would not go along with a plank in the platform calling for an immediate peace, the Copperheads opposed him, yet they did not have enough votes to deny him the nomination. But they still had enough standing in the party to have their way with the platform. After the general was easily nominated on the first ballot, Vallandigham made a motion, in a placating gesture, that the nomination be made unanimous. Although forced to accept McClellan, the peace wing was able to arrange the selection of George H. Pendleton, an Ohio Copperhead, as the nominee for vice president. Pendleton, Heintzelman observed, was as vehement as Vallandigham in opposing the war.[40]

At the Sherman House, Copperhead delegates came to visit and plot strategy with Vallandigham. Heintzelman too had a "pleasant talk" and shared a drink and ate breakfast with Vallandigham. For this he was severely criticized by a few newspapers and a number of Midwestern Republicans. In celebration of McClellan's nomination and of what the Democrats perceived to be an electoral landslide in November, there was "great cheering," and after dark, as Heintzelman watched from the Tremont Hotel, a large torchlight parade, with marching bands and flags waving, wound its way through the city. There was also a colorful fireworks display and endless speeches that were "very abusive to the President."[41]

At a meeting with Indiana Copperheads, Heintzelman was promised that there would be "no organized resistance to the draft," though the Hoosiers refused to rule out "disturbances at a few places." In another meeting with an aide of Gov. Horatio Seymour of New York, the general was pressured to publicly proclaim himself a Democrat. "I told him that I belonged to neither of the great parties, . . . that I went for the Union and for the whole Union," he wrote. On leaving Chicago, he stopped at the Cook County courthouse to watch as a "thousand voices" sang the "Flag of the Union." Back in Columbus, and reflecting on the Chicago convention, he seemed pleased that he had met "a great many leading politicians and distinguished men."[42]

By the late summer of 1864, war weariness continued to grip the nation. There were few Union victories, only stalemates and failures. Both Richmond and Atlanta stood defiant, and Northern morale sank to a new low. Endless and unfathomable Union casualties, the worst of the war, were being reported from the Army of the Potomac. With the November election becoming a referendum on the war, many concluded that Lincoln was doomed. Even the president himself thought that he was unlikely to be reelected. Yet the day after McClellan received the Democratic nomination, news arrived in Chicago that Sherman, after weeks of terrible fighting, had taken Atlanta. In Columbus a few days later, Heintzelman watched as the city celebrated and a one-hundred-gun salute was fired. His only regret was that the fall of Atlanta had not been announced while the Democrats were in session. "It would have been a bombshell in their camp," he wrote. A few days later he learned that John Hunt Morgan, while preparing an attack into eastern Tennessee, had been surprised and killed by a Union raiding party at Greeneville. Earlier in May he had read where the dashing "Cavalier of Dixie," Gen. J. E. B. Stuart had been killed by General Sheridan's bluecoat cavalry at Yellow Tavern in the Virginia woods. In August news reached Columbus that Admiral Farragut had taken Mobile Bay.[43] Then word came that Sheridan, winning three victories in a row, had swept through the Shenandoah Valley, the breadbasket of Virginia, destroying everything in his path.

But for Heintzelman personally, there was little opportunity to celebrate. In Columbus persistent rumors and complaints continued to circulate that he and his staff had become too cozy with a number of leading Copperheads. Criticism reached a crescendo when Governor Brough openly accused Colonel Lathrop of Copperhead sympathies and speaking disrespectfully of Lincoln. In defense of his best friend, Heintzelman turned on Brough with wrath and vehemence, referring privately to the governor as an indecisive War Democrat who had opportunistically switched to the Republican Party. Even worse, Brough was "Falstaff," a "spy and informer," as well as a philanderer who flaunted his mistress in public. The general argued that Lathrop had been a loyal Whig before becoming a Republican and that he was even Radical in many of his beliefs, having urged as early as January 1861 the recruitment of blacks into the Union Army; Lathrop had even helped raise a black regiment in Kentucky. Moreover, he had always defended Lincoln. Heintzelman was even forced to fend off complaints that he too was soft on the Copperheads and disloyal. "If I have not established my loyalty, I had better quit the country," he angrily retorted.[44]

At breakfast on September 12, Major Johnson handed Heintzelman a telegram from the War Department that the general could "scarcely believe." Lathrop was being sent back to the 17th Infantry. Even worse, Johnson was being dismissed "for speaking disrespectfully of the President." Realizing that Brough was the source of much of Stanton's misinformation, Heintzelman rushed to the Capitol to confront the governor. In a heated exchange in which Heintzelman bluntly told the governor his charges were "utterly false and very absurd," Brough admitted that he was the "spy and informer."[45]

A few days after writing Stanton a long letter defending both Lathrop and Johnson, he met with Ohio senator John Sherman, brother of General Sherman, at the state fair in Columbus and complained about Brough. Sherman's only response was that the governor's actions were certainly "extraordinary."[46] Heintzelman also encouraged Lathrop, whom he argued had "served the country industriously and faithfully," to not only protest to Stanton but also personally go and see Brough and explain his views while appealing to as many influential friends as possible. Although it was doubtful that Johnson could be saved, the situation with Lathrop was different.

At the state fair Heintzelman did not help matters when he again met with Vallandigham and two other leading Copperheads, George E. Pugh and Gen. George Washington Morgan. Heintzelman had always admired Morgan, who had fought with Sam Houston during the Texas Revolution and had a distinguished career in the U.S. military. A boyhood friend of Vallandigham and an outspoken opponent of emancipation, Morgan had quarreled with Sherman during the Atlanta Campaign and resigned his commission, returning to Ohio to campaign actively for McClellan.[47]

Heintzelman's troubles with the Northern Department seemed endless. Although the draft was progressing quietly, with Ohio even exceeding its quota, he received a flood of telegrams on September 20 regarding a major crisis at Sandusky, where there had been an attempt to seize the arsenal and free the twenty-five hundred prisoners on Johnson's Island. Thirty raiders from Canada, mostly paroled or escaped Confederate soldiers along with a few Copperheads and some sailors armed with Bowie knives and revolvers, had captured two steamers, the *Island Queen* and *Philo Parsons*, near Bass Island in Lake Erie. Receiving the news, Stanton telegraphed Heintzelman to "proceed immediately to Johnson's Island." Learning that the boats had been scuttled in Canadian waters, the prison was secure, and the *Michigan*, the only warship on Lake Erie, was patrolling the area, Heintzelman canceled plans to go there personally. But when word reached him that sixty-seven-year-old Maj. Gen. Ethan Allen Hitchcock, an intimate of Lincoln and Stanton who was in charge of prisoner exchanges, was scheduled to meet him in Sandusky, he changed his mind and caught the train for Lake Erie.[48]

Arriving in Sandusky, he was met by General Hitchcock, and the two retired to a hotel room where they put on their uniforms and immediately took a boat to the island. Before walking ashore, they boarded the *Michigan* to interview two prisoners, Charles H. Cole, a captain in Forrest's cavalry corps who had been held at Johnson's Island before escaping to Canada, and a man named Robinson, who had also been arrested. Cole, who was apprehended at a Sandusky hotel, said that most of the men in the attempted rescue were Copperheads from the Midwest posing as mechanics and laborers. The leader of the grandiose scheme was John Yates Beall, and the idea for the raid had come from the highest echelons of the Rebel government in Richmond. Beall had been directed in the rescue scheme by Jacob Thompson, former secretary of the interior under James Buchanan. Both Heintzelman and Hitchcock were sure a case could be made against Thompson, and they recommended that an extradition request be sent to the Canadian government.[49]

That night a tornado roared over Johnson's Island from the west, partly destroying a building, blowing down a large part of the perimeter fence, and uprooting over one hundred trees. At one of the barracks, the winds swept away the stairs to the second story, and fifty men tumbled out and onto the ground in the darkness. The storm was so violent that it broke the glass in the pilothouse of the island's steamboat. The torrential winds even swept much of the water out of Sandusky Bay, and for hours it was impossible to reach the island. Examining the damage at the prison the next day, Heintzelman learned that Rebel general Isaac Trimble wanted to present him with a petition outlining a number of complaints. Heintzelman also talked again with General Beall, Mrs. Abadie's brother, and met briefly with Thomas Randolph Harrison, the son of William Mortimer Harrison. Heintzelman had met the older Harrison at the Riverside Plantation when he first arrived at the James River following the Union retreat from Malvern Hill in July 1862. An aide to Brig. Gen. Richard Brooke Garnett, young Harrison had been badly wounded and taken prisoner during Pickett's Charge on the third day at Gettysburg. His father, who had taken the family from the James River to Baltimore, had written asking that Heintzelman inquire into his son's well being. Heintzelman also spoke with Brig. Gen. John Wesley Frazer, who said that because he had surrendered Cumberland Gap without a fight, his fellow Rebel officers were "rather down on him."[50]

Back in Columbus and realizing that his time as commander of the Northern Department was probably drawing to a close, Heintzelman found time for personal reflection. "I cannot have many more years to live and would be glad to have some quiet home to spend them," he wrote on his fifty-ninth birthday. The Civil War had clearly mastered the old general. Rumors persisted that General Hooker was being sent to relieve him. Such rumors were probably true, he thought, and Stanton was to blame. Sure enough, on September 29 he picked up a copy of the *Cincinnati Gazette* and learned that he was being replaced.[51] With no word from Washington, the next day he found more articles in other newspapers saying that Hooker would arrive soon. "I have not been radical enough—won't arrest people without orders. . . . They can't make me radical. I will do what I think best for the country and not for a party. I have served my country too long to now commence to serve a party," he defiantly stated. After dining on pigeon that evening, he went to breakfast the next morning and learned that Hooker had arrived at the hotel. "He soon came in and we took breakfast together," Heintzelman recorded. Hooker carried with him General Orders No. 263, dated September 28, 1864, sending Heintzelman to Wheeling on the east bank of the Ohio River in the new state of West Virginia, there to await orders. It was "as nice a piece of petty spite as I have seen," he recorded. That afternoon, as the Camp Chase band arrived to serenade him, Heintzelman issued orders, as was the custom in the army, relinquishing command. In the evening he began to pack his personal belongings, including his journals and books, for the trip east. Three days later, as Margaret and Mary departed for Buffalo, he caught the Central Ohio and Steubenville Railroad for Wheeling, a "drunken, lawless, notorious town" and "a sort of Botany Bay," where there was "nothing to do."[52]

Only hours after checking in at the McClure House in the newly designated West Virginia capital, Heintzelman made a courtesy call on the state's first governor, Arthur Ingram Boreman. Back at the hotel a committee of politicians and local dignitaries arrived to invite him to a Union meeting at the Ohio County courthouse in Wheeling that evening. After newly elected U.S. senator Waitman T. Willey made a lengthy speech, Heintzelman was introduced as the "hero of Malvern Hill" and invited to address the large assemblage. Although somewhat embarrassed at the introduction, since the III Corps had borne little of the fighting at that battle, he agreed to say a few words, telling the crowd "that peace could only be obtained by a vigorous prosecution of the war." McClellan's election would bring an "armistice" and "the destruction of the Union and eternal war," which "our children's children will not see the last of." It was the first partisan political meeting he had ever attended. He was pleased to read a few days later that the *New York Times* noted his "little speech," since they had "never bothered to notice what he had done earlier in the war."[53] But that October there was no toast on the anniversary of the Battle of Huamantla, as had been his custom for eighteen years.

With the first snows of the season, Heintzelman took a skiff across the Ohio River to visit Maj. Gen. Edward Otho Cresap Ord, who was living at the small village of Bellaire.[54] Ord had been with him in the Washington defenses during the first winter of the war. In 1862 he had been wounded at Corinth, Mississippi, and at Petersburg he had been seriously wounded while commanding the XVIII Corps.

As the winter darkness reached Wheeling and more snows blanketed the town and the hills along the Ohio River, the general enjoyed long afternoon naps and sleigh rides through the woods, which brought back memories of happier and simpler times when he was a young officer in Buffalo. He rode out along the National Road to see a monument honoring Henry Clay. He took long, slow walks on his crippled feet to Wheeling Creek to watch the young people of the town ice skate. As was his custom ever since his marriage, he spent endless hours religiously answering Margaret's long letters from Buffalo and Washington. Lathrop, who was still in Ohio, also wrote, and there was a "long and loyal letter" from Albert Lowry at the Vallecillo mines in Nuevo León detailing the extent of the contraband trade on the Rio Grande and the flow of Confederate cotton into Mexico. During the long evenings, he spent much of his time following the war in the newspapers. The Rebels had been decisively defeated in Tennessee, first at Franklin and then at Nashville. Sherman was deep in Georgia and heading for the sea at Savannah. Grant, who did not have Sherman's abilities, he thought, was still at Petersburg. "I would rather be doing almost anything than stay here," Heintzelman wrote in early November, yearning to be with either Grant or Sherman. Kept in Wheeling by the "whim . . . of a tyrant," he grew increasingly impatient and angry.[55]

From Wheeling the general carefully watched the progress of the most important political campaign in American history. In September it was thought that Lincoln was unelectable. By October many Republicans had successfully, at least in the Northern imagination, tied McClellan to the Democratic Party's peace platform. Foreshadowing the general election, early returns from state races in Pennsylvania, Ohio, and Indiana, bolstered by the soldier vote, were decisively Republican. As November neared, many continued to accuse the Democrats and Little Mac of disloyalty and treason. Recalling McClellan's ineptness during the Peninsula Campaign, some Republicans even claimed he was a Copperhead himself.

As the election drew near, Heintzelman was serenaded and cheered at his hotel, and he even agreed to join in a Union torchlight parade. Following the crowd in a buggy past the three-story State Capitol, he was happy to see that many of the homes had hung out patriotic illuminated lanterns. Flags flew, people lined the streets, and cheers greeted the marchers. He seemed especially joyous when a young girl rushed up to present him with a bouquet of flowers. Two weeks later, following a sizeable Copperhead demonstration of the "unwashed democracy," during which a number of Peace Democrats became intoxicated and engaged in a number of "rows" with local Republicans, he agreed to give a speech in Richtown, an impoverished section of Wheeling where large numbers of German immigrants had settled. Despite his contempt for Stanton and Halleck, he badly wanted Lincoln reelected and the war pursued to the end, but he did not like people calling McClellan seditious. McClellan was not "disloyal," nor could his failures be attributed to "treachery or treason." He became particularly perturbed when letters arrived from Republican newspaper editors in the Midwest asking him for information that would confirm the Democratic candidate as a traitor. Although Heintzelman had never questioned McClellan's loyalty, he was forced to admit that Little Mac did have friends who were subversive. Seeing the Copperheads parading the streets of Wheeling, he granted that the Democrats might win Kentucky, but he was hoping that McClellan would carry "no state." If Lincoln could win a clear mandate, it "will then kill traitors."[56]

November 8, 1864, election day in Wheeling, was cold and overcast with a few snowflakes as people gathered quietly at the polls. The next evening everything at the McClellan Club was dark, while the noisy and festive procession in front of the Union Club told the results. Lincoln had won the popular vote in the country by 403,000 ballots and the electoral vote by a margin of 212 to 21. McClellan had only managed to carry New Jersey, Delaware, and Kentucky. Little Mac was "a dead cock in the pit," Heintzelman concluded.[57]

Still bored and depressed in Wheeling and itching for a field command, the general complained that his hair was falling out and that he was becoming bald, "the first indication I have had that I am growing old." Blaming the "tyrant" Stanton for his exile and realizing that a field command now was out of the question, he fondly yearned to return to Washington, where he could be with Margaret and Mary and closer to the war in Virginia. Once, after a long nap in late January, he awoke to the clatter of artillery in the street. "The sight of the guns, carriages and men make me feel like the war horse when he hears the trumpet," he wrote. "It made me wish to go with them." With Grant hammering at the gates of Petersburg and Sherman preparing to march north from Savannah into the Carolinas, he felt that the war could not last much longer. Senator Sherman promised to intervene with Lincoln on his behalf; Governor Curtin agreed to do what he could; and Thomas Wrightson sent a petition to the president protesting Heintzelman's treatment. But all was to little avail, and the general remained at Wheeling. "It is a poor reward for near 40 years service and three brevets and a crippled arm from a Rebel bullet," he despondently wrote a few days before Christmas.[58]

After obtaining ten days' leave, he traveled east to Washington to see Margaret and Mary, then steamed up the Hudson River to see Charles at West Point. He was proud of his son, who was rooming with Loyall Farragut, the son of Admiral Farragut, and was doing well academically, though Samuel Peter complained that he had too many demerits. By early December 1864 he was back at Wheeling for a "dull Christmas eve," during which he spent several hours watching ice skaters on Wheeling Creek while the fate of the nation was decided elsewhere. There was little doubt that he remained, as he often noted, "in the clutches of a tyrant," and he promised to use all his influence to displace Stanton. Even news that he was being brevetted a major general in the Regular Army for gallantry and meritorious service for his leadership at the Battle of Williamsburg did not mollify his anger. Convinced that Stanton was out to get him, he noticed that several other generals, including Hooker, Schofield, and Hancock, were also brevetted and that, although their meritorious conduct was after the Peninsula Campaign, their brevets were dated earlier than his. His only consolation seemed to be that he was perceived as somewhat of a hero back home at Manheim in Lancaster County, Pennsylvania. About this time, good news came from Arizona that the silver mines were reopening. He was also pleased when Gen. Zenas Bliss arrived in Wheeling looking for investors to purchase a large tract of land in the burgeoning oil fields of western Pennsylvania. Always inclined to invest in any capitalistic venture regardless of the risk, Heintzelman gave Bliss several thousand dollars.[59]

Beginning in January 1865, Heintzelman was assigned to court-martial duty in Wheeling, but there were no cases to be heard and the court adjourned. He was convinced it had been convened by Stanton out of spite just to keep him in Wheeling and away from Washington. During the second week of February, he was ordered to Cairo, Illinois, "the worst place in the country," for another court-martial.[60] Pausing at Columbus during a snowstorm, he visited briefly with Lathrop before continuing on to Cincinnati, where he changed cars for Cairo. After a thirty-six-hour train trip, he arrived in the river town at the confluence of the Mississippi and Ohio rivers. With several members of the court still en route, he took long walks through the town, along the river levee, and to the Presbyterian church. With Heintzelman presiding as president, the court was finally able to convene at the St. Charles Hotel by mid-February. Distinguished members of the court were Maj. Gen. David Hunter, who had presided over the highly publicized court-martial of Fitz John Porter; Maj. Gen. Silas Casey, whose division had borne the brunt of the Confederate attack on the first day at Fair Oaks; and Brig. Gen. John Baille McIntosh, who had lost a leg five months earlier at Winchester, Virginia, and whose brother, James, a Confederate general, had been killed at Pea Ridge, Arkansas. Col. William McKee Dunn, who had once been an aide to McClellan, completed the court. Brig. Gen. Eleazer Arthur Paine, an Ohioan 1839 West Point graduate, and who Heintzelman had known as a young officer in Florida during the Second Seminole War, was the first on trial.

Only days after gathering at Cairo, everyone agreed the venue should be changed to Paducah, Kentucky, some fifty miles upstream at the confluence of the Ohio and Tennessee rivers. Walking up Washington Street to the Continental Hotel in Paducah, Heintzelman could not help but notice the large earthworks ringing the town. He also noticed several burned and bullet-scarred buildings, all evidence of General Forrest's raid the previous year. Taking quinine and whiskey to ward off malaria, he instead came down with a case of diarrhea that turned into dysentery. Unable to consume any food and frequently confined to bed, the general had a difficult time presiding over the court. Even a keg of beer sent to his room by the local physician did not help. Heintzelman was still in Paducah on February 22, when one hundred guns were fired to commemorate the capture of Charleston and Columbia, South Carolina. "Our flag now floats from Sumter," he proudly recorded. It was not until the second week of March, with the work of the court finally concluded, that Heintzelman was able to leave the small river town. "I for one was delighted to turn my back on Paducah," he wrote while steaming up the Ohio River.[61] Taking on bales of tobacco at Galaconda, Illinois, and stopping at Evansville, Indiana, where several members of the court-martial caught a train for Washington, he continued upriver by boat to Louisville, though still sick.

Weak and still ill, Heintzelman reached Cincinnati, where he immediately sought out Dr. Tripler. With his health improved somewhat, he remained in the city for over a week. Feeling better but still ill, he telegraphed Margaret to join him in Wheeling as soon as possible. By late March he was back at the same room at the McClure House but spent most of the time in bed. His spirits were instantly lifted at noon on April 3, when an officer excitedly rushed into his room to say the telegraph was alive with news that Lee had evacuated Petersburg, the Rebel government had fled Richmond, and black Union cavalrymen were already in the streets of the Confederate capital. By the time Heintzelman reached the hotel lobby, several people were already in the streets with flags flying, and in a few minutes a band began to play. There was "great rejoicing in the city," he wrote. Church bells rang out and a large crowd assembled at the Ohio County courthouse. "This virtually ends the war," he concluded.[62] The next day Margaret arrived on the Baltimore and Ohio, and the two took a walk to the impressive suspension bridge spanning the Ohio River, then a buggy ride out the National Road. Even more exciting news came on April 10 when word reached Wheeling that Lee had surrendered to Grant at Appomattox Court House.

But five days later, on April 15, tragic news arrived from Washington. President Lincoln was dead at the hands of twenty-seven-year-old actor, pro-Confederate fanatic, and recreant assassin John Wilkes Booth. Flags that had flown in triumphant celebration only days earlier were now draped in black, and the church bells that tolled so gleefully now rang out in somber mourning. Shops and businesses were closed, and the "whole city was horrified." After reading every newspaper he could get his hands on and attending a eulogy for the slain president at the courthouse, Heintzelman was able to obtain twenty days' leave. Leaving Wheeling the very afternoon his request was approved, he went first to Pittsburgh, where space he found on a sleeping car, then across the Allegheny Mountains to Harrisburg to see Governor Curtin, who was busy making arrangements to receive Lincoln's body at the capital. In Philadelphia he decided to proceed on to New York to visit Charles at West Point. Arriving at the academy, he sent a note to Charles, who hurried to the hotel to spend the evening. Both Samuel Peter and Margaret were overjoyed to see their son, who had grown so much and was more mature since departing for the academy. After watching a review of the troops, Samuel Peter once again walked over the parade ground and went with Charles to the academy chapel to see the flags and black crepe honoring the dead president. The night before leaving West Point, he learned that Gen. Joe Johnston had surrendered to Sherman in a farmhouse at Durham Station, North Carolina. The terms given to the Rebels were so liberal, the newspaper said, that the new president, Andrew Johnson, had revoked them. Heintzelman was furious at Sherman, who must have been "crazy"; it was Jeff Davis who "dictated the terms and not Sherman," he sarcastically commented.[63]

Four days later the Heintzelmans were back in New York City on a "raw and cold" day as great crowds assembled before City Hall to view the president's open coffin. Later an even larger crowd gathered for a glimpse of the president's casket during a four-hour funeral procession. From there Samuel Peter and Margaret went on to Philadelphia and West Chester to see Elizabeth and Juliana, then to Washington, where he found Mary had draped the entrance to their house in black crepe. After three months of "exile," he went to the War Department, where Stanton was in a good mood and surprisingly "very gracious." The secretary of war said he wanted to put Heintzelman on active duty but asked if he did not need additional time to spend with his family. In Virginia the assassin Booth had been killed, and from Arizona came the news that his good and "fearless" friend and business partner, William Wrightson, was dead at the hands of Apaches. Wrightson had "few superiors," and "his word was better than most people's bond," Heintzelman wrote. His death was certain to be a "great loss to Arizona." When "will these human fiends be exterminated?" he asked in anger. "I wish I were out there to exterminate the race."[64] He wrote Thomas Wrightson a letter of condolence and again urged Stanton to send troops to protect the Arizona mines.

In Washington during the second week of May, with the war at last over, the streets were full of thousands of soldiers. The western men in Sherman's army were easily detectable, he noticed, by their awkward manners as they stood at shop windows gawking. The following week he visited with both Grant and Sherman, fresh from their victories in Virginia and North Carolina. Grant was "stiff and cold," but Sherman was warm and cordial. It was the first time he had seen Sherman since First Bull Run. Visiting President Johnson at the White House, he found the Tennessean "quite courteous."[65]

From a review stand along Pennsylvania Avenue, Heintzelman had watched for two days the "Grand Review" of first Grant's Army of the Potomac, then Sherman's Army of the Tennessee. With the armed might of the Republic on display under regimental flags embroidered with the names of a hundred bloody battles flapping in the sunshine, it was all a "grand pageant," a "magnificent sight," he thought. Thousands of spectators lined the avenue as regiment after regiment of cavalry, artillery, and infantry marched by, giving the "appearance of a vast moving panorama." He was especially delighted to see what remained of his "Old Corps." On the second day, as Sherman's long-striding infantry came swinging by, some of the spectators began to sing "John Brown's Body." Within minutes the soldiers had picked up the lines, and thousands of voices were soon thundering the great marching song of the Union armies. It was a scene not to be witnessed again in "this age."[66]

In early June Heintzelman was invited to help dedicate markers to commemorate First and Second Bull Run. Leaving the depot on Maryland Avenue at sunrise in a car that had been built especially for President Lincoln, he chatted with a number of old grizzled generals and correspondents as the excursion train made its way across the Virginia countryside, past luxuriant green fields as well as bare chimneys and rotting log huts. At Fairfax Station, carriages and horses waited to convey the dignitaries. Riding on horseback to Fairfax Court House, then on to Centreville, and finally along the Warrenton Turnpike to the stone bridge spanning Bull Run, he was at the battlefield by noon. Heintzelman thought it most appropriate that the site for the marker to commemorate the first battle was atop Henry House Hill, just north of the spots where Griffin's and Ricketts's batteries had stood and the scene of some of the most furious fighting. By the bleached and weathered white bones of the dead artillery horses, he could see exactly where Ricketts's battery had stood. Hymns were sung, poems were read, and the blue-clad 5th Pennsylvania Heavy Artillery paraded by, after which a red sandstone marker, twenty-one feet tall and completed the previous day, was dedicated. Inscribed on the pyramid-shaped monument were the simple words: "To the Memory of the Heroes who fell in defence of their country, June 21, 1861." After a few veterans, including such men from his old division as Orlando Willcox and Addison Farnsworth, had spoken, Heintzelman was called on for a few remarks "amid vociferous cheers" by the soldiers and spectators. "His profession was [that of a] soldier, not a speaker," the general said simply. Reflecting on the difficult days of Reconstruction that lay ahead, he concluded by declaring that "he was in favor of justice first and mercy afterwards." "Gen. Heintzelman was greatly interested on [*sic*] these grounds and 'fought the battle o'er again,'" the *New York Times* reported. "The dedicatory services were of a simple but impressive character."[67] At the conclusion of the ceremonies, the dignitaries posed for Alexander Gardner. Walking over the battlefield afterward, he was saddened to see so many skeletons of soldiers still unburied, and he was sorry that more veterans of the battle had not been present, especially Ricketts and Griffin.

Later he hurried over to Groveton for the dedication of a second, similar marker to commemorate Second Bull Run, but he arrived too late. Walking along the railroad cut where Colonel Grover had made his furious charge on the second day of the battle, he saw more broken skulls, rotting cartridge boxes, tin plates, canteens, and even hats and fragments of clothing and belts. Time and the elements had not erased the carnage of war. Even the trees still showed the scars of the battle.[68] After riding some thirty-six miles on horseback and then a rattling train ride back to Washington in the darkness, the general was home by midnight, tired and exhausted but contented. He had not been on horseback for over eighteen months, and he was stiff and sore for a week.

In late July, after a month in summer camp, Charles, sunburned and even more mature than before, arrived on furlough from West Point. Samuel Peter took great pride in his son, who was near the top of his class. During the three weeks Charles remained in Washington, the two strolled down Pennsylvania Avenue to have their photographs taken together and to visit important political and military figures.[69]

As Presidential Reconstruction began to take shape, Texas again came to dominate Heintzelman's thoughts. He met with Matías Romero, the debonair Mexican ambassador to the United States, and a senator he failed to identify who asked if he would be interested in an "expedition to root out the French" in Mexico.[70] Declining the unofficial offer to command an army rumored to number as many as seventy thousand men that would be sent to the Mexican border, Heintzelman, remembering back to the Cortina War, felt the real reason for such a large army in Texas was to stop Americans from invading Mexico, not to expel the French. Besides, he argued, ten thousand men were more than enough to guard the Rio Grande.

But at the same time he remained interested in Arizona Territory and the mines. After reading a pamphlet Mowry had written entitled *Arizona and Sonora*, he again became convinced that the Heintzelman Mine at Cerro Colorado was "the richest in the country." He also took time to communicate with Zenas Bliss and press for the sale or lease of the oil tract they had purchased in western Pennsylvania. Bliss, who was on leave at Providence, Rhode Island, then later at Albany, had "done nothing," he complained. In the meantime he became embroiled in a legal suit when Eva Smith, daughter of Confederate major Albert Smith, sued for $8,375 in back rent and the recovery of the Smith home in Washington that the Heintzelmans had occupied since the beginning of the war. Hoping to have the dwelling confiscated as a result of Smith's disloyalty, Heintzelman was forced to hire a local attorney. "Now is the time to teach those returned Rebels a lesson," he vengefully wrote.[71] Learning that Smith had taken the loyalty oath and that the judge hearing the case had ruled against the general, he asked that the decision be appealed, certain the judge was a Southern sympathizer.

In early July, when the *Washington Daily National Intelligencer* began publishing Capt. F. C. Adams's version of the Battle of Fair Oaks in a series of articles entitled "The Story of a Trooper," he became embroiled in a war of words with the author. Adams, who had been a volunteer aide-de-camp to General Franklin, asserted that on the afternoon of the first day of the battle, General Keyes had sent an urgent request to Heintzelman for reinforcements, to which he did not respond for nearly an hour. The delay, Adams asserted, had caused "serious injury" to Keyes's II Corps. The "unaccountable delay" was the result of "a misunderstanding between Generals Heintzelman and Keyes" about rank, he wrote. To Heintzelman, the article amounted to little more than an "ill tempered and violent attack." Inquiring further, he concluded that Adams must have got his "venom" while at Franklin's headquarters. Franklin, he knew, had always been jealous of the fact that Heintzelman outranked him, possessing "a bitter hatred" about it, and as a consequence he had been most imprudent in his remarks.[72]

Forced to dig out his journal and papers, Heintzelman spent several hours preparing a lengthy rebuttal, which appeared in the newspaper a few days later. Noting that Adams's account of the battle was "full of errors," he argued that there had never been "any misunderstanding between General Keyes and myself" about rank. Heintzelman admitted that he had received a note from one of Keyes's aides at 2 P.M., but he had "immediately ordered up Kearney's and Hooker's troops." Five days later Adams responded with a letter that attacked Heintzelman personally. The general's delay at Seven Pines was inexcusable, Adams charged, and his reaction to the initial article was "prompted by that same spirit of insubordination which found you disobeying orders and got you into so much troubled water on the Peninsula." Should the general desire, Adams could publicize even worse things about his performance at Savage's Station. Heintzelman responded a few days later with a lengthy letter in which he reproduced the note he had received from Keyes. He also reasserted the fact that he had rushed reinforcements to the front as soon as possible. "I have no hesitation in leaving my reputation, whilst commanding the gallant 3d army corps on the Peninsula, in the hands of the future historian," he concluded.[73] If Adams attempted to respond, the newspaper did not publish his rebuttal, and the matter disappeared into a mountain of other Civil War controversies, accusations, and counter-accusations that would engulf the conflict's historiography.

The Civil War would remain the pivotal event of Heintzelman's life. Strolling through the streets of Washington on the fourth anniversary of First Bull Run, he was disappointed that not a single individual he met had been at the battle. Later, however, he was saddened to meet an unnamed veteran who had lost both legs at Second Bull Run. He also took time to visit the War Department to remind Stanton that he was "unemployed and wanted to be put on duty." He was willing to go to Texas, he said, if given a command independent of Philip Sheridan. On August 28, after hearing that he had been mustered out of volunteer service, he took a leisurely stroll by the Executive Mansion for a baseball game on the south lawn. With four thousand spectators looking on, the Athletics of Philadelphia easily defeated the National Baseball Club of Washington. Although the game was anything but "extraordinary," he returned again the next day as the National Club did better but still lost to Atlantic of Brooklyn.[74]

Hearing rumors that he might be sent to New Mexico Territory, he immediately put in for six months' leave. In early September, after being granted a much shorter absence, he left with Mary during a rainstorm in a crowded train for Baltimore and Philadelphia, where they paused for a tour of Independence Hall. It was then on to West Chester to see Juliana and Maria, then by train to Lancaster and a two-hour buggy ride to Manheim, where he took a room at the Black Horse Tavern opposite "our old house, where I was born." One of his first visits was to the cemetery where the family tombstones were still in good order. A new church had been constructed east of the burial ground, and the old parochial schoolhouse across the street had been torn down. The owner of the Heintzelman home on Main Street invited the general and his daughter into the house for a visit. Samuel Peter also walked with Mary through what remained of the family orchard that he so fondly remembered from childhood, but all the trees except a single "old . . . apple tree" were dead. In the evening a number of the town's more prominent citizens called, but there were few people he recognized.[75]

From Manheim, where local residents were still referring to him as "Sourdough Sam," he went on to Lancaster, where he rode out to Wheatland, the stately home of the aging former president James Buchanan. Although Buchanan had handled secession abysmally, from the time he had assisted Heintzelman in gaining admittance to West Point forty-three years earlier, Samuel Peter had always been grateful to the lifelong bachelor and workaholic. He also found time for a "pleasant visit" with Thaddeus Stevens at his modest brick row-house in Lancaster. Indefatigable, egalitarian, and powerful as chairman of the House Ways and Means Committee, Stevens was a brilliant lawyer and a firebrand abolitionist who possessed a commitment to racial equality far in advance of his time. Like so many others in Washington in 1865, Stevens was struggling to shape the course of the nation. From Lancaster Samuel Peter went on to Harrisburg for a visit with Governor Curtin and a walk with Mary to the Capitol to see the portraits of all the Pennsylvania governors. By September 10 he was back in Washington.

In late September Poston arrived, and the two rushed off to see Secretary of State Seward to continue to press for troops for Arizona and to have Richard C. McCormick, secretary of the territory, made governor. Sent to see President Johnson, they found the White House full of Southerners, men and women, asking for pardons, a few of whom Heintzelman recognized but refused to acknowledge. After waiting five hours, the two were referred back to Seward. Later, over drinks at Willard's Hotel, Senator Weed of New York agreed to press Secretary of War Stanton on the issue.[76]

In late September Heintzelman and Poston made their way to New York by train for a meeting with several mining executives about the future of the Arizona mines. Although devastated over the death of their brother William, Thomas and George Wrightson, along with their sister and father, were in the city. With so much uncertainty in Arizona, little could be decided, though the mines continued to be worked by Mexican employees. There was time for a visit to Brady's photographic gallery and Fredericks's daguerrean studio, which Heintzelman thought the best in the city. He also walked with Poston down Fifth Avenue for a visit to the Travelers' Club and later took a carriage ride through Central Park with Poston and his daughter. The park was full of spectators waiting for Prof. Thaddeus Lowe to inflate one of his balloons. As twenty thousand onlookers gazed in amazement, the balloon soared several hundred feet into the air, after which a man then dangled from the gondola. Heintzelman also attended a Union veterans dinner to make a short speech, which he thought was well received. Public speaking, which had been so painful for most of his life, was now becoming a pleasure, and he was elated when old friends from Pennsylvania offered to run him for governor. Although they were sure he would be elected, Heintzelman wondered on what ticket they hoped he would campaign. Besides, he mused, "I am too poor to be governor and no politician."[77]

Back in Washington in September, Margaret handed him Special Orders No. 520, signed by General Grant. Samuel Peter would not be going to New Mexico after all but to Hart's Island in New York Harbor to join the 17th U.S. Infantry. Although he had spent a lot of time in New York, he admitted that he "had no idea what kind of a place Hart's Island is." On the anniversary of the Battle of Huamantla a few days later, he left Washington in a rainstorm on the steamer *Fairfax*. After a pleasant, uneventful trip up the coast, he arrived in New York on the afternoon of September 13. With the last boat having already left for Hart's Island, he was walking down Liberty Street when he heard a stable boy exclaim, "There goes the great general."[78] Looking up, he spotted General Scott passing by in a carriage. It was the last time he would ever see the old general.

After finding the quarters on Hart's Island "cheerful" and "quite cozy," he was able to hire a seventeen-year-old African American to assist with his horses and assorted chores. Margaret arrived from Washington, and the Northeast autumn proved to be a pleasant respite from the grinding war years. There was shopping in the city and nightly visits to the theater. In early November the couple hurried up the Hudson by train to visit Charles at West Point, and Samuel Peter took yet another nostalgic stroll across the parade ground. Back in New York City, and with the pleasant fall weather continuing, he and Margaret were again able to spend evenings at the theater, take long carriage rides through Central Park, and visit the various art galleries, one of which featured a "most vulgar" statue of Napoleon. Thomas Wrightson arrived to say that the Heintzelman Mine had been abandoned and that Arizona was "all doubt and uncertainty." When General Grant arrived in the city, Heintzelman sent the band of the 17th Infantry to serenade him at the Union Club on Fifth Avenue. He also made frequent visits to the Union League Club on East Seventeenth Street, where in his vanity, he loved to be introduced as one of the heroes of the war. When Maj. Gen. Frederick Steele, his subordinate from Fort Yuma, arrived from the Rio Grande frontier, the two went to the horse races and later had a long talk about "Brownsville and Matamoros" and stirring events on the Texas-Mexico border.[79] Fitz John Porter arrived in the city from Colorado looking well, and the two chatted about the war. With Margaret, he went to one of the art galleries to see the German-born Albert Bierstadt's highly romanticized yet strikingly vivid paintings of the Rocky Mountains.

In New York he managed to keep an eye on Reconstruction politics. Disloyal Rebels must be punished, he asserted, even "whole communities" if they "permit treason." Blacks in the South must be given "the same rights as the whites . . . though not to include suffrage at least not at the present." When Samuel R. Wells, editor of the *American Phrenological Journal*, invited him to write a brief autobiography for the magazine, Heintzelman jumped at the occasion and was delighted when the sketch appeared two months later. Wells also wrote a striking and very complimentary psychological profile, saying that the general possessed a "remarkable temperament." Forced to fend for himself from the time he entered West Point, he had learned to "adapt himself to any condition in which he may be placed." Heintzelman was "reasonably cautious, but never timid." He was "kind, considerate, and without malice or revenge." Moreover, he was "ambitious, very sensitive in regard to his reputation, and . . . no man who knows him well, questions his motives where moral principles are involved." Intellectually, Heintzelman was a "good observer and a good thinker," Wells wrote in conclusion.[80]

At a gathering in the city, he met Judge J. F. Cowan, a prominent lawyer who lived across the Hudson River in Englewood Cliffs, New Jersey, and when Margaret returned to Washington, Samuel Peter spent Christmas with the Cowan family, taking the opportunity to enjoy a long carriage ride along the New Jersey Palisades high above the Hudson. Initially, he was very impressed with the judge, and in the months to come, the Heintzelmans became frequent guests in the Cowans' lavish and "handsome stone house." After an uneventful and boring New Year's Day, he visited with former president Millard Fillmore, who was in the city, though Heintzelman had often criticized his stance on the war. On January 10 he accompanied Admiral Farragut to the traditional Tammany Hall dinner in the building where Andrew Jackson had dined in 1819. With Margaret back in Washington, he was often bored and lonely, so much so that he even took time to visit with his old adversary from Fort Yuma, one-armed Brig. Gen. "Fighting Tom" Sweeny. Twice wounded early in the Civil War, Sweeny had led a division during the Atlanta Campaign before being court-martialed for calling his corps commander, Maj. Gen. Grenville M. Dodge, a "God-damned liar" and a "cowardly son of a bitch." Like Heintzelman, Sweeny closed out the war without a command. A leading member of the Fenians, who were actively planning an invasion of Canada, Sweeny had virtually given up on his army career, and Heintzelman jokingly referred to him as the Fenian secretary of war.[81] In February Heintzelman visited with Joseph Hooker, who had suffered a stroke while at a reception for General Grant in New York City three months earlier. Hooker looked frail and sickly, requiring the constant assistance of a valet. Part of his face was paralyzed, and he could barely use his right arm and leg. Heintzelman noted too that his speech was slurred and that he could sign his name only by guiding the pen with both hands.[82] Heintzelman did not think "Fighting Joe" would ever be able to command an army or even ride a horse again, and he felt very bad for him.

Back in Washington on leave in late February, he went to see Stanton and found him to be "very gracious."[83] Two weeks later he was able to see President Johnson and then General Grant, who said that the 17th Infantry was not being sent to the Rocky Mountains to fight Indians, as had been speculated, but to either Texas or Mississippi. Finally in late March, after returning to New York with Margaret, Samuel Peter learned that his regiment was destined for Texas, though to what part of the state he did not know, only that he was to have eight companies and was to embark as soon as possible. Although he was ambivalent about returning there, especially since Margaret would not be accompanying him this time, he was anxious to be in the field again. The vast and untamed expanses of the Lone Star State once again beckoned him to the Southwest.

THIRTEEN

The Turmoil of Texas Reconstruction

WITH CHARLES AT WEST POINT and Mary away at school in West Chester, Pennsylvania, Margaret declined to go to Texas. Capt. Solon Lathrop, who had returned to the ranks of the 17th Infantry, along with his wife, Elizabeth, and their daughter, Maggie, would be making the long trip to the Lone Star State. On April 8, with the regimental band playing in a light drizzle, Heintzelman departed New York with several officers of the regiment aboard the steamer *Mariposa*. Within hours, most of the troops in the regiment followed on the *Mary Benton* and the *Raleigh*. Once away from shore, the *Mariposa* began to roll badly in the heavy seas, and many of the soldiers became sick. As the small ship was tossed about on the open waters, Heintzelman could not help but remember the long trip around Cape Horn on the *Rome* in 1849. Able to make 240 miles in the first twenty-four hours, the *Mariposa* was soon past Cape Hatteras, however, and the weather calmed. Five days out of New York, the steamer eased around Key West and into the balmy gulf. Entering the Mississippi River at midnight on April 15, the steamer churned slowly upriver past several slower ships. Passing Fort Jackson and Fort St. Philip before dusk, Heintzelman ordered the regimental band to play as the black garrisons crowded the dank parapets of the two historic fortresses. By the army barracks on the river below New Orleans in a heavy fog the next morning, the band again struck up a lively tune. At 10 A.M. on April 17, the *Mariposa* eased into the docks at New Orleans.[1]

In the Crescent City most of the officers scurried off to the fashionable St. Louis Hotel, while the troops marched to the barracks. Although Federal soldiers seemed to be everywhere in the city, New Orleans had not changed much since Heintzelman had seen it last in December 1860. Meeting briefly with Philip Sheridan, he was invited to stay at the general's headquarters. The five-foot, five-inch tall "Little Phil," largely because of his cavalry exploits in the Shenandoah Valley during the war, had become a hero in the North. Heintzelman liked Sheridan, whom Lincoln described as "a brown, chunky chap, with a long body, short legs, not enough neck to hang him, and such long arms that if his ankles itch he can skratch [*sic*] them without stopping."[2] Sheridan had the tough task of maintaining law and order in Louisiana and Texas while pressuring the French into leaving Mexico.

Heintzelman took time to visit with Gen. E. R. S. Canby and his wife, Louisa Hawkins. He also spoke at length with Maj. Gen. Stephen Gano Burbridge, who had just arrived in the city from a lengthy trip through northeastern Texas and Louisiana. Heintzelman had liked Burbridge ever since the loyal Kentuckian had crushed Morgan's cavalry at Cynthiana, Kentucky, while Heintzelman was in Columbus. Burbridge said both Texas and Louisiana were full of recalcitrant Rebels, many of whom were hostile and unwilling to concede defeat. When he had reached New Orleans, he told Heintzelman, a Southern zealot had attacked him with a Bowie knife, and the general had shot the man dead.[3] Burbridge, along with Sheridan and Canby, cautioned their friend that he was likely to have a difficult time in Texas.

At midmorning on April 20, after three days in New Orleans, Heintzelman and several companies of the 17th Infantry departed for Galveston on the steamer *Clinton.* After passing down the coast and around Point Bolivar in a heavy fog, he rushed ashore at Galveston to see Maj. Gen. Horatio Gouverneur Wright, commanding the Department of Texas. From Wright he learned that his headquarters would be at San Antonio, where several companies of the 17th Infantry were to be stationed.

The regiment that arrived in Texas was a mere skeleton of its former self. Having sustained heavy losses with the Army of the Potomac during the final months of the war in Virginia, the 17th Infantry was now reliant on men who "represented the scum of society." Despite a vigorous recruiting campaign, most of the companies remained understrength, and the officers quarreled among themselves over rank and privileges. In Galveston many of the soldiers became rousingly drunk and began fights. In one instance a soldier in the regiment accosted a former slave on the street and demanded that he pay a dollar "for services rendered" in his emancipation. In another incident several intoxicated men from the regiment threatened a black man with a bayonet for no apparent reason. The following day more drunken soldiers initiated a series of fights with recently discharged black soldiers, and when a race riot threatened to engulf the city, General Wright was forced to declare Galveston's liquor establishments off limits, a consequence of which being that soldiers began breaking into stores and saloons at gunpoint. Compared to the rowdies of the 17th Infantry, many residents openly stated their preference for the 10th U.S. Colored Infantry, which had formerly garrisoned the city.[4]

With Wright, Heintzelman took a buggy ride out to the railroad bridge that connected the island to the mainland to examine the "quite extensive" earthworks General Magruder, who had been sent to Texas after the Peninsula Campaign, had thrown up during the war.[5] He could also see the damage from the battle of January 1, 1863, when Magruder had recaptured the city. Even the house in which Wright was living, and where Heintzelman stayed during his brief respite, had been badly damaged.

The two took a short ride to the customhouse, where Brig. Gen. Edgar M. Gregory had installed the headquarters of the Freedman's Bureau. Established by Congress as a branch of the army to provide relief for thousands of refugees and to supervise the affairs of newly freed slaves, the Bureau of Refugees, Freedmen, and Abandoned Lands had been operating in Galveston since September 1865. Gregory had carved the Lone Star State into eighteen administrative subdivisions, most of them in the eastern and upper gulf coast regions of the state, where large numbers of African Americans were concentrated. Although he initially reported a willingness by planters to cooperate with the bureau, as Gregory became better acquainted with the situation in Texas, he became more concerned about the fate of the freed people.

Confrontations were inevitable, and Gregory, a college-educated Yankee Protestant who was also an avowed abolitionist, had come under fire in Texas by former secessionists. With the passions of war still very much alive in the state, both he and Wright admitted that chaos and disorder were likely to prevail for sometime. Texas, Heintzelman soon realized, was different from the other states of the conquered South. During the war, Federal armies had remained on its periphery, occupying only Galveston, a few coastal towns, the Lower Rio Grande Valley, and El Paso in far West Texas. Prior to the summer of 1865, Houston, San Antonio, Austin, and the interior had not seen any conquering armies in blue. Despite having lost thousands of its finest young men on a hundred distant battlefields, Texas remained proud and defiant. The *Houston Tri-Weekly Telegraph* perhaps best captured the obstinacy in Texas: "The Southern people, one and all, do not lie down, confess ourselves felons, acknowledge the vast superiority of the North, and express our humble thankfulness for their great condescension. . . . [W]e declare, simply and categorically, that we are not whipped, not half whipped. . . . [W]e are determined to whip them. . . . [W]e are determined to get again the control of the Federal Government." In referring to former Confederates, Heintzelman also captured the mood in Texas: "They would rebel again if they had the slightest hope."[6]

In June 1865 President Johnson appointed a militant Unionist and former congressman, Andrew Jackson Hamilton, as provisional governor of the state. Perhaps more provocative than any of Johnson's other appointments, Hamilton soon incurred the intense animosity of many white Texans. Prior to the war, the six-foot-tall, broad-shouldered "Colossal Jack," as Hamilton was known, had represented the Western District of Texas in the House of Representatives while Heintzelman was at Camp Verde. Persecuted and fearful of being hanged for his Unionist pronouncements, Hamilton had fled Austin during the night for Mexico in 1862. Commissioned a brigadier general and appointed military governor of Texas, he returned with the Union Rio Grande Expedition in late 1863. Possessing little real authority, he left the state a second time only to return with the Union Army in the summer of 1865. As Hamilton struggled to set up a government in Austin, General Sheridan sent the army across the vast Texas landscape. Moving west from Louisiana, two black regiments occupied Marshall on June 18; two days later another Federal force moved into Houston. Attired in a sailor's blouse and a blue jacket agleam with gold, and with his long blond hair set off by a red tie, the flamboyant Col. George Armstrong Custer arrived in San Antonio and Austin with five cavalry regiments. By this time Union forces had already occupied Brownsville, the Lower Rio Grande Valley, and various posts as far upriver as Ringgold Barracks at Rio Grande City. By the end of 1865, as many as fifty thousand soldiers were in Texas, half of them African Americans.

As Heintzelman was on his way to Texas, Hamilton struggled but failed to prevent the resurgence of the Democrats and the antebellum economic elite. So bad was the situation that many Texans, some of them former slaveholders, argued that emancipation was unconstitutional and stubbornly refused to liberate their slaves. In some instances, former slaves who dared to leave their former owners became fugitives to be hunted down like antebellum runaways. In some counties in East Texas, planters formed secret societies that hanged disobedient blacks. Defiant former Confederates, many still in their gray uniforms, seemed to be everywhere. With elections in early January 1866, the prewar power structure was restored, and when delegates assembled in Austin a month later for a constitutional convention, it was evident that prominent prewar secessionists, though forced to share the spotlight with moderate Unionists, were poised to regain control of the state. James Webb Throckmorton, a transplanted Tennessean who had campaigned against disunion but had gone on to serve in the Confederate Army, was elected president of the convention. Although accepting the abolition of slavery and agreeing to basic black civil rights, the delegates refused to affirm African American suffrage.

Yet during the few days he spent in Galveston, Heintzelman saw evidence of how affairs in Texas had changed when he watched a black regiment on parade. He also enjoyed dinner with General Lee's "Old Warhorse," James Longstreet, perhaps the most conciliatory of the Confederate generals. If the topic of Seven Pines, the furious battles of the Seven Days, or Second Bull Run came up at the dinner, Heintzelman did not mention it in his journal. Later he learned that much of his baggage, while setting in the quartermaster's warehouse near the docks, had been plundered. Two boxes of wine were broken open and the wine stolen. Angry, he convened a board of inquiry that fixed the theft on three recruits, but they had already deserted.

On the afternoon of April 28, Heintzelman boarded the *Crescent* for Indianola. After a lengthy delay in loading baggage and horses, the small steamer headed down the gulf coast. By daylight the next morning, the vessel was through Pass Cavallo, across the choppy waters of Matagorda Bay, and had arrived at Indianola. While the men of the 17th Infantry went into camp on the edge of town in a misty rain, Heintzelman and the regiment's officers and their wives hurried off to the modish Casimir House, only one block from where the Galveston and New Orleans steamers docked in Lavaca Bay. Except for the wharves that Magruder had burned during the war, the town had not changed much since Heintzelman had seen it last in 1860. After watching the troops march off the next morning, he commandeered an ambulance from the army depot and set off for Port Lavaca, where he caught the San Antonio and Mexican Gulf Railroad for Victoria. In anticipation of a Union invasion, Magruder had destroyed much of the railroad, but the tracks had been repaired. Churning along the gulf coast at ten miles an hour, the train arrived in Victoria on the evening of April 30. Heintzelman booked a room at the Union House, while many of the officers and their wives took rooms at the more fashionable Globe Hotel on the north side of De León Square. He learned the next morning that many of the women, complaining of fleas, bedbugs, and grime, had fled the hotel in the night for the army camp on the outskirts of town.

After seeing off most of the regiment the next morning, Heintzelman too splashed across the Guadalupe River and with John, a young black man he had hired as a servant, took up the long march for San Antonio. The trip inland reminded him of his first trek to San Antonio seven years earlier. Margaret and the children had been along then, and everyone was excited to be in a new and exotic land. The long, dusty trek this time was different. His family was scattered in the East, and Heintzelman admitted he was so depressed he "could not stand it." A good officer, he rationalized, one sworn to duty, honor, and country, did not question orders, and he plodded on. After bivouacking on the sandy banks of Coleto Creek, the next day the column pushed on to Yorktown, where part of the 18th New York Cavalry was camped. Before daybreak the next morning, he was on the road again but, taking a wrong turn, wound up in the "dilapidated" and "strongly rebel" community of Helena, where he found more New York cavalrymen. Jostling on toward the northwest, past Sulphur Springs and ahead of the slower moving infantry, he arrived in San Antonio early on the afternoon of May 12. Unpacking his personal belongings at the Menger Hotel, he was horrified to discover that a box of his valuable papers was badly water damaged. Although he spent hours trying to dry the documents, he found over one hundred prized photographs covered with a black mold, while several of his valuable personal journals were damaged and numerous other papers ruined. The box, he learned, had been accidentally dumped into the harbor at Indianola.[7]

After assuming command of the Central District of Texas and setting up his office in General Twiggs's old headquarters, Heintzelman was able to visit with several antebellum friends, including Frances and Ludovic Colquohn and Mary and Samuel Maverick. As he had done before the war, he took a leisurely buggy ride down the San Antonio River to Mission Concepcion and San José, "a miserable ruin though still used and with a few of the lowest class of Mexicans about." Later at a picnic at San Pedro Springs on June 19 to celebrate the emancipation of the slaves in Texas, he watched "an ex-rebel Capt. . . . dancing among'st the negroes." Stupefied, Colquohn was sure the man had to be a "Yankee abolitionist." He was also pleased when a number of prominent German Texans invited him to the Casino Club, the city's first social club and theater. "The Germans here are as a general thing," he wrote, "better educated than you will find in any other city in the Union." Old friends from Camp Verde rode into town to call at his headquarters. He enjoyed further picnics at San Pedro Springs and on the banks of Salado Creek. Although he yearned for the family life he had enjoyed in Washington, he felt very much at home in the Alamo city. Margaret wrote from Washington to say that the courts had ruled in their favor, and they would not have to compensate Eva Smith for the back rent she had demanded. Nevertheless, the house had to be vacated, so Margaret was going to Buffalo.[8]

While in San Antonio, Heintzelman kept a close watch on the ever-evolving political scene in the state and the nation. On June 25, voters, by a decisive margin of 49,277 to 12,168, chose Throckmorton over a Unionist ticket led by former governor Elisha M. Pease. The Eleventh Legislature took office six days later, and on August 9 Throckmorton was inaugurated. Studying the new governor's inaugural speech in the newspaper, Heintzelman liked what he read. "We must let Southern people have some human nature," he commented.[9] When the Texas legislature, dominated by former secessionists, abruptly tried to return the state to the status quo antebellum, the general began to change his mind. From the time he arrived, he grew increasingly uncomfortable with Reconstruction in Texas.

Heintzelman took a special interest in the Fourth of July celebration that year, the first of the postwar parades in the city, which he saw as symbolizing the reunification of the country. Although he persuaded a few city officials to participate, not one former secessionist "put out a flag or joined the celebration." Realizing a majority of "the American part of the population is rebel" and bitterly secessionist, he feared a public disturbance. With the procession starting and ending at Military Plaza, the city's two fire companies marched along with the Laborer's Association, a liberal group of German workers. The parade also featured the ordnance sergeant's young daughter as the Goddess of Liberty, while other young ladies represented different states. The German population of the city was in a festive mood, and Samuel Bell, a strong Unionist, waved a large American flag from a carriage as the parade paused in front of the Menger Hotel. There on Alamo Plaza, Heintzelman asked that the Declaration of Independence be read, after which the army fired a salute. Those assembled also listened attentively to a patriotic speech by Charles Anderson, another Texan Unionist whom Heintzelman had known before the war. At least one Confederate sympathizer, Vinton James, was not impressed, however: "The people of southern persuasion viewed this 1866 4th of July celebration with sullen looks and silence and utter helplessness and bitter disappointment."[10]

Responding to the demands of merchants, Heintzelman agreed to assist in reestablishing the mail service between San Antonio and El Paso, though he realized the risk to couriers would be great. In late June James Holliday arrived in San Antonio with the first eastbound stage; two days later the first stage rolled west. At the eastern end of Limpia Canyon near Barilla Spring, just east of Fort Davis, the stage was met by Chief Espejo and one hundred Mescalero warriors. Although the guards were able to escape, the conductor, Tom Davis, shot himself as the Apaches closed in on him. Only by garrisoning the posts along the route could it be made secure, Heintzelman realized, and in late July eight companies of the 4th Cavalry were sent to occupy several of the trans-Pecos forts. He also worked to reestablish several posts on the northwestern frontier of the state.[11]

A few days after the Fourth of July celebration, Polocarpio Rodriguez, his friend and guide from Camp Verde, rode into town to say that he still had a box of the Heintzelmans' crockery, which had been left at Camp Verde in December 1860. Two weeks later Rodriguez came in again, reporting that he had been out "after Indians" and had found a new route that would cut 100 miles off the current 652-mile journey to El Paso. He also invited Heintzelman to his ranch northwest of San Antonio near Bandera to "spend a few days" hunting and fishing.[12]

In early October 1866, along with his friend Samuel Maverick, Heintzelman rode north into the Hill Country. Arriving at the Ganahl home at Zanzenberg, or Center Point, where he had spent many pleasant evenings in 1859–60, Virginia Ganahl, whose secessionist husband was in Brownsville, sent for Rodriguez, who rode through the night to join his friend. After breakfast the next day, the three men set out on a fishing trip up the Guadalupe River, after which they conversed into the night over ice cream at Zanzenberg. The next day they rode through the cedar-crowned hills to Rodriguez's 420-acre ranch along Privilege Creek east of Bandera. They then pressed on to Camp Verde, where Heintzelman found the post largely deserted and little more than a "cattle rancho." Only an Irish family was living on the grounds, and most of the buildings were dilapidated and falling down. The fences, sutler's store, and even Heintzelman's bathhouse were all gone. Before departing for San Antonio, he enjoyed another fishing excursion and a bountiful catch of trout, catfish, perch, and even a large turtle. Rodriguez and Maverick also found time to shoot several turkeys. "Polly is one of the best Mexicans I ever met with and I parted from him with regret," Heintzelman wrote upon returning to San Antonio.[13]

By late July there were several deaths from cholera at Galveston, and the alarm spread across the state. In mid-August a senior officer of the 17th Infantry, Maj. Peter William Livingston Plympton, died of the dreaded disease, and Heintzelman knew it was only a matter of time before it spread to San Antonio.[14] Following heavy rains, or what Heintzelman called "real cholera weather," in late August, several deaths were reported in San Antonio. Admitting that "the town is in great excitement about the cholera," he did not believe the news at first, but then five deaths were confirmed the next day in the poorer southern part of the city along the river. Almost immediately orders went out for the cavalry to establish a camp along the Medina River west of San Antonio, in what was thought to be a healthier climate.[15] A flood that inundated the community on the night of September 10 did not help, and citizens and soldiers were forced to flee their homes in the night. The water was two feet deep in the army quarters, and several horses and mules drowned. Two days later Heintzelman reported that the soldiers had begun to contract cholera and die. The epidemic was so bad that fourteen citizens were buried in San Antonio in a single day.

With no treatment of its raw sewage and a contaminated water system, San Antonio had experienced cholera outbreaks in 1833 and again in 1849, but the epidemic of 1866 was one of the worst. On October 16 the wife of 1st Lt. Frederick W. Bailey became ill in the evening, died before morning, and was buried in the afternoon. The next day the couple's infant son was dead, and Bailey followed a second coffin to the cemetery. "What a change 24 hours have made in the prospects of his life," Heintzelman wrote of the grief-stricken young officer. Taking no chances, the remainder of the cavalry was sent southwest to the Medina River, and within days two companies of the 17th Infantry and Heintzelman's headquarters followed. For the next month, in the rain and heat, the disease raged out of control in San Antonio, with several deaths each day. Army hospitals were full, and scarcely a day passed that several soldiers did not succumb to the disease. With profuse watery diarrhea, vomiting, and leg cramps accompanied by rapid loss of body fluids, many soldiers became so dehydrated that they went into shock, with death following within hours. Burials were hastily made in shallow graves. For the first time since arriving in Texas, Heintzelman was thankful that Margaret and Mary had not accompanied him. On September 19 seventeen new cases were reported, and eight people died before evening. Even in the army camps along the Medina, four or five soldiers were dying each day.[16] It was not until cooler weather arrived in early October that the disease abated.

Amid this deadly epidemic, Heintzelman received a letter from Governor Throckmorton inviting him to Austin, and in early September he left for the capital. Riding past large corn and cotton fields on the edge of the Blacklands Prairie, more "beautiful and more cultivated" than he had ever imagined existed in the state, he reached New Braunfels the first night and took a room at a "miserable house." Crossing the Guadalupe River early the next morning, he reached the Colorado River at Austin by sunset. Rather than wait on the south bank until morning, he placed his valuables in his pants pocket, tied his pants into a bundle on his head, and attempted to wade across the river. In the darkness he came close to being swept away and drowned in the strong current. Assisted by two Mexicans with ropes, he was finally able to reach the north bank in safety, where he built a fire and sent for soldiers from the Austin garrison.[17]

Able to find a room at the Avenue House on Congress Avenue, he slept the night on a mattress of cornhusks. The next morning he spent several hours with the governor. Although most of their discussion centered on Indian affairs, Heintzelman was suspicious of Throckmorton's real intentions. Called "Throcky" by the army in Texas, the governor's request for a more vigorous pursuit of raiding Indians was really a thinly veiled plea to move the U.S. "troops out of the settlements," Heintzelman concluded. White Texans, the governor said, were being antagonized by "unrestrained" black troops. That afternoon Heintzelman met with a party of unnamed "Union men" who warned that if the black troops were indeed withdrawn from many of the communities, as Throckmorton was asking, "no Union or Freeman's life would be safe." Texas was far "more disloyal than when the [Twiggs] surrender took place," they said.[18] The next day he was invited to appear before the state senate but opted for a tour of the Texas

"Lunatic Asylum" instead. On September 7 he hurried back to San Antonio, where the cholera was said to be growing worse.

Well into the fall, the governor continued to write Heintzelman complaining of Indian raids on the frontier west and northwest of San Antonio. Specifically, Throckmorton wanted two companies of cavalry stationed at Jacksboro, where they could help stop raids coming out of Indian Territory. More cavalry should be stationed at Fort Mason too, while two companies should make camp in northeastern Comanche County. The troops at Jacksboro could eventually be stationed at Fort Belknap, and those in Comanche County could eventually regarrison Camp Cooper, the governor went on to suggest. Before Heintzelman was willing to act, though, Sheridan, who downplayed the dangers posed by Indians on the frontier, wanted evidence that the more-settled portions of the state were safe first. Using the "greatest care," Heintzelman was to undertake "a full investigation." Sheridan did not like or trust Throckmorton and most former Confederates in the state. "If a white man is killed by the Indians . . . the greatest excitement will take place, but over the killing of many freemen in the settlements, nothing is done," he commented.[19]

If U.S. soldiers could not be sent to protect the frontier settlements, Throckmorton wanted to raise one thousand volunteers. The governor was besieged with letters and petitions from frontier communities and individuals asking that he take action against the hostile Comanches. Many of these were from former Confederates, who volunteered their services and urged him to create a frontier militia army as soon as possible. Some even recommended that John R. Baylor, an Indian-hating, fire-eating former Confederate colonel and secessionist, should command the force. After President Johnson discussed the situation at a cabinet meeting, Secretary of War Stanton agreed that assistance should be provided. On October 26 Heintzelman wrote Throckmorton to say that "the movement of troops towards the Frontier has commenced." With Sheridan expected to arrive in Texas in a few days, Heintzelman promised that the military would "do all that is necessary for the protection of the border counties."[20]

In less than two weeks Sheridan authorized stationing the 6th Cavalry to guard the frontier line from the Red River to Camp Cooper and the 4th Cavalry to patrol the frontier from Fort Clark to Fort Mason. Eventually, almost the entire 6th Cavalry would be sent to Jacksboro, while five companies of the 4th Cavalry went to Fort Mason. Three companies of cavalry were stationed at Fort Clark to guard the area west of San Antonio. Troops already at Fort Inge and those along the Rio Grande would remain in place. The 17th Infantry would garrison Hempstead, Brenham, Houston, and Galveston. In addition, four hundred recruits from Carlisle Barracks, expected to embark from New York in the next few weeks, were to join the cavalry in Texas.[21] A company of black cavalry being recruited in New Orleans could also be sent to the Lone Star State if needed.

At the same time, Sheridan, who was annoyed by this constant demand for soldiers, read in the *Waco Valley Register* that Throckmorton remained adamant about recruiting Texans to help guard the frontier. "Now as I have ordered to the frontier double the number of men the legislature thought necessary, I cannot see any good excuse for the employment of this volunteer force," Sheridan bluntly telegraphed the governor.[22] An army of Texans on the frontier or anywhere else would not be tolerated.

When General Wright left Texas in the fall of 1866, considerable confusion developed in the army high command. George Washington Getty was the highest-ranking general in Texas, but he was at the Rio Grande, seriously ill, and reluctant to assume command. Consequently, in the third week of September, Sheridan telegraphed Heintzelman to take charge. Five days later, however, word came that Getty had recovered and would assume command after all. Yet two weeks later Getty telegraphed to say that he was leaving Texas and that Heintzelman should proceed to Galveston to take charge. Learning that Heintzelman was leaving San Antonio, the German press in the community praised him as "a true supporter of the Johnson policy" and someone who had done "everything to please his conservative friends." After William Menger hosted a small reception and dinner in his honor at the Menger Hotel on the evening of October 17, Heintzelman packed his personal belongings and rode out of San Antonio in a light rain at midmorning the next day. After reaching Sulphur Springs the first evening, the next day he hurried over rutted and muddy roads to Yorktown, where he spent the eighty-fifth anniversary of the British surrender at Yorktown in 1781. Riding on to Victoria and then to Indianola, he took a room at the Casimir Hotel before leaving on a revenue cutter for Galveston the next day. Going ashore on the island, he found the Lathrops—Solon, Elizabeth, and their daughter, Maggie—sick but anxiously awaiting his arrival.[23] Taking a room at the Island City Hotel, he issued orders on October 24 assuming command of the District of Texas. A few weeks later he came down with chills and fever, everyone fearing that he might have contracted cholera, but recovered quickly and was back on duty within a week.

In Galveston his mood was buoyed when Margaret wrote that she had decided to join him in Texas after all. When she shipped the family piano and her sewing machine at an exorbitant cost of $150, Samuel Peter made plans to meet her in New Orleans. By November, however, when he wrote that he had moved in with the Lathrops to save money on rent, Margaret wrote to say that she was "utterly opposed to living two families in one house" and had decided to "stay North." If she "chooses to come, well and good and if not, I must get along," Samuel Peter defiantly recorded. Margaret also wrote Elizabeth asking for $800 the Lathrops owed them. Hurt by her sister's curtness, Elizabeth angrily responded by saying that she would pay the money, even if she had to "sell her diamonds and silver."[24]

Heintzelman found Galveston markedly different from Austin and San Antonio, where he had been greeted by large numbers of loyal Union citizens. Even in those cities, the secessionist element was not that bitter. But in Galveston he complained to Rep. Thaddeus Stevens, "your uniform draws scowls from the men and more decided demonstrations from the women." Arriving in the "rebel town," he remembered uneasily how a number of leading ladies had hissed when "Yankee Doodle" was played. After five months in the seaside community, he had made friends with only one "rebel family" and had not been "invited to any social gatherings."[25]

Elizabeth Lathrop, despite her excessive moodiness and social elitism, appears to have had a great deal of influence on Heintzelman and his decision making. Shortly after she informed him of a quarrel she was having with the wife of Col. Henry Ashfield Ellis of the 17th Infantry, who had temporarily replaced Brig. Gen. Joseph Barr Kiddo in charge of the Freedman's Bureau in Texas, Heintzelman replaced Ellis with Abner Doubleday. "It has created quite an excitement," Heintzelman admitted. Colonel Ellis, who vehemently argued that he had done nothing wrong, defiantly refused to be relieved and even declined to accept any communications from the district commander. When Heintzelman threatened to have him arrested, Ellis finally acquiesced. As commander of the 17th Infantry, Ellis was to report to his regiment in San Antonio. When Doubleday refused to become involved in the growing and embarrassing feud, Heintzelman named Lathrop as acting assistant commissioner of the bureau. Rumors circulated widely in Galveston that Elizabeth had instigated the appointment because she had vindictively "wanted to exile her greatest feminine enemy from her social circle in Galveston." Such intrigue seriously tarnished Heintzelman's already ebbing reputation as an effective military commander.[26]

Indeed, Heintzelman's problems seemed to escalate daily with the continued wide-scale brutalization of freedmen and anyone associated with the Freedman's Bureau. When a former Unionist was jailed at Belton in Bell County, Heintzelman refused to intervene, and a mob took the man out and hanged him. When Throckmorton complained that troops had been sent into the community, Heintzelman assured the governor that it was only "temporary" and that the troops would be withdrawn. So bad was the situation in East Texas that he published orders from the adjutant general in Washington that authorized the "arrest [of] those committing crimes in states that were in rebellion when civil officers have failed or seem unwilling to act."[27]

When a rambunctious former Confederate complained that black soldiers at Victoria had arrested him and confiscated his goods, Governor Throckmorton asked Heintzelman to intervene. Examining the case closely, the general concluded that, though "many illegal and unlawful acts have been committed," he had no authority to intervene since the soldiers were "under the charge of the Freedman's Bureau."[28] When two other black soldiers were accused of murdering a man named William Walker in Victoria, Throckmorton demanded that they be arrested and tried by civil authorities. Heintzelman agreed to allow an investigation of the killing, and when a Victoria County grand jury returned a murder indictment shortly thereafter, the case was turned over to General Sheridan. By the time Sheridan agreed to turn the soldiers over to local authorities, they had already left Texas, been discharged in Baltimore, and could not be found.[29]

Trouble also flared at Brenham, a rough and brawling railroad town between Houston and Austin. There, Capt. Samuel A. Craig, a dedicated agent of the Freedman's Bureau committed to Reconstruction, was doing everything possible to protect blacks and bureau schoolteachers who were subjected to continuous verbal and physical abuse. Stationed in Brenham at the time was Company E, 17th Infantry commanded by Capt. George William Smith. The unit had previously been stationed in Galveston, where they had gained a well-earned reputation for "drinking, whoring, and fighting."[30]

Tensions in Brenham peaked when Craig arrested D. L. McGary, a fire-eating former secessionist and local newspaper editor who had howled against the captain and the Yankee occupiers ever since the Freedman's Bureau had arrived in town. On the night of September 7, 1866, matters came to a violent climax when a number of marauding, half-drunk soldiers invaded an African American ball, after which they interrupted a similar gathering of whites and a gun battle erupted in which two of the soldiers were wounded. Failing to apprehend the assailants, the soldiers set fire to a store and a saloon, the flames spreading throughout the night to consume the entire business district of the town.[31] White citizens of Brenham were outraged, demanding that the soldiers responsible be punished. Throckmorton protested to Sheridan, who arrived in Texas to confer with Heintzelman and investigate the incident. He directed Heintzelman not to remove the soldiers from the town or allow any of them to be arrested, though Captain Smith and Captain Craig were transferred to other counties.

More trouble came three months later at Seguin in Guadalupe County. In this riverside community, William Longworth, a judge from nearby Wilson County who was working as an agent for the Freedman's Bureau, was doing everything possible to assist and protect freedmen in the area. As unpopular in the county as Captain Craig was in Brenham, Longworth feared for his life. When he and another bureau agent were indicted by a local grand jury for illegal gambling, Craig vowed to protect the judge and all other Freedmen's Bureau employees. Acting under Heintzelman's orders, the captain demanded that the district clerk, James Wilcox, give up the papers in the Longworth case. When Wilcox closed his office rather than turn over the papers, Craig threatened to arrest him and take him to San Antonio for prosecution. When Wilcox finally surrendered the keys, Craig entered the courthouse, took the papers, and destroyed them. "If these things are to be allowed then the holding of courts and the attempt to exercise civil power by civil authorities is 'a miserable farce,'" Guadalupe County officials declared to Throckmorton, who demanded to know under whose orders Craig had acted.[32]

Within weeks Craig was indicted by a Guadalupe County grand jury. Seguin District Judge John Ireland was furious that a Federal officer had dared to invade his courthouse. Born and educated in Kentucky, Ireland had been a member of the Texas Secession Convention and had enlisted as a private in the Confederate Army, eventually rising to the rank of lieutenant colonel. Although he demanded that Craig be arrested and punished, the Guadalupe County sheriff, knowing that a platoon of bluecoats were in the community and were determined to protect Craig, was reluctant. But after the cavalry platoon returned to San Antonio, Ireland noticed Craig on the street and was heard to say, "Why isn't that God damn Yankee thief arrested, yet?"[33] Shortly thereafter, Craig was indeed arrested and thrown into the county jail. Within hours, the captain's friends took his plea for assistance to San Antonio, where Col. John Porter Hatch's 4th U.S. Cavalry was stationed.

The news from Seguin helped convince Heintzelman that the military must do everything possible to protect the Freedman's Bureau in Texas. In this instance he threatened to have the newly elected officials in Guadalupe County arrested. If the military did not take action, "not one of them [bureau agents] can perform his duties for an hour." Not a single "Union man or Freedman would be safe a day were it not for the wholesome fear there is of the military." When Hatch telegraphed Galveston for instructions, Heintzelman ordered him to send a company of cavalry to Seguin to secure Craig's release. An 1845 West Point graduate, Hatch was a dedicated and seasoned Civil War veteran decorated for bravery at South Mountain during the Antietam Campaign. Not hesitating, he sent a lieutenant with forty-five cavalrymen galloping east to Seguin, where they surrounded the Guadalupe County courthouse and set Craig free. The captain, who had grown wealthy by speculating in oil stock in Pennsylvania, decided to immediately retire from the army and left the state. As far as he was concerned, Guadalupe County had "gone to the devil."[34]

As Craig departed Texas, Judge Ireland, who Heintzelman claimed was "notoriously disloyal," went after the district commander with a vengeance. In mid-December 1866 the sheriff of Galveston County arrived at army headquarters with an arrest warrant, but Heintzelman refused to recognize the warrant and turned the man away. "I won't obey the arrest," he defiantly wrote. "I am here on duty by military authority and cannot obey this summons without orders from superior military authorities." Moreover, the "present disturbed condition of the country" would not allow him to leave his post. Knowing that "a strong feeling" existed in Texas "against all officers who have been in any way instrumental in sustaining the U. S. laws, particularly those connected with the Freedman's Bureau," he was determined not to capitulate.[35]

In the escalating controversy, Heintzelman sought the advice and assistance of the U.S. attorney for the Eastern District of Texas, David G. Baldwin. Three days before Christmas, Baldwin came to the island on the train from Houston, and the two discussed the case at length over dinner. Realizing that Baldwin was determined to defend him at all costs, Heintzelman took an instant liking to the hardnosed attorney, writing that he was the "only congenial man I have met in Texas." Baldwin agreed that Ireland was "notoriously disloyal," a "mischief maker," and acting under the "counterfeit robes of 'civil authority.'" Moreover, he had no problem defending "those who uphold the flag of our nation." For Heintzelman to be arrested would be similar to President Johnson being "dragged from a cabinet council on civil process for signing the death warrant of the [Lincoln] conspirators." In early January 1867 Heintzelman met again with Baldwin to talk and plot a strategy. Baldwin had little sympathy for those who had failed "in succession, nullification, secession and armed rebellion." He reassured Heintzelman that he had "acted as an officer of the government of this nation" and that his conduct was "proper and becoming [of] a heroic officer who loves his country and his country's laws."[36]

Writing to Representative Stevens and Sen. Ben Wade that the life of a "Union man or Freedman" in Texas was of little value, Heintzelman vowed to have the last word in the legal feud. "Texas must have a military governor," he proclaimed. Moreover, criminals should be tried by a military commission. The "great mass of the people are loyal, or at least they are anxious for quiet to attend to their private affairs, but dare not . . . be civil to Union men or they are marked in their social and business relationships," he informed Stevens. Moreover, the hanging of two "respectable citizens" at Belton was yet another reason why he would not submit himself to civil judgment. "I would not deem my life safe in the hands of the Texas authorities." If necessary, Baldwin would evoke the prewar case of *Ableman v. Booth*, in which the U.S. Supreme Court had ruled unanimously that individual states had lost their inherit sovereignty once they joined the Union. Men such as Ireland could use a good "dose" of Roger B. Taney, the "Southern rights man," since the "Rebs" were "great sticklers for the Constitution," Baldwin rationalized.[37] Although the case continued to hang over his head, Ireland finally gave up any attempt to have the district commander arrested.

Heintzelman had been in Galveston for only a few weeks when he learned that Brig. Gen. Charles Griffin was arriving to relieve him in command of the District of Texas. Although Heintzelman was the oldest colonel in the army, Griffin had held his brevet rank longer, and he was left no alternative but either to retire or to return to the 17th Infantry, eventually choosing the latter. Sheridan became convinced that Heintzelman had gone too far in placating former secessionists when, in November 1866, he returned some old cannon to Galveston. Mayor Charles H. Leonard, speaking for "every Texian," wrote to thank him for his courtesy for the "relics . . . so identified with the history of our State." Heintzelman was not "an aggressive leader" in Sheridan's eyes, and his "kindness, consideration, and sympathy to the former Confederates" was counterproductive.[38] He needed an officer with energy and a different political philosophy, and he chose General Griffin. A splendid combat officer, Griffin had served with distinction at First Bull Run and during the Peninsula Campaign. In addition, he had commanded infantry brigades at Fredericksburg and Chancellorsville, and during the furious fighting in the final year of the war, he had gained the confidence of both Grant and Sheridan. Yet Griffin, Heintzelman pointed out to anyone who would listen, had not even been born when he entered West Point in 1822.

As was his custom in times of crisis, Heintzelman turned to his political friends in Washington, among them Sen. James Root Doolittle, Republican from Wisconsin. Doolittle had visited Texas in early December 1866, and the two had spent an evening together discussing the progress of Reconstruction in the state. Since the colonel had not been furnished by Sheridan with any rationale for his removal, there "must have been some prejudices and unfounded reports made against me," he told the Wisconsin senator. Although Texas was "filled with un-reconstructed rebels," this had not prevented him from "treating them in a kind and conciliating manner," Heintzelman admitted. He blamed his old adversary Stanton. His "long service and attention to duty weigh nothing" against Stanton's "ill will," he dejectedly concluded. It was "as great an outrage as he has yet been guilty of." In a letter to Rep. Glenni William Scofield of Pennsylvania, he outlined his military career and wrote of how badly he had been treated.[39] In the rough and tumble world of Texas Reconstruction politics, Heintzelman had simply been caught between former secessionists, who were vigorously trying to turn the clock back to 1861, and an army controlled by Radical Republicans determined to reform what they perceived as a wayward and sinful South.

Out of courtesy, Heintzelman wrote Throckmorton saying that he had been relieved and thanking the governor for his "uniform courtesy towards me during the short time I have been in command." He assured him that Griffin was "an officer disposed to aid you in the defense and protection of the frontier." In response, Throckmorton offered an equally conciliatory, warm, and "handsome" letter saying that Heintzelman's departure would be a great loss and "sad for the people of the state." But the ultra-conservative *Galveston Daily News* wrote a blistering editorial expressing shock that Throckmorton could "express regret" at the loss of a scoundrel who saw himself above the law. Heintzelman was no friend of the conservatives. He was a Radical, and would always be so.[40]

Although no longer in command, Heintzelman became involved in another potentially explosive incident that January. Ashbel Smith, a leader in the Texas Democratic Party, stopped in Galveston on his way to New Orleans to say that he was heading a party of leading Texans on their way to the Crescent City to accompany the remains of Gen. Albert Sidney Johnston back to Texas for reburial. To many Texans , the reinterment of General Johnston, with all the pomp and pageantry the Lone Star State could muster, would not only honor a fallen hero but also epitomize their defiance to Federal authority. In Galveston, the Board of Aldermen and Mayor Charles H. Leonard began making plans for an elaborate funeral procession.[41]

Seeing the details for the cortege in the local newspapers, General Griffin fired off a letter to the mayor. "Although there is a sacredness surrounding the remains of all deceased persons which makes it exceedingly delicate to interfere with their funeral celebrations, it becomes my duty owing to the position that Gen'l Johnston occupied towards the United States Government during the latter period of his life, to forbid the funeral procession." A tough Civil War veteran, Griffin was bellicose and outspoken, and he early on clashed consistently with conservative forces in the state. "If the body can be taken quietly, without any ringing of bells, public or popular demonstrations, from the point of its arrival, direct to the point of its departure from the city, no objections will be made."[42] It was evident that the attitude of the U.S. Army in Texas was hardening toward the Throckmorton government.

At his headquarters in New Orleans, Sheridan remained unsympathetic to the complaints of conservative Texas Democrats, and he cheered Griffin's actions. Brilliant but ruthless himself, Sheridan had allegedly arrived in Galveston after a fatiguing inspection tour of the Rio Grande frontier and had checked into a local hotel. Approached by a stranger who wished to know what the general thought of Texas, the five-foot, four-inch Sheridan slapped the dust off his uniform and replied: "If I owned hell and Texas, I would rent Texas out and live in hell!" This flippant "hell and Texas" remark rapidly became newspaper copy throughout the state. In rebuttal, one small newspaper praised the general for sticking up for his place of origin.[43]

General Griffin ordered Heintzelman to make sure the funeral procession did not proceed as the city fathers planned. Although far less radical than Griffin, Heintzelman agreed that former secessionists should not be allowed to parade the remains of his old West Point classmate through the streets of the city. "A program for the funeral procession of Gen. A. S. Johnston for tomorrow came out in the paper," he wrote in his journal. "Gen. Griffin prohibited it. I am to see it carried out. It has created quite an excitement."[44]

Although three companies of the 17th Infantry and one of the 117th Colored Troops were in the city at the time, many of the leading citizens of Galveston were determined to defy General Griffin and Federal authorities. "Great excitement prevails" in Galveston, a correspondent wired the *New Orleans Picayune*. While "the bayonet might restrict a demonstration," the *Galveston Daily News* reported, Federal authorities could never "restrain the natural feelings of the human heart." Ferdinand Flake, publisher of English- and German-language newspapers in Galveston, was furious at Griffin. Although a Unionist before the war, Flake had formed a friendship with former Confederates, and he had been one of the first to suggest that the city honor the legacy of the fallen Confederate hero of Shiloh.[45] The *Galveston Daily News* was far more hostile, calling on the citizens of the city to show their respect for General Johnston and their defiance of General Griffin by their silence. Every business would close while Johnston's remains were in the city.

Early on January 24, the steamer *Matagorda*, with the Texas delegation and Johnston's body onboard, arrived in Galveston. When Griffin and Heintzelman met with Smith and the delegation, they agreed that the casket would remain in a warehouse on the wharf during the night, followed by a simple procession to the Episcopal church, where the burial service would be read two days later. Under Griffin's instructions, Mayor Leonard agreed to issue an order: "There shall be no music by bands, ringing or tolling of bells, public or private demonstrations of any organized associations in the procession."[46]

Throughout the day, Johnston's casket lay on a bed of flowers at the Central Wharf as thousands of citizens—men, women, and children—

arrived to view the bier. Throngs of people, some in tears, passed by the casket for hours. Even about thirty-five African Americans came to pay their respects. Twenty-eight "old grey-haired men, . . . with tears rolling down their cheeks," agreed to "watch the remains on the wharf until the time came for the removal," the *Daily News* reported.[47]

On Saturday, January 25, the day of the funeral procession, citizens awoke to find a cold norther sweeping across the bay and the army out in force. All the banks and businesses were closed and draped with mourning, as were most private homes. Much to his alarm, Heintzelman learned that the Galveston firemen who would be marching in the procession had not only draped their engine with black crepe but also would be in uniform. Using Mayor Leonard as an intermediary, he warned that such a demonstration would be in violation of General Griffin's orders and the army would have to intervene, if necessary.[48] Leonard was left no alternative but to visit the engine houses and counsel the firemen not to appear in uniform. Grudgingly, they acquiesced.

At 9 A.M. Heintzelman watched as thousands of citizens made their way toward the Central Wharf. Thirty minutes later a hearse, decorated with long black plumes and pulled by four black horses, arrived, and the coffin was carried from the warehouse by the Texas delegation. Without direction and in silence, the crowd formed a column of twos and moved off. All along the Strand and Centre Street, hundreds of citizens, mostly women and children, in the cold and wind came forth to join the procession. Others, unable to find a place in the long line, moved parallel along the sidewalks. More and more people joined the procession as the cortege moved up Centre Street, then along Market Street to the depot of the Galveston and Houston Railroad. Nearby, "the whole width of the street . . . was packed with the seething mass of human beings," a newspaper reported.[49]

A special engine and several cars, all draped with mourning array, waited at the depot. A number of prominent ladies from Galveston boarded the train to accompany Johnston's casket to Houston, where another ceremony would be held before the remains were finally interred in Austin several days later. As the whistle blew and the train edged away from the platform, Heintzelman was greatly relieved to have the potentially explosive episode behind him.[50]

In March 1867, when Mayor Leonard was defeated in a hotly contested election because, Heintzelman thought, he had been too "civil to officers and Yankees," the colonel concluded that there was little hope for Texas. In late April a former Confederate decided to entertain several Federal officers at a local restaurant with a drunken rendition of the "Bonny Blue Flag," for which the officers had him arrested and tied up for several hours.

The next month a brawl broke out at a Union rally in a public park when the black speaker and other African Americans were attacked by former secessionists. So bad was the situation that Heintzelman feared a riot.[51]

During this time, Heintzelman took time to write a couple of letters to the *Army and Navy Journal*, a publication he had religiously subscribed to for twenty years. Looking out across the choppy waters of Galveston Bay, he envisioned a better way to defend the nation's harbors. Knowing that harbor defense was a perplexing problem, he recommended constructing several "strong, heavy vessels, with the hatches so prepared that they can easily be made water-tight." Ballasted properly and anchored in position, they could be connected by heavy chains and sunk, if necessary, to obstruct the entrance to any harbor. Mines, or what were called torpedoes at the time, could be positioned in advance of the vessels, and in the rear, armored gunboats with revolving turrets, similar to that on the *Monitor*, could be stationed. After reading several letters to the *Army and Navy Journal* criticizing the cost of maintaining regimental bands in the army, he also wrote a short article recommending that bands be retained.[52]

A few months previous, in early November 1866, he was saddened to read in the *New York Times* that his lifelong friend and valued chess partner, Charles Stuart Tripler, had died in Cincinnati on October 20. He had always admired the New York–born Tripler, who had risen to become medical director of the Army of the Potomac and been brevetted a brigadier general for his services during the war. Dr. Tripler had lanced Margaret's breast twenty years earlier, and he had twice operated on Mary's leg. By Christmas Lt. Henry Norton, who had been assigned to the 17th Infantry, arrived for a festive party at the Lathrop home in Galveston. Three days later Heintzelman read in a New Orleans newspaper that his close friend and business partner Hermann Vollrath Ehrenberg, "a true man," had been murdered in California. It was sad, he said, "to read [of] the deaths of one after another of our old Arizona friends." He hastily compiled an emotional obituary, complete with several biographical errors, that was published five days later in *Flake's Weekly Galveston Bulletin* under the heading "Death of Herman Ehrenberg, the Metallurgist." The obituary was picked up and later published by the *New York Times*. Ehrenberg's death, he wrote, "will be deplored by his many friends at the East, and by none more than by those who have profited by his scientific attainments and labors. . . . It is a sad end, after spending so many years among all the tribes from Oregon to Mexico, to fall at last by the paw of the savage."[53] Three months later Poston wrote to say that the Sonora Exploring and Mining Company had "been sold out by the sheriff," and Heintzelman realized that he had "lost all I had in it." Only his interest in the Santa Rita Company remained of his once-promising mining interests in Arizona. Always the schemer, Poston came up with the idea of making Heintzelman president of the Southern Pacific Railroad—"I am familiar with the route and well known to Californians and Texans," he mused in his journal—but the plan went nowhere.[54]

More-immediate concerns came from Port Lavaca, where several companies of the 17th Infantry, while on their way to the frontier, began pillaging the community. The thievery did not stop until a black company stationed at the port was able to restore order. Problems of a personal nature also complicated Heintzelman's stay in Texas. In what he called "vindictive rascality," Lathrop was relieved by Sheridan from the Freedman's Bureau in Galveston and ordered to San Antonio. But the colonel worried more about Elizabeth than Solon. Elizabeth, irritable and moody, was sick and at times lost "all self control." There is little joy, Heintzelman remarked, living "in a house with a half crazed woman." Despite her insistence on a ridiculously lavish lifestyle and a tendency to be a malicious gossiper, she was, he thought, "one of the most kind hearted people in the world." Elizabeth wanted to return to Buffalo, but Heintzelman feared that if she did, Solon, who was known to drown himself in alcohol when lonely and depressed, would "soon go to the dogs."[55]

No sooner had Lathrop arrived in San Antonio than a feud developed with his commander, Maj. John Sanford Mason. Solon had asked for a short leave to return to Galveston to bring Elizabeth, Maggie, and the family's personal belongings to San Antonio, but Mason denied the request. In response, Lathrop took a large dose of laudanum while consuming alcohol, becoming drunk, irrational, and "very noisy and abusive" toward Mason, for which he was arrested and charged. When tempers and egos finally calmed, Mason agreed to drop the charges, and Heintzelman even persuaded Griffin to destroy the papers in the case. Realizing that a "single glass of ale upsets his mind," Heintzelman wrote Lathrop in San Antonio to "let every kind of liquor alone." In Galveston Elizabeth was "overcome" by the news from San Antonio, and Heintzelman spent an entire afternoon trying to calm her. On February 8, when Elizabeth had "another of her crazy turns," the colonel approached General Griffin asking that as a personal favor, he overrule Mason and grant Lathrop a short leave. Griffin, who was a close friend of Mason, would only say that Lathrop had been drunk again and that "there are two sides to every question."[56]

In the cold and damp Galveston winter, Heintzelman came down with another severe case of gout. At first he was unable to use his left foot, then his right foot also began to pain him. The discomfort was so intense that he could barely sleep at night. In addition, he wrote, "I never saw affairs in such disorder as . . . in my department." Continuing to suffer, he remained hobbled for weeks. By early April he was determined to leave

Galveston as soon as possible.[57] His only consolation came in letters, first from Margaret with news from Buffalo, then Mary, who wrote from West Chester, Pennsylvania, to say that she was not only academically first in her class but also first in her school. Charles, who was in his final year at West Point, was also doing well, but his letters were infrequent.

In early March Senator Wade and other Radical Republicans in Congress brought Presidential Reconstruction to an end by passing the First Reconstruction Act. The Southern states were divided into military districts, each placed under the command of the army; Texas and Louisiana were to be part of the Fifth Military District. Five months later General Sheridan, upon the recommendation of General Griffin, declared Governor Throckmorton "an impediment to the reconstruction of the state" and removed him from office.[58]

In Galveston Heintzelman read in the *Army and Navy Journal* that he was scheduled to be forcibly retired from the military. Any officer who had reached the age of sixty-two or had served forty-five years in the military could be involuntarily retired, and the colonel would be sixty-two on October 30, 1867. General Grant, who had never liked him, was undoubtedly to blame, he concluded. Complaining that he could not live on a "pittance . . . out of the Army," he urged Margaret to see Grant personally, but when she did, the general in chief refused to change the order. He also sought help from Rep. Gilman Marston of New Hampshire. A Dartmouth College and Harvard Law School graduate, Marston had recruited the 2nd New Hampshire Infantry, which had been part of Heintzelman's division at Bull Run. During the Peninsula Campaign he had fought bravely at Williamsburg and had been with Heintzelman in the Washington defenses in late 1862 and 1863. Heintzelman told Marston that he had no desire to leave the army and that he could not live on a salary equal to that of a second lieutenant. If he were "forcibly retired as a colonel," he would be forced to "give up my life long friends and acquaintances and bury myself and family from the world in some cheap out of the way village." He also complained to Sen. Edgar Cowan of Pennsylvania. Except for the "lameness of the right arm from a rebel bullet received at the first Bull Run," he told the senator, he was "competent to perform any military duty." An "unwarranted prejudice has been excited against me in some high quarters." Realizing that any officer disabled in battle could retire at his volunteer rank, Heintzelman hoped that if necessary, he could leave the army as a major general and thus receive a retirement pension that would enable him to live comfortably.[59] Tired of Galveston and the harsh realities of Texas Reconstruction, he applied for a leave, which was promptly granted.

On April 30, 1867, in what he realized was probably his last muster, Heintzelman ordered a "colored company put with the others and it was decidedly in the best order." Six days later he issued orders relinquishing command of the 17th Infantry and departed on the *Crescent* for New Orleans, where he took the New Orleans, Jackson, and Northern Railroad out of "rebeldom" to Cincinnati. After a brief visit with Thomas Wrightson, he hastened east to West Chester to see sisters Juliana and Maria, both old and decrepit now, and Mary, who was continuing to do well in school. He was leaving West Chester when a messenger overtook him with a note that Juliana was seriously ill and that he should return at once. Rushing back, he learned that his sister had died an hour earlier. After a hastily arranged funeral, Samuel Peter went on to Philadelphia to meet Margaret, who he found tired but looking "very well." Memories of his bad experience in Texas and the death of his beloved sister were set aside when the couple traveled north for Charles's graduation at West Point. Seeing his son march across the parade ground in his dress uniform brought back fond memories of his own graduation forty-five years earlier. He was overcome with nostalgic pride. Afterward, the Heintzelmans traveled north and west to the Stuart home at Park Place in Buffalo for some badly needed rest and relaxation.[60]

FOURTEEN

Back in Washington

BACK IN WASHINGTON IN JULY 1867, Heintzelman met with Thaddeus Stevens, who inquired about the practicality of dividing Texas into two or more states. Still bitter at the former Confederates there, Heintzelman liked the idea and suggested the Brazos River as a possible boundary for two new states. He also met with Benjamin Butler and Nathaniel Banks as well as General Grant, who said the colonel was being considered for temporary duty in New York City until he could be officially retired. Heintzelman was also able to see President Johnson, but the president, as usual, professed to know little of what the army had planned for him.[1]

At the Astor House in New York in early October, a number of dignitaries assembled for a sumptuous dinner to celebrate the creation of Arizona Territory. R. C. McCormick, secretary for the territory, was returning to the Southwest, and there were toasts, more toasts, and endless long-winded speeches. Saying he was the "grandson of a pioneer who crossed the Blue Ridge with Daniel Boone," Charles Poston gave a lengthy history of Arizona, recalling how Heintzelman, "a brave old veteran," had established Fort Yuma, or what Poston called "Tophet," or hell. Despite all the cheers, few in the room, except Heintzelman, Poston, and two or three career army officers, had even been to Arizona.[2]

While Heintzelman was in New York, a yellow fever epidemic raged out of control in Texas. Only hours after presiding over a meeting at the Cooper Union, shocking news arrived from the Lone Star State in a telegram from New Orleans. His lifelong friend Solon Lathrop, forty-four, had died of yellow fever on October 7 at Victoria. Lathrop had been on his way from San Antonio to Indianola when he had received orders to stop at Victoria because of the epidemic on the coast. Worried about Elizabeth and Maggie, he telegraphed Lt. Henry Norton to hurry to her side and bring her "out of Texas" as soon as possible. Within days Norton wired back that he had arrived in Victoria but that he too had been stricken with the dreaded disease. It was not until early December, after young Norton had recovered, that the lieutenant arrived in New York with Elizabeth and Maggie. Solon's remains followed for interment in Buffalo's Forest Lawn Cemetery.[3]

On a "sad" wedding anniversary in 1867, Heintzelman learned that before he could retire, he was being sent back to the 17th Infantry in Texas. "I don't want to return to Texas . . . before re-construction is complete," he wrote while heading to Washington to protest the order to General Grant. In a snowstorm in the capital in early December, he went as far as to say that he did not want "anything to do with re-construction." After complaining to a "most friendly" Grant of his new assignment, he went again to the White House to complain to President Johnson of "how badly" he "had been treated."[4] Although the president was hoping Heintzelman would continue to assist with Reconstruction, he agreed that the colonel could be assigned to a retirement board in New York, where he would be responsible for little more than examining disabled officers.

Heintzelman had always loved the sights and sounds of New York City, and since the retirement board met infrequently, the winter of 1867–68 proved to be a pleasant respite from the stress of military duty and Washington politics. He played "draw poker" with old friends from the Civil War and the western frontier, attended lectures with Margaret and Mary at the Cooper Union on Astor Place, and visited the city's numerous art galleries, the theater, and church. He also had time to keep up with his investments, including his interest in oil lands in Western Pennsylvania, the Southern Pacific Railroad, a chemical works in New Jersey, the Vallecillo silver mines in Mexico, and what was left of the Santa Rita Mining Company in Arizona. At social events Margaret and Mary were his constant companions. Mary, who was pampered but who he loved dearly, sometimes got on his nerves, however. "Mary is full of whims and . . . her mother yields to them," he wrote. Margaret, he insisted, has "made a baby of her and it is hard for her to change." Letters from Charles, who was stationed at Fort Kearny, Nebraska, told of pursuing Indians and the rigors of army life on the western frontier. Charles, however, did not like the army, and he wrote of resigning and "going to a foreign land," an idea his father found asinine.[5]

By the summer of 1868, the family had moved from the Metropolitan Hotel in Manhattan to a house across the Hudson River at Bergen Point, New Jersey. Again he was able to visit Manheim and Lancaster, but he was back in New York in time for General Hooker's appearance before the retirement board in September. Heintzelman was shocked by his old division commander's appearance, and he even thought Hooker's "mind [was] very much impaired."[6]

Hoping for promotion to brigadier general and still resisting the thought of retirement, Heintzelman traveled to Washington in January 1869 to see President Johnson again and lobby several sympathetic senators and influential politicians, including the old New York Peace Democrat Horatio Seymour, who agreed to petition for his promotion. While there, he made his way down Pennsylvania Avenue to Capitol Hill for a "noisy and undignified" session of the Senate. He later watched as the Electoral College proclaimed Ulysses Grant the eighteenth president. Samuel Peter was on his way back to his hotel when Margaret handed him the order he had dreaded—he was being forcibly retired.[7] At the White House he queried the president as to where the "suggestion to retire me came from," but Johnson would say only that it was "no good to tell." After Grant's inauguration on March 5, 1869, he learned that the new president had made several appointments to brigadier general, but he was not among them. Heintzelman had never liked Grant, who was "filling offices with his relatives and personal friends."[8] There were even rumors, he wrote, that Grant had been drunk again. In May, however, there was some good news. Although he was being retired, it would be at his Civil War volunteer rank of major general.

In early May 1869 Heintzelman was back in New York, where he was cheered at an annual meeting of the veterans of the III Corps of the Army of the Potomac. When Charles arrived by train from Omaha, Nebraska, the young lieutenant and the old general set out for what proved to be a delightful visit to Richmond, Virginia. After visiting the Confederate White House, they hired a carriage and rode through the burned-out district of the city and the ruins of the Tredegar Iron Works. The 17th Infantry, which was stationed in the city at the time, was on dress parade, and in the evening the officers and the regimental band, along with a crowd of citizens, came to serenade the regiment's old commander. Later, while onboard a steamer on the James River, Heintzelman spotted places such as Drewery's Bluff and Bermuda Hundred, familiar names to many veterans of the Army of the Potomac. At City Point he and Charles caught the railroad to the "old dilapidated town" of Petersburg, where they hired a carriage for a tour of the battlefield.[9] Back on the James, Samuel Peter pointed out Harrison's Landing, and he and Charles talked endlessly of that terrible and bloody summer of 1862. After stopping briefly at Norfolk, father and son steamed up the Chesapeake to Baltimore, then returned to Washington by train.

Back in New York City, Heintzelman talked at length to Judge Cowan about assuming the presidency of a large lumber company, and he even made a four-day trip to Cumberland, Maryland, to inspect the company's timberlands. He also entered into discussions with John C. Frémont about an executive position with the proposed Memphis and El Paso Railroad Company, which was planning to build a transcontinental railroad across the Desert Southwest to California. Cowan optimistically assured him that he could make at least ten thousand dollars a year from the lumber business and the railroad. The judge also had plans for starting an insurance company and was considering him as president or vice president.[10]

On July 4, 1869, Heintzelman put on his uniform and joined other "old" officers of the Army of the Potomac, including Sheridan and Meade, for a ceremonious march down Broadway. Later in the reviewing stand, he talked briefly with George McClellan, and at a well-attended and festive banquet in the evening, he heard an excellent address by scholarly Joshua Lawrence Chamberlain, hero of Little Round Top, who was now governor of Maine. During the course of the evening, several of the old veterans became roaring drunk.[11]

Three weeks later Heintzelman met ex-governor James Throckmorton of Texas at the office of the Memphis and El Paso Railroad. Heintzelman's main interest, however, remained in mining, especially after he was elected president of the Defiance Silver Mining Company, with holdings at Georgetown, Colorado. In Arizona the Santa Rita Mining Company was fifty thousand dollars in debt, and Charles Poston and Thomas Wrightson were unable to raise sufficient capital to keep it in operation. Hearing that Hooker's wife had recently died, leaving her husband a sizeable fortune, he approached the aging and infirm general about investing in the company, but Hooker was not interested.[12] Heintzelman still hoped to recover some of his mining investments, for Poston was negotiating to sell the company to a Spanish corporation for as much as one million dollars.

In Mexico Lowry, whom Heintzelman was coming to mistrust, was failing to turn a profit at the Vallecillo mines. Yet the retired officer remained convinced there was money to be made in mining. He insisted that his stock in the Vallecillo Company was worth ten thousand dollars, but Margaret argued that it was not worth more than five hundred. Another financial setback came in late November 1869, when he learned that a storm had caused property damage of fifty thousand dollars at the Defiance Mining Company, and there was little hope of recovering his investment there. Heintzelman's rather elaborate lifestyle, which included at least two servants, forced him to confess that he was "living beyond my means and running in debt everyday." On his twenty-fifth wedding anniversary in December, he remarked in his journal that he was poorer than when he was first married. He had been in New York for six months and had not "made one cent." By December the insurance company and the lumber company still had not been organized, and he felt that "Cowen had talked a good deal . . . but will not do much for me."[13] His only income remained his army pension.

In February 1870 a telegram carried the sad news that Margaret's aging mother had died, and the family hurried west to Park Place in Buffalo for the funeral. Heintzelman remained concerned about Elizabeth Lathrop, who appeared "to have entirely lost control of her mind."[14] The death of her husband in Texas and now her mother was simply too much for her, he realized.

After attending the annual meeting of the veterans of the Army of the Potomac in Philadelphia in April 1870, Heintzelman complained of fatigue and of growing old. A few days later, however, he traveled to West Chester to see Maria, and the two took a carriage drive out in the countryside to plant violets on Juliana's grave.

By that time, with his appointment as president of Cowan's Mutual Guaranty Life Insurance Company and an office at 98 Broadway, he at last had a monthly salary, but living in a rented house in Brooklyn, he continued to complain of being in debt. The only good news came from Charles, who had been promoted to first lieutenant and who was on Gen. Edward R. S. Canby's staff. Ever since the Mexican War, Heintzelman had considered Canby one of the most honest and decent men in the army. In the late summer Charles arrived in New York after an eleven-day train trip from Portland, Oregon. Considering his nearly six-month sea voyage around Cape Horn to reach California in 1849–50, Samuel Peter could only marvel at how the railroad had transformed western travel. In September Charles's visit was followed by the arrival of Dr. John Summers, his wife Caroline, and their daughter Carrie. While reminiscing about their careers in the antebellum army, Heintzelman was forced to confess that he did not much like the insurance business. His heart remained with the military, though, and on his sixty-fifth birthday he proudly put on his uniform and followed Adm. David Farragut's casket to Woodlawn Cemetery in the rain. Heintzelman too was growing old, and he even forgot to celebrate the Battle of Huamantla with a toast.

By December 1870 he was coming to have serious doubts about the future of the Guaranty Insurance Company. Although a number of prominent individuals, including Maj. Gen. William S. Rosecrans, had been persuaded to invest in the company, few policies had been sold. A newspaper editor had even attacked the company as a fraud, and there was talk of selling out. "We will hope for better times next year," he wrote on New Year's Eve.[15]

Heintzelman yearned to find a permanent home "for the few remaining years I can expect to live." More and more he was thinking of settling at San Diego, California, as soon as the Southern Pacific Railroad was complete. He had always liked the sunny and invigorating southern California climate and had maintained his property in the ocean-side community. Moreover, he took pride in knowing that a post of the Grand Army of the Republic had been established there and named in his honor. His interest in the West was heightened after attending a stirring lecture on the "Colorado canons" by Maj. John Wesley Powell at the Packer Institute in January 1871. Within a month Heintzelman had given up on the Guaranty Insurance Company and was trying to find a way to transfer its policies to another company. Soon, all that remained was to consult a lawyer and "wind up."[16] By March the Mutual Guaranty Life Association was no more.

In May, following a veterans' meeting in Boston, Heintzelman returned to New York, where he had a long talk with Sylvester Mowry about the Arizona mines. He would later learn of Mowry's death at the age of thirty-eight in London, where he had gone seeking medical attention. "His has been a strange career," Heintzelman wrote. "He managed to have plenty of money and followed no regular business." Later he traveled down to Fortress Monroe, Virginia, where Dr. Summers was stationed, and the two men rode up the Peninsula through the woods, past familiar landmarks, to Yorktown for the dedication of the national cemetery. At a small hotel there, he reminisced with several Civil War veterans, including one Rebel who had been in General Magruder's army, and became even more convinced that his "information . . . was correct, and we should have advanced without a siege as I wished."[17]

After he and Margaret spent several days at the mineral baths at Berkeley Springs along the Potomac River in northern West Virginia, where Samuel Peter bathed his aching feet and legs in the medicinal waters, the couple returned to Carlisle, Pennsylvania, by railroad to unveil a monument to the soldiers from Cumberland County who had died during the Civil War. As the old general signaled with his hand, flags were dropped around the monument, and the crowd cheered.[18] He spent his sixty-sixth birthday in Harrisburg, complaining of rheumatism and feeling "like an old man," but he later managed a buggy ride into the countryside with his old friend Simon Cameron. Back in New York, he remained undecided as to where he wanted to spend his remaining years, but he was thinking of San Diego still, possibly Philadelphia, or even some small community by the beach in Delaware.

By Christmas, 1871, the family was back in Washington. Suffering from asthma and rheumatism, Samuel Peter also complained that one shoulder was lower than the other and that his old wound from First Bull Run did not permit complete use of his right arm. His feet also kept him lame for weeks at a time, and he was now walking with a cane. Early in January 1872 he heard that Maria, who had lived near West Chester with a niece and nephew for the last thirteen years, was ill and refusing to see a physician. Ever since he had received a depressing letter from his sister written on December 25 saying that it would probably be her last Christmas, he had been concerned for her well being. Leaving Washington, he spent the night in Wilmington, Delaware, before hurrying on to West Chester, where he learned that his sister had died a few hours earlier of pneumonia. He shed few tears, only confessing that her "death saved her much suffering." After arranging for a simple funeral, which she had requested, Samuel Peter attended the burial of his last sister in the Quaker Cemetery at Birmingham on the Brandywine battlefield. Our "family are all scattered," he sadly reflected. "I have an infant at San Diego and one at Buffalo."[19]

In Washington in February 1872, he was visited by a delegation from Texas that included ex-governor Edward Clark and the old Unionists John Hancock and George W. Pascual. They had lengthy discussions about Texas politics, mining in Mexico, and "doings on the Rio Grande." The Texans reported that there were serious problems on the border with raiding Mexican bandits, including Juan Cortina, and as the commanding officer during the Cortina War, they hoped Heintzelman would testify before the House Foreign Affairs Committee "about the troubles on the Rio Grande." Although growing old and decrepit, Heintzelman could not keep his mind off Texas and the Southwest. Hearing that Tucson had a population of three thousand, he realized how the region was being transformed. In his leisure moments he read a book on the exploration of Yellowstone, and although he was unable to invest, he remained interested in a copper mining company that had purchased thirty thousand acres of land in Texas.[20]

Samuel Peter also took great pride in his son's military career. Charles was offered a professorship in civil engineering at Cornell, but he politely declined. He "don't fancy small western colleges," his father wrote. But in Heintzelman's imagination there was always the lure of the West. He visited with the one-armed Major Powell and continued to attend lectures on the exploration of the Colorado River. Powell even gave him twenty to thirty stereoscopic views of the Grand Canyon. Heintzelman, who had first heard of the Grand Canyon when he was at the Yuma Crossing some twenty years earlier, was so inspired that he dug out his journals covering his long sojourn at Fort Yuma and read the entries he had made during his trip down the river in 1852. He even copied and gave Powell a portion of his journal on his descent of the river as well as the account he had written of the frightening desert earthquake of November 1852. In the process he became convinced that he was "probably the first white man [to have] ever descended" the Colorado.[21] Heintzelman also took time to reread the text of the Treaty of Guadalupe-Hidalgo, the Gadsden Purchase, and Emory's *Boundary Report.* In June he visited with several Arizona Indians that his friend Gen. Oliver O. Howard, one of his brigade commanders from First Bull Run, brought to Washington. The natives included Apaches, Pimas, Maricopas, Papagos, and his old friends, the Yumas. "The true way to deal with an Indian," he reflected, "is to tell him what he must do and what you will do and that if he don't you will make him. That was my policy and it was successful. I never promised an Indian only what I could perform and took care to do so."[22]

In August 1872, with Margaret by his side, he traveled through the night by train south into Virginia, past "familiar names," to Lynchburg, then on to Christianburg, Newport, Blacksburg, and across the Appalachian Mountains to Mountain Lake in Giles County. There Gen. Herman Haupt, the Union Civil War engineering genius, ran a hotel along the banks of a picturesque mountain lake. In the refreshing and invigorating mountain air, Heintzelman walked, cane in hand, to a nearby waterfall for a picnic and to the top of a nearby "hillock" for a fine view of the countryside. There were few visitors with whom to converse, and unable to find a newspaper, he found his stay relaxing but dull.[23]

Thinking of Arizona and the Heintzelman Mine at Cerro Colorado, he wrote his old friend Charles Poston saying that he hoped to "visit his friends at San Diego and to pass his remaining years on the Pacific." Somehow, Heintzelman still thought "that something would come from the mine for his family as his income would die with him." But the mine, Poston wrote, could "be jumped by any wandering vagabond."[24]

In October 1872 he was in New York for a reunion of the Army of the Potomac, and in November, upon learning that George Meade was dead of pneumonia in Philadelphia, he left by train with President Grant and Sherman for the funeral. Back in Washington he thought again of moving west to San Diego, but instead he settled into a house on M Street in the capital. There, old friends from Texas and comrades from the Civil War came to call. One was Francis W. Latham, the customs collector from Brazos Santiago who he had befriended in Brownsville during the Cortina War. In late December Heintzelman went to the White House to see President Grant and Secretary of State Hamilton Fish to lobby for Arizona and Colorado City. He also met with Thomas P. Robb and Congressman John Hancock, who had arrived from Texas, and they had long discussions about the continuing problems on the border. Robb recalled having spoken with Gen. George Thomas about the possibility of the U.S. Army following Mexican raiders across the Rio Grande. To do so would mean war, Thomas remarked, but "Heintzelman did it."[25]

Surprisingly, on December 31, 1872, Heintzelman's journal, which he had kept so religiously for forty years since he had been a young cadet on the plain at West Point, ends abruptly. In a cold Washington rain he had called on Congressman Hancock, and the two "had a long talk [about] the situation on the Rio Grande." Reflecting the popular Texas attitude at the time, Hancock favored "the military occupation of the Mexican side of the river." In the final analysis, Heintzelman concluded, Hancock was "about right."[26]

During the last decade of his life, Samuel Peter spent much of his time corresponding with and visiting old comrades from the Army of the Potomac, reliving not only First Bull Run but also the entire Peninsula Campaign and Second Bull Run. He was particularly irked when Gen. Joseph E. Johnston published his Civil War recollections, in which he described the second day of the Battle of Fair Oaks as little more than a "skirmish." To prove Johnston wrong, Heintzelman dug out copies of his battle and casualty reports, went back through his journals, and wrote to the War Department to determine exactly how many men he had in his command at the time. He also corresponded with veterans of the battle and assisted his friend, George W. Mindil, in writing a pamphlet on Fair Oaks that contradicted much of what Johnston had written.[27] When the publication appeared in print, Heintzelman rushed to deposit a copy in the Library of Congress. He also began gathering information for Mindil on the Battle of Williamsburg, remaining convinced that Williamsburg was one of the most important battles of the Civil War, in fact "in a moral sense the most important." He agreed with Union veterans and future historians that one of the greatest mistakes McClellan made during the Peninsula Campaign was his reluctance to throw the Army of the Potomac at Yorktown. He also remained convinced that Fair Oaks opened the road to Richmond, and had McClellan given him permission to advance on the Confederate capital, the III Corps, if properly reinforced, could have taken the city. Heintzelman was also excited to receive complimentary copies from the Comte de Paris of his two-volume *History of the Civil War in America.* He had retained enough knowledge of French from West Point to read the books, which he found accurate and "beautifully done."[28]

Heintzelman remained in Washington and never saw Texas, Arizona, or California again, though he was able to fulfill a lifelong desire in 1876 when he, Margaret, and Mary made what his friend Poston called a "long cherished visit to Europe." The Heintzelmans toured the historic sites of London before crossing the English Channel to visit Paris and then Rome. Back in the United States, he remained active in veterans' groups and was on the finance committee of the National Association of Veterans of the Mexican War when the gray-haired warriors met in February in Baltimore on

Washington's Birthday in 1878. Besides listening to twenty-one speeches and a letter from Jefferson Davis, such occasions were often moments of sadness, for one of the first orders of business was a somber reading of the names, often long, of members of the club who had died since the last meeting. In 1878 there was also one last visit to his boyhood home in Manheim. Invited by several of the borough's leading citizens, Heintzelman remained in the community for two weeks. The visit was said to have "aroused considerable enthusiasm among some of the residents," during which the old general was cheered heartedly and was even serenaded by the Manheim Liberty Band. From the steps of the house where he was born on South Main Street, now owned by a local dentist, he addressed a sizeable crowd.[29] Heintzelman thanked the citizens for their public recognition of him through the years and noted with pride the many changes the town had undergone since his last visit. Yet he was saddened that so many of his old friends were either dead or had moved away.

Knowing that he did not have many years left to live, in May 1875 he dictated his last will and testament, giving all his possessions, real and personal, to Margaret. Samuel Peter Heintzelman, a man of "intense nature" and "vehement action," slipped quietly into unconsciousness and died at the age of seventy-four at his residence in Washington in the early morning hours of May 1, 1880. With the Stars and Stripes in the capital at half-staff, an elaborate funeral was conducted by Rev. John B. Paxton at the Presbyterian church on New York Avenue two days later. Pallbearers included his old friends Gen. William Tecumseh Sherman, Gen. James B. Ricketts, Gen. Benjamin Alvord, Gen. William McKee Dunn, Gen. David Hunter, Gen. Joseph K. Barnes, and Gen. Joseph Jones Reynolds. After the funeral Heintzelman's body was escorted to the Sixth Street depot by a detachment of marines, the Marine Corps Band, and two companies of the 2nd Artillery. Margaret was too ill and grief stricken to make the trip to Buffalo, but Mary accompanied her father's remains. The midnight train of the New York, Lake Erie, and Western Railroad took them through a soft spring landscape, arriving in Buffalo at 8 a.m. on May 4. Covered in quilted black satin and draped with an American flag, his casket was met at the depot by a detachment of the 10th Infantry and carried to City Hall, where it lay in state in a darkened vestibule. For seven hours a long, steady stream of mourners filed past the open casket to view the old general, while flags in the city flew at half-staff and public offices remained closed. Dressed in his blue uniform, it was said that "his strongly marked features were calm and natural looking." Shortly before three in the afternoon, a large military procession formed outside. At the head of the long and impressive funeral cortege marched the 74th New York National Guard and a detachment of the 10th Infantry. Pallbearers and his casket were followed by a riderless horse with reversed boots in the stirrups led by an army sergeant. Next came family and mourners in carriages, followed by the 65th New York National Guard, members of the Buffalo City Council, municipal officers, and a multitude of citizens. At Forest Lawn Cemetery overlooking Delaware Avenue and Park Lake, Samuel Peter Heintzelman was laid to rest next to his infant son.[30]

The seventy-four-year-old general had fought his last battle. Poston, perhaps, put it best when he wrote of his friend, "He was an honest man, a brave soldier, and in manners as simple as a child."[31]

Notes

Abbreviations Used in Notes

AAG	Assistant Adjutant General
AGO	Adjutant General's Office
CAH	Center for the Study of American History, University of Texas at Austin
CWLSB	Cortina War Letters-Sent Book
CWOB	Cortina War Order Book
FYLSB	Fort Yuma Letters-Sent Book
GO	General Orders
HJ	Heintzelman Journals, Heintzelman Papers and Journals, Manuscript Division, Library of Congress, Washington, D.C.
HN	Heintzelman Notebooks, Heintzelman Papers and Journals, Manuscript Division, Library of Congress, Washington, D.C.
HP	Heintzelman Papers and Journals, Manuscript Division, Library of Congress, Washington, D.C.
HPD	Heintzelman Pocket Diaries, Heintzelman Papers and Journals, Manuscript Division, Library of Congress, Washington, D.C.
HQB	"Quartermaster Book, 1836–1841," May 18, 1836, Heintzelman Papers and Journals, Manuscript Division, Library of Congress, Washington, D.C. [Heintzelman Quartermaster Book]
HWPJ	"Journal of S. P. Heintzelman, U.S. Army, while a Cadet in the Military Academy, West Point, New York, from Jan. 1, 1825 to Aug. 2, 1826," Special Collections, USMA [Heintzelman West Point Journal]
JAGO	Judge Advocate General's Office
LC	Manuscript Division, Library of Congress, Washington, D.C.
LR	Letters Received
LS	Letters Sent
NA	National Archives, Washington, D.C.
OR	War Department, *The War of the Rebellion: The Official Records of the Union and Confederate Armies*, 128 vols. (Washington, D.C.:

	Government Printing Office, 1889). All references are to series 1 unless otherwise noted.
PR	Post Returns
RNBP	Richmond National Battlefield Park, Richmond, Va.
RG	Record Group
RR	Regimental Returns
SO	Special Orders
TSA	Texas State Archives, Austin
USMA	U.S. Military Academy, West Point, N.Y.
USAMHI	U.S. Army Military History Institute Archives, Carlisle Barracks, Pa.
VHS	Virginia Historical Society, Richmond, Va.

Introduction

1. For Heintzelman's interest in fine art, see HJ, Feb. 21, 1842, June 2, Aug. 23, Nov. 1843, Apr. 5, 1844, Feb. 19, 20, 1847, Jan. 29, Feb. 12, 1848. For his interest in Shakespeare and literature, see HJ, Aug. 26, Dec. 20, 1842, Feb. 16, 1843, Oct. 26, Dec. 30, 1846, Jan. 18, Mar. 14, 1847, Jan. 17, 1848, Mar. 26, 1849, Aug. 3, 30, 1852, Oct. 3, 1853, Jan. 30, 1854, July 26, 1866. For his love of opera and the theater, see HJ, July 10, Sept. 26, Dec. 13, 1842, Jan. 4, Sept. 3, 5, 19, 1843, Feb. 26, Apr. 25, June 27, 1844, July 8, 1845, Jan. 21, 22, 23, May 25, Nov. 26, 1847, Apr. 30, 1848, Apr. 20, 1859. For his astronomy interests, see HJ, Aug. 9, 1842, Sept. 8, 1847.

2. Blackwell, *Heintzelman's Journal*, v.

3. HJ, Dec. 8, 1865. Except for a brief period in early 1849, while Heintzelman was at sea on his way to California, the journals are, with patience and perseverance, readable. This particular portion of the journal is difficult, if not impossible, to read since he wrote in pen on both sides of thin paper and the ink bled through the paper, partly obscuring the opposite side.

Five pencil sketches made by Heintzelman from 1821 to 1825; seventy-nine drawings completed for engineering courses at West Point; along with a map of Fort Yuma, California; miscellaneous papers relating to Arizona; and reports of the Sonora Exploring and Mining Company that were in manuscript holdings of the library at the U.S. Military Academy in 1972 have been misplaced and were not available to the author. Marie T. Capps to Robert W. Rose Jr., Oct. 25, 1972, Heintzelman File, Special Collections, USMA.

4. North, *Samuel Peter Heintzelman;* Thompson, *Fifty Miles and a Fight;* Sacks, *Be It Enacted*, 90; Sears, *George B. McClellan;* Sears, *To the Gates of Richmond;* Hennessy, *Return to Bull Run;* Davis, *Battle at Bull Run.*

1. Duty, Honor, Country

1. HJ, Oct. 25, 1842.

2. Heiges, "Heintzelman Visits His Hometown," 88; HJ, Dec. 29, 1831; Hostetter, "Major Samuel Peter Heintzelman," 58.

3. Heiges, "Heintzelman Visits His Hometown," 88. See also Fulton and Mylin,

Index to the Will Books and Interstate Records. In 1810 Manheim had a population of 1,282, including eight free persons of color. Third Census (1810), Lancaster County, Pa., NA. Heintzelman was always close to his two older sisters—Maria, who was born on July 25, 1800, and Juliana, who was born on May 24, 1802. A brother, H. Wagner, came into the world on July 30, 1804, but died three months later. Another brother, Henry, was born on December 8, 1807. A younger sister, Ann Elizabeth, named after her mother, was born in 1810. Yet another sister, Susan, was born during the War of 1812 but died at the age of four weeks.

4. HJ, Mar. 16, 1833. For a short time during his early life, Samuel Peter, along with his younger brother, Henry, lived briefly with an uncle near Pottsville in the Blue Mountains of east central Pennsylvania.

5. James Buchanan to J. C. Calhoun, Feb. 27, 1822, West Point Application Papers of Samuel Peter Heintzelman, AGO, RG 94, NA; David May et al. to Calhoun, Jan. 17, 1822, ibid.; Samuel P. Heintzelman to Calhoun, Apr. 9, 1822, ibid.; Heintzelman to L. Thomas (quoting Buchanan), Feb. 19, 1861, HP. See also Calhoun to Heintzelman, Mar. 23, 1822, HP.

6. Pappas, *To the Point,* 152.

7. Ibid., 115.

8. Ambrose, *Duty, Honor, Country,* 103, 165.

9. A. I. Measonton to S. G. Blunt, June 3, 1880, Heintzelman Cullum File, Special Collections, USMA; HJ, Feb. 18, 1825.

10. Pappas, *To the Point,* 106.

11. Ibid., 104.

12. HWPJ, Jan. 5, 6, 15, 1825. This particular journal was donated to West Point by General Heintzelman's grandson, Gen. Stuart Heintzelman. All other journals by Samuel Peter Heintzelman were donated by his daughter, Mary, to the Library of Congress. Physics was called "natural philosophy" at the time.

13. Pappas, *To the Point,* 163; HWPJ, Mar. 19, 1825.

14. HWPJ, Sept. 5, 1825.

15. HJ, Jan. 8, Feb. 5, Apr. 13, July 6, 1825.

16. HWPJ, Jan. 26, 1825. Minor would die at an early age in 1833. Loyal to the South, Mercer would become a brigadier general in the Confederate Army. Parks would go on to become a chaplain and professor at West Point before dying in July 1853. Dancy would resign from the army in 1861 to serve the Confederacy.

17. HWPJ, July 4, 1825.

18. Pappas, *To the Point,* 157; HWPJ, Sept. 17, 18, 1825.

19. HWPJ, July 9, Oct. 29, 1825; [Sibley], "Recollections of Cadet Life," *Popular Monthly,* 14.

20. Pappas, *To the Point,* 169, 173;

21. Cullum, *Biographical Register,* 372–74; Roland, *Albert Sidney Johnston,* 14; James Barbour to Heintzelman, July 12, 1826, HP; HJ, June 22, 1825; HWPJ, July 2, 1826.

22. HWPJ, July 17, 1826; HJ, Oct. 10, 15, 1825.

23. HJ, Dec. 26, 1825, May 19, Oct. 19–29, 1826, Dec. 9, 1828. While at West Point Heintzelman had corresponded regularly with his brother. Later, while keeping his journal at Fort Gratiot, he mentions sending his brother money.

24. HJ, Feb. 8, 1829.

25. "Court-Martial Proceedings in the Case of Lt. Samuel Peter Heintzelman" (AA-187), June 17–July 3, 1831, JAGO, RG 153, NA. Other members of the court were Brig. Gen. John Roger Fenwick, 4th Artillery; Col. William MacRea, 2nd Artillery; Col. William Lindsay, 3rd Artillery; Lt. Col. William Jenkins Worth, 1st Artillery; Maj. Matthew Mountjoy Payne, 4th Artillery; Lt. Col. Ichabod Crane, 4th Artillery; Lt. Col. Alexander Cummings, 2nd Infantry; and Maj. Alexander Ramsay Thompson, 2nd Infantry. First names are from Heitman, *Historical Register*, vol. 1.

26. "Court-Martial Proceedings," JAGO.

27. HJ, Sept. 26, Nov. 19, 20, 22, 25, 29, 1831, Feb. 19, 22, Apr. 9, 1832.

28. HJ, Sept., 8, 18, 21, 25, Oct. 29, Dec. 12, 1832, Jan. 1, 3, 18, 1833.

29. HJ, Mar. 15, 16, 20, 1833.

30. HJ, July 17, 25, 27, 1833.

31. HJ, July 15, Sept. 2, 1834; RR, 2nd Infantry, June–Aug. 1834, AGO, RG 94, NA.

32. HJ, Dec. 31, 1834, Jan. 1, 3, 12, 1835.

33. HJ, Sept. 30, 1835.

34. HJ, Dec. 8, 18, 1835; RR, 2nd Infantry, Jan.–July 1836, AGO, RG 94.

35. HJ, Apr. 22, 1836. See also HQB, May 18, 1836.

36. HJ, June 29, 1836. See also HQB, June 7, 1836.

37. HJ, Feb. 21, 1842; HQB, Aug. 1836–Mar. 1838. See also "Letter Book, 1841–1842," HP. For Heintzelman's travels from January 1841 to March 1843, see his letters in "Army Service Records, 1841–1846," Military Papers, HP.

38. HJ, Jan. 1, 1842; RR, 2nd Infantry, Jan. 1841–Jan. 1842, AGO, RG 94.

39. HJ, Jan. 1, 1842. See also HJ, Feb. 21, 1842.

40. HJ, Jan. 16, May 26, June 3, 1842. Heintzelman's brief stay in Tallahassee is mentioned by an unnamed army officer in "Recollections of Florida and the South," *Catholic World* 54 (Feb. 1892), 702.

41. HJ, June 18, July 10, 1842.

42. HJ, July 30–31, 1842.

43. HJ, Aug. 1, 1842.

44. HJ, Aug. 9, 11, 18, 22, 24, 28, 1842.

45. HJ, Sept. 24, 26, 28, 1842.

46. HJ, Oct. 24–26, 1842.

47. HJ, Nov. 21, Dec. 11, 25, 1842, Jan., 15, 1843.

48. HJ, Feb. 16, 19, 23, Apr. 24, 26, 1843; RR, 2nd Infantry, Apr. 1843, AGO, RG 94.

49. HJ, July 27, 30, Aug. 10, 31, Sept. 30, 1843. Frederick Douglass and Charles Lenox Remond had spoken at a large gathering in Buffalo six weeks earlier, on August 13, 1843. "George Washington Jonson—Buffalo Diarist," The Buffalonian, http://www.buffalonian.com/diaries/jonsondex.html.

50. HJ, Oct. 20, Dec. 14, 31, 1843, June 24, 1844.

51. HJ, Feb. 6, July 6, 1844.

52. HJ, Oct. 15, Nov. 30, 1844, Mar. 12, 1845. The 1850 census for San Diego County, California, lists Margaret Heintzelman as twenty-five, which would indicate that she was probably born in 1825. Diane North states that she was born December 1,

1819. The date on the 1850 census is suspect since Charles, age five, is listed as being born in New York, though he was actually born in Detroit, Michigan. North, *Samuel Peter Heintzelman,* 190. Margaret's vanity may help explain the census discrepancy in her age. Her tombstone in Forest Lawn Cemetery in Buffalo, New York, does not give a birth date.

53. HJ, Mar. 12, 1845.

54. HJ, June 13, Sept. 12, 1845; RR, 2nd Infantry, July–Sept. 1845, AGO, RG 94.

2. To the Halls of Montezuma

1. HJ, Sept. 14, Dec. 29, 1845, May 14, 1846.

2. HJ, June 9, 14, 1846; RR, 2nd Infantry, June–July 1846, AGO, RG 94. See also "Letter Book," June 10–Oct. 31, 1846, HP.

3. HJ, June 14, 21, Aug. 28, 1846.

4. HJ, Aug. 28, 1846.

5. HJ, Sept. 30, 1846.

6. HJ, Oct. 26, 1846.

7. HJ, Dec. 7, 1846.

8. HJ, Dec. 11, 16, 1846.

9. HJ, Dec. 25, 1846.

10. HJ, Jan. 7, 1847.

11. HJ, Jan. 12, 14, 16, Feb. 13, 1847.

12. HJ, Mar. 2, 1847.

13. HJ, Apr. 11, 13, 1847.

14. HJ, Apr. 18, June 17, 1847; RR, 2nd Infantry, May–June 1847, AGO, RG 94.

15. HJ, July 27, 1847.

16. HPD, July 27, 1847. A wedding notice appeared in the *Buffalo Commercial Advertiser* on July 28, 1847. Born in Lebanon, New Hampshire, Lathrop had come to Buffalo where he became a partner in the firm of Jewett, Thomas and Company, a large publishing company that owned the *Commercial Advertiser.* He was said to have been a "cheerful, good natured and kindly man." *Buffalo Commercial Advertiser,* Oct. 28, 1867.

17. HPD, Aug. 4, 1847; HJ, Aug. 4, Sept. 14, 1847; S. P. Heintzelman to G. W. Cullum, June 4, 1860, Heintzelman Cullum File, USMA. The soldier was buried in a shallow grave in a garden the next day.

18. HJ, Oct. 2, 1847.

19. Kenly, *Memoirs of a Maryland Volunteer,* 319–20.

20. HJ, Sept. 29, 1847.

21. HJ, Oct. 4, 1847. In his journal Heintzelman confuses the execution of the Mier prisoners at Salado in the "Black Bean Incident" on March 25, 1843, with the death of other Mier prisoners at Perote of typhus in the winter of 1843–44.

22. HPD, Oct. 9, 1847; HJ, Oct. 10, 1847. See also Webb, *Texas Rangers,* 118; and Johannsen, *To the Halls of the Montezumas,* 135–36.

23. HJ, Oct. 10, 1847. See also Bauer, *Mexican War,* 331.

24. HJ, Oct. 12, 1847.

25. HJ, Oct. 19, 22, 1847; HPD, Oct. 19, 21, 1847.
26. HJ, Dec. 3, 9, 1847; RR, 2nd Infantry, Dec. 1847, AGO, RG 49.
27. HJ, Dec. 13, 1847, Jan. 26, 29, Feb. 12, 1848.
28. HJ, Dec. 31, 1847.
29. HJ, Jan. 16, Feb. 10, 1848.
30. HJ, Mar. 29, Apr. 1, 1848.
31. HJ, Apr. 2, 1848.
32. HJ, June 3, 1848; RR, 2nd Infantry, Apr.–May 1848, AGO, RG 94.
33. HPD, May 21, 28, June 9, 1848; HJ, June 10, July 11, 1848.
34. HJ, Jan. 5, 1866.

3. Hell Burned Out

1. HPD, July 28, 1848; HJ, July 30, 1848; RR, 2nd Infantry, July 1848, AGO, RG 94, NA. On April 27, 1865, the USS *Sultana* was carrying more than two thousand former Union prisoners of war and crew when it exploded ninety miles south of Memphis, killing one-third of those onboard.

2. HPD, Aug. 10, 1848; HJ, Aug. 22, 1848. Unfortunately, none of these images appear to have survived.

3. HJ, Aug. 23, 1848. See also McFeely, *Frederick Douglass*, 157.

4. HJ, Sept. 17, Oct. 1, 1848.

5. B. Riley to Heintzelman, Oct. 29, 1848, HP; HJ, Nov. 6, 8, 9, 18, 23, Dec. 6, 1848. Companies C, G, and I, with Colonel Riley, sailed on the *Iowa*, while Companies A and F embarked on the *Mary* and *Adeline*. RR, 2nd Infantry, Nov., 1848, AGO, RG 94, NA; Battalion Returns, Cos. D & H, 2nd Infantry, Dec. 1848, in RR, AGO, RG 94, NA; Woodward, *Journal of Lt. Thomas W. Sweeny*, 23.

6. Heintzelman to R. Jones, Mar. 3, Apr. 6, 1849, LR, AGO, RG 94, NA; HJ, Dec. 14, 1848.

7. Woodward, *Journal of Lt. Thomas W. Sweeny*, 34–36; HPD, Dec. 24, 1848; HJ, Dec. 24, 1848.

8. HJ, Jan. 12, 22, Feb. 9, 1849; Geo. C. Westcott to Heintzelman, Feb. 12, 1849, HP; Woodward, *Journal of Lt. Thomas W. Sweeny*, 45.

9. HJ, Apr. 2, 1849.

10. HJ, Apr. 10, 20, 1849.

11. HJ, Apr. 21, July 19, 1849; Woodward, *Journal of Lt. Thomas W. Sweeny*, 48.

12. HJ, Oct. 31, Nov. 28, 1849; N. C. Ferrell, "A list of lots belonging to Major S. P. Heintzelman in the town of San Diego," July 17, 1857, Research Library, San Diego Historical Society, San Diego, Calif.

13. HJ, Feb. 8, 1850, July 27, 1854.

14. HJ, Apr. 23–24, 1849.

15. HJ, May 26, 27, 31, Nov. 8, 1849; Seventh Census (1850), San Diego County, Calif., NA.

16. HJ, Apr. 28, Oct. 24, 1849, Feb. 21, 1850.

17. Edward Canby to Heintzelman, May 9, 1849, HP; HJ, Dec. 22, 1849, Mar. 26, Apr. 1, 1850.

18. HJ, Mar. 28, Apr. 1, 1850; Pitt, *Decline of the Californios*, 43, 46.

19. HJ, Oct. 28, 1849.

20. HJ, May 10, May [June] 3, 1850; RR, 2nd Infantry, Apr.–May 1850, AGO, RG 94.

21. HJ, July 2, 1850.

22. Canby to Heintzelman, July 4, 1850, HP. See also Heintzelman to W. H. Emory, Aug. 6, 1850, HP; Battalion Returns, Cos. D & H, 2nd Infantry, in Post Returns, Fort Yuma, Oct. 1850, AGO, RG 94; and T[homas] Sweeny to Ell[en Swain Sweeny], Jan. 26, 1851, Sweeny Letterbook, Sweeny Papers, Huntington Library, San Marino, Calif. Heintzelman was not the first army officer to arrive at the Yuma Crossing. Lt. Amiel Weeks Whipple of the Corps of Topographical Engineers, escorted by Lt. Cave Johnson Couts and Company A, 1st Dragoons and a small detachment from the 2nd Infantry, had crossed the Colorado Desert with the help of Quechan Indians, arriving at Yuma Crossing at the end of September 1849. While Whipple set up a crude astronomical observatory on the California side of the Colorado River atop the small hill on which Heintzelman would later construct Fort Yuma, Couts built a small outpost just downriver near present Winterhaven on the California bank, calling it Camp Calhoun in honor of Sen. John C. Calhoun of South Carolina. Whipple, Couts, and their men remained at the crossing until December 1, 1849. McPherson, *From San Diego to the Colorado;* Edwards, *Whipple Report;* Senate, *Report of the Secretary of the Interior*, 31st Cong., 1st sess., S. Doc. 34.

23. Heintzelman to Canby, Aug. 24, 1850, FYLSB, HP; HJ, Aug. 26, 29, Sept. 17, 1850.

24. Smith, *Borderlander*, 225, 294, 296; Clifford E. Trafzer, *Yuma: Frontier Crossing of the Far Southwest* (Wichita: Western Heritage Books, 1980), 76; Smith, "John Joel Glanton," 9–16; Heintzelman to Canby, Sept. 29, Oct. 20, 1850, FYLSB, HP.

25. Heintzelman to Canby, Nov. 27, 1850, Feb. 18, 1851, FYLSB, HP.

26. Blackwell, *Heintzelman's Journal*, Jan. 8, Feb. 16, 1851; Heintzelman to Secretary of War, Nov. 27, 1850, LR, AGO, RG 94, NA. See also PR, Fort Yuma, Oct. 1851, AGO, RG 393, NA. The originals of most of Heintzelman's official letters written from Fort Yuma and copied in his FYLSB also survive in LR, RG 94, and LR, RG 393.

27. Heintzelman to Canby, Dec. 24, 1850, FYLSB, HP.

28. Heintzelman to Canby, Jan. 7, 1851, ibid.; Heintzelman to A. H. Wilcox, Jan. 22, 1851, FYLSB; Heintzelman to Canby, Jan. 24, 1851, FYLSB, HP. See also Ciruzzi, "'Phoenix' Revisited"; Derby, *Report on the Opening of the Colorado; San Francisco Alta California*, Apr. 26, 1852; Heintzelman to Geo. H. Derby, Jan. 8, 1851, FYLSB, HP; and Lewitt, "Steam Navigation on the Colorado River," 3.

29. Lingenfelter, *Steamboats on the Colorado River*, 5; Blackwell, *Heintzelman's Journal*, Jan. 14, 20, 24, 1851; E. D. Townsend to Heintzelman, Jan. 23, 1852, LR, AGO, RG 94, NA; Townsend to Heintzelman, Jan. 19, 1852, ibid.; Heintzelman to Townsend, Apr. 6, 1853, ibid.; Heintzelman to C. S. Merchant, Jan. 27, 1851, FYLSB, HP. See also Wagoner, *Early Arizona*, 308.

30. Bee, "Quechan," 86–88.

31. Blackwell, *Heintzelman's Journal*, Feb. 21, 1851; Heintzelman to Canby, Dec. 11, 1850, FYLSB, HP.

32. Blackwell, *Heintzelman's Journal,* Feb. 20, 21, Mar. 8, Apr. 8, Apr. 18, 1851; Heintzelman to J. Hooker, Oct. 22, 1851, LR, Dept. of the Pacific, AGO, RG 393, NA.

33. HJ, Dec. 11, 1842; Blackwell, *Heintzelman's Journal,* Mar. 9, Apr. 7, 13, 1851.

34. Blackwell, *Heintzelman's Journal,* Feb. 12, 13, 1851; Heintzelman to Canby, Mar. 10, 1851, FYLSB, HP. See also Wagoner, *Early Arizona,* 134. Heintzelman learned that the mission had been overrun and destroyed by hostile Indians. Much of this information was incorporated into a lengthy report he sent to the adjutant general. "The rough stone foundations of the houses, with their earthen ruins could be clearly traced," he wrote. "The buildings appear to have been made of mud between upright poles or forks to support the roof. The charred ends we dug up with the remains of a copper urn shaped vessel of the capacity of about a quart. There were 8 or ten buildings 15 to 20 feet nearly square, irregularly placed, covering an area of about an acre and including the site of the present commanding officers' quarters." Heintzelman to Townsend, July 15, 1853, LR, AGO, RG 94, NA.

35. Royce Oatman to Heintzelman, Feb. 15, 1851, in Rice, "Captivity of Olive Oatman," 109. The original letter is in the Hubert Howe Bancroft Papers, Bancroft Library, University of California at Berkeley. The letter was sent by Capt. Gilbert Cole Smith from Camp Grant, Arizona, to Bancroft in 1877. Rice provides no explanation of how Smith came in possession of the letter.

36. Blackwell, *Heintzelman's Journal,* Feb. 25, 27, 1851; Heintzelman to C. S. Merchant, Mar. 11, 1851, FYLSB, HP. Heintzelman's information came from a party of immigrants who had stopped at the Pima Villages on their way west. The Pimas said fifteen Maricopas had met the Oatmans on top of "a difficult ascent," where part of the wagon had to be unloaded. At first the Indians seemed friendly and had sat down to smoke, but when the Oatmans relaxed their vigil, they were attacked with clubs. Lorenzo Oatman, who was only stunned, crawled off into bushes after the Indians left. Two days later he was found by an immigrant party who, upon hearing of the attack, had turned back. Heintzelman also reported that the immigrants had seen a Maricopa Indian with a bag containing some of the clothing of the Oatman children. The Maricopas denied any part in the massacre, he wrote, saying the Apaches were to blame. Heintzelman to Merchant, Mar. 27, 1851, FYLSB, HP.

37. *San Francisco Alta California,* Apr. 12, 1851; *San Francisco Herald,* Apr. 25, 1851; and miscellaneous newspaper clippings accompanying E. A. Hitchcock to R. Jones, July 28, 1851, LR, AGO, RG 94, NA.

38. *San Francisco Alta California,* July 24, 1851; Heintzelman to Townsend, July 15, 1853, LR, AGO, RG 94, NA; Heintzelman to J. Hooker, Aug. 21, 1851, FYLSB, HP. See also Heintzelman to Editor, *San Francisco Alta California,* June 17, 1851, in LR, Dept. of the Pacific, AGO, RG 393, NA; R. B. Stratton, *Captivity of the Oatman Girls* (Lincoln: University of Nebraska Press, 1983), 85–159; and Martin, *Yuma Crossing,* 159–68.

39. Blackwell, *Heintzelman's Journal,* Feb. 20, 1851, Nov. 11, 1852; Heintzelman to Townsend, July 15, 1853, LR, AGO, RG 94, NA.

40. Blackwell, *Heintzelman's Journal,* Apr. 22, 1851. For Sweeny, see Moriarty, "Fighting Tom Sweeny." The trial, in which Sweeny was acquitted, resulted from the young lieutenant bucking and gagging a private (Lawrence Kearney) so severely that

he died five days later. On the recommendation of superiors, Heintzelman had requested the case be heard in a civil court. Private Kearney had been found intoxicated and unconscious, and when brought before Sweeny, the lieutenant had him arrested, whereupon the soldier was heard to say, "that damned one-arm son-of-bitch, pity he didn't lose the other arm too."

41. Heintzelman to F. Steele, June 17, 1851, FYLSB, HP; Blackwell, *Heintzelman's Journal*, Mar. 15, Apr. 22, 1851; Heintzelman to J. Hooker, Aug. 21, 1851, LR, Dept. of the Pacific, AGO, RG 393, NA; "Charges and Specifications Preferred against Asst. Surgeon Henry L. Hewit, U.S. Army," June 17, 1851, ibid.; Heintzelman to Hooker, Aug. 21, 1851, ibid. See also E. A. Hitchcock to R. Jones, July 28, 1851, LR, AGO, RG 94, NA.

42. Blackwell, *Heintzelman's Journal*, Mar. 9, 1851.

43. Heintzelman to Canby, Mar. 23, 1851, FYLSB, HP; Heintzelman to N. Lyon, Apr. 10, 185, ibid.; Heintzelman to H. Thorn, Apr. 10, 1851, ibid.; Heintzelman to I. L. Folsom, Apr. 10, 1851, ibid.; Heintzelman to T. W. Sweeny, June 4, 1851, ibid.

44. Heintzelman to J. Hooker, Aug. 22, 1851, LR, Dept. of the Pacific, AGO, RG 393, NA; Heintzelman to R. Jones, June 16, 1851, FYLSB, HP.

45. Heintzelman to J. Hooker, Aug. 28, 1851, LR, Dept. of the Pacific, AGO, RG 393, NA. See also Heintzelman to Townsend, Aug. 21, 1852, FYLSB, HP.

46. Heintzelman to Hooker, Oct. 8, 1851, FYLSB, HP; Heintzelman to Hooker, Nov. 14, 1851, ibid.; Heintzelman to D. Davidson, Nov. 23, 28, 1851, ibid. Upon reaching the Colorado River, Davidson was to send Sweeny back to the coast with the empty wagons and mules. Each man was given sixty rounds of ammunition.

47. Murry to Heintzelman, Nov. 18, 1851, LR, Dept. of the Pacific, AGO, RG 393, NA; Heintzelman to D. Davidson, Nov. 23, 1851, ibid.; Murry to Heintzelman, Dec. 4, 1851 ibid.

48. Blackwell, *Heintzelman's Journal*, Dec. 18, 1851; Murray to Davidson, Dec. 4, 1851, LR, Dept. of the Pacific, AGO, RG 393, NA; Heintzelman to J. Hooker, Nov. 28, 1851, ibid.; Heintzelman endorsement on D. Davidson to Heintzelman, Dec. 18, 1851, ibid. Lieutenant Murray reported that he was being constantly harassed by the Yumas and that on his way from San Diego, Jager had been attacked by about two hundred Yuma less than two miles below the post, wounding the ferryman three times. Davidson had arrived at the Colorado River on the afternoon of December 3 after a difficult crossing on the southern trail across the mountains, during which most of the grain bound for the post had been lost. At Fort Yuma he found Maj. Henry Lane Kencrick of the 2nd Artillery and fifty to sixty men who were escorting the Sitgraves Expedition in a "destitute condition." Some of the men were suffering from scurvy and had been living for weeks on mule meat. After consulting all the officers present, Davidson concluded that there were barely enough provisions to get the command to San Diego. Weber, *Richard H. Kern*, 182–83.

49. *San Diego Herald*, Oct. 16, 1851; Heintzelman to Hooker, Oct. 21, 1851, LR, Dept. of the Pacific, AGO, RG 393, NA. The feud between the two officers had begun when Davidson brought charges against Heintzelman in October 1851. Heintzelman to Hooker, Oct. 10, 1851, LR, Dept. of the Pacific, AGO, RG 393, NA. For Davidson's protest of his treatment by Heintzelman and his general court-martial, see Davidson

to Townsend, Oct. 19, 1851, ibid. For Heintzelman's response, see Heintzelman to Townsend, Oct. 30, 1851, ibid.; and Heintzelman to Townsend, Nov. 13, 1852, ibid. As late as the Civil War, Heintzelman was still referring to Davidson as a "coward." HJ, Nov. 8, 1864. In fact, Davidson was ordered cashiered for cowardice during the war but was able to get the sentence reduced to a reprimand contingent on his resignation.

50. Heintzelman to J. Hooker, Nov. 28, 1851, FYLSB, HP; Heintzelman to Hooker, Nov. 28, 1851, LR, Dept. of the Pacific, AGO, RG 393, NA; Heintzelman to F. Steele, Dec. 7, 1851, ibid.; Heintzelman to Steele, Dec. 30, 1851, ibid. See also Blackwell, *Heintzelman's Journal*, Dec. 21, 1851; and Heintzelman to C. P. Couts, Dec. 29, 1851, FYLSB, HP.

51. "Proceedings of a Council of War Convened in the Valley Los Coyotes," Dec. 23, 1851, LR, Dept. of the Pacific, AGO, RG 393, NA. Documents at the Arizona Historical Society indicate that Warner sometimes used the name Juan José. J. J. Warner Papers, Arizona Historical Society Library, Tucson.

52. Blackwell, *Heintzelman's Journal*, Dec. 24, Dec. 25, 1851; "Proceedings of a Council of War Convened in the Valley Los Coyotes," Dec. 23, 1851, LR, Dept. of the Pacific, AGO, RG 393, NA; Woodward, *Journal of Lt. Thomas W. Sweeny*, 241; *San Diego Herald*, Dec. 25, 1851, Jan. 10, 1852; *San Francisco Alta California*, Jan. 14, 1852; Heintzelman to R. Jones, LR, AGO, RG 94, NA. Antonio Garra, a mission-educated Indian and the leader of the uprising, was later executed in San Diego. For Smith's congratulations to Heintzelman, see Townsend to Heintzelman, Jan. 16, 1852, HP.

53. Blackwell, *Heintzelman's Journal*, Dec. 30, 1851; Townsend to Heintzelman, Jan. 16, 1852, Heintzelman Cullum File, USMA. For Heintzelman attempting to obtain an additional brevet, see S. H. Lathrop to Jefferson Davis, Apr. 2, 1853, LR, AGO, RG 94, NA; and Blackwell, *Heintzelman's Journal*, Nov. 25, 28, 1852.

54. Blackwell, *Heintzelman's Journal*, Feb. 3, 1852.

55. Heintzelman to Townsend, Feb. 8, 1852, LR, Dept. of the Pacific, AGO, RG 393, NA; Heintzelman to R. Jones, Feb. 29, 1852, FYLSB, HP. Heintzelman's column comprised Company E, 1st Dragoons and Companies C, D, H, and I, 2nd Infantry.

56. Heintzelman to Townsend, Feb. 29, 1852, LR, Dept. of the Pacific, AGO, RG 393, NA; and Heintzelman to R. Jones, Feb. 9, 1852, LR, AGO, RG 94, NA. When the latter letter reached Washington, Gen. Winfield Scott forwarded it to the secretary of war, noting that it was "interesting."

57. Blackwell, *Heintzelman's Journal*, Feb. 29, Mar. 4, 1852, Jan. 11, 1853; Heintzelman to R. Jones, Feb. 8, 29, 1852, LR, AGO, RG 94, NA. See also Heintzelman to E. D. Townsend, Mar. 24, 1852, FYLSB, HP.

58. Blackwell, *Heintzelman's Journal*, Mar. 16, Mar. 28, 1852; Heintzelman to Townsend, Apr. 4, 1852, FYLSB, HP. See also "Table of Scouts at Fort Yuma in 1852," LR, AGO, RG 94, NA; and Heintzelman to Townsend, July 15, 1853, ibid. For references to sandstorms at Fort Yuma, see HPD, Feb. 20, Mar. 7–11, 15, 17, May 12–13, 1853.

59. Heintzelman to Townsend, Apr. 24, 1852 (second letter), Nov. 16, 1853, FYLSB, HP.

60. Lingenfelter, *Steamboats on the Colorado River*, 5. The boats were built on frames constructed in San Francisco. After being fitted out in San Diego, the *Sierra Nevada*

had sailed for the mouth of the Colorado on February 17, 1853. Leavitt, "Steam Navigation on the Colorado River," 3.

61. Edward H. Fitzgerald to Heintzelman, Mar. 6, 1852, LR, Dept. of the Pacific, AGO, RG 393, NA; Heintzelman to Townsend, Mar. 24, Apr. 4, 1852, ibid.; PR, Fort Yuma, Mar. 1852, AGO, RG 94, NA; Heintzelman to Jones, Apr. 4, 1852, LR, ibid.; Woodward, *Journal of Lt. Thomas W. Sweeny*, 151–52, 251; Martin, *Yuma Crossing*, 169; Blackwell, *Heintzelman's Journal*, Mar. 6, 9, 1852; Heintzelman to Townsend, Mar. 25, 1852, FYLSB, HP. Those killed included Sgt. Isaiah B. Taylor; Pvts. Philip Knoth, William A. McCluhan, George Betts, John Simmons, A. Burrows; and a mule-skinner named Benjamin McCoy.

62. Heintzelman to Townsend, Nov. 29, 1852, FYLSB, HP. *Capacity* had sailed from San Francisco on August 2. It was followed by *General Patterson*, which arrived at the mouth of the river in early July 1853, some eighteen days out of San Diego. See also *San Diego Herald*, Apr. 30, 1852.

63. Heintzelman to Townsend, Sept. 3, Oct. 17, Nov. 29, Dec. 4, 26, 1852, Jan. 23, Apr. 6, June 24, 1853, FYLSB, HP; Heintzelman to Townsend, Jan. 20, 1854, LR, AGO, RG 94, NA; E. A. Hitchcock to S. Cooper, Jan. 22, 1854, ibid.

64. Heintzelman to Townsend, Apr. 4, 1852, FYLSB, HP.

65. Heintzelman to Townsend, Apr. 24, May 11, 1852, ibid.

66. Heintzelman to Townsend, May 18, 1852, ibid.

67. Heintzelman to Townsend, June 5, 29, 1852, ibid.

68. Heintzelman to Townsend, June 27, 29, July 25, Aug. 15, 1852, ibid.

69. Heintzelman to Townsend, June 27, Aug. 21, 26, 1852, ibid.; Heintzelman to Armijo, Aug. 24, 1852, ibid.

70. Heintzelman to Townsend, Aug. 26, 1852, ibid. See also Blackwell, *Heintzelman's Journal*, Aug. 25–26, 1852.

71. Heintzelman to Townsend, Aug. 26, 1852, FYLSB, HP.

72. Heintzelman to Townsend, Sept. 25, 1852, ibid.

73. Heintzelman to Townsend, Oct. 2, 1852, ibid.

74. Heintzelman to Townsend, Oct. 11, 1852 (two letters), ibid.

75. Heintzelman to Townsend, May 29, 1853, ibid.

76. Heintzelman to Townsend, Sept. 2, 1853, ibid.

77. Heintzelman to Townsend, Aug. 15, 1852, LR, Dept. of the Pacific, AGO, RG 393, NA. See also Heintzelman to Townsend, Mar. 4, 1853, FYLSB, HP.

78. "Message from the President of the United States Transmitting Report in Regard to Indian Affairs on the Pacific," *Congressional Record*, 34th Cong., 3rd sess., 1859, 112–14. See also HJ, July 16, 1853; and Heintzelman to Townsend, July 15, 1853, LR, AGO, RG 94, NA.

79. Heintzelman to "My Dear Margaret," Nov. 1, 1852, HP; Blackwell, *Heintzelman's Journal*, Oct. 26, 1852, Jan. 11, 1853; Heintzelman to Townsend, Oct. 27, 1852, LR, Dept. of the Pacific, AGO, RG 393, NA; E. D. Townsend to Heintzelman, Nov. 29, 1852, AGO, RG 94, NA.

80. Heintzelman to E. D. Townsend, July 15, 1853, LR, ibid.; Blackwell, *Heintzelman's Journal*, Nov. 29, 30, 1852; T[homas] Sweeny to El[len Sweeny], Dec. 27, 1852, Sweeny Letterbook, Huntington Library. Also of interest is "Sketch of a Reconnaissance

of the Lower Part of the Colorado River by Bvt. Maj. S. P. Heintzelman, U.S. Army, in Jany. 1851 & Oct. 1852," LR, AGO, RG 94, NA. While at Fort Yuma, Heintzelman's journal and pocket diary are replete with references to minor earthquakes. For example, see HPD, Mar. 19, Apr. 2, May 10, June 16, 1853. See also Le Conte, "Account of Some Volcanic Springs," 1–6; and Strand, "Mud Volcanoes, Faults, and Earthquakes."

81. Blackwell, *Heintzelman's Journal*, Sept. 25, 1852.

82. Ibid., Mar. 30, 1852; "Proceedings of a Board of Inspection," Apr. 15, 1852, LR, AGO, RG 94, NA; Heintzelman to Jones, Mar. 25, 1852, ibid.; Heintzelman to Townsend, May 11, 1852, LR, Dept. of the Pacific, AGO, RG 393, NA.

83. Blackwell, *Heintzelman's Journal*, Jan. 12, 1853; PR, Fort Yuma, June and July 1852, AGO, RG 393, NA; Heintzelman to Townsend, Jan. 12, 1853, FYLSB, HP.

84. Heintzelman to Townsend, June 12, 1852, FYLSB, HP.; Blackwell, *Heintzelman's Journal*, June 9, 1852; Feb. 1, 10, 1853; J. B. Magruder to Townsend, Feb. 1, 1852, LR, AGO, RG 95, NA; Heintzelman to Townsend, June 12, 1852, LR, Dept. of the Pacific, AGO, RG 393, NA. The best account of Captain Craig's death can be found in Bartlett, *Personal Narrative*, 2:142–45. See also Faulk, "Letter from John R. Bartlett," 208–10.

85. Heintzelman to Townsend, June 12, 1852, FYLSB, HP; Blackwell, *Heintzelman's Journal*, June 12, 16, 1852; Heintzelman to Townsend, June 27, 1852, LR, Dept. of the Pacific, AGO, RG 393, NA; Davidson et al. to Townsend, July 16, 1852, ibid. Lt. George Horatio Derby would later quip: "One of our Fort Yuma men died and unfortunately went to hell. He wasn't there one day before he telegraphed for his blankets." "Lt. George Horatio Derby," San Diego History, http://www.sandiegohistory.org/bio/derby/derby.htm.

86. Heintzelman to J. R. Bartlett, June 11, 1852, FYLSB, HP; Bartlett, *Personal Narrative*, 2:153; John R. Bartlett to "My Dear Major," July 6, 1852, HP.

87. *Tucson Arizona Weekly Star*, May 13, 1880. See also J. J. Warner to Heintzelman, Apr. 12, 1853, J. J. Warner Papers, Arizona Historical Society Library.

88. Blackwell, *Heintzelman's Journal*, June 19, Aug. 30, 1852, Feb. 20, Apr. 3, 15, May 2, July 29, Oct. 3, 31, 1853.

89. Heintzelman to Right Reverend Bishop of California, Jan. 10, Mar. 10, 1853, FYLSB, HP.

90. Lingenfelter, *Steamboats on the Colorado River*, 11–15.

91. Heintzelman to "My Dear Margaret," Nov. 1, 1852, HP.

92. Blackwell, *Heintzelman's Journal*, Jan. 3, May 4, 20, Sept. 20, Oct. 10, 1853; Wagoner, *Early Arizona*, 309; Stephen W. Patzman, "Louis John Frederick Jaeger: Entrepreneur of the Colorado River," *Arizonian* 4 (Spring 1963): 32–34; Hargett, "Pioneering at Yuma Crossing," 331–35. When other officers showed an interest in the area across the Colorado River from Fort Yuma, Heintzelman deviously told them it was to be set aside as a reservation for the Yumas.

93. Blackwell, *Heintzelman's Journal*, Sept. 1, 1852, Apr. 4, 1853.

94. Heintzelman to Townsend, Aug. 26, 1852, LR, Dept. of the Pacific, AGO, RG 393, NA; HJ, May 3, Nov. 11, 1853, Apr. 8, 25, 1854.

95. Heintzelman to H. S. Burton, Apr. 8, 1854, LR, Dept. of the Pacific, AGO,

RG 393, NA; Heintzelman to Townsend, Apr. 26, 1854, FYLSB, HP. On filibustering activities in Baja California and Sonora, see E. A. Hitchcock to S. Cooper, Dec. 15, 1853, enclosing clippings from the *San Francisco Alta California*, Dec. 1, 8, 13, 15, 1853, LR, AGO, RG 94, NA. See also May, *Manifest Destiny's Underworld*, 40–42; and Gerson, *Sad Swashbuckler*, 54–56.

96. L. R. Bailey, ed., *The A. B. Gray Report: Survey of a Route on the 32nd Parallel for the Texas Western Railroad, 1854* (Los Angeles: Westernlore, 1963), 134.

97. HJ, Oct. 10, 12, 15, 1853, June 30, 1854. See also James Bradas O'Neil, *To Die But Once: The Story of a Tejano* (New York: Knight Publications, 1935), 30; Sandwich, *Great Western*, 33–38; Elliott, "Great Western," 109–20. The transcription of Heintzelman's Arizona journal by Creola Blackwell for some reason does not include the entries from January 1 to July 16, 1854, when he was still at Fort Yuma. In the late summer of 1853, Heintzelman recorded that "Antonio" had arrived with servants and "camp women." HPD, Aug. 27, 1853.

98. HJ, June 5–6, 1854; J. K. F. Mansfield, Fort Yuma Miscellaneous Notes, Mansfield Papers, Middlesex County Historical Society, Middletown, Conn.; Frazer, *Mansfield on the Condition of the Western Forts*, 146–49. Somewhat impressed, Mansfield filled an entire page in a small leather notebook with a brief history of the Great Western.

99. HJ, July 11, 1854; Goff, *Charles D. Poston*, 10–11; Martin, *Yuma Crossing*, 179; Sacks, *Be It Enacted*, 9.

100. HJ, June 21, 1854; PR, Fort Yuma, July 1854, AGO, RG 393, NA.

101. HJ, Aug. 13, 1854.

102. HJ, Aug. 28, 1854. Many years later an American remembered seeing Heintzelman in Acapulco at the time. See *Appletons' Journal*, Sept., 16, 1871, 324.

103. *Appletons' Journal*, Sept., 16, 1871, 324. See also David I. Folkman Jr. *The Nicaragua Route* (Salt Lake City: University of Utah Press, 1972), 23–42.

104. HJ, Sept. 8, 12, 30, Dec. 6, 29, 1854.

4. Arizona and Silver

1. HJ, Feb. 28, 1855; Heintzelman to S. Cooper, Feb. 12, Mar. 31, 1855, LR, AGO, RG 94, NA; SO 18, Mar. 18, 1855, ibid.; Heintzelman, Request for Compensation, n.d., ibid.

2. HJ, Mar. 9, 1855; Heintzelman to G. W. Cullum, Dec. 18, 1865, Heintzelman Cullum File, USMA.

3. Heintzelman to Cooper, June 7, 1855, LR, AGO, RG 94, NA.

4. HJ, Sept. 22, 24, Oct. 28, Nov. 1, 1855; Freeman, *R. E. Lee*, 1:362; Warner, *Generals in Blue*, 330.

5. HJ, Oct. 28, Nov. 7, 19, 1855.

6. HJ, Dec. 14, 24, 1855; Report of Board of Inspections, Heintzelman to I. N. G. Whistler, Oct. 2, 6, 28, 1856, LR, AGO, RG 94, NA; Heintzelman, GO 32, July 3, 1856, ibid.; Heintzelman, GO 44, Sept. 12, 1856, ibid.; Heintzelman to E. Backus, Sept. 18, 1856, ibid.; Heintzelman, GO 49, Sept. 27, 1856, ibid.; Heintzelman to Backus, Oct. 23, 1856, ibid.

7. North, *Samuel Peter Heintzelman*, 14, 22; HJ, Mar. 7, 24, 1856.

8. HJ, Aug. 4, 1854.

9. HJ, Aug. 10, 13, 17, 27, Sept. 1, 1856, HJ, Jan. 31, Mar. 1, 1857. See also *Sonora and the Value of its Silver Mines.*

10. Th. G. Hibben to J. Floyd, Jan. 3, 1859, LR, AGO, RG 94, NA; HJ, Apr. 15, 22, 1857. See also Ives, *Report upon the Colorado River of the West.*

11. HJ, May 21, 1857.

12. HJ, Aug. 25–26, 1857.

13. HJ, Sept. 26, 1857.

14. HJ, Nov. 3, 1857.

15. HJ, Nov. 8, Dec. 7, 10, 1857.

16. HJ, Nov. 26, 10, 21, 1857.

17. HJ, Jan. 2, 1858; Edwards, *Story of Colt's Revolver*, 347–49.

18. HJ, Jan. 24, Feb. 8, Feb. 12, 1858. Tombstone data, Forest Lawn Cemetery, Buffalo, N.Y. (courtesy of Charles E. Chambers). See also HPD, Feb. 11, 14, 1858.

19. HJ, Mar. 1, 1858. See also Sacks, *Be It Enacted*, 15.

20. L. Anderson et al. to James Buchanan, Jan. 1858, HP; Washington McLean et al. to James Buchanan, Jan. 1858, ibid.; Eli Cook et al. to "the President," ibid.; Wm. Bigler et al. to John B. Floyd, Jan. 20, 1858, HP.

21. HJ, Mar. 28, 1858. See also HPD, Apr. 5, 6, 1858. Having lost everything in the Panic of 1857, Lathrop also wanted to go to Arizona, where Heintzelman had promised him a job with the mining company. It was said Lathrop had been "suddenly transferred from affluence to comparative poverty, retaining nothing of his former wealth." *Buffalo Commercial Advertiser*, Oct. 28, 1857.

22. HJ, Apr. 10, 1858; Heintzelman to Irvin McDowell, Apr. 10, 1858, LR, AGO, RG 94, NA. Heintzelman even enclosed Ehrenberg's latest map, *Sonora & the Gadsden Purchase.*

23. HJ, Apr. 14–15, 1858.

24. SO 67, Apr. 29, 1858, HP; HJ, Apr. 30, 1858.

25. HJ, May 2, 1858.

26. HPD, May 27, 1858; HJ, May 26, 1858. Eunice Tripler, wife of Dr. Charles S. Tripler, who performed the operation, later wrote that her husband had operated on Mary for "hip-joint disease" and that the Heintzelmans were "most grateful." Tripler, *Eunice Tripler*, 140.

27. HJ, June 4, 15, 23, 1858. See also HPD, June 14, 20, 1858. While on lengthy marches or journeys, Heintzelman always calculated mileages in his pocket diary. See, for example, HPD, June 12, 1858.

28. HJ, July 6, 8, 1858. See also HPD, June 28–29, July 3–7, 1858.

29. HPD, Aug. 12, 14, 14, 1858; HJ, Aug. 3, 1858; North, *Samuel Peter Heintzelman*, 53. See also Van Tramp, *Prairie and Rocky Mountain Adventures*, 723–24.

30. North, *Samuel Peter Heintzelman*, 107; Heintzelman to Samuel Cooper, Sept. 1, Oct. 1, Nov. 1, Dec. 31, 1858, LR, AGO, RG 94, NA. See also Wagoner, *Early Arizona*, 386.

31. Van Tramp, *Prairie and Rocky Mountain Adventures*, 723–24; North, *Samuel Peter Heintzelman*, 40. The method of extraction used was that European-barrel amal-

gamation. The plant could process only about 1.5 tons of ore a day. Six dry stamps, a steam arrastra, a reverberatory furnace with four barrels, a retort, and one refining furnace, together with a ten-horsepower engine, made up the entire operation. Edwards, *Story of Colt's Revolver*, 348.

32. North, *Samuel Peter Heintzelman*, 41, 120; HJ, Sept. 29, Nov. 7, 1858. Even so, Heintzelman attended the Fiesta de San Agustin in Tucson. HPD, Aug. 28, 1858.

33. North, *Samuel Peter Heintzelman*, 90; HJ, Sept. 25, 1858.

34. HPD, Oct. 27, 1858; HJ, Aug. 31, Oct. 5, 1858.

35. North, *Samuel Peter Heintzelman*, 132–33, 162; HJ, Nov. 24, 25, 1858, Jan. 5, 1859. The *Weekly Arizonian* was the first newspaper established in what is today Arizona.

36. HJ, Jan. 1, Jan. 26, Mar. 8, 1859; HPD, Jan. 9, 12, 15–16, 18, 20, 23–25, 1859. These artifacts, like so many others, were probably destroyed in the fire that engulfed a large part of the Smithsonian Institution on the afternoon of January 24, 1865. *Harper's Weekly*, Feb. 11, 1865.

37. HPD, Jan. 12, 15–16, 18, 20, 23–25, 1859.

38. HJ, Feb. 17, 22, Mar. 3, 1859.

39. HJ, Mar. 4, 22, 1859.

5. Texas and the Cortina War

1. HJ, Mar. 31, Apr. 9, 16, 1859.

2. Thompson, *Fifty Miles and a Fight*, 60; HPD, Apr. 21, 1859.

3. HJ, Apr. 23, 1859; Thompson, *Fifty Miles and a Fight*, 61.

4. Weisinger, "Globe House" (articles courtesy of Charles Spurlin, Victoria College).

5. Heintzelman to S. Cooper, May 1, 1859, LR, AGO, RG 94, NA. "Maj. S. P. Heintzelman with family, USA," arrived at the Menger Hotel on May 3, 1859, the *San Antonio Daily Herald* noted.

6. SO 31, May 11, 1859, HP; Thompson, *Fifty Miles and a Fight*, 68. See also HPD, May 7, 1859.

7. Thompson, *Fifty Miles and a Fight*, 69–70.

8. S. B. Lathrop to J. B. Floyd, June 5, 1859, LR, AGO, RG 94, NA. The article was signed by "H. E.," probably Hermann Ehrenberg. *Tubac Weekly Arizonian*, n.d.

9. SO 34, May 11, 1859, HP; Thompson, *Fifty Miles and a Fight*, 78. See also HPD, May 24, 1859.

10. Thompson, *Fifty Miles and a Fight*, 80.

11. D. E. Twiggs to L. Thomas, Jan. 11, 1859, in U.S. House, *Difficulties on the Southwestern Frontier*; HPD, June 13–14, 16, 1859; Thompson, *Fifty Miles and a Fight*, 83. See also GO 1, Feb. 5, 1859, in *Difficulties on the Southwestern Frontier*, 8.

12. Boyd, *Noble Brutes*, 56–66; Hunter, *Old Camp Verde;* Post Returns, Camp Verde, AGO, RG 393, NA.

13. Thompson, *Fifty Miles and a Fight*, 88, 110–11.

14. Heintzelman to *Scientific American*, Sept. 28, 1859, HP. See notes in HPD, Jan. 3, July 31, Nov. 24, 1859.

15. Thompson, *Fifty Miles and a Fight*, 97, 109; William Ballantyne et al. to the

President of the United States, n.d., LR, AGO, NA; G. F. Towle to A. J. Hamilton, Jan. 16, 1860, ibid. .

16. Rodriguez, *Tejano Son of Texas*, 21–26; *Message from the President of the United States*, 22.

17. HPD, Aug. 19, 1859.

18. SO 103, Nov. 12, 1859, HP. See also HPD, Nov. 13, 1859.

19. Heintzelman to J. P. Taylor, Feb. 27, 1861, HP; SO 105, Nov. 15, 1859, HP; Twiggs to Secretary of War, Nov. 12, 16, 1859, LR, AGO, RG 94, NA; Twiggs endorsement, Nov. 15, 1859, on "Abstract of Ordnance and Ordnance Stores on Hand at Brazos Santiago," Sept. 30, 1859, ibid.

20. Twiggs to Secretary of War, Nov. 17, 21, 1859, LR, AGO, RG 94, NA.

21. Thompson, *Fifty Miles and a Fight*, 118; HPD, Oct. 13, 1859; W. G. Tobin to Runnels, Nov. 16, 1859, Sam Houston Papers, TSA; Heintzelman to T. A. Washington, Nov. 23, 1859, CWLSB, HP; SO 113, Dec. 10, 1859, HP. See also HJ, Nov. 22, 1859.

22. HJ, Nov. 29, Dec. 2, 1859; HPD, Nov. 29, 1859; Heintzelman to Washington, Nov. 28, Dec. 7, 1859, CWLSB, HP.

23. HPD, Dec. 5, 1859.

24. *Corpus Christi Ranchero*, Nov. 26, 1859; W. G. Tobin to Richard H. Runnels, Nov. 16, 1859, Sam Houston Papers, TSA.

25. *Corpus Christi Ranchero*, Dec. 3, 1859; Heintzelman to Robert E. Lee, Mar. 1, 1860, in House, *Trouble on Texas Frontier*, 36th Cong., 1st sess., 6. See also Thompson, *Fifty Miles and a Fight*, 33.

26. *Brownsville American Flag*, Nov. 26, 1859; *Corpus Christi Ranchero*, Dec. 3, 1859; Heintzelman to Lee, Mar. 1, 1860, in House, *Trouble on Texas Frontier*, 6. For a copy and discussion of this particular *pronunciamiento*, see Thompson, *Juan Cortina*, 19–28.

27. HJ, Dec. 11, 1859.

28. HJ, Dec. 10–12, 1859; Thompson, *Juan Cortina*, 22.

29. HJ, Dec. 16, 1859.

30. Ibid.; *Dallas Herald*, Jan. 4, 1860.

31. *Dallas Herald*, Jan. 4, 1860. See also HPD, Dec. 14–15, 1859; Heintzelman to Washington, Dec. 16, 1859, CWLSB, HP.

32. HJ, Dec. 16, 1859; Ford, *Rip Ford's Texas*, 268.

33. Heintzelman, "List of Persons Killed by Cortinas," in House, *Trouble on Texas Frontier*, 75; Heintzelman to Washington, Dec. 16, 1859, CWLSB, HP.

34. Heintzelman to S. Cooper, Dec. 18, 1859, CWLSB, HP; HJ, Dec. 16, 1859.

35. HPD, Dec. 17, 1859; Orders 4, Dec. 17, 1859, CWOB, HP.

36. HPD, Dec. 21, 1859; Heintzelman to Lee, Mar. 1, 1860, in House, *Trouble on Texas Frontier*, 8.

37. HJ, Dec. 26, 1859.

38. Ford, *Rip Ford's Texas*, 270.

39. Ibid., 272.

40. *New Orleans Daily Picayune*, Jan. 22, 1860; Heintzelman to Washington, Dec. 27, 1859, CWLSB, HP; Heintzelman to Lee, Mar. 1, 1860, in House, *Trouble on*

Texas Frontier, 9. An outline of the different engagements of the Cortina War can be found in GO 11, Nov. 23, 1860, HP.

41. There is no additional mention of these historically valuable records, and it is presumed they were either lost or destroyed.

42. HJ, Dec. 27, 1859; HPD, Dec. 27, 1859; Heintzelman to G. W. Cullum, Dec. 18, 1865, Heintzelman Cullum File, West Point.

43. Thomas, *Fort Davis and the Texas Frontier*, 24–25.

44. Noah Cox to Heintzelman, Dec. 27, 1859, HP; Heintzelman to Cooper, Dec. 27, 1859, CWLSB, HP; HJ, Dec. 31, 1859.

45. Heintzelman to Wm. G. Tobin, Jan. 2, 1860, CWLSB, HP; HJ, Dec. 30, 1859, Jan. 1, 1860; Heintzelman to Washington, Dec. 30, 1859, CWLSB, HP; Ford, *Rip Ford's Texas*, 276.

46. HJ, Jan. 2–7, 1860.

47. HJ, Jan. 2–6, 1860.

48. Heintzelman to Jno. Withers, Jan. 29, 1860, CWLSB, HP; HJ, Jan. 16, 1859; Withers to Heintzelman, Jan. 4, 1860, HP; "Orders to Ángel Navarro and Richard Taylor," Jan. 2, 1860, in Williams and Barker, *Writings of Sam Houston*, 7:395–96; *San Antonio Daily Herald*, Jan. 5, 1860; Heintzelman to Tobin, Jan. 16, 1860, CWLSB, HP.

49. HJ, Jan. 23, 1860. As a major in the Confederate Army of New Mexico, Lockridge would die at the Battle of Valverde on February 21, 1862, after promising his men he would "make his wife a shimmy" from the Federal banner waving over Fort Craig. Baylor, *Into the Far, Wild Country*, 77–82; Fornell, "Texans and Filibusters," 417–27; *San Antonio Daily Herald*, May 6, 1859, quoting the *New Orleans Bee*, n.d.; *New Orleans Daily Picayune*, Jan. 7, 1860.

50. HJ, Jan. 26, 31, 1860.

51. HJ, Feb. 10, 1860; Heintzelman to Withers, Feb. 10, 1860, CWLSB, HP. See also Orders 10, Feb. 8, 1860, CWOB, HP; and Orders 11, Jan. 28, 1860, ibid.

52. Heintzelman to Lee, Mar. 1, 1860, in House, *Trouble on Texas Frontier*, 10. Even at the time there was considerable confusion over exactly what happened at La Bolsa. Perhaps the best initial accounts are Ford to Heintzelman, Feb. 8, 1860, HP; and Loomis Langdon to Heintzelman, Apr. 28, 1860, HP. See also Heintzelman to Withers, Apr. 29, 1860, CWLSB, HP.

53. Ford, *Rip Ford's Texas*, 285–86.

54. Heintzelman to Withers, Apr. 29, 1860, CWLSB, HP.

55. Heintzelman to Lee, Mar. 1, 1860, in House, *Trouble on Texas Frontier*, 11.

56. Heintzelman to Ford, Feb. 4, 1860, HP; HJ, Feb. 8, 1860. See also Heintzelman to Ford, Feb. 5, 1860, HP; Heintzelman to A. T. Lee, Feb. 4, 1860, HP; Heintzelman to Stoneman, Feb. 4, 1860, HP; Heintzelman to Joaquin Arguilles, Feb. 11, 1860, CWLSB, HP; and Langdon to Heintzelman, Feb. 4, 1860, LR, AGO, RG 94, NA. For specifics on the incident, see Thompson, *Fifty Miles and a Fight*, 188–91.

57. HJ, Feb. 15, 1860; Ford, *Rip Ford's Texas*, 295. See also George Stoneman and John S. Ford to C. W. Thomas, Mar. 18, 1860, in House, *Trouble on Texas Frontier*, 80–81; Stoneman to Heintzelman, Mar. 18, 1860, HP; Stoneman to Heintzelman, Mar. 19, 1860, HP; Heintzelman to Stoneman, Mar. 18, 1860, HP; and Ford to Heintzelman, Mar. 18, 1860, HP.

58. Heintzelman to Withers, Mar. 25, 1860, CWLSB, HP.

59. García to "General of Brigade," Mar. 11, 1860, HP; Heintzelman to García, Mar. 11, 1860, HP; Heintzelman to Stoneman, Mar. 12, 1860, HP; HJ, Apr. 6, 1860. See also Arnold, *Jeff Davis's Own*, 276–77. For details, see Thompson, *Fifty Miles and a Fight*, 125–26; and Ford, *Rip Ford's Texas*, 296–97.

60. H. L. Scott to "Dear Sir," Feb. 1, 1860, HP; HJ, Mar. 24, 1860. Lt. Col. Henry Lee Scott, writing from army headquarters in New York, copied a portion of General Scott's endorsement on Heintzelman's report of December 27, 1859: "This is the report of a brilliant affair in which Major Heintzelman distinguished himself as he has done often many years before. I beg to ask a brevet for him—in small part to compensate for the outrage done him by the War Department, which took [Silas] Casey, a junior and inferior captain, from the same regiment [2nd Infantry] March 3, 1855, and made him lieutenant colonel of the 9th Infantry."

61. Heintzelman to Lee, Mar. 1, 1860, in House, *Trouble on Texas Frontier*, 13–14.

62. Ibid., 15–62. A month after the Battle of Rio Grande City, for example, Kelsey, the largest merchant in that town, wrote José San Roman that "Cortina took from me and damaged otherwise near five thousand worth of Mds." Kelsey promised to "make a claim on Uncle Sam for a pile . . . whether I get it or not." True to his word, he submitted claims amounting to $31,757. John Kelsey to José San Roman, Jan. 26, 1860, San Roman Papers, CAH; John P. Kelsey to "Commanding Officer at Ringgold Barracks," Jan. 27, 1860, in House, *Trouble on Texas Frontier*, 38.

63. R. E. Lee to Heintzelman, Feb. 20, 1860, quoting GO 2, HP.

64. Rister, *Robert E. Lee in Texas*, 119. See also Robert E. Lee to [Mary] Lee, Apr. 1, 1860, in Francis Raymond Adams Jr., "An Annotated Edition of the Personal Letters of Robert E. Lee, April 1856 to April 1861" (Ph.D. diss., University of Maryland, 1955), 598.

65. R. E. Lee to Ándres Treviño, Apr. 2, 1860, in Jenkins, *Robert E. Lee on the Rio Grande*, 12–13; Lee to "Civil and Military Authorities of the City of Reynosa, Mexico," Apr. 7, 1860, in ibid., 13–14; Lee to G. García, Apr. 12, 1860, in ibid., 20–21. Most of the letters in this collection are from House, *Trouble on Texas Frontier.* See also Heintzelman to Manuel Treviño, Apr. 3, 1860, CWLSB, HP.

66. R. E. Lee to Heintzelman, Apr. 30, 1860, quoting SO, n.d., HP; Lee to George McKnight, Apr. 11, 1860, in Jenkins, *Robert E. Lee on the Rio Grande*, 19–20.

67. HJ, Apr. 9, 1860; Francisco Zepeda to Lee, Apr. 8, 1860, in House, *Trouble on Texas Frontier*, 86–87.

68. Dunn, "KGC in Texas," 543–69; Bridges, "Knights of the Golden Circle," 287–302; Crenshaw, "Knights of the Golden Circle," 23–50; *Galveston Weekly News*, Feb. 16, 1861; HJ, Apr. 12, 1860. See also May, *Manifest Destiny's Underworld*, 43–44. As many as one hundred of the filibusters were led by the notorious William Robertson "Big Bill" Henry, the grandson of Patrick Henry and who had been shot in the leg during the skirmish with Cortina at La Bolsa. Henry was later killed during a gunfight in San Antonio's Main Plaza in 1862. May, *Manifest Destiny's Underworld*, 43; Thompson, *Fifty Miles and a Fight*, 126–27.

69. HJ, May 7, 1860. A street in Brownsville was later named for Heintzelman, but in the 1970s the name was changed to honor a local college administrator. No

one on the Texas Southmost Board of Trustees could remember a man by the name of Heintzelman ever having anything to do with Fort Brown. Bruce Aikens, interview with author, Apr. 17, 2000.

70. Lee to [Mary] Lee, May 2, 1860, in Adams, "Personal Letters of Robert E. Lee," 625.

71. HJ, May 28, 30, 1860.

72. HJ, Sept. 19, 1860.

73. Jeremiah Galvan to Heintzelman, June 24, 1860, HP; Stoneman to Heintzelman, July 8, 1860, HP.

74. A. Williams to Heintzelman, Dec. 10, 1860, HP.

75. Ford to Heintzelman, Nov. 20, 1860, HP; HJ, Nov. 26, 1860.

76. HJ, Dec. 18, 1860.

77. HJ, Dec. 31, 1860.

6. Debacle at Bull Run

1. HJ, Jan. 1, 1861; Hall, *Confederate Army of New Mexico*, 138.

2. HJ, Jan. 2, 9, 1861.

3. HJ, Jan. 9, 1861.

4. HJ, Jan. 14, 1861.

5. Thompson, *Texas and New Mexico on the Eve of the Civil War*, 196; HJ, Jan. 26, 1861.

6. SO 60, Feb. 27, 1861, HP; Cozzens, *General John Pope*, 30–31.

7. HJ, Mar. 1, 1861.

8. HJ, Feb. 25, 1861. Heintzelman kept a copy of the orders dismissing Twiggs for "treachery to the flag of his country." GO 5, Mar. 1, 1861, HP. See also *New York Times*, Mar. 5, 1861.

9. HJ, Mar. 14, 1861.

10. HJ, Mar. 2, 1861.

11. HJ, Mar. 4, 1861; *New York Times*, Mar. 5, 1861.

12. HJ, Mar. 5, 1861. See also Nelligan, *Custis-Lee Mansion*, 20–25.

13. HJ, Apr. 16, 19, 1861; SO 98, Apr. 8, 1861, HP.

14. E. D. Townsend to Heintzelman, Apr. 17, 1861, *OR*, 51(1):598; HJ, Apr. 27, 1861.

15. GO 20, May 8, 1861, HP; Simon Cameron to Heintzelman, May 27, 1861, HP; HJ, May 7, 1861. See also HJ, May 2, 1861.

16. Furgurson, *Freedom Rising*, 206–208, 233, 352.

17. HJ, May 9, 1861; *Harper's Weekly*, May 25, 1861.

18. HJ, May 13, 1861.

19. Cameron to Heintzelman, May 14, 27, 1861, HP; HJ, May 13, 15, 17–19, 1861. See also Heintzelman to G. W. Cullum, Dec. 18, 1865, HP. The original of this letter and an accompanying outline of Heintzelman's military career are in the library at West Point.

20. James B. Fry, SO 5, June 3, 1861, *OR*, 51(1):396.

21. Leech, *Reveille in Washington*, 80; Cooling, *Symbol, Sword, and Shield*, 35–36.

22. Heintzelman greatly admired Winfield Scott, who had dominated Mexico and whose service in the army went back to before the War of 1812. Although well past his prime, Scott, who stood six feet, five inches tall and weighed close to 350 pounds, was one of the greatest soldiers of his age. Possessing a powerful intellect, he had served every president from Jefferson to Lincoln.

23. Heintzelman to L. Thomas, July 20, 1861, *OR,* 2:40. Heintzelman outlined much of his Civil War career in a letter to AAG E. D. Townsend, Nov. 30, 1864, HP.

24. HJ, May 25, 1861; GO 1, May 28, 1861, HP. See also Randall, *Colonel Elmer Ellsworth,* 257–62.

25. HJ, May 25, 1861.

26. GO 1, May 28, HP; GO 13, 1861, HP; HJ, June 17, 19, 1861.

27. HJ, June 11, 1861.

28. HJ, June 6, 1861.

29. Williams, *Lincoln and His Generals,* 21.

30. HJ, June 8, 1861.

31. HJ, June 14, 29, July 1, 3–4, 1861; GO 13, July 8, 1861, HP.

32. De Peyster, *Obituary Notice of Maj.-Gen. Samuel Peter Heintzelman,* 8.

33. *Battle of Bull Run,* 29; HJ, July 15, 1861.

34. HJ, July 16, 1861.

35. HJ, July 18, 1861; *Battle of Bull Run,* 28; "Notes Taken on the Advance to Bull Run, July 16 to July 21, 1861," n.d., HP.

36. O. B. Willcox to C. McKeever, July 17, 1861, *OR,* 2:309; O. B. Willcox to J. B. Fry, July 18, 1861, ibid., 310. See also Comte de Paris, *Civil War in America,* 232–33.

37. Heintzelman Testimony, Dec. 24, 1861, in *Battle of Bull Run,* 29.

38. "Notes Taken on the Advance to Bull Run," n.d., HP; Heintzelman to Mrs. M. H., July 18, 1861, HP.

39. Leech, *Reveille in Washington,* 100.

40. "Notes Taken on the Advance to Bull Run," n.d., HP; HJ, Sept. 1, 1861.

41. W. B. Franklin to C. McKeever, July 28, 1861, *OR,* 2:405–406.

42. Aldrich, *History of Battery A,* 19; Rhodes, *All for the Union,* 26. See also McDonald, "*We Shall Meet Again,*" 46–47.

43. Alonzo F. Bidwell to [J. H. Hobart] Ward, July 29, 1861, *OR,* 2:413; Mark H. Dunnell to O. O. Howard, July 26, 1861, ibid., 421; Francis S. Fiske, "Second New Hampshire Regiment at Bull Run," USAMHI.

44. Davis, *Battle at Bull Run,* 182–83; Comte de Paris, *Civil War in America,* 242. See also Heintzelman to Jas. B. Fry, July 31, 1861, *OR,* 2:402–404. Heintzelman kept a copy of this letter for his files.

45. HJ, Sept. 1, 1861.

46. Davis, *Battle at Bull Run,* 172–73.

47. Charles Griffin Testimony, Jan. 14, 1861, in *Battle of Bull Run,* 168; Willcox, *Forgotten Valor,* 290; James B. Ricketts Testimony, Apr. 3, 1862, in *Battle of Bull Run,* 243.

48. HJ, Sept. 1, 1861; Willcox, *Forgotten Valor,* 290; Heintzelman Testimony, Dec. 24, 1861, in *Battle of Bull Run,* 30; P. G. T. Beauregard to S. Cooper, Aug. 26 [Oct. 14], 1861, *OR,* 2:494; William F. Barry to J. B. Fry, July 23, 1861, ibid., 347; O. B. Wilcox to Thomas, Sept. 3, 1861, ibid., 408–409; J. E. B. Stuart to Joseph E. Johnston, July 26,

1861, ibid., 483; "Return of Casualties in the Third Division, Army of Northeastern Virginia, at the Battle of Bull Run," July 21, 1861, ibid., 405. See also Heintzelman to Fry, July 31, 1861, ibid., 402–404. This same letter can be found in HP. Casualties from all Federal brigades are given in McDonald, *"We Shall Meet Again,"* 187–96.

49. Griffin Testimony, Jan. 14, 1861, in *Battle of Bull Run*, 169, 172.

50. Ricketts Testimony, Apr. 3, 1862, in ibid., 243. In the attack on Ricketts's battery, the 7th Georgia lost 153 of 580 men. For Ricketts's imprisonment, the mistreatment of his wife in Richmond, and his release, see HJ, Dec. 23, 1861.

51. After the First Battle of Bull Run, Heintzelman wrote to Sen. Morton S. Wilkinson and Rep. Cyrus Aldrich of Minnesota praising Colonel Gorman for his bravery under fire and urging that he be made a brigadier general. Heintzelman to Morton S. Wilkinson and Cyrus Aldrich, Aug. 23, 1861, HP; Wilkinson and Aldrich to Heintzelman, Aug. 15, 1861.

52. Mathless, *Voices of the Civil War: First Manassas*, 124, 125 (Thatcher quote). See also Heintzelman to Fry, July 31, 1861, *OR*, 2:403.

53. A. F. Bidwell to [J. H. Hobart] Ward, July 25, 1861, *OR*, 2:412.

54. Heintzelman to Fry, July 31, 1861, ibid., 403; HJ, Sept. 1, 5, 1861. See also miscellaneous newspaper obituary, n.d., HP; and "Notes on Gen. [John Watts] de Peyster's Article—'Heintzelman: The First Commander of the III Corps,'" n.d., HP.

55. HJ, Sept. 1, 1861; Howard quoted in Mathless, *Voices of the Civil War: First Manassas*, 145.

56. Heintzelman to Fry, July 31, 1861, *OR*, 2:403; Miscellaneous newspaper obituary, HP; de Peyster, *Obituary Notice of Maj.-Gen. Samuel Peter Heintzelman*, 9; "Notes on Gen. de Peyster's Article," n.d., HP.

57. HJ, Sept. 1, 1861.

58. Heintzelman to Fry, July 31, 1861, *OR*, 2:404.

59. Ibid. See also HJ, Sept. 5, 1861.

60. Rhodes, *All for the Union*, 22, 26–27.

61. HJ, Sept. 6, 1861.

62. Ibid.

63. Heintzelman to Fry, July 31, 1861, *OR*, 2:405 (an original draft can be found in HP); "Return of Casualties in the Third Division," July 31, 1861, ibid.

7. Red Mud of Virginia

1. Leech, *Reveille in Washington*, 111.

2. HJ, Sept. 1, 1861.

3. SO 51, July 30, 1861, HP; SO 10, Aug. 14, 1861, HP; AAG to Heintzelman, Aug. 13, 1861, HP; HJ, Sept. 13, 1861.

4. HJ, Sept. 13, 1861. William Wrightson had written Secretary of War Simon Cameron in March 1861, following the evacuation of two companies of dragoons from Fort Buchanan, asking that cavalry again be assigned to the post. In his attempt to persuade Cameron to act, Wrightson included five extracts of letters written from Tubac in January and February 1861. W. Wrightson to Cameron, Mar. 8, 1861, LR, AGO, RG 94, NA.

5. HJ, Sept. 23, 1861.

6. Sears, *George B. McClellan*, 107–109.

7. Leech, *Reveille in Washington*, 112; Sneden, *Images from the Storm*, 10. The fort was named for Brig. Gen. Nathaniel Lyon, who was killed at Wilson's Creek, Missouri, on August 10, 1861. No visible remains of the fort exist today. See Cooling and Owen, *Mr. Lincoln's Forts*, 60–64.

8. Sneden, *Images from the Storm*, 17; HJ, Dec. 25, 30, 1861.

9. Robert Knox Sneden Diary, Apr. 2, 1862, July 27, 1863, Robert Knox Sneden Diary and Papers, VHS; GO 1, Mar. 16, 1862, HP; Heitman, *Historical Register*, 1: 520, 556, 575, 671, 709, 731, 752. Heine would later transfer to the staff of Brig. Gen. David B. Birney. He was replaced by Pennsylvania-born 1st Lt. Orlando G. Wagner, an 1859 West Point graduate who had been serving in the Topographical Engineers.

10. HJ, Nov. 2, 1861; Leech, *Reveille in Washington*, 110–11.

11. HJ, Sept. 30, 1861; I. B. Richardson to S. P. Heintzelman, Oct. 19, 1861, *OR*, 5(1):249; Isaac Moses to John Sedgwick, Nov. 11, 1861, *OR*, 51(1):504.

12. Heintzelman to S. Williams, Nov. 13, 1861, *OR*, 5:413–14; Henry B. Todd to Heintzelman, Nov. 21, 1861, *OR*, 5:419–20.

13. Chas. P. Stone to S. Williams, Oct. 29, 1861, *OR*, 5:293–99.

14. HJ, Sept. 21, 1861.

15. HJ, Sept. 22, Oct. 8, 10, Nov. 20, 25, 1861.

16. HJ, Nov. 11, 1861. See also Sears, *George B. McClellan*, 132.

17. HJ, Nov. 7, 1861, Oct. 7, Nov. 22, 1863; Heintzelman to Edgar Cowan, Jan. 28, 1867, HP; "Notes on Gen. [John Watts] de Peyster's Article—'Heintzelman: The First Commander of the III Corps,'" n.d., HP. For references to "Contrabands," see also HJ, Oct. 31, Dec. 9, 16, 31, 1861, Jan. 2, 3, 1862.

18. HJ, Nov. 30, Dec. 16, 30, 1861. .

19. HJ, Jan. 15, 23, 1862.

20. HJ, Dec. 16, 1861; Tap, *Over Lincoln's Shoulder*, 103.

21. "Notes on Gen. de Peyster's Article," n.d., HP.

22. McClellan quoted in McPherson, *Ordeal by Fire*, 236.

23. Tap, *Over Lincoln's Shoulder*, 71, 79; HJ, Feb. 10, May 22, 1862.

24. Heintzelman Testimony, Dec. 24, 1861, in *Battle of Bull Run*, 31; HJ, Dec. 24, 1861. The committee, which met in secret, even interrogated the president about Mary Lincoln's alleged Southern sympathies.

25. HJ, Dec. 31, 1861; *New York Times*, Jan. 3, 1862. Sketching the scene was Alfred R. Waud, artist for *Harper's Weekly*. On the far right of the sketch, Heintzelman is clearly identifiable. Ray, *"Our Special Artist,"* 88–89.

26. Sneden, *Eye of the Storm*, 14. The perceptive Sneden would be Heintzelman's most valuable cartographer.

27. HJ, Dec. 24, 1861, Jan. 9, 22, Feb. 21, 1862. For Heintzelman's concern regarding Sumner, see HJ, Dec. 16–17, 20, 28.

28. HJ, Jan. 13, 21, 1862.

29. HJ, Nov. 25, Dec. 6, 1861.

30. HJ, Dec. 28, 1861.

31. Simpson, *Hood's Texas Brigade*, 76–77; HJ, Jan. 29, 1862. See also HPD, Jan. 29, 1862.

32. HJ, Dec. 28, 1861.

33. HJ, Feb. 15, 24, 1862.

34. HJ, Jan. 27, 1862.

35. Haydon, *Military Ballooning*, 294.

36. T. S. C. Lowe to R. B. Marcy, Mar. 6, 1862, *OR*, ser. 3, 3:271; HJ, Feb. 21, 27, Mar. 4–6, 1862. See also HPD, Mar. 6, 1862.

37. HJ, Mar. 4, 1862; Sears, *Gates of Richmond*, 6–7.

38. Sears, *George B. McClellan*, 159–60; HJ, Mar. 8, 1862.

39. HJ, Mar. 8, 1862; Sears, *George B. McClellan*, 159–60.

40. Tap, *Over Lincoln's Shoulder*, 113.

41. Welcher, *Union Army*, 802, 805, 813.

42. Wainwright, *Diary of Battle*, 38.

43. Sears, *George B. McClellan*, 163–64.

44. HJ, Mar. 13, 1862. This was after it was learned the *Virginia* "was probably disabled by the *Monitor*."

45. Sneden Diary, Mar. 20, 1862, VHS; HJ, Mar. 16, 20, 1862. See also Wert, *Sword of Lincoln*, 65–66.

46. Sneden, *Eye of the Storm*, 24.

47. Ibid., 25.

48. Ibid., 28.

49. Sneden Diary, Mar. 23, 1862, VHS; HJ, Mar. 24, 1862; HPD, Mar. 23, 1862.

50. Sears, *Gates of Richmond*, 28.

51. Sneden, *Images from the Storm*, 30.

52. HJ, Mar. 25, 1862

53. McClellan to Heintzelman, Mar. 21, 1862, HP.

54. HJ, Mar. 26–28, 1862; McClellan to Heintzelman, Mar. 22, 1862, *OR*, 2(1):6. Sneden Diary, Mar. 27, 1862, VHS; S. Williams to Heintzelman, Mar. 28, 1862, *OR*, 11(3):42. See also McClellan to Heintzelman, Mar. 28, 1862, in Sears, *Civil War Papers of George B. McClellan*, 218–19; McClellan to Heintzelman, Mar. 28, 1862, *OR*, 11(3):43; and HN, Mar. 27, 1862. Two of Heintzelman's notebooks, dating from March 1862 to October 1863, are far more detailed than any of his pocket diaries that cover the Peninsula Campaign. Although not as descriptive as his journals, the notebooks are a valuable source for the advance against Richmond, Second Bull Run, and events in the fall of 1863. The first several pages of both notebooks were badly damaged when a box containing the general's journals, pocket diaries, notebooks, and over a hundred photographs accidentally fell into the harbor at Indianola, Texas, in May 1866. HJ, May 4, 1866.

55. Heintzelman to McClellan, Mar. 29, 1862, *OR*, 11(3):47; HJ, Mar. 30, 1862.

56. HJ, Mar. 29, 1862.

57. McClellan to Heintzelman, Apr. 4, 1862, HP.

58. McClellan to Heintzelman, Apr. 3, 4 (two letters), 1862, HP; HJ, Apr. 3, 1862.

59. HJ, Apr. 5, 1862; Sears, *Gates of Richmond*, 39.

60. Ibid., 36. See also Sneden Diary, Apr. 3, 1862, VHS.

61. Sneden, *Eye of the Storm*, 38.

62. Ibid., 39; HJ, Apr. 5, May 6, 1862.

63. Wainwright, *Diary of Battle*, 37; HN, Apr. 11, 1862.

64. Sears, *Gates of Richmond*, 42; Sneden, *Eye of the Storm*, 43.

65. HJ, Apr. 23, May 4, 1862. See also Heintzelman to McClellan, Mar. 29, 1862, *OR*, 11(3):47. According to Sneden, Heintzelman estimated Magruder's force at this time to be around thirteen thousand. *Eye of the Storm*, 41.

66. Sears, *Gates of Richmond*, 37; Sneden Diary, Apr. 17, 1862, VHS; HJ, Apr. 5, 1862.

67. Charles S. Hamilton to Samuel Breck, Mar. 20, 1864, Lincoln Papers, LC; HN, May 2, 1862.

68. HJ, Apr. 30, 1862. See also P. Kearny to "My Dear Parker," May 3, 1862, in Kearny, *Letters from the Peninsula*, 56–57.

69. Kearny, *Letters from the Peninsula*, 85, 127, 146.

70. HJ, Apr. 6, 1862; Haydon, *Military Ballooning*, 318–21; Sneden, *Images from the Storm*, 41; HN, Apr. 18, 1862.

71. Sneden, *Eye of the Storm*, 45–46; Sears, *Gates of Richmond*, 54; HJ, Apr. 10, 1862.

72. Sneden, *Eye of the Storm*, 45; HJ, Apr. 13, 1862.

73. HJ, Apr. 23, Aug. 20, 1862; HN, Apr. 26, 1862. For Heintzelman's other observations on Yorktown, see HJ, July 15, 1862, June 28, 1871.

74. Sneden, *Eye of the Storm*, 56; Sears, *Gates of Richmond*, 57.

75. Sneden Diary, Apr. 13, 1862, VHS.

76. Sneden, *Eye of the Storm*, 47.

77. Sneden Diary, Apr. 13, 17, 1862, VHS; Sneden, *Eye of the Storm*, 44.

78. Sneden Diary, Apr. 17, 1862, VHS; Heitman, *Historical Register*, 2:993; HN, Apr. 22, 1862.

79. HJ, Apr. 29, 1862.

80. Warner, *Generals in Blue*, 492; HJ, Apr. 12, 1862; *New York Daily Tribune*, May 1, 1862; HN, Apr. 28, 1862.

81. *New York Daily Tribune*, May 2, 9, 1862; Bosse, *Civil War Newspaper Maps*, 18–19; *New York Herald*, Apr. 22, 1862; Sneden, *Eye of the Storm*, 53; HJ, Apr. 18, 23, 1862; Ray, *"Our Special Artist,"* 33–36, 93–103.

82. HJ, Apr. 15, 30, 1862; Sears, *George B. McClellan*, 180–81; Sears, *Gates of Richmond*, 57–58.

83. Williams to Heintzelman, May 2, 1862, HP.

84. Sneden, *Eye of the Storm*, 55–56; Lowe, "Balloons with the Army of the Potomac," 372; Evans, *War of the Aeronauts*, 216; HN, May 1, 1862. Heintzelman thought the shell was from an 8-inch Columbiad being used as a mortar. Evans mistakenly placed this event during the Battle of Williamsburg. Lowe clearly states in his recollections: "I could see readily that I could be of no service at Williamsburg, both armies being hidden in a great forest. Therefore, General McClellan at the close of the battle sent orders to me to proceed with my outfit including all the balloons, gas-generators, the balloon-inflating boat, gunboat, and tug up the Pamunkey River, until I reached White House and the bridge crossing the historic river, and join the army which would be there as soon as myself."

85. Heintzelman to George W. Mindil, July 24, 1874, George W. Mindil Papers, USAMHI; Sneden, *Eye of the Storm*, 57; Lowe, "Balloons with the Army of the

Potomac," 370; Evans, *War of the Aeronauts*, 212; HJ, May 4, 1862; HN, May 4, 1862. See also HN, May 3, 1862.

86. Sneden, *Eye of the Storm*, 58.

87. HJ, May 3, 4, 1862; Sears, *Gates of Richmond*, 61–62; Heintzelman to McClellan, May 7, 1862, *OR*, 11(2):456–57. Heintzelman retained a copy of this letter, as he did most other important battle reports, for his files.

88. HJ, May 4, 1862. See also Heintzelman to Mindil, July 24, 1874, Mindil Papers, USAMHI; *New York Daily Tribune*, May 5, 1862.

89. Sneden, *Eye of the Storm*, 61; HJ, May 6, 1862. See also HN, May 4, 1862.

8. A Crisis in Our Affairs

1. R. B. Marcy to Heintzelman, May 4, 1862 (2:30 P.M.), HP; McClellan to Heintzelman, May 4, 1862, HP; Sneden, *Eye of the Storm*, 62.

2. Sears, *Gates of Richmond*, 70. See also Sneden, *Images from the Storm*, 60–61.

3. HN, May 4, 1862; Sneden, *Eye of the Storm*, 64.

4. Dubbs, *Defend This Old Town*, 83–84.

5. HJ, May 6, 1862.

6. Ibid. See also HN, May 6, 1862.

7. Heintzelman to Mindil, July 14, 1874, Mindil Papers, USAMHI; HN, May 6, 1862.

8. Hastings and Hastings, *A Pitiless Rain*, 64.

9. Hooker quoted in Heintzelman to McClellan, May 7, 1862, *OR*, 11(2):458; HJ, Mar. 14, 18, 1863.

10. Hooker to Chauncey McKeever, May 10, 1862, *OR*, 11(2):467; HN, May 5–6, 1862; Heintzelman to R. B. Marcy, May 5, 1862, *OR*, 2(1):454; Heintzelman to McClellan, May 7, 1862, *OR*, 11(2):459.

11. Dubbs, *Defend This Old Town*, 139–41.

12. Heintzelman to McClellan, May 7, 1862, *OR*, 11(2):458.

13. Marston quoted in Heintzelman to McClellan, May 7, 1862, *OR*, 11(2):459–60.

14. Heintzelman to McClellan, May 7, 1862, *OR*, 11(2):459; HN, May 6, 1862; Dubbs, *Defend This Old Town*, 130.

15. Heintzelman to McClellan, May 7, 1862, *OR*, 11(2):458; Mathless, *Voices of the Civil War: The Peninsula*, 90.

16. Heintzelman to McClellan, May 7, 1862, *OR*, 11(2):458–59. See also de Peyster, *Personal and Military History of Philip Kearny*, 281; and Herbert, *Fighting Joe Hooker*, 87.

17. Page quoted in Mathless, *Voices of the Civil War: The Peninsula*, 90–91.

18. Sears, *Gates of Richmond*, 75 (quotes); Dubbs, *Defend This Old Town*, 130; Mathless, *Voices of the Civil War: The Peninsula*, 89; Hastings and Hastings, *A Pitiless Rain*, 88.

19. HN, May 6, 1862; J. H. B. Jenkins to Mary [A. Benjamin], May 17, 1862, Henry C. Hoar Papers, William and Mary College, Williamsburg, Va. (typescript, RNBP).

20. Kearny, *Letters from the Peninsula*, 60.

21. Heintzelman to McClellan, May 7, 1862, *OR*, 2(1):459; de Peyster, *Personal and Military History of Philip Kearny*, 272; Kearny, *Letters from the Peninsula*, 62.

22. Haydon, *For Country, Cause, & Leader*, 235.

23. Heintzelman to McClellan, May 7, 1862, *OR*, 2(1):459.

24. HJ, May 19, 1862; Dubbs, *Defend This Old Town*, 174; *OR*, 11(1):454–56; Sears, *Gates of Richmond*, 82; *New York Times*, May 19, 1862. See also Heintzelman to J. G. Barnard, Mar. 23, 1863, HP; and Heintzelman to M[argaret] S. Heintzelman, May 6, 1862 (telegram), HP.

25. De Peyster, *Personal and Military History of Philip Kearny*, 295; HN, May 6, 1862.

26. HJ, May 6, 1862.

27. HJ, May 1, 1863. For a thorough analysis of casualties at the Battle of Williamsburg, see Dubbs, *Defend This Old Town*, 186–89. See also Wainwright, *Diary of Battle*, 55; Sears, *Gates of Richmond*, 82–83; and HJ, May 8, 10, 13, 1862. The general also discusses the "fearful" casualties in a letter to Margaret a few days after the battle. Heintzelman to Mrs. M. S. Heintzelman, May 14, 1862, HP. For his recollections of the battle, see Heintzelman to J. Watts de Peyster, Apr. 19, 1869, HP; and Heintzelman to de Peyster, Apr. 20, 1869, HP. Casualties are roughly calculated in HN, May 15, 1862.

28. HJ, May 6, 10, 1865; Hudson, *Civil War Williamsburg*, 24, 29; Dubbs, *Defend This Old Town*, 182; HN, May 6, 1862.

29. Dubbs, *Defend This Old Town*, 231. For Sneden's watercolor of the Mercer home and the nearby brick female seminary, both of which were used as hospitals for Union wounded, see *Images from the Storm*, 65; and Hudson, *Civil War Williamsburg*, 26–27.

30. HJ, May 12, 17, June 24, Aug. 23, 1865; *New York Daily Tribune*, May 15, 1862.

31. HJ, May 10, 12–13, 16, 20, 1862. "It is astonishing that even American history can be written so falsely and unjustly," the *New York Daily Tribune* wrote on May 15. Hancock's affair "was but a skirmish," the *Tribune* continued on May 16. "On the left, Heintzelman was compelled to fight a great battle of vastly more consequences than Bull Run," fighting for "six hours against the odds of three to one and against odds that disciplined troops never before encountered," the article went on to say.

32. HJ, May 11, 1862; Philip Kearny to Oliver S. Halsted, May 15, 1862, Lincoln Papers, LC. "I wish to bear testimony to the splendid conduct of Hooker's and Kearny's divisions under command of Gen. Heintzelman in the battle of Williamsburg," McClellan wrote. *New York Daily Tribune*, May 17, 1862.

33. HJ, May 17, 19, 1862. The unnamed officer, obviously from Kearny's division, while complaining of "favoritism, intrigue and confusion" in the Army of the Potomac, said that Heintzelman was "as stupid as antediluvian, although perhaps not a coward," and that he kept "at a distance from the balls." *New York Times*, May 17, 1862. The language and wording in the letter are amazingly similar to that found in Kearny's letters to his wife and other close colleagues.

34. HJ, May 11, 1862; *Speeches of William Curtis Noyes, Daniel S. Dickinson, and Lyman Tremain.*

35. HJ, May 6, 1862.

36. HN, May 10, 1862.

37. HJ, May 10, 1862; Sneden, *Images from the Storm*, 67; HN, May 12, 1862; Sears, *Gates of Richmond*, 85–86.

38. HJ, May 23, 1862. When the supply base was later abandoned, the White House Plantation was burned by some malicious and disobedient soldiers of the 93rd New York Infantry.

39. *Rochester Union & Advertiser*, June 5, 1862.

40. Sears, *Gates of Richmond*, 88–89; HJ, May 14–16, 1862; Sneden, *Images from the Storm*, 68; S. Williams to Heintzelman, May 13, 1862, HP.

41. S. Williams to Heintzelman, May 18, 1862, *OR*, 11(3):181; HN, May 18, 1862; Sneden, *Images from the Storm*, 69–70; S. Williams to Heintzelman, May 10, 1862, HP; *Rochester Union & Advertiser*, June 4, 1862; Alvan Beach to "Dear Sister," June 3, 1862, RBHP.

42. HJ, May 19, 1862.

43. HJ, [May 21], 1862; Sneden, *Images from the Storm*, 71.

44. HJ, [May 21], 1862. See also Sears, *Gates of Richmond*, 93–94.

45. HJ, [May 21], 1862; Sears, *Gates of Richmond*, 113.

46. Heintzelman to Henry Wilson, May 21, 1862, HP; HJ, May 21, 1862. Ernest McKay, in his biography *Henry Wilson*, makes no mention of Heintzelman's brief relationship with the senator.

47. Sears, *Gates of Richmond*, 110.

48. Marcy to Heintzelman, May 23, 24 (two letters), 25, 1862, HP; HJ, May 24–25, 1862; HN, May 25, 1862.

49. HJ, May 26, 1862.

50. HN, May 26, 27, 1862.

51. Savage's problems did not end with the Seven Days Battles. His wife died a few months later, and his house burned to the ground. Savage Family File, RNBP.

52. Heintzelman to Marcy, June 7, 1862, *OR*, 11(1):812–23; Mindil, *Battle of Fair Oaks*, 1–2; Heintzelman to George W. Mindil, June 8, 1874, Mindil Papers, USAMHI. Both Heintzelman and Hooker judged Mindil's article, which corrected much of what Johnston had written in his *Narrative of Military Operations, Directed, during the Late War between the States* (New York: D. Appleton, 1874) to be the most thorough and objective they had seen on the battle.

53. Sears, *Gates of Richmond*, 120; *New York Daily Tribune*, June 5, 1862; *New York Times*, June 3, 1862; HN, May 30, 1862. For Wilkeson on the Peninsula, see Crozier, *Yankee Reporters*, 239–40.

54. HN, May 30, 1862; Heintzelman, "Battle of Seven Pines," n.d., HP; Mindil, *Battle of Fair Oaks*, 2; Heintzelman to Marcy, June 7, 1862, *OR*, 11(1):813.

55. *U.S. Army and Navy Journal*, Oct. 31, 1874; *New York Daily Tribune*, June 2, 3, 1862; Sears, *Gates of Richmond*, 125; Squire Tuttle to "Dear Brother," June 12, 1862, Squire Tuttle Letters and Diary, USAMHI.

56. Heintzelman to George W. Mindil, June 8, Nov. 4, 1874, Mindil Papers, USAMHI. Heintzelman was later critical of Casey's testimony before the Joint Committee on the Conduct of the War, when Casey claimed that he had held his ground

for three hours. "Why if Gen. Casey's division held its ground so gallantly for three hours did he come to my Hd. Qrs. the next day and ask me to be as easy on them (the troops) as I could be," he wrote. Heintzelman, "Battle of Seven Pines," n.d., HP.

57. Sears, *Gates of Richmond*, 129; Sears, *George B. McClellan*, 194.

58. Heintzelman, "Battle of Seven Pines," n.d., HP. These rough notes were evidently prepared while contemplating his testifying before the Joint Committee on the Conduct of the War.

59. Heintzelman to "Comd'g Officer at the Entrenchments near Burnt Chimnies [*sic*]," May 31, 1861, Naglee Family Papers, Bancroft Library, University of California at Berkeley; Heintzelman to McClellan, May 31, 1861 (9:15 P.M.), *OR*, 51(1):646; R. B. March to E. V. Sumner, May 31, 1861, *OR*, 11(3):203.

60. Heintzelman to McClellan, May 31, 1861 (8:45 P.M.), *OR*, 51(1):645–46; Heintzelman to Marcy, May 31, 1861, ibid.; HJ, May 31, 1862; John H. B. Jenkins to Mary A. Benjamin, June 5, 1862, Hoar Papers, William and Mary College (typescript, RNBP); Haydon, *For Country, Cause, & Leader*, 246. See also McClellan to Heintzelman, May 31, 1862, HP; and Heintzelman to Mrs. S. P. Heintzelman, June 1, 1862, HP.

61. Heintzelman to Marcy, June 7, 1862, *OR*, 11(2):817; HJ, Feb. 28, 1866.

62. Sears, *Gates of Richmond*, 131; Heintzelman to Mindil, June 8, 1862, Mindil Papers, USAMHI; Marks, *Peninsula Campaign*, 201; Letter of Darius Vasbinder, *G.A.R. National Tribune*, July 8, 1901 (typescript, RNBP).

63. Heintzelman to Mindil, July 24, 1874, Mindil Papers, USAMHI.

64. Samuel A. Craig Diary, [May 31, 1862], USAMHI, transcript.

65. Mindil, *Battle of Fair Oaks*, 5–6.

66. Sears, *Gates of Richmond*, 136; Mindil, *Battle of Fair Oaks*, 9.

67. Mindil, *Battle of Fair Oaks*, 5; *New York Daily Tribune*, June 5, 1862. The *New York Times* stated that Heintzelman had been wounded. The newspaper later said, however, that the initial "report proved to be without foundation." *New York Times*, June 2, 1862.

68. HJ, May 31, 1861; Heintzelman to Marcy, June 7, 1862, *OR*, 11(2):814.

69. Heintzelman to Marcy, June 7, 1862, *OR*, 11(2):815; Heintzelman to Mindil, June 8, 1874, Mindil Papers, USAMHI; D. B. Birney to Heintzelman, June 3, 1862, HP; P. Kearny to Heintzelman, June 2, 1862, HP; *New York Daily Tribune*, June 6, 1862.

70. Marks, *Peninsula Campaign*, 190–93.

71. McClellan to Heintzelman, May 31, 1862 (5 P.M.), *OR*, 11(3):203; Heintzelman to McClellan, May 31, 1862 (8:45 P.M.), *OR*, 51(1):646; Heintzelman to McClellan, May 31, 1862 (9:15 P.M.), ibid., 647.

72. Heintzelman to Mindil, July 24, 1874, Mindil Papers, USAMHI; Mindil, *Battle of Fair Oaks*, 11; HJ, June 1, 1862.

73. HJ, May 31, 1862; Symonds, *Joseph E. Johnston*, 172; Newton, *Joseph E. Johnston and the Defense of Richmond*, 198.

74. Heintzelman to Mindil, July 24, 1874, Mindil Papers, USAMHI; Sears, *Gates of Richmond*, 138.

75. Sears, *Gates of Richmond*, 138.

76. Howard, *Autobiography*, 2:251.

77. Heintzelman to McClellan, June 1, 1862 (8:30 A.M.), *OR*, 51(1):649.

78. R. B. Marcy to Edwin M. Stanton, June 1, 1862, ibid., 648. See also Bellard, *Gone for a Soldier*, 81.

79. HJ, June 2, 1863.

80. McClelland quoted in Sears, *Gates of Richmond*, 145; HJ, June 2, 11, 1862. "You have done what I expected of you," McClellan also wrote. McClellan to Heintzelman, May 31, 1862, *OR*, 11(3):203; McClellan to Heintzelman, May 31, 1862, in Sears, *Civil War Papers of George B. McClellan*, 218–19.

81. HJ, June 2, 1862.

82. Bellard, *Gone for a Soldier*, 84–86.

83. Mindil, *Battle of Fair Oaks* 14; Heintzelman to Mindil, June 8, 1874, Mindil Papers, USAMHI; *New York Daily Tribune*, June 26, 1862.

84. *New York Daily Tribune*, June 26, 1862; *New York Times*, June 4, 5, 1862.

85. HJ, June 4, 8–9, 1862. "I buried a nephew yesterday, an acting captain in the New York 100th, whose body I recovered way in front of the bastioned fort beyond Casey's headquarters," Samuel Wilkeson wrote in the *New York Daily Tribune* on June 10, 1862. The captain had been "shot in the breast and lay in advance of all the dead on the field." Wilkeson would later lose his own son at Gettysburg, for which he would become much embittered toward the army. HJ, Feb. 28, 1866; Crozier, *Yankee Reporters*, 360–61.

86. Heintzelman to A. V. Colburn, June 2, 1862 (9 A.M.), *OR*, 51(1):654.

87. Heintzelman to General Marcy, June 2, 1862 (11:45 A.M.), ibid.; Joseph Hooker to C. McKeever, June 2, 1862, HP; Heintzelman to Mindil, June 8, 1874, Mindil Papers, USAMHI.

88. Sears, *George B. McClellan*, 195–96.

89. Mindil, *Battle of Fair Oaks*, 15.

90. *New York Times*, June 2, 1862.

9. Seven Harrowing Days

1. HJ, June 10, 1862. The sketch is not part of HP.

2. HJ, June 4, 1862.

3. HJ, June 2, 11, 1862.

4. HJ, June 12, 19, 1862.

5. HJ, June 15, 1862. Conkling, who commanded the 84th New York Infantry during the Shenandoah campaign, was the brother of Roscoe Conkling, representative from New York and the former mayor of Utica. *Biographical Directory of the American Congress*, 1009.

6. McClellan to Mary Ellen McClellan, June 9, 1862, in Sears, *Civil War Papers of George B. McClellan*, 293; Sears, *Gates of Richmond*, 160; HJ, June 8, 12, 19, 22, 24, 1862. Lisboa served as ambassador from 1859 to 1864. Lucia Harrington, e-mail message to author, Feb. 9, 2005.

7. HJ, June 5, 1862.

8. HJ, June 6, 19–20, 1862.

9. HJ, June 16–17, 1862. Birney went on to serve with distinction during the

war, even coming to command the III Corps after Gen. Dan Sickles was wounded at Gettysburg.

10. HJ, June 6, 17, 23, 1862.

11. HJ, June 22, 1862.

12. HJ, June 13, 1862.

13. Heintzelman to Williams, July 18, 1862, *OR,* 2(2):96; Burton, *Extraordinary Circumstances,* 42–43. Heintzelman kept a draft of this letter for his personal files. See also HJ, June 25, 1862.

14. Sears, *Gates of Richmond,* 186.

15. C. Grover to Jos. Dickinson, July 8, 1862, *OR,* 2(2):121; Joseph Hooker to Chauncey McKeever, July 14, 1862, ibid., 108–10; Heintzelman to General Marcy, June 25, 1862, ibid., 11(3):254; Burton, *Extraordinary Circumstances,* 47; Heintzelman to Williams, July 18, 1862, *OR,* 2(2):96.

16. G. A. De Russy to AAG, June 25, 1862, *OR,* 2(2):104; Burton, *Extraordinary Circumstances,* 48.

17. HJ, June 25–26, 1862; Burton, *Extraordinary Circumstances,* 47; Marcy to Heintzelman, June 25, 1862 (two orders), HP; McClellan to Heintzelman, June 25, 1862, HP.

18. HJ, June 26, 1862.

19. Heintzelman to Marcy, June 26, 1862, HP. In response to McClellan's article, "The Peninsular Campaign," published in *Century Magazine* in May 1885 (and later published as part of the *Battles and Leaders* collection), Mary Heintzelman used this particular letter to refute McClellan's claim that when he asked for reinforcements, all the corps commanders south of the Chickahominy "thought the enemy so strong in their respective fronts as to require all their force to hold their positions." See McClellan, "Peninsula Campaign," 180.

20. HJ, June 13, 1862.

21. HJ, June 26, 1862.

22. Sears, *Gates of Richmond,* 249.

23. Ibid.; HJ, June 27, 1862; Burton, *Extraordinary Circumstances,* 149; Wert, *Sword of Lincoln,* 107. Wert uses the Heintzelman quote as the title for his chapter on Seven Pines and the Seven Days.

24. HJ, June 27–28, 1862.

25. Sears, *Gates of Richmond,* 256; Joseph Hooker to Chauncey McKeever, June 27, 1862, *OR,* 11(3):265; HJ, June 30, 1862.

26. Sneden, *Eye of the Storm,* 68–69.

27. Ibid., 74; Marks, *Peninsula Campaign,* 238; Burton, *Extraordinary Circumstances,* 203; Georgia soldier quoted in Sears, *Gates of Richmond,* 283. Over a year later, many skeletons along with tons of ammunition and entrenching tools could be seen at Savage's Station. *Richmond Dispatch,* Oct. 26, 1863.

28. Heintzelman to [Margaret Heintzelman], July 2, 1862, HP.

29. Sneden, *Eye of the Storm,* 70.

30. Sears, *Gates of Richmond,* 272.

31. McClellan, "Peninsula Campaign," 183; Heintzelman to L. Thomas, Apr. 11, 1863, HP; HJ, June 30, 1862. See also Heintzelman to Williams, July 21, 1862, HP.

32. Heintzelman to [Margaret Heintzelman], July 2, 1862, HP; Sneden, *Eye of the Storm,* 81; Squire Tuttle to "Dear Brother," July 12, 1862, Squire Tuttle Letters and Diary, USAMHI.

33. Burton, *Extraordinary Circumstances,* 244.

34. Heintzelman to Williams, July 21, 1862, *OR,* 2(2):99; Sears, "Glendale," 16.

35. Sneden, *Images from the Storm,* 91; Sears, "Glendale," 22; John A. Faller to "Dear Folks," July 12, 1862, John and Leo Faller Letters, RNBP, typescript.

36. HJ, June 30, July 3, 1862; Sneden, *Eye of the Storm,* 98; Heintzelman to [Margaret Heintzelman], July 2, 1862, HP; Heintzelman to Williams, July 21, 1862, *OR,* 2(2):100. A copy of Heintzelman's battle report can also be found in HP.

37. Heintzelman to Williams, July 21, 1862, *OR,* 2(2):100; Sears, "Glendale," 23; Haydon, *For Country, Cause, & Leader,* 260.

38. Hooker quoted in Burton, *Extraordinary Circumstances,* 304.

39. Sears, "Glendale," 19; Thomas, "Battle of Glendale," 821.

40. Heintzelman to Williams, July 21, 1862, *OR,* 2(2):101; HJ, June 30, 1862.

41. Heintzelman to Williams, July 21, 1862, *OR,* 2(2):102; HJ, July 2–3, 1862.

42. Haydon, *For Country, Cause, & Leader,* 265–66. See also Wert, *Sword of Lincoln,* 118–19.

43. Sneden, *Images from the Storm,* 95.

44. Sneden, *Eye of the Storm,* 94–95; HJ, June 30, 1862; Heintzelman to Williams, July 24, 1861, HP.

45. Porter, "Battle of Malvern Hill," 416; Sneden, *Images from the Storm,* 97.

46. Averell, "With the Cavalry," 432; Sneden, *Images from the Storm,* 97.

47. For III Corps losses , see Heintzelman to Williams, July 24, 1862, HP.

48. Sneden, *Eye of the Storm,* 98.

49. Ibid., 100.

50. HJ, July 2, 1862; Heintzelman to [Margaret Heintzelman], July 2, 1862, HP.

51. Sneden, *Eye of the Storm,* 102; HJ, July 4–5, 1862; Edwin M. Stanton to Heintzelman, July 6, 1862, *OR,* 51(1):716; Sears, *Gates of Richmond,* 226–27. For a detailed sketch of the defenses of the III Corps at Harrison's Landing, see "Position of the 3rd Corps, A. P., at Harrison's Landing, James River, Virginia, July 9, 1862," Sneden Papers, VHS.

52. Donald, *Lincoln,* 359; HJ, July 8, 1862; Sneden, *Eye of the Storm,* 104.

53. Lincoln, "Memorandum on Interviews with Generals in the Army of the Potomac," July 9, 1862, Lincoln Papers, LC; HJ, July 9, 1862; Sears, *Gates of Richmond,* 350. For the strength of the III Corps after Malvern Hill by regiment, see Heintzelman to S[eth] Williams, July 15, 1862, HP.

54. Sneden, *Eye of the Storm,* 106–107. See also Scarborough, *Diary of Edmund Ruffin,* 399–400. Ironically, the owner of the plantation, a widow named Cox, had taken refuge at Harrison's Landing.

55. HJ, July 15, 1862.

56. HJ, July 31, 1862.

57. HJ, July 29, 1862; John A. Faller to "Dear Folks," July 12, 1862, Faller Letters, RNBP, typescript. For Heintzelman's opposition to withdrawing the Army of the Potomac from the Peninsula, see Sears, *George B. McClellan,* 241.

58. Margaret Heintzelman to Abraham Lincoln, Aug. 9, 1862, Lincoln Papers, LC; Heintzelman to E. M. Stanton, July 26, 1862, HP. Although Samuel Peter's letter to Margaret has been either lost or destroyed, his thoughts are reflected in his journal entries.

59. HJ, July 6, 11, 15, 1862.

60. HJ, July 20, Aug. 7, 1862. This photograph has been published. See *Lee Takes Command*, 74–75; and Thompson, *Fifty Miles and a Fight*, 41.

61. McClellan to Halleck, Aug. 5, 1862, *OR*, 1:77–78.

62. Sneden, *Eye of the Storm*, 113.

63. McClellan to Heintzelman, Aug. 19, 1862, *OR*, 12(3):599.

10. Failure at Second Bull Run

1. McClellan to Heintzelman, Aug. 20, 1862, *OR*, 12(3):607.

2. HJ, Aug. 26 [22], 1862.

3. R. B. Marcy to J. Pope, Sept. 5, 1862, *OR*, 51(1):788.

4. HJ, Aug. 23, 1862.

5. Ibid.; Strother, *Diaries*, 89; HJ, Aug. 26, 1862.

6. Cozzens, *General John Pope*, 116.

7. Ibid.; T. C. H. Smith to Heintzelman, Aug. 26, 1862, *OR*, 12(1):70; HJ, Aug. 27, 1862.

8. H. J. Bliss to Nelson Taylor, Aug. 28, 1862, *OR*, 12(2):450–51.

9. Hennessy, *Return to Bull Run*, 117–18.

10. Strother, *Diaries*, 89; Cozzens, *General John Pope*, 115; Bellard, *Gone for a Soldier*, 130.

11. Sneden, *Eye of the Storm*, 121–22; Hennessy, *Return to Bull Run*, 132–34; HJ, Aug. 31, 1862; M. Wm. Burns to Nelson Taylor, Sept. 5, 1862, 12(2):452–53. See also Heintzelman, "Second Bull Run Notes," Aug. 28, 1862, HP. These notes were probably prepared later in anticipation of testifying before the Joint Committee on the Conduct of the War.

12. *New York Daily Tribune*, Aug. 29, 1862; HJ, Aug. 31, 1862.

13. Heintzelman, "Second Bull Run Notes," Aug. 28, 1862, HP; Sneden, *Eye of the Storm*, 120; Vandiver, *Mighty Stonewall*, 361; Robertson, *Stonewall Jackson*, 557; Strother, *Diaries*, 91.

14. Heintzelman, "Second Bull Run Notes," Aug. 29, 1862, HP; Heintzelman to E. D. Townsend, Apr. 19, 1879, HP. For a sketch of III Corps's headquarters, see Sneden, *Eye of the Storm*, 125.

15. HJ, Aug. 29, 1862.

16. Heintzelman to George D. Ruggles, Oct. 21, 1862, *OR*, 12(2):413. See also Jno. Pope to Heintzelman, Aug. 28, 1862, ibid., 75 (copy in HP).

17. C. Grover to Jos. Dickinson, n.d., ibid., 439. See also Heintzelman to Ruggles, Oct. 21, 1862, ibid., 413.

18. C. Grover to Jos. Dickinson, n.d., ibid., 439–40. See also "Return of Casualties in the Union Forces, Commanded by Maj. Gen. John Pope, during the Operations August 16–September 2, 1862," n.d., ibid., 258.

19. Kearny quoted in Mathless, *Voices of the Civil War: Second Manassas*, 117.

20. HJ, Aug. 30, 1862; SO 10, Aug. 30, 1862 (midnight), HP.

21. Gibbon, *Personal Recollections*, 62–63. See also Heintzelman to Ruggles, Oct. 21, 1862, *OR*, 12(2):413; and Cozzens, *General John Pope*, 168.

22. Hennessy, *Return to Bull Run*, 311. See also Heintzelman, "Second Bull Run Notes," Aug. 30, 1862, HP.

23. Sneden, *Eye of the Storm*, 125; Strother, *Diaries*, 95–96; Cozzens, *General John Pope*, 176.

24. Martin, *Second Bull Run Campaign*, 247; HJ, Aug. 30, 1862.

25. Sneden, *Eye of the Storm*, 127.

26. Geo. D. Ruggles to Heintzelman, Aug. 30, 1862, HP.

27. Gibbon, *Personal Recollections*, 66–67.

28. Heintzelman, "Second Bull Run Notes," Aug. 30, 1862, HP; Heintzelman to Ruggles, Oct. 21, 1862, 12(2):414.

29. Confederate soldier quoted in Hennessey, *Return to Bull Run*, 441.

30. HJ, Aug. 30, 1862; Heintzelman to Ruggles, Oct. 21, 1862, *OR*, 12(2):414.

31. Sneden, *Images from the Storm*, 128.

32. Joseph Hooker to Chauncey McKeever, Aug. 31, 1862, 12(2):437; HJ, Aug. 31, Sept. 1, 1862, HP.

33. Jno. Pope to Major General Halleck, Sept. 1, 1862, 12(2):82–83.

34. See Sneden, *Images from the Storm*, 129.

35. Heintzelman to Ruggles, Oct. 21, 1862, 12(2):414; T. C. H. Smith to General [Heintzelman], Sept. 1, 1862, HP; Pope to Heintzelman, Sept. 1, 1862, HP.

36. De Peyster, *Personal and Military History of Philip Kearny*, 461–62; Sneden Diary, "Death of General Kearny," n.d., VHS. Specifics of the Battle of Chantilly, or Ox Hill, can be found in Welker, *Tempest at Ox Hill;* and Taylor, *He Hath Loosed the Fateful Lightning*.

37. Sneden wrote that the body had been "robbed of money, watch, diamonds, and everything valuable." There is no corroborating evidence, however, that Jackson's men looted the corpse. Sneden, *Eye of the Storm*, 132. See also HJ, Sept. 2, 1862; Hennessy, "Thunder at Chantilly," 58; and Hennessy, *Return to Bull Run*, 450. For Kearny's last report, see Kearny to Ruggles, Aug. 31, 1862, *OR*, 12(2):415–17. The inscription on the south end of the Kearny monument in Washington reads: "GAVE HIS LEFT ARM AT CHURUBUSCO, MEXICO AUGUST 18, 1847 AND HIS LIFE AT CHANTILLY, VIRGINIA SEPTEMBER 1, 1862."

38. Heintzelman to Ruggles, Oct. 21, 1862, *OR*, 12(2):414; Sneden, *Eye of the Storm*, 130. See also Bellard, *Gone for a Soldier*, 145. Winfield Scott called Kearny "the bravest man I ever met, and a perfect soldier."

39. HJ, Aug. 31, 1862.

40. HJ, Sept. 4, 1862; Cozzens, *General John Pope*, 201; Jno. Pope to G. W. Cullum, Jan. 27, 1863, *OR*, 12(2):47.

41. "Return of Casualties in the Union Forces Commanded by Maj. Gen. John Pope, during the Operations August 16–September 2, 1862," *OR*, 12(2):257–58; H. W. Halleck to E. M. Stanton, Nov. 25, 1862, ibid., 8.

42. Hennessy, *Return to Bull Run*, 464.

11. A City of Shoulder Straps

1. Sneden Diary, Sept. 10, 1862, VHS; HJ, Sept. 15, 1862.

2. HJ, Sept. 7, 16, 18, 1862. On October 7, 1862, expecting a desperate fight near Winchester, Virginia, McClellan had telegraphed Halleck requesting reinforcements, including Heintzelman's old corps. George B. McClellan to Henry W. Halleck, Oct. 7, 1862, Lincoln Papers, LC.

3. R. Butler Price to Chauncey McKeever, Sept. 25, 1862 *OR,* 19(2):3–4; HJ, Sept. 20, 23, 1862.

4. N. C. McLean to J. Stahel, Sept. 29, 1862, *OR,* 19(2):5–6; HJ, Sept. 25–26, 31 [Oct. 1], 1862; Joseph Kargé to Heintzelman, Oct. 1, 1862, *OR,* 19(2):8; Heintzelman to Sigel, Oct. 7, 1862, ibid., 9.

5. HJ, Oct. 14, 1862.

6. HJ, Sept. 10, 1862; C. H. Porter, GO 11, Dec. 6, 1862, *OR,* 21:836; GO 2, Sept. 12, 1862, HP; GO 20, Jan. 1, 1863, HP.

7. HJ, Nov. 3, 1862.

8. Tripler, *Eunice Tripler,* 140, 143.

9. HJ, Oct. 31, 1862.

10. Edmund J. Davis to Heintzelman, Aug. 8, 1862, HP.

11. Ibid.; HJ, Nov. 4, 9, Dec. 6, 1862.

12. HJ, Dec. 6, 1862.

13. HJ, Oct. 16–17, 1862.

14. Leech, *Reveille in Washington,* 211, 220; HJ, Dec. 10, 1862, Jan. 29, 1863.

15. Heintzelman to J. G. Parke, Jan. 14, 1863, *OR,* 21:970.

16. J. G. Barnard to Heintzelman, Jan. 7, 1863, *OR,* 21:954–55; "Abstract from Return of the Department of Washington, Maj. Gen. Samuel P. Heintzelman, Commanding, for Feb. 28, 1863," *OR,* 25(2):112; J. G. Barnard to Heintzelman, Mar. 31, 1863, ibid., 177.

17. Testimony of Gen. S. P. Heintzelman, Dec. 5, 1862, *OR,* 12(1):74–75.

18. Testimony of Gen. S. P. Heintzelman, Dec. 12, 1862, *OR,* 12(2):900–902; HJ, Jan. 22, 24, 1863.

19. HJ, Dec. 15–17, 25, 1862.

20. HJ, Jan. 5, 1863; Heintzelman to G. W. Cullum, Jan. 3, 1863, *OR,* 21:706–707; Heintzelman to J. G. Parke, Dec. 29, 1862, ibid., 898; J. J. Abercrombie to Heintzelman, Dec. 31, 1862, ibid., 923.

21. Horatio Nelson Taft Diary, Jan. 1, 1863, LC; HJ, Jan. 2, 1863.

22. HJ, Oct. 15, 18, 24, 1862.

23. HJ, Jan. 28, 1862. Before the war the three-story red-brick building had been the home of John B. Floyd, the former secretary of war and Virginia politician who became a general in the Confederate Army.

24. *Washington Daily Morning Chronicle,* Jan. 31, 1863. Heintzelman seemed perturbed that Forney or one of his editors had used "was" instead of "were," "there" instead of "their," and misspelled Kearny as "Kearney," a common mistake at the time.

25. Taft Diary, Jan. 13, 1863, LC; HJ, Feb. 16, 1863.

26. HJ, Mar. 20, 1863.

27. *Battle of Bull Run,* 346–66; Tap, *Over Lincoln's Shoulder,* 156–59; HJ, Feb. 17, 1863.

28. Ramage, *Gray Ghost,* 63–76; Siepel, *Rebel,* 74–77. Only twenty-five years old at the time, Stoughton was the youngest general in the Union Army.

29. Heintzelman to General Schenck, May 14, 1863, *OR,* 51(1):1041; Cooling, *Symbol, Sword, and Shield,* 144; Ramage, *Gray Ghost,* 36–119.

30. HJ, Mar. 21–22, 1863.

31. HJ, Mar. 23, Apr. 13, 1863.

32. HJ, Jan. 15, Apr. 18, 25, 1863. See also Abraham Lincoln, "Memorandum on West Point Recommendations," Apr. 23, 1863, Lincoln Papers. LC; and various letters in West Point Application Papers of Charles Heintzelman, AGO, RG 94, NA.

33. HJ, May 3–4, 7, 20, 1863.

34. HJ, June 13, 15, 17, 25, 1863; Heintzelman to Halleck, June 25, 1863, *OR,* 27(3):323. See also J. G. Barnard to Heintzelman, Mar. 31, 1863, *OR,* 25(2):177–85; and Heintzelman to Halleck, May 17, 1863, ibid., 499–500.

35. HJ, Apr. 19, June 10, 1863; Sneden Diary, June 9, 1863, VHS.

36. J. G. Barnard to Heintzelman, June 25, 1863, *OR,* 27(3):331.

37. Halleck to Heintzelman and George G. Meade, July 26, 1863, *OR,* 27(1):102; Stanton to Halleck, June 30, 1863, *OR,* 27(3):429; Heintzelman to Stanton, June 30, 1863, ibid., 429–30; Barnard to Heintzelman, July 4, 1863, ibid., 526.

38. Cooling, *Symbol, Sword, and Shield,* 157; Sneden Diary, June 15, 1863, VHS; HJ, June 30, 1863.

39. Sneden Diary, June 30, 1863, VHS; HJ, June 16, 20, 23, 1863.

40. HJ, June 28, 1863.

41. HJ, July 3–4, 1863; Sneden Diary, July 7, 1863, VHS.

42. HJ, July 18, Aug. 31, 1863.

43. HJ, July 5, 17, 1863.

44. HJ, July 8, 22, 1863.

45. HJ, July 11, 15, Aug. 19, Sept. 6–7, 25, 1863. Governor Gurley died on the way west and was replaced by John N. Goodwin.

46. HJ, Aug. 20, 1863.

47. HJ, Aug. 29, 1863.

48. J. H. Taylor to C. R. Lowell, Aug. 15,1863, *OR,* 29(2):53; HJ, Sept. 17, 1863.

49. Mosby, *Memoirs,* 259–65; D. C. McCallum to Halleck, Oct. 2, 1863, *OR,* 29(2):253.

50. HJ, Sept. 28, 1863; A. A. Humphries to Heintzelman, Aug. 10, 1863, *OR,* 29(2):23; Elias M. Greene to J. H. Taylor, ibid., 255–56. From his headquarters in Alexandria, Brig. Gen. John P. Slough with 867 infantry was responsible for protecting the railroads nearer Washington.

51. Heintzelman endorsement on C. H. Potter to J. H. Taylor, Oct. 3, 1863, *OR,* 29(1):203. Halleck concurred with the recommendation, and Stanton ordered Keays dismissed.

52. Heintzelman to Halleck, Oct. 2, 1863, *OR,* 29(2):253–54; HJ, Oct. 2, 1863; Mosby, *Memoirs,* 265–66.

53. Lee, *Wartime Washington,* 186; HJ, Oct. 6, 1863.

54. HJ, Oct. 15, 17, 19, 1863.

55. HJ, Oct. 6, 1863.

56. HJ, Nov. 3, Dec. 3, 1863.

57. HJ, Nov. 25, 1863. For Heintzelman advising the War Department on Texas, see Heintzelman to Stanton, July 15, 1864, HP. See also Heintzelman to [William] Dennison, Nov. 15, 1864, HP.

58. Taft Diary, Dec. 20, 1863, LC.

59. HJ, Jan. 2, 1864.

60. HJ, Jan. 12–13, 1864; E. D. Townsend to Heintzelman, Jan. 12, 1864, HP; GO 17, Jan. 12, 1864, HP.

61. For example, all but thirty-five men from the 128th Illinois, a regiment recruited from the "Butternut" counties of southern Illinois, had deserted early in 1863. When other Illinois regiments learned of the Emancipation Proclamation, half the men left their units, arguing that the war had become one of slave liberation rather than preservation of the Union.

62. Klement, *Limits of Dissent,* 150–60.

63. HJ, Jan. 15, 1864.

12. Copperheads and Prison Camps

1. HJ, Jan. 20, 1864.

2. Klement, *Copperheads in the Middle West,* 275–76.

3. *Columbus Daily Ohio State Journal,* Feb. 2, 1864; McPherson, *Ordeal by Fire,* 448–49.

4. Churchill, "Liberty, Conscription, and a Party Divided," 295.

5. Speer, *Portals to Hell,* 46–47; HJ, Jan. 26, 1864.

6. Speer, *Portals to Hell,* 148–49; HJ, Feb. 21, 1864.

7. HJ, Feb. 12, 1864.

8. Heintzelman to B. F. Butler, Feb. 17, 1864, HP; HJ, Feb. 18, 1864. The letter to Butler is also in *OR,* 51(1):1287–89. See also HJ, Feb. 17, Apr. 1, 1864.

9. HJ, Feb. 25, 1863. See also *Cincinnati Daily Enquirer,* Feb. 26, 1864.

10. Halleck to Heintzelman, Mar. 2, 1864, *OR,* ser. 3, 4:149; Heintzelman to Halleck, Apr. 8, 1864, ibid., 221–22.

11. Heintzelman to Halleck, Mar. 5, 1864, ibid., 155.

12. HJ, Mar. 7, 16, 1864; Lambert, "Basil Wilson Duke," 498; Warner, *Generals in Gray,* 77; HJ, Oct. 8, 1864. Heintzelman kept several newspaper clippings relating to this incident for his files. See "A Noted Guerilla Chieftain Feasted in Our City," "The Case of Basil Duke," and "Not So," n.d., HP.

13. Julius White to Heintzelman, Mar. 28, 1864, *OR,* 32(3):178; Heintzelman to White, 29, 1864, ibid., 190; Heintzelman to Captain Hill, ibid.; HJ, Mar. 29, Apr. 1, 1864. See also Tibbals, "'There has been a serious disturbance at Charleston,'" 10–16. Details of the Coles County revolt can be found in the *Daily Ohio State Journal,* Mar. 28, Apr. 4, 5, 7, 1864. For the Copperhead view of what happened, see *Dayton Daily Empire,* Apr. 1, 1864. The *Chicago Tribune,* a Republican publication, and the *Chicago Times,* a Copperhead organ, also covered the Coles County violence in considerable

detail. See also *Cincinnati Daily Enquirer*, Mar. 31, Apr. 1, 4, 1864; and Barry, "Charleston Riot," 82–106.

14. James Oakes to Heintzelman, Mar. 30, 1864, *OR*, 32(3):198; Heintzelman to C. H. Potter, Mar. 30, 1864, ibid., 198; Halleck to Heintzelman, Apr. 8, 1864, *OR*, 33:826; Sherman to Heintzelman, May 31, 1864, *OR*, 38:368.

15. Halleck to Heintzelman, Apr. 8, 1864, *OR*, 33:826.

16. McAdams, *Rebels at Rock Island*, 45–55; Speer, *Portals to Hell*, 155, 174; Heintzelman to Halleck, July 5, 1864, *OR*, 37(2):70.

17. Heintzelman to Halleck, July 5, 1864, *OR*, 37(2):71; Sherman to Heintzelman, *OR*, 38(4):368. Most of this same document is in *OR*, 39(2):164.

18. Heintzelman to Halleck, Aug. 15, 1864, *OR*, 39(2):255–56; *Daily Ohio State Journal*, Mar. 22, 1864.

19. Heintzelman to Halleck, Apr. 1, 1864, *OR*, 32(3):218. Hearing such rumors, Brig. Gen. Henry D. Terry had proceeded to Ontario and, with Canadian authorities, had gone to Rondeau on the north shore of Lake Erie, where the vessel in question was located and found to be unarmed. Terry did report, however, that "many rebel refugees" were organizing at Windsor. Henry D. Terry to Carroll H. Potter, Mar. 29, 1864, ibid., 219.

20. Davis, *Official Military Atlas of the Civil War*, plate 65; Speer, *Portals to Hell*, 77–78, 184–85; HJ, Apr. 1, 1864.

21. Heintzelman to Halleck, Apr. 2, 1864, *OR*, 32(3):236; HJ, Mar. 23, Apr. 22, 29, June 12, 1864; Klement, *Limits of Dissent*, 183–85; Heintzelman to Halleck, Mar. 29, 1864, *OR*, 32(1):629.

22. *Daily Ohio State Journal*, Jan. 19, Apr. 19, 26, May 7, 1864. See also Heintzelman to W. S. Rosecrans, June 14, 1864, William Starke Rosecrans Papers, Special Collections, University of California, Los Angeles.

23. Speer, *Portals to Hell*, 75–77, 197–98.

24. HJ, June 8, 24, 1864. The Copperhead *Dayton Daily Empire* reported Vallandigham's return on June 16, 1864, as did most Midwestern newspapers, including the *Cincinnati Daily Enquirer*, June 18, 1864.

25. HJ, June 14–15, 1864; Klement, *Limits of Dissent*, 275–76.

26. Klement, *Limits of Dissent*, 276; HJ, June 17, 1864.

27. Lincoln to Brough and Heintzelman, June 20, 1864, Lincoln Papers, LC. The envelope contains the statement "Not Sent." See also HJ, June 15, 1864; and Klement, *Limits of Dissent*, 276–77.

28. HJ, June 29, 1864; Klement, *Copperheads in the Middle West*, 194–95.

29. *History of Delaware and Ohio*, 248–49. See also *Daily Ohio State Journal*, May 28, 1864.

30. HJ, May 7, Aug. 19, 1864.

31. HJ, July 4, 1864.

32. *Daily Ohio State Journal*, May 12, 13, 1864; HJ, May 9, 13, 1864.

33. HJ, Aug. 15, 1864.

34. HJ, July 26, Sept. 5, 1864.

35. HJ, Aug. 6, Sept. 9, 1864.

36. HJ, Aug. 15, 1864; Halleck to Heintzelman, Apr. 23, 1864, *OR*, 33:955.

37. S. G. Burnbridge to Heintzelman, Aug. 12, 1864, *OR*, 39(2):243; Henry B. Carrington to S. H. Lathrop, Aug. 24, 1864, ibid., 295; Carrington to Lathrop, Aug. 24, 1864, ibid., 296; Halleck to Heintzelman, Aug. 28, 1864, ibid., 312.

38. Heintzelman to Halleck, Sept. 3, 1864, ibid., 341. See also *Cincinnati Daily Enquirer*, Aug. 30, 1864.

39. Speer, *Portals to Hell*, 71–72, 181–82. See also Levy, *To Die in Chicago*, 349–64.

40. Sears, *George B. McClellan*, 374; *Daily Ohio State Journal*, Aug. 30, 31, Sept. 1, 1864.

41. Edwin M. Stanton to Heintzelman, Sept. 11, 1864, HP; HJ, Aug. 30, 1864; Sherman, *Recollections of Forty Years*, 293–94.

42. Sherman, *Recollections of Forty Years*, 342; HJ, Sept. 2, 1864.

43. HJ, Aug. 17, Sept. 3, 1864. For his views on Sherman's "March to Sea," see Heintzelman to E. D. Mansfield, Nov. 23, 1864, HP.

44. HJ, Sept. 12, 1864; Heintzelman to E. M. Stanton, Sept. 16, 1864, HP. See also "Extract of Telegram Received from Stanton," n.d., HP; and GO 64, Sept. 17, 1864, HP.

45. HJ, Sept. 12, 1864.

46. HJ, Sept. 16, 1864.

47. Klement, *Limits of Dissent*, 246; Warner, *Generals in Blue*, 333–34; HJ, Sept. 13, 1864.

48. Stanton to Heintzelman, Sept. 20, 1864, *OR*, 39(2):426; Heintzelman to Stanton, Sept. 20, 1864, ibid.; HJ, Sept. 22–23, 1864.

49. Frohman, *Rebels on Lake Erie;* HJ, Sept. 23–24, 1864; Downer, "Johnson's Island," 108–109. For the Southern account of the attempt to rescue the Johnson Island prisoners, see "The Plan to Rescue the Johnston's [*sic*] Island Prisoners: Captain Robert D. Minor's Report," *Southern Historical Society Papers* 23 (Jan.–Dec. 1895): 283–90, Southern Crossroads, http://www.csa-dixie.com/csa/prisoners/t67.htm. (This Web site also includes other items pertaining to the Johnson Island prison as well as other prisoner-of-war compounds in the Northern Department.) For his part in the scheme, Yates was later apprehended and hanged.

50. HJ, Sept. 24–25, 1864; Judith Ledbetter, Charles City County Historical Society, Charles City, Va., telephone conversation with author, July 12, 2004; John M. Coski, Museum of the Confederacy, Richmond, Va., telephone conversation with author, July 12, 2004; Bob Krick, RNBP, interview by author, July 12, 2004; Christine Joyce, curator, Shirley Plantation, Va., interview by author, June 19, 2004.

51. HJ, Sept. 29–30, 1864. The news was also briefly reported in the *Daily Ohio State Journal*, October 3, 4, 1864; and *Cincinnati Daily Enquirer*, Oct. 5, 1864. See also Herbert, *Fighting Joe Hooker*, 289.

52. HJ, Sept. 30, Oct. 1, 4, Dec. 26, 1864; E. D. Townsend, GO 263, Sept. 28, 1864, *OR*, 39(2):515. The orders are reprinted in *Daily Ohio State Journal*, Oct. 4, 1864.

53. HJ, Oct. 4, 14, 1864.

54. HJ, Oct. 7, 1862.

55. HJ, Nov. 7, 14, 16, 19, 1864.

56. HJ, Oct. 12, 27, Nov. 5, 1864.

57. HJ, Nov. 9, 1864.

58. HJ, Nov. 20, Dec. 18, 1864, Jan. 29, 1865. Five years later Heintzelman was still angry at Stanton for his "exile" at Wheeling. See Heintzelman to Rosecrans, Mar. 16, 1870, Rosecrans Papers.

59. SO 429, Dec. 3, 1864, HP; HJ, Dec. 4, 24, 1864, Jan. 1, 12, 30, Mar. 9, 21, 1865. For other complaints against Stanton, see Heintzelman to J. A. Garfield, Jan. 21, 1865, HP.

60. HJ, Feb. 4, 1865.

61. HJ, Feb. 22, Mar. 10, 1865.

62. HJ, Apr. 3, 1865. For Heintzelman's views on ending the war, see Heintzelman to the Editor, *New York Times*, Dec. 28, 1864, HP.

63. HJ, Apr. 15, 27, 1865.

64. HJ, Apr. 27–28, May 22, 1865.

65. HJ, May 6, 1865.

66. HJ, May 23–24, 1865; Marszalek, *Sherman*, 355–57; *Daily National Intelligencer*, May 22–25, 1865; McPherson, *Ordeal by Fire*, 486.

67. *Washington Daily National Intelligencer*, June 12, 1865; *New York Times*, June 12, 13, 1865. For other articles by reporters covering the dedication, see *Washington Evening Star*, June 12, 1865; *New York Herald*, June 13, 1865; and *Harpers Weekly*, July 1, 1865.

68. HJ, June 10, 1865. After receiving several complaints of human remains remaining unburied on the battlefield, in June 1866 the army sent a party to collect as many of the bones of the Union dead as possible. Sam'l R. Fisher to Gen. Meigs, June 16, 1866, Dedication File, Manassas National Battlefield Park, Manassas, Va. For another photograph of the dedication of the monument at the First Bull Run battlefield, see Davis, *Battle of Bull Run*, 58.

69. HJ, July 31, Aug. 24, 1865.

70. HJ, July 3, 1865.

71. HJ, June 30, July 5, 9, 1865.

72. *Daily National Intelligencer*, July 26, 27, Aug. 9, 1865; HJ, July 30, Aug. 8–9, 27, 1865.

73. *Daily National Intelligencer*, Aug. 1, 5, 9, 1865.

74. HJ, July 21, Aug. 28–30, 1865. On being mustered out of volunteer service, see GO 135, Aug. 24, 1865, HP.

75. HJ, Sept. 7, 1865.

76. HJ, Sept. 28, 1865.

77. HJ, Mar. 3, 1866.

78. HJ, Sept. 27,1865.

79. HJ, Nov. 13, 17, 1865.

80. HJ, Dec. 5, 1865; [Heintzelman], "Samuel P. Heintzelman," 37–38.

81. HJ, Dec. 16, 25, 1865, Jan. 5, 10, 1866. Indeed, a few days later, when Sweeny led the Fenians on a half-hearted invasion of Canada, he was dismissed from the army. On November 8, 1866, he was restored to duty.

82. Herbert, *Fighting Joe Hooker*, 291.

83. HJ, Feb. 5, 1866.

13. The Turmoil of Texas Reconstruction

1. HJ, Apr. 13–17, 1866.

2. Hutton, *Phil Sheridan and His Army*, 2.

3. HJ, Apr. 18, 1866.

4. Richter, "'Best to Go in Strong-Handed,'" 137–39. See also *Flake's Daily Galveston Bulletin*, Apr. 25, 26, 27, 1866; and *Galveston Daily News*, Apr. 26, 1866.

5. HJ, Apr. 26, 1866.

6. Wooster, *Texas and Texans in the Civil War*, 185; *Houston Tri-Weekly Telegraph*, Jan. 9, 1867; HJ, July 4, 1866.

7. HJ, May 2, 4, 11–12, 15–16, 1866; *Dallas Herald*, May 26, 1866.

8. HJ, Apr. 12, June 6, 9, July 25, 27, Aug. 10, 1866. Heintzelman described Mary Maverick in his journal as a "pleasant middle aged woman."

9. Moneyhon, *Texas after the Civil War*, 52; HJ, Aug. 14, 1866.

10. HJ, July 4, 9, 1866; Sobré, *San Antonio on Parade*, 39.

11. HJ, June 28, July 19, 1866; Austerman, *Sharps Rifles and Spanish Mules*, 203; *Galveston Daily News*, July 26, 1866; Heintzelman to R. M. Morris, June 5, 1866, LS Letterbook, District of Texas and Subdistrict of San Antonio, AGO, RG 393, NA. See also HP, July 26, 1866.

12. HJ, July 25, 1866.

13. HJ, Oct. 10–13, 1866.

14. HJ, July 30, Aug. 2, 15, 1866. Heintzelman had always liked Plympton, a West Point graduate who had been brevetted for gallantry at the Battle of Valverde in New Mexico Territory early in the war.

15. HJ, Sept. 3, 4, 1866; SO 4, Sept. 6, 1866, LS Letterbook, AGO, RG 393, NA; SO 9, Sept. 15, 1866, ibid.; SO 11, Sept. 17, 1866; ibid.

16. HJ, Sept. 14, 16, 22, 24–25, 1866. See also Heintzelman to J. H. Lyons, Oct. 1, 1866, LS Letterbook, Central District of Texas and Subdistrict of San Antonio, AGO, RG 393, NA.

17. Heintzelman to Throckmorton, Aug. 28, 1866, Throckmorton Papers, TSA; *Dallas Herald*, Sept. 22, 1866; HJ, Sept. 4–5, 1866.

18. HJ, Sept. 5–6, 1866.

19. Elliott, *Leathercoat*, 138; Sheridan to Heintzelman, Oct. 15, 1866, Throckmorton Papers, TSA; Rister, *Border Command*, 32; Hutton, *Phil Sheridan and His Army*, 25.

20. J. B. Walker et al. to Governor Throckmorton, Sept. 3, 1866, Throckmorton Papers, TSA; Jno. A. Wallace to W. B. Knox, Sept. 24, 1866, ibid.; Heintzelman to Throckmorton, Oct. 26, 1866, ibid.

21. Sheridan to Heintzelman, Nov. 6, 1866, Throckmorton Papers, TSA; Elliott, *Leathercoat*, 142–43; HJ, Nov. 6, 1866; Sheridan to Throckmorton, Nov. 3, 1866, Throckmorton Papers, TSA.

22. Sheridan to Throckmorton, Oct. 9, Nov. 11, 1866, Throckmorton Papers, TSA; Stanton to Throckmorton, n.d., in *Dallas Weekly Herald*, Oct. 11, 20, 1866; Elliott, *Leathercoat*, 141.

23. Richter, *Overreached on All Sides*, 141; HJ, Sept. 22, Oct. 23, 1866; *Galveston Tri-Weekly News*, Nov. 2, 1866.

24. HJ, Nov. 13, 1866, Jan. 14, 1867.

25. Heintzelman to Thaddeus Stevens, Feb. 16, 1867, HP; HJ, Oct. 30, 1866.

26. HJ, Nov. 4, 21–23, Dec. 12, 1866; Richter, *Overreached on All Sides*, 142–43.

27. Heintzelman to Throckmorton, Sept. 3, 1866, Throckmorton Papers, TSA. See also Heintzelman to Throckmorton, Sept. 12, 1866, LS Letterbook, Central District of Texas and Subdistrict of San Antonio, AGO, RG 393, NA; GO 44, July 6, 1866, in *Dallas Herald*, Nov. 17, 1866.

28. Heintzelman to Throckmorton, Sept. 29, 1866, Throckmorton Papers, TSA; Heintzelman to Throckmorton, Sept. 14, 1866, ibid. These same letters are in LS Letterbook, Central District of Texas and Subdistrict of San Antonio, AGO, RG 393, NA.

29. Robert D. Tippett to Throckmorton, Aug. 20, 1866, Throckmorton Papers, TSA; Heintzelman to Throckmorton, Sept. 12, 1866, LS Letterbook, Central District of Texas and Subdistrict of San Antonio, AGO, RG 393, NA; Richter, *Army in Texas during Reconstruction*, 63–64.

30. Morris, *Life and Wars of General Phil Sheridan*, 277.

31. Richter, *Overreached on All Sides*, 128, 131; Richter, "Brenham Fire of 1866," 287–314; Richter, *Army in Texas during Reconstruction*, 64–65. McGary's *Banner* boasted of subscription rates of three dollars a year for loyal Southern whites and six dollars for "Yankees, Carpetbaggers, and Scalawags."

32. John P. White et al. to Throckmorton, Oct. 8, 1866, Throckmorton Papers, TSA; Richter, *Overreached on All Sides*, 134.

33. Ireland quoted in Richter, *Overreached on All Sides*, 135. After being removed by Sheridan as an "impediment to Reconstruction," Ireland was elected to the legislature, where he gained the sobriquet "Oxcart John" for his opposition to giving railroads land and subsidies. He was elected governor in 1882 and reelected in 1884.

34. HJ, Dec. 8, 1866; J. P. Hatch to AAG, Dec. 11, 1866, HP. See also Heintzelman to W. C. Wiseman, July 26, 1866, LS Letterbook, Central District of Texas and Subdistrict of San Antonio, AGO, RG 393, NA.

35. James Wilcox to Sheriff of Galveston County, Dec. 11, 1866, HP; HJ, Dec. 20–22, 1866; Heintzelman statement, Dec. 21, 1866, HP.

36. HJ, Dec. 23, 1866; D. J. Baldwin to Heintzelman, Dec. 29, 1866, HP.

37. HJ, Dec. 8, 20, 1866; Heintzelman to Thaddeus Stevens, Feb. 16, 1867, HP; *Galveston Daily News*, Jan. 10, 1867; *New Orleans Daily Picayune*, Jan. 10, 1867; Baldwin to Heintzelman, Dec. 29, 1866, HP.

38. *Galveston Tri-Weekly News*, Nov. 21, 1866; Richter, *Army in Texas during Reconstruction*, 70. The two "old" cannon were not the "Twin Sisters" of San Jacinto fame, as one might speculate. Jeff Dunn, e-mail to author, Mar. 9, 2005.

39. Heintzelman to J. R. Doolittle, Dec. 12, 1866, HP; HJ, Nov. 30, 1866; Heintzelman to Geo. W. Schofield, Jan. 12, 1867, HP; Heintzelman to Edgar Cowan, Jan. 28, 1867, HP.

40. Heintzelman to Throckmorton, Dec. 1, 1866, Throckmorton Papers, TSA; HJ, Dec. 9, 1866; *Dallas Herald*, Dec. 29, 1866; *New Orleans Daily Picayune*, Jan. 6, 1867; *Galveston Daily News*, Jan. 18, 1862.

41. Thompson, "When General Albert Sidney Johnston Came Home," 453–78.

42. Chas. Griffin to C. H. Leonard, cited in *Flake's Daily Galveston Bulletin*, Jan. 25, 1867. Sadly, General Griffin fell victim to the devastating yellow fever epidemic that began in Galveston and swept the Texas gulf coast and hinterland in the summer of 1867, killing thousands, including the general and his son on Sept. 15, 1867.

43. Hutton, *Phil Sheridan and His Army*, 22.

44. HJ, Jan. 24, 1867.

45. *New Orleans Daily Picayune*, Jan. 26, 1867; *Galveston Daily News*, n.d., quoted in Johnston, *Life of Albert Sidney*, 706; *Flake's Daily Galveston Bulletin*, Jan. 25, 1867.

46. *Flake's Daily Galveston Bulletin*, Jan. 26, 1867.

47. *Galveston Daily News*, Jan. 26, 1867.

48. HJ, Jan. 25, 1867; *Flake's Daily Galveston Bulletin*, Jan. 26, 1867.

49. *Galveston Daily News*, Jan. 26, 1867.

50. Ibid. See also *Dallas Herald*, Feb. 16, 1867.

51. HJ, Apr. 22, May 14–15, 1867.

52. [Heintzelman], "Harbor Defences," 588–89; HJ, Apr. 14, 1867. Several articles appeared in the *Army and Navy Journal* after Heintzelman mentioned writing a response on March 12, 1867. The short article that appeared on April 13, 1867, and signed "Pleutz" appears to match his ideology and writing style, though he may be the author of a second article entitled "Bands in the Army," which appeared on April 20.

53. HJ, Nov. 3, Dec. 28, 1866; *Flake's Weekly Galveston Bulletin*, Jan. 2, 1867; *New York Times*, Jan. 10, 1867. Ehrenberg scholar James E. Crisp has astutely observed that the *New York Times*, in reprinting the obituary, replaced the word "paw" with "hand." Crisp, "In Pursuit of Herman Ehrenberg," 435. The Library of Congress has the only hard copy of this particular issue of *Flake's Weekly Galveston Bulletin*. James E. Crisp to author, Dec. 29, 2003.

54. HJ, Apr. 19, May 10, 1867.

55. *Galveston Daily News*, Jan. 3, 1867; HJ, Jan. 6, 13–14, 22, 1867.

56. HJ, Jan. 26, Feb. 3, 10, 1867.

57. HJ, Feb. 4, Apr. 9, 1867.

58. Moneyhon, *Texas after the Civil War*, 75–76.

59. *Army and Navy Journal*, Jan. 19, 1867; HJ, Jan. 10, 28, Apr. 21, 1867; Heintzelman to G. Marston, Jan. 29, 1867, HP; Heintzelman to Edgar Cowan, Jan. 28, 1867, HP.

60. HJ, Apr. 30, June 3–5, 7, 13–14, 19, 1867.

14. Back in Washington

1. HJ, July 12, 18–19, 24, 1867.

2. *New York Daily Tribune*, Oct. 2, 1867.

3. Heintzelman to E. D. Townsend, Oct. 11, 1867, HP; HJ, Oct. 10, Dec. 6, 1867, Mar. 14, 1868; *Buffalo Commercial Advertiser*, Oct. 14, 28, 1867; *Galveston Daily News*, Oct. 12, 1867. The *Galveston Daily News*, in announcing Lathrop's death a second time in its October 17 edition, reported him to be "respected and esteemed as a judicious and humane officer."

4. HJ, Dec. 5, 11, 31, 1867.

5. HJ, July 1, 18, Oct. 3, 1868.

6. HJ, Sept. 25, 1868.

7. GO 47, Apr. 28, 1869, HP; GO 7, Feb. 28, 1869, HP. See also HJ, Feb. 10, 1869; George W. Woodward et al. to the President, Dec. 11, 1868, HP; Woodward et al. to the President, Dec. 11, 1869, HP; Edmund L. Gould et al. to the President, Jan. 13, 1869, HP; Horatio Seymour to Pres. Johnson, Dec. 11, 1868, HP; Millard Fillmore to Heintzelman, Dec. 17, 1868, HP; Washington McLean to [Andrew Johnson], Dec. 22, 1868, HP; T. Wrightson to H. Groesbeck, Dec. 23, 1868, HP; and Heintzelman to Johnson, Dec. 11, 1868, HP.

8. HJ, Feb. 26, Mar. 12, 1869. For his retirement at the rank of major general, see GO 47, Apr. 29, 1869, HP.

9. HJ, May 17–18, 1869.

10. HJ, Aug. 19, 1869.

11. HJ, July 9, 1869.

12. HJ, Apr. 12, 1870.

13. HJ, Nov. 21, Dec. 6, 9, 1869, Apr. 19, 1870.

14. *Buffalo Express*, Feb. 7, 1870; HJ, Mar. 25, 1870.

15. HJ, Dec. 31, 1870. See also Heintzelman to Rosecrans, July 12, 1870, William Starke Rosecrans Papers, Special Collections, University of California, Los Angeles.

16. HJ, Dec. 31, 1870, Jan. 14, 28, 1871.

17. HJ, May 18, June 28, Oct. 22, 1871.

18. HJ, Aug. 18, 1871.

19. HJ, Jan. 6, 1872.

20. HJ, Feb. 14, Apr. 3, 1872.

21. HJ, Apr. 23, May 17, 1872. Heintzelman, of course, had no knowledge of Hernando de Alarcon's ascent and descent of the lower Colorado River as part of Francisco Vasquez de Coronado's expedition in 1540.

22. HJ, June 25, 1872.

23. HJ, Aug. 10, 12–14, 1872.

24. *Tucson Arizona Weekly Star*, May 13, 1880.

25. HJ, Nov. 15, 19, Dec. 14, 30, 1872; *Tucson Arizona Weekly Star*, May 13, 1880.

26. HJ, Dec. 31, 1872. Since Heintzelman left no indication that he was ending his journal in December 1872, it is probable that he continued with yet another book and that somehow it was lost in the years that followed. Possibly, Mary chose, for unknown personal reasons, not to donate it to the Library of Congress along with her father's other papers.

27. Heintzelman to George W. Mindil, Nov. 29, 1873, Mindil Papers, USAMHI; Mindil, *Battle of Fair Oaks*, 1–16. See also O. M. Poe to Heintzelman, June 3, 1874, Mindil Papers, USAMHI; and Heintzelman to Mindil, July 21, 1864, ibid. Joseph E. Hooker, however, wrote Mindil agreeing with Johnston's assessment of Fair Oaks. Highly critical of McClellan as well as Halleck, who he called the "evil geniuses of our war," Hooker recalled observing Johnston during the Seminole and Mexican wars and remembering him "as the best field soldier I had ever seen." Hooker to Mindil, Jan. 12, 1875, ibid.

28. Heintzelman to Mindil, Nov. 29, 1873, Mindil Papers, USAMHI; Heintzel-

man to Mindil, June 8, 1874, ibid. The lengthy study was later published in English in three volumes in the United States.

29. *Tucson Arizona Weekly Star*, May 13, 1880; *Manheim Sentinel*, Aug. 6, 1875; Heintzelman to Rufus Ingalls, Mar. 16, 1876, HP; *Annual Reunion of the National Association of Veterans of the Mexican War held in Baltimore, Md., Feb. 22, 1878* (Thos. J. Brashears: Washington, D.C., 1878), copy in William Watts Hart Davis Papers, Beinecke Library, Yale University, New Haven, Conn.; *Manheim Sentinel*, Aug. 26, 1898. In December 1882, when the Civil War veterans in Manheim met to organize what became Post No. 300 of the Grand Army of the Republic, the chapter was named in Heintzelman's honor.

30. Will of S. P. Heintzelman, May 17, 1875, Research Library, San Diego Historical Society, San Diego, Calif.; *New York Times*, May 2, 4, 1880; Poston, "In Memoriam"; *Manheim Sentinel*, May 7, 1880; "Maj. Gen. Samuel P. Heintzelman," misc. newspaper obituary, n.d., HP; *Eleventh Annual Reunion of the Association of the Graduates of the U.S. Military Academy*, 103–104; *Return of the Graduates of the U.S. Military Academy, June 9, 1881* (East Saginaw: E. W. Lyon, 1881), 35–36; *Biographical Register of the Officers and Graduates of the U.S. Military Academy*, 372–74; De Peyster, *Obituary Notice of Maj.-Gen. Samuel P. Heintzelman*, 6–14; *Buffalo Commercial Advertiser*, May 3, 4, 13, 1880. See also Forest Lawn Cemetery, http://www.forest-lawn.com. Heintzelman's friends, Bennett Riley and Millard Fillmore, are also buried in the cemetery.

Margaret Stuart Heintzelman died on August 9, 1893, at Boyce, Virginia, in the countryside west of Washington. She was buried next to her husband in Buffalo's Forest Lawn Cemetery three days later. Mary Heintzelman, their beloved daughter, who struggled most of her adult life to protect her father's Civil War reputation, died on March 24, 1927, and was also buried in Buffalo next to her parents. North, *Samuel Peter Heintzelman*, 190; *Buffalo Courier*, Aug. 13, 1893; Tombstone data and photographs, Forest Lawn Cemetery (courtesy of Charles E. Chambers).

Capt. Charles Stewart Heintzelman, after serving in Texas and at various posts in Florida and the trans-Mississippi, died of disease only ten months after his father on February 17, 1881, at the age of thirty-five in Washington, D.C. *Buffalo Commercial Advertiser*, Mar. 3, 1881.

The Heintzelmans' grandson, Stuart "Tommy" Heintzelman, born in New York City in 1876 and educated abroad and at Groton, Connecticut, graduated from West Point in 1899. He served in the Philippines, the Boxer Rebellion, and as a military instructor at Princeton University in 1916. He fought with the American Expeditionary Force at St. Mihiel during World War I and was an observer with the French Army and later on the Italian front during the winter of 1917. He received a number of French and Italian medals, including the Croix de Guerre and the Order of the Crown. He was promoted to brigadier general in 1922 and major general in 1931. Gen. Stuart Heintzelman died at Hot Springs, Arkansas, July 6, 1935. *Sixty-Seventh Annual Report of the Association of Graduates of the United States Military Academy*, 209–12.

31. *Tucson Arizona Weekly Star*, May 13, 1880.

Bibliography

Manuscripts and Archival Collections

Agricultural Census (1860). Cameron County, Tex. National Archives, Washington, D.C.

Battalion Returns. Companies D, H (2nd Infantry). Adjutant General's Office. Record Group 94. National Archives, Washington, D.C.

Beach, Alvan. Typescript. Richmond National Battlefield Park. Richmond, Va.

Bradley, Charles E. Papers. Special Collections, Alderman Library, University of Virginia, Charlottesville.

Brownsville City Council Minutes (1850–59). City Secretary's Office, Brownsville, Tex.

Cameron County Commissioner's Court Minutes (1848–62). County Clerk's Office, Brownsville, Tex.

Cameron County District Court Minutes (1849–1914). Office of the District Clerk, Brownsville, Tex.

Craig, Samuel A. Diary (transcript). U.S. Army Military History Institute, Carlisle Barracks, Pa.

Davis, William Watts Hart. Papers. Beinecke Library, Yale University, New Haven, Conn.

Ehrenberg, Hermann. *Map of the Gadsden Purchase, Sonora, and Portions of New Mexico, Chihuahua, and California* (1854). Arizona Historical Society Library, Tucson.

Eighth Census (1860). National Archives, Washington, D.C.: Arizona County, N.M. Terr.; Bandera County, Tex.; Bexar County, Tex.; Cameron County, Tex.; San Diego County, Calif.

Ford, John S. Memoirs. Center for the Study of American History, University of Texas at Austin.

Hawley, Edmund. Letters. U.S. Army Military History Institute, Carlisle Barracks, Pa.

Heintzelman, Samuel Peter. Papers and Journals. Manuscripts Division, Library of Congress, Washington, D.C.: Journals, 1825–72; Letterbooks, 1836, 1841–42, 1846, 1850–54, 1859–60, 1862; Military Papers (Orders, Furloughs, Commissions, Circulars, Field Returns, Casualty Lists), 1822–69; Miscellaneous Correspondence, 1830–85; Miscellaneous Newspaper Clippings, 1860–80; Notebooks,

1862–63; Pocket Diaries, 1832–33, 1847–50, 1853–65; Survey Books, 1833, 1851–52; Telegrams, 1861–65, 1878.

———. Will and List of Property. Research Library, San Diego Historical Society, San Diego, Calif.

———. "Journal of S. P. Heintzelman, U.S. Army, while a Cadet in the Military Academy, West Point, New York, from January 1, 1825, to August 2, 1826." Special Collections, U.S. Military Academy Library, West Point, N.Y.

Heintzelman Cullum File. Special Collections, U.S. Military Academy Library, West Point, N.Y.

Hidalgo County Commissioner's Court Minutes (1852–1912). Rio Grande Valley Historical Collection, University of Texas Pan American Library, Edinburg.

Hidalgo County District Court Minutes (1853–1912). Rio Grande Valley Historical Collection, University of Texas Pan American Library, Edinburg.

Hoar, Henry C. Papers. Archives, William and Mary College, Williamsburg, Va.

Houston, Sam. Papers. Record Group 301, Texas State Archives, Austin.

Kingsburg, Gilbert. Papers. Center for the Study of American History, University of Texas at Austin.

Letters Received, Adjutant General's Office. Record Group 94, National Archives, Washington, D.C.

Letters Received, Central District of Texas and Subdistrict of San Antonio. Record Group 393, National Archives, Washington, D.C.

Letters Received, Military District of Washington (March 1862–December 1864). Record Group 393, National Archives, Washington, D.C.

Letters Sent, Military District of Washington (March 1862–December 1864). Record Group 393, National Archives, Washington, D.C.

Letters Sent Book, Army of the Potomac, Heintzelman's Division (October 1861–62). Record Group 393, National Archives, Washington, D.C.

Letters Sent Letterbook, Central District of Texas and Subdistrict of San Antonio. Record Group 393, National Archives, Washington, D.C.

Lincoln, Abraham. Papers. Manuscript Division, Library of Congress, Washington, D.C.

Lowe, Thaeddeus Sobieski Constantine. Papers. Manuscript Division, Library of Congress, Washington, D.C.

McClellan, George B. Papers. Manuscript Division, Library of Congress, Washington, D.C.

Mindil, George W. Papers. U.S. Army Military History Institute, Carlisle Barracks, Pa.

Moore, William A. Reminiscences. U.S. Army Military History Institute, Carlisle Barracks, Pa.

Naglee Family. Papers. Bancroft Library, University of California, Berkeley.

Nichols, Charles. H. Papers. Library of Congress, Washington, D.C.

Plumb, Edward Lee. Papers. Archives, Stanford University, Palo Alto, Calif.

Post Returns, Adjutant General's Office. Record Group 393, National Archives, Washington, D.C.: Camp Verde, Tex.; Fort Brown, Tex.; Fort Duncan, Tex.; Fort Yuma, Calif.; Ringgold Barracks, Tex.

Regimental Returns, Adjutant General's Office. Record Group 94. National Archives, Washington, D.C.: 1st Infantry, 2nd Infantry, 3rd Infantry.

Rosecrans, William Starke. Papers. Special Collections, University of California, Los Angeles.

Rosenkranz, Frasier. Letters. U.S. Army Military History Institute, Carlisle Barracks, Pa.

San Roman, José. Papers. Center for the Study of American History, University of Texas at Austin.

Seventh Census (1850). National Archives, Washington. D.C.: Bexar County, Tex.; Cameron County, Tex.; San Diego County, Calif.

Sneden, Robert Knox. Diary and Papers. Virginia Historical Society, Richmond.

Starr County Commissioner's Court Minutes (1852–1923). Rio Grande Valley Historical Collection, University of Texas Pan American Library, Edinburg.

Texas Adjutant General's Records. Texas State Archives, Austin.

Third Census (1810). National Archives, Washington, D.C.: Lancaster County, Pa.

Throckmorton, James W. Papers. Texas State Archives, Austin.

Tuttle, Squire. Letters and Diary. U.S. Army Military History Institute, Carlisle Barracks, Pa.

Warner, J. J. Papers. Arizona Historical Society Library, Tucson.

Warren, E. Willard. Papers. Duke University Library, Durham, N.C.

West Point Application Papers of Samuel Peter Heintzelman. Adjutant General's Office. Record Group 94, National Archives, Washington, D.C.

West Point Application Paper of Charles Heintzelman. Adjutant General's Office. Record Group 94, National Archives, Washington, D.C.

Government Publications

Emory, William H. *Report of the United States and Mexican Boundary Survey, Made under the Direction of the Secretary of the Interior.* 34th Cong., 1st sess.

Ives, Joseph Christmas. *Report upon the Colorado River of the West, explored in 1857 and 1858 by Lt. Joseph C. Ives, Corps of Topographical Engineers, under the direction of the Office of Exploration and Surveys, A. A. Humphreys, Captain Topographical Engineers, in Charge.* Washington, D.C.: Government Printing Office, 1861.

Message from the President of the United States to the Two Houses of Congress at the Commencement of the Second Session of the Thirty-Fifth Congress. 35th Cong., 2nd sess., 1858, Exec. Doc. 2, vol. 2.

Reports of the Committee of Investigation sent in 1873 by the Mexican Government to the Frontier of Texas. New York: Baker and Godwin, 1875.

U.S. House. *Difficulties on the Southwestern Frontier.* 36th Cong., 1st sess., H. Doc. 52.

U.S. House. *Message from the President of the United States Transmitting Report in Regard to Indian Affairs on the Pacific.* 34th Cong., 3rd sess., H. Doc. 76.

U.S. House. *Organization of Territory of Arizona.* 34th Cong., 3rd sess., H. Rpt. 117.

U.S. House. *Reconnaissance of Routes from San Antonio to El Paso.* 31st Cong., 1st sess., S. Doc. 64.

U.S. House. *Texas Frontier Troubles.* 44th Cong., 1st sess., H. Doc. 81.

U.S. House. *Trouble on Texas Frontier.* 36th Cong., 1st sess., H. Doc. 127.

U.S. Senate. *Hostilities on the Rio Grande.* 36th Cong., 1st sess., S. Doc. 21.

U.S. Senate. *Report of the Secretary of the Interior.* 31st Cong., 1st sess., S. Doc. 34.

War Department. *War of the Rebellion: A Compilation of the Official Records of the Union and Confederate Armies.* 128 vols. Washington, D.C.: Government Printing Office, 1889.

Books

Acken, J. Gregory, ed. *Inside the Army of the Potomac: The Civil War Experience of Captain Francis Adams Donaldson.* Mechanicsburg, Pa.: Stackpole, 1998.

Adams, Michael C. C. *Fighting for Defeat: Union Military Failures in the East, 1861–1865.* Lincoln: University of Nebraska Press, 1992.

Aldrich, Thomas M. *The History of Battery A: First Regiment Rhode Island Light Artillery in the War to Preserve the Union, 1861–1865.* Providence: Snow and Farnham, 1904.

Altshuler, Constance Wynn, ed. *Latest from Arizona: The Hesperian Letters, 1859–1861.* Tucson: Arizona Pioneers' Historical Society, 1969.

———. *Cavalry Yellow & Infantry Blue: Army Officers in Arizona between 1851 and 1886.* Tucson: Arizona Historical Society, 1991.

Amberson, Mary Margaret McAllen, et al. *I Would Rather Sleep in Texas: A History of the Lower Rio Grande Valley & the People of the Santa Anita Land Grant.* Austin: Texas State Historical Association, 2003.

Ambrose, Stephen E. *Duty, Honor, Country: A History of West Point.* Baltimore: Johns Hopkins University Press, 1999.

———. *Halleck: Lincoln's Chief of Staff.* Baton Rouge: Louisiana State University Press, 1962.

Arnold, James R. *Jeff Davis's Own: Cavalry, Comanches, and the Battle for the Texas Frontier.* New York: John Wiley and Sons, 2000.

Austerman, Wayne. *Sharps Rifles and Spanish Mules: The San Antonio–El Paso Mail.* College Station: Texas A&M University Press, 1985.

Averell, William Woods. *Ten Years in the Saddle.* Edited by Edward K. Eckett and Nicholas J. Amato. San Rafael, Calif.: Presidio, 1978.

Ball, Durwood. *Army Regulars on the Western Frontier, 1848–1861.* Norman: University of Oklahoma Press, 2001.

Barnard, John G. *The Peninsular Campaign and its Antecedents as Developed by the Report of Maj. Gen. George B. McClellan.* New York: D. Van Nostrand, 1864.

Barnard, John G., and W. F. Barry. *Report of the Engineer and Artillery Operations of the Army of the Potomac from Its Organization to the Close of the Peninsular Campaign.* New York: D. Van Nostrand, 1863.

Barrett, Edwin S. *What I Saw at Bull Run.* Boston: Beacon, 1886.

Bartlett, John Russell. *Personal Narrative of Explorations and Incidents in Texas, New Mexico, California, Sonora, and Chihuahua Connected with the United States Boundary Commission during the Years 1850, '51, '52, and '53.* Chicago: Rio Grande Press, 1965.

Battle of Bull Run: Extracted from U.S. Congress, Joint Committee on the Conduct of the War. Millwood, N.Y.: Kraus Reprint, 1977.

Bauer, K. Jack. *The Mexican War: 1846–1848.* New York: Macmillan, 1974.

Bausman, Lottie M. *A Bibliography of Lancaster County, Pennsylvania, 1743–1912.* Philadelphia: Patterson and White, 1916.

Bay, Betty. *Historical Brownsville: Original Townsite Guide.* Brownsville: Brownsville Historical Association, 1980.

Baylor, George Wythe. *Into the Far, Wild Country: True Tales of the Old Southwest.* Edited by Jerry Thompson. El Paso: Texas Western Press, 1996.

Beatie, R. H., Jr., *Road to Manassas: The Growth of Union Command in the Eastern Theatre from the Fall of Fort Sumter to the First Battle of Bull Run.* New York: Cooper Square, 1961.

Bellard, Alfred. *Gone for a Soldier.* Edited by David Herbert Donald. Boston: Little, Brown, 1975.

Biographical Directory of the American Congress, 1774–1949. Washington, D.C.: Government Printing Office, 1950.

Biographical Register of the Officers and Graduates of the U.S. Military Academy at West Point, N.Y. Vol. 1. Boston: Riverside, 1891.

Blackwell, Creola, transc. *Samuel P. Heintzelman's Journal: 1851–1853, Fort Yuma.* Yuma, Ariz.: Yuma County Historical Society, 1989.

Blake, Henry N. *Three Years in the Army of the Potomac.* Boston: Lee and Shepard, 1865.

Bosse, David. *Civil War Newspaper Maps: A Historical Atlas.* Baltimore: Johns Hopkins University Press, 1991.

Boyd, Eva Jolene. *Noble Brutes: Camels on the American Frontier.* Plano, Tex.: Republic of Texas Press, 1995.

Brooks, Nathan Covington. *A Complete History of the Mexican War, 1846–1848.* Chicago: Rio Grande Press, 1965.

Burton, Brian K. *Extraordinary Circumstances: The Seven Days Battles.* Bloomington: Indiana University Press, 2001.

Butterworth, Samuel F. *Arizona Mining Company.* N.p., 1864.

Campbell, Randolph B. *Grass-Roots Reconstruction in Texas.* Baton Rouge: Louisiana State University Press, 1997.

Carpenter, John A. *Sword and Olive Branch: Oliver Otis Howard.* New York: Fordham University Press, 1999.

Casdorph, Paul D. *Prince John Magruder: His Life and Campaigns.* New York: John Wiley & Sons, 1996.

Chatfield, W. H. *Twin Cities of the Border and the Country of the Lower Rio Grande.* New Orleans: E. P. Brandao, 1893.

Cheeseman, Bruce S., ed. *My Dear Henrietta: Hiram Chamberlain's Letters to His Daughter, 1846–1866.* Kingsville: King Ranch, 1993.

Clarke, Dwight L. *Stephen Watts Kearny: Soldier of the West.* Norman: University of Oklahoma Press, 1961.

Clement, Edward Henry. *The Bull Run Rout: Scenes Attending the First Clash of Volunteers in the Civil War.* Cambridge: John Wilson and Son, 1909.

Coker, Caleb, ed. *The News from Brownsville: Helen Chapman's Letters from the Texas Military Frontier, 1848–1852*. Austin: Texas State Historical Association, 1992.

Comte de Paris. *History of the Civil War in America*. Vol. 1. Philadelphia: Jos. H. Coates, 1875.

Conyngham, David Porter. *The Irish Brigade and Its Campaigns*. New York: Fordham University Press, 1994.

Cook, Joel. *The Siege of Richmond: A Narration of the Military Operations of Major-General George B. McClellan*. Philadelphia: George W. Childs, 1862.

Cooling, Benjamin Franklin, III. *Symbol, Sword, and Shield: Defending Washington during the Civil War*. Hamden, Conn.: Archon, 1975.

Cooling, Benjamin Franklin, III, and Walton H. Owen II. *Mr. Lincoln's Forts: A Guide to the Civil War Defenses of Washington*. Shippensburg, Pa.: White Mane, 1988.

Copeland, Fayette. *Kendall of the Picayune*. Norman: University of Oklahoma Press, 1943.

Coski, John M. *The Army of the Potomac at Berkeley Plantation: The Harrison's Landing Occupation of 1862*. N.p., 1989.

Cox, Joseph D. *The Second Battle of Bull Run as Connected with the Fitz-John Porter Case*. Cincinnati: Peter G. Thomson, 1882.

Cozzens, Peter. *General John Pope: A Life for the Nation*. Urbana: University of Illinois Press, 2000.

Crouch, Barry. *The Freedman's Bureau and Black Texans*. Austin: University of Texas Press, 1992.

Crozier, Emmet. *Yankee Reporters, 1861–65*. New York: Oxford University Press, 1956.

Cullen, Joseph C. *The Peninsula Campaign 1862: McClellan and Lee Struggle for Richmond*. Harrisburg, Pa.: Stackpole, 1973.

Cullum, George W. *Biographical Register of the Officers and Graduates of the U.S. Military Academy at West Point, N.Y., from Its Establishment, in 1802, to 1890*. Vols. 1, 3. Cambridge, Mass.: Riverside, 1891.

Current, Richard Nelson. *Lincoln's Loyalists: Union Soldiers from the Confederacy*. Boston: Northeastern University Press, 1992

Daddysman, James W. *The Matamoros Trade: Confederate Commerce, Diplomacy, and Intrigue*. Cranbury, N.J.: University of Delaware Press, 1984.

Davis, Burke. *Jeb Stuart: The Last Cavalier*. New York: Wings, 1957.

Davis, George B., et al., *The Official Military Atlas of the Civil War*. New York: Gramercy, 1983.

Davis, William C. *Battle at Bull Run: A History of the First Major Campaign of the Civil War*. Baton Rouge: Louisiana State University Press, 1977.

Dawes, Rufus. *Service with the Sixth Wisconsin Volunteers*. Edited by Alan T. Nolan. Madison: State Historical Society of Wisconsin, 1962.

Dawson, Joseph G. *Army Generals and Reconstruction: Louisiana, 1862–1877*. Baton Rouge: Louisiana State University Press, 1982.

De Cordova, J. *Texas: Her Resources and Her Public Men*. Waco: Texian Press, 1969.

De Leon, Arnoldo. *They Called Them Greasers: Anglo Attitudes towards Mexicans in 19th Century Texas*. Austin: University of Texas Press, 1983.

———. *Mexican Americans in Texas: A Brief History*. Arlington Heights, Ill.: Harlan Davidson, 1992.

De Peyster, John Watts. *The Anniversary Address Delivered before the Third Corps Union, 5th May, 1875, the Glorious Old Fighting Third Corps, as We Understand It.* New York: Atlantic, 1875.

———. *Obituary Notice of Maj.-Gen. Samuel P. Heintzelman, First Commander of the Third Army Corps.* New York: Charles H. Ludwig, 1881.

———. *Personal and Military History of Philip Kearny, Major-General United States Volunteers.* New York: Rice and Gage, 1869.

———. *With the Army of the Potomac: Address Delivered after the Anniversary Dinner of the Third Corps Union, 5th May, 1887, at the Hotel Windsor, New York.* New York: n.p., 1887.

Derby, George H. *Derby's Report on the Opening of the Colorado, 1850–1851.* Albuquerque: University of New Mexico Press, 1969.

De Trobriand, Regis. *Four Years with the Army of the Potomac.* Translated by George K. Dauchy. Boston: Ticknor and Fields, 1989.

Dobie, J. Frank. *A Vaquero of the Brush Country.* Austin: University of Texas Press, 1965.

Donald, David Herbert. *Lincoln.* New York: Simon and Schuster, 1995.

Doubleday, Abner. *My Life in the Old Army: The Reminiscences of Abner Doubleday.* Edited by Joseph E. Chance. Fort Worth: Texas Christian University Press, 1998.

Dowdey, Clifford. *The Seven Days: The Emergence of Lee.* Boston: Little, Brown, 1964.

Dubbs, Carol Kettenburg. *Defend This Old Town: Williamsburg during the Civil War.* Baton Rouge: Louisiana University Press, 2002.

Eby, Cecil D., Jr., ed. *A Virginia Yankee in the Civil War: The Diaries of David Hunter Strother.* Chapel Hill: University of North Carolina Press, 1961.

Eckenrode, H. J., and Bryan Conrad. *George B. McClellan.* Chapel Hill: University of North Carolina Press, 1941.

Edge, Frederick Milnes. *Major-General McClellan and the Campaign on the Yorktown Peninsula.* London: Trubner, 1865.

Edwards, E. I., ed. *The Whipple Report: Journal of an Expedition from San Diego, California, to the Rio Colorado, from September 11 to December 11, 1849.* Los Angeles: Westernlore, 1961.

Edwards, William B. *The Story of Colt's Revolver: The Biography of Col. Samuel Colt.* Harrisburg, Pa.: Stackpole, 1957.

Eleventh Annual Reunion of the Association of the Graduates of the U.S. Military Academy at West Point, New York, June 17, 1880. East Saginaw: E. W. Lyon, 1880.

Elliott, Claude. *Leathercoat: The Life of James W. Throckmorton.* San Antonio: Standard Printing, 1938.

Emmett, Chris. *Texas Camel Tales.* Austin: Steck-Vaughn, 1969.

Evans, Charles M. *War of the Aeronauts: A History of Ballooning in the Civil War.* Mechanicsburg, Pa.: Stackpole, 2002.

Fifth Annual Reunion of the National Association of Veterans of the Mexican War held in Baltimore, Md., February 22, 1878. Washington, D.C.: Alexander M. Kenaday, 1878.

Fischel, Edwin C. *The Secret War for the Union: The Untold Story of Military Intelligence in the Civil War.* Boston: Houghton Mifflin, 1996.

Folkman, David I., Jr. *The Nicaragua Route.* Salt Lake City: University of Utah Press, 1972.

Ford, John Salmon. *Rip Ford's Texas.* Edited by Stephen B. Oates. Austin: University of Texas Press, 1963.

Fornell, Earl Wesley. *The Galveston Era: The Texas Crescent on the Eve of Secession.* Austin: University of Texas Press, 1876.

Frazer, Robert W. *Forts and Supplies: The Role of the Army in the Economy of the Southwest, 1846–1861.* Albuquerque: University of New Mexico Press, 1983.

———. *Forts of the West.* Norman: University of Oklahoma Press, 1965.

———, ed. *Mansfield on the Condition of the Western Forts, 1853–54.* Norman: University of Oklahoma Press, 1963.

Freeman, Douglas Southall. *R. E. Lee: A Biography.* New York: Scribner's Sons, 1934.

Frohman, Charles E. *Rebels on Lake Erie.* Columbus: Ohio Historical Society, 1965.

Fry, James B. *McDowell and Tyler in the Campaign of Bull Run, 1861.* New York: Van Nostrand, 1884.

Fulton, Eleanor Jane, and Barbara Kendig Mylin, comps. *An Index to the Will Books and Interstate Records: Lancaster County, Pennsylvania, 1729–1850.* Book 50, Vol. 1. N.p., 1936.

Furgurson, Ernest B. *Freedom Rising: Washington in the Civil War.* New York: Alfred A. Knopf, 2004.

Gallagher, Gary W., ed. *The Richmond Campaign of 1862: The Peninsula & the Seven Days.* Chapel Hill: University of North Carolina Press, 2000.

Garrison, Nancy Scripture. *With Courage and Delicacy, the Civil War on the Peninsula: Women and the U.S. Sanitary Commission.* New York: Da Capo, 1996,

Garza, Israel Cavazos. *Diccionario Biografico de Nuevo León.* Monterrey: Universidad Autonoma de Nuevo León, 1984.

Gerson, Noel B. *Sad Swashbuckler: The Life of William Walker.* Nashville: Thomas Nelson, 1976.

Gibbon, John. *Personal Recollections of the Civil War.* Dayton, Ohio: Morningside, 1988.

Goff, John S. *Charles D. Poston.* Cave Creek, Ariz.: Black Mountain, 1995.

Goldfinch, Charles W., and Jose T. Canales. *Juan N. Cortina: Two Interpretations.* New York: Arno, 1974.

Goss, Thomas J. *The War within the Union High Command: Politics and Generalship during the Civil War.* Lawrence: University Press of Kansas, 2003.

Govan, Gilbert E., and James W. Livingwood. *A Different Valor: Joseph E. Johnston.* New York: Konecky & Konecky, 1956.

Grimm, Agnes. G. *Llanos Mestenas, Mustang Plains.* Waco: Texian, 1972.

Hall, Martin H. *Confederate Army of New Mexico.* Austin: Presidial, 1978.

Hastings, Earl C., Jr., and David Hastings. *A Pitiless Rain: The Battle of Williamsburg, 1862.* Shippensburg, Pa.: White Mane, 1997.

Haydon, Charles B. *For Country, Cause, & Leader: The Civil War Journal of Charles B. Haydon.* Edited by Stephen W. Sears. New York: Ticknor & Fields, 1993.

Haydon, F. Stansbury, *Military Ballooning during the Early Civil War.* Baltimore: Johns Hopkins University Press, 1941.

Hays, Gilbert Adams, comp. *Under the Red Patch: Story of the Sixty-Third Regiment*

Pennsylvania Volunteers, 1861–1864. Pittsburgh: Sixty-Third Pennsylvania Volunteers Regimental Association, 1908.

Hazen, William B. *A Narrative of Military Service.* Huntington, W.Va.: Blue Acorn, 1993.

Hebert, Rachel Bluntzer. *The Forgotten Colony, San Patricio de Hibernia.* Burnet, Tex.: Eakin, 1981.

Heitman, Francis B. *Historical Register and Dictionary of the United States Army, from Its Organization, September 29, 1789, to March 2, 1903.* 2 vols. Washington: Government Printing Office, 1903.

Hennessy, John J. *The First Battle of Manassas: An End to Innocence, July 18–21, 1861.* Lynchburg: H. E. Howard, 1989.

———. *Return to Bull Run: The Campaign and Battle of Second Manassas.* New York: Simon & Schuster, 1993.

Herbert, Walter H. *Fighting Joe Hooker.* Lincoln: University of Nebraska Press, 1999.

Hesseltine, William B., and Hazel C. Hesseltine. *The Blue and the Gray on the Nile.* Chicago: University of Chicago Press, 1961.

Hicken, Victor. *Illinois in the Civil War.* Urbana: University of Illinois Press, 1991.

History of Delaware and Ohio. Chicago: O. L. Baskins, 1880.

Holden, Edward S., ed. *Biographical Register of the Officers and Graduates of the U.S. Military Academy at West Point, New York.* Cambridge, Mass.: Riverside, 1901.

Howard, Oliver Otis. *Autobiography of Oliver Otis Howard, Major General United States Army.* 2 vols. New York: Baker and Taylor, 1907.

Hudson, Carson O., Jr. *Civil War Williamsburg.* Williamsburg: Colonial Williamsburg Foundation, 1997.

Hudson, Linda S. *Mistress of Manifest Destiny: A Biography of Jane McManus Storm Cazneau, 1807–1878.* Austin: Texas State Historical Association, 2001.

Hughes, W. J. *Rebellious Ranger: Rip Ford and the Old Southwest.* Norman: University of Oklahoma Press, 1964.

Hunter, J. Marvin. *Old Camp Verde, the Home of the Camels: A Romantic Story of Jefferson Davis' Plan to Use Camels on the American Frontier.* Bandera, Tex.: Frontier Times, 1948.

Hurlbert, William Henry. *General McClellan and the Conduct of the War.* New York: Sheldon, 1864.

Hutton, Paul Andrew. *Phil Sheridan and His Army.* Lincoln: University of Nebraska Press, 1985.

Ives, Joseph Christmas. *Report upon the Colorado River of the West, Explored in 1857 and 1858 by Lt. Joseph C. Ives, Corps of the Topographical Engineers, under the Direction of the Office of Exploration and Surveys, A. A. Humphreys, Captain, Topographical Engineers, in Charge.* Washington, D.C.: Government Printing Office, 1861.

Jackson, Jack. *Los Mestenos, Spanish Ranching in Texas, 1721–1821.* College Station: Texas A&M University Press, 1986.

Jacob, Kathryn Allamong. *Testament to Union: Civil War Monuments in Washington, D.C.* Baltimore: Johns Hopkins University Press, 1998.

Jenkins, John H., ed. *Robert E. Lee on the Rio Grande: The Correspondence of Robert E. Lee on the Texas Border, 1860.* Austin: Jenkins, 1988.

Johannsen, Robert W. *To the Halls of the Montezumas: The Mexican War in the American Imagination.* New York: Macmillan, 1974.

Johnston, R. M. *Bull Run: Its Strategy and Tactics.* Boston: Houghton Mifflin, 1913.

Johnston, William Preston. *The Life of Gen. Albert Sidney Johnston.* Austin: State House Press, 1997.

Kearney, Milo, ed. *More Studies in Brownsville History.* Brownsville: Pan American University at Brownsville, 1989.

———, ed. *Still More Studies in Brownsville History.* Brownsville: University of Texas at Brownsville, 1991.

———, ed. *Studies in Brownsville History.* Brownsville: Pan American University at Brownsville, 1991.

Kearney, Milo, and Anthony Knopp. *Boom and Bust: The Historical Cycles of Matamoros and Brownsville.* Austin: Eakin, 1991.

Kearny, Philip. *Letters from the Peninsula: The Civil War Letters of General Philip Kearny.* Edited by William B. Styple. Kearny, N.J.: Belle Grove, 1988.

Kelly, Pat. *River of Lost Dreams: Navigation on the Rio Grande.* Lincoln: University of Nebraska Press, 1986.

Kenly, John Reese. *Memoirs of a Maryland Volunteer: War with Mexico in the Years 1846–8.* Philadelphia: J. B. Lippincott, 1873.

Kirsch, George B. *Baseball in Blue and Gray: The National Pastime during the Civil War.* Princeton, N. J.: Princeton University Press, 2003.

Klement, Frank L. *The Copperheads in the Middle West.* Chicago: University of Chicago Press, 1960.

———. *The Limits of Dissent: Clement L. Vallandigham and the Civil War.* New York: Fordham University Press, 1998.

———. *Lincoln's Critics: Copperheads of the North.* Shippensburg, Pa.: White Mane, 1999.

Lang, Theodore F. *Loyal West Virginia from 1861 to 1865.* Huntington, W.Va.: Blue Acorn, 1998.

Lash, Jeffrey N. *Destroyer of the Iron Horse: General Joseph E. Johnston and Confederate Rail Transport, 1861–1865.* Kent, Ohio: Kent State University Press, 1991.

Lea, Tom. *The King Ranch.* 2 vols. Boston: Little, Brown, 1959.

Lee, Elizabeth Blair. *Wartime Washington: The Civil War Letters of Elizabeth Blair Lee.* Edited by Virginia Jeans Laas. Urbana: University of Illinois Press, 1991.

Lee, Richard M. *Mr. Lincoln's City: An Illustrated Guide to the Civil War Sites of Washington.* McLean, Va.: EPM Publications, 1981.

Lee Takes Command: From the Seven Days to Second Bull Run. Alexandria, Va.: Time-Life Books, 1984.

Leech, Margaret. *Reveille in Washington, 1860–1865.* New York: Harper & Brothers, 1941.

Levy, George. *To Die in Chicago: Confederate Prisoners at Camp Douglas, 1862–65.* Gretna, La.: Pelican, 1999.

Lingenfelter, Richard E. *Steamboats on the Colorado River, 1852–1916.* Tucson: University of Arizona Press, 1978.

Livermore, Thomas. *Numbers and Losses in the Civil War in America: 1861–1865.* Bloomington: Indiana University Press, 1957.

Longstreet, James. *From Manassas to Appomattox: Memories of the Civil War in America.* Philadelphia: J. P. Lippincott, 1896.

Lyon, William H. *Those Old Yellow Dog Days: Frontier Journalism in Arizona, 1859–1912.* Tucson: Arizona Historical Society, 1994.

Magruder, John. *Major-General Magruder's Report of his Operations on the Peninsula and the Battles of "Savage Station" and "Malvern Hill," near Richmond.* Richmond, Va.: Charles H. Wynne, 1862.

Maguire, Thomas Miller. *The Campaigns in Virginia, 1861–62.* London: W. H. Allen, 1891.

Malsch, Brownson. *Indianola: The Mother of Western Texas.* Austin: State House Press, 1988.

Marks, J. J. *The Peninsula Campaign in Virginia, or Incidents and Scenes on the Battle-Fields and in Richmond.* Philadelphia: J. B. Lippincott, 1864.

Marszalek, John F. *Sherman: A Soldier's Passion for Order.* New York: Free Press, 1993.

Martin, David G. *Second Bull Run Campaign: July–August 1862.* Conshohocken, Pa.: Combined Books, 1997.

Martin, Douglas D. *Yuma Crossing.* Albuquerque: University of New Mexico Press, 1954.

Marvel, William. *Burnside.* Chapel Hill: University of North Carolina Press, 1991.

Mathess, Paul, ed. *Voices of the Civil War: First Manassas.* Richmond, Va.: Time-Life Books, 1997.

———, ed. *Voices of the Civil War: The Peninsula.* Richmond, Va.: Time-Life Books, 1997.

———, ed. *Voices of the Civil War: Second Manassas.* Alexandria, Va.: Time-Life Books, 1995.

May, Robert E. *Manifest Destiny's Underworld: Filibustering in Antebellum America.* Chapel Hill: University of North Carolina Press, 2002.

McAdams, Benton. *Rebels at Rock Island: The Story of a Civil War Prison.* DeKalb: Northern Illinois University Press, 2000.

McCall, George Archibald. *The Seven Day's Contest. Pennsylvania Reserves. General McCall's Report and Accompanying Documents.* New York: Office of the Rebellion Record, 1864.

McClellan, George B. *McClellan's Own Story: The War for the Union.* New York: Charles Webster, 1887.

McComb, David G. *Galveston: A History.* Austin: University of Texas Press, 1986.

McDonald, JoAnna M. *"We Shall Meet Again": The First Battle of Manassas (Bull Run), July 18–21, 1861.* Shippensburg, Pa.: White Mane, 1999.

McFeely, William S. *Frederick Douglass.* New York: Norton, 1991.

McKay, Ernest. *Henry Wilson: Practical Radical, a Portrait of a Politician.* Port Washington, N.Y.: Kennikat, 1971.

McKinney, Tim. *West Virginia Civil War Almanac.* Charleston, W.Va.: Pictorial Histories Publishing, 1998.

McKnight, William Mark. *Blue Bonnets o'er the Border: The 79th New York Cameron Highlanders.* Shippensburg, Pa.: White Mane, 1998.

McPherson, James. *Battle Cry of Freedom: The Civil War Era.* New York: Oxford University Press, 1988.

———. *Ordeal by Fire: The Civil War and Reconstruction.* Boston: McGraw-Hill, 2001.

McPherson, William, ed. *From San Diego to the Colorado in 1849: The Journal and Maps of Cave J. Couts.* Los Angeles, 1932.

Meagher, Thomas Francis. *Memoirs of Gen. Thomas Francis Meagher Comprising Leading Events of His Career.* Worcester, Mass.: Messenger, 1892.

Metz, Leon. *Border: The U.S.-Mexico Line.* El Paso: Managan, 1989.

Miller, William J. ed., *The Peninsula Campaign of 1862: Yorktown to the Seven Days, Volume I.* Campbell, Calif.: Savas-Woodbury, 1995.

Mindil, George W. *The Battle of Fair Oaks: A Reply to General Joseph E. Johnston.* Philadelphia: n.p., 1874.

Moe, Richard. *The Last Full Measure: The Life and Death of the First Minnesota Volunteers.* New York: Henry Holt, 1993.

Mombert, Jacob Isidor. *An Authentic History of Lancaster County in the State of Pennsylvania.* Lancaster: J. E. Barr, 1869.

Moneyhon, Carl H. *Republicanism in Reconstruction Texas.* Austin: University of Texas Press, 1980.

———. *Texas after the Civil War: The Struggle of Reconstruction.* College Station: Texas A&M University Press, 2004.

Moneyhon, Carl, and Bobby Roberts. *Portraits of Courage: A Photographic History of Louisiana in the Civil War.* Fayetteville: University of Arkansas Press, 1990.

Monroy, Douglas. *Thrown among Strangers: The Making of Mexican Culture in Frontier California.* Berkeley: University of California Press, 1990.

Morris, Roy, Jr. *Sheridan: The Life and Wars of General Phil Sheridan.* New York: Crown, 1992.

Morrison, James L., Jr. *"The Best School": West Point, 1833–1866.* Kent, Ohio: Kent State University Press, 1986.

Mosby, John S. *Memoirs of John S. Mosby.* Boston: Little, Brown, 1917.

Naglee, Henry Morris. *Reconnaissance from Bottom's Bridge to Seven Pines, May 24, 25, and 26, 1862, Made by Naglee's Brigade.* Philadelphia: Collins Printer, 1863.

———. *Report of Brig. Gen. Henry M. Naglee: Commanding First Brigade, Casey's Division, Army of the Potomac.* Philadelphia: Collins, 1862.

Nelligan, Mary H. *Custis-Lee Mansion: The Robert E. Lee Memorial.* Washington, D.C.: National Park Service, 1962.

Newton, Steven H. *The Battle of Seven Pines, May 31–June 1, 1862.* Lynchburg, Va.: H. E. Howard, 1993.

———. *Joseph E. Johnston and the Defense of Richmond.* Lawrence: University Press of Kansas, 1998.

Nevins, Allan, ed. *A Diary of Battle: The Personal Journals of Colonel Charles S. Wainwright, 1861–1865.* New York: Da Capo, 1998.

Nicolay, John G. *The Outbreak of Rebellion.* New York: Charles Scribner's Sons, 1992.

North, Diane M. T, ed. *Samuel Peter Heintzelman and the Sonora Exploring and Mining Company.* Tucson: University of Arizona Press, 1980.

Olliff, Donothon C. *Reforma Mexico and the United States: A Search for Alternatives to Annexation, 1854–1861.* University: University of Alabama Press, 1986.

Pappas, George S. *To the Point: The United States Military Academy, 1802–1902.* West Point, N.Y.: Praegar, 1993.

Pennsylvania Reserves in the Peninsula: General McCall's Official Reports of the Part Taken by his Division in the Battles of Mechanicsville, Gaines' Mills, and New Market Cross Roads. N.p., n.d.

Pierce, Frank Cushman. *A Brief History of the Lower Rio Grande Valley.* Menasha, Wis.: George Banta Publishing, 1917.

Pingenot, Ben E. *Paso del Aguila: A Chronicle of Frontier Days on the Texas Border as Recorded in the Memoirs of Jesse Sumpter.* Austin: Encino, 1969.

Pitt, Leonard. *The Decline of the Californios: A Social History of the Spanish-Speaking Californians, 1846–1890.* Berkeley: University of California Press, 1971.

Pope, John. *The Military Memoirs of General John Pope.* Edited by Peter Cozzens and Robert I. Girardi. Chapel Hill: University of North Carolina Press, 1998.

Rafuse, Ethan S. *McClellan's War: The Failure of Moderation in the Struggle for the Union.* Bloomington: Indiana University Press, 2005.

———. *A Single Grand Victory: The First Campaign and Battle of Manassas.* Wilmington, Del.: Scholarly Resources, 2002.

Ramage, James A. *Gray Ghost: The Life of Col. John Singleton Mosby.* Lexington: University of Kentucky Press, 1999.

Ramsdell, Charles William. *Reconstruction in Texas.* Austin: University of Texas Press, 1970.

Randall, Ruth Painter. *Colonel Elmer Ellsworth: A Biography of Lincoln's Friend and First Hero of the Civil War.* Boston: Little, Brown, 1960.

Ray, Frederic E. *"Our Special Artist": Alfred R. Waud's Civil War.* Mechanicsburg, Pa.: Stackpole, 1974.

Report of the Judge Advocate General on "The Order of American Knights" alias "The Sons of Liberty," a Western Conspiracy in Aid of the Southern Rebellion. Washington, D.C.: Daily Chronicle Printing, 1864.

Rhodes, Elisha Hunt. *All for the Union: The Civil War Diary and Letters of Elisha Hunt Rhodes.* Edited by Robert Hunt Rhodes. New York: Orion, 1985.

Richter, William L. *The Army in Texas during Reconstruction.* College Station: Texas A&M University Press, 1987.

———. *Overreached on All Sides: The Freedman's Bureau Administrators in Texas, 1865–1868.* College Station: Texas A&M University Press, 1991.

Ridgway, James M., Jr. *Little Mac: Demise of an American Hero.* N.p.: XLibris, 2000.

Rister, Carl Coke. *Border Command: General Phil Sheridan and the West.* Norman: University of Oklahoma Press, 1944.

———. *Robert E. Lee in Texas.* Norman: University of Oklahoma Press, 1946.

Robertson, Brian. *Wild Horse Desert: The Heritage of South Texas.* Edinburg, Tex.: New Santander Press, 1985.

Robertson, James I., Jr. *Stonewall Jackson: The Man, the Soldier, the Legend.* New York: Macmillan, 1997.

———, ed. *The Civil War Letters of General Robert McAllister.* New Brunswick, N.J.: Rutgers University Press, 1997.

Robinson, John C. *Obituary Notice of Maj. Gen. Samuel P. Heintzelman, First Commander of the Third Army Corps.* New York: C. H. Ludwig, 1881.

Rodriguez, José Policarpo. *The Old Guide: Surveyor, Scout, Hunter, Indian Fighter, Ranchman, Preacher.* Dallas, n.d.

Rodriguez, Rudi R. *A Tejano Son of Texas: An Autobiography of José Policarpio Rodriguez.* TexasTejano.com, 2002.

———. *A Tejano Son of Texas: A Record of José Policarpio Rodriguez.* San Antonio: TexasTejano.com, 2002.

Roland, Charles P. *Albert Sidney Johnston: Soldier of Three Republics.* Austin: University of Texas Press, 1964.

Ropes, John G. *The Army under Pope.* New York: Charles Scribner's Sons, 1882.

Rosenbaum, Robert J. *Mexicano Resistance in the Southwest: "The Sacred Right of Self-Preservation."* Austin: University of Texas Press, 1981.

Sacks, B. *Be It Enacted: The Creation of the Territory of Arizona.* Phoenix: Arizona Historical Foundation, 1964.

Sandwich, Brian. *The Great Western: Legendary Lady of the Southwest.* El Paso: Texas Western Press, 1991.

Sayner, Donald B., and Robert P. Hale, comp. *Arizona's First Newspaper: "The Weekly Arizonian."* Tucson: Arizona Historical Society, n.d.

Scarborough, William Kauffman, ed. *The Diary of Edmund Ruffin: The Years of Hope, April, 1861–June, 1863.* Vol. 2. Baton Rouge: Louisiana State University Press, 1976.

Schutz, Wallace J., and Walter N. Trenerry. *Abandoned by Lincoln: A Military Biography of General John Pope.* Urbana: University of Illinois Press, 1990.

Scott, Robert Garth, ed. *Fallen Leaves: The Civil War Letters of Major Henry Livermore Abbott.* Kent, Ohio: Kent State University Press, 1991.

Sears, Stephen W., ed. *The Civil War Papers of George B. McClellan, Selected Correspondence, 1860–1865.* New York: Ticknor & Fields, 1989.

———. *George B. McClellan: The Young Napoleon.* New York: Ticknor & Fields, 1988.

———. *To the Gates of Richmond: The Peninsula Campaign.* New York: Ticknor & Fields, 1992.

Sherman, John. *John Sherman's Recollections of Forty Years in the House, Senate, and Cabinet: An Autobiography.* Chicago: Werner, 1895.

Sherman, William Tecumseh. *Memoirs of General William T. Sherman.* Westport, Conn.: Greenwood, 1957.

Siepel, Kevin H. *Rebel: The Life and Times of John Singleton Mosby.* New York: Da Capo, 1997.

Silber, Nina, and Mary Beth Sievens, eds. *Yankee Correspondence: The Civil War Letters between New England Soldiers and the Home Front.* Charlottesville: University Press of Virginia, 1996.

Simpson, Brooks D. *Let Us Have Peace: Ulysses S. Grant and the Politics of War and Reconstruction, 1861–1868.* Chapel Hill: University of North Carolina Press, 1991.

Simpson, Harold B. *Cry Comanche: The 2nd U.S. Cavalry in Texas, 1855–1861.* Hillsboro, Tex.: Hill College Press, 1979.

———. *Hood's Texas Brigade: Lee's Grenadier Guard.* Waco: Texian, 1960.

Sixty-Seventh Annual Report of the Association of Graduates of the United States Military Academy at West Point, New York, June 11, 1936. Newburg, N.Y.: Moore Printing, 1936.

Skelton, William B. *An American Profession of Arms: The Army Officer Corps, 1784–1861.* Lawrence: University Press of Kansas, 1992.

Small, Harold Adams. *The Road to Richmond: The Civil War Letters of Major Abner R. Small.* Edited by Harold Adams Small. New York: Fordham University Press, 2000.

Smith, Gustavus. *The Battle of Seven Pines.* New York: C. G. Crawford, 1891.

Smith, Ralph Adam. *Borderlander: The Life of James Kirker, 1793–1852.* Norman: University of Oklahoma Press, 1999.

Smith, Thomas T. *Fort Inge: Sharps, Spurs, and Sabers on the Texas Frontier, 1849–1869.* Austin: Eakin, 1993.

———. *The Old Army in Texas: A Research Guide to the U. S. Army in Nineteenth-Century Texas.* Austin: Texas State Historical Association, 2000.

———. *The U.S. Army & the Texas Frontier Economy, 1845–1900.* College Station: Texas A&M University Press, 1999.

Sneden, Robert Knox. *Eye of the Storm: Written and Illustrated by Private Robert Knox Sneden.* Edited by Charles F. Bryan Jr. et al. New York: Free Press, 2000.

———. *Images from the Storm.* Edited by Charles F. Bryan Jr. et al. New York: Free Press, 2001.

Snell, Mark A. *From First to Last: The Life of Major General William B. Franklin.* New York: Fordham University Press, 2002.

Sobré, Judith Berg. *San Antonio on Parade.* College Station: Texas A&M University Press, 2003.

Sonora and the Value of Its Silver Mines, Report of the Sonora Exploring and Mining Co., Made to the Stockholders, December, 1856. Cincinnati: Railroad Record Printers, 1857.

Speeches of William Curtis Noyes, Daniel S. Dickinson, and Lyman Tremain at the Great Union War Ratification Meeting Held at the Cooper Institute in the City of New York, October 8, 1862. N.p., n.d.

Speer, Lonnie R. *Portals to Hell: Military Prisons of the Civil War.* Mechanicsville, Pa.: Stackpole, 1997.

Stillman, Devereux. *Charles Stillman, 1810–1875.* New York: n.p., 1956.

Stout, Joseph A., Jr. *Schemers & Dreamers: Filibustering in Mexico, 1848–1921.* Fort Worth: Texas Christian University Press, 2002.

Stratton, R.B. *Captivity of the Oatman Girls.* Lincoln: University of Nebraska Press, 1983.

Strother, David Hunter. *The Diaries of David Hunter Strother: A Virginia Yankee in the Civil War.* Edited by Cecil D. Eby Jr. Chapel Hill: University of North Carolina Press, 1998.

Stutler, Boyd. *West Virginia in the Civil War.* Charleston, W.Va.: Education Foundation, 1966.

Swanberg, W. A. *Sickles the Incredible.* Gettysburg: Stan Clark Military Books, 1991.

Swift, Roy L. *Three Roads to Chihuahua: The Great Wagon Roads that Opened the Southwest, 1823–1883.* Austin: Eakin, 1988.

Swinton, William. *Army of the Potomac.* New York: Konecky & Konecky, 1995.

Symonds, Craig L. *Joseph E. Johnston: A Civil War Biography.* New York: W. W. Norton, 1992.

Tap, Bruce. *Over Lincoln's Shoulder: The Committee on the Conduct of the War.* Lawrence: University Press of Kansas, 1998.

Taylor, John M. *William Henry Seward: Lincoln's Right Hand.* New York: HarperCollins1991.

Taylor, Paul. *He Hath Loosed the Fateful Lightning: The Battle of Ox Hill (Chantilly), September 1, 1862.* Shippensburg, Pa.: White Mane, 2003.

Thomas, Stephen. *Fort Davis and the Texas Frontier: Paintings by Captain Arthur T. Lee, Eighth U.S. Infantry.* College Station: Texas A&M University Press, 1976.

Thompson, Jerry. *Henry Hopkins Sibley: Confederate General of the West.* Natchitoches: Northwestern State University Press, 1987.

———. *Juan N. Cortina and the Texas-Mexico Frontier, 1859–1877.* El Paso: Texas Western Press, 1994.

———, ed. *Fifty Miles and a Fight: Major Samuel Peter Heintzelman's Diary of Texas & the Cortina War.* Austin: Texas State Historical Association, 1998.

———. *Sabers on the Rio Grande.* Austin: Presidial, 1974.

———, ed. *Texas and New Mexico on the Eve of the Civil War: The Mansfield and Johnston Inspections, 1858–1861.* Albuquerque: University of New Mexico Press, 2001.

Thrapp, Dan L. *Encyclopedia of Frontier Biography.* 3 vols. Spokane, Wash.: Arthur H. Clark, 1990.

Tripler, Eunice. *Eunice Tripler: Some Notes of Her Personal Recollections.* New York: Grafton, 1910.

Twelfth Annual Return of the Graduates of the U.S. Military Academy, June 9, 1881. East Saginaw, Mich.: E. W. Lyon, 1881.

Tyler, Ronnie. *Santiago Vidaurri and the Southern Confederacy.* Austin: Texas State Historical Association, 1973.

Utley, Robert M. *Frontiersmen in Blue: The United States Army and the Indian, 1848–1865.* New York: Macmillan, 1962.

Van Deusen, Glyndon G. *Thurlow Weed: Wizard of the Lobby.* New York: Da Capo, 1969.

Vandiver, Frank. *Mighty Stonewall.* New York: Macmillan, 1988.

Van Tramp, John C. *Prairie and Rocky Mountain Adventures or Life in the West.* Columbus, Ohio: Segner & Condit, 1870.

Vayssade, Martin Reyes, comp. *Cartografia Historica de Tamaulipas.* Ciudad Victoria: Instituto Tamaulipeco de Cultura, 1990.

Wagoner, Jay J. *Early Arizona: Prehistory to Civil War.* Tucson: University of Arizona Press, 1954.

Wainwright, Charles S. *A Diary of Battle: The Personal Journals of Colonel Charles S. Wainwright, 1861–1865.* Edited by Allan Nevins. New York: Hardcourt, Brace, & World, 1962.

Waller, John L. *Colossal Hamilton of Texas.* El Paso: Texas Western Press, 1968.

Warner, Ezra J. *Generals in Blue: Lives of the Union Commanders.* Baton Rouge: Louisiana State University Press, 1977.

———. *Generals in Gray: Lives of the Confederate Commanders.* Baton Rouge Louisiana State University Press, 1959.

Watkins, Clara. *Kerr County, Texas, 1856–1976.* Hill Country Preservation Society, 1975.

Webb, Alexander S. *The Peninsula, McClellan's Campaign of 1862.* New York: Charles Scribner's Sons. 1882.

Webb, Walter Prescott. *The Texas Rangers: A Century of Frontier Defense.* Austin: University of Texas Press, 1965.

Weber, David J. *Richard H. Kern: Expeditionary Artist in the Far Southwest, 1848–1853.* Albuquerque: University of New Mexico Press, 1985.

Welcher, Frank J. *The Union Army, 1861–1865: Organization and Operation, Volume I: Eastern Theater.* Bloomington: Indiana University Press, 1989.

Welker, David A. *Tempest at Ox Hill: The Battle of Chantilly.* New York: Da Capo, 2002.

Wert, Jeffrey D. *The Sword of Lincoln: The Army of the Potomac.* New York; Simon & Schuster, 2005.

Wheeler, Richard. *Sword over Richmond: An Eyewitness History of McClellan's Peninsula Campaign.* New York: Fairfax, 1986.

Widder, Keith R. *Reveille till Taps: Soldier Life at Fort Mackinac.* Mackinac Island, Mich.: TriKraft, 1972.

Willcox, Orlando B. *Forgotten Valor: The Memoirs, Journals, & Civil War Letters of Orlando B. Willcox.* Edited by Robert Garth Scott. Kent, Ohio: Kent State University Press, 1999.

Williams, Amelia W., and Eugene C. Barker, eds. *The Writings of Sam Houston, 1813–1863.* 8 vols. Austin: Jenkins Publishing, 1970.

Williams, T. Harry. *Lincoln and His Generals.* New York: Knopf, 1952.

Woodman, Lyman L. *Cortina, the Rogue of the Rio Grande.* San Antonio: Naylor, 1950.

Woodward, Arthur, ed. *Journal of Lt. Thomas W. Sweeny, 1849–1853.* Los Angeles: Westernlore, 1956.

Woodridge, Ruby A., and Robert B. Vezzetti. *Brownsville: A Pictorial History.* Norfolk, Va.: Donning, 1982.

Wooster, Robert. *Soldiers, Sutlers, and Settlers: Garrison Life on the Texas Frontier.* Texas A&M University Press, 1987.

Wooster, Ralph A. *Texas and Texans in the Civil War.* Austin: Eakin, 1995.

Wormley, Katharine Prescott. *The Other Side of War with the Army of the Potomac.* Boston: Ticknor, 1889.

Wright, Marcus J. *Texas in the War, 1861–1865.* Edited by Harold B. Simpson. Hillsboro, Tex.: Hill College Press, 1965.

Articles

Ames, John Worthington. "The Second Bull Run." *Overland Monthly* 8 (1872).

Averell, William W. "With the Cavalry on the Peninsula." In *Battles and Leaders of the Civil War.* Vol. 2. 1887. Reprint, New York: Castle, 1956.

Baldridge, Lillian W. "Cattle Bandit Extraordinary." *Cattlemen* 34 (June 1947).

Barney, James M. "The Establishment of Old Fort Yuma." *Sheriff Magazine*, June 1954.

Barry, Peter J. "The Charleston Riot and Its Aftermath: Civil, Military, and Presidential Responses." *Journal of Illinois History* 7 (Summer 2004).

Bee, Robert L. "Quechan." In *Handbook of North American Indians, Vol. 10 (Southwest).* Washington, D.C.: Smithsonian Institution, 1983.

Bibb, Leland E. "William Marshall: 'The Wickedest Man in California,' a Reappraisal." *Journal of San Diego History* 22 (Winter 1976).

Blake, Kellee L. "Ten Firkins of Butter and Other 'Traitorous' Aid." *Prologue* 30 (Winter 1998).

Bridges, C. A. "The Knights of the Golden Circle: A Filibustering Fantasy." *Southwestern Historical Quarterly* 44 (January 1941).

Broussard, Edward J. "The Origins of the McLane-Ocampo Treaty of 1859." *Americas* 14 (1958).

Churchill, Robert. "Liberty, Conscription, and a Party Divided: The Sons of Liberty Conspiracy, 1863–1864." *Prologue* 30 (Winter 1998).

Cirruzzi, Canice G. "'Phoenix' Revisited: Another Look at George Horatio Derby." *Journal of San Diego History* 26 (Spring 1980).

Crenshaw, Ollinger. "The Knights of the Golden Circle: The Career of George Bickley." *American Historical Review* 47 (October 1941).

Crimmins, M. L. "An Episode in the Texas Career of General David E. Twiggs." *Southwestern Historical Quarterly* 41 (October 1937).

Crisp, James E. "In Pursuit of Herman Ehrenberg: A Research Adventure." *Southwestern Historical Quarterly* 102 (April 1999).

Darrow, Caroline Baldwin. "Recollections of the Twiggs Surrender." In *Battles and Leaders of the Civil War.* Vol. 1. 1887. Reprint, New York: Castle, 1956.

Davenport, Harbert. "General José María Jesús Carbajal." *Southwestern Historical Quarterly* 55 (April 1952).

Dennis, Frederick E. "The 8th New Jersey: How It Faced the Music at the Battle of Williamsburg." *National Tribune*, September 16, 1886.

Dougherty, William E. "An Eyewitness Account of Second Bull Run." *American History Illustrated* (December 1966).

Downer, Edward T. "Johnson's Island." In *Civil War Prisons.* Kent, Ohio: Kent State University Press, 1992.

Duffen, William A., ed. "Overland Via 'Jackass Mail' in 1858: The Diary of Phocion R. Way." *Arizona and the West* 2 (Spring 1960).

Dunn, Roy Sylvan. "The KGC in Texas, 1860–1861." *Southwestern Historical Quarterly* 70 (Spring 1967).

Elliott, J. K. "The Great Western: Sarah Bowman, Mother and Mistress to the U.S. Army." *Journal of Arizona History* 30 (Spring 1989).

Ellis, Richard E. "Duff Green." In *Encyclopedia of Southern History.* New York: Simon and Schuster, 1993.

Evans, Thomas H. "At Malvern Hill." *Civil War Times Illustrated* (December 1967).

Faulk, Odie B., ed. "A Letter from John R. Bartlett at Camp Yuma, 1852." *Journal of Arizona History* 6 (Winter 1965).

Fornell, Earl W. "Texans and Filibusters in the 1850s." *Southwestern Historical Quarterly* 59 (April 1956).

Fowler, Robert H., ed. "Mary Lincoln or Mrs. Heintzelman." *Civil War Times Illustrated* 6 (May 1967).

Franklin, W. B. "Rear-Guard Fighting during the Change of Base." In *Battles and Leaders of the Civil War.* Vol. 2. 1887. Reprint, New York: Castle, 1956.

Geer, John. "Fighting at Fair Oaks." *National Tribune*, June 4, 1914.

Glavecke, Adolphus. "The Story of Old Times." In *Twin Cities of the Border and the Lower Rio Grande*, by W. H. Chatfield. New Orleans: E. P. Brandao, 1893.

Goldsmith, W. L. "Who Killed Gen. Phil Kearney?" *Confederate Veteran*, June 1907.

Goss, Warren Lee. "Yorktown and Williamsburg." In *Battles and Leaders of the Civil War.* Vol. 2. 1887. Reprint, New York: Castle, 1956.

Hargett, Janet L. "Pioneering at Yuma Crossing: The Business Career of L. J. F. Jaeger, 1850–1887." *Arizona & the West* 25 (Winter 1983).

Heiges, George L. "Gen. S. P. Heintzelman Visits His Hometown of Manheim." *Journal of Lancaster County Historical Society* 68 (1964).

Heintzelman, Mary. "General Heintzelman in the Peninsula Campaign." *Century Illustrated Monthly Magazine* 30 (May–October 1885).

[Heintzelman, Samuel Peter]. "Harbor Defences." *Army and Navy Journal, and Gazette of the Regular and Volunteer Services* 4 (1866–67).

———. "Samuel P. Heintzelman." *American Phrenological Journal and Life Illustrated* 43 (February 1866).

Hennessy, John. "Thunder at Chantilly: The Second Manassas Campaign Closes amidst Blood and a Torrent." *North and South* 3 (March 2000).

Hingo, Don. "Texas' First Aristocracy: Robber or Robin Hood." *Houston Genealogical Journal* 7 (1989).

Holbrook, Arthur. "With the First Wisconsin at Williamsburg." In *War Papers Being Read before the Commanderey of the State of Wisconsin Military Order of the Loyal Legion of the United States*, vol. 3. Wilmington, N.C.: Broadfoot, 1993.

Hostetter, A. K. "Major Samuel Peter Heintzelman." *Historical Papers and Addresses of Lancaster County Historical Society* 17 (1913).

Hunt, Henry J. "Report of Light Battery M, Second Artillery, U.S.A., under Command of Major Henry J. Hunt." N.p., n.d.

Hunter, J. T. "Captain J. T. Hunter Tells of the Cortina War." *Hunter's Magazine* 2 (November 1911).

Kent, William C. "Sharpshooting with Berdan." *Civil War Times Illustrated*, May 1976.

Kilmer, George. "The Army of the Potomac at Harrison's Landing." In *Battles and Leaders of the Civil War.* Vol. 2. 1887. Reprint, New York: Castle, 1956.

Knox, Edward B. "The Capture of Alexandria and the Death of Ellsworth." In *Military Essays and Recollections*, vol. 2. Wilmington, N.C.: Broadfoot, 1992.

Kroeker, Marvin E. "William B. Hazen." In *Soldiers West: Military Biographies from the Military Frontier.* Lincoln: University of Nebraska Press, 1987.

Lambert, Paul F. "Basil Wilson Duke." In *Encyclopedia of the Confederacy.* Vol. 2. New York: Simon and Schuster, 1993.

Lammons, Frank Bishop. "Operation Camel: An Experiment in Animal Transportation in Texas, 1857–1860." *Southwestern Historical Quarterly* 61 (July 1957).

Lamont, Eneas N. "Second Bull Run." *Philadelphia Weekly Times*, March 1, 1881.

Le Conte, J. L. "Account of Some Volcanic Springs in the Desert of the Colorado in Southern California." *American Journal of Science* 19 (1855).

Lewitt, Francis Hale. "Steam Navigation on the Colorado River: Experimentation and Development, 1850–1864." *California Historical Society Quarterly* 22 (March 1943).

Long, J. W., Jr. "The Origin and Development of the San Juan Island Boundary Controversy." *Pacific Northwest Quarterly* 43 (1952).

Longstreet, James. "'The Seven Days,' Including Frayser's Farm." In *Battles and Leaders of the Civil War*. Vol. 2. 1887. Reprint, New York: Castle, 1956.

Lowe, Thaddeus S. C. "Balloon Army Service." *Scientific American*, February 2, 1895.

Lowe, T. S. C. "The Balloons with the Army of the Potomac." In *The Photographic History of the Civil War*, vol. 8. Edited by Francis Trevelyan Miller. New York: Review of Reviews, 1911.

Lyster, Henry F. "Recollections of the Bull Run Campaign." In *War Papers: Being Papers Read before the Commandery of the State of Michigan, Military Order of the Loyal Legion of the United States*, vol. 1. Wilmington, N.C.: Broadfoot, 1993.

McClellan, George B. "The Peninsula Campaign." In *Battles and Leaders of the Civil War*. Vol. 2. 1887. Reprint, New York: Castle, 1956.

Marten, James. "True to the Union: Texans in the U.S. Army." *North & South: The Magazine of Civil War Conflict* 3 (November 1999).

Miller, James Cooper. "With McClellan on the Peninsula." *Civil War Times Illustrated*, June 1969.

Moriarty, James Edward. "Fighting Tom Sweeny: The California Years." *Journal of San Diego History* 26 (Summer 1980).

Muther, Kay. "'The Devil Is Coming': Paddle-Wheelers on the Colorado." *Wild West* 17 (August 2004).

Pope, John. "The Second Battle of Bull Run." In *Battles and Leaders of the Civil War*. Vol. 2. 1887. Reprint, New York: Castle, 1956.

Porter, Fitz John. "The Battle of Malvern Hill." In *Battles and Leaders of the Civil War*. Vol. 2. 1887. Reprint, New York: Castle, 1956.

Poston, Charles D. "In Memoriam: Major-General Samuel P. Heintzelman." *Tucson Arizona Weekly Star*, May 13, 1880.

Rice, William B. "The Captivity of Olive Oatman: A Newspaper Account." *California Historical Society Quarterly* 21 (June 1942).

Richter, William L. "The Brenham Fire of 1866: A Texas Reconstruction Atrocity." *Louisiana Studies* 14 (Winter 1975).

———. "'It Is Best to Go in Strong-Handed': Army Occupation of Texas, 1865–1866." *Arizona and the West* 27 (1985).

Rippy, J. Fred. "Border Troubles Along the Rio Grande, 1848–1860." *Southwestern Historical Quarterly* 23 (October 1919).

Robins, W. T. "Stuart's Ride around McClellan." In *Battles and Leaders of the Civil War*. Vol. 2. 1887. Reprint, New York: Castle, 1956.

Sacks, B. "Charles Debrille Poston: Prince of Arizona's Pioneers." *Smoke Signal* 7 (Spring 1963).

———. "The Creation of the Territory of Arizona." *Arizona and the West* 5 (Spring–Summer 1963).

———. "Sylvester Mowry: Artilleryman, Libertine, Entrepreneur." *American West* 3 (Summer 1964).

Sears, Stephen W. "Glendale: Opportunity Squandered." *North and South*, December 2001.

Secrest, William B. "Wozencraft." *Real West* 24 (October–December 1981).

Shearer, Ernest C. "The Carvajal Disturbances." *Southwestern Historical Quarterly* 55 (October 1951).

Shook, Robert W. "The Battle of the Nueces, August 10, 1862." *Southwestern Historical Quarterly* 66 (July 1962).

[Sibley, Henry Hopkins]. "Recollections of Cadet Life Forty Years Ago." *Popular Monthly*, July 17, 1883.

Slater, John S. "Scenes at Malvern Hill." *Philadelphia Weekly Times*, December 11, 1880.

Smith, Gustavus W. "Two Days of Battle at Seven Pines." In *Battles and Leaders of the Civil War*. Vol. 2. 1887. Reprint, New York: Castle, 1956.

Smith, Ralph A. "John Joel Glanton: Lord of the Scalp Range." *Smoke Signal* 6 (1962).

Strand, Carl L. "Mud Volcanoes, Faults, and Earthquakes of the Colorado Delta before the Twentieth Century." *Journal of San Diego History* 27 (Winter 1981).

Thomas, Emory M. "Battle of Glendale." In *Historical Times Illustrated Encyclopedia of the Civil War*. New York: Harper & Row, 1986.

Thompson, Jerry. "The Many Faces of Juan Nepomuceno Cortina." *South Texas Studies* 2 (1991).

———. "'Near 106 Yesterday: It Has Been a Cool Summer': Samuel P. Heintzelman Views Yuma Crossing and Arizona Territory." *Journal of Arizona History* 41 (Autumn 2000).

———. "When General Albert Sidney Johnston Came Home to Texas: Reconstruction Politics and the Reburial of a Hero." *Southwestern Historical Quarterly* 103 (April 2000).

Tibbals, Richard K. "'There Has Been a Serious Disturbance at Charleston . . .': The 54th Illinois vs. the Copperheads." *Military Images* 21 (July–August 1999).

Von Schweinitz, Helga. "Hermann Ehrenberg, Fighting for Texas." *True West* 33 (April 1986).

Weisinger, Sidney R. "Globe House." *Victoria Advocate*, February 3. 10, 17, 1974.

Wert, Jeffry D. "Battle of Malvern Hill." In *Historical Times Illustrated Encyclopedia of the Civil War*. New York: Harper & Row, 1986.

———. "Engagement at Oak Grove." In *Historical Times Illustrated Encyclopedia of the Civil War*. New York: Harper & Row, 1986.

Winfrey, Dorman H. "Fort Clark." In *Frontier Forts of Texas*. Waco: Texian, 1968.

Newspapers

Brownsville, Tex.

American Flag

Bandera Americana

Daily Ranchero

Daily Ranchero and Republican
Fort Brown Flag
Buffalo, N.Y.
Commercial Advertiser
Courier
Express
Cincinnati, Ohio
Daily Commercial
Daily Enquirer
Daily Gazette
Daily Times
Chicago, Ill.
Times
Daily Tribune
Post
Clarksville, Tex.
Northern Standard
Columbus, Ohio
Daily Ohio State Journal
Corpus Christi, Tex.
Ranchero
Dallas, Tex.
Herald
Dayton, Ohio
Daily Empire
Galveston, Tex.
Daily Civilian
News
Tri-Weekly News
Flake's Weekly Galveston Bulletin
Houston, Tex.
Tri-Weekly Telegraph
Indianola, Tex.
Commercial Bulletin
Lebanon, Pa.
Lebanon Advertiser
Manheim, Pa.
Sentinel
New Orleans, La.
Daily Delta
Daily True Delta
Bee
Daily Picayune
Picayune
New York, N.Y.

Frank Leslie's Illustrated Newspaper
Herald
Times
Philadelphia, Pa.
Inquirer
Weekly Times
Rochester, N.Y.
Democrat & American
Union & Advertiser
San Antonio, Tex.
Alamo Express
Daily Herald
Herald
Ledger
San Diego, Calif.
Herald
San Francisco, Calif.
Alta California
Tubac, Ariz.
Weekly Arizonian
Tucson, Ariz.
Arizona Weekly Star
Weekly Arizonan
Victoria, Tex.
Advocate
Washington, D.C.
Daily Morning Chronicle
Daily National Intelligencer
National Tribune

Dissertations and Theses

De Blasio, Mario. "Sonora Exploring and Mining Co., 1856–1861." Master's thesis, University of Arizona, 1949.

Douglas, James Ridley. "Juan Cortina: El Caudillo de la Frontera." Master's thesis, University of Texas, 1992.

Gray, Leroy P. "The Economic History of the Lower Rio Grande Valley, 1820–1875." Ph.D. diss., Harvard University, 1942.

Gray, Ronald Norman. "Edmund J. Davis: Radical Republican and Reconstruction Governor of Texas." Ph.D. diss., Texas Tech University, 1976.

Hargett, Janet Lee. "Louis John Frederick Jaeger: Entrepreneur at Yuma Crossing." Master's thesis, University of Arizona, 1967.

Heidler, Jeanne Twiggs. "The Military Career of David Emanuel Twiggs." Ph.D. diss., Texas Christian University, 1987.

Lackman, Howard. "George Thomas Howard, Texas Frontiersman." Ph.D. diss., University of Texas, 1954.

Marcum, Richard T. "Fort Brown, Texas: A History of the Border Post." Ph.D. diss., Texas Tech University, 1964.

Sellers, Rosella A. "The History of Fort Duncan, Eagle Pass, Texas." Master's thesis, Sul Ross College, 1960.

Shook, Robert W. "Federal Occupation and Administration of Texas, 1865–1870." Ph.D. diss., North Texas State University, 1970.

Thompson, James Heaven. "A Nineteenth Century History of Cameron County, Texas." Master's thesis, University of Texas, 1965.

Townsend, Stephen A. "The Rio Grande Expedition, 1863–1965." Ph.D. diss., University of North Texas, 2001.

White, J. L. "Founder of Fort Yuma: Excerpts from the Diary of Major Samuel P. Heintzelman, U.S.A., 1849–1852." Master's thesis, University of San Diego, 1975.

Index

ISBN-13: 978-1-58544-535-6
ISBN-10: 1-58544-535-5